THE
HANDBOOK

**The Unofficial and Unauthorised Guide to the
Production of *Doctor Who***

Volume One

THE
HANDBOOK

The Unofficial and Unauthorised Guide to the
Production of *Doctor Who*

David J Howe
Stephen James Walker
Mark Stammers

Volume One

First published in England in 2005 by
Telos Publishing Ltd
5A Church Road, Shortlands, Bromley, Kent, BR2 0HP
www.telos.co.uk

Telos Publishing Ltd values feedback. Please e-mail us with any comments
you may have about this book to: feedback@telos.co.uk

This edition 2016

ISBN: 978-1-84583-941-3

Previously published in a different form in seven volumes
by Virgin Publishing Ltd, 1992, 1993, 1994, 1995, 1996, 1997.
And in one volume by Telos Publishing Ltd, 2005.

British Library Cataloguing in Publication Data.
A catalogue record for this book is available from the British Library.

Dedication

The seven volumes that comprised the original Handbook series were dedicated to a number of people. We feel it is only right to repeat those dedications here. So this book is dedicated to:

Ian K McLachlan, David Auger, Tony and Nikki Jordan, Martin Wiggins, the memory of Jon Pertwee, Ted, Sheila, Alan, Robert and Caroline, Alison, Anita Cotis, Mark Stammers, Andrew Pixley, Susan, Julie, Teresa and Kimberlie, everyone who ever contributed to *The Frame*, Nicole Adams (aka Suki), Claire.

Acknowledgements

First Doctor: For this incredible feat of researching the past we are, as always, indebted to numerous people who helped along the way. This time thanks must go to Keith Barnfather and Reeltime Pictures, David Auger, Michael Imison, Dallas Jones, Barry Newbery, Andrew Pixley, Marc Platt, Paul Scoones, Neil Somerville and Trevor White of the BBC Written Archives Centre, Martin Wiggins, John Wiles and all unsung *Doctor Who* fanzine editors and writers everywhere.

Second Doctor: For help in delving into the era of the second Doctor we are grateful to Andrew Pixley (as always), and also Keith Barnfather, Bobi Bartlett, Martin Baugh, David Brunt, Terrance Dicks, Sean Gaffney, Sean Gibbons, David Auger, Christopher Heer, Evan Hercules, Susan James, Sylvia James, Dallas Jones, Lighthope, Peter Ling, David Maloney, Ian McLachlan, John Peel, Jon Preddle, Darren Primm, Steve Roberts, Alex Rohan, Paul Scoones, Damian Shanahan, Roger Stevens, Jan Vincent-Rudzki, Patrick White, Martin Wiggins, the BBC Written Archives Centre and all *Doctor Who* fanzine editors everywhere.

Third Doctor: For help in delving into the era of the third Doctor we are grateful to, as always, Andrew Pixley, and also to James Acheson, Keith Barnfather and Reeltime Pictures, Bobi Bartlett, Jeremy Bentham and *In-Vision*, Paul Bernard, Richard Bignell, Allister Bowtell, David Brunt, Terrance Dicks, Sandra Exelby, David Auger, Gary Gillett, Simeon Hearn, Richard Hollis, Caroline John, David Myerscough-Jones, Barbara Kidd, Barry Letts, Jon Pertwee, Jon Preddle, Christine Rawlins, Tim Robins, Gary Russell, the Skaro Team, Elisabeth Sladen, Mark Stammers, Ken Trew, Jan Vincent-Rudzki, Martin Wiggins and all *Doctor Who* fanzine editors everywhere.

Contents

Authors' Note to the Telos Edition

The Handbook series, originally published by Virgin Publishing in the 1990s, was a great success, not only for us as authors, but also for the publishers. For the first time, we had the scope to delve into some of the minutiae and detail of the production of the *Doctor Who* series, and collect it all together in a series of books that, we hoped, would complement our larger format, illustrated volumes, collectively known as the 'decades' books.

In 2003, Telos Publishing released a new and updated edition of *The Television Companion*, a programme guide that collected together as much information about the actual televised *Doctor Who* stories as possible: the plots, the cliff-hanger endings, cast and crew, location and recording information, and review commentaries. Into that volume we added material from the 'Stories' sections of the seven original Handbooks, to make it even more comprehensive. That material is therefore omitted here, to avoid excessive duplication between the two books.

For this book, we have not extensively re-worked the remainder of the material from the original Handbooks: we have presented it in the same Doctor-by-Doctor format as before. Some corrections and updates have been made to the text to remove inadvertent mistakes, small instances of repetition etc. Also, some material cut from the published versions of those earlier volumes for reasons of space has been reinstated here. Most notably, there is the entire 'Script to Screen' section on the first Doctor story *The Ark*, which appeared only in heavily truncated form in the original Handbook. The extensive Production Guide to the first Doctor's era also has several more entries this time, and some of the other chapters have small embellishments to them as well. We have not, however, added large amounts of material to cover new developments that have occurred since the original volumes were written – such as the production of new audio adventures of the fifth, sixth, seventh and eighth Doctors by Big Finish – as these have already been comprehensively documented elsewhere.

At the time of writing this introduction, there is also a new series of *Doctor Who* due for transmission on BBC1 in 2005 ... something we've been awaiting with bated breath since 1989! Again, this book does not cover the production of the new series – look out for another Telos Publishing title, *Back to the Vortex*, for information on that.

Our aim here is to complete the picture with regard to *Doctor Who* on television from 1963 to 1996, and provide a complement to *The Television Companion* by chronicling the behind-the-scenes history of the first eight Doctors. We hope you enjoy reading, or re-reading, it as much as we enjoyed writing it.

David J Howe
Stephen James Walker
Mark Stammers

Doctor Who Story Checklist

SEASON ONE (1963 – 1964)

The Doctor played by William Hartnell
100,000 BC (A)
The Mutants (B)
Inside the Spaceship (C)
Marco Polo (D)
The Keys of Marinus (E)
The Aztecs (F)
The Sensorites (G)
The Reign of Terror (H)

SEASON TWO (1964 – 1965)

Planet of Giants (J)
The Dalek Invasion of Earth (K)
The Rescue (L)
The Romans (M)
The Web Planet (N)
The Crusade (P)
The Space Museum (Q)
The Chase (R)
The Time Meddler (S)

SEASON THREE (1965 – 1966)

Galaxy 4 (T)
Mission to the Unknown (T/A)
The Myth Makers (U)
The Daleks' Master Plan (V)
The Massacre of St Bartholemew's Eve (W)
The Ark (X)
The Celestial Toymaker (Y)
The Gunfighters (Z)
The Savages (AA)

The War Machines (BB)

SEASON FOUR (1966 – 1967)

The Smugglers (CC)
The Tenth Planet (DD)
The Doctor played by Patrick Troughton
The Power of the Daleks (EE)
The Highlanders (FF)
The Underwater Menace (GG)
The Moonbase (HH)
The Macra Terror (JJ)
The Faceless Ones (KK)
The Evil of the Daleks (LL)

SEASON FIVE (1967 – 1968)

The Tomb of the Cybermen (MM)
The Abominable Snowmen (NN)
The Ice Warriors (OO)
The Enemy of the World (PP)
The Web of Fear (QQ)
Fury from the Deep (RR)
The Wheel In Space (SS)

SEASON SIX (1968 – 1969)

The Dominators (TT)
The Mind Robber (UU)
The Invasion (VV)
The Krotons (WW)
The Seeds of Death (XX)
The Space Pirates (YY)
The War Games (ZZ)

SEASON SEVEN (1970)

The Doctor played by Jon Pertwee
Spearhead from Space (AAA)
Doctor Who and the Silurians (BBB)
The Ambassadors of Death (CCC)
Inferno (DDD)

SEASON EIGHT (1971)

Terror of the Autons (EEE)
The Mind of Evil (FFF)
The Claws of Axos (GGG)
Colony In Space (HHH)
The Dæmons (JJJ)

SEASON NINE (1972)

Day of the Daleks (KKK)
The Curse of Peladon (MMM)
The Sea Devils (LLL)
The Mutants (NNN)
The Time Monster (OOO)

SEASON TEN (1972 – 1973)

The Three Doctors (RRR)
Carnival of Monsters (PPP)
Frontier In Space (QQQ)
Planet of the Daleks (SSS)
The Green Death (TTT)

SEASON ELEVEN (1973 – 1974)

The Time Warrior (UUU)
Invasion of the Dinosaurs (WWW)
Death to the Daleks (XXX)
The Monster of Peladon (YYY)
Planet of the Spiders (ZZZ)

SEASON TWELVE (1974 – 1975)

The Doctor played by Tom Baker
Robot (4A)
The Ark in Space (4C)
The Sontaran Experiment (4B)
Genesis of the Daleks (4E)
Revenge of the Cybermen (4D)

SEASON THIRTEEN (1975 – 1976)

Terror of the Zygons (4F)
Planet of Evil (4H)
Pyramids of Mars (4G)
The Android Invasion (4J)
The Brain of Morbius (4K)
The Seeds of Doom (4L)

SEASON FOURTEEN (1976 – 1977)

The Masque of Mandragora (4M)
The Hand of Fear (4N)
The Deadly Assassin (4P)
The Face of Evil (4Q)
The Robots of Death (4R)
The Talons of Weng-Chiang (4S)

SEASON FIFTEEN (1977 – 1978)

Horror of Fang Rock (4V)
The Invisible Enemy (4T)
Image of the Fendahl (4X)
The Sun Makers (4W)
Underworld (4Y)
The Invasion of Time (4Z)

SEASON SIXTEEN (1978 – 1979)

The Ribos Operation (5A)
The Pirate Planet (5B)
The Stones of Blood (5C)
The Androids of Tara (5D)
The Power of Kroll (5E)
The Armageddon Factor (5F)

SEASON SEVENTEEN (1979 – 1980)

Destiny of the Daleks (5J)
City of Death (5H)
The Creature from the Pit (5G)
Nightmare of Eden (5K)
The Horns of Nimon (5L)

Shada (5M)

SEASON EIGHTEEN (1980 – 1981)

The Leisure Hive (5N)
Meglos (5Q)
Full Circle (5R)
State of Decay (5P)
Warriors' Gate (5S)
The Keeper of Traken (5T)
Logopolis (5V)

SEASON NINETEEN (1982)

The Doctor played by Peter Davison
Castrovalva (5Z)
Four To Doomsday (5W)
Kinda (5Y)
The Visitation (5X)
Black Orchid (6A)
Earthshock (6B)
Time-Flight (6C)

SEASON TWENTY (1983)

Arc of Infinity (6E)
Snakedance (6D)
Mawdryn Undead (6F)
Terminus (6G)
Enlightenment (6H)
The King's Demons (6J)

TWENTIETH ANNIVERSARY SPECIAL (1983)

The Five Doctors (6K)

SEASON TWENTY-ONE (1984)

Warriors of the Deep (6L)
The Awakening (6M)
Frontios (6N)
Resurrection of the Daleks (6P)
Planet of Fire (6Q)

The Caves of Androzani (6R)
The Doctor played by Colin Baker
The Twin Dilemma (6S)

SEASON TWENTY-TWO (1985)

Attack of the Cybermen (6T)
Vengeance On Varos (6V)
The Mark of the Rani (6X)
The Two Doctors (6W)
Timelash (6Y)
Revelation of the Daleks (6Z)

SEASON TWENTY-THREE (1986)

The Trial of a Time Lord (7A/7B/7C)

SEASON TWENTY-FOUR (1987)

The Doctor played by Sylvester McCoy
Time and the Rani (7D)
Paradise Towers (7E)
Delta and the Bannermen (7F)
Dragonfire (7G)

SEASON TWENTY-FIVE (1988 – 1989)

Remembrance of the Daleks (7H)
The Happiness Patrol (7L)
Silver Nemesis (7K)
The Greatest Show In the Galaxy (7J)

SEASON TWENTY-SIX (1989)

Battlefield (7N)
Ghost Light (7Q)
The Curse of Fenric (7M)
Survival (7P)

THE TELEVISION MOVIE (1996)

The Doctor played by Paul McGann
Doctor Who

THE FIRST DOCTOR

David J Howe
Mark Stammers
Stephen James Walker

Foreword

The arrival of the elderly figure of the Doctor in a junkyard at 76 Totter's Lane heralded the start of a ground-breaking British television success story that would continue from the transmission of that first episode on Saturday 23 November 1963 right up to the present day.

The seeds of this success were sown in the spring of 1962, when the idea of mounting an ongoing science fiction series was first mooted within the BBC. The BBC's television service was not long out of its infancy then. Less than sixteen years had passed since it was reinstated after its wartime hiatus, and less than seven since it first encountered competition in the form of the new ITV network. The launch of its second channel, BBC2, was still some two years away. Over the past decade, it had however made enormous technical advances; had come to rival and then overtake the radio service in terms both of its popularity and of its resources; and had firmly established itself as one of the foremost programme-making institutions in the world.

The advent of ITV, and its initial ratings triumph, had acted as a catalyst that had caused the BBC completely to re-evaluate its output, aiming to broaden its popular appeal whilst retaining its commitment to quality. The Sixties was to be one of its most artistically successful decades as, under Director-General Hugh Carleton Greene, it cast off its former, rather stuffy, highbrow image and became a creative hothouse turning out a multitude of innovative, challenging and highly-acclaimed programmes across its entire range of production.

One way in which it did this was to bring in visionary new personnel such as the charismatic Canadian producer Sydney Newman, whose recent achievements at the independent ABC TV had included the popularisation of an entirely new style of drama – 'kitchen sink drama', as the critics dubbed it – dealing with contemporary social issues of relevance to ordinary working-class viewers; not to mention the creation a number of highly successful individual series such as, most notably, *The Avengers*.

It was under Newman's guidance, and with his active contribution and participation, that the format of *Doctor Who* was devised. It was a perfect example of the new style of programming for which he was striving; a style that eschewed the tried-and-trusted in favour of the innovative and the experimental; a style that matched the spirit of the bright new decade.

The Sixties was to be a period of great change and success for Great

Britain. British pop music – especially the Mersey-beat groups led by the Beatles – would end America's domination of rock 'n roll. The fashionable would no longer look only to Paris for their clothes but also to London's King's Road and Carnaby Street, to new designers like Mary Quant and Biba. Attitudes towards the roles of the sexes were fast changing as people questioned long-established social codes, whilst the ever-present threat of nuclear war between the two super-powers, the Soviet Union and the United States of America, was leaving its mark on the collective psyche. Mankind was also taking its first faltering steps into space, turning what had so recently been science fiction into fact. If Man could now leave the Earth, surely he might one day walk on other worlds?

It was against this background and into this context that *Doctor Who* was born, to take its place – alongside its most famous monsters, the Daleks – as one of the greatest products and most widely-recognised icons of British popular culture.

Join us for a journey back in time to the swinging Sixties, and to the golden age of television.

William Hartnell
In His Own Words

ON HIS EARLY LIFE:

'All my spare coppers were spent on visits to the cinema. I revelled in the serials of Pearl White and the exploits of Tarzan. But my real guiding star was Charlie Chaplin. He influenced me more than any other factor in taking up acting as a career.'

Quoted by Peter Haining in *Doctor Who – A Celebration*, **original source unknown.**

'I was born in North Devon. Little place called Seaton.* A very old family. 300 years of us.

'I ran away from school at an early age. I had written to Stanley Wootton, at Treadwell House, Epsom, got myself a job as an apprentice with him to ride and become a jockey. After … I suppose it was a year or so, I suddenly started to put on weight and Stanley Wootton said it wouldn't do and he thought I ought to get out and take up another profession. Yes. So my second desire, immediate desire, was the theatre. Naturally I wanted to couple the two, but there it was – I was unable to do so.

'I suppose I associated myself with a lot of reading matter over a period. Shakespeare and other playwrights. And I was always in the school concerts and things like that. I was just mad keen on the theatre and horses, and those were the two things that I wanted in life, and unfortunately it didn't turn out that way.

'My first job in the theatre was luckily to be with Sir Frank Benson, a wonderful Shakespearean actor and teacher whom we all of course called at that period Pa Benson.

'After leaving the Benson company I was like any other actor, I

---

* It is now known that this was untrue. Hartnell was born in London, the illegitimate son of a single mother, but concealed this fact from journalists throughout his later life.

suppose. I had to take a job on tour and earn my living the best way I could, which I did. I was on tour doing once-nightly and twice-nightly shows for fourpence a week and living in back rooms.

'My first appearance in the West End was a very modest entrance on my part, I think. I was understudy when I first appeared and, you know, sort of general dog's body. I understudied such personalities as Ernest Truex in *Good Morning Bill*, which was a Robert Courtneidge production, and Ralph Lynn in his light comedies and farces. Charles Heslop, who was in musicals, and also a farcical actor. And Bud Flanagan, Chesney Allen. And a well-known actor when I was a boy, Lawrence Grossmith.'

Interviewed by Roy Plomley on 2 August 1965 for BBC Radio's *Desert Island Discs*.

'Sir Frank Benson's Company was good training. Not only in Shakespeare, but in keeping fit! Sir Frank Benson believed in keeping his actors in good health and we were organised into hockey teams and cricket sides.'

Quoted by Peter Haining in *Doctor Who – A Celebration*, original source unknown.

'In 1924 I ran away from school to join Sir Frank Benson's Shakespearean Company. I later persuaded my parents to allow me to go on tour; at that time I was just seventeen. After I left Benson's Company, I stayed on the road for another six years, touring with various modern productions, old and new. In the years 1928-29 I did a tour in Canada, came back to England and found things pretty tough so crashed into pictures, but as I was unknown as a film actor I had to start all over again. And many of the agents who saw me so often in their offices began to think that I was quite a comic. They roared and laughed at my persistence and confidence.'

William Hartnell writing in 1946 for *British National's Film Review*.

'I reasoned that my light comedy style was much more fitted for British talkies than their American counterparts, so I returned to England. But now I think that decision was completely wrong.

'I often hovered near directors so that I could learn the business of film-making. I was always on hand, too, in case another actor was suddenly needed. Although this strategy worked on occasions, and I did get bigger "bit" parts, it did not lead to stardom. If fact, after crowd work for two years, I was told by a casting director that I had not got a "film face". I remember, incidentally, that Laurence Olivier was also a neighbour at the film casting offices as we all sought vainly for work.'

Quoted by Peter Haining in *Doctor Who – A Celebration*, original source unknown.

ON HIS EARLY FILM ROLES:

'I can't remember my very first film appearance. But I must admit that I was two years in crowd scenes before I was ever allowed to appear in a film. I was then in numerous films, "Quickies" of those days, where if you had ten pages of dialogue in one take and if you fluffed, well, you had to ad lib and then carry on. No retakes. Couldn't afford it.'

Interviewed by Roy Plomley on 2 August 1965 for BBC Radio's *Desert Island Discs*.

'One day I found myself playing in a comedy lead in a "Quickie" called *I'm an Explosive*, directed by Adrian Brunel. Other leads at this period were *Follow the Lady* (Fox), *Seeing is Believing* (Paramount), *Nothing Like Publicity* (Radio). On my discharge from the Army I had to pick up anew the threads of my career. I kicked off again playing a valet-cum-thief opposite Oliver Wakefield in *The Peterfield Diamond*, then an old London taxi-cab driver in *Flying Fortress* (which I enjoyed very much as it was a character part). Then came a small cameo in *Sabotage at Sea*, and a comedy lead in *The Dark Tower*, from there to Ealing Studios to play *The Bells Go Down*, directed by Bill Dearden. I played Dallow in *Brighton Rock* at the Garrick Theatre. This play certainly helped me up a few rungs. During its run, Carol Reed tested me for the part of the Sergeant in *The Way Ahead*. Since then I have starred in four pictures made by British National Limited; *Strawberry Roan*, and *The Agitator*, *Murder in Reverse*, and *Appointment with Crime*.'

William Hartnell writing in 1946 for *British National's Film Review*.

ON HIS DISCHARGE FROM THE ARMY:

'The strain of training was too much. I spent twelve weeks in an army hospital and came out with a terrible stutter. The Colonel said, "Better get back to the theatre. You're no bloody good here." I had to start all over again. I was still only a spit and a cough in the profession and now I had a stutter which scared the life out of me!'

Interviewed in 1965 for the *Sunday Mirror*.

ON HIS 'TOUGH GUY' ROLES:

'Anyone can be horrific by gumming on lumps of hair and wax and by putting cotton wool up their nostrils to look like an ape, but I think the real shudder-creating villain is the one who looks the same as other men, except for the eyes, and the eyes ought to reveal just how rotten to the core the heavy is, with subtle graduations such as "forced into crime by mental instability" or "gone to the bad through evil surroundings" or "not a bad chap at heart but just lacking in strength of character." It's a fascinating study.'

Quoted by Peter Haining in *Doctor Who – A Celebration*, original source unknown.

'I'm tired of being the eternal "tough guy" of British films. Asking me to play this type of role in the first place was about as practical as asking Danny Kaye to play Napoleon on Elba!

'Somehow I've managed to scrape through, but after five years of it I can clearly see the danger signal ahead. I'm certain picturegoers are sick and tired of seeing me pull horrid faces before the cameras, and that if I don't change my style very soon, I shall soon find myself a has-been!

'It's not generally realised that forty-five of my sixty films are comedies and that I was a leading "Quota Quickie" funny man.'

Interviewed by D McFadden for *Picturegoer*, edition dated 26 May 1945.

'I got fed-up playing the bullying sergeant-major. People, complete strangers, would come up to me in pubs and bellow "Get yer 'air cut!"'

Interviewed for *Reveille*, edition dated 7-13 January 1965.

ON HIS ROLE AS SERGEANT MAJOR BULLIMORE IN
THE ARMY GAME:

'I stayed with that series for the first year, and then I thought I would give it a rest and try and do something else. I was away from it for two years, back making films. And then I quite by accident met the producer again in a train going one evening, and he asked me if I'd come back to the show. So I said yes, at a price. And he agreed and I went back for another year. Then I thought, well, I'd better leave now before I do go into a mental home.'

Interviewed by Roy Plomley on 2 August 1965 for BBC Radio's *Desert Island Discs.*

ON BEING CAST AS THE DOCTOR:

'All my life I've wanted to play an older character part in films, or in a play, and I've never been allowed to. Except just on one occasion prior to being offered this part, Doctor Who. After a second reading for Lindsay Anderson I was given the part of an old boy in *This Sporting Life*, where the lead was played and shared by Robert Harris and Rachel Roberts, both superb artists. And I was just playing this sort of bone idle, out of work, on the dole, ill old man called Dad who had a great ambition in life in earlier days to be a rugger player, and to be a good professional player, make a success of his life. Unfortunately he ended up, as it were, in the gutter, and rather an ill and useless old man, but in this young boy he saw something; he saw something of himself. Yes. And therefore he … I think he used his influence with the club managers and associates to get this boy a chance, give him a chance.

'And playing this part, strangely enough, led to the part of Doctor Who. Because it turned out that after I had played Doctor Who for several months Verity Lambert, my producer, a very charming and lovable person, finally confessed to me that she'd seen this film and she had decided that there was her Doctor Who.'

Interviewed by Roy Plomley on 2 August 1965 for BBC Radio's *Desert Island Discs.*

'I was "resting" when my son-in-law, who is also my agent, approached me about playing the part. I hadn't worked for the BBC since steam radio twenty-five years ago, and I didn't fancy the idea of returning to state control so late in life.

'My son-in-law – Terry Carney, son of George Carney, the variety artist – was quite right, the role was exactly me. For only the second time in thirty-seven years – the film *This Sporting Life* was the last – I had the opportunity to play an old man.

'What's more, the part required some thought, unlike *The Army Game* and most of the other rubbish I've been associated with in the past. I've not been offered the sort of work I've wanted, due I think to past disagreements I've had with producers and directors over how parts should be played.

'Financially and otherwise I am much better off now. I didn't like the initial script and I told them so. It made the old man too bad tempered. So they gave me carte blanche to introduce more humour and pathos into the part.

'I can hardly believe the break from playing servicemen has come, but now that it has happened, it's for good. I'll never play a uniformed part again.'

Interviewed in 1964 for syndication in local newspapers.

'I wanted to get away from military roles. That's why I was so pleased to be offered Dr Who.'

Interviewed for the *Daily Mirror*, edition dated 23 April 1966.

'The moment this brilliant young producer, Miss Verity Lambert, started telling me about *Doctor Who* I was hooked.'

Quoted in *The Making of Doctor Who* by Malcolm Hulke and Terrance Dicks, original source unknown.

ON THE MAGIC OF *DOCTOR WHO*:

'Apart from there being no sex or swearing, the treatment is very adult. But aiming it at the kids first was a masterstroke. Around tea time it's the children who decide what is seen on TV, not the parents. On the other hand, it is something mums and dads can watch as well without cringing.'

Interviewed in 1964 for syndication in local newspapers.

'The programme is a success because we keep it as a children's programme.

'The scriptwriters sometimes try to make Dr Who use expressions like "centrifugal force," but I refuse. If it all gets too technical, the children don't understand and they lose interest. After all, it's an adventure story, not a scientific documentary. And Dr Who isn't a scientist. He's a wizard.'

Interviewed for *Reveille*, edition dated 7-13 January 1965.

'After we remade the first episode, I decided that the show would run for five years. That was my assumption then, two-and-a-half years ago, and I think my assumption is still pretty right.

'If it does continue for that long, then I shall have had enough.

'I hope that before we finish the series that we shall be able to make it in colour. I feel this would enhance the programme.'

Interviewed for the *Western Daily Press and Bristol Mirror*, edition dated 14 December 1965.

'To me, kids are the greatest audience – and the greatest critics – in the world. When I knew it was a children's programme, I thought "I must really make something of this."'

Interviewed for the *Daily Mirror*, edition dated 23 April 1966.

'I predicted it would run for at least five years. I was universally scoffed at – by the press and the producers.

'It was magical. Children don't think of space as magical anymore.'

Interviewed by Michael Wynn Jones for the *Radio Times*, edition dated 30 December 1972 – 5 January 1973.

'It may look like hindsight now, but I knew – I just knew – that *Dr Who* was going to be an enormous success. Don't ask me how. Not everybody thought as I did. I was laughed at and mocked a good deal for my initial faith in the series. But I believed in it. I remember telling producer Verity Lambert right at the start: "This is going to run for five years." And now it's ten years old.

'We did it forty-eight weeks a year in those days. You know, I couldn't go out into the High Street without a bunch of kids following me. I felt like the Pied Piper.

'People really used to take it literally. I'd get letters from boys swotting for O Levels asking complicated questions about time-ratio and the TARDIS. Dr Who might have been able to answer them. I'm afraid I couldn't.

'But *Dr Who* is certainly a test for any actor. Animals and children are renowned scene-stealers and we had both – plus an assortment of monsters that became popular in their own right. Look at the Daleks. They started in the second series and were an immediate success.

'I remember once when I was asked to open a local fete I dressed in my *Dr Who* clothes and turned up in an old limousine owned by a friend. I'll never forget the moment we arrived. The children just converged on the car cheering and shouting, their faces all lit-up. I knew then just how much *Dr Who* really meant to them.'

Interviewed by David Gillard for the *Radio Times Doctor Who* special, published 1973.

'I think that if I live to be ninety, a little of the magic of *Doctor Who* will still cling to me.'

Quoted in *The Making of Doctor Who* by Malcolm Hulke and Terrance Dicks, original source unknown.

ON PLAYING THE DOCTOR:

'With rehearsals every day, it's just like being on tour. I live in digs near the studios all week and only go home at weekends.

'I give the rest of the cast my experience and they help me memorise my lines.

'I hope the series runs for another five years, because that is about as long as I give myself in this business. After that, I shall retire. After all, I'm not 21 anymore.'

Interviewed in 1964 for syndication in local newspapers.

'I see Dr Who as a kind of lama. No, not a camel. I mean one of those long-lived old boys out in Tibet who might be anything up to eight hundred years old, but look only seventy-five.'

Interviewed for *Reveille*, edition dated 7-13 January 1965.

'I'm the High Lama of the Planet. Although I portray a mixed-up old man, I have discovered I can hypnotise children. Hypnosis goes with the fear of the unknown. I communicate fear to children because they don't know where I'm going to lead them. This frightens them and is the attraction of the series.

'I am hypnotised by *Dr Who*. When I look at a script I find it unbelievable, so I allow myself to be hypnotised by it. Otherwise I would have nothing to do with it.

'Everyone calls me Dr Who and I feel like him. I get letters addressed to me as "Mr Who" and even "Uncle Who". But I love being this eccentric old man. I love it when my grand-daughter, Judith, calls me "barmy old grandad".

'I can see this series going for five years at least. It has already been sold in Australia, New Zealand and Canada, so my audience is getting bigger every week.

'I am getting more money than I've ever earned in my life.'

Interviewed for the *Sunday Mirror*, edition dated 7 February 1965.

'I am fortunate to be given *carte blanche* with the role. This allows me tremendous range to improve and build on the original outline of Dr Who.

'I think I represent a cross between the Wizard of Oz and Father Christmas. Yet I am always adding fragments to the part, always trying to expand it.'

Interviewed for the *Daily Express*, date unknown.

'Last year I was invited by Whitehall to be VIP guest of honour at a Battle of Britain display near Doncaster. I put on my Doctor Who clothes and appeared in a colourful battle of the Daleks – with planes dropping bombs etc. There were 11,000 people there. Kids smashed barriers to get near me. But the greatest moment for me was to be entertained afterwards by 150 of Britain's most famous flyers.'

Interviewed in 1966, source unknown.

'I love playing to children, because you can't pull the wool over their eyes. And when they write to me, you know, it's the truth, the whole truth and nothing but the truth.

'I don't mind being typecast again, even if it's in a bath-chair for the rest of my life.

'They give me pretty well *carte blanche*; and as a matter of fact Verity has said that when the time comes they will give me a bath-chair free. So I said I might take her up on that one day.'

Interviewed by Roy Plomley on 2 August 1965 for BBC Radio's *Desert Island Discs*.

'When children write to me they demand sometimes over and above what I can provide, but I send them a photograph and sign it and answer some of their letters. One little child wrote to me not so long ago, which is rather charming, she told me in her letter how much she liked the show, and she ended up by saying "When I grow up will marry you" – aged 4½!'

Interviewed by Roy Plomley on 2 August 1965 for BBC Radio's *Desert Island Discs*.

'I find there is a great appeal in playing older parts. In this story I am 750 years old, because I am a man from the future, and I label myself "The High Lama of the Planets". To the viewer, I appear as a man between 60 and 70.'

Interviewed for the *Western Daily Press and Bristol Mirror*, edition dated 14 December 1965.

'I'm signed up until next October. And the BBC have flatteringly said that they'll keep it on as long as I'm willing to continue. But I want a change in conditions. It's not a question of money, the BBC pay me very well, though I work bloody hard for it.

'But you can never escape from the character – that's the agony of being Dr Who.

'When I was in films, you worked hard for twelve or sixteen weeks, but when you'd finished, it was gone, in the bag.

'Dr Who has given me a certain neurosis – and it's not easy for my wife to cope with. I get a little agitated, and it makes me a little irritable with people.

'In fact, Dr Who seems to be taking over.

'I get nine weeks off a year. But it takes me two weeks to unwind from the part. What I would like for the next contract is something like Dr Finlay. He runs for twenty-six episodes and then gets a twenty-six-week break.

'Once or twice I've put my foot down with a new director and told him "I know how to play Dr Who and I don't want you to intrude on it or alter it."'

Interviewed for the *Daily Mirror*, edition dated 23 April 1966.

'It was like manna from heaven to get away from uniformed parts. The original Doctor was pig-headed and irascible, certainly, but there was also an element of magic in him – and that was what I tried to bring out.'

Interviewed by Michael Wynn Jones for the *Radio Times*, edition dated 30 December 1972 – 5 January 1973.

ON MAKING STORY SUGGESTIONS:

'The idea of doing a Western story was my idea. Children will always adore cowboys and Indians. And I'd like to see characters from children's books come into the series.'

Interviewed for the *Daily Mirror*, edition dated 23 April 1966.

'Your letter to me I found very interesting but first let me say you could not have two Doctor Whos.

'I myself suggested this some four years ago by having a son. The idea was for me to have a wicked son, both looked alike and both had a TARDIS and travelled in time and space. In fact I would have had to play a dual role when meeting up with him.

'This idea was not acceptable to the BBC so I forgot it very quickly. But I still think it would have worked and been exciting for the children.'

William Hartnell writing in July 1968 in a letter to fan Ian McLachlan.

ON HIS DEPARTURE FROM *DOCTOR WHO*:

'I think three years in one part is a good innings and it is time for a change.'

Quoted in a BBC press release dated 6 August 1966.

'Basically I left *Dr Who* because we did not see eye to eye over the stories and too much evil entered into the spirit of the thing. *Dr Who* was always noted and spelled out to me as a children's programme, and I wanted it to stay as such, but I'm afraid the BBC had other ideas. So did I, so I left. I didn't willingly give up the part.'

William Hartnell writing in July 1968 in a letter to fan Ian McLachlan.

'It is a long time ago now, and I think my hurt has healed, although I must say the events of those last few months are engraved on my heart.'

Quoted by Peter Haining in *The Doctor Who File*, purportedly from an interview conducted in April 1969 by John Ball, actual provenance uncertain.

'I was upset at coming out of *Dr Who*. But I didn't agree with what was happening to him. There was too much violence creeping into the series.

'It's too adult. It's meant for children, not grown-ups.

'There are lots of things you could learn from it now to start a major war.

'I've stopped watching. So have a lot of children – that's what I hear. They keep saying to me, "When are you coming back?"

'But it's all so different now.'

Interviewed in 1970 for a newspaper, details unknown.

ON OUTER SPACE:

'Space travel? Quite honestly it scares me stiff. I haven't the slightest wish to get in a rocket and zoom through the stratosphere. Somebody else can be the first man on the moon. It doesn't interest me at all.

'If God had wanted us to live on Mars, he'd have put us there in the first place. I prefer life on Earth.'

Interviewed for *Reveille*, edition dated 7-13 January 1965.

'Certainly I believe there is life on other planets – and they know there's life here but don't have the technology to get through.'

Interviewed by Michael Wynn Jones for the *Radio Times*, edition dated 30 December 1972 – 5 January 1973.

ON HIS HOME LIFE:

'My favourite pastimes are work, recreation, fishing, horse-riding and reading.'

William Hartnell writing in 1946 for *British National's Film Review*.

'My leisure interests before getting the part of Dr Who were strictly down to earth – gardening, fishing, sitting down and horse racing.

'I've been married thirty-nine years, and all of them to the same woman.'

Interviewed in 1964 for syndication in local newspapers.

'My grand-daughter Judith, who is seven, will probably be a TV producer one day. With Doctor Who in the middle of some terrible global disaster she'll ask me what I've done with that pretty tall hat I was wearing in the previous scene.

'I'm a countryman at heart. I love fishing, especially sea fishing for bass. I have a couple of rods down at Newhaven and go there whenever I get the chance.

'My favourite exercise is chopping wood.

'My wife and I are both keen bird-watchers. During the big freeze a few winters back, you'd be amazed at all the different birds which came to visit us. We kept them alive during that cold weather.

'We found out what food each bird liked, and got it for them somehow.

'Everyone has to escape somehow. Some people do it through TV. My escape is the English countryside, which I love.

'Nothing would ever make me leave it to explore life on some other planet.'

Interviewed for *Reveille*, edition dated 7-13 January 1965.

ON LIFE AFTER *DOCTOR WHO*:

'How lovely to be interviewed for a television feature. I thought people had forgotten me.

'Before I went into *Dr Who* I was always given sergeant-major parts like the one in *The Army Game*. I thought playing Dr Who would break my image. It didn't people still think of me as Dr Who or a bad-tempered sergeant major.

'Recently I was in *Softly, Softly* playing an ordinary old man. You've no idea how marvellous that was for a change.

'I read a lot of play-scripts. When I find the right one, I'm hoping I'll be able to put it on in the West End.'

Interviewed in 1968 for a newspaper, details unknown.

'For your information, the original Dr 'Who', which I think is me, is still running, and has reopened in New Zealand, Iran and Jamaica.

'My fan mail is still coming along, also, some from Australia, posted to the BBC.

'Of course you may use our names on the Fan Club notepaper, but keep my address to the blackout, in other words, to yourself.

'Also, let me add, I have had a nervous breakdown which has lasted nearly two years and am only just getting on my feet again. My wife has had to take the brunt of my illness, and no better nurse I can assure you.

'At the moment on holiday in Ireland.

'It was my own fault, much too long without a proper rest.

'A lot of parts come my way but, of little use to an ill man. Anon.

'Carry on and bless you together with fans.'

William Hartnell writing in a letter dated 11 August 1969 to *Doctor Who* Fan Club Secretary Graham Tattersall.

ON HIS RETURN TO TV IN THE ITV PLAY *CRIME OF PASSION*:

'I was ill for eighteen months. It was a double affair – pleurisy and a nervous breakdown.

'Now I'm back in the acting business. But I don't say "Yes" to everything. I turn things down if I don't think they're right.

'I would like to get back to more TV, but it is difficult because you don't always get the parts you want.

'And, of course, they fight shy about engaging expensive actors.'

Interviewed in 1970 for a newspaper, details unknown.

William Hartnell
As Others Saw Him

CHRISTOPHER BARRY (DIRECTOR):

'I remember, unfortunately, that William Hartnell had a rather old fashioned attitude to race. Also, by the time I came back to work with him on some of the later episodes, he thought he was "the Doctor", not William Hartnell. But all the cast had assumed their characters' personalities, and it's a great short-cut on any series or serial if the actors know their roles. They will then tell the director, "This is what I ought to be doing," or "ought not," and if you disagree with them it's up to you to convince them. That's perfectly healthy – you stop rehearsal and talk about it.'

Interviewed by David J Howe and Rosemary Howe in 1987 for *The Frame* Issue 1.

IAN STUART BLACK (WRITER):

'I thought he was an excellent actor. I think I first became aware of him when I saw a little scene he had done in a British film called *Odd Man Out*. He was on screen for only about two or three minutes in a ninety-minute picture, playing the part of a bartender who was under great strain, and in that short space of time he really caught my attention and impressed me with his abilities. Then of course my children used to watch him in *Doctor Who*. So when I came to write for him I was very pleased.

'I've heard it said that Hartnell could be irritable, and that's true. Certainly he could be irritable with some of the younger actors and actesses in *Doctor Who* whom he didn't consider to be totally professional. You have to remember that the series was taking people who at the time were fairly unknown and still learning the business, although some of them became stars later on, and I think that every now and again he felt mildly irritated. In a sense he was carrying some of them. As far as I was concerned, though, his professionalism excused any sort of personal attitude he might have had. I didn't know him very well, but I liked him. He just took the script and he acted it.'

Interviewed by Stephen James Walker in 1992 for *The Frame* Issue 23 & 24.

DOUGLAS CAMFIELD (DIRECTOR):

'To be perfectly honest, Bill could be difficult to work with. He was cantankerous, wilful, dogmatic and never suffered fools gladly. But life was never dull in his company and he was generous and encouraging if he knew that, like him, you put the good of the programme above all. He had "star quality" in abundance, and brought a special magic to the part. He "created" the Doctor and provided the yardstick against which every other actor who plays the part is measured. He helped me to get started as a director and I owe him a great deal. He was a remarkable man and I shall never forget him.'

Interviewed by Gary Hopkins in 1979 for *The Doctor Who Review* Issue 1.

ANN CARNEY (DAUGHTER):

'His grandchildren had given him a new interest in the younger generation, as they always do older people. He never had a son, so I was the only one, and Paul (his grandson) had stimulated a different approach to children. Their interest in the modern space age etc was reflected in his interest in that type of programme.'

Interviewed for *The Time Scanner* Issue 2, published in 1985.

FRANK COX (DIRECTOR):

'William Hartnell seemed to me to hate rehearsing. He had a great problem learning the lines, and if he found a biggish speech, of half a page or so, he would say "Christ. Bloody *Macbeth*!" My impression was that he loved being the Doctor, especially when it involved opening bazaars etc., but that he was insecure about his ability to do the work. William Russell was a great help to me, mediating between the irascible old Hartnell and the trembling novice director, Cox. It was all a nightmare quite honestly.'

Interviewed by Ian K McLachlan for *TARDIS* Volume 7 Number 1.

RAYMOND CUSICK (DESIGNER):

'Bill Hartnell took acting very seriously, and was desperate as an actor to do *Doctor Who* – and then all the mail that came in was for the Daleks, some fibreglass model! I remember him telling me that the company which manufactured the Dalek playsuits sent a representative down to his house to give him one of them. He said, "I don't know why they brought this bloody thing down to me. What do I want a bloody Dalek for?"

'He was funny, Bill Hartnell, but on the face of it he didn't appear to have any sense of humour. For instance, we were all sitting around drinking coffee one day and reminiscing about our time in the theatre, recalling all the embarrassing things which had gone wrong during shows we'd been involved with, and he couldn't understand why we thought these things were funny!

'He started telling us a story, very seriously. Apparently he had been touring in a play with an actor-manager who was an alcoholic – a Henry Irving type, a real ham. In one scene, the actor-manager's character was supposed to have an argument with Hartnell's character and then leave the room through a door, where he would meet two other characters and they would discover what was happening – this was the denouement of the play. Anyway, one night, when the actor-manager came to make his exit, instead of going through the door he opened a big wardrobe next to it and went in! Hartnell stood there waiting for him to come out, because it didn't lead anywhere, but he didn't come out. The two actors outside were given a cue and came in, and they just had to busk it – to make it up as they went along! After the curtain came down, they all rushed over to the wardrobe, opened the door, and there he was, fast asleep! "What happened?" they asked him. "Well, my dears, I came inside here, shut the door, and suddenly it was dark. So I thought I'd sit down and have a rest." Hartnell was absolutely serious when he told us this but, by the time he'd finished, we were falling about, it was so funny.'

Interviewed by Stephen James Walker and David J Howe in 1991 for *The Frame* Issue 21 & 22.

GERRY DAVIS (STORY EDITOR):

'I got on well with Billy Hartnell. I discovered it was no good confronting him, because as soon as you did he'd get angry. There was a lot of anger in him. What I would do was, having the necessary knowledge, talk about something to do with his past.

'For example, there was the occasion of the chair. He came onto the set, took one look at this chair, and said, "This is ridiculous – I can't sit in this chair, it's wrong! Take it away – and I won't do anything until it's taken away." They used to send for me, and I'd come down and say, "What's the matter?" He said, "Look at this. It's an insult, and completely wrong for the scene." So I replied, "Doesn't it look familiar to you? When Barrymore played his 1925 *Hamlet* he used a chair identical to that!" And Hartnell paused, thought, and then said, "Oh yes, I saw him." So we talked about Barrymore for five minutes, and then I said, "Well, sorry to disturb you, you'd better get on with the scene. But first we must get rid of that chair!" And he looked at me and said, "Oh no, that's fine, nothing wrong with that!"

'He was very nice to me and took a great interest in me, always asking after my daughters. It was the make-up and costume people he bullied.'

Interviewed by Richard Marson in 1987 for *Doctor Who Magazine* No. 124.

MICHAEL CRAZE (ACTOR):

'Mr Hartnell, god rest his soul, was a devil! He was a bit overpowering, quite frankly. I found him just difficult to work with. I don't think he wanted to leave. I think the powers-that-be got fed up and said "Let's change the whole format," and they redrafted the whole thing.'

Interviewed by Gordon Roxburgh for *TARDIS* Volume 7 Number 4.

MICHAEL FERGUSON (DIRECTOR):

'I liked him a lot and got on quite well with him, possibly because I had already worked with him as an assistant floor manager. The AFM really has to get on well with everyone, otherwise it can made life very difficult. I had always looked after Bill on *The Mutants* and I found him very co-operative. He could be cantankerous, he could be snappy, he could be a bit huffy sometimes, but that was something I found not particularly remarkable then and I find even less remarkable now when I think of the burdens borne by the lead actor of a major and popular series.'

Interviewed by Stephen James Walker in 1991 for *The Frame* Issue 18.

HEATHER HARTNELL (WIFE):

'The cast all got on awfully well. Of course he had his favourites. He loved

Bill Russell, who was the first of his assistants, and Peter Purves who joined later. He got on awfully well with Bill Russell and Jackie Hill and Carole Ann Ford, who was his grand-daughter in the beginning. Oh! They all got on well together. Well, they had to, because they were making it in a very tiny studio and they were all on top of each other; they had to get on well together or else they would have come to blows I would imagine!

'He loved the historical stories because, like all actors, he loved dressing up in great gay clothes. He loved stories like the French Revolution one and *Marco Polo* and things like that, because they all had gorgeous, glamorous clothes. I don't know what his favourite story was. Perhaps *Marco Polo*, because they had great fun doing that. But of course his favourite monster had to be the Daleks. The point was that somehow he could get the better of all the other monsters, but the Daleks always popped up again! And William felt that he was never going to get the better of them.

'The performances that he was really proud of were in films, particularly a film called *The Way Ahead* and a film called *The Yangtse Incident*; they were service films. He loved doing *Doctor Who*, though. He absolutely adored it, because he always loved children and always had a way with them. He used to stay five nights a week in a little flat in London and then come home to Mayfield, where we lived, at the weekend. I used to drive over and meet him at Tunbridge Wells station, and the local children got to know that he'd arrive at Tunbridge Wells on a Saturday morning and they'd be waiting for him. It was very like the Pied Piper of Hamlyn, walking through the streets down to the car park. They knew it was him, and if he went into a shop they would wait outside, then follow him again. Well of course he loved it because they were children; he loved children.'

Interviewed for *No, Not the Mind Probe* Issue 1, published January 1985.

WARIS HUSSEIN (DIRECTOR):

'William Hartnell was Verity Lambert's idea for the role of the Doctor, but at first he was quite reluctant to accept it. We took him out to lunch one day and I had to talk literally non-stop to try to convince him. He had a number of worries. He had recently done a series – *The Army Game* – and didn't really want to get involved with something else which took up so much of his time. Also, he didn't quite know if he wanted to play such a peculiar character. He seemed to think that, by asking him to play the part of an eccentric, we were implying that he was eccentric himself – which of course he was! Ultimately, though, he agreed, and that was due largely to these diplomatic approaches from Verity and me, so I feel fairly strongly that I was very influential there.

'William was very much a prejudiced person, and I had a strong suspicion that he was prejudiced about me to start with. What was interesting, though, was that he never allowed it to interfere with his work, and gradually he came to like me a great deal, so in a way you could say there was something achieved through that! Once he realised that I knew what I was doing he really was supportive. He never, ever made things difficult for me, which he could have done if he'd wanted to. I had a lot of respect for the man. I think everyone's entitled to their opinions; but if you can change some of them, all for the better.'

Interviewed by Stephen James Walker and David J Howe in 1990 for *The Frame* **Issue 16.**

INNES LLOYD (PRODUCER):

'Bill had been in the role for a long time. He was getting on and he was getting tired. I thought that the tiredness and the irascibility were not going to be good a) for the show and b) for him – for him, mostly – and I would always have advised him to leave. I remember taking him home after the party on his last night, at about one in the morning. I told him "Bill, now you can have a rest" and he said "Yes, I'll be very pleased."

'I also recall him saying to me – though I don't know if he said it to anyone else – "There's only one man in England who can take over, and that's Patrick Troughton"! I think he was happy when he heard that Pat would be doing it.'

Interviewed by Stephen James Walker and Peter Linford in 1990 for *The Frame* **Issue 14.**

DEREK MARTINUS (DIRECTOR):

'Hartnell was very quick to size me up; he did that with all the new directors. He was a pretty formidable figure, with a good track record in films, and he liked to present himself as an imposing, knowledgeable sort of guy. He definitely liked to be the star.

'I remember Hartnell saying to me during one of the earlier episodes that he had been told he could go on as the Doctor for as long as he liked, that he had *carte blanche* over the scripts, and that when he finished the series was finished. He really believed he was the series, poor chap. He could not envisage it existing without him. He said "How can they replace Doctor Who? It's called *Doctor Who*, and if I don't do it, that's the end of it. They keep asking me to carry on, but I don't know how long I'll do it."'

Interviewed by Stephen James Walker and David J Howe in 1991 for *The Frame* **Issue 21 & 22.**

RICHARD MARTIN (DIRECTOR):

'William Hartnell disliked quite a lot but worked like a white man and worried like Reagan's bodyguard.'

Interviewed by Ian K McLachlan in 1983 for *TARDIS* **Volume 8 Number 2.**

WILLIAM RUSSELL (ACTOR):

'Billy was marvellous, very professional. He had all the switches in the TARDIS marked out exactly in his mind, and he thought up the idea about the Doctor always getting my name wrong. Billy wasn't at all like the Doctor off set. He was a very professional actor who just did his job, in his own way.'

Interviewed by Graeme Wood, John Brand and Andy Lennard in 1984 for *The Merseyside Local Group Megazine* **Volume 2 Issue 17.**

JULIA SMITH (DIRECTOR):

'Mr Hartnell was a terrific professional and totally dedicated to the part he was playing. At times I think he honestly believed he was Doctor Who. Any actor supporting a series over a number of years gets very weary, and his age must have added to this. He was finding it difficult to remember lines, which was one of the reasons he was given two companions instead of one. He was also given very athletic things to do by a lot of the writers and, as a director, one had to save him as much as possible.'

Interviewed in 1982 by Ian K McLachlan for *TARDIS* **Volume 7 Number 2.**

PETER PURVES (ACTOR):

'I liked Bill a lot. I thought he was a smashing bloke. Very difficult to work with, but he was a perfectionist in his own way and it came out as rattiness with directors and producers. He had a strong sense of what was wrong and what was right. He did have a bit of trouble learning his lines sometimes and used to get them wrong on takes, but that sort of thing happens and I still think he was the best Doctor by a long way. I had a very good relationship with Bill and he used to take me and my wife out for meals. He was a lovely man. Very entertaining and, I think, a very good actor.'

Interviewed in 1986 for *Flight Through Eternity* No. 2.

'Television acting is really quite confined, and he would always hold his hands up in front of his chest, because if they were down by his sides and he was in close-up you wouldn't see them. If he made a gesture it wouldn't be a big one, because again that would take his hands out of shot. Instead, he used to make all those neat little gestures of his.'

Interviewed in 1990 for the British Satellite Broadcasting *Doctor Who* weekend.

DONALD TOSH (STORY EDITOR):

'Bill was a hardened old pro, but he was also getting on in years. Time and time again he had the weight of the explanation to do, so as to make the whole thing acceptable and believable. He would stray away from the script and bumble and ad-lib his way through so that at times we tore our hair and there were some great old fights. However, usually when we came to look at the finished product, Bill had made it sense and it looked fine.

'John Wiles and I had many battles royal with him, but that is true of any long-running programme – there are always arguments with the star. Bill cared very, very deeply for the programme. He was desperately sorry when the time came and he had to give it up. The success that *Doctor Who* has lived on since it began is greatly due to what Bill Hartnell brought to the programme.

'I think towards the end he almost began to lose the dividing line between his own reality and the fantasy reality of the Doctor. There were times when one knew he was going to be difficult and one had to head off trouble if one could, for our schedule was terribly tight and time was always at a premium. I recall once at a read-through Bill had a long and complicated speech which was absolutely vital, and I knew that he was going to ask for it to be rewritten or cut. As soon as the read was over I rushed across and congratulated him. I told him that it was a vital speech and he had read it quite beautifully, and that I had written it especially for him. Everyone likes sudden and surprising flattery so he was slightly taken aback, then smiled, said "Thank you" and went away and learned every word, and on transmission delivered it absolutely perfectly.'

Interviewed by Jan Vincent-Rudzki, Stephen Payne and Ian Levine in 1978 for *TARDIS* Volume 3 Number 3.

EDMUND WARWICK (ACTOR WHO DOUBLED FOR HARTNELL):

'He was incredibly kind. He wanted me to be good in the part, obviously, and so when we weren't rehearsing he spent a lot of his spare time showing me exactly how he held his head and how he stood, which was very generous of him really because actors are not all that kind as a rule.

'He could be tetchy, but when he wanted to help he was most helpful. The thing that made him tetchy was when scripts were not up to scratch.

'When Hartnell was there, he really was the most important person of the lot. Things went according to the way Hartnell wanted them to go, rather than anything else.'

Interviewed by John Bowman in 1989 for *The Frame* Issue 10.

JOHN WILES (PRODUCER):

'He wasn't as old as he thought he was. When he was with me he treated himself almost as a 75 year old. It may well have been that he was physically not in the best of health and so could not learn lines. Consequently, studio days could be absolute purgatory for everybody. If Bill was in an unhappy state then it put everyone into a terrible state.

'Eventually my directors devised a code for me. They would turn to their production assistant and say, "You had better phone the designer," which meant, "Get John down here quick," so that Bill wouldn't know I'd been summoned.

'One day I got a call from the studio to say that all the dressers had come out on strike! Now this was a cataclysmic start to a day in the studio where you depend on all your back-up all the time. Bill had simply offended his dresser, who had then complained, and so the entire staff had walked out. And this was on the *one* day you had to get an entire episode recorded. So there were those kind of pressures all the time.

'Peter Purves was very supportive and helped as much as he could. I imagine it must have been very nerve-wracking for him, in that he never knew from one day to the next what was coming from Bill.

'The feeling from above was that the show worked as it was, and would continue to run as long as Bill Hartnell played the Doctor. So perhaps I was mad for wanting to change it. But our audience research had shown the production office that many adults watched the show and so I felt we could do better than we were doing.

'I do remember suggesting to Bill once that we take the TARDIS to a planet where there is no gravity and no oxygen – where he would have to wear a spacesuit. You never heard such an uproar in all your life ...'

Interviewed by Jeremy Bentham in 1983 for *Doctor Who Monthly* Winter Special 1983/84.

ANNEKE WILLS (ACTRESS):

'As you have probably heard from other people, Bill Hartnell was a very tricky character. Very, very tricky. So the rest of the cast would stick together, and have a sort of reality check! His departure was all pretty emotional, I think, and rather difficult.'

Interviewed by Stephen James Walker in 1991 for *The Frame* Issue 20.

Character – The First Doctor

The character of the Doctor was devised by BBC Head of Drama Sydney Newman in April 1963. His staff had by this point already done a considerable amount of work on developing a proposed new science fiction series, but it was Newman himself who decided that the central character ought to be, as he later put it:

> A man who is 764 years old – who is senile but with extraordinary flashes of intellectual brilliance. A crotchety old bugger – any kid's grandfather – who had, in a state of terror, escaped in his machine from an advanced civilisation on a distant planet which had been taken over by some unknown enemy. He didn't know who he was any more, and neither did the Earthlings, hence his name, Dr Who. He didn't know precisely where his home was. He did not fully know how to operate the time-space machine.
>
> In short, he never intended to come to our Earth. In trying to go home he simply pressed the wrong buttons – and kept on pressing the wrong buttons, taking his human passengers backwards and forwards, and in and out of time and space.'

The earliest contemporary description of the Doctor's character appeared in a format document prepared during the early part of April 1963 by BBC staff writer/adaptor C E Webber, in consultation with Newman and with the Head of the Script Department, Donald Wilson. It read as follows:

DR WHO

> A frail old man lost in space and time. They give him this name because they don't know who he is. He seems not to remember where he has come from; he is suspicious and capable of sudden malignance; he seems to have some undefined enemy; he is searching for something as well as

fleeing from something. He has a 'machine' which enables them to travel together through time, through space, and through matter.

The same document later went on to give a description of the part that the Doctor would play within the continuity of the stories:

He remains a mystery. From time to time the other three discover things about him, which turn out to be false or inconclusive (i.e. any writer inventing an interesting explanation must undercut it within his own serial-time, so that others can have a go at the mystery). They think he may be a criminal fleeing from his own time; he evidently fears pursuit through time. Sometimes they doubt his loss of memory, particularly as he does have flashes of memory. But also, he is searching for something which he desires heart-and-soul, but which he can't define. If, for instance, they were to go back to King Arthur's time, Dr Who would be immensely moved by the idea of the Quest for the Grail. That is, as regards him, a Quest Story, a Mystery Story, and a Mysterious Stranger Story, overall.

While his mystery may never be solved, or may perhaps be revealed slowly over a very long run of stories, writers will probably like to know an answer.

Shall we say:

The Secret of Dr Who: In his own day, somewhere in our future, he decided to search for a time or for a society or for a physical condition which is ideal, and having found it, to stay there. He stole the machine and set forth on his quest. He is thus an extension of the scientist who has opted out, but he has opted farther than ours can do, at the moment. And having opted out, he is disintegrating.

One symptom of this is his hatred of scientists, inventors, improvers. He can get into a rare paddy when faced with a cave man trying to invent a wheel. He malignantly tries to stop progress (the future) wherever he finds it, while searching for his ideal (the past). This seems to me to involve slap up-to-date moral problems, and old ones too.

In story terms, our characters see the symptoms and guess at the nature of his trouble, without knowing details; and always try to help him find a home in time and space.

Wherever he goes he tends to make ad hoc enemies; but also there is a mysterious enemy pursuing him implacably every when: someone from his own original time, probably. So, even if the secret is out by the fifty-second episode, it is not the whole truth. Shall we say:

The Second Secret of Dr Who: The authorities of his own (or some other future) time are not concerned merely with the theft of an obsolete machine; they are seriously concerned to prevent his monkeying with time, because his secret intention, when he finds his ideal past, is to destroy or nullify the future.

If ever we get this far into Dr Who's secret, we might as well pay a visit to his original time. But this is way ahead for us too. Meanwhile, proliferate stories.

Sydney Newman, when presented with a copy of Webber's document, made a number of handwritten annotations to it, indicating that he was less than happy with some of these suggestions for the Doctor's character. Beside the section headed 'The Secret of Dr Who' he wrote:

Don't like this at all. Dr Who will become a kind of father figure – I don't want him to be a reactionary.

Beside 'The Second Secret of Dr Who' he commented simply:

Nuts!

Newman's idea for the character was that he should be an old man who, although grumpy and partly senile, would have a heart of gold; and who, far from hating scientists and inventors, would regard 'science, applied and theoretical, as being as natural as eating.'

The next version of the format document, dated 15 May 1963, contained the following revised description of the Doctor's character and of his relationship with his companions (one of whom was to have been called Cliff):

DR WHO

About 650, a frail old man lost in space and time. They give him this name because they don't know who he is. He seems not to remember where he comes from, but he has flashes of garbled memory which indicated that he was involved in a galactic war, and still fears pursuit by some undefined enemy. He is suspicious of the other three, and capable of sudden malignance. They want to help him find himself, but Cliff never quite trusts him.

All the other suggestions, including the 'Secrets of Dr Who' had by this point been dropped.

The character was further refined over the following weeks. The finalised version of the format document, produced by story editor David Whitaker around early July 1963 and sent out to freelance writers to invite them to submit ideas to the series, contained the following description:

DOCTOR WHO:

A name given to him by his two unwilling fellow travellers, Barbara Wright and Ian Chesterton, simply because they don't know who he is and he is happy to extend the mystery surrounding him. They do know that he is a Doctor of Science and that he is over sixty. He is frail-looking but wiry and tough like an old turkey and this latter is amply demonstrated whenever he is forced to run away from danger. His watery blue eyes are continually looking around in bewilderment and occasionally suspicion clouds his face when he assumes his decisions are being opposed by his earthly 'passengers'. He can be enormously cunning once he feels he is being conspired against and he sometimes acts with impulse more than reasoned intelligence. He can be quite considerate and wise and he responds to intelligence eagerly. His forgetfulness and vagueness alternate with flashes of brilliant thought and deduction. He has escaped from the 50th Century because he has found life at that time to be unpleasant and he is searching for another existence into which he can settle. Insofar as his operation of the 'ship' is concerned he is much like the average driver of a motor car in that he is its master when it works properly and its bewildered slave when it is temperamental. Because he is somewhat pathetic, his grand-daughter and the other two continually try to help him find 'home' but they are never sure of his motives.

It was during July 1963 that William Hartnell was cast as the Doctor. Unlike some of his successors, he had little initial input into the development of the character, being content to be guided by the requirements of the scripts and by the wishes of his producer and directors. He did however recall in a later interview that he considered the Doctor to be 'too bad tempered' as depicted in the series' untransmitted pilot episode, and that he told the production team as much. Sydney Newman also disliked the rather arrogant, supercilious Doctor of the pilot, feeling that he was not 'funny' or 'cute' enough, and asked that the character be softened in the remount for transmission.

The Doctor's costume was also changed between the pilot and the remount, from a plain dark suit and tie to a more eccentric outfit with a high wing collar and cravat. These formal, Edwardian-style clothes, together with the wig of long white hair that Hartnell was asked to wear for the role, helped to set the Doctor apart from the norm of paternal, lab-coated boffins who had been a stock feature of children's adventure serials in the past. Even more innovative was the fact that he was as an alien time traveller from an advanced civilisation. While it was hardly unexpected for a science fiction series to involve extraterrestrial life-forms, to have an alien as the central figure was a very novel idea indeed. This aspect of the Doctor's background was first made clear to viewers in the following speech that he delivered in the first transmitted episode, *An Unearthly Child*:

'Have you ever thought what it's like to be wanderers in the fourth dimension? Have you? To be exiles? Susan and I are cut off from our own planet, without friends or protection. But one day we shall get back. Yes, one day, one day.'

This is one of the few references ever made to the Doctor's desire, as mooted in the early format documents, to return 'home'. His principal motivation in the transmitted stories seems to be, rather, to explore the universe and to see its many wonders. Whenever his 'ship', the TARDIS, materialises in a new location, he is always eager to venture outside and find out what fresh mysteries and wonders lie in store. This passion for discovery appears to be, at times, almost a compulsion; in the opening episode of the second story, *The Mutants* (sometimes referred to as *The Daleks* to avoid confusion with the Third Doctor story of the same title), it leads him to play a deception on his three travelling companions – Ian, Barbara and his granddaughter Susan – so that they will be forced to go along with his plan to visit a mysterious city that he has seen in the distance.

Plainly he likes to get his own way; and his confidence in his own abilities is such that it occasionally borders on the arrogance of the untransmitted pilot. 'The mind will always triumph,' he announces at one point during *The Mutants*. 'With me to lead them, the Thals are bound to succeed'. In the early part of the first season, he can indeed be regarded more as an anti-hero than as an out-and-out hero. While he is essentially a kindly, sentimental, compassionate character, and while he certainly mellows quite considerably with the passage of time, he can often be brusque and irritable, and at times even violent – displaying perhaps the flashes of 'sudden malignance' described in early versions of the series' format document.

This Doctor is not one who sees himself as some sort of crusader against universal evil, nor one who goes looking for trouble. Certainly he is a humane man, who regards life in all its various forms as something to be valued and respected and who consistently sides with the wronged and the oppressed against the forces of tyranny and evil; but he does not actively court confrontation and conflict. His concern for the safety of himself and Susan, and later for that of his human travelling companions, means that he is quite content on occasion to withdraw from a dangerous situation and let discretion be the better part of valour.

Nor does he seek to stand out from the crowd; on the contrary, he prefers to remain in the background and keep a low profile. Whether he be on an alien planet like Marinus or Xeros or on Earth in a historical period such as the French Revolution or the American Wild West era, he always endeavours to assimilate the local customs and win the acceptance of the indigenous population. He is, in short, an observer rather than an active participant – unless forced by circumstances to become involved.

The necessity for the Doctor to remain an observer arose largely out of the attitude that producer Verity Lambert and story editor David Whitaker took towards the concept of time travel. This was set out by Whitaker in a reply of 1 May 1964 to a letter received from a viewer, Mr R Adams of Quinton, Birmingham:

> Undoubtedly one must look at time as a roadway going uphill and down the other side. You and I are in the position of walking along that road, whereas Doctor Who is in the position of being placed on top of the hill. He can look backward and he can look forward, in fact the whole pattern of the road is laid out for him. But you will appreciate of course that he cannot interfere with that road in any way whatsoever. He cannot divert it, improve it or destroy it. The basis of time travelling is that all things that happen are fixed and unalterable, otherwise of course the whole structure of existence would be thrown into unutterable confusion and the purpose of life itself would be destroyed. Doctor Who is an observer. What we are concerned with is that history, like justice, is not only done but can be seen to be done. Where we are allowed to use fiction, of course, is that we allow the Doctor and his friends to interfere in the personal histories of certain people from the past. We can get away with this provided they are not formally established as historical characters. We cannot tell Nelson how to win at the Battle of the Nile because no viewer would accept such a hypothesis.

However, we can influence one Captain on board a minor ship in Napoleon's armada.

As far as going into the future, learning facts, and returning to relay them, I am not sure that society is prepared to accept something until it is ready for it. There have been many long-sighted predictions in the world which have been ignored. Much of science fiction as written in the twenties and thirties is now established scientific fact today; such as space travel, for example; and H G Wells in *The War of the Worlds* came very near to future truths.

This rationale of time travel came to the fore on a number of occasions during the series' first season, most notably in *The Aztecs* when Barbara was seen to discover the futility of attempting to overturn the Aztecs' tradition of human sacrifice. Dennis Spooner, when he took over from David Whitaker as story editor, adopted a rather more flexible approach, indicating in his story *The Time Meddler* that the Doctor's opposition to changing established history was a matter of personal policy rather than a belief that to do so was impossible. The whole concept of the Monk character introduced in that story depended upon the fact that history could indeed be altered and redirected onto a new course. Even under this more flexible regime, however, it remained the case that the Doctor was fiercely opposed to such meddling, as evidenced in his attitude towards the Monk – who, apart from Susan, was the only other character from the Doctor's own planet to be seen during this era of *Doctor Who*.

Further evidence of David Whitaker's philosophy – which was of particular importance in the early development of the Doctor's character – can be gleaned from the following essay, entitled 'Who is Dr Who?', written for the *Dr Who Annual* published in 1965:

After Sir Isaac Newton came Dr Albert Einstein. After Einstein came Dr Who. His is the master-mind that spans all spatial infinity and all temporal eternity in his strange small ship, the TARDIS.

No one knows where he came from. He is human in shape and speech and manner. He appears to be old and feeble and at the same time young and strong and active, as though the normal processes of ageing had passed him by.

Inclined to be absent-minded and forgetful, he is also very much subject to fits of impatience whenever his will is thwarted and whenever his ideas are doubted. He likes his own way all the time and can sulk like any baby when he doesn't get it. He is, after all, a citizen of all Space and Time and that must make a man feel there's nothing much he doesn't know.

He is mostly very gentle and kind-hearted and he has the utmost respect for life of any kind, small and feeble or monstrous and mighty. He has seen more specimens of living creatures than any other person in the history of all the worlds and his heart is big enough to respect every one of the countless forms life has taken in all the ages and all the worlds.

A planet in our galaxy would seem to have been his original home, but he has journeyed so many millions of miles and covered so many millions of years back into the past and forward into the future, that perhaps even the good Doctor himself does not much remember his origins ...

The TARDIS holds within itself many marvellous inventions which would be scientific miracles in many of the spheres Dr Who has visited. To him, they are commonplace tools and instruments, methods of doing what he wants to do.

Headlong he passes, in his TARDIS, through all of Space and Time. Where is he going? What is his objective? What goal draws him on through the endless spheres, the millions of ages? No one knows. Perhaps he himself has long forgotten, so distant, in our years, is the time when he first set out on his odyssey. Are his voyages haphazard and merely satisfying the urge to travel everywhere and see everything, or is he seeking something definite? Again, no one knows.

Ceaselessly and restlessly he moves on, along the infinite strands of energy that criss-cross all Space-Time. There is the deep and always unsatisfied curiosity of the scientist in him. There is the love of all life which fights against its surroundings.

Strange as his many adventures and experiences have been, how strange will be that time and place, no matter how far away or how distant in time, that point in Infinity-Eternity when, at long last, Dr Who will reach his final goal and find that for which he is searching.

Mysterious and other-worldly though his origins may be, the Doctor's physical capabilities appear to be not much greater than those of a human being from Earth. He is actually rather frail, suffering all the aches and pains of old age, and often carries a walking stick given to him by Kublai Khan, a fellow sufferer, in the first season story *Marco Polo*. Mentally, however, his powers are somewhat superior. He delights in his ability to outwit his opponents, such as when, in *The Space Museum*, the Morok Governor of the museum tries to interrogate him with a mind-reading device and he projects an extraordinary series of false images onto the screen. He can even sense sometimes when an evil presence is nearby, as he indicates in *The War Machines*; and it is revealed in *The Sensorites* that he has a certain degree of telepathic ability.

At times, it must be said, his successes appear to result more from luck than from good judgment. He tends to muddle his way through situations, and often has a slightly bewildered air about him. If he seems a near-charlatan in some of his earlier stories, then in some of the later ones he could even be thought slightly senile, as Ian actually speculates in *The Rescue*. Indeed, there are aspects of his behaviour – such as his occasional bursts of almost hysterical laughter – that appear positively manic.

This trait of endearingly absent-minded bumbling was largely William Hartnell's contribution to the role. Hartnell regarded *Doctor Who* as a children's programme first and foremost, and was always looking for ways of making the Doctor more appealing to that audience. It was he who, for instance, came up with the idea that the Doctor should often get his companion Ian's surname wrong: so instead of saying 'Chesterton' he would call him anything from 'Chesserman' (in *The Mutants*) to 'Chatterton' (when remembering him in *The Massacre of St Bartholomew's Eve*). It was he, too, who gave the Doctor his indignant 'humphs!' and his frequent high-pitched chuckles. As his widow Heather later recalled, 'I know Bill would have liked to have put more comedy into the part, and to a degree he did try with those exasperated little coughs and splutters.'

Hartnell saw the Doctor as a wizard-like figure rather than a scientist. He was convinced that he knew better than the series' writers how the character should be played, and would actively resist the inclusion of obscure or technical terms in his dialogue. Writer Donald Cotton recalled sharing a taxi with him on one occasion and being asked if, instead of writing lines for the Doctor, he could in future simply give an indication of what he wanted the character to say and leave it to the actor to come up with the actual words.

Part of Hartnell's motivation in this regard may well have been to lessen the very considerable burden of dialogue that he, as the series' lead, had to carry in each episode. He was by this stage of his career finding it increasingly difficult to memorise his lines, and he lacked the advantage afforded to actors in later years of being able to stop for frequent retakes (video editing being a technically difficult and expensive process to achieve in the mid-Sixties.) There is however no doubt that he had very strong views as to how the Doctor should speak and behave, and that much of the character's on-screen appeal, which made him a hero to millions of children worldwide, was down to the actor's own skilful and engaging performance.

Aside from the aforementioned mellowing, and the refinements of interpretation made by Hartnell in his performance, no radical changes in the characterisation of the Doctor occurred during the three years of the actor's tenure in the role. The description given in the format guide sent out to writers towards the end of the first Doctor's era was much the same as that in the one prepared by David Whitaker in 1963 – and in some respects harked back to the even earlier C E Webber version. It read as follows:

DR WHO

A name given by the first travelling companions because neither he nor they knew who he was. He is 650 years old. Frail but wiry and tough like an old turkey – this is demonstrated when he is forced to run from danger. He has an air of bewilderment and occasionally a look of utter malevolence clouds his face as he suspects his travelling companions of being part of some giant conspiracy he cannot understand. He has flashes of garbled memory which indicate he was involved in a galactic war and still fears some undefined enemy. Because he is somewhat 'pathetic' his friends continually try to help him but are now and again bewildered by his mental agility and superior intellect – they are never quite sure of his 'motives' in dealing with a situation. He is vague – inquisitive. Has an interest in people and problems to do with people and civilizations. His ability to deal with highly complex problems, both scientific and menacing, comes, not really from intellect, but from experience and great age.

He and his two companions must be the pivot around which any story revolves – their relationship in the different ways they deal with the situation.

He is fond, in an uncle's way, of his two companions. Ben he finds somewhat meddlesome, and irritating in the expressions he uses (Cockney), amusing because of his cautiousness.

Polly represents much that he finds annoying in modern girl – her flippancy, independence and her impulsiveness. Nevertheless he feels protective towards her.

Even in his last story, *The Tenth Planet*, the Doctor has lost none of his restlessness and curiosity, ushering his companions out of the TARDIS to investigate even though he knows that they have arrived in 'the coldest place on Earth' – Antarctica. Nor has his moral courage diminished, as is evident from the outrage he expresses at the Cybermen's unfeeling nature: 'Love, pride, hate, fear! Have you no emotions, sir?' However, when he collapses part-way through the story, apparently exhausted, and later speculates that his old body might be 'wearing a bit thin', it becomes clear that something very unusual is happening. This is confirmed in the closing moments of the final episode, when he demonstrates perhaps his most remarkable and unexpected ability of all and undergoes a complete transformation of his physical appearance …

Establishing the Myth

Every era of *Doctor Who* brings new elements to the series' developing mythology. Story after story, new facts are invented by the programme's writers and added to what is already known of the Doctor's universe. Some new pieces of this ever-growing jigsaw puzzle interlock neatly with what has gone before, while others fit so poorly that the viewer is forced to start rebuilding the picture from scratch. Many hard-core *Doctor Who* fans expend great amounts of time and energy trying to find an order that gives all the seemingly contradictory facts and storylines some kind of logical continuity.

The three most enduring elements of *Doctor Who*'s mythology were all introduced within the space of the first two stories. These were the TARDIS, the Daleks and of course the good Doctor himself.

Of the three, the Doctor is by far the most mysterious. There are however a number of tantalising clues given during the first Doctor's era which reveal some insights into the time traveller's background.

One of the most enigmatic aspects of the character is his name. Susan refers to him as 'Grandfather' or occasionally, when speaking to others, as 'the Doctor'. When Ian, one of Susan's teachers at Coal Hill School, addresses him as 'Doctor Foreman' in *100,000 BC*, the Doctor's brow creases as he mutters 'Eh? Doctor who? What's he talking about?', leaving little doubt that this is not his name – Susan has apparently taken the surname Foreman for the purposes of the school records, presumably because 'I M Foreman' is the name on the doors of the junkyard where the TARDIS stands. The only instance of the Doctor being called 'Doctor Who' is in *The War Machines*, where the computer WOTAN and its controlled human slaves use the term; although, in *The Gunfighters*, when Bat Masterson asks him 'Doctor who?', the Doctor does respond 'Yes, quite right!'

In *The Dalek Invasion of Earth*, the Doctor berates the human resistance fighter Tyler for calling him 'Doc': 'I prefer "Doctor",' he explains to the weary rebel. The Doctor also tells his companion Steven not to use this diminutive form, but it takes the astronaut slightly longer to get used to the idea.

The term 'Doctor' does not denote a medical qualification. In *100,000 BC*, he says, 'I'm not a Doctor of medicine'; in *Marco Polo* he tells Kublai Khan the same thing; in *The Aztecs*, he corrects the assumption that he is a medical man by explaining that he is 'a scientist and an engineer – a builder of things, not a healer'; and in *The Rescue* he tells Ian, after giving him a cursory medical examination, 'It's a pity I didn't get that degree, isn't it?'

Equally mysterious is the character's background. First of all there is his grand-daughter, Susan. There is little doubt that she is indeed his grand-daughter, and that this is not simply an unusual term of affection. In *Inside the Spaceship* he refers to himself as being Susan's grandfather and in *The Sensorites* he again clearly states that she is his own grand-child. He also demonstrates obvious familial affection for the girl. What is never explained is the whereabouts of the Doctor's own son or daughter – as, if he has a grand-daughter, he must have had at least one child of his own. This of course assumes that his race reproduces in the same way as ours, but there is never any suggestion to the contrary. The Doctor's decision to leave Susan on Earth with David Campbell at the end of *The Dalek Invasion of Earth* could otherwise seem rather thoughtless; or, at any rate, could leave David in for a shock if he and Susan ever decided to have children!

What is known for sure is that the Doctor and Susan are not from Earth. 'Susan and I are cut off from our own planet, without friends or protection,' the Doctor tells Ian and Barbara in *100,000 BC*. Susan adds that she was 'born in another time, another world'; and in *Marco Polo*, when asked how far away her home is, she says that it is 'as far as a night star'. In *The Sensorites*, she confirms: 'Grandfather and I don't come from Earth. It's ages since we've seen our planet. It's quite like Earth, but at night the sky is a burnt orange, and the leaves on the trees are bright silver.' At the end of the same story, she asks the Doctor when they will return to their own planet, and her tells her, 'I don't know, my dear, this old ship of mine seems to be an aimless thing.'

There are other pointers to their alien origins, too, like the Doctor not knowing what cricket is when the TARDIS materialises in the middle of a Test Match at the Oval in *The Daleks' Master Plan*. In *The Mutants*, he states, 'I was once a pioneer amongst my own people'; and, again, in *The Daleks' Master Plan*, he describes himself as 'a citizen of the universe – and a gentleman to boot!' In *The Rescue*, Barbara tells Vicki that the Doctor is 'from a different age, a different planet altogether.'

This is about all we ever learn of the origins of the Doctor and Susan, although Carole Ann Ford (who played Susan) once revealed that the cast had developed their own ideas as to why the pair were travelling about as they were. They had postulated that their own planet had undergone some violent natural catastrophe, like an earthquake or a volcano, and that they had fled in order to survive. No reference was made to this in the televised stories, however, and in fact it was arguably contradicted by the Doctor's meeting with another of his race – the Monk in *The Time Meddler*. The Monk, like the Doctor, is a renegade in search of excitement – but in his case the excitement is derived not from exploring the universe and seeing its wonders but from interfering with the course of history for the sake of his own amusement. The Monk crosses paths with the Doctor once more in *The Daleks' Master Plan*, and is still meddling and interfering; but no other members of the Doctor's race appear or are mentioned during the era of the first Doctor.

At the start of the series, the Doctor and Susan have been living in 20th Century England for five months, and Susan is distraught at the prospect of having to leave. The suggestion is that she and her grandfather have previously led a very unsettled, nomadic life to which she has little wish to return. In *Marco Polo*, she says 'One day we'll know all the mysteries of the skies, and we'll stop our wanderings.' During the course of the transmitted stories, details of a number of their earlier adventures are revealed. These include a visit to the planet Quinnis in the fourth universe, where they nearly lost the TARDIS (this was four or five journeys prior to *Inside The Spaceship*); a meeting with Gilbert and Sullivan (from whom the Doctor acquired the coat borrowed by Ian at the end of *Inside the Spaceship*); witnessing the metal seas of Venus (as mentioned by Susan in *Marco Polo*); and a trip to the planet Esto, where the plants communicate by thought transference (*The Sensorites*).

The Doctor has met Pyrrho, the inventor of scepticism (*The Keys of Marinus*); travelled to Henry VIII's court, where he threw a parson's nose at the King in order to be sent to the Tower of London and thereby regain the TARDIS (*The Sensorites*); and encountered Beau Brummell ('He always said I looked better in a cloak.') (*The Sensorites*). He claims to have taught a boxer (or possibly wrestler) called the Mountain Mauler of Montana (*The Romans*) and seems to be well-known in contemporary London, being accepted without question by senior civil servant Sir Charles Summer and by the scientific community working on the WOTAN project (*The War Machines*). It can also be surmised that he has previously visited Earth at the time of the French Revolution, as Susan asserts in *The Reign of Terror* that this is his favourite period in the planet's history – a fact that might explain her own desire in *100,000 BC* to borrow a book on the subject from Barbara, and her subsequent assertion that details in it are incorrect.

Despite his alien origins, the Doctor seems to have a physiology very much akin to that of a man from Earth. In *Inside the Spaceship*, he cuts his head when thrown to the floor of the TARDIS and, although the viewer never actually sees any blood or (this being the era of black and white TV) what colour it is, there are no comments of surprise from Barbara when she dresses the wound. In *The Mutants*, the Doctor appears to be at least as susceptible as his companions to radiation sickness, if not more so. In *The Sensorites*, he is attacked by an unseen assailant and knocked unconscious by a blow above his heart, suggesting that his internal organs are akin to a human's, too. His respiration seems to act in the same way as ours – he is quickly overcome by fumes in a burning farmhouse in *The Reign of Terror* and even dislikes London's night air, judging from his protective handkerchief and the cough he gives the first time he is seen in *100,000 BC*. Of course, the cough could be the result of smoking too much, as later in the same story he produces a pipe and matches; but as he is never again seen to smoke after he loses these in the Stone Age, perhaps it is not a regular habit.

In *The War Machines*, the character Professor Brett speaks of the Doctor's brain as being 'human', and in *The Sensorites* the Doctor actually refers to himself and his companions as 'we humans' when speaking of the difference between their eyes and those of cats. Similarly, in *The Savages*, he tells a guard harassing a defenceless Savage: 'They are men; human beings, like you and me.' In this context however he is clearly using the term 'human' as a figure of speech, or as shorthand for 'humanoid', rather than as a reference to a native of the planet Earth.

The Doctor appears to be elderly, and all the evidence is that this is exactly what he is. He has bad eyesight, needing the use of either pince-nez glasses or a monocle for close-up work. He also tires quickly, needs sleep and rest in order to recover and uses a walking stick to aid his progress. He even faints on several occasions. He complains of rheumatism in *Marco Polo*, and again in *The Space Museum* when he is subjected to the Moroks' freezing process. He tells Ian that he always gets rheumatism when cold, and yet also comments that throughout the freezing process his mind stayed active and alert – a clear difference between himself and his human companion.

If the Doctor's body seems weak and frail, then his mind is anything but. He displays an enormous intellect and a great wealth of knowledge on a wide range of different subjects. In *The Sensorites*, for example, he can reel off from memory the melting points of steel and molybdenum, and knows not only that the antidote to atropine poison is caffeine citrate but also how to make it. In *The Ark*, he even concocts a cure for the common cold virus.

He works out how to operate a complicated mechanism to escape from a Dalek cell in *The Dalek Invasion of Earth*, and frequently bamboozles his opponents with his wit and charm, always leaving himself with the advantage. Despite all this, there is no mention at all of the Doctor's age or of any special alien powers – unless one includes the implication in *The Sensorites* that he and Susan are both partially telepathic.

In fact the first suggestion of any special abilities comes in *The Web Planet*, when the Doctor uses his large, blue-stoned ring to open the TARDIS doors. 'This ring isn't merely decorative,' he explains to Ian. In *The Daleks' Master Plan*, he puts the ring to a similar purpose to overcome the Monk's jamming of the TARDIS lock mechanism. Later, in *The War Machines*, he uses it to help him hypnotise Dodo, leading one to believe that he has some aptitude in that direction.

Of course, the most startling ability of all is revealed right at the end of the first Doctor's era, when at the conclusion of *The Tenth Planet,* he collapses on the floor of the TARDIS and undergoes a complete change of physical appearance – a feat no human could possibly achieve. The result of this remarkable metamorphosis is the second Doctor, who subsequently comments that without the TARDIS, he couldn't have survived the process.

Like the Doctor, the TARDIS keeps many of its secrets to itself, but during the first Doctor's era viewers do learn a surprising amount about its properties, size and facilities.

The ship's name is revealed in the first episode of *100,000 BC* to be an acronym made up by Susan from the initials of Time And Relative Dimension In Space – a term that apparently describes the craft and what it does. The inference is that this is the only 'TARDIS' (and the name does not enter into regular use until the fifth story, *The Keys of Marinus*, the more usual appellation being simply 'the ship'). Nothing is said in *The Time Meddler* to contradict this, as the Monk's vessel is referred to both by the Doctor and by the Monk as a time-ship, and not as a TARDIS – it is the Doctor's companions Vicki and Stephen who assume that its name is the same. In *The Daleks' Master Plan*, however, the Doctor does himself refer to the Monk's machine as a TARDIS.

The fact that the ship is dimensionally transcendental – bigger inside than out – is established from the outset, but exactly how this paradox is achieved is left to the viewer's imagination.

Also quickly established is the fact that the police box exterior is simply a disguise. When the travellers leave the ship to explore the Stone Age in *100,000 BC*, the Doctor and Susan both remark upon its failure to change its appearance. Susan later explains that the ship's exterior should change to suit its surroundings wherever it lands. It has in the past been an ionic column and a sedan chair, amongst other things. The implication is that this is the first time this particular malfunction has occurred – the TARDIS had disguised itself as a police box as this was a commonplace sight in London in 1963.

The precise details of the ship's interior lay-out and of its instrument panels and contents vary from story to story, suggesting that its dimensions may be in some way unstable.

Inside the Spaceship reveals more of its secrets than perhaps any other story. From the main control room – which is the first room one enters from the external doors – there is a connecting lobby area, with at least two adjoining bedrooms. In the main control room, one wall is taken up with the fault locator – a bank of computers monitoring and checking the operation of the ship. Each component has a reference number, and the numbers of failed components appear on a read-out (K7, for example, is the fluid link).

The centre of the room is dominated by a hexagonal control console, at the apex of which is a transparent, instrument-filled column, which rises and falls during flight (and also rotates on occasion, usually with the ship is at rest). The heart of the TARDIS is held under the column, and when the column rises it shows the extent of the power thrust. Should the column come all the way out, then the power would escape; and the Doctor comments that even if a small fraction of it were to escape, then it would blow the occupants to atoms. Exactly what the power is and how it is contained is unclear, however.

The control room also has a monitor screen, which gives a black and white picture – the Doctor explains in *The Keys of Marinus* that he has a colour screen but that it is temporarily out of order. In *Planet of Giants*, the screen explodes, requiring a hasty – and unseen – replacement for the following adventure. There are also chairs, ornaments and other bits and pieces dotted about the control room.

In the lobby there is a food machine which, as revealed in *The Mutants*, can supply any food in any combination in a form that looks like a small, foil-wrapped chocolate bar. The machine also supplies water that comes sealed in a plastic bag (although in *The Space Museum* it arrives in a glass tumbler, which Vicki promptly breaks). The bedrooms have contoured sleeping couches, which swing down from the walls; and the presence of six buttons on a wall panel suggests that there are either six beds, or three beds that each have one button to lower and one to raise them.

In *The Web Planet*, the viewer sees for the first time the 'fourth wall' of the TARDIS control room. It seems to house two alcove-like spaces full of ornaments and clutter; and it is here that the Doctor operates the doors by passing his ring in front of a light on one of the pieces of equipment. Also in *The Web Planet*, the central console is seen to spin round, and the TARDIS doors open and close apparently of their own volition. When an inquisitive Zarbi ventures inside, it is repelled by some unknown force.

In *Inside the Spaceship*, Susan remarks upon the fact that the TARDIS is silent, implying that this is highly unusual and that it is normally active all the time. There is a faint vibration inside when it is in flight and this ceases when it arrives at its destination. As Ian and Barbara discover in *100,000 BC*, the exterior vibrates slightly while at rest. Perhaps the most intriguing suggestion is that TARDIS may actually be sentient. This comes in *Inside the Spaceship* when the ship itself attempts to warn the Doctor of the peril into which he has inadvertently placed himself and his fellow travellers. Although the Doctor is initially adamant that the machine cannot think for itself, he is later forced to consider the possibility that it might.

One area of initial inconsistency in the depiction of the TARDIS concerns the noise it makes on leaving one location and arriving in another. When it departs from London in the first episode of *100,000 BC*, a strident roaring is heard inside the control room. This gives way to a raucous cacophony during flight and fades out altogether on arrival in the Stone Age. When the ship dematerialises again at the end of the story, the roaring is heard outside but there is no subsequent materialisation noise inside – just the tail end of the dematerialisation whine, as before. In line with this, when the Doctor sets the controls to dematerialise in the first episode of *The Mutants*, the initial phase of the noise is heard inside (although the take off is subsequently aborted due to an apparent malfunction). The dematerialisation noise is also heard outside the ship at the end of this story. At the beginning of *The Keys of Marinus*, *The Reign of Terror*, *Planet of Giants* and *The Dalek Invasion of Earth*, however, no noise is heard outside when the TARDIS materialises; and its dematerialisation is also silent at the end of *The Keys of Marinus* and *Planet of Giants*. (No dematerialisation occurs at the end of *The Reign of Terror*). It is not until the end of *The Dalek Invasion of Earth* that a fairly consistent pattern emerges whereby the roaring noise is heard both inside and outside the ship, both when it materialises and when it dematerialises.

Amongst the other titbits of information revealed about the TARDIS during the first Doctor's era are: that it is impossible for the ship to crash (*Inside the Spaceship*); that it has a defence mechanism (*Inside the Spaceship*); that it has a memory bank to record all its journeys (*Inside the Spaceship*); that its doors should never open in flight (*Inside the Spaceship* and *Planet of Giants*); that its danger signal sounds like a fog horn or klaxon (*Inside the Spaceship* and *Planet of Giants*); that the interior is susceptible to movement of the exterior (*Inside the Spaceship*, *The Romans*, *The Web Planet*); that the outer shell is light enough to be lifted by several men and carried on a wooden cart (*Marco Polo*); that the external doors cannot be forced open from outside as this would 'disturb the field of dimensions inside the ship' (*The Sensorites*); that the lock is 'an electronic miracle' (*The Sensorites*), requires not only a key but also 'knowledge' to operate (*Marco Polo*) and has twenty-one different positions, only one them correct, so that if the wrong combination is used the whole lock fuses (*The Mutants*); that the ship can materialise inside a moving object (*The Sensorites*) and travel through solid matter (*The Rescue*); that it has some kind of loudspeaker system enabling the Doctor to address someone outside (*The Dalek Invasion of Earth*, *The Daleks' Master Plan*); and that anyone can operate the controls if properly instructed (*The Daleks*, *The Rescue* and *The Daleks' Master Plan* to name just three stories in which examples occur).

The Monk's ship is said in *The Time Meddler* to be a 'Mark Four' and to have originated some fifty years later than the Doctor's, from which it differs in that for example its control console stands on a raised dais and that it has an automatic drift control which allows it to stay suspended in space with absolute safety. When at the end of the story the Doctor removes its dimensional control, its interior dimensions contract to occupy the same space as the exterior. Components from the Monk's ship are only partly compatible with the Doctor's, however, as is demonstrated in *The Daleks' Master Plan* when the Doctor attempts to wire the Monk's directional control into his own control console and causes an explosion.

The other major element of *Doctor Who* mythology established right at the start of the first Doctor's era was the Daleks. In their first story, it is revealed that they are the mutated survivors of a civil war on the planet Skaro, which finished some 500 years beforehand when a neutron bomb was detonated. The Doctor deduces that the Daleks – then called Dals – were teachers and philosophers while the Thals, their opponents in the war, were warriors. After the bomb was dropped, both races underwent a cycle of mutation. In the Thals' case this came full circle, so that they are now a race of physically handsome humanoids, dedicated to farming and peace. The Daleks, on the other hand, retreated into their city and built machines in which to live and travel. They became the warriors.

The Thals seem now to have lost most of their technological skills – that is assuming they ever had any – although they are obviously able somehow to make the anti-radiation drugs that they give to the time travellers. The Daleks on the other hand have flourished in this respect. Their city is constructed from gleaming metal and glass, and the machines in which they live are powered by static electricity picked up from the floors. They are able to grow food and to analyse and synthesise drugs. They have cameras that can produce both moving and still pictures; vibration detectors; and a nuclear reactor that provides the power for their city.

The Daleks' casings are themselves also very advanced. They each have an eye-stalk with a dilating lens; a sucker arm that can operate machinery, open doors via a swipe mechanism and hold paper and trays with ease; and a gun that can either paralyse or kill, depending on its setting, and that is powerful enough to scorch metal.

Only once is a brief glimpse afforded of the creature inside the casing. When the Doctor and Ian remove the top of one of the machines, they hear a moist sucking sound and see a sight that brings a look of extreme distaste to both their faces. They then remove the creature from its casing, wrap it in a cloak and throw it onto the floor nearby, where a withered, claw-like appendage pushes its way into view.

Further evidence of what the creature is like can be gleaned from the fact its casing is sufficiently spacious for Ian to climb inside in its place, and from the nature of the equipment that he finds once there. He discovers that there are numerous levers and switches; and, when the eye lens has been cleared of the mud placed on it to trap the creature in the first place, he is able to see out, suggesting some sort of screen or periscope device. His voice is also synthesised into a Dalek-like grate, suggesting that the Dalek speaks aloud. Logically therefore these creatures must have limbs, eyes, a mouth (with lips and tongue, both needed to form words), vocal cords and possibly also lungs.

At the conclusion of the story, the Daleks are deactivated and left on Skaro, apparently dead. When they next appear, in *The Dalek Invasion of Earth*, the Doctor speculates that this is a million years in their past, in the 'middle period' of their history when they are a space-faring race and have invaded Earth in the 22nd Century. If this is indeed the case – and it is possible the Doctor may be mistaken – one can only presume that the planet Skaro must have undergone several rises and falls of civilisation in its history.

What is most telling is that in *The Dalek Invasion of Earth*, the Daleks have gone from being just one of a number of alien races that the Doctor encountered during the series' first season – others being the Sensorites, the brain creatures in the city of Morphoton, the Voords and the Thals – to being the most evil race in the universe. In behind-the-scenes terms, this change was of course prompted by the massive surge of popularity that the Daleks had enjoyed since their debut appearance, which required them to be developed from one-off characters into recurring villains.

In *The Dalek Invasion of Earth*, the viewer learns that the Daleks can now (or could then, depending on one's perspective) travel through space; move on non-metallic surfaces; and condition humans to work for them. They seem also for the first time to have a hierarchy, based on the colour scheme of their casings. One, possibly the captain of their space ship, has a shaded dome and alternately shaded panels on its base unit, and another, apparently the commander of the entire invasion force, has a black dome and base unit and is referred to as 'the Dalek Supreme' or, on occasion, 'the Black Dalek'. All the Daleks in this story are mounted on a wider skirt section than in *The Mutants* and have on their backs a saucer-shaped attachment, which Ian suggests could account for their greater mobility.

Also seen in this story is the Slyther – a 'pet' of the Black Dalek, used to keep guard in their mine. It is revealed that the Daleks have direct communication with each other and that they are light enough to be lifted up by several humans. In the process it is seen that they have a smooth, flat base – with no wheels – suggesting some form of hover or anti-gravity capability.

By the time of their third story, *The Chase*, the Daleks have a time machine and are able to follow the Doctor's progress through time and space in an attempt to destroy him. Then, in *The Daleks' Master Plan*, they are seen to have formed a temporary alliance with a number of other races in a plan to take over the Earth's galaxy using a powerful weapon known as the Time Destructor. When the Doctor turns this weapon against them at the end of the story, time runs backwards and their casings split open, leaving the embryonic Dalek creatures – looking something akin to star-fish – floundering on the surface of the planet Kembel.

Like *The Mutants* and *The Dalek Invasion of Earth*, *The Daleks' Master Plan* reveals more about the Daleks than is actually seen on screen. It is now clear that they are in fact one of the dominant forces in the universe, with a large and effective power base. In the light of this, it is perhaps not surprising that the Doctor keeps crossing paths with them. This, however, was to be the last of the first Doctor's battles with the creatures from Skaro, and further revelations would have to await later eras of the series' history.

Of the other creatures and aliens that appeared in *Doctor Who*'s first three years, many had the potential to develop into recurring adversaries. The Zarbi and the Menoptra from *The Web Planet*, for example, featured in stories in the *Doctor Who* annuals and in comic strips in *TV Comic*. None, though, flourished as the Daleks had done. In fact, apart from the Daleks, the Meddling Monk was the only adversary who returned for a second TV appearance during the first Doctor's era. As that era drew to a close, however, another monster race appeared that was ultimately to rival the Daleks in popularity: the Cybermen.

In *The Tenth Planet*, it is revealed that the Cybermen were originally humanoids from the planet Mondas – Earth's 'twin planet'. Aeons ago, Mondas drifted away from the solar system on a journey through space. During this journey, the inhabitants started experimenting with cybernetics and replacing their limbs and organs with machine parts. Now Mondas has returned to the solar system and is drawing energy away from the Earth. The Cybermen intend to destroy the Earth to safeguard their own planet's existence, and to take with them the occupants of a South Pole space tracking station for conversion into further Cybermen.

Like the Daleks, the Cybermen would go on to make many return appearances in later eras of *Doctor Who*'s history. It also appears that the Doctor may have encountered them prior to *The Tenth Planet*, as he knows in advance that the planet approaching the Earth will be its twin, and that the tracking station will shortly be receiving visitors.

During the era of the first Doctor, all the most important elements of *Doctor Who*'s enduring mythology were established and developed. As a basis from which to progress, it provided an almost perfect formula: a mysterious stranger, a powerful and unpredictable time machine and a race of evil killers who would stop at nothing to achieve their aims.

Production Diary

This chapter takes the form of a diary chronicling the production of *Doctor Who* during the first Doctor's era, concentrating in particular on the steps that led up to the series' BBC TV debut in 1963 and on its formative and highly turbulent first year, when it had not only to establish itself with the viewing public but also to contend with considerable hostility from certain quarters within the BBC itself. All passages reproduced from contemporary memos and correspondence are quoted verbatim, save for spelling and clarificatory changes of a minor nature. The sender and the main recipient are always identified but, for reasons of space, details of other copy recipients are generally omitted.

The story begins in the spring of 1962 when responsibility for making all the BBC's plays, series and serials rested with the Drama Department, within which a large number of staff producer/directors were employed to take charge of individual projects. The scripts, on the other hand, were the province of the Script Department, which had the task of commissioning and developing material to meet the needs not only of Drama but also of many of the other production departments.

Acting Head of Drama at this time was Norman Rutherford. He had been temporarily promoted to the post in September 1961 pending the arrival of a permanent successor to the long-serving and highly-respected Michael Barry, who had left the BBC earlier in the year. Head of the Script Department was fifty-one year old writer, producer and director Donald Wilson, who had joined the BBC in 1955 after a successful career in the film industry.

Wilson's principal staff consisted of eight script editors – each responsible for a specific area of programming – and ten writer/adaptors, supported by a team of more junior readers and researchers. The Department was always on the lookout for fresh source material for television adaptation, and in May 1960 Wilson had established the Monitoring Group, later known as the Survey Group, the objective of which was 'to cover and report on current work in other media, in order that we may keep ourselves fully informed about writing and writers likely to be useful to us here.' The media covered were radio, films, stage plays, books and commercial television. The Group reported its findings at regular Script Department meetings, and the practical pursuit of new talent was then delegated to the editor concerned.

It was around March 1962 that Eric Maschwitz, the Head of Light Entertainment for BBC TV, asked Donald Wilson to have the Survey Group prepare a report on the literary genre of science fiction, the aim being to determine whether or not this would constitute a suitable source for 'a series of single-shot adaptations.' The task was delegated by Wilson to Donald Bull, the script editor for drama, and his colleague Alice Frick; and it is to their report that *Doctor Who*'s earliest roots can be traced ...

APRIL 1962

Wednesday 25: Alice Frick sends Donald Wilson two copies of the report that she and Donald Bull have prepared. She suggests to his secretary Gwen Jones that one of them be retained for duplication and circulation with the next Survey Group minutes, and that the other be passed direct to Eric Maschwitz.

The report is three-and-a-half pages long. It describes the survey's scope as follows:

> In the time allotted, we have not been able to make more than a sample dip, but we have been greatly helped by studies of the field made by Brian Aldiss, Kingsley Amis and Edmund Crispin, which give a good idea of the range, quality and preoccupations of current SF writing. We have read some useful anthologies, representative of the best SF practitioners, and these, with some extensive previous reading, have sufficed to give us a fair view of the subject. Alice Frick has met and spoken with Brian Aldiss, who promises to make some suggestions for further reading. It remains to be seen whether this further research will qualify our present tentative conclusions.

After making the general observations that 'SF is overwhelmingly American in bulk' and 'largely a short story medium' in which 'the interest invariably lies in the activating idea and not in character drama', the report goes on to describe a number of distinct sub-genres: 'the simple adventure/thriller'; the more sophisticated type of story which 'takes delight in imaginative invention, in pursuing notions to the farthest reaches of speculation'; 'the large field of what might be called the Threat to Mankind, and Cosmic Disaster'; and finally 'satire, comic or horrific, extrapolating current social trends and techniques'. Of these sub-genres, the report identifies 'Threat and Disaster' as being the one most commonly exploited by British writers and the one most suitable for TV adaptation.

> We thought it valuable to try and discover wherein might lie the essential appeal of SF to TV audiences. So far we have little to go on except *Quatermass, Andromeda* and a couple of shows Giles Cooper did for commercial TV. These all belong to the Threat and Disaster school, the type of plot in which the whole of mankind is threatened, usually from an 'alien' source. Where the threat originates on Earth (mad scientists and all that jazz) it is still cosmic in its reach. This cosmic quality seems inherent in SF; without it, it would be trivial. Apart from the instinctive pull of such themes, the obvious appeal of these TV SF essays lies in the ironmongery – the apparatus, the magic – and in the excitement of the unexpected. *Andromeda*, which otherwise seemed to set itself out to repel, drew its total appeal from exploiting this facet, we consider. It is interesting to note that with *Andromeda*, and even with *Quatermass*, more people watched it than liked it. People aren't all that mad about SF, but it is compulsive, when properly presented.

> Audiences – we think – are as yet not interested in the mere exploitation of ideas – the 'idea as hero' aspect of SF. They must have something to latch on to. The apparatus must be attached to the current human situation, and identification must be offered with recognisable human beings.

> As a rider to the above, it is significant that SF is not itself a wildly popular branch of fiction – nothing like, for example, detective and thriller fiction. It doesn't appeal much to women and largely finds its public in the technically minded younger groups. SF is a most fruitful and exciting area of exploration – but so far has not shown itself capable of supporting a large population.

> This points to the need to use great care and judgment in shaping SF for a mass audience. It isn't an automatic winner. No doubt future audiences will get the taste and hang of SF as exciting in itself, and an entertaining way of probing speculative ideas, and the brilliant imaginings of a writer like Isaac Asimov will find a receptive place. But for the present we conclude that SF TV must be rooted in the contemporary scene, and like any other kind of drama deal with human

beings in a situation that evokes identification and sympathy.

The report goes on to conclude that 'television science fiction drama must be written not by SF writers, but by TV dramatists' and that 'the vast bulk of SF writing is by nature unsuitable for translation to TV'. It adds that Bull and Frick 'cannot recommend any existing SF stories for TV adaptation', but that 'Arthur Clarke and John Wyndham might be valuable as collaborators' on any future projects.

Friday 27: Having obtained Donald Wilson's agreement, his secretary Gwen Jones sends a copy of the report to Eric Maschwitz.

MAY 1962

Tuesday 1: Donald Bull writes to Jean LeRoy of the literary agency David Higham Associates Ltd, thanking her for sending him some science fiction stories by her client John Christopher. Bull's letter reflects the conclusions of the Survey Group report, asserting that the broad TV audience is not yet ready for 'the more fanciful flights of SF' in stories such as the author's *Christmas Roses*, but that there are 'considerable immediate opportunities ... for using John Christopher's specialised knowledge and talent in conjunction with our future schemes, possibly in collaboration with a skilled TV dramatist ...'

Monday 14: Donald Baverstock, the Assistant Controller of Programmes for BBC television, sends Eric Maschwitz a memo of thanks for letting him see the Survey Group report:

> You describe it as interesting and intelligent. I would go further and say that it seems to me exactly the kind of hard thinking over a whole vein of dramatic material that is most useful to us.
>
> I gather that Donald Bull and Alice Frick were responsible for it and I hope HSDTel will thank them.

Tuesday 15: Maschwitz forwards Baverstock's memo to Donald Wilson (HSDTel in the BBC's internal shorthand) after adding a handwritten note conveying his own 'admiring thanks'.

A few days later, following further discussion of the report, Alice Frick and Script Department colleague John Braybon are asked to prepare a follow-up, identifying some specific science fiction stories suitable for TV adaptation.

JUNE 1962

Saturday 9: The BBC transmits in its early evening slot the first of six weekly, half-hour episodes of a science fiction serial entitled *The Big Pull*, written specially for TV by Robert Gould. The story concerns an alien invasion precipitated by the return to Earth of a manned American space capsule which has passed through the Van Allen belt of deadly radioactive particles. The serial's producer/director is Terence Dudley.

Sunday 24: ABC TV, one of the ITV companies, screens an hour-long science fiction play entitled *Dumb Martian*, adapted from a story by John Wyndham, in its regular *Armchair Theatre* slot. It is presented as a prelude to a new thirteen-part anthology series, *Out of this World*, due to begin the following Saturday.

Thursday 28: A new BBC science fiction serial entitled *The Andromeda Breakthrough* – a sequel to the previous year's *A for Andromeda* – begins its run with the first of six weekly, forty-five- to fifty-minute episodes.

Saturday 30: ABC's *Out of this World* begins, becoming the first science fiction anthology series ever screened on British TV. It has been given the go-ahead by ABC's drama supervisor, Sydney Newman, who is a lifelong fan of science fiction and has previously produced a number of children's serials in that genre, including one based partly on Jules Verne's *Twenty Thousand Leagues under the Sea* for CBC in his native Canada, and the popular *Pathfinders in Space* and its two sequels for ABC. He is currently being forced to serve out the final months of his contract with ABC before leaving to join the BBC as their new Head of Drama, having accepted an invitation to do so shortly after Michael Barry's departure in the autumn of 1961.

JULY 1962

Saturday 14: *The Big Pull* finishes its run in the BBC's early evening slot.

Wednesday 25: John Braybon and Alice Frick present their report to Donald Wilson. The introduction reads:

> It is not the purpose of the comments below to suggest that a science fiction series should, or should not, be undertaken.

However, during the course of the past eight weeks, we have read some hundreds of science fiction stories; in general, they have been of the short story variety, so beloved by the current science fiction generation of authors. Included in the attached list are a number of titles each together with a brief synopsis. They have been chosen as potentially suitable for adaptation to television because they fulfil one, or all, of the following requirements:

1. They do not include Bug-Eyed Monsters.

2. The central characters are never Tin Robots (since the audience must always subconsciously say 'My goodness, there's a man in there and isn't he playing the part well')

3. They do not require large and elaborate science fiction type settings since, in our considered opinion, the presentation of the interior of a space-ship, or the surface of another planet, gives rise to exactly the same psychological blockage as the above-mentioned Robots and BEMs. (In our opinion, this has already resulted in the failure in the current ITV series, which has included *The Yellow Pill*, *Dumb Martian* and *Little Lost Robot*.)

4. They do provide an opportunity for genuine characterisation and in most cases, they ask the audience to suspend disbelief scientifically and technologically on one fact only, after which all developments follow a logical pattern.

Because of the above restrictions, we consider that two types of plot are reasonably outstanding, namely those dealing with telepaths, see *Three to Conquer* in the attached list, and those dealing with time travelling, see *Guardians of Time*. This latter one is particularly attractive as a series, since individual plots can easily be tackled by a variety of script-writers; it's the *Z Cars* of science fiction.

The stories covered by Braybon and Frick in the main body of their report are *Guardians of Time* by Poul Anderson, *Three to Conquer* by Eric Frank Russell, *Eternity Lost* by Clifford Simak, *Pictures Don't Lie* by Catherine MacLean, *No Woman Born* by C L Moore, *The Cerebrative Psittacoid* by H

Nearing Jnr and *The Ruum* by Arthur Forges. The report concludes:

> An SF serial or series is a possibility. A number of possible stories have already been tackled (with varying degrees of success) by ITV; e.g. *The Imposter*, *Dumb Martian*, *The Cold Equations*. Best bets are: *Three to Conquer* (rights are available, we're told) and *Guardians of Time*.

AUGUST 1962

Donald Wilson appoints Vincent Tilsley as Drama Script Supervisor to achieve a stronger liaison and better co-operation between the Script Department and the Drama Department.

NOVEMBER 1962

Thursday 8: A science fiction serial entitled *The Monsters* begins its run on BBC TV. Its four, forty-five- to fifty-minute weekly episodes are written by Vincent Tilsley with playwright Evelyn Frazer. The story, inspired by a *Panorama* documentary about the Loch Ness Monster, concerns the exploits of a honeymooning zoologist who sets out to investigate some reported sightings of strange creatures in a remote English lake and ends up uncovering a threat to the very survival of mankind. The serial's director is Mervyn Pinfield.

Thursday 29: The final episode of *The Monsters* is transmitted.

DECEMBER 1962

Wednesday 12: Sydney Newman finally takes up post at the BBC, beginning his five year contract as Head of Drama. The appointment of this charismatic, highly outspoken Canadian is viewed with considerable scepticism by some of the more traditional elements within the BBC, where senior posts have traditionally been the preserve of upper-class establishment types. His superiors meanwhile are looking to him to revitalize his Department's output in much the same way as he did at ABC; and this is no easy task, as he will recall in a later interview:

> 'I'll be perfectly frank. When I got to the BBC and I looked my staff over, I was really quite sick, because most of the

directors there were people whose work I just did not like. I thought it was soft and slow and had no edge. Believe me, I had a bad Christmas, because I didn't know what to do – how to change those people who were stuck in their old ways, many of them having done their first television work at Alexandra Palace in 1938! Nice guys, willing guys, but most of them were just rigid!'

JANUARY 1963

Early in the new year, Newman receives some welcome news from the BBC's Controller of Programmes:

'When I turned up early in January 1963, after the Christmas week, I was called into Kenneth Adam's office, and Kenneth said "Sydney, I've got some great news. DG" – that is Hugh Carleton Green, the Director General – "has convinced the Government to allow the BBC to do a second channel, and we're going to go on the air one year from now. So you have an increase in budget of 40 per cent!"

'Of course, that opened the door – I could then hire people whose work I liked. So I put the word around, and many of the directors and writers who had worked for me at ABC – Philip Saville, Ted Kotcheff, Peter Luke and so on – came over to join me at the BBC.'

During the course of this month, Sydney Newman disbands the BBC Children's Department. For the foreseeable future all children's drama programmes would be made by the Drama Department.

FEBRUARY 1963

Newman puts in hand some radical changes to the organisation and working methods of the Drama Department, which now becomes the Drama Group:

'When I got to the BBC and saw the whole of it, I thought "I can't control all this by myself." So I broke the Drama Group down into three separate departments – Series, Serials and Plays – and appointed to each of them a Head who would exercise the direct control and do my bidding.'

One of the most important changes initiated by Newman is the phasing out of the traditional producer/director role in favour of the production team approach already established in a number of the ITV companies but hitherto adopted only infrequently within the BBC. The producer will now be invariably an executive rather than a director and will have full artistic and financial control over a particular project. Staff or freelance directors will be brought in to handle individual programmes or episodes on a one-off basis. The other permanent member of the production team will be a relatively junior story editor, who will have responsibility for finding and working with writers to provide the scripts.

These changes, which will take place over the following three months, will render the Script Department largely obsolete, and it will consequently be abolished.

MARCH 1963

Sydney Newman discusses with Donald Baverstock, now designated Chief of Programmes for BBC1, and Joanna Spicer, the Assistant Controller (Planning) Television, the requirement for a new drama serial to fill the early Saturday evening slot between the sports round-up *Grandstand* and the pop music show *Juke Box Jury*. What is needed is something that will appeal equally well to the respective audiences of both these highly popular programmes and so bridge the gap between them. Previously the slot has been filled with a wide variety of different shows such as the science fiction serial *The Big Pull*, a Francis Durbridge thriller and the comedy antics of *The Telegoons*.

Newman has considered a number of different possibilities – including, according to his later recollection, a series about two boys in a boys' school – but eventually decided on a science fiction idea. (It is possible he may have been involved in developing a series along these lines just before he left ABC; Howard Thomas, the Managing Director of that company, will later incorrectly assert in his autobiography *With an Independent Air* that *Doctor Who* was actually conceived while Newman was working there.)

Newman outlines his idea in general terms to Baverstock and Spicer, and they react very favourably. He then asks Donald Wilson, at this point still serving as Head of the Script Department, to come up with suggestions for a suitable format for a 52-week science fiction series comprised of a number of shorter serials.

Tuesday 26: Wilson convenes a meeting in his office to discuss ideas for the proposed new series, taking as a starting point the Survey Group reports on science fiction prepared in 1962. Present are John Braybon, Alice Frick and another Script Department writer/adaptor, Cecil Edwin Webber. Webber –

generally referred to by the nickname 'Bunny' – has been on the Department's staff for some time and has previously been responsible for many successful children's dramas, including some popular adaptations of Richmal Crompton's *Just William* books.

Wednesday 27: John Mair, who as Senior Planning Assistant (I) is responsible for the allocation of studio time within the BBC's television service, sends a memo to Joanna Spicer seeking details of the proposed new series.

Friday 29: Alice Frick sends Donald Wilson a note recording the main points of the meeting held three days earlier:

> The following devices were discussed:
>
> 1. Time Machine: Donald Wilson suggested if this were used, it should be a machine not only for going forward and backwards in time, but into space, and into all kinds of matter (e.g. a drop of oil, a molecule, under the ocean, etc.)
>
> 2. Flying Saucer: Alice Frick thought this might be a more modern vehicle than a time machine, much discussed at present, and with a considerable body of literature concerning it. It would have the advantage of conveying a group of people (i.e. the regular cast of characters.)
>
> 3. Computer: Donald Wilson thought this should be avoided, since it was the *Andromeda* device.
>
> 4. Telepathy: This is an okay notion in modern science, and a good device for dealing with outer space inhabitants who have appropriated human bodies (e.g. *Three to Conquer* by Eric Frank Russell).
>
> 5. John Braybon suggested that the series should be set in the future, and that a good device would be a world body of scientific trouble-shooters, established to keep scientific experiments under control for political or humanistic reasons.
>
> Ideas:
>
> A good many possible (and probably some impracticable!) ideas for themes and content were discussed, among them

some published works – *Guardians of Time* by Poul Anderson and *Three to Conquer* by Russell.

Some recent scientific discoveries or developments whose uses are still not known nor explored were mentioned, e.g. the Laser Beam. We all thought that the use of seven or eight such 'new' ideas, one for each short serial, could make a 52-week series.

Bunny Webber brought forward the idea of the continuance of thought; the idea that great scientists of the past might continue in some form of existence and could be contacted to discover further advances they had made, ideas they might bring to current discoveries, thought, etc.

Donald Wilson introduced a discussion of human creativity, the presence in the world of the human capacity to initiate original thought, to create new concepts, ideas, etc, the immeasurable and inexplicable work and productivity of genius. This led on to a discussion of energy, the difference between scientific energy, which can be measured, and human energy, which cannot.

Format:

Donald Wilson said that the series must be based on a group of regular characters, some of whom would be employed in major roles in one limited serial, others in the next, according to the needs of the different stories. He felt this was essential to establishing a loyalty audience. He suggested that, for the time-slot, two young teenagers should be included. Alice Frick advanced the opinion that children of that age were more interested in characters who are older than themselves, in the early twenties. Braybon and Webber supported this idea. Young children could be introduced occasionally, but should not be among the regulars.

The major problems in format are, how to involve a part of a permanent group in widely differing adventures, and how to transport them believably to entirely disparate milieux.

The meeting ended with Alice Frick assigned to making this report and Bunny Webber asked to suggest a cast of viable characters, which is attached hereto.

Webber's note, headed 'Science Fiction', begins as follows:

Characters and Setup

Envisaged is a 'loyalty programme', lasting at least 52 weeks, consisting of various dramatised SF stories, linked to form a continuous serial, using basically a few characters who continue through all the stories. Thus if each story were to run six or seven episodes there would be about eight stories needed to form fifty-two weeks of overall serial.

Our basic setup with its loyalty characters must fulfil two conditions:

1. It must attract and hold the audience.

2. It must be adaptable to any SF story, so that we do not have to reject stories because they fail to fit into our setup.

Suitable characters for the five o'clock Saturday audience.

Child characters do not command the interest of children older than themselves. Young heroines do not command the interest of boys. Young heroes do command the interest of girls. Therefore, the highest coverage amongst children and teenagers is got by:

THE HANDSOME YOUNG MAN HERO (First character)

A young heroine does not command the full interest of older women; our young hero has already got the boys and girls; therefore we can consider the older woman by providing:

THE HANDSOME WELL-DRESSED HEROINE AGED ABOUT 30 (Second character)

Men are believed to form an important part of the five o'clock Saturday (post-*Grandstand*) audience. They will be interested in the young hero; and to catch them firmly we should add:

THE MATURER MAN, 35-40, WITH SOME 'CHARACTER' TWIST (Third character)

Nowadays, to satisfy grown women, Father-Figures are introduced into loyalty programmes at such a rate that TV begins to look like an Old People's Home: let us introduce them ad hoc, as our stories call for them. We shall have no child protagonists, but child characters may be introduced ad hoc, because story requires it, not to interest children.

Under the heading 'What are our three chosen characters?', Webber's note goes on to propose that the regulars should be 'the partners in a firm of scientific consultants' known as:

'THE TROUBLESHOOTERS'

Each of them is a specialist in certain fields, so that each can bring a different approach to any problem. But they are all acutely conscious of the social or human implications of any case, and if the two men sometimes become pure scientist and forget, the woman always reminds them that, finally, they are dealing with human beings. Their Headquarters or Base illustrates this dichotomy: it consists of two parts: 1. a small lab fitted with way-out equipment, including some wondrous things acquired in previous investigations and 2. an office for interviews, homely, fusty, comfortable, dustily elegant: it would not have been out of place in Holmes's Baker Street.

After a brief discussion of the series' villains, suggesting that these be created on an ad hoc basis unless a recurring adversary should happen to emerge in the development of the stories, Webber's note concludes with a section headed 'Overall Meaning of the Serial.' This echoes the reports prepared in 1962 in stressing that science fiction on TV should be much more character-based than in literature; should have some 'feminine interest' added; and should 'consider, or at least firmly raise' serious moral and philosophical questions.

APRIL 1963

Sydney Newman considers the notes by Frick and Webber, which have been passed on to him by Donald Wilson, and makes a number of handwritten annotations to them. He dislikes Frick's idea of featuring a flying saucer, expressing the view that it is 'Not based in reality – or too Sunday press.' He also summarily rejects the idea of a future team of scientific trouble-shooters, writing simply 'No' against this point in Frick's note. In the margin beside Webber's suggestions on possible characters he writes: 'Need a kid to get into trouble, make mistakes.' Concerned that the series should be partly educational, he notes that within the proposed team of scientists 'no-one has to require being taught.' He also criticises Webber's suggestions on villains as being 'corny.'

Newman's overall reaction to the ideas put forward by Wilson's team is that they are too highbrow and unimaginative, very much in the mould of old-fashioned BBC family drama from which he is keen to break away. He himself favours a format more akin to that of the *Pathfinders...* serials he produced at ABC, following in the long tradition of children's cliff-hanger adventures pioneered in the cinema and on radio and since continued on television – an area of science fiction completely overlooked in the Script Department reports of 1962, even though the BBC had itself produced a number of earlier serials in this vein, such as *Stranger from Space* (two seasons, 1951 and 1952), *The Lost Planet* (1954) and *Return to the Lost Planet* (1955).

Newman does however approve of the idea of a time-space machine, which will carry a group of contemporary characters 'backwards and forwards in time and inward and outward in space,' as he will later recall:

> All the stories were to be based on scientific and historical facts as we knew them at that time.
>
> Space also meant outer space, intergalactic travel, but again based on understood fact. So no bug-eyed monsters, which I had always thought to be the cheapest form of science fiction.
>
> Re time. How wonderful, I thought, if today's humans could find themselves on the shores of England seeing and getting mixed up with Caesar's army in 54 BC, landing to take over the country; be in burning Rome as Nero fiddled; get involved in Europe's tragic Thirty Years War; and so on.
>
> That was the scheme, so how to dress it up?'

Although content to go along with Webber's 'Handsome Young Man Hero' and 'Handsome Well-dressed Heroine', Newman insists that a young teenager be added to the regular team. And in place of Webber's 'Maturer Man', he devises the character who will become the focal point of the series: a frail and grumpy old man called the Doctor, who has stolen the time machine from his own people, an advanced civilisation on a far-distant planet.

As Newman later recalls (although no contemporary documentation exists to confirm this), he conveys these ideas in a memo to Donald Wilson.

Following the demise of the Script Department, Newman has now appointed Wilson as Head of the new Serials Department – the Department that will be responsible for making the series.

Friday 26: Drama Group administrator Ayton Whitaker replies on Donald Wilson's behalf to the memo that John Mair sent Joanna Spicer on 27 March. Noting that the new series is due to be recorded in Studio D at the BBC's Lime Grove Studios in west London, he goes on to describe the intended production and transmission dates and the requirements for special facilities such as back projection (BP):

> I understand that facilities are available for recording the Saturday serial weekly in Studio D on Fridays, starting from 5 July (Week 27), the first transmission to be in Week 31 on Saturday 27 July.

> The serials, which will in all run for 52 weeks, will average six episodes, and each serial will require one week's filming at the Television Film Studios. For the most part this filming will be confined to special effects, but artists, with therefore attendant wardrobe and make-up facilities, will be required on occasions. The first two serials are each of four episodes. Serial 1 will be recorded from Weeks 27-30 (transmitted Weeks 31-34), Serial 2 recorded Weeks 31-34 (transmitted Weeks 35-38), Serial 3 recording to start Week 35 (transmitted Week 39 onwards). A week's filming at the Television Film Studios will therefore be required in Weeks 26, 30 and 34.

> Moving and Still BP will be required in the studio on all recording days, so there should be a block booking for 52 weeks, starting on the Friday of Week 27. Inlay and overlay will also be required as a regular facility.

> The serials will cost £2,300 per episode, and an additional £500 will be needed to build the space/time machine which will be used throughout the 52 weeks.

Whitaker is informed that the Design Department should have sufficient capacity to handle the new series, provided that the work involved does not exceed 500 man-hours on the first episode and 350 man-hours on subsequent episodes.

MAY 1963

Around the beginning of May, staff producer/director Rex Tucker is asked to take charge of the series pending the appointment of a permanent producer under Sydney Newman's new production team regime. Tucker – a veteran who joined BBC radio in the thirties and transferred to TV in the fifties, specialising in children's drama and classic serials – is summoned to a meeting in Newman's office, where the format of the new series is explained to him. Also present is Richard Martin, an inexperienced young director who has just been assigned to the newly-established Serials Department after completing the internal directors' training course. It is expected that Tucker will direct the first story and that Martin will direct some of the other early episodes.

In subsequent discussions, the series is given the title *Doctor Who*. (Actor and director Hugh David, a friend of Tucker's, will later assert that it was Tucker who came up with the title. Tucker himself, however, will maintain that it was Newman.)

As the organisational changes initiated by Newman steadily reach fruition, the remains of the old Script Department are redesignated as the Television Script Unit. Bunny Webber, meanwhile, continues to be involved in *Doctor Who*'s development. Early in the month, he drafts a document headed 'General Notes on Background and Approach', intended primarily as a guide for prospective writers. It begins by setting out the basic format now established for the series:

> A series of stories linked to form a continuing serial; thus if each story ran six or seven episodes there would be about eight stories needed for fifty-two weeks of the serial. With the overall title, each episode is to have its own title. Each episode of 25 minutes will begin by repeating the closing sequence or final climax of the preceding episode; about halfway through, each episode will reach a climax, followed by blackout before the second half commences (one break).

> Each story, as far as possible, to use repeatable sets. It is expected that BP will be available. A reasonable amount of film, which will probably be mostly studio shot for special effects. Certainly writers should not hesitate to call for any special effects to achieve the element of surprise essential in these stories, even though they are not sure how it would be done technically: leave it to the Effects people. Otherwise work to a very moderate budget.

The document goes on to give a brief description of each of the series' four regular characters. Apart from the one for 'Dr Who' himself, these are:

BRIDGET (BIDDY)

A with-it girl of 15, reaching the end of her Secondary School career, eager for life, lower-than-middle class. Avoid dialect, use neutral accent laced with latest teenage slang.

MISS MCGOVERN (LOLA)

24. Mistress at Biddy's school. Timid but capable of sudden rabbit courage. Modest, with plenty of normal desires. Although she tends to be the one who gets into trouble, she is not to be guyed: she also is a loyalty character.

CLIFF

27 or 28. Master at the same school. Might be classed as ancient by teenagers except that he is physically perfect, strong and courageous, a gorgeous dish. Oddly, when brains are required, he can even be brainy, in a diffident sort of way.

Webber next summarises some of the other main aspects of the series:

QUALITY OF STORY

Evidently, Dr Who's 'machine' fulfils many of the functions of conventional science fiction gimmicks. But we are not writing science fiction. We shall provide scientific explanations too, sometimes, but we shall not bend over backwards to do so, if we decide to achieve credibility by other means. Neither are we writing fantasy: the events have got to be credible to the three ordinary people who are our main characters, and they are sharp-witted enough to spot a phoney. I think the writer's safeguard here will be, if he remembers that he is writing for an audience aged fourteen … the most difficult, critical, even sophisticated, audience there is, for TV. In brief, avoid the limitations of any label and use the best in any style or category, as it suits us, so long as it works in our medium.

Granting the startling situations, we should try to add meaning; to convey what it means to be these ordinary human beings in other times, or in far space, or in unusual physical states. We might hope to be able to answer the question: 'Besides being exciting entertainment, for 5 o'clock on a Saturday, what is worthwhile about this serial?'

DR WHO'S 'MACHINE'

When we consider what this looks like, we are in danger of either science fiction or fairytale labelling. If it is a transparent plastic bubble we are with all the lowgrade spacefiction of cartoon strip and soap-opera. If we scotch this by positing something humdrum, say, passing through some common object in the street such as a night-watchman's shelter to arrive inside a marvellous contrivance of quivering electronics, then we simply have a version of the dear old Magic Door.

Therefore, we do not see the machine at all; or rather it is visible only as an absence of visibility, a shape of nothingness (Inlaid, into surrounding picture). Dr Who has achieved this 'disappearance' by covering the outside with light-resistant paint (a recognised research project today). Thus our characters can bump into it, run their hands over its shape, partly disappear by partly entering it, and disappear entirely when the door closes behind them. It can be put into an apparently empty van. Wherever they go, so contemporary disguise has to be found for it. Many visual possibilities can be worked out. The discovery of the old man and investigation of his machine would occupy most of the first episode, which would be called:

NOTHING AT THE END OF THE LANE

The machine is unreliable, being faulty. A recurrent problem is to find spares. How to get thin gauge platinum wire in BC 1566? Moreover, Dr Who has lost his memory, so they have to learn to use it, by a process of trial and error, keeping records of knobs pressed and results (this is fuel for many a long story). After several near-calamities they institute a safeguard: one of their number is left in the machine when the others go outside, so that at the end of an agreed time, they can be fetched back into their own era. This provides a suspense element in any given danger: can they survive till the moment of recall? Attack on recaller etc.

Granted this machine, then, we require exciting episodic stories, using surprising visual effects and unusual scenery, about excursions into time, into space, or into any material state we can make feasible. Hardly any time at all is spent in the machine: we are interested in human beings.

OVERALL CONTINUITY OF STORY

Besides the machine, we have the relationship of the four characters to each other. They want to help the old man find himself; he doesn't like them; the sensible hero never trusts Dr Who; Biddy rather dislikes Miss McGovern; Lola admires Cliff ... these attitudes developed and varied as temporary characters are encountered and reacted to. The old man provides continuing elements of *Mystery*, and *Quest*.

The document continues with a more detailed discussion of the Doctor's function within the stories and proposes two 'Secrets of Dr Who'. It then concludes as follows:

The first two stories will be on the short side, four episodes each, and will not deal with time travel. The first may result from the use of a micro-reducer in the machine which makes our characters all become tiny. By the third story we could first reveal that it is a time-machine; they witness a great calamity, even possibly the destruction of the Earth, and only afterwards realize that they were far ahead in time. Or to think about Christmas: which seasonable story shall we take our characters into? Bethlehem? Was it by means of Dr Who's machine that Aladdin's palace sailed through the air? Was Merlin Dr Who? Was Cinderella's Godmother Dr Who's wife chasing him through time? Jacob Marley was Dr Who slightly tipsy, but what other tricks did he get up to that Yuletide?

On receiving a copy of this latest format document, Sydney Newman again records his reactions by making a number of handwritten annotations to it. At the end of the opening paragraph he notes that each episode should close with a 'very strong cliff-hanger.' Much of the section headed 'Quality of Story' he considers 'not clear.' He is concerned that the proposed depiction of the Doctor's time machine is 'not visual', adding that a 'tangible symbol' is needed. He is pleased with the paragraph discussing the unreliability of the time machine, but greatly dislikes the description of the Doctor's role within the stories. As before, his overall reaction is largely negative.

I don't like this much – it all reads silly and condescending. It doesn't get across the basis of teaching of educational experience – drama based upon and stemming from factual material and scientific phenomena and actual social history of past and future. Dr Who – not have a philosophical arty-science mind – he'd take science, applied and theoretical, as being as natural as eating.

Thursday 9: Owen Reed, Head of Children's Programmes for BBC Television, sends a memo to Donald Wilson strongly recommending Leonard Chase as a director for *Doctor Who?* [sic]. He points out that Chase 'has worked closely with Webber and has exactly the right flair for bold and technically adventurous "through the barrier" stuff.'

Monday 13: Ayton Whitaker circulates a memo indicating that the start of the new Saturday serial has been postponed by four weeks, and that recording will now begin on Friday 2 August.

Wednesday 15: After further discussion with colleagues involved in the project, Bunny Webber completes a revised draft of the format document. This is essentially a précis of the previous version – running to one-and-a-half pages rather than three-and-a-half – but takes Newman's comments into account. All the material under the heading 'Overall Continuity of Story', including the 'Secrets of Dr Who', has now been dropped. The young girl is no longer named Biddy; instead, Webber suggests a number of different names – Mandy, Gay, Sue, Jill, Janet and Jane – of which he appears to consider Mandy and Sue the front runners. The most significant changes of substance occur in the description of the Doctor's time machine, which now reads as follows:

THE MACHINE

Dr Who has a 'machine' which enables them to travel together through space, through time and through matter. When first seen, this machine has the appearance of a police box standing in the street, but anyone entering it is immediately inside an extensive electronic contrivance. Though it looks impressive, it is an old beat-up model which Dr Who stole when he escaped from his own galaxy in the year 5733; it is uncertain in performance and often needs repairing; moreover, Dr Who has forgotten how to work it, so they have to learn by trial and error.

The new idea for the ship's outward appearance has been suggested by Anthony Coburn, another BBC staff writer whom Donald Wilson has allocated to work on the series. Coburn has had the idea after seeing a police box while out walking near his office.

Also rather different in this version of Webber's document is the proposed outline for the first story:

THE FIRST STORY

> Mandy/Sue meets the old man wandering in fog. He takes her to a police box in street. Entering the box, she finds herself inside this large machine; directly she leaves it she is again in street outside police box. Cliff and Lola, who have been to a late meeting at the school, come across Mandy/Sue and the old man. She shows them the machine. They are all reduced in size, to about one-eighth of an inch tall, and the story develops this situation for four episodes within the school science laboratory. The next story will begin with their regaining normal size, and at once start them on another adventure.

On this occasion it is Donald Wilson who makes handwritten annotations to Webber's work. These consist mainly of minor changes of wording, although he puts a cross right through the description of the Doctor's character, indicating that he considers this in need of more extensive revision. He also chooses the name Sue for the young girl character, striking out Webber's other suggestions, and changes the heading of the paragraph about the Doctor's time machine from 'The Machine' to 'The Ship'.

Thursday 16: Another draft of the format document is produced. Again Wilson makes some handwritten annotations to it, and a further draft is typed up the same day to incorporate these changes. The document then reads as follows:

'DR WHO'

> General Notes on Background and Approach for an Exciting Adventure-Science Fiction Drama Series for Children's Saturday Viewing.

> A series of stories linked to form a continuing 52-part serial; each story will run from between 4 and 10 episodes. Each episode of 25 minutes will have its own title, will reach a

climax about halfway through, and will end with a strong cliff-hanger.

APPROACH TO THE STORIES

The series is neither fantasy nor space travel nor science fiction. The only unusual science fiction 'angle' is that four characters of today are projected into real environments based on the best factual information of situations in time, in space and in any material state we can realise in practical terms.

Using unusual exciting backgrounds, or ordinary backgrounds seen unusually, each story will have a strong informational core based on fact. Our central characters because of their 'ship' may find themselves on the shores of Britain when Caesar and his legionnaires landed in 44 BC; may find themselves in their own school laboratories but reduced to the size of a pinhead; or on Mars; or Venus; etc etc.

The series, by the use of the characters in action stories, is designed to bridge the gap between our massive audience who watch sport on Saturday afternoon and those teenagers who watch *Juke Box Jury*.

CHARACTERS

Our four basic characters:

SUE

15, working-class, still at school; a sharp intelligent girl, quick and perky. She makes mistakes, however, because of inexperience. Uses the latest teenage slang. Has a crush on Cliff and regrets that his name is the same as Cliff Richard whom she now thinks is a square.

CLIFF

27, red-brick university type, the teacher of applied science at Sue's school. Physically perfect, a gymnast, dexterous with his hands.

MISS MCGOVERN

23, a history mistress at the same school. Middle class. Timid but capable of sudden courage. Admires Cliff, resulting in undercurrents of antagonism between her and Sue.

These are the characters we know and sympathise with, the ordinary people to whom extraordinary things happen. The fourth basic character remains always something of a mystery …

DR WHO

A name given to him by his three earthly friends because neither he nor they know who he is. Dr Who is about 650 years old. Frail looking but wiry and tough like an old turkey – is amply demonstrated whenever he is forced to run from danger. His watery blue eyes are continually looking around in bewilderment and occasionally a look of utter malevolence clouds his face as he suspects his earthly friends of being part of some conspiracy. He seems not to remember where he comes from but he has flashes of garbled memory which indicate that he was involved in a galactic war and still fears pursuit by some undefined enemy. Because he is somewhat pathetic his three friends continually try to help him find his way 'home', but they are never sure of his motives.

THE SHIP

Dr Who has a 'ship' which enables them to travel together through space, through time, and through matter. When first seen, this ship has the appearance of a police telephone box standing in the street, but anyone entering it finds himself inside an extensive electronic contrivance. Though it looks impressive, it is an old beat-up model which Dr Who stole when he escaped from his own galaxy in the year 5733; it is uncertain in performance; moreover, Dr Who isn't quite sure how to work it, so they have to learn by trial and error.

FIRST STORY

The Giants

Four episodes of turbulent adventure in which proportion and size are dramatized

Leaving the secondary modern school where they work at the end of Parents Day, the applied science master, Cliff, and the history mistress, Miss McGovern, come across Sue in the fog. She asks them to help her find the home of a strange old man (Dr Who) who is lost.

To their surprise they find that his home is apparently a police box. To their further amazement they discover that its shabby exterior conceals a vast chromium and glass interior of a kind of space ship. They become locked in. Through the pressing of wrong buttons the ship convulses itself, breaking away from its moorings (no exteriors of this, please). More wrong buttons pressed and they discover that the ship has the capacity to transport them into time, space and other seemingly material worlds. In fact they get a preview of this.

The first episode ends when they find themselves in Cliff's own school laboratory. To their horror they have been reduced to the size of pinheads. 'All we have to do' says Sue 'is to get back to the ship.' Miss McGovern (somewhat hysterically) 'That's all! At our present size the door is equivalent to two miles away!'

Three more episodes follow to complete this first story in which their dreaded enemies turn out to be the other students and teachers who are of normal size and who might step on them at any moment. This adventure ends about two-thirds through the fourth episode and a new adventure begins.

Prepared by:
Donald Wilson
C E Webber
Sydney Newman

16 May 1963

Monday 20: Sydney Newman, now satisfied with the format document, sends a copy of it to Chief of Programmes Donald Baverstock with the following memo:

> This formalises on paper our intentions with respect to the new Saturday afternoon serial which is to hit the air on 24 August. As you will see, this is more or less along the lines of the discussion between you and me and Joanna Spicer some months ago.
>
> Those of us who worked on this brief, and the writers we have discussed assignments with, are very enthusiastic about it. If things go reasonably well and the right facilities can be made to work, we will have an outstanding winner.

Baverstock later tells Newman that the series is 'looking great.'

Tuesday 21: Ayton Whitaker sends John Mair a memo indicating that, owing to the previously notified four week postponement in recording of the series' first episode, the planned pre-filming at the BBC's Television Film Studios in Ealing should also be put back by four weeks. Filming for the first story should therefore take place in week commencing Saturday 20 July (Week 30 in BBC production terms).

Later the same day, Whitaker sends Mair another memo, requesting that filming for the first story now be brought forward by two weeks to week commencing 6 July as there is to be an experimental pilot episode of the series recorded on Friday 19 July. If this pilot proves successful, it will form the first transmitted episode on Saturday 24 August; if it proves unsuccessful, however, there will be two weeks remaining in which to resolve any technical problems before the previously scheduled first recording date of Friday 2 August.

Tuesday 28: Rex Tucker sends a memo to Donald Wilson expressing the view that the facilities available at Lime Grove Studio D will be inadequate for recording of such a technically complex production as *Doctor Who*.

Friday 31: Donald Wilson discusses Rex Tucker's memo of 28 May with Ian Atkins, who as Controller of Programme Services for Television has overall responsibility for the BBC's studio facilities. Ayton Whitaker is also present and later in the day produces a note of the meeting. Atkins agrees that, with its 'old fashioned lighting equipment,' Studio D is 'virtually the worst possible studio for such a project.' Other options are considered, including using either TC2 or TC5 at Television Centre which, because of their smaller size, would require recording over two days rather than one, with a concomitant increase in artists' fees. Donald Wilson decides that this is unacceptable and that the larger TC3 or TC4 should be used for the first serial – unless TC2 and TC5 can both be used together on the same day, with the artists moving between them as required. It is also agreed that Studio 2 at Riverside could be acceptable for the second serial, provided that new inlay equipment has been installed by then as anticipated.

By the end of May, *Doctor Who*'s production team has gained an additional member in the person of associate producer Mervyn Pinfield. Pinfield has worked in the BBC's television service since its earliest days in the thirties and is particularly expert in technical matters. His job will be to co-ordinate and advise on the technical aspects of *Doctor Who*'s realisation, drawing in part on his experience of directing the science fiction serial *The Monsters* the previous November.

JUNE 1963

Whilst development of the series' format has been progressing, Rex Tucker has been turning his attention to other aspects of the production. He has approached composer Tristram Cary to see if he would be willing to provide both the theme tune and the incidental music for the first serial, and has asked Hugh David if he would be interested in taking on the role of the Doctor. David however has declined, disliking the high public profile he has gained as a result of a recent stint as a regular in the Granada TV series *Knight Errant*.

Anthony Coburn has meanwhile started work on the series' second story, another four-parter, in which he proposes that the Doctor's time machine should journey back to the Stone Age. Coburn – full name James Anthony Coburn – has been on staff at the BBC ever since coming to England from his native Australia, where he worked as a butcher's assistant before turning to writing.

Tuesday 4: Donald Wilson sends Sydney Newman a full synopsis for Webber's story *The Giants*, promising that draft scripts for the first two episodes will be ready by the end of the week.

Webber's synopsis refers back to the 16 May format guide for the opening part of the first episode. It goes on to describe how in the later episodes the four travellers find themselves back in Cliff's classroom but reduced to one-sixteenth of an inch tall. A biology class is in progress and Cliff and Sue, having become separated from Lola and the Doctor, face a variety of dangers including a caterpillar, a boy carving his initials in a desk with a compass point, and a spider in a matchbox. They eventually make their way over to a microscope and position themselves under the lens, where they are spotted first by the pupils and then by the teacher.

By recording their voices onto tape and playing them back at a slower speed, so as to compensate for the change in pitch resulting from their miniaturisation, Cliff and Sue are able to communicate with the 'giants' and explain their predicament. The 'giants' and the 'minis' then co-operate in rescuing Lola, who has set out on a valiant but hopeless attempt to find Sue and Cliff. The travellers are returned to the police box just in time to avert an impending danger (which Webber suggests might be the threat of the ship being eaten by a mouse).

Friday 7: Sydney Newman briefly discusses with Donald Wilson and John Mair the problem regarding the unsuitability of Lime Grove D for recording of *Doctor Who*. It now appears that this will be the only studio available on the dates required for the first two serials. It is agreed that Mair will talk to Ian Atkins to ascertain how difficult it would be to have the facilities there adapted to make them more suitable.

Monday 10: Sydney Newman, having made a number of handwritten annotations to Bunny Webber's synopsis of *The Giants*, returns it to Donald Wilson with a memo summarising his reactions. He comments that 'the four episodes seem extremely thin on incident and character' and that Webber has 'forgotten that his human beings, even though miniscule, must have normal sized emotions.' The memo continues:

> Items involving spiders etc get us into the BEM school of science fiction which, while thrilling, is hardly practical for live television. In fact what I am afraid irritated me about the synopsis was the fact that it seemed to be conceived without much regard for the fact that this was a *live* television drama serial. The notion of the police box dwindling before the policeman's eyes until it's one-eighth of an inch in size is patently impossible without spending a tremendous amount of money.

> There are also some very good things in the synopsis, like the invention of the use of the microphone and microscope to enable our central characters to communicate with the normal size people.

> I implore you please keep the entire conception within the realms of practical live television.

(Newman's comments about 'live television' here are presumably figurative rather than literal, referring to the fact that the series is to be recorded largely continuously, as if live. *Doctor Who* has been planned from the outset as a recorded programme – a fact that Newman recognizes in earlier correspondence.)

Bunny Webber has by this time completed draft scripts for the first two episodes of *The Giants*. On the basis of these, however, Donald Wilson and Rex Tucker have decided to reject the story. This is partly because they realise that even radical reworking will fail to overcome Newman's objections (Tucker will later offer the opinion that Webber was too good a writer to 'write down to the level required') but mainly because the necessary 'giant' effects will now be impossible to achieve given that the production is to be restricted to Studio D, where amongst other problems the cameras cannot take either wide-angle or zoom lenses.

Wilson has concluded that, in view of the shortage of time now remaining before the planned recording dates, Anthony Coburn's story should be moved forward from second place to first in the running order. He has asked Coburn to adapt the first episode of his story accordingly, drawing on Webber's draft for ideas. He has also given him the task of writing in due course a replacement second story, again in four episodes.

Ayton Whitaker sends a memo to John Mair summarising the planned production dates and budgets for these first two serials. He ends with the following note headed 'Subsequent Serials':

> While the first two serials of this 52 week series of serials can be produced in Studio D, a change of studio will almost certainly be required for some of the later ones. This change should be to (in order of preference): (i) TC2 & TC5; (ii) TC3 *or* TC4; (iii) Riverside 2. We would be glad if this change could be made in time for recording the third serial.

Tuesday 11: Donald Wilson goes on leave to take a holiday in Norway.

Rex Tucker sends Ayton Whitaker a 'blocked-out schedule' for production of the first serial, starting with pre-filming for the pilot episode in week commencing 6 July and ending with recording of the fourth and final episode either in week commencing 10 August or in week commencing 17 August depending on whether or not the pilot episode has proved acceptable for transmission. In his covering memo, Tucker notes that he has taken 19 July as the optimum date for recording of the pilot episode but that if the whole schedule is shifted 'a day or two earlier or (*preferably*) later' it would not matter as there is a week in hand at the end before he is due to go on leave. He adds:

The post-recording of the special music on the video tape *after* the latter is made (a special and essential facility Donald Wilson agreed with me) prevents the pilot (1) date coming much closer to the second recording date than the fortnight which (for other reasons) I know you consider necessary.

The playback immediately following recordings is for me to brief the composer. It is essential for the pilot (1) recording and very desirable after the others.

Wednesday 12: John Mair and Ian Atkins discuss the continuing problem of *Doctor Who*'s studio allocation. It is suggested that specialist inlay equipment could be transferred from TC2 to Riverside 2 to enable the series to be made in the latter.

Thursday 13: John Mair sends a memo to Ian Atkins. He reports that Donald Baverstock is unwilling to have inlay equipment transferred from TC2 to Riverside 2 as suggested, as this would deprive the popular satirical show *That Was the Week That Was* of the facility. He also reports that the Drama Group have now agreed that the first eight episodes of *Doctor Who* can be made in Lime Grove D and that Baverstock wishes to see how this works out before deciding whether or not a move is necessary. Baverstock does wish to know, however, what the cost and other implications would be of installing specialist inlay equipment in Riverside 2; if the answers are satisfactory, he might reconsider that studio being used on a permanent basis.

Richard Levin, the Head of Television Design, sends a memo to Joanna Spicer for the attention of John Mair, protesting at the demands which the new series will place on his Department:

So far there are *no* accepted scripts for the series – at least if there are we have not seen any.

The designer allocated for the series – and I have no substitute – does not return from leave until Monday of Week 26 and I am not prepared to let him start designing until there are four accepted scripts in his hands. The first filming cannot take place within four weeks of this.

I also understand that the series requires extensive model-making and other visual effects. This cannot be undertaken under four weeks' notice and, unless other demands are withdrawn, I estimate the need would be for an additional four effects assistants and 400 sq ft of additional space.

To my mind, to embark on a series of this kind and length in these circumstances will undoubtedly put this Department in an untenable situation and, as a natural corollary, will throw Scenic Servicing Department for a complete 'burton'. This is the kind of crazy enterprise which both Departments can well do without.

Ayton Whitaker sends a memo to Sydney Newman's deputy, Assistant Head of Drama Group Norman Rutherford – Newman himself having, like Donald Wilson, gone away on leave at this point – recommending that if the series' previously-stated production requirements cannot be met, as would appear to be the case from Richard Levin's comments, then the Drama Group should make no further compromise in its attempts to meet the planned first transmission date of 24 August but should 'ask for postponement ... until such time as *we* are ready.'

By the end of the week, another major development has occurred with the arrival at Television Centre of *Doctor Who*'s permanent producer, Verity Lambert. She has been appointed to the post by Sydney Newman after his first choice, Don Taylor, turned it down. As Newman will later recall, she is exactly the kind of young, go-ahead person he wants in charge of the series:

When Donald Wilson and I discussed who might take over the responsibility for producing the show, I rejected the traditional drama types, who did the children's serials, and said that I wanted somebody, full of piss-and-vinegar, who'd be prepared to break rules in doing the show. Somebody young with a sense of 'today' – the early 'Swinging London' days.

I phoned Verity Lambert, who had been on my *Armchair Theatre* staff at ABC. She had never directed, produced, acted or written drama but, by god, she was a bright, highly intelligent, outspoken production secretary who took no nonsense and never gave any. I offered her the job and after Donald Wilson met her she joined us. I have a vague recollection that Donald Wilson at first sniffed at Verity Lambert's 'Independent' ways. Knowing both of them, I knew they would hit it off when they got to know one another better. They did.

Lambert's office is in Room 5014 on Television Centre's fifth floor (the floor allocated for use by the Drama Group), where she begins to acquaint herself with the work already carried out on the series. She has been sent in advance by Newman a copy of the format document and also a copy of a report published by ABC describing the results of a study carried out by two educationalists into children's reactions when viewing episode seven of *Pathfinders to Venus*.

Staff director Waris Hussein is also assigned to *Doctor Who* around this time to handle the second story.

Monday 17: A meeting takes place between production and servicing personnel with a view to reaching agreement over *Doctor Who*'s requirements. A two week postponement in production has now been decided upon, with initial pre-filming for the pilot episode put back to week commencing 20 July. Anthony Coburn's draft script for the first episode of serial one is now available, and those for the other three are confidently expected to be completed by 26 June. It is agreed that the series' filming, costume and make-up requirements can all be met without difficulty, both in the short term and in the long term. Although Richard Levin has specified that scenic design work for serial one cannot get underway until all four scripts are available, this should cause no difficulties provided that their completion is not delayed. To meet Levin's request for an extra four effects assistants and 400 square feet of space, however, would add approximately £40 to the cost of each episode. James Bould, the Design Manager, points out that the design and construction of the space/time machine will be particularly time consuming.

Tuesday 18: John Mair sends Joanna Spicer a memo recording the outcome of the previous day's meeting. He concludes:

> 1. It is clear … that provided the script dates are met we could handle recording on a weekly basis from Week 33 of the first two serials, carrying us up to Week 40, all in Studio D.

> 2. The question to be decided is whether to do this before the long-term studio problem has been solved. It seems unlikely that this can be done by June 26; and it seems therefore that we can either:

> > (a) Ask Head of Drama Group to accept D on a continuing basis for the present, with an assurance that we will try to provide Riverside 2 as and when possible, but no certainty that in fact it can be done.

Transmission would then start in Week 37;

(b) Postpone the start of production for, say, another six weeks, and decide the Riverside 2 issue before we launch out on a continuing basis. If we did that, transmission would not start before Week 43. We should have to fill with further repeats – e.g. *Dark Island*.

3. My own feeling is that the long-term studio basis should be settled first, and that we should do all we can to do this before June 26, or as soon thereafter as we possibly can.

Ian Atkins speaks to D M B Grubb – designated Senior Assistant, Planning, Television – who agrees to report by 26 June on the implications of specialist inlay equipment being installed in Riverside 2.

Ayton Whitaker sends a memo to Terence Cook, the Acting Drama Organiser for Television, requesting that arrangements be made for an experimental session to take place in Lime Grove D between 10.30 am and 5.30 pm on Friday 19 July. The purpose of this session is to test the viability of achieving the dematerialisation of the Doctor's ship without recourse to inlay, using the previously untried 'roll back and mix' technique of rewinding the videotape between shots and performing a mix between two separately recorded images:

In all aspects our requirements are minimal, i.e. design: a police or 'phone box, plus a little additional stock; technical requirements: two cameramen, simple lighting. We shall also require one vision mixer and one scene hand.

NB This experimental session is for technical purposes and is quite distinct from the pilot recording two weeks later.

Whitaker also sends a memo to Bill Patterson, Assistant Head of Studio Management, requesting on Rex Tucker's behalf that Noel Lidiard-White be assigned as the vision mixer for the first serial, or Rachel Blayney if he is not available.

Other preferences expressed by Tucker for the first serial are to have Crew 1 or 4 as the camera crew, Graham Sothcott as Technical Operations Manager, Jack Brummett or Jack Clayton as Sound Supervisor and, in order of preference, Sam Barclay, Gerry Millerson, Geoff Shaw or Phil Ward as Lighting Supervisor.

Thursday 20: Donald Baverstock, Joanna Spicer and John Mair meet to discuss the problems regarding the servicing of the new series.

James Mudie, the Head of Scenic Servicing for Television, sends Mair the following memo:

> The present late information/drawing/properties plot situation is so bad that I feel you should think twice before proceeding with a weekly series of this nature. If you decide to proceed and the series falls in arrears with scripts, can I have an assurance that it will be withdrawn? If you cannot give this assurance and you decide to proceed as planned, I consider you are likely to endanger the rest of the planned output.

Friday 21: Mair sends Spicer a memo informing her that since the previous day's meeting he has heard from Assistant Head of Drama Group Norman Rutherford that Baverstock has now given his agreement for the new series to be started once four scripts are available. As previously stated, this should be by 26 June. In the event of a delay, further repeats can be scheduled as a stop-gap. He also reports that he has now heard it will be a year before specialist inlay equipment can be installed in Riverside 2, and that the cost would be £5,000. He continues:

> I am frankly not very happy about the idea of starting this series without Drama knowing the continuing studio basis on which they are to operate. I suspect that unless we tell them they will instruct their script-writers – and they are struggling to get some scripts written – to write on the assumption that they can use extensive visual effects, tricks etc. For the same reason I feel we have to let them know whether additional Effects Assistants are likely to be available in the long run or not.

Monday 24: By the beginning of this week, the final member of *Doctor Who*'s production team has been appointed in the person of David Whitaker. He has spent the past six years on the staff of the recently-abolished Script Department, most recently as the assistant script editor responsible for Sunday plays, and is already fully conversant with the background to *Doctor Who*. His office, which he shares with fellow BBC story editor Barry Thomas, is in a caravan parked outside Television Centre.

Spicer sends Baverstock a memo, attaching the one of 20 June from Mudie to Mair:

This had not arrived when we had our discussion last Thursday: but it supports my statement to you that I feel we ought not to embark on this series until there are an agreed number of scripts completed and accepted for servicing requirements.

A.H.D.G.(Tel) [Assistant Head of Drama Group Norman Rutherford] informed S.P.A.(I) [Mair] after our meeting with you that you had accepted the series subject to the availability of four scripts. I hope you will agree that, before we give pre-recording facilities, these scripts must have reached the servicing departments and have been fully discussed with them and then with us.

I think the real danger is that scripts will fall behind again after this delivery of the first four. From our meeting, however, I understood that you would be prepared to drop the series after eight if things go badly.

A.C.P.S.(Tel) [Ian Atkins' assistant, Leonard Miall] has informed S.P.A.(I) that it would cost £5,000 to buy specialist inlay equipment for Riverside 2 and that the equipment would have to be installed in a room adjacent to the gallery, not in the gallery itself.

It seems definite therefore that we must inform H.S.D. (Tel) [Donald Wilson] that all the episodes which they are now planning must be written for Studio D.

Tuesday 25: Terence Cook replies to Ayton Whitaker's memo of 18 June, telling him that as 'the whole production is awaiting the arrival of four scripts, and there is a stand-still on all facilities pending this moment,' no progress can be made on arranging the requested experimental session for 19 July.

Coburn has now completed a draft script for the second episode of serial one, which he has decided to assign the working title *The Tribe of Gum*. He has given the male schoolteacher the new name Mr Chesterton and has amended the young girl's name to Susan Forman. The script contains no dialogue for the Stone Age characters as the intention is that they will communicate merely by grunts. He sends the script to David Whitaker with the following letter:

I meant you to have this on Monday morning, but I have

found out one thing about the cave man that you might pass on to any learned anthropologists you know – and I am sure you number many amongst your closest friends – and it is this. They must have been very much smaller than ourselves. This fact I deduce, not from a close study of their implements, nor by using my Scobonomometer in Hachendorff's Test of the Plutonium content of their left elbows ... but by knowing how bloody difficult it is to get into their skins.

And lastly, I rather think that, wordwise, this one might be a little too long. I'm a lousy timer. See what you think.

Son of the son of the son of the son of the son of the ad infinitum, firemaker,

Tony

Verity Lambert has a meeting with Head of Design Richard Levin and Design Manager James Bould. Levin backs down from his previous stand and agrees that scenic design work can now go ahead on the basis of just the two scripts currently available, given that no new sets are to be required for the other two episodes of the story.

D M B Grubb sends a memo to Ian Atkins explaining that the reason no inlay equipment can be installed in Riverside 2 until the following year is that all resources are currently tied up in providing the additional studios and facilities required for the forthcoming launch of BBC2. He indicates that the cost of the new equipment would be (contrary to the figure previously quoted) around £3,500.

Rex Tucker holds auditions in Television Centre Room 2119 for the roles of Susan Forman and Miss McGovern. The audition list reads:

Susan: Maureen Crombie, Anna Palk, Waveney Lee, Anneke Wills (not seen), Heather Fleming, Christa Bergman (to be considered in her absence), Camilla Hasse, Ann Casteldini.

Miss McGovern: Phillida Law, Penelope Lee, Sally Holme.

Tucker will many years later recall that he decided to cast 'an Australian girl' as Susan.

Wednesday 26: Coburn has now completed a draft script for the third episode of *The Tribe of Gum*, but the fourth is not expected to be ready until Friday 28.

Verity Lambert and David Whitaker both dislike Coburn's story and, despite the problems already caused by the unavailability of scripts, seriously consider rejecting it. Coburn is asked to carry out a substantial rewrite. Around the same time, Lambert approaches Terence Dudley – the producer responsible for the earlier Saturday serial *The Big Pull* – to see if he would be willing to write a replacement first story, but he declines.

Lambert sends a memo to Pauline Mansfield-Clark, Head of Artists' Bookings, to set out the basis on which the series' cast should be engaged:

> Will you please note that the four principals in the above series, i.e. Dr Who, Mr Chesterton, Miss McGovern, Susan Foreman, should be booked on the following basis: for the pilot to be recorded on Friday 2 August (rehearsals to start on 26 July) on a two thirds payment to be made up to a full payment if it is transmitted, with an option for 51 weekly episodes, the first to start rehearsals on Monday 14 August, with a further option for one extra week should the pilot not be transmitted. To confirm our telephone conversation, there will be no recording or rehearsals during Christmas week, which will mean adding a week on to the total.
>
> Will you please note that all the small parts for the first four episodes should be booked for the pilot on a two thirds payment, to be made up to a full payment on transmission, and for three weekly episodes (rehearsals to start on Monday 14 August) at full payment with an option for a further week at the end of this period should the pilot not be transmitted.
>
> Artists may be required from time to time to do pre-filming, and bookings for this should be taken direct from the director concerned.

It will subsequently be agreed that the fifty-two week contracts for the regulars should be subdivided into four option periods of eight weeks, twelve weeks, sixteen weeks and sixteen weeks respectively, rather than two periods of one week and fifty-one weeks as Lambert has suggested.

Thursday 27: Sydney Newman, having now returned from leave, learns of the behind-the-scenes wrangling that has gone on in his and Donald Wilson's absence. He has a heated phone conversation with Joanna Spicer in which Spicer alleges that the Serials Department has failed to follow correct

BBC procedures in setting up the new series; that the production team has been carrying out auditions and making other preparations without her authorization; and that the series' ambitious nature will place unreasonable demands upon the servicing departments. Later in the day, Newman sends Spicer a memo headed 'Dr Who Hassle', which begins as follows:

> Your comments of today on the "phone absolutely flabbergasted me and I take exception to most of what you said. We are trying to get a new children's serial out economically and quickly and from what I can see the Serials Department of this Group has acted in complete accordance with all the standard Corporation procedures.

The memo then summarises some of the key steps in the development of the series to date, before concluding:

> In view of the above, and since the first recording date is only five weeks away, do you wonder that we are anxious not to be held up? We have got to cast four people who must wear well over something like 52 episodes.

> I cannot understand from the mass of correspondence that has gone on about this project why permission is still required from your office. At no time have I received from Ch.P.(1). [Baverstock], or anybody else, the notion that the project was ever even vaguely in doubt. Especially as we have in the main held to the limitations stated on 26 April. While I may be ignorant of some of the finer points of Corporation routine, it is apparent that Ayton Whitaker and others in my Group are not. I am, therefore, surprised at what seems to me a last minute hold up. After all, it was only H.Tel.Des. [Levin] who dug his heels in about the scripts and he changed his mind two days ago.

> You may assume only that I intend to get drama programmes out on time and within budget. That my attitude to you and to Corporation routine will never be less than correct.

Spicer subsequently has a meeting with her Head of Department and Donald Baverstock in which a change is agreed to the early Saturday evening schedule: instead of two twenty-five minute children's programmes, broadcast between 5.00 pm and 5.50 pm, there will in future be only one half hour one, broadcast between 5.20 pm and 5.50 pm. This change will take place on 28 September and the new slot will be filled initially with the cartoon series *Deputy Dawg*; *Doctor Who* will then take over from 9 November onwards.

Friday 28: John Mair's deputy Alan Shallcross sends Spicer a memo reporting that Richard Levin and the Design Manager have now studied the first three scripts for *The Tribe of Gum* and have confirmed that they can meet the servicing requirements based on the previously agreed production dates. They are however unable to accept the requested experimental session on Friday 19 July.

Spicer, meanwhile, sends Baverstock a memo noting the outcome of their meeting the previous day. She also has a meeting with Sydney Newman and Kenneth Adam, the Controller of Programmes for Television, and later sends Newman a memo recording the decisions taken. In view of the change in the Saturday evening schedule, production of *Doctor Who* is to be postponed for a further eight weeks and the episode length increased from 25 minutes to 30. The pilot episode is to be recorded on Friday 27 September and the subsequent episodes weekly from Friday 18 October, all in Lime Grove D. The budget per episode is set at £2,300 and Newman is asked to make a formal request if the producer still wishes to use extensive visual effects which will entail the cost of extra staff, space and equipment. In addition, Newman is asked to confirm that the 'space time machine which is to be used throughout the series' cannot be financed on the standard budget.

Later in the day, at a Programme Management Board meeting, Sydney Newman protests at the change of episode length, pointing out that it has always been planned as 25 minutes. Ronald Waldman, the General Manager of Television Enterprises, also favours that length as it is better for overseas sales purposes. It is agreed that the episode length should be the subject of further discussion.

JULY 1963

Monday 1: The production team are informed of the postponement of the series. They quickly realise that Rex Tucker will no longer be able to direct *The Tribe of Gum* as the new production dates cut across the period when he is due to take a holiday in Majorca. It is therefore agreed that Waris Hussein will now direct the first story and Tucker the second.

Tucker subsequently phones composer Tristram Cary to tell him that, as a result of this change of plan, he will no longer be required to provide the music for *The Tribe of Gum*.

Verity Lambert and Waris Hussein dislike Tucker's casting ideas for the four regulars and, during the course of July, set about making their own choices. Actors considered for the role of the Doctor include Cyril Cusack (who is David Whitaker's suggestion) and Leslie French (who is favoured by Mervyn Pinfield and by Lambert herself). Lambert eventually decides to approach fifty-five year old character actor William Hartnell, having been impressed by his performances in the Granada TV comedy series *The Army Game* and in the film *This Sporting Life*. She contacts his agent – Hartnell's own son-in-law, Terry Carney, of the Eric l'Epine Smith agency – who, although a little reluctant to recommend a part in a 'children's programme', realises that this might be just the thing the actor needs to break out of his type-casting as a tough guy army officer or crook. Carney visits Hartnell at his home in Mayfield, Sussex and discusses the idea with him, taking along a copy of the draft first script for his perusal. Hartnell's reaction is initially quite positive, and he agrees to a meeting with Lambert and Hussein. His remaining reservations are then overcome, and he accepts the role of the Doctor.

The role of Ian goes to Russell Enoch, who uses the stage name William Russell. He is another actor whom Verity Lambert has admired for some time and is well known for his portrayal of Sir Lancelot in the Sapphire Films series *The Adventures of Sir Lancelot*. His BBC credits include *Suspense: The Patch Card*, *Moonstrike*, *Jane Eyre* (directed by Rex Tucker), *A Song of Sixpence*, *Nautilus* and *Adventure Story*.

Jacqueline Hill, a former model whose BBC credits include *Maigret*, *The Man from Room 13*, *The Watching Cat* and *The Six Proud Walkers* and whose husband, Alvin Rakoff, is an old friend of Verity Lambert's, is cast as Barbara after Lambert sees her at a party.

A number of actresses are considered for the role of Susan. These include Jackie Lane (then working under the name Jackie Lenya), whom Lambert and Hussein have seen appearing in recent episodes of the soap opera *Compact*. Lane loses interest however when she learns that the series is to run for a year, being disinclined to commit herself to one job for that length of time. The role eventually goes to twenty-three year old Carole Ann Ford after Hussein spots her on a monitor at Television Centre and recommends her to Lambert. Ford has been acting since an early age. She has appeared in a number of films, including *Mix Me a Person* and *Day of the Triffids*, and in TV series including ATV's *Emergency Ward 10* and, for the BBC, *Moonstrike*, *Compact* and *Man on a Bicycle*.

Tuesday 2: Ayton Whitaker sends a memo to John Mair setting out proposed new dates for filming at Ealing for the first three stories. He adds that an additional £500 will still be needed for building of the space/time machine and that a one day experimental session is still desired for Friday 19 July.

Ayton Whitaker also phones Design Manager James Bould and points out that the production team are awaiting the allocation of a designer so that they can explain their requirements for the space/time machine.

Wednesday 3: Ayton Whitaker sends a further memo to John Mair explaining that as the Design Department are unable to service the experimental session planned for 19 July, and as the technical adviser for the session is due to go on leave on 20 July, it should be postponed until Friday 13 September.

Anthony Coburn has left the staff of the BBC at the end of June following the demise of the Script Department. David Whitaker therefore briefs the Copyright Department to commission him to continue working on his two stories on a freelance basis. It has been agreed that the second story, with the working title *The Robots*, will now be a six-parter rather than a four-parter.

Friday 5: Head of Copyright R G Walford sends Coburn a contract for his ten episodes. At David Whitaker's request, it is made clear in the contract that the initial idea of *Doctor Who* and its four basic characters are the property of the BBC. Coburn is to receive the standard script fee of £225 for each of his episodes. Walford's letter continues:

> I understand that in this case you would like the payments for the initial fees for the ten programmes to be paid in the form of twelve monthly payments beginning on 1 August 1963 (so that in effect they will replace payments which you would have had in your staff contract as a scriptwriter/adaptor which has recently been terminated).

Donald Baverstock confirms that the episode length of *Doctor Who* will, after all, be 25 minutes. Sydney Newman conveys this information in a memo to Donald Wilson.

During the course of this week, both Verity Lambert and Mervyn Pinfield have made further calls to James Bould to enquire if he is yet in a position to allocate a designer to *Doctor Who*. He has told them that he may be able to do so on the following Monday.

Monday 8: Coburn receives his contract and signs it 'James A Coburn.'

Shortly after this, Coburn delivers to David Whitaker a revised script for the first episode of *The Tribe of Gum*. Concerned at the possible sexual connotations of a young schoolgirl travelling alone with an old man, he has suggested making Susan an alien of royal blood from the same planet as the Doctor and renaming her Suzanne.

David Whitaker passes the script on to Verity Lambert with the following note:

Tony has improved episode one very much – particularly regarding CHESTERTON.

He agrees to the change of any names we wish.

I have discussed the whole business with him and we have agreed he shall push on and finish all four of the scripts before we get down to going through each one with the minor changes.

He feels that the 'Gums' ought to talk.

I have some reservations about this episode, this newly rewritten one, but all in all it flows much better. Tony has inserted some details about Suzanne regarding her own existence which we ought to consider, for they are important. Doctor Who, as you will read, tells that (or hints that) Suzanne has some sort of royal blood. This gives Dr Who and Suzanne good reason to leave their own environment, of course, but I think we must discuss this carefully with Tony when we go through the scripts with him.

Regarding Doctor Who, I feel that he should be more like the old Professor that Frank Morgan played in *The Wizard of Oz*, only a little more authentic. Then we can strike some of the charm and humour as well as the mystery, the suspicion and the cunning. Do you agree with this idea?

The insertion of Suzanne as a princess or whatever can be carried off quite well but I think it ought to be done in a rather lighter way. Also I think Chesterton is a couple of shades too beefy in attacking Doctor Who.

Minor reservations then, but this is a better script. The cliff-hanger isn't as good as Tony's earlier one.

In subsequent discussions with Coburn, the idea of Suzanne being a princess is dropped. Instead, it is decided that she should be the Doctor's granddaughter. Her name is finally fixed as Susan Foreman, and those of the two teachers as Ian Chesterton and Barbara Wright. It is however agreed that the Stone Age tribe should have dialogue. Whitaker will later describe this as 'the hardest decision we had to make' with regard to the tribe.

Tuesday 9: David Whitaker briefs the Copyright Department to commission Canadian writer John Lucarotti to provide the series' third story, a seven-parter with the working title *A Journey to Cathay*. Lucarotti has been suggested as a potential contributor to *Doctor Who* by Sydney Newman, who is an old friend of his. He lives and works in Majorca and makes only occasional visits to England, so most of his subsequent discussions with David Whitaker will be conducted over the phone. Waris Hussein has been assigned to direct Lucarotti's story.

Wednesday 10: Verity Lambert again phones James Bould about the allocation of a designer to the series, and is told that Peter Brachacki has been detailed to handle the first four episodes and the design of the space/time machine. At present, however, Brachacki is largely tied up on other programmes.

In the afternoon, Lambert, Mervyn Pinfield and Waris Hussein have a preliminary meeting with Brachacki. Brachacki can spare only half an hour and informs the production team that he will be completely unavailable for the next two weeks.

Friday 12: Verity Lambert asks the Music Copyright Department to contact the New York agent of the avant-garde French electronic music composers Jacques Lasry and Francois Baschet with a view to commissioning them and their group, Les Structures Sonores, to provide fifteen to twenty seconds of opening title music for *Doctor Who*. Les Structures Sonores typically create their music by such techniques as playing glass rods mounted in steel.

David Whitaker has by this time prepared a revised version of the series' format document. This is based on the 16 May version but has been updated to take account of more recent developments. The following new paragraphs have been added to the section headed 'Approach to the Stories':

> It is emphasised that the 'ship' may transport the four characters backwards or forwards, sideways into lesser or greater dimensions or into non-gravitational existence or invisibility etcetera, but once arrived into the different place and time the four characters have only their intelligence and ingenuity upon which to rely. They cannot produce a 'ray gun' to reduce a horde of Picts and Scots, nor can they rely upon specialised drugs to cure a Greek philosopher.

> It is also emphasised that the four characters cannot make history. Advice must not be proffered to Nelson on his battle tactics when approaching the Nile, nor must bon mots be put into the mouth of Oscar Wilde. They are four people plunged

into alien surroundings armed with only their courage and cleverness.

The character outline for Doctor Who now states that he is aged 'over sixty' rather than 'about 650' and the one for Susan has been amended to read as follows:

> The Doctor's grand-daughter, aged fifteen. She is a sharp, intelligent girl, quick and perky. She makes mistakes, however, because of inexperience. Addicted to 20th Century contemporary slang and likes pop records – in fact, she admires the life teenagers enjoy in 1963. At the beginning of the story, she has persuaded her grandfather to stay in 1963 so that she can go to school and create at least one complete section of experience. Since she has been visiting all sorts of existences and places with her grandfather, Susan has a wide general knowledge and on some subjects can be brilliantly factual. On other matters, she is lamentably ignorant. She has something of a crush on Ian Chesterton.

The paragraph on the Doctor's ship has also undergone substantial revision, and now reads:

> Doctor Who has a 'ship' which can travel through space, through time and through matter. It is a product of the year 5733 and cannot travel forward from that date (otherwise the Doctor and Sue could discover their own destinies), the authorities of the 50th Century deeming forward sight unlawful. This still enables Ian and Barbara (and the audience) to see into environments and existences far beyond the present day. The ship, when first seen, has the outward appearance of a police box, but the inside reveals an extensive electronic contrivance and comfortable living quarters with occasional bric-a-brac acquired by the Doctor in his travels. Primarily, the machine has a yearometer, which allows the traveller to select his stopping place. In the first story, however, the controls are damaged and the 'ship' becomes uncertain in performance, which explains why Ian and Barbara, once set upon their journey, are never able to return to their own time and place in their natural forms.

The revised document continues as follows:

> The first story of four episodes, written by Anthony Coburn,

begins the journey and takes the four travellers back in time to 100,000 BC to mid-Palaeolithic man, and it is in this story that the 'ship' is slightly damaged and forever afterwards is erratic in certain sections of its controls.

The second story of six episodes, written by Anthony Coburn, takes the travellers to some time approximately near the 30th Century, forward to the world when it is inhabited only by robots, where humanity has died away. The robots themselves, used to a life of service, have invented a master robot capable of original thought but, realising the dangers, have rendered their invention inoperative, even though it means they must sink into total inertia. The travellers, unaware of this situation, bring the robots and then the new invention 'to life' and face the dangers inherent in a pitiless computer.

Since this is primarily a series of stories concerning people rather than studio effects, and the original characters and backgrounds have been prepared already, the writer will be asked to submit a storyline from which he will be commissioned. This need not go into fractional detail – three or four pages of quarto ought to be sufficient to express the idea.

Technical advice is available insofar as what may or may not be achieved in the studio, but every endeavour will be made to meet the requirements of your story. There is a certain film budget, not extensive but sufficient to cover most contingencies, and the episodes will be Ampexed so that a 'stop and start' may be achieved if desired.

Writers may consult the story editor who will work out their plots and situations with them and arrange meetings with the associate producer who acts as the arbiter on technical and factual detail.

David Whitaker has sent this revised document to a number of freelance writers and writers' agents. 'They were all friends,' he will later recall, 'or otherwise friends of friends, who were then recommended to me ... People I knew I could trust not only to produce a good story within the restrictions we had, but also who could produce their story to a very tight deadline.'

Writers so far invited to submit storylines are: Malcolm Hulke, Peter

Yeldham, Robert Stewart (who will later write under the name Robert Banks Stewart), Terry Nation, Alan Wakeman, John Bowen and Jeremy Bullmore, and Barbara Harper.

Monday 15: Ayton Whitaker sends John Mair a memo listing the working title, director and number of episodes for each of the first three stories. He confirms that the second and third stories will each require five days' filming at Ealing, in weeks commencing 26 October (Week 44) and 7 December (Week 50) respectively, and concludes:

> In the event of the pilot recording in Week 39 being considered suitable for transmission, we will record part two of *The Tribe of Gum* in Week 42 and bring all subsequent recordings forward by one week until the Friday of Week 51 when we should record part one of *A Journey to Cathay*. We would then not record in Christmas week (Week 52), but record part two of *A Journey to Cathay* on the Friday of Week 1, as already planned. This arrangement cannot be put into effect until after the pilot recording has been assessed.

> I understand that Studio D will probably be going out of commission for conversion in December; I would be glad to know as soon as possible which will be the replacement studio for *Dr Who* as it will clearly have a bearing on facilities available for *A Journey to Cathay*.

Tuesday 16: C E Webber is paid a staff contribution fee of £187 10s 0d for the two scripts he wrote for his rejected story *The Giants*.

Wednesday 17: Verity Lambert sends Donald Wilson a memo recording her concern that the limited availability of designer Peter Brachacki has so far made it impossible to discuss with him in detail the requirements for the design of the first story and of the Doctor's time/space machine. She concludes:

> As we have been prepared to discuss in detail the design of the machine as from 2 July, I hope we will not be asked to make any compromises owing to shortage of effort in the Design Department.

Donald Wilson subsequently writes to Richard Levin, the Head of Design, conveying the substance of Lambert's memo and continuing:

I should add that at the beginning of June, before I went away, I saw James Bould and told him of the special problems involved in *Dr Who*. We discussed possible designers and he told me there would be difficulty in obtaining the ideal man at that moment. There was no doubt in my mind when I heard of the postponement of the programme that a designer would be made available in time, particularly as everyone clearly understood the necessity for your Department to design and execute the space machine as early as possible.

If the circumstances are as reported in Miss Lambert's note, it seems to me that this project, which is designed to run for 52 weeks, is not getting the necessary attention. We are constantly being asked for earlier information to help in design problems; the information is available, and has been available for some time. I would like to ask you now that one designer for the whole project of 52 weeks be agreed with Miss Lambert, with whatever assistance may be required, because we shall wish to maintain the same style of design throughout, however varied the different stories may be.

Monday 22: Donald Wilson holds a meeting with Richard Bright, the Television Publicity Organiser, to discuss promotion of *Doctor Who*.

David Whitaker is continuing to liaise with Anthony Coburn on his scripts for the first two stories. No-one on the production team is particularly enthusiastic about *The Tribe of Gum*, but it is too late for a replacement story to be found. Coburn's other story, which he has given the title *The Robots*, has undergone a number of revisions, and is now set on an alien planet rather than on a future Earth.

Tuesday 23: Richard Bright circulates a memo to his publicity colleagues attaching a copy of the format document for *Doctor Who* and reporting on the previous day's meeting with Donald Wilson. Likening the format to that of *Tim Frazer*, an earlier BBC drama which also consisted of a series of serials, he notes:

This is the first time we have undertaken a 52-part serial. It will be rather on the *Tim Frazer* pattern – a series of stories of varying lengths, each one starting during the last episode of the previous one. It will go on the air at 5.20-5.45 on Saturdays and is planned for family viewing with special attention to the 11-14 group.

After briefly summarising the intended transmission and production dates and the subject matter of the first three stories and giving the names of the four principal cast members, Bright continues:

> Of the production team the producer, Verity Lambert, is a twenty-seven year old girl who has done a lot of commercial TV over here and has worked in the USA for David Susskind. She has been put on programme contract for a year to handle this serial. The two directors, Waris Hussein and Rex Tucker, will be in charge of alternate stories beginning with Hussein on No. 1. Anthony Coburn is writing the first two stories and the third will be written by John Lucarotti who has written a lot of television in the USA, Canada and commercial over here.

> This would obviously be an important part of C.P Tel's [Kenneth Adam] autumn plans announcement and A.H.P. [the Assistant Head of Publicity] may decide to have a press launching when the first episode has been finally approved.

John Mair sends Sydney Newman and Donald Wilson a memo explaining that, due to previously unanticipated coverage of an athletics meeting in Moscow the previous Saturday, transmission of both *Deputy Dawg* and *Doctor Who* has been put back a further week. The first episode of *Doctor Who* is now therefore due to go out on Saturday 16 November.

Ronald Waldman, the General Manager of Television Enterprises, sends R G Walford, the Head of Copyright, a memo informing him of a dispute which has arisen with a company called Zenith Film Productions Ltd. Zenith have for some time been trying to interest the Children's Department and latterly Television Enterprises in commissioning a proposed new puppet series called *The Time Travellers*, devised by Martin and Hugh Woodhouse, the principal writers of the first season of Gerry Anderson's *Supercar* in 1959/60, but Waldman has turned the proposal down as being 'much too similar for comfort' to *Doctor Who*. Zenith are now claiming that the idea for *Doctor Who* has been stolen from them.

Thursday 25: Walford writes to Kenneth Cleveland, the legal adviser to Zenith, denying that the idea for *Doctor Who* has been taken either directly or indirectly from *The Time Travellers*:

> The first important point which I must make is that this *Dr Who* series was devised jointly by Sydney Newman and Donald Wilson and I have ascertained that at the time when they

worked it out they had no knowledge whatever of the suggested puppet series *The Time Travellers*. The scriptwriter of the first ten episodes of *Dr Who* is Anthony Coburn who likewise had no knowledge whatever of *The Time Travellers*. He was commissioned in the usual way as an outside writer to write scripts on the basic format which Sydney Newman and Donald Wilson devised and which of course the BBC owns.

Ronnie has already told you that he himself had no knowledge of *Dr Who*. *Dr Who* was of course never thought of in terms of a puppet series, and as Ronnie said in his letter of 16 July 'this is a large organisation and many things happen in the area of the creation of programme ideas which take a long time to come to the surface.'

The next important point to emphasise is that while, as Ronnie stated, *the idea* of the two programmes is similar, i.e. the idea of crossing time barriers, the two series are themselves completely different, one being for puppets and the other for live actors, and there could be no possibility of there being plagiarism of any sort.

Walford goes on however to offer Zenith 'a special *ex gratia* payment of 100 guineas, this being without prejudice and on the understanding that while we admit no legal liability we make the offer as a gesture of goodwill.'

Ian Atkins' assistant Leonard Miall sends him a memo to let him know that John Mair has now indicated that *Doctor Who* will be recorded in Lime Grove D on a permanent basis, and that the scripts will be tailored accordingly.

Tuesday 30: Donald Wilson circulates his own note of the preliminary promotion meeting held on 22 July. This summarises in more detail the points recorded by Richard Bright in his memo of 23 July and includes the revised first transmission date of 16 November.

Wednesday 31: The four regular cast members are issued with their contracts for the series.

David Whitaker briefs the Copyright Department to commission from writer Terry Nation a six-part story entitled *The Mutants*. This is on the strength of a detailed storyline that he has submitted under the earlier working title *The Survivors*. Nation's agents, Associated London Scripts, have negotiated a higher-than-usual fee of £262 per episode. His story is intended as the fourth in the series' running order, to be directed by Rex

Tucker.

Whitaker also circulates a note giving a brief summary of the plot of each of the first four stories:

> Sufficient information is given of the flavour of each story to avoid possible future duplication of periods of history or environments by Saturday evening films, US or foreign television shows and so on, securing for *Doctor Who* an additional strength in its constantly varying locales, costumes and motivations.

Around this time, writer Alan Wakeman is also commissioned to write one episode as a pilot for a story entitled *The Living World,* the production team having been unable to decide on the basis of his storyline whether or not it might be suitable for the series. In the event, nothing comes of this. Wakeman is paid a fee of £75 for the work he has carried out.

By the end of the month, the idea of commissioning Les Structures Sonores to provide the series' opening music has been abandoned. At the suggestion of Lionel Salter, Head of TV Music, Verity Lambert has since had a meeting with Desmond Briscoe, Head of the Radiophonic Workshop, and explained that what she is seeking is something radiophonic, with a strong beat, which will sound 'familiar but different.' She has also expressed a desire for the theme to be written by Ron Grainer – a top TV composer who has provided memorable signature tunes for series such as *Maigret* and *Steptoe and Son*. Briscoe has been able to arrange this without difficulty as Grainer has only recently finished collaborating with the Workshop on *Giants of Steam*, a programme about railways.

AUGUST 1963

Thursday 1: Kenneth Cleveland of Zenith Films replies to R G Walford's letter of 25 July. He argues that plagiarism is not ruled out simply by the fact that *The Time Travellers* is intended for puppets and *Doctor Who* for live action, and requests a round table meeting between his clients and Sydney Newman, Donald Wilson and Ronald Waldman.

Friday 2: Mervyn Pinfield goes on leave.

Verity Lambert sends E Caffery, the BBC's Assistant Head of Copyright, a memo confirming that Ron Grainer is to provide the opening and closing music for *Doctor Who* in conjunction with the Radiophonic Workshop:

Perhaps you could arrange a contract for him to compose approximately one minute of music at the opening and one minute of music at the closing, making a total of two minutes in all. I understand from Mr Grainer that because he will be working in conjunction with the Radiophonic Workshop, the BBC will automatically have some rights in any music produced.

Wednesday 7: William Hartnell visits Television Centre to have a make-up test and be measured for his costume.

Thursday 8: R G Walford replies to Kenneth Cleveland's letter of 1 August, reiterating that *Doctor Who* has been developed completely independently of Zenith's *The Time Travellers*:

> I am not saying that because one series related to puppets and the other to actors there could be no plagiarism, but simply that in this particular case the facts were such that neither series could possibly have been derived directly or indirectly from the other, so that any similarities that there may be could only be the result of coincidence, and such coincidences would not of course amount to plagiarism.

Walford goes on to reject Cleveland's request for a meeting.

David Whitaker sends the following memo to Ayton Whitaker arguing that the recording of *Doctor Who* in Lime Grove D on a permanent basis will 'badly restrict the variation of stories so necessary for the maintenance of the entertainment level':

> We badly need a serial about our four running characters being reduced in size. This requires inlay and could make effective use of overlay. I know the difficulties of black and white separation are not lost upon you nor the fact that these can be overcome in the right studio. I have had great experience of these techniques, having worked with Graeme Muir on over forty different productions employing inlay for which I wrote the scripts. I am very loathe to abandon the idea of a 'miniscule' adventure for *Doctor Who* without asking you what chances there are of eventual transfer from D to a studio capable of handling the visual effects which are, after all, an integral part of this project.

David Whitaker also sends E Caffery a memo stating that Terry Nation's story *The Mutants* is to be extended from six episodes to seven:

> Group producer Miss Lambert and I agree that Mr Nation's
> story is better expressed with the additional episode.

Around this time, Terry Nation delivers his first draft scripts to David
Whitaker. The working title of the story has at this point been changed to
Beyond the Sun, although it subsequently reverts to *The Mutants*. The
production team consider the scripts and Whitaker discusses them with
Nation, making a number of suggestions for rewrites. Consideration is given
to dropping this story back to fifth in the running order, subject to obtaining
the necessary facilities to mount a 'miniscules' story in the fourth slot.

Verity Lambert sends a memo to Jack Kine, one of the Heads of the
Visual Effects Department (a separate unit within the Design Department),
requesting that he provide a model of a 'Frank Lloyd Wright type of
building' for filming on 28 October. This is to appear at the close of the final
episode of *The Tribe of Gum*, in the scene leading into *The Robots*, to depict the
travellers' new arrival point.

Monday 12: Waris Hussein contacts the BBC Radiophonic Workshop to brief
them on the series' special sounds requirements. The man assigned to meet
these requirements is Brian Hodgson. His biggest challenge on this first
story is the sound effect to accompany the dematerialisation of the Doctor's
ship, which Anthony Coburn has now named TARDIS – standing for Time
and Relative Dimension in Space. He is inspired with an idea while out
visiting a local cinema and later creates the effect by recording and then
manipulating the sound of him scraping his front door key along the strings
of an old upright piano at the Workshop.

Donald Wilson sends Sydney Newman a memo conveying his
continuing dissatisfaction with *Doctor Who*'s studio allocation. Although it
has previously been accepted that the series should be made in Lime Grove
D, and the first four stories have been tailored accordingly, Wilson argues
that a better result could be achieved with more advanced facilities:

> These four stories cover a wide variation in time (100,000 BC
> to 30,000 AD) and space, but for so long as we are operating
> from D we shall not be able to introduce the third variant,
> that of size. I am particularly anxious that we should mount
> the 'miniature' adventure of *Dr Who*. Ideally this should be
> No. 4 in the series (starting recording on Friday 14 February
> 1964). Would you support an application for TC3, TC4 or
> Riverside 1 to be made available to us for Friday 14 February
> 1964 and the five successive Fridays? Of course if we could

have one of these studios for story No. 3 (20 December 1963) and continue on a permanent basis, so much the better.

I feel most strongly that *Dr Who* must from time to time explore the full range of technical resources, otherwise we shall lay ourselves open to criticism for lacking in imagination and boldness.

Tuesday 13: Newman replies to Wilson's memo of the previous day:

You've got me wrong man! When I agreed to Studio D, I was led to believe that this studio contained all the technical facilities *Dr Who* required. It was only after the realisation that Studio D was inefficient for our purposes that I suggested we tried to 'live with it' for a while.

I'll do the best I can about getting the proper 'inlay, overlay' studio for the 'diminutive' size *Doctor Who*.

Thursday 15: Carole Ann Ford has a make-up test and costume fitting at Television Centre.

Saturday 17: Carole Ann Ford appears as a guest on the pop music programme *Juke Box Jury*.

Monday 19: Mervyn Pinfield returns from leave.

Tuesday 20: The first filming for *Doctor Who* – the creation of the series' opening title sequence – takes place on Stage 3A at the BBC's Television Film Studios in Ealing. The sequence has been designed by Bernard Lodge of the BBC Graphics Unit and makes use of a technique known as howl-around, which involves pointing a TV camera at a screen displaying the camera's own output and then filming the resultant feedback patterns. As Lodge recalls in a later interview, he has been inspired to use this technique by the pioneering work of a man named Ben Palmer:

'Quite a lot of howl-around footage already existed as a technical guy called Ben Palmer had been experimenting and had produced these patterns for a drama called *Amahl and the Night Visitors*. Although the pattern generation was a purely electronic process it had been recorded on film. They had yards and yards of this experimental footage and I was asked to go down to Ealing and watch through it all with Verity Lambert.'

Lambert's initial idea was that Lodge should create some animated lettering of the words 'Doctor Who' to be superimposed over the existing footage, but Lodge convinced her that the studio should be set up again so that the words could be fed into the picture electronically:

> 'What I didn't realise was that the simple shape of the words, the two lines of fairly symmetrical type, would actually generate its own feedback pattern. We shot a whole lot of new cloudy abstract stuff as well, but in the end I think we used one piece from the old *Amahl* footage – the very nice opening line which comes up the screen then breaks away. I can't take credit for that.'

The generation of the howl-around effect for this studio session has been supervised by a technician named Norman Taylor. Lodge subsequently takes the completed footage away and has it edited together into the finished sequence.

Having agreed with Lodge a rough timing for the sequence, Ron Grainer has meanwhile been working on his theme music. He has written a fairly simple score while on holiday in Portugal and has since discussed it with Delia Derbyshire, the Radiophonic Workshop composer assigned the task of committing it to tape. Keen that the music should be in keeping with the visuals, he has used expressions like 'windbubble and clouds' when describing the sort of sounds he envisages. Derbyshire and her assistant, Dick Mills, have created these sounds using sine and square wave generators, a white noise generator and a special beat frequency generator. The tune has been put together virtually note by note – each 'swoop' in the music being a carefully-timed hand adjustment of the oscillators – and the sounds have been cut, shaped, filtered and manipulated in various ways to prepare the tracks for mixing and synchronization.

Wednesday 21: Jacqueline Hill has a make-up test and costume fitting at Television Centre.

Verity Lambert discusses the first story's design requirements in detail with Peter Brachacki, who is now free of his other commitments.

Thursday 22: Verity Lambert sends a memo to James Bould, the Design Organiser, noting that *Doctor Who*'s fourth story will be either a futuristic one or an adventure concerning 'people who are greatly reduced in size', and that 'extensive use of electronic and scenic effects' will be required. She continues:

> I understand that George Djurkovic has made a detailed study of the Swedish entry for the Montreaux Festival, which

concerned new techniques in this field. In the circumstances, I think George Djurkovic would be particularly useful to us on either of these two stories, and, if he is available, I would like to request that he be allocated to us.

Lambert now has a new office in Room 5017 of Television Centre, just two doors along from her old one. She has also been assigned a secretary, who is in Room 5016.

Friday 30: Rex Tucker goes on leave to take his holiday in Majorca. It has however been decided by this stage that when he returns on 23 September he will no longer be involved with *Doctor Who*. He has never been entirely happy working on the series and has now been reassigned to direct a prestigious Giles Cooper adaptation of Flaubert's *Madame Bovary* for transmission in March 1964. 'Much more the sort of thing I had done in the past,' he will later recall.

SEPTEMBER 1963

Monday 2: David Whitaker receives from writer Malcolm Hulke proposed outlines for two six-part stories: one set in Roman-occupied Britain around 400 AD and the other, entitled *The Hidden Planet*, set on a planet in the same orbit as the Earth but out of view on the opposite side of the sun.

Monday 9: By the beginning of this week, the first transmission of *Doctor Who* has been postponed again, to Saturday 23 November.

Tuesday 10: Revised versions of the scripts for episodes one and three of *The Tribe of Gum* are sent out to the cast, who previously received drafts of all four episodes.

Tuesday 12: Verity Lambert sends a memo to R W Bayliff, the Head of Technical Operations for Television Studios, requesting permission for Norman Taylor to be given a credit on the pilot episode for his electronic howl-around effects.

Friday 13: The experimental session originally scheduled for 19 July finally takes place in Lime Grove D, the purpose being to try out the effect of the dematerialisation of the Doctor's ship. A problem immediately arises when it is discovered that the police box prop is too tall to fit into the service lift by which scenery is transported up to the studio.

Monday 16: David Whitaker circulates a note containing synopses of the stories now planned to fill the first six slots in the series' running order. The first three are, as before, *The Tribe of Gum*, *The Robots* and *A Journey to Cathay*. The fourth, however, is now a four-part 'miniscules' story by writer Robert Gould, and is described by Whitaker as follows:

> 'Tardis' transports Doctor Who and his party back to 1963 but reduced down to one sixteenth of an inch in size. One room becomes a world of frightening proportions, one carpet an impenetrable jungle, where 'dust storms' are minor concerns. The immense difficulties of finding food and water, the death that can result from the sudden falling cigarette ash, the terrifying creatures that inhabit the new world in which they find themselves make up an unusual and thrilling adventure.

The fifth slot is now occupied by Terry Nation's *The Mutants*, while the sixth has been set aside for one of the Malcolm Hulke stories, summarised by Whitaker in the following terms:

> The travellers are set down in a Britain of 400 AD, when the Romans are just about to retire from the island. The Romans leave behind them an authority which intends to carry on their civilisation but this is opposed by a group of people who see profit in destruction and disorder. This latter group are excellent allies for invading Saxons, completely opposed to anything Roman. Doctor Who and his friends are involved in a struggle at a time when the blank pages of history occur, in an adventure full of excitement and action.

Waris Hussein is still expected to direct the first, third and fifth stories, while Christopher Barry – a young but experienced staff director who joined the BBC in 1955 after starting his career in the film industry – has been pencilled in for the second and sixth and Richard Martin for the fourth. Whitaker concludes:

> These six stories, covering thirty-four episodes, are, as has already been stated, not finalised – however they do provide a statement of flavour and intention. The first, second, third and fifth serials have been commissioned and are in various stages of development – the first being complete, the second being half written in draft, the third in preparation and the fifth delivered in draft. Serials four and six are in discussion stages.

Waris Hussein is definite for the first and third serials but the
actual deployment of Christopher Barry and Richard Martin
has yet to be finalised.

Wednesday 18: R W Bayliff replies to Verity Lambert's memo of 12
September declining permission for Norman Taylor to receive an on-screen
credit. This is on the grounds that his electronic effects fall short of meeting
the established policy requirement of being 'both artistic and substantial, or
of significant interest to viewers.'

Composer Norman Kay, conducting a group of seven musicians, records
the incidental music for *The Tribe of Gum* between 6.00 pm and 10.00 pm in
the Camden Theatre.

Thursday 19: A day of filming is carried out on Stage 3A at Ealing for the
first story.

Friday 20: The series' regular cast take part in a *Radio Times* photocall at
Television Centre, on a mock-up of the junk yard set for the pilot episode. It
begins at 3.00 and is due to last an hour.

Editing of the Ealing film footage is carried out for the pilot episode. This
is to be continued on the first three days of the following week.

Saturday 21: Waris Hussein and the cast begin rehearsals for the pilot
episode, *The Tribe of Gum: An Unearthly Child*. The venue is a Drill Hall at 117
Walmer Road, London W2 – one of a number of West London halls used
regularly by the BBC for rehearsal purposes.

Monday 23: A further four days' preliminary rehearsal begins for the pilot
episode.

By the beginning of this week, Verity Lambert and David Whitaker have
decided that Anthony Coburn's *The Robots* and Terry Nation's *The Mutants*
should swap places in the planned running order. This is mainly because
design work now needs to get underway on the second story and Nation's
scripts are the only ones ready. The production team are dissatisfied with
the work so far carried out by Coburn on *The Robots* and have asked for
further rewrites.

The current intention is that, after the six-part Malcolm Hulke story
pencilled in as the sixth in the running order, the remainder of the 52-week
season should be broken down into two seven-parters and one four-parter.
Terry Nation is to be asked to contribute the second of the seven-parters – a
historical story entitled *The Red Fort* – but the other two slots remain to be
filled.

During the course of this week, it is decided that only the individual episode titles will appear on screen and not the overall story titles, which will now be used for production purposes only.

Tuesday 24: Terry Nation is commissioned to write *The Red Fort*. This is to be a seven-part historical story set during the Indian Mutiny and will see the four time travellers becoming involved in events which took place on 11 May 1857 at the so-called Red Fort in Delhi. The target delivery date for the scripts is 16 December.

Friday 27: The pilot episode is camera rehearsed and recorded in Lime Grove D. The total cost of the episode (estimated at 18 November 1963) is £2,143 3s 3d.

It has yet to be decided how *Doctor Who*'s visual effects requirements will be serviced on a long-term basis, so the interior of the Doctor's ship has been constructed from Peter Brachacki's designs by a firm of freelance contractors, Shawcraft Models (Uxbridge) Ltd. The set has a number of unusual aspects, including its size – it takes up almost half the studio – and a large hexagonal unit suspended from the ceiling. The central control console is the dominant feature, with its six instrument panels and transparent central column. Brachacki's reason for having a console of this sort is that the ship is supposed to be capable of operation by a single pilot. He initially hoped to create special controls, moulded to the pilot's hands, but this proved too expensive so standard switches and dials have been used instead. Budgetary restrictions have also ruled out some of the designer's other ideas, such as having translucent wall panels that would pulsate during flight. One feature that has been afforded, however, is a distinctive pattern of indented circles on the walls. Brachacki's intention in using a geometric shape is to create a timeless feel, and he has chosen circles simply due to the fact that the plastic from which he made his original design model of the set happened to have circles on it. The central column of the control console is designed to rise, fall and rotate, but it frequently jams in the studio, causing hold-ups during camera rehearsals. The doors of the set also prove very difficult to open and close.

The costume supervisor assigned to the first story is Maureen Heneghan and the make-up supervisor Elizabeth Blattner.

Monday 30: By the beginning of this week, Sydney Newman has arranged to view a recording of the pilot episode. He jots down a number of comments on the back of two pages of the script. These range from technical instructions (such as 'Music to be very loud' at the start of the episode, 'Tremble camera' with reference to the scene of the dematerialisation of the Doctor's ship and 'End credits too big and roll credits faster' at the close), through relatively minor observations on the direction and scripting ('Bad profile of girl – can she be more cheeky? – too dour,' 'Lay off her profiles' and 'What does she draw?') to more substantive criticisms ('Old man – not funny enough,' 'They don't act as if he's locked her in box' and, again, 'Old man ain't cute enough.')

Newman subsequently takes Verity Lambert and Waris Hussein out to lunch and tells them that the pilot is unacceptable for transmission. The episode will therefore have to be remounted, as already planned on a contingency basis.

A meeting is held in Lambert's office to discuss special effects requirements for *The Mutants*. Present are Lambert, Mervyn Pinfield, David Whitaker, Christopher Barry (who has now been assigned to direct this story), designer Barry Newbery, lighting supervisor Geoff Shaw and secretary Susan Pugh.

Although *Doctor Who* has always been planned as a fifty-two week series, Chief of Programmes Donald Baverstock has yet to give his formal approval for it to continue beyond the first four episodes.

OCTOBER 1963

Wednesday 2: H Wilson, designated Film Operations Manager II, makes arrangements at Verity Lambert's request for a show copy of the pilot episode to be made available for the remount on 18 October.

Tuesday 8: Production assistant Douglas Camfield learns that scenery due to be delivered the previous day to the Television Film Studios at Ealing has yet to arrive. On making enquiries, he discovers that this is due to a lack of transport and a lack of staff at Television Centre to load it onto a van. The scenery eventually arrives at 3.40 pm and Camfield authorises the scene crew to work overtime to get it ready for the start of filming the following day.

Wednesday 9: Three days' filming begins at Ealing to complete all the film inserts required for the second, third and fourth episodes of *The Tribe of Gum*. Camfield directs some of these scenes himself, on Waris Hussein's behalf.

Thursday 10: Donald Wilson sends a lengthy memo to Donald Baverstock, Joanna Spicer, Sydney Newman and Richard Levin about the 'special effects effort' required on *Doctor Who*. After summarising discussions and correspondence to date on this issue, he protests that no extra visual effects staff have yet been provided for the series and that Programme Services are working on the basis that it is 'to be tailored to normal Saturday afternoon series level.' He continues:

I do not know what 'normal Saturday afternoon series level' may mean, but if it means that the effort required to build the space ship for *Dr Who* is abnormal, then it seems to me that I should have been told so and I would then have informed everybody that the serials could not be done on these terms and we should therefore have to withdraw the project.

What happened in fact was that a certain amount of effort was bought outside to make it possible for the pilot to be recorded on 27 September. The work was defective and this was one of the reasons why we determined that the pilot episode could be very much improved if it was done again. It was not until the deficiencies appeared that I myself realised that the effort we had asked for was not being provided and could not be provided in the future without a large weekly sum of money over and above the agreed budget.

Wilson goes on to argue for an immediate decision to be taken on the continuation of the series beyond the first four episodes:

As a result of the pilot, we have engaged the artists for the four running characters according to the option terms set out in their contracts, and have two further serials in writing.

If we begin recording weekly on 18 October without a decision being made about the continuation we will be able, given the £800 promised by A.C.(Planning), to complete the first four episodes and the filming of the special effects for the second serial, but if we do not make a decision until after the third recording there will not be time enough to have the design effort and building ready for continuous production after number four. In other words, we would have to cease production for a period of three weeks after the decision is made, during which time we would have to continue paying the four running artists at the rate of £550 a week. We would also be unable to cast the second serial.

To sum up, I think we should commit ourselves to at least eleven episodes on the basis of the existing pilot. (Eighteen episodes would be more satisfactory from the budgeting point of view.) We know that subsequent episodes will be better than this pilot if the effort is available and in view of the changes we have now made in script and characterisation.

But in my professional opinion what we have here is something very much better both in content and in production value than we could normally expect for this kind of money and effort.

Friday 11: Christopher Barry sends David Whitaker a note of his initial thoughts on the scripts for *The Mutants*. He begins:

Here are some general comments on the serial, but there are two important facets of the Thals' and the Daleks' characters which should be borne in mind throughout all re-writing.

The Thals should have a death urge – or, at any rate, little will to live – in contrast to the Daleks who, hideously mutilated though they are, wish to survive, dominate, and perpetuate their ghastly species. They should be frightened for their ability – or lack of ability – to survive, and it is this fear that drives them to suspicious hatred of strangers.

The Thals should be absolutely unable to take command of their own destiny, or even of any situation in which they find themselves, until our four come along and befriend/are befriended by them.

Barry then goes on to give a number of detailed comments on points of dialogue and description in Terry Nation's scripts.

Monday 14: Four days' preliminary rehearsal begins for the remount of *The Tribe of Gum: An Unearthly Child*. The venue for the series' rehearsals has now been changed to a Drill Hall at 239 Uxbridge Road, just a few minutes' walk from Lime Grove Studios.

Wednesday 16: Donald Baverstock decides on the basis of the pilot episode, which he has now viewed, that he is willing to give the go ahead to thirteen episodes of *Doctor Who*. John Mair, whose official designation has now changed from Senior Planning Assistant (I) to Planning Manager (Forward), is asked to 'state what extra programme allowance will be required to finance the special effects requirements and the operating effort needed to work them in the studio' so that Baverstock can decide by the end of the week whether or not he can agree to the consequent increase in the series' budget.

Friday 18: The remount of *The Tribe of Gum: An Unearthly Child* is camera rehearsed and recorded in Lime Grove D. Its total cost is £2,746.

It has by this point been decided that Peter Brachacki is unsuited to working on *Doctor Who,* and Verity Lambert has asked for a different designer to be allocated to the series. (Brachacki is in any case unwell and is soon to be admitted to hospital for an operation.) Two designers, Barry Newbery and Raymond P Cusick, have been asked to take over from Brachacki, handling stories on an alternate basis. Newbery's first task on *The Tribe of Gum* has been to have all the sets for the first episode rebuilt from Brachacki's plans as – despite Lambert's instructions to the contrary – only the set of the interior of the Doctor's ship has been retained from the pilot recording, the others having all been junked.

Director Christopher Barry sends David Whitaker a memo of further, more considered comment on the scripts for the first two episodes of *The Mutants*. He concludes:

> It seems that Terry Nation feels that once he has told the audience something the characters need no longer react to the situation. He is continually having them accept a situation in a most undramatic manner, and therefore losing a lot of potential value.
>
> I shall in due course be reading more carefully the remaining five scripts, but thought you would rather have what comments I have been able to produce so far in time for the weekend.

A major crisis arises for *Doctor Who* when Donald Baverstock sends Donald Wilson the following memo just before going on leave for three weeks:

> I am told that a first examination of your expenditure on the pilot and of your likely design and special effects requirements of later episodes, particularly two, three and four, shows that you are likely to overspend your budget allocation by as much as £1,600 and your allocation of man-hours by as much as 1,200 per episode. These figures are arrived at by averaging the expenditure of £4,000 on the spaceship over thirteen episodes. It also allows for only £3,000 to be spent on the expensive space creatures and other special effects. It does not take account of all the extra costs involved in the operation of special effects in the studio.
>
> Last week I agreed an additional £200 to your budget of £2,300 for the first four episodes. This figure is now revealed to be totally unrealistic. The costs of these four will be more

than £4,000 each – and it will be even higher if the cost of the spaceship has to be averaged over four rather than thirteen episodes.

Such a costly serial is not one that I can afford for this space in this financial year. You should not therefore proceed any further with the production of more than four episodes.

I am asking A.C.(P) Tel. [Joanna Spicer] and P.M.F. [John Mair] to examine with everyone concerned the exact realistic costs of this serial so far and the costs we should have to face if it were to continue.

In the meanwhile, that is for the next three weeks while I am away, you should marshall ideas and prepare suggestions for a new children's drama serial at a reliably economic price. There is a possibility that it will be wanted for transmission from soon after Week 1 of 1964.

Sydney Newman receives a copy of this memo and immediately notes that the cost of the Doctor's ship was supposed to be £3,000 spread over fifty-two weeks, not £4,000 spread over thirteen.

Monday 21: Four days' preliminary rehearsal begins for *The Tribe of Gum: The Cave of Skulls*.

Tuesday 22: The implications of Donald Baverstock's memo of the previous Friday are now being considered. At Joanna Spicer's request, John Mair sends her a memo detailing some of the background to *Doctor Who*'s production, focusing in particular on its budget and costs. With regard to the interior of the Doctor's ship, he notes that 'this was originally to cost £500; the producer was told it would cost £3,000; in the event it appears to have cost nearly £4,000' but that Donald Wilson had always planned its cost to be spread over the full fifty-two episodes and kept within the original £2,300 budget.

Spicer subsequently holds a meeting with Mair, Donald Wilson, Verity Lambert, James Bould, Jack Kine and others to discuss the situation. She explains that Baverstock would be prepared to accept a run of thirteen episodes of *Doctor Who*, but only if he can afford it. She asks Wilson and Lambert to examine the possibility of making thirteen episodes within a budget of £2,500 each (£32,500 in total), from which £75 per episode (£975 in total) would go towards the cost of interior of the Doctor's ship, £200 per episode (£2,600 in total) would be used to employ an outside contract scenic effects firm and £500 per episode (£6,500 in total) would be the Design

Department's budget allocation (DDBA in BBC terminology). The man-hours allocation would be 500 per episode (6,500 in total) and Lambert would have to gain clearance from James Mudie, Head of Scenic Servicing, if an unusually large proportion of the total was to be used up on any one episode. A special allocation would be made to pay off the remainder of the cost of the set of the Doctor's ship.

Wilson and Lambert are confident that the series can be produced within these limits. They agree to consider the matter in more detail and respond shortly. This marks the beginning of a week of intensive meetings and discussions between Wilson, Lambert and other members of the production team.

During the course of the week, David Whitaker prepares a new story listing, which indicates that the plans for the year-long run are now as follows: *The Tribe of Gum* (four episodes) by Anthony Coburn; *The Mutants/Beyond the Sun* (seven episodes) by Terry Nation; *Marco Polo/A Journey to Cathay* (seven episodes) by John Lucarotti; an untitled 'miniscules' story (four episodes) by Robert Gould; *The Robots/The Masters of Luxor* (six episodes) by Anthony Coburn; an untitled historical story (seven episodes) by Whitaker himself; *The Hidden Planet* (six episodes) by Malcolm Hulke (this having been substituted for Hulke's historical story set in Britain around 408 AD); *The Red Fort* (seven episodes) by Terry Nation; and a futuristic story (four episodes) still to be decided.

It is subsequently concluded that, given Donald Baverstock's decision to accept only thirteen episodes for the time being, a two-part story will have to be slotted in after *The Mutants*. This will have to be written by Whitaker himself as it is now too late for a suitable story to be found and commissioned from a freelance writer. It will also have to be confined to the interior of the Doctor's ship as there is no money available for additional scenery to be designed and constructed.

Also around this time, a less significant development occurs when the title of the first story is changed from *The Tribe of Gum* to *100,000 BC* (the likely reason being that the Palaeolithic tribe is no longer given a name in the final version of Anthony Coburn's scripts). As it has previously been decided that only the individual episode titles are to appear on screen and not the overall story titles, this creates no difficulty with regard to the recording already carried out.

It has now been agreed that Christopher Barry and Richard Martin should share responsibility for directing *The Mutants*. Directors for the later stories have yet to be assigned at this point.

Richard Martin sends the following memo to Verity Lambert, Mervyn Pinfield, David Whitaker and Christopher Barry:

At the back of my mind there is a worry. This is the

vagueness of the ship itself, whose qualities and possibilities *must*, I think, be understood and accepted by the audience before the adventures of its occupants are given credence. Therefore here is some phoney science for your agreement/disagreement.

The ship is out of time but in space. The entrance is in both time and space. This entrance (the phone box) can best be described as a time/space ship gangplank. Or compression-decompression (comparison-decomparison) chamber.

The only way to pass down the gangplank is by an effort of will. Therefore if you are afraid or doubtful all you would find is the inside of a phone box, and if you stayed inside you would have a bad headache from the intercellular electronic pulses forming the mental link. Therefore it is not easy to get in and out of the ship. For those unused to it, traumatic.

The unit producing the band waves which form the time/space penetrator beams and the electronic computer to control this force are the two main pieces of machinery, the third being a service unit to take humans with it in their environment – oxygen, food etc. This is of strictly limited dimensions as every square foot supported out of time and space needs great energy!

The outside appearance of the machine is a police box because when the machine is made and before it goes critical it is given an anchor in a definite age and space, without which there can be neither past nor future, and the time/space traveller would go mad – or meet God. Therefore its occupant must tie the machine to some definite anchor. This is the most complete of all its functions and one which Dr Who has only dared to do once when he originally escaped. When he does this again it could well be the end of the series – or at least a good reason to alter the external shape if desired.

Agreement on these basic rules I feel is necessary to the right use of the ship – the internal limit of it and the handling and mending of the controls and their appearance.

None of these ideas is taken up by the production team.

Wednesday 23: John Mair sends Donald Wilson a memo recording the main points of the previous day's meeting chaired by Joanna Spicer.

Friday 25: *100,000 BC: The Cave of Skulls* is camera rehearsed and recorded in Lime Grove D. Its total cost is £4,307.

Spicer sends Wilson a memo setting out in detail the financial basis on which she has asked him and Lambert to consider making *Doctor Who*.

Monday 28: Four days' preliminary rehearsal begins for *100,000 BC: The Forest of Fear*.

Five days' shooting of film inserts for *The Mutants* begins at Ealing.

Tuesday 29: Mair sends Spicer the following memo:

> As a result of further intensive discussions the costs of *Dr Who* appear to come out as follows:
>
> *Part I (four episodes)*
>
> Actual costs are not yet available for all four episodes, but on present reckoning it seems that:
>
> (a) The spaceship cost £4,328 in all. The programme budget can contribute 14 x £75 = £1,050. Net sum to be met from special funds is therefore £3,278.
>
> (b) The pilot, and episodes one and two together, cost a total, above the budget and above a sum equivalent to the original allocation of 350 man-hours, of £782. It is thought however that when the costs of the remaining two episodes come in, they will be well below the man-hour allocation, and much of this £782 can be paid for from DDBA.
>
> *Part II (seven episodes)*
>
> There is every hope that this can now be managed within a budget of £2,500 and 500 man-hours per episode.

Wilson and Lambert have a meeting with Spicer in which they agree to *Doctor Who* being taken forward on the basis proposed on 22 October.

Wednesday 30: James Mudie writes to Joanna Spicer drawing her attention to the memo he sent John Mair on 20 June protesting at the demands placed on his Department by *Doctor Who*'s scenic servicing requirements. He adds that the design drawings for the second story, which were due on 24 October, have yet to be received, and concludes:

> In these circumstances, you may wish to call a halt to the series before the output of the service as a whole is jeopardised by this production.

Spicer, meanwhile, sends the following memo to Kenneth Adam and (to be seen on his return) Donald Baverstock:

> I held a detailed discussion of the problems of, and future plans for, *Dr Who* on 22 October on the basis of Ch.P.BBC1's [Baverstock] wish to schedule thirteen programmes in this serial, as an initial stage, subject to a proper method of servicing being found and subject to acceptable cost.
>
> H.Serials.D.Tel. [Donald Wilson] and Miss Lambert followed up this meeting by further detailed discussions and came to see me yesterday with the position as it now appears.
>
> The details are as follows; and I recommend that these episodes are acceptable on this basis:
>
>> 1. The pilot programme was made on an allocation of £2,300 which has already been covered in the BBC1 Pilot Fund for this financial year.
>>
>> 2. Thirteen episodes of *Dr Who* are offered to us in three parts of four episodes, seven episodes and two episodes respectively.
>>
>> The allocation for each programme would be £2,500; and in addition a special grant of £3,278 would be made for the provision of the special model space machine.
>>
>> Out of her £2,500 allocation per episode the producer will contribute £75 for this model. She will also set aside £200 per episode within which her requirement for scenic effects will be met by employment of the

outside contract firm.

The producer also intends to set aside £500 a week for the cost of sets etc, in the studio and for the filming sessions.

3. Each episode will be allocated seven days' designer effort and five hundred man-hours. The producer is fully informed about the use of man-hours and states that the programme can be successfully planned on this basis.

She will expect the designer to inform her if on any occasion the script, as first presented to him, requires more effort than this. It is then open to the producer to ask for an increase from within her programme allocation, subject always to H.S.S.Tel. [James Mudie] being able to handle this.

I hope it can now be agreed that H.Serials.D.Tel. can plan the serial on this basis. These thirteen episodes would thus run weeks 48-7 inclusive; and discussions could be held in good time about a continuation of the serial.

Approval is subsequently given for production to proceed on this basis, resolving the crisis that has threatened *Doctor Who* with cancellation before the first episode has even been transmitted. One consequence of the agreement reached is that the BBC's Visual Effects Department will have only minimal involvement in *Doctor Who* during the first Doctor's era. Instead, all the series' special props and effects will be designed by the scenic designer and realised by specialist freelance contractors such as Shawcraft.

Thursday 31: Richard Martin sends David Whitaker a three-page memo of comment on the script for the fifth episode of *The Mutants*.

A short video insert is recorded for *100,000 BC: The Forest of Fear* in Lime Grove D. This is for the scene where the caveman Za is attacked by a tiger (unseen).

NOVEMBER 1963

Friday 1: *100,000 BC: The Forest of Fear* is camera rehearsed and recorded in Lime Grove D. Its total cost is £2,181.

A meeting is held between Controller of Programme Services Ian Atkins, Head of Scenic Servicing James Mudie, Assistant Head of Scenic Servicing Tony Reeves, Assistant Head of Design I Beynon-Lewis and designer Raymond Cusick to discuss the sets for *The Mutants*. Atkins decides that the interior of the Doctor's ship should be redesigned as it is currently too heavy and too difficult to put up and take down in the studio. Reeves later conveys this decision to Verity Lambert, who replies that although she has no objection to the set being redesigned in this way, the costs should be borne by the Design Department rather than by the series itself as the fault lies with the original designer, Peter Brachacki.

The same day, Lambert produces an amended version of the Donald Wilson promotional note of 30 July, taking account of the changes agreed over the previous fortnight. The note no longer refers to the series running for fifty-two weeks but lists the first three stories, *100,000 BC*, *The Mutants* and *Inside the Spaceship*, the latter of which it describes with the single sentence: 'Dr Who and his companions find themselves facing a terrifying situation within the ship itself.' The note goes on to name the writers and directors for the three stories, indicating that Paddy Russell has been assigned to direct *Inside the Spaceship*, and concludes:

> NB It is absolutely essential that the fact that the spaceship, from the exterior, looks like a police telephone box, should remain completely confidential.

Monday 4: Four days' preliminary rehearsal begins for *100,000 BC: The Firemaker*.

Tuesday 5: Donald Wilson is informed that plans to publicise the first episode of *Doctor Who* with a photograph on the front cover of the BBC's listings magazine *Radio Times* have been dropped, partly due to a lack of confidence in the series on the part of Controller of Programmes Kenneth Adam (C.P.Tel.). Wilson sends the following memo to the editor of *Radio Times*:

> I am unhappy to hear today that the proposal to give *Dr Who* the front page of *Radio Times* had now been abandoned. It was particularly distressing to hear that one reason given was lack of confidence in the programme at Controller level. I assure you that this does not exist and if you have a word with C.P.Tel. I know he will express enthusiasm. I myself

believe that we have an absolute knock-out in this show and that there will be no question but that it will run and run.

I would be most grateful, if it is not too late, for the decision against it to be reversed, and that will help me to get this show off to a good start.

The *Radio Times* cover photo for the week 23-29 November will in the event be of Kenneth Horne from the radio comedy series *Beyond our Ken*, although *Doctor Who* will be prominently mentioned in the cover text and will be featured within the magazine in the form of two photographs and a short article. The series will also be promoted in the previous week's edition as a forthcoming attraction.

Wednesday 6: James Mudie sends Beynon-Lewis a memo reminding him of Ian Atkins' decision that the interior of the Doctor's ship should be redesigned and asking him to take this forward as a matter of urgency 'as in its present form it is obstructing the night setting operations for the whole of the Television Service.'

Thursday 7: Joanna Spicer responds to Mudie's memo of 30 October. She notes the developments that have occurred since the meeting she chaired on 29 October and expresses the hope that 'the situation in which your memo of 30 October was written no longer obtains.'

Raymond Cusick queries with Verity Lambert the instructions he has been given to redesign the interior of the Doctor's ship and shows her a copy of the previous day's memo from Mudie to Lewis. Lambert speaks to Design Manager James Bould and asks where the money and man-hours are to be found for this, reiterating her strong view that they should not come out of *Doctor Who*'s own allocation. She also sends a memo to Donald Wilson informing him of these developments and concluding:

I would like to mention that I only found out about the redesign of the spaceship having been put into operation because the designer called me to check. No copy of Mr Mudie's memo was sent to me and instructions were issued to the designer without reference to me in spite of the fact that no provision of man-hours or money has been made for this by anybody up to the present time.

Friday 8: *100,000 BC: The Firemaker* is camera rehearsed and recorded in Lime Grove D. Its total cost is £2,316.

Monday 11: Four days' preliminary rehearsal begins for *The Mutants: The Dead Planet.*

Friday 15: *The Mutants: The Dead Planet* is camera rehearsed and recorded in Lime Grove D.

This episode is the first to feature costumes designed by Daphne Dare, who has now been assigned as *Doctor Who*'s regular costume supervisor. The make-up is designed, as for *100,000 BC*, by Elizabeth Blattner. Subsequent make-up designers for the first year of stories will be Ann Ferriggi, Jill Summers and Sonia Markham, the latter of whom will go on to handle the make-up for the great majority of the first Doctor's stories.

Sydney Newman sends the following memo, marked 'Strictly Confidential', to Donald Wilson:

> I talked to Donald Baverstock this morning about *Dr Who* and am happy to tell you he is very keen about what he has heard about the serial.

> He is worried about money and was unable to commit himself at this time to the continuation of the serial beyond thirteen. I would suggest that sometime next week you give him a ring and … go and see him for a decision. If you handle him right I am sure everything will be OK.

Saturday 16: A trailer for *100,000 BC: An Unearthly Child* is transmitted at 5.40 pm on BBC TV.

Monday 18: Four days' preliminary rehearsal begins for *The Mutants: The Survivors.*

Verity Lambert sends Donald Wilson a memo giving estimated total cost figures, and actual design cost figures, for all four episodes of *100,000 BC*. These indicate that the series is operating well within budget and should certainly be able to pay off its outstanding commitment to the cost of the Doctor's ship by the end of the initial thirteen episodes.

The *Doctor Who* production office has now been moved to Room 512 of Threshold House, a BBC-owned building overlooking Shepherd's Bush Green in west London.

Tuesday 19: A serious problem has by this point been discovered with the previous Friday's recording of *The Mutants: The Dead Planet*: talk-back from the production assistant's headphones (i.e. the sound of messages relayed to him from the director in the control gallery) has been picked up by the studio microphones and is clearly audible on the soundtrack of the episode.

Having viewed the episode, Donald Wilson has decided that this 'induction' is 'so bad as to make the recording unsuitable for transmission.' It is agreed that the episode will have to be completely re-recorded on 6 December, in the slot originally intended for recording of the fourth instalment of *The Mutants*. All subsequent episodes will therefore be put back one week, but recording will still be six clear weeks ahead of transmission. This change of plan will also allow for model filming of the Dalek city to be redone, as the production team were unhappy with the model that Shawcraft built for the original recording of the episode.

Thursday 21: David Whitaker sends Donald Wilson a memo, headed 'Confidential', to convey some information he feels he is unable to give to Verity Lambert 'because of a personal friendship between her and Jacqueline Hill':

> Jackie told me in confidence that she has been offered a film which will begin immediately after her current engagement on *Doctor Who* is terminated, with the proviso that the BBC have an option on her services. Apparently the problem is that with the re-recording of episode one of Serial B, because the talk-back interfered, this will add another week on to the current contract, but from what I gather, no additional week's contract has been arranged by the Corporation with her.

> She told me that she was informed that there would be an extra week added on to the current commitment and felt that Verity would only ask her to do this because of their personal friendship, and she told me that she was not prepared to sacrifice her film simply for one extra week. It is not for me to decide whether or not this is reasonable, and neither do I wish to raise any mountains where mole hills exist, but it is surely right to let you know so that you can anticipate the situation. I hope I can be kept out of it.

> It may be symptomatic of a gradual lessening of confidence that the four contracted actors and actresses have in the serial itself. I think they are afraid that it is going to be taken off, and what worries me is that it will eventually affect their performances. Already I sense a certain laissez-fair attitude, and I would dearly love to stop this at birth. The only solution I can see is, of course, to tell them that the serial will continue after thirteen weeks, or not, as the case may be. Perhaps it is the indecision which is really making them feel insecure.

I hope I am right in writing to you on this subject, which I
hope you will treat in confidence.

After receiving this memo, Wilson recommends to Donald Baverstock that a
further thirteen episodes of *Doctor Who* be given the go-ahead.

A press conference to launch the series is held at 5.00 pm in Room 222 at
the Langham, a BBC-owned building opposite Broadcasting House in
London's West End. Present are Wilson, Whitaker, Lambert and the four
regular cast members.

Friday 22: Baverstock accepts Wilson's recommendation and sends him a
memo authorising him to take up options for a further thirteen episodes,
with a budget of £2,300 each. He adds:

It is likely that I should be able to make a decision on the
option to take up another thirteen, making thirty-nine in all,
sometime early in the New Year.

The Mutants: The Survivors is camera rehearsed and recorded in Lime Grove
D. Its total cost is £2,796. The cast and crew are shocked to learn of the
assassination of US President John F Kennedy in Dallas, Texas.

The set of the interior of the Doctor's ship has now been redesigned and
is somewhat simpler than before, omitting altogether the large hexagonal
unit that previously hung from the ceiling between the central console and
the main doors.

Saturday 23: *100,000 BC: An Unearthly Child* is transmitted on BBC TV.
Viewers in certain areas of the country are unable to receive the transmission
due to a widespread power failure.

Monday 25: Four days' preliminary rehearsal begins for *The Mutants: The
Escape*.

Tuesday 26: An additional day's shooting of film inserts for *The Mutants*
takes place on Stage 2 at Ealing.

Wednesday 27: Donald Wilson sends the following telegram to Sydney
Newman, who is currently staying at the Warwick Hotel in New York, USA:

DOCTOR WHO OFF TO A GREAT START EVERYBODY
HERE DELIGHTED REGARDS DONALD

Friday 29: *The Mutants: The Escape* is camera rehearsed and recorded in Lime

Grove D. Its total cost is £2,232.

Saturday 30: *100,000 BC: The Cave of Skulls* is transmitted on BBC TV. It is preceded by a repeat of *100,000 BC: An Unearthly Child*, which has been slotted into the evening's schedule for the benefit of those viewers affected by the power cut on 23 November.

DECEMBER 1963

Monday 2: Four days' preliminary rehearsal begins for re-recording of *The Mutants: The Dead Planet*.

One day's shooting of film inserts for *The Mutants* takes place at Ealing.

David Whitaker briefs the Copyright Department to commission the scripts for the six part story *The Hidden Planet* from writer Malcolm Hulke.

Tuesday 3: Verity Lambert sends a memo to Head of Artists' Bookings Pauline Mansfield-Clark enquiring if there is any possibility of changing the option terms of the regular cast's contracts:

> At present we have taken up the first option for eight and the second option for twelve weeks; our next two options are for sixteen weeks each. Ideally if we could issue a third option to run six weeks, bringing us to a total of twenty-six, and two further options to run thirteen weeks each, this would bring us into line with the Planning Department. I do not see any reason why the money should be altered, but this is something that probably you will have to go into in detail with the agents.

Lambert goes on to ask if separate contracts could be issued to extend the second option period from twelve weeks to thirteen in order to allow for the re-recording of *The Mutants: The Dead Planet*.

Thursday 5: Lambert sends Controller of Programme Services Ian Atkins a memo reminding him of the difficulties presented for *Doctor Who* by the antiquated facilities and lack of space in Lime Grove D and requesting that the studio be allocated four ring pedestal cameras rather than, as at present, two ring pedestals and two of the more cumbersome ordinary pedestals, which 'are heavy to move and ... cannot easily move up and down in vision, thereby imposing further restrictions on both director and cameraman and end product.'

Friday 6: *The Mutants: The Dead Planet* is re-recorded in Lime Grove D. This re-recording was not budgeted for; however, the cost – £2,817 – is largely confined to the artists' fees as all scenery etc can be reused from the original recording.

Saturday 7: *100,000 BC: The Forest of Fear* is transmitted on BBC TV.

Monday 10: Four days' preliminary rehearsal begins for *The Mutants: The Ambush.*

Friday 13: *The Mutants: The Ambush* is camera rehearsed and recorded in Lime Grove D. Its total cost is £2,641.
   The recording medium on this occasion is 35mm film rather than videotape; a departure from the norm requested by the production team in order to facilitate the unusually complex editing required.

Saturday 14: *100,000 BC: The Firemaker* is transmitted on BBC TV.

Monday 17: Four days' preliminary rehearsal begins for *The Mutants: The Expedition.*

Thursday 19: *Junior Points of View* shows a clip of the fight scene between Kal and Za from *100,000 BC: The Fire Maker*, but overdubbed with a wrestling commentary by Kent Walton.

Friday 20: *The Mutants: The Expedition* is camera rehearsed and recorded in Lime Grove D. Its total cost is £2,223.

Saturday 21: *The Mutants: The Dead Planet* is transmitted on BBC TV.

Monday 23: A photo shoot with the Daleks is carried out around Shepherd's Bush in London.

Saturday 28: *The Mutants: The Survivors* is transmitted on BBC TV.

Monday 30: Four days' preliminary rehearsal begins for *The Mutants: The Ordeal.*

Tuesday 31: Chief of Programmes Donald Baverstock sends Donald Wilson a memo committing himself to accepting a further ten episodes of *Doctor Who* after the twenty-six already accepted. The budget per episode will remain at £2,300. Baverstock continues:

I mentioned that I need from you now an outline of the future storylines with their locations in space and time. I hope that in these you will brighten up the logic and inventiveness of the scripts. In the episodes already recorded we have seen Dr Who and his daughter, though ageless and miraculously clever, reduced to helpless unscientific ordinariness once they left their spaceship, whereas even the two lay characters should have appeared incredibly knowledgeable to such people as the Cave Dwellers and the Country Dwellers outside the blasted city. Any ordinary man of the mid-20th Century returning to, say, the Marco Polo age could hardly help making assertions all the time which would sound to the 14th Century Chinese or Venetians like mad ludicrous prophesies. Likewise, the characters of the past and the future should also have appeared more strikingly and differently ingenious – the one more often reminding us of lost simple knowledge; the other of credible skills and capacities that can be conceived likely in the future.

I suggest that you should make efforts in future episodes to reduce the amount of slow prosaic dialogue and to centre the dramatic movements much more on historical and scientific hokum.

JANUARY 1964

Friday 3: *The Mutants: The Ordeal* is camera rehearsed and recorded in Lime Grove D. Its total cost is £1,919.

Saturday 4: *The Mutants: The Escape* is transmitted on BBC TV.

Monday 6: Four days' preliminary rehearsal begins for *The Mutants: The Rescue*.

Sydney Newman sends Verity Lambert a memo of comment after watching *The Mutants: The Escape*. Despite reservations about the Daleks' adversaries, the blond-haired Thals, his reaction is very positive:

Congratulations are due to you and those working with you on the splendid progress being made on *Doctor Who*. Many, many people have told me how much they enjoy it.

Despite the blond faeries this last episode, *The Escape*

contained one very marvellous thing which you should attempt to duplicate as often as possible. I am referring to the *demonstration* of intelligence by our four heroes – you know the way they figured out how the Daleks operated their machines and how to disable them.

Tuesday 7: Donald Wilson sends Donald Baverstock a memo containing synopses of the next three stories due into production, which at this point are *Inside the Spaceship* (now to be directed by Richard Martin rather than by Paddy Russell or by Mervyn Pinfield who had been suggested as her replacement), *Marco Polo* (to be directed by Waris Hussein) and *The Hidden Planet* (to which a director has still to be assigned). The concluding scenes of *Marco Polo*, leading into *The Hidden Planet*, are described as follows:

> … the travellers repossess their ship and land in a country which, at first sight, could well be England. The cycling policeman they see on their scanner screen however, once out of sight, behaves in a most extraordinary fashion, a way which leaves no doubt that wherever the TARDIS has landed, it is certainly not 20th Century England.

The Hidden Planet itself is then summarised as follows:

> Without knowing it, the space and time travellers have landed on a planet identical to Earth; the Tenth Planet on the other side of Earth's sun. The glass of fashion has a different reflection, the mould of form an altered pattern, yet both have sprung from the same roots as their counterparts on Earth. Thus, Doctor Who and his friends find themselves in a world where every parallel is in fact a paradox that comforts whilst it mocks. Primarily, the male sex is insisting on equality and the vote. The leader of the ruling (and female) class is, to all intents and purposes, Barbara's double. When Barbara is kidnapped by the male rebels, she is forced to assume her double's identity, while Doctor Who, Susan and Ian find themselves caught up not only in the violent struggle for male suffrage but in a web of intrigue and suspicion.

Thursday 9: J J Stringer, an administrator in Programme Planning, sends Donald Wilson a memo informing him that while it is acceptable within any given financial year for savings on one episode to be carried forward to help finance others, 'it is not possible to carry forward savings from one year to the next.' This means that the first eighteen episodes of *Doctor Who* – i.e.

those currently due to be transmitted before week commencing 4 April 1964 (Week 14) – must be 'financially self-balancing, as no savings on these can be carried forward, neither can overspending be offset by savings in the following year.' He goes on to note that as the series' allocated budget up to the end of 1963 was fully spent, 'expensive programmes in January/March must be financed by savings within the same quarter.'

It has now been decided that Waris Hussein should direct all seven episodes of *Marco Polo*. Previously, Richard Martin has been due to direct episodes four and six.

William Hartnell appears on *Junior Points of View* in an interview about the Daleks recorded the previous day.

Friday 10: *The Mutants: The Rescue* is camera rehearsed and recorded in Lime Grove D. Its total cost is £2,634.

This episode is the first to utilise the 'roll back and mix' technique experimented with on 13 September 1963 for the effect of the police box dematerialising. The effect proves very difficult to achieve and will be used less than half a dozen times on *Doctor Who* during the sixties.

Saturday 11: *The Mutants: The Ambush* is transmitted on BBC TV.

Monday 13: Four days' preliminary rehearsal begins for *Inside the Spaceship: The Edge of Destruction*.

Five days' shooting of film inserts for *Marco Polo* begins on Stage 3B at Ealing.

A permanent production office has by this time been set up for *Doctor Who* in Rooms 505, 506 and 507 of Union House – the building directly adjoining its previous location, Threshold House.

Wednesday 15: At Verity Lambert's request, David Whitaker sends Donald Wilson a memo setting out audience size and audience reaction figures for *100,000 BC* and for each of the first three episodes of *The Mutants*. *100,000 BC*, including the repeat of the first episode, has registered an average audience of 12% (i.e. 6 million viewers) and an average audience reaction figure of 58.25; *The Mutants* has so far done even better, reaching by the third episode an audience of 18% (9 million viewers) and an audience reaction figure of 62.

Friday 17: *Inside the Spaceship: The Edge of Destruction* is camera rehearsed and recorded in Lime Grove D. Its total cost is £1,480.

Saturday 18: *The Mutants: The Expedition* is transmitted on BBC TV.

Monday 20: Four days' preliminary rehearsal begins for *Inside the Spaceship: The Brink of Disaster*.

Tuesday 21: The production team have by this point decided to abandon Terry Nation's historical story *The Red Fort*. They ask him instead to write a six-part replacement story with a futuristic theme. Nation agrees that, in view of the shortage of time remaining before the planned production dates, he will complete and deliver his scripts within the space of four weeks. Whitaker arranges to help him with weekly or bi-weekly discussions.

Friday 24: *Inside the Spaceship: The Brink of Disaster* is camera rehearsed and recorded in Lime Grove D. Its total cost is £1,506.

Saturday 25: *The Mutants: The Ordeal* is transmitted on BBC TV.

Monday 27: Four days' preliminary rehearsal begins for *Marco Polo: The Roof of the World*.

Friday 31: *Marco Polo: The Roof of the World* is camera rehearsed and recorded in Lime Grove D. Its total cost is £2,687.

FEBRUARY 1964

Saturday 1: *The Mutants: The Rescue* is transmitted on BBC TV.

Monday 3: Four days' preliminary rehearsal begins for *Marco Polo: The Singing Sands*. William Hartnell is ill and unable to take part.

David Whitaker visits Terry Nation's home for a script conference on the writer's new six-part story, which he has decided to call *The Keys of Marinus*. They discuss the first four episodes in depth and work out the set, filming and casting requirements as far as possible.

Tuesday 4: Whitaker sends William Hartnell a letter wishing him a speedy recovery.

Whitaker also has a meeting with writer Robert Gould in which they discuss at length the difficulties of the 'miniscules' idea. Whitaker asks Gould to submit another story proposal instead. Gould says that he has had an idea about a planet where plants treat people the way that people normally treat plants, and that he will let Whitaker know if this works out.

Two of the four Dalek props made by Shawcraft for *The Mutants* have now been put into storage, along with the control panels from their city, in the BBC's special effects store at Ealing. Jack Kine of the Visual Effects

Department has decided that there is no room for the other two to be stored so, rather than let them be broken up, the production team decide to donate them to Dr Barnardo's children's homes.

Thursday 6: David Whitaker collects from Terry Nation's home the draft script for the first episode of *The Keys of Marinus*.

Friday 7: *Marco Polo: The Singing Sands* is camera rehearsed and recorded in Lime Grove D. Its total cost is £1,618.

Saturday 8: *Inside the Spaceship: The Edge of Destruction* is transmitted on BBC TV. A scene in which Susan violently and repeatedly stabs a pair of scissors into the mattress of her bed will subsequently be criticised internally at the BBC on the grounds that it could easily be copied by children. Verity Lambert will admit that its inclusion was a mistake and give an undertaking that nothing similar will occur in future.

Sunday 9: Robert Gould sends Whitaker a card to let him know that he has decided against proceeding with his idea for a story about a planet where the roles of people and plants are reversed.

Monday 10: Four days' preliminary rehearsal begins for *Marco Polo: Five Hundred Eyes*.

Tuesday 11: Whitaker collects from Nation's home the draft script for the second episode of *The Keys of Marinus*.

Wednesday 12: David Whitaker sends Assistant Head of Copyright E Caffery a memo seeking advice about a request made to the production office by A R Mills, Deputy Editor of publishers Frederick Muller Ltd, for permission to produce novelisations of 'several of the *Doctor Who* stories.' Mills had previously contacted writer Terry Nation about this 'but now thought it better to come to the fountain head, so to speak.' Whitaker has explained to Mills that *Doctor Who* is the property of the BBC and that he is unable to release any copies of scripts at this stage. 'I closed the meeting,' Whitaker notes, 'by saying that I would endeavour to find out, in the next few days, if the BBC was willing to grant permission for publication.'
    Frederick Muller Ltd will later publish three novelisations: *Doctor Who in an exciting adventure with the Daleks* by David Whitaker (1964), *Doctor Who and the Zarbi* by Bill Strutton (1965) and *Doctor Who and the Crusaders* by David Whitaker (1966).

Thursday 13: Donald Baverstock, at a meeting with Donald Wilson to discuss the Serials Department's offers for the July/September quarter, agrees in principle that *Doctor Who*'s four regular cast members can now be firmly engaged right up to the end their fifty-two week contracts. Production is to continue uninterrupted and Baverstock will consider at a later date a proposal made by Wilson for a six week break in transmission at some point during the run. Baverstock agrees a budget for the last sixteen episodes of £2,380 per episode if outside stock film hire is involved or £2,300 per episode as before if film requirements can be serviced from within the BBC. He also agrees to consider separately a bid by Wilson for extra money to make a four part 'miniscules' story.

Friday 14: *Marco Polo: Five Hundred Eyes* is camera rehearsed and recorded in Lime Grove D. Its total cost is £1,958.

Saturday 15: *Inside the Spaceship: The Brink of Disaster* is transmitted on BBC TV.

Monday 17: Four days' preliminary rehearsal begins for *Marco Polo: The Wall of Lies*.

Terry Nation delivers to David Whitaker his draft scripts for the third and fourth episodes of *The Keys of Marinus*.

Tuesday 18: Donald Baverstock sends Donald Wilson a memo recording the points agreed at their meeting on 13 February.

The BBC's two remaining Daleks appear on *Hi There!*, a BBC programme starring popular Australian entertainer Rolf Harris.

Thursday 20: Sydney Newman is sent a memo by the Head of Business for Television Enterprises, who asks how long *Doctor Who* is due to continue and whether or not there are any plans to resurrect the phenomenally popular Daleks.

Friday 21: *Marco Polo: The Wall of Lies* is camera rehearsed and recorded in Lime Grove D. Its total cost is £2,317.

Saturday 22: *Marco Polo: The Roof of the World* is transmitted on BBC TV. It is promoted with a photograph on the front cover of this week's edition of *Radio Times* – the first time *Doctor Who* has been accorded this privilege. The photograph shows the Doctor (William Hartnell) with Marco Polo (Mark Eden) and the Mongol warlord Tegana (Derren Nesbitt).

Sunday 23: William Russell writes to his agent, T Plunkett Green, raising a number of grievances about his role in the series.

Monday 24: Four days' preliminary rehearsal begins for *Marco Polo: Rider from Shang-Tu*.

Donald Wilson replies on Sydney Newman's behalf to the memo of 20 February from the Head of Business for Television Enterprises. He informs him that there is now a firm commitment to fifty-two weeks of *Doctor Who* and continues:

> We have in mind, of course, to try and resurrect the Daleks, but with the writing we at present have in hand it is hardly likely to happen until well on in the summer.

> I am asking Verity Lambert to keep you informed both of the continuation dates for the programme and of any possible exploitation ideas, including the return of the Daleks.

T Plunkett Green writes to Wilson conveying the grievances that his client William Russell has raised with him. First, Russell is irritated that two of the guest cast rather than the regulars were pictured with William Hartnell on the previous week's *Radio Times* front cover; secondly, he feels that recent scripts have given him, and his fellow regulars, an insufficiently substantial role in the action; thirdly, he is concerned that a six minute scene, largely involving him, was added to *The Wall of Lies* only the day before the episode was recorded, leaving him very little time to learn and rehearse it.

Tuesday 25: Terry Nation has now completed his draft scripts for all six episodes of *The Keys of Marinus*, and these have been formally accepted by the production team.

At David Whitaker's request, Assistant Head of Copyright E Caffery writes to Malcolm Hulke's agent, Harvey Unna, to inform him that the scripts for *The Hidden Planet* are unacceptable in their present form and will have to be abandoned unless Hulke is prepared to rewrite them completely.

Whitaker also briefs the Copyright Department to commission from writer John Lucarotti a four-part historical story entitled *The Aztecs*.

Wednesday 26: John Crockett, a BBC staff director who has been brought in to handle episode four of *Marco Polo* before taking full responsibility for *The Aztecs*, sends David Whitaker a list of ideas for subsequent historical stories. The list reads as follows:

Jack Cade/Peasants' Revolt/Pilgrimage of Grace

Viking Raids on Britain

The '45 and Bonnie Prince Charlie

Drake/Armada

Raleigh/Colonisation

Globe Theatre/Burbage/Alleyne/Plague/Puritans

Australian Convict Settlement

Roman Invasion of Britain   )
Or   ) c.f. Alfred Duggan
Defeat of Romans in Britain)

Crusades/Richard I

Akhnaton/and his downfall

Guelphs & Ghibellines   )
)
Medici (Leonardo, Michelangelo, Savanarola or Borgias   )
Florence

)
Benvenuto Cellini   )

Covered Wagons

18th to early 19th Century Cornish smugglers and wreckers

Boadicea

Friday 28: *Marco Polo: Rider from Shang-Tu* is camera rehearsed and recorded in Lime Grove D. Its total cost is £2,821.

Donald Wilson replies in apologetic terms to T Plunkett Green's letter of 24 February. He explains that many shots of the four regulars were taken at the *Radio Times* photocall for *Marco Polo* and that the production side had 'confidently expected' one of these to be used on the cover. The magazine makes its own decisions, however, and Wilson can only complain after the event – which he is now doing. On the question of the series' scripts, he continues:

I know that Verity Lambert has discussed all this very thoroughly in the last two days with all four principals and I believe that now they are feeling much happier about what she has been able to tell them of our future plans. As you will now know, it is agreed that we should continue *Dr Who* for at least fifty-two weeks. This gives us a chance to work much further ahead on scripts and make sure that we do not again have to plunge into an unprepared job.

I assure you that I will, myself, be watching very carefully to make sure that neither William Russell's or our own interests suffer from scripts which do not use his talents to the maximum.

Lambert sends Wilson a memo informing him that up to the end of the financial year the production team will have had to write off one script by Alan Wakeman (the trial episode of *The Living World*) and six by Malcolm Hulke (*The Hidden Planet*). If *Doctor Who* were to be discontinued after its initial fifty-two week run they would also have to write off 'a six-part serial by Anthony Coburn which has been accepted but which needs further work on it' (*The Masters of Luxor*). She adds that they are currently considering commissioning a four-part serial from writer Margot Bennett to act 'as a cover' in case TC1 proves unavailable or 'the "miniscule" story falls through,' and that this might also have to be written off if the series were to be discontinued.

David Whitaker has by this point commissioned a six-part future-based story entitled *The Sensorites* from writer Peter R Newman and has himself undertaken to write a six-part historical story set in 16th Century Spain after the Armada. Terry Nation has also agreed to write a six-part story concerning a future Dalek invasion of Earth, thus meeting the ever-growing demand for a return appearance by the series' most popular monsters. Moris Farhi is another writer currently in discussion with the production team.

The planned running order for the stories after *Marco Polo* is now: *The Keys of Marinus* (six episodes) by Terry Nation, to be directed by John Gorrie; *The Aztecs* (four episodes) by John Lucarotti, to be directed by John Crockett; *The Sensorites* (six episodes) by Peter R Newman, to be directed by Mervyn Pinfield; David Whitaker's historical story (six episodes), to be directed by Gerald Blake; a 'miniscules' story (four episodes), yet to be commissioned, to be directed by Richard Martin; and Terry Nation's Dalek story (six episodes), director yet to be assigned.

Saturday 29: *Marco Polo: The Singing Sands* is transmitted on BBC TV.

MARCH 1964

Monday 2: Four days' preliminary rehearsal begins for *Marco Polo: Mighty Kublai Khan*.

Harvey Unna writes to E Caffery to convey his client Malcolm Hulke's concern at being asked to make substantial revisions to his scripts for *The Hidden Planet*. He points out that the scripts adhere closely to the storyline, which was agreed with the production team in advance, and that the requested revisions constitute an unreasonable departure from this.

Friday 6: *Marco Polo: Mighty Kublai Khan* is camera rehearsed and recorded in Lime Grove D.

Saturday 7: *Marco Polo: Five Hundred Eyes* is transmitted on BBC TV.

Monday 9: Four days' preliminary rehearsal begins for *Marco Polo: Assassin at Peking*.

Tuesday 10: Caffery replies to Unna's letter of 2 March, refuting the assertions made by Hulke about the requested revisions to his scripts for *The Hidden Planet*:

> In our opinion, and subject to the suggestions already made about it, there is nothing basically wrong with the storyline. It is the scripts – and their treatment of the storyline – which proved unacceptable and which need completely rewriting to bring them up to acceptance standards. Given Mr Hulke's contention that we are not adhering to the storyline and that he has already done what he was asked to do – a contention with which we cannot agree – is there really any point in continuing? In view of this impasse, is not the only sensible and practical solution to pay Mr Hulke for the work he has done and call the whole project off? Whilst Mr Hulke is free to rewrite the scripts on the basis proposed in my letter of 25 February, there can surely be no useful point in continuing in the face of such fundamental disagreement between the production unit and the writer.

Hulke subsequently agrees to continue working on his scripts and rewrite them as suggested by the production team. Episode two of the story subsequently acquires the working title *Year of the Lame Dog*.

Friday 13: *Marco Polo: Assassin at Peking* is camera rehearsed and recorded in Lime Grove D. The start of the day's work is delayed when the lift required to transport a camera dolly to the studio breaks down and has to be hastily repaired. A further fifteen minute hold up occurs when the studio fireman refuses to let camera rehearsals get underway due to his concern over a clutter of electrical equipment left in the fire gangways. A compromise is eventually reached on this.

Saturday 14: *Marco Polo: The Wall of Lies* is transmitted on BBC TV.

Monday 16: Four days' preliminary rehearsal begins for *The Keys of Marinus: The Sea of Death*.

Writer John Lucarotti is making good progress on his scripts for *The Aztecs*, but illness prevents him from bringing them in to the production office as he had planned. He agrees to come in the following day instead.

David Whitaker makes an appointment to see writer Dennis Spooner at 11.00 am on 18 March to discuss the possibility of him contributing a story about the French Revolution. This would act as a replacement for Whitaker's own Spanish Armada story.

Whitaker also visits rehearsals. He later reports to Verity Lambert, who is absent from the office this week, that they are going well and that the cast like director John Gorrie.

In addition, Whitaker sends some stills from *Doctor Who* to A R Mills of Frederick Muller Ltd, who are taking forward their plans to publish novelisations based on the series. Mills promises to return them by the end of the week.

Tuesday 17: David Whitaker briefs the Copyright Department to commission Terry Nation's new Dalek story, which at this point is referred to as *The Daleks*. It will shortly afterwards be given the new working title *The Return of the Daleks*. The target delivery date for the scripts is 19 June 1964.

John Lucarotti spends the day at the production office. His scripts for *The Aztecs* are two-thirds finished, and he works all day on the remainder.

Whitaker, meanwhile, completes some rewrites on episode four of *The Keys of Marinus* to remove the Doctor from the plot and thereby allow William Hartnell a week's holiday.

The BBC are currently considering a proposal from the *Daily Express* newspaper to run a regular cartoon strip based on *Doctor Who*. Jacqueline Hill, however, has considerable reservations about her likeness being used for this.

Wednesday 18: Whitaker meets Dennis Spooner to discuss the French Revolution idea. Spooner agrees to submit a storyline in two weeks' time.

Whitaker also sends copies of the completed scripts for *The Aztecs* to Design Manager James Bould.

Donald Wilson attends rehearsals to see a run-through of the episode due to be recorded in two day's time. He has only three minor comments on the dialogue, and Whitaker agrees to take these on board. Subsequently Wilson talks to Jacqueline Hill and the rest of the regular cast about the *Daily Express* proposal for a *Doctor Who* cartoon strip.

Whitaker speaks to William Russell about giving him a holiday from the series and suggests that this could fall during the French Revolution story, due to be made in July and August. Russell agrees to leave it to him.

Whitaker also makes arrangements with John Gorrie for Carole Ann Ford to be released from rehearsals on 13 April as she will be needed at Ealing for the shooting of some film inserts for *The Aztecs*. These are designed to cover for Ford's planned absence on holiday during the period when episodes two and three of that story are in production.

Mervyn Pinfield sends Wilson a memo explaining the reasons for the late start of recording the previous Friday. He notes that the problem of electrical equipment is an old and continuing one, as 'a certain quantity of equipment is permanently allocated to Studio D and it has to be kept in the studio, there being absolutely no other area to accommodate it.' He adds that this problem is particularly acute 'when the studio is chock full of sets' and concludes:

> Of course, the only real remedy is not to fill the studio area with sets and to leave a reasonable amount of room for this lighting equipment, but last Friday's production was, perhaps, the most complicated set-wise that we have yet had in the *Doctor Who* series.
>
> With the aim of reducing the possibility of a future delay of this description, perhaps the designers could be made more aware of this aspect of the problem.

Friday 20: *The Keys of Marinus: The Sea of Death* is camera rehearsed and recorded in Lime Grove D.

Saturday 21: *Marco Polo: Rider from Shang-Tu* is transmitted on BBC TV.

Monday 23: Four days' preliminary rehearsal begins for *The Keys of Marinus: The Velvet Web*.

David Whitaker briefs the Copyright Department to commission from writer Louis Marks a storyline for a possible 'miniscules' story to replace Robert Gould's.

Thursday 26: Whitaker sends Donald Wilson a memo refuting a charge made by Gould that Terry Nation's script for *The Screaming Jungle*, the third episode of *The Keys of Marinus*, plagiarises his idea for a story about a planet where plants treat people the way that people normally treat plants. Whitaker sets out the key stages in the development and writing of Nation's story and continues:

> I spoke to Terry Nation this morning on the telephone and a summary of his words is as follows:
>
>> That the conception of an episodic serial (three or four different adventures in one serial) arose from combined discussions.
>>
>> That episode one was entirely his creation, with only minor suggestions.
>>
>> That episode two arose out of combined discussion – the 'throwing' of ideas back and forwards.
>>
>> That episode three began with a suggestion from me that he wrote a 'House that Jack Built' story – some house or place that was full of booby-traps. Since episodes one and two had been basically interior sets, he wished to tell a story more 'out in the open' to give the designer a chance for different settings. It was his own idea to speed up Nature's process and have some of our principal artists battling with vegetation rather than with alien people.
>>
>> Episode four started with an idea from me to change the climate (from the hot jungle of episode three to a snow region). The rest came out of general discussion.
>>
>> Episodes five and six arose out of general discussion, although episode six was totally the author's.
>
> Terry Nation is prepared to write to you himself with the relevant dates in confirmation of this, if necessary.
>
> In conclusion, I can only say that Robert Gould at no time discussed his idea in any detail with me. My reaction after our meeting on 4 February was to repeat his 'plants treating people as people treat plants' comment to Miss Lambert, who agreed

with me that it might be too near *The Day of the Triffids* by John Wyndham but that we would wait to see the storyline.

Friday 27: *The Keys of Marinus: The Velvet Web* is camera rehearsed and recorded in Lime Grove D.

Saturday 28: *Marco Polo: Mighty Kublai Khan* is transmitted on BBC TV.

Monday 30: Four days' preliminary rehearsal begins for *The Keys of Marinus: The Screaming Jungle*.

APRIL 1964

Thursday 2: David Whitaker briefs the Copyright Department to commission from Dennis Spooner the six scripts for his French Revolution story, now entitled *The Reign of Terror*.

Friday 3: *The Keys of Marinus: The Screaming Jungle* is camera rehearsed and recorded in Lime Grove D. Severe problems are encountered with the scenery during the recording of this episode. Head of Scenic Servicing James Mudie later puts this down to lateness of the design drawings, which was due in turn to lateness of the scripts.

Saturday 4: *Marco Polo: Assassin at Peking* is transmitted on BBC TV.

Monday 6: Four days' preliminary rehearsal begins for *The Keys of Marinus: The Snows of Terror*.

Tuesday 7: Verity Lambert sends Donald Wilson the following memo:

> As we discussed, I would like to put forward the following suggestion for a break in transmission of *Doctor Who* for the six weeks of 1 August to 5 September inclusive.
>
> We would, of course, continue recording *Doctor Who* during this period and, therefore, when transmissions commenced again on 12 September, we would be ten weeks in hand. This would mean that, if the series should continue for the following year, we would be able to have a break in recording of five weeks after 23 October (Week 43), and we would commence recording again in Week 48 with five weeks in hand.

For the six weeks that we are not transmitting *Doctor Who*, we will provide a six part serial at approximately the same budget as *Doctor Who* to be recorded from Weeks 27 to 32 inclusive. David Whitaker and I are, at present, discussing ideas for this and we hope to let you have something definite by the end of next week.

Friday 10: *The Keys of Marinus: The Snows of Terror* is camera rehearsed and recorded in Lime Grove D.

Sydney Newman sends Verity Lambert the following memo:

> May I encourage you to do something in future episodes of *Doctor Who* to glamorize the title, occupation etc of an engineer.

> Nowadays for a kid to want to become a scientist is really hot stuff, but to become a technologist or an engineer – which the country needs in millions – is without prestige. Engineers, of course, are people who repair cars, aeroplane engines, run atomic energy plants etc. Another way of putting it is an emphasis on the applications of science rather than on pure science by itself.

> If you can help do this I think it will do the country a lot of good.

Nothing comes of this suggestion.

Saturday 11: *The Keys of Marinus: The Sea of Death* is transmitted on BBC TV.

Monday 13: Four days' preliminary rehearsal begins for *The Keys of Marinus: Sentence of Death*.

Film inserts for *The Aztecs* are shot at Ealing.

Tuesday 14: David Whitaker sends Verity Lambert a memo setting out his ideas for the second season of *Doctor Who*, on the assumption that the series 'will be renewed for a full fifty-two week period':

> The first thing of importance to say is that the fewer writers we employ the better. It is quite obvious that Terry Nation, for example, has improved his approach to the serial and to the four running characters, although he had to write his second serial very speedily. I think a nucleus of writers would

ensure that the characters did have growth and added dimension.

This is the way I suggest the future fifty-two weeks to be set up:

Serial A	Past	Spanish Armada	6 parts
Serial B	Future	(Possibly Malcolm Hulke)	6 parts
Serial C	Past	Egyptian	4 parts
Serial D	Future		6 parts
Serial E	Sideways		4 parts
Serial F	Future	(Possibly Tony Coburn)	6 parts
Serial G	Past	American Civil War	6 parts
Serial H	Future		4 parts
Serial I	Past	Roman	4 parts
Serial J	Future		6 parts

What I suggest is this. That at some time in the summer when the plans are clear, we ask two or three writers to attend a planning conference. That we discuss which characters are going to continue in *Doctor Who*; the way they are to develop; and the subjects we would like treated. (Obviously the above list is merely a suggestion.) Then I think we should put authors' names beside certain serials and in this way we can have a grand plan of operations. Writers will be able to see a year's work ahead of them and will know in plenty of time what their delivery date situation is, and their subject, and finally it will be very much easier to devise the ending and the beginning of new serials when the writers are able to co-operate with each other. At the moment I am entirely responsible for the linking of one serial into another, and while this may work well enough I feel that the more original ideas we have the better. If we are guaranteeing a year's work in the shape of, say, a promise of two serials to a writer, then he is going to be prepared to contribute ideas to the project as a whole.

I recommend that we make Terry Nation the senior writer, insofar as future subjects are concerned. He has worked very well for us and his writing is obviously improving. His figures are certainly the highest so far of all the writers and my suggestion is that he be offered three serials in the new fifty-two weeks. Secondly, I suggest that there be a senior 'past' writer who is offered two serials. This will then leave five serials only, and I suggest that they are split up between no more than four writers.

As you can see from my list above, I have suggested places where we can use scripts we have bought, like the Malcolm Hulke future serial, and Tony Coburn's robot serial.

Wednesday 15: Evelyn M Thomas, designated Editorial Assistant Publicity, sends the BBC's Publications Executive a memo confirming that, 'subject to the usual agreement being reached concerning the BBC's right to approve content and format', there is no objection in principle to a proposal from Souvenir Press Ltd to publish a *Daleks Annual*, based on contributions from Terry Nation and BBC illustrations, or to the proposal from Frederick Muller Ltd to produce *Dr Who and the Daleks*, written by David Whitaker based on Terry Nation's scripts. The Head of Films Television has agreed that reasonable facilities may be granted to Souvenir Press to view telerecordings of episodes and arrange for stills to be taken from them.

These are just the first of many product proposals that will soon see a whole host of *Doctor Who*-related and, in particular, Dalek-related merchandise appearing in the nation's toyshops.

Thursday 16: Chief of Programmes Donald Baverstock sends Donald Wilson the following memo regarding the continuation of *Doctor Who* beyond its initial fifty-two week production run:

> Present commitments, as I understand them, commit us to transmission of *Doctor Who* until the end of October this year. Provided you can assure me that, after a full examination of the problems ahead, you will find it possible to obtain a sufficient variety of good new storylines, I am willing to agree in principle that *Doctor Who* should continue for three months beyond the end of October. In contracting the four artists for this period I suggest you should also obtain options at the same fees for a further three months.

Friday 17: *The Keys of Marinus: Sentence of Death* is camera rehearsed and recorded in Lime Grove D.

Saturday 18: *The Keys of Marinus: The Velvet Web* is transmitted on BBC TV.

Monday 20: Four days' preliminary rehearsal begins for *The Keys of Marinus: The Keys of Marinus*.

BBC2 begins transmission.

Friday 24: *The Keys of Marinus: The Keys of Marinus* is camera rehearsed and recorded in Lime Grove D.

Saturday 25: *The Keys of Marinus: The Screaming Jungle* is transmitted on BBC1.

Monday 27: Four days' preliminary rehearsal begins for *The Aztecs: The Temple of Evil.*

Tuesday 28: Kenneth Adam, the Director of Television, sends a memo to Stuart Hood, the Controller of Programmes for Television, conveying the concerns of fellow members of the BBC's Board of Management about the direction *Doctor Who* is taking:

> The 'creepiness' is laid on rather thick and there are so many refugees from Attica or, if you prefer, the Eisteddfod wandering about. If it is to survive, it needs a touch of discipline – especially in the writing; they couldn't really be so stupid by now as always to split up the way they do when danger threatens. Even my 3½ year old grand-daughter remarked on it on Saturday.

Hood subsequently passes a copy of this memo on to Sydney Newman, and Newman raises the matter with Donald Wilson.

Thursday 30: John Mair, Planning Manager (Forward), responds to a request from Joanna Spicer, Assistant Controller (Planning) Television, for recommendations regarding 'the Studio D situation with particular reference to *Dr Who.*' He explains that there are two problems currently faced by the production: first, the studio is to be taken out of service from 1 to 16 August inclusive to allow for work to be carried out on the sound equipment and to meet requests from the electricians' trade union for improved ventilation at studio gallery level; secondly, the lack of storage facilities for technical equipment means that space has to be allowed for this on the floor of the studio itself, leading to setting and rigging difficulties and potential union demarcation disputes.

Mair goes on to note that *Doctor Who*'s claim to one of the big Television Centre studios has previously been thought unjustified, but that he undertook some time ago to try to transfer it to the Centre during the summer months due to the excessive heat in Studio D. Consequently the series is due to be in TC4 for the six Fridays from 7 August to 11 September inclusive. Donald Wilson has also agreed that it can be moved into Lime Grove G for the four weeks prior to that, and Mair is hopeful that Verity Lambert will be prepared to accept this studio on a longer-term basis. The series could be moved to a larger studio if an exchange could be arranged with another show that similarly recorded just one day a week, but the only shows which follow that pattern are situation comedies and BBC2's *Thriller* serial, which are unsuited to being made in Studio D. He concludes:

> Given all these complexities, my recommendations would be:
>
> a) that we make TC3/4 available to *Dr Who* in the immediate future as and when possible, and subject to a guarantee that no last minute move will be made later than four weeks before production;
>
> b) that we put *Dr Who* into G and then TC3/4 as already agreed up to Week 37; and
>
> c) that we review the whole position in the light of autumn needs (which will by then be more clearly known) about two months before *Dr Who* is due to move out of the Centre in Week 38, unless we can do so earlier.

MAY 1964

Friday 1: *The Aztecs: The Temple of Evil* is camera rehearsed and recorded in Lime Grove D.

Saturday 2: *The Keys of Marinus: The Snows of Terror* is transmitted on BBC1.

Monday 4: Four days' preliminary rehearsal begins for *The Aztecs: The Warriors of Death*.

Wednesday 6: Donald Wilson sends Sydney Newman the following response to Kenneth Adam's memo of 28 April:

> I myself have been concerned about D.Tel.'s [Adam] points, particularly his last one, and some three weeks ago I urged on Verity the necessity for making sure a) that our leading characters don't appear to be simply stupid and b) that the thrills should be genuine and lead directly out of a strong

situation and not be added for kicks. When I last spoke about this serial to you if you remember I made the point that the kind of writers with the necessary invention are not always necessarily the best in terms of characterisation and dialogue, but we must keep trying.

I made a copy of D.Tel.'s note and will make sure that both Verity and David Whitaker see it.

Friday 8: *The Aztecs: The Warriors of Death* is camera rehearsed and recorded in TC3.

Sydney Newman sends Stuart Hood the following memo about the points raised by Kenneth Adam:

> Donald and I were on to this three or four weeks ago and rather forcefully brought these to Verity's attention. The scripts are what is difficult!

Saturday 9: *The Keys of Marinus: Sentence of Death* is transmitted on BBC1.

Monday 11: Four days' preliminary rehearsal begins for *The Aztecs: The Bride of Sacrifice*.

Wednesday 13: Verity Lambert sends Donald Wilson a memo commenting on John Mair's suggestion that Lime Grove G could become *Doctor Who*'s regular studio. She informs him that neither *The Aztecs* nor *The Sensorites* could be made there as they will require large composite sets and cannot be radically rewritten at this late stage. Although Studio G is larger in area than Studio D, it is long and narrow in shape and therefore accommodates only simple box sets. This makes it unsuitable for a drama series like *Doctor Who*, which depends greatly on having solid and sizeable sets – particularly for the historical stories. She concludes:

> If we were to move into Studio G, which certainly is inadequate for our design requirements, we would have to impose even more severe restrictions on our writers than we are doing at the moment. I can only say that this will obviously be detrimental to the series as a whole.

> As you already know, I am certainly not in favour of staying in Studio D, even if we are allowed to do so. The restrictions in D involve technical facilities and working conditions. We have struggled along for six months in this studio and have

made compromises of all kinds. The sound equipment is inadequate, old fashioned and worn out. The cameras do not take any wide angle lenses or any zooms. The lighting equipment makes life almost impossible for the lighting supervisor and, because of the heat, unbearable for everybody else in the studio.

Friday 15: *The Aztecs: The Bride of Sacrifice* is camera rehearsed and recorded in TC3.

Saturday 16: *The Keys of Marinus: The Keys of Marinus* is transmitted on BBC1.

Tuesday 19: Three days' preliminary rehearsal begins for *The Aztecs: The Day of Darkness.* (The rehearsal room has been closed on Monday 18 as it is Whit Monday.)

Wednesday 20: Sydney Newman sends Chief of Programmes Donald Baverstock a memo in which he outlines the problems currently facing *Doctor Who* and proposes a six week break in transmission after the conclusion of *The Sensorites* on Saturday 25 July:

> (1) The contracts of the main lead characters expire on 24 October. It is urgent that we renew on the basis of run-of-programme. In short, they should be contracted for as long as the programme continues, subject to our giving them between six and twelve weeks' notice. May I urgently request that you agree with this on the understanding that we will continue *Dr Who* until such time as you give us warning that it should stop – such warning to be as short a period of cancellation time as we can negotiate with the four stars.

> (2) On the assumption that you agree generally with the above it is proposed that we stop producing *Dr Who* for six weeks at the expiry of the present contracts. Since this comes at very much of a peak time of the year, I would like to recommend that we take *Dr Who* off the air from Weeks 32 to 37 inclusive, but continue the recordings to enable programmes to continue from the resumption in Week 38 during the winter months.

> Relating to an earlier conversation on this problem, we have found it impossible to plan the production of another serial to fill in the six-week summer gap, due largely to the shortage of studio facilities and production staff.

(3) The most vexing problem of all is studio facilities. Studio D has worked against the best interests of *Dr Who*, has tired the cast, has not allowed for sufficient camera rehearsal, the heat is unbearable, it has no proper technical gimmicks, and so on. At any rate, I understand the deficiencies of the studio have been recognised and it is being withdrawn for use as a drama studio. Studio G, because of its somewhat ridiculous proportions, is unacceptable. Riverside 1 or the Television Centre studios are what remain as being suitable. I have gone into the question of seeing what single play series or weekly series can be switched about to make room for *Dr Who* and have come to the irrevocable conclusion that none can. Unless the proper studio can be allocated for *Dr Who* from Week 38 (the start of *The Return of the Daleks*) I think it would be better that I recommended its cancellation. I can't bear to see this potentially marvellous programme go down the drain through inadequate support.

In general, Donald, I am proposing going off the air for six weeks in the summer in order to achieve a six-week break in the autumn. This will enable us to lick our wounds, consider the future with possible changes in cast, script, etc so that we can go on with the series with more promise than any idea we have yet thought of.

Baverstock subsequently approves a break in transmission, but stipulates that this must last for only four weeks and start from week commencing 12 September (Week 38) rather than from week commencing 1 August (Week 32). Dennis Spooner's French Revolution contribution, *The Reign of Terror*, will therefore form the closing story of the first season rather than the opening story of the second. Baverstock is furthermore unwilling to renew the series on an indefinite basis, agreeing only that it can continue transmission up to the end of January 1965.

Over the next few weeks, the production team discuss this situation and convey their thoughts to Donald Wilson. They have been considering making changes to the series' format and cast for its second year – in particular, they have been thinking of dropping the character of Barbara, thus reducing the number of regulars from four to three, and replacing Susan with another, younger girl – but Baverstock's indecision over the series' long-term future raises doubts as to whether or not this is worthwhile. Wilson summarises these considerations in the following discussion document:

We intend to continue recording until Week 43, then break recording for four weeks. This arrangement puts back our final transmission date of the current programme to Week 51 so only one more six-part serial will be required to take us up to the end of January. It is quite clearly not worth rethinking in terms of cast or format for one more six-part serial. I doubt even if the break in recording is necessary after Week 43. Moveover, there is no point in obtaining new scripts beyond the present limit unless and until we have decided on any changes in format and cast. One of our troubles has always been (from a design point of view) in getting scripts early enough. If we are to make changes starting with the first recording date of the new series, which date is in Week 48, i.e. week commencing 21 November, we must have the scripts for the first new serial completed by 1 October. I estimate, therefore, that the latest commissioning date for this serial ... must be not later than 7 July. At this date we shall have the artists engaged only up to the end of the present recording period, namely 23 October.

If we are to lose any members of the cast – and our present thinking is that we may well drop the Jackie Hill character altogether and replace Carole Ann Ford with another younger girl – this must be decided upon in time so that we can write into *The Return of the Daleks* serial (the last in the first year's programme) the scenes which will make these changes work from then on. This serial is at present being written by Terry Nation and he is naturally anxious for an early decision.

In short, if we are to continue only to the end of January we will not make any changes in format or cast because it won't be worthwhile. If we are to change the format and cast we must decide to do so not later than 7 July.

Wilson is in one respect mistaken in this memo: the number of episodes required to take transmission up to the end of January 1965 would be seven, not six.

Thursday 21: John Mair sends Joanna Spicer a further memo about *Doctor Who*'s studio allocation. He begins:

As spoken, in discussion with H.Serials.D.Tel. [Wilson] yesterday he explained that Serial G of *Dr Who* (production Weeks 22-27) is really too close to be rewritten for Studio G.

He is having difficulty in any case with one or two of the storylines and he would prefer to accept D in certain weeks, even given the problems there, than to risk further disruption by trying to get the whole rewritten in terms of sets.

On the other hand, I am sure we must not because of union problems leave it in D any more than is essential. I have therefore said that I would recommend:

Weeks 22, 23TC3
Week 24D
Week 25TC4
Week 26D
Week 27D unless, as seems possible, the producer can manage G for this particular production. This she will confirm.

You accepted that in the circumstances we should work on this basis.

Mair goes on to note the previously-agreed arrangement that the first four episodes of Serial H – *The Reign of Terror* – will be made in Studio G and the other two in TC4, and that all four episodes of Serial J – the 'miniscules' story – will be made in the latter.
    The scripts for the four-part 'miniscules' story have now been commissioned from writer Louis Marks. It is known for a time simply as *The Miniscules*, but is later given the title *Planet of Giants*.

Friday 22: *The Aztecs: The Day of Darkness* is camera rehearsed and recorded in Lime Grove D.

Saturday 23: *The Aztecs: The Temple of Evil* is transmitted on BBC1.

Monday 25: Four days' preliminary rehearsal begins for *The Sensorites: Strangers in Space*.

Friday 29: *The Sensorites: Strangers in Space* is camera rehearsed and recorded in TC3.

Saturday 30: *The Aztecs: The Warriors of Death* is transmitted on BBC1.

JUNE 1964

Monday 1: Four days' preliminary rehearsal begins for *The Sensorites: The Unwilling Warriors*.

Thursday 4: Discussions have been continuing over the past fortnight with regard to *Doctor Who*'s long-term studio allocation. Sydney Newman has asked Donald Wilson and Verity Lambert to consider the possibility of using the small Television Centre studio TC2 and compensating for the reduction in space by recording each episode over two days rather than one (an idea first proposed as early as the end of May 1963). Lambert sends Wilson a memo pointing out that this would mean spending one day shooting on a large composite set and the other on all the more minor sets, therefore doubling the number of occasions on which scenery had to be put up and taken down in the studio. She adds that under the terms of the BBC's agreement with the actors' union Equity it would mean paying some £250 extra in fees to the cast for each episode. It would also necessitate an increase in camera rehearsal and recording time. She ends:

> The above-the-line costs of a two day operation are, in fact, not great, but I think that the below-the-line costs will be quite considerable.
>
> My own feelings are that this would be a very unsatisfactory way of doing *Doctor Who* from both a monetary and an artistic point of view.

It is subsequently agreed that *Doctor Who* will continue to be recorded one day per week and that Studio 1 at Riverside will be made available for it from the start of *The Return of the Daleks*.

Friday 5: *The Sensorites: The Unwilling Warriors* is camera rehearsed and recorded in TC3.

Saturday 6: *The Aztecs: The Bride of Sacrifice* is transmitted on BBC1.
    Dalek actor Kevin Manser opens a fete for Dr Barnardo's in one of the Daleks donated to them by the BBC.

Monday 8: Four days' preliminary rehearsal begins for *The Sensorites: Hidden Danger*.

Friday 12: *The Sensorites: Hidden Danger* is camera rehearsed and recorded in Lime Grove D.

Saturday 13: *The Aztecs: The Day of Darkness* is transmitted on BBC1.

Monday 15: Four days' preliminary rehearsal begins for *The Sensorites: A Race Against Death*.

Doctor Who's first ever location filming takes place on a poplar-lined lane at White Plains, Tile House Lane, Denham, Buckinghamshire and on a lane and field at Isle of Wight Farm, Gerrards Cross, Buckinghamshire. The filming consists of some silent inserts for *The Reign of Terror* of the Doctor walking towards Paris. The Doctor, seen only from a distance, is played by Brian Proudfoot, who has spent most of the previous Friday learning to imitate William Hartnell's walk.

Tuesday 16: Three days' shooting of film inserts for *The Reign of Terror* begins on Stage 3A/B at Ealing. The first two days are devoted to live action work and the third, Thursday 18 June, to model shots of a farmhouse burning down for the end of the first episode.

Friday 19: *The Sensorites: A Race Against Death* is camera rehearsed and recorded in TC4.

Saturday 20: *The Sensorites: Strangers in Space* is transmitted on BBC1.

Monday 22: Four days' preliminary rehearsal begins for *The Sensorites: Kidnap*.

Friday 26: *The Sensorites: Kidnap* is camera rehearsed and recorded in Lime Grove D.

Saturday 27: *The Sensorites: The Unwilling Warriors* is transmitted on BBC1.

Monday 29: Four days' preliminary rehearsal begins for *The Sensorites: A Desperate Venture*.

JULY 1964

Friday 3: *The Sensorites: A Desperate Venture* is camera rehearsed and recorded in Lime Grove D.

Saturday 4: No episode of *Doctor Who* is scheduled for this evening as the sports programme *Grandstand* is extended to cover the cricket Test Match between England and Australia and the finals of the Wimbledon tennis tournament. The gap between recording and transmission is therefore restored to the position before *The Mutants: The Dead Planet* had to be remounted.

Monday 6: Four days' preliminary rehearsal begins for *The Reign of Terror: A Land of Fear*.

Friday 10: *The Reign of Terror: A Land of Fear* is camera rehearsed and recorded in Lime Grove G.
This is the first episode since the pilot to feature sets designed by someone other than Barry Newbery or Raymond Cusick. Roderick Laing has been brought in to handle *The Reign of Terror* in order to ease the workload on the two regulars.

Saturday 11: *The Sensorites: Hidden Danger* is transmitted on BBC1.

Monday 13: Four days' preliminary rehearsal begins for *The Reign of Terror: Guests of Madame Guillotine*.

Friday 17: *The Reign of Terror: Guests of Madame Guillotine* is camera rehearsed and recorded in Lime Grove G.

Saturday 18: *The Sensorites: A Race Against Death* is transmitted on BBC1.

Monday 20: Four days' preliminary rehearsal begins for *The Reign of Terror: A Change of Identity*.

Friday 24: *The Reign of Terror: A Change of Identity* is camera rehearsed and recorded in Lime Grove G. Director Henric Hirsch collapses outside the studio control room shortly before recording is due to begin, and John Gorrie is hastily brought in to take over from him for the rest of the evening.

Saturday 25: *The Sensorites: Kidnap* is transmitted on BBC1.

Monday 27: Four days' preliminary rehearsal begins for *The Reign of Terror: The Tyrant of France*.

Thursday 30: One day's shooting of film inserts for *Planet of Giants* takes place at Ealing.
It has now been over two months since Sydney Newman first raised with Donald Baverstock the question of *Doctor Who*'s long-term future, and still

no decision has been taken. The start of the series' second season has meanwhile been put back to 31 October, three weeks later than originally planned. The production team have concluded that, if there remains a real possibility of the series being discontinued at the end of January 1965, a four part story will be required for transmission after *Planet of Giants* and *The Return of the Daleks*. This presents them with a number of difficulties, not least of which is that there is no four-part story currently commissioned; they have been thinking of using Malcolm Hulke's *The Hidden Planet*, now rewritten as a five-parter, to launch the new production block.

The production team have now abandoned the idea of writing Barbara out of the series but still intend to replace Susan with another, younger girl. To this end they have prepared the following document headed 'Proposed Elimination of Susan from *Doctor Who* Series':

> Doctor Who and his group return to Earth in the year 2042. They find the planet occupied by the Daleks. The plague and famine that preceded the invasion destroyed 90% of the Earth's population. Nearly all who survived are prisoners in Dalek working parties.
>
> In London one small group is attempting to overthrow the invaders. Doctor Who and his party become involved with this group. Prominent amongst them is David Somheim. In an early battle Susan becomes his companion.
>
> The enormity of the world catastrophe has a marked effect on Susan's character. She grows more adult as she realises that the *individual* is the society. She begins to find her place in time and space. David Somheim is dedicated to overthrowing the Daleks in order to build a new world. Some of his feeling is transmitted to Susan who, no longer a child, is unwittingly seeking an objective.
>
> David and Susan fall in love. For Susan this presents another problem. She knows that sooner or later the space travellers must move on and that she must go with them. She must leave David behind. And she must forget her ideals of a new world. She is bound too tightly to her grandfather to think of leaving him.
>
> However, Doctor Who is aware of her growing womanhood. He knows that he must make the decision as to whether she continues to travel with him or not.

In the closing scenes of the final episode, Susan prepares to leave with her grandfather. Inside the ship Barbara, Ian and Doctor Who prepare for their journey. Doctor Who watches Susan and David on the scanner, and then presses the control to close the doors. He talks to Susan telling her that she has grown up and that she no longer needs him. Susan, in spite of her sadness at saying goodbye to her grandfather, is happy to remain with David and to start her new life.

Inside the ship Doctor Who's sadness at leaving Susan is obvious to the others. They leave as soon as possible. During the course of their new journey they discover that there is a stowaway aboard, a fifteen year old girl whom they have already befriended. In spite of their concern, they know that there is no going back. In any case Ian and Barbara both realise that in time she may help Doctor Who to forget the loss of Susan.

Friday 31: *The Reign of Terror: The Tyrant of France* is camera rehearsed and recorded in Lime Grove G.

AUGUST 1964

Saturday 1: *The Sensorites: A Desperate Venture* is transmitted on BBC1.

Monday 3: Four days' preliminary rehearsal begins for *The Reign of Terror: A Bargain of Necessity*. The regular venue for the series' rehearsals has now been changed to the London Transport Assembly Rooms, a training establishment opposite Television Centre, as the Drill Hall at 239 Uxbridge Road has been criticised by cast and production team alike for its poor facilities.

Thursday 6: Verity Lambert sends the Serials Department Organiser a memo with the heading 'Renewal of Artists' Contracts for *Doctor Who*' in which she points out that the need for a decision on *Doctor Who*'s long-term future is becoming increasingly pressing:

If we could get an OK for a further thirteen weeks from 2 January, I would at least be able to take out contracts for thirteen weeks with an option for a further thirteen. I have a feeling that, if we wait for much longer, we will find ourselves in the position of losing our artists, which can only lead to a certain amount of chaos at the end of our next serial.

We will not be renewing Carole Ann Ford's contract, but I would like to retain the other three principals. I therefore would be most grateful if we could have a decision on the continuance of *Doctor Who* as soon as possible.

Friday 7: *The Reign of Terror: A Bargain of Necessity* is camera rehearsed and recorded in TC4.

The recording of this episode is covered by a film crew working on a documentary called *Short Circuit – The Park*.

Saturday 8: *The Reign of Terror: A Land of Fear* is transmitted on BBC1.

Monday 10: Four days' preliminary rehearsal begins for *The Reign of Terror: Prisoners of Conciergerie*.

The BBC's two remaining Daleks are lent out this week to appear in a recording of a BBC light entertainment show starring comedian Roy Kinnear.

Tuesday 11: Verity Lambert follows up her memo of the previous Thursday by preparing the following discussion document:

NOTES

On the effect of not having a decision as to whether we continue after the end of January.

1. If we continue to the end of January, we have to provide a four week serial, since the last transmission of the Daleks is on 2 January.

> a) I really do not see what kind of an approach I can make to artists' agents at this point on the basis of a four week extension.

> b) William Hartnell has already had an offer. William Russell's agent is going ahead on the understanding that his client's contract finishes on 23 October. The best offer I can make at this point is a four week extension with no guarantee of the serial continuing thereafter.

CONCLUSIONS:

If a four week extension is the best that Baverstock can offer us, I feel that we should terminate *Doctor Who* at the end of this present series.

2. We had intended to write the character of Susan out, and this has been done in the Dalek serial, the first recording of which is on 18 September. Filming for this serial takes place on 23 August to 28 August. If we are only continuing for four weeks, or if we finish at the end of this series, there does not seem to be any point in writing Susan out.

a) We, therefore, have to rewrite the serial which goes into production in five weeks' time.

b) If the series is to continue, we have to develop a character in this serial which we intend to take Susan's place. This means that, in the next week to ten days, we have to look for and cast somebody who, to all intents and purposes, may continue at least for six months next year. We cannot approach any artist on the basis of a six weeks' engagement if, in fact, we are intending a six months' engagement. We, therefore, have to take out options.

CONCLUSIONS:

If we do not have a decision within the next two weeks as to at least a thirteen week extension, we will not be able to write Susan out and we will be stuck with the prospect of renewing her contract for next year when we have no desire to do so. The best we can do under the circumstances is to write the part of the new girl out of the present serial. This will involve considerable rewriting and it will also present us with the problem of introducing the new girl.

3. We also have the problem of commissioning a four part serial when we do not want to. We have a five part serial which we would have put in. It means that we have now the prospect of commissioning a serial in which we may have to introduce the new girl or we may not have to introduce the new girl: we may have to write in the part of Susan or we

may not have to write in the part of Susan.

The information for this serial will be required eight weeks before our first recording date, which is scheduled for Week 50, i.e. 4 December 1964. This means that the information for the serial will be required at the latest by 12 September. This, of course, means commissioning it now.

I think this is an absolutely insoluble problem unless we can get a decision one way or another.

Wednesday 12: Verity Lambert sends Planning Manager (Forward) John Mair a memo summarising the problems set out in her discussion document. She ends:

I am really not trying to force a decision on this, but I think it would be a pity to jeopardise scripts if, in fact, there is any intention at all to carry on *Doctor Who* after the end of January.

John Mair subsequently sends Chief of Programmes Donald Baverstock a memo describing the problems put to him by Verity Lambert and concluding:

There appear to be three possible lines you could take.

a) You could stop transmission after Serial K, in Week 1. This would save possible contractual trouble with the artists, but would mean rewriting Serial K at short notice to make it suitable for a 'farewell' one. Replacement would be difficult at such short notice.

b) You could stop at end January. This would involve the problems described above.

c) You could continue to end March.

My own feeling is that an equivalent audience-puller will be difficult to find and a new series in any case unwise to launch in the middle of a winter when audience figures are particularly important, and that *Dr Who* should now go on till end March.

(Sample audience figures are attached. The series is doing less well than it did during last winter, but the drop may be at least partly seasonal.)

The search for a replacement should begin now, so that you are able to make a choice by say November/December on what to put in after March 1965.

Mair also sends Sydney Newman a memo briefly outlining the problems. He explains that Baverstock would like the cast's existing contracts to be extended by four weeks but that 'Verity Lambert is afraid that the agents will either ask exorbitant sums or refuse.' He adds that he has asked Lambert to get the agents' reactions, after which he will report back to Baverstock.

Thursday 13: A further day's shooting of film inserts for *Planet of Giants* takes place at Ealing.

Friday 14: *The Reign of Terror: Prisoners of Conciergerie* is camera rehearsed and recorded in TC4.
    Donald Baverstock has a meeting with Verity Lambert in which he finally agrees to renew *Doctor Who* for thirteen weeks, with the possibility of a further thirteen after that. Later the same day, he sends her a memo recording the outcome of the meeting. With regard to the regular cast, he notes:

> I agreed that you should renew contracts for three of the principals (and negotiate a new one for the artist who will now play the fourth) for a further thirteen weeks, with an option on thirteen more beyond that. This will take transmissions to 21 March. It is important that you should not assume the necessity for an automatic increase in fees. Negotiations should aim initially at no increase. If increases are demanded, I would like to be informed so that I can decide whether or not to agree them ...

> No plans should be made, please, which might involve commitment to productions beyond these thirteen (other than options for us to decide) without prior discussion with me.

Music for episodes one and two of *Planet of Giants* is recorded.

Saturday 15: *The Reign of Terror: Guests of Madame Guillotine* is transmitted on BBC1.

Monday 17: Four days' preliminary rehearsal begins for *Planet of Giants: Planet of Giants.*

Following Donald Baverstock's agreement to renew *Doctor Who* for at least thirteen weeks, Verity Lambert chooses actress Pamela Franklin to replace Carole Ann Ford as the series' fourth regular cast member. Franklin is to be introduced in Terry Nation's Dalek story, now retitled *The Dalek Invasion of Earth*, playing a human resistance fighter named Jenny (originally called Saida).

Lambert sends Head of Artists' Bookings Pauline Mansfield-Clark a memo asking her to offer William Hartnell, William Russell and Jacqueline Hill new contracts on the basis agreed by Baverstock, and to offer Pamela Franklin a contract on the same basis but also covering the six episodes of *The Dalek Invasion of Earth*. She requests that Mansfield-Clark let her know if the established regulars' respective agents demand an increased fee, or if Franklin's agent asks for a higher fee than Carole Ann Ford's.

Derek Hoddinott of the Publicity Department has informed Lambert that he has seen in a newspaper that there is a beat group calling itself 'Doctor Who and the Daleks.' He is told that this is not a breach of copyright and that Lambert thinks it would be good publicity for the programme.

Wednesday 19: Lambert sends Baverstock a memo reporting the outcome of the approaches made to the regulars' agents:

> WILLIAM HARTNELL has turned down the offer completely. He would like a six months' contract with no options at 250 guineas per episode. This is 25 guineas more than he is getting at the present time.
>
> WILLIAM RUSSELL'S agent is away on holiday. In his absence, the contract for thirteen with an option of a further thirteen would be acceptable on the following terms. William Russell feels that his fee should be brought into line with William Hartnell's. He is, at the present time, getting 150 guineas a week and this would mean a raise in salary of approximately 75 guineas.
>
> JACQUELINE HILL would accept the offer of thirteen programmes with an option of a further thirteen at a salary of 200 guineas per episode. Her present salary is 105 guineas per episode and this would mean a raise of 95 guineas (I think

there would be some room for negotiation in this particular case.)

We have not tried to negotiate on any of the above. As you can see, it would mean a considerable increase in money.

Baverstock calls a meeting with Lambert to discuss the situation and then sends her the following memo recording his reactions:

1) That as a first step you should talk with the three principals and mention that if they were to hold to their demands for such very large increases, you might have difficulty in recommending a continuation of the series beyond January, with the same cast. Of the three, Hartnell and Russell would be more valuable to you than Jacqueline Hill. But you thought it possible that none of them might prove indispensable. If the two men were to show willingness to sign again for their present fees (or with only a nominal increase), I mentioned to you that I would be willing to consider a commitment for six months, rather than for three with an option for three.

2) That I would agree to face the replacement of *Dr Who* for a period of six weeks, from 2 January, with another short serial (preferably science fiction) if you would need this time to restore *Dr Who* with a totally new or partly new group of principals after the end of the run which finishes in January.

3) That it would be unwise to attempt to establish the new girl as a permanent member of the cast in the last episode of the present series already booked.

Baverstock goes on to inform Lambert that he has decided, on reflection, that it would be wrong of him to act as her adviser 'on matters of negotiations and of such professional details', and that she should consult instead with Elwyn Jones, the BBC's Head of Series. Jones is currently deputising for Sydney Newman as both Newman and Donald Wilson are away from the office on holiday.

Later in the day, Lambert has a discussion with Jones and then sends him the following memo:

After careful consideration, I have decided, based on the premise that we can get permission to continue *Doctor Who* for six months, that it would be best to meet William Hartnell's demand for six months' contract at 250 guineas per episode.

As far as William Russell and Jacqueline Hill are concerned, we will try and negotiate contracts with them on the basis of a nominal rise of between £10 and £20 per episode. If this is not acceptable, we will write these two artists out at the end of the present series.

Bearing in mind that negotiations with the latter two artists may take a little time, I think, if we could keep the six weeks' break which Chief of Programmes BBC1 agreed with me this morning, this would alleviate the situation as to commissioning future scripts.

Thursday 20: Verity Lambert, director Richard Martin and a group of Daleks spend the morning visiting well-known London landmarks – including the Planetarium and Westminster Bridge with the Houses of Parliament in the background – for a press photocall. The aim is to publicise the Daleks' imminent return and also the fact that *The Dalek Invasion of Earth* is to be the first *Doctor Who* story to feature extensive location shooting.

Lambert later has a further discussion with Elwyn Jones about the situation regarding the regular artists' contracts. Jones supports most of the proposals she has made, but is unwilling to recommend a six week break in transmission after *The Dalek Invasion of Earth*. Instead, he suggests that if William Russell and Jacqueline Hill have to be written out, William Hartnell should carry the main burden of the action on his own for three or four episodes. Lambert confirms that this would be possible and Jones then conveys their conclusions in a memo to Donald Baverstock, recommending that he now 'concede the existence of this programme for six months rather than for three with an option for three.'

In the light of the decisions already taken, Lambert has by this time requested that *The Dalek Invasion of Earth* be rewritten so that Jenny is no longer established as a regular character but relegated to a more minor, one-off role (which will eventually be played by actress Ann Davies). The new regular will now be introduced in the first story of the new production block, but Pamela Franklin is no longer in the running for the role.

Friday 21: *Planet of Giants: Planet of Giants* is camera rehearsed and recorded in TC4.

Elwyn Jones sends Verity Lambert a memo informing her that Donald Baverstock, in accordance with the recommendation put to him the previous day, has now agreed to renew *Doctor Who* for six months, rather than for three with an option for three as before.

Saturday 22: *The Reign of Terror: A Change of Identity* is transmitted on BBC1.

Sunday 23: Six days' pre-filming begins for *The Dalek Invasion of Earth*. The first five days are on location in London – the first major location shoot ever carried out for *Doctor Who*.

Monday 24: Four days' preliminary rehearsal begins for *Planet of Giants: Dangerous Journey*.

Verity Lambert sends Head of Artists' Bookings Pauline Mansfield-Clark a memo informing her of the decision taken by Donald Baverstock the previous Friday and asking her to negotiate contracts with Jacqueline Hill and William Russell on the basis that they can be offered a raise of between ten and twenty-five guineas per episode each, but no more. She adds:

> As far as the options are concerned, we will leave it to you to
> do the best deal you can with their agents, but I am not averse
> to tying them both up for 26 weeks with no option.

Lambert also writes to Donald Wilson at his holiday home in Southwold, Suffolk, to inform him of the conclusions reached 'after the dramas of the last ten days.' She apologises for having disturbed him in the middle of his leave, but notes that 'things were a bit fraught here.'

Tuesday 25: Music for episodes three and four of *Planet of Giants* is recorded between 6.30 pm and 10.30 pm in studio 2 at Maida Vale.

Friday 28: *Planet of Giants: Dangerous Journey* is camera rehearsed and recorded in TC4.

Saturday 29: *The Reign of Terror: The Tyrant of France* is transmitted on BBC1.

Monday 31: Four days' preliminary rehearsal begins for *Planet of Giants: Crisis*.

David Whitaker, now starting to look for stories to use in the series' second production block, briefs the Copyright Department to commission from writer Dennis Spooner the scripts for a four-part historical adventure entitled *The Romans*.

SEPTEMBER 1964

Friday 4: *Planet of Giants: Crisis* is camera rehearsed and recorded in TC4.

Saturday 5: *The Reign of Terror: A Bargain of Necessity* is transmitted on BBC1.

Monday 7: Four days' preliminary rehearsal begins for *Planet of Giants: The Urge to Live*.

Friday 11: *Planet of Giants: The Urge to Live* is camera rehearsed and recorded in TC4.

Saturday 12: *The Reign of Terror: Prisoners of Conciergerie* is transmitted on BBC1.

Monday 14: Four days' preliminary rehearsal begins for *The Dalek Invasion of Earth: World's End*.

Camera tests are held at 11.15 am for the role of the new companion to replace Susan. The two actresses under consideration are Maureen O'Brien – one of whose former teachers at the Central School of Speech and Drama, now working at the BBC, has brought her to Verity Lambert's attention – and Denise Upson. The part eventually goes to the former. O'Brien has most recently been working as one of the founder members of the Everyman Theatre in her native Liverpool. She is initially reluctant to accept the *Doctor Who* role, but does so partly to be with her London-based boyfriend (later her husband).

Friday 18: *The Dalek Invasion of Earth: World's End* is camera rehearsed and recorded. This is the first episode to be recorded in *Doctor Who*'s new regular studio, Riverside 1. Assistant floor manager Christina Lawton subsequently prepares the following report on the day's proceedings:

> Only the marvellously efficient and willing co-operation of the scene crew made the day possible – complex and exceptionally filthy sets to handle with a lot of reconstruction of trick pieces. Only one run achieved before recording time. Three scheduled recording breaks plus two extra arising from the transposing of shot 56. Very slow start to camera rehearsal until it was proved that planned tracking lines had some validity. Floor Assistant Ray Day was most reliable and quick.

Production assistant Jane Shirley adds the following summary of the retakes required during the evening's recording:

> Shot 56   Taken out of seq at actor's request. Producer's
>   agreement. Retake – actor missed cue.

Shots 24-26	Actor out of pos.
Shot 32 on	Re-start – actor jumped cue.
Shot 42 on	Re-start here. 1. Actor dried. 2. Box did not fall.
Shot 59	Retake – 1. Camera didn't make position in time – actor off marks. 2. Extra long pause interpreted as dry!
Shots 69A-73	Telecine mistimed.
Shot 74	Camera off pos.

Monday 21: Four days' preliminary rehearsal begins for *The Dalek Invasion of Earth: The Daleks.*

Thursday 24: David Whitaker has by this time got down to work in earnest on finding and commissioning stories for *Doctor Who*'s second production block. It has been agreed that he himself should write the first of these, a two-parter which will introduce the Doctor's new companion. An early name considered for the character is Tanni, and Whitaker's draft scripts will bear the title *Doctor Who and Tanni* before the story is subsequently renamed *The Rescue.*

This story will mark Whitaker's own departure from the series' production team, as he has now decided to move on to other work. His successor is to be Dennis Spooner, whose *The Romans* is to be the second story of the new production block and who on 6 August began a period of trailing Whitaker to 'learn the ropes' of the story editor's job. Spooner has been working as a freelance writer since the early fifties, when he abandoned an unsuccessful career as a stand-up comic. His earliest TV scripts were for half-hour sitcoms, but he has since gone on to work prolifically on a wide variety of different shows including *Hancock, The Avengers, No Hiding Place* and Gerry Anderson's puppet series *Fireball XL5* and *Stingray.*

It has now been decided that Malcolm Hulke's *The Hidden Planet* should be finally written off as unsuitable. Whitaker sends Hulke's agent, Harvey Unna, a letter in which he explains the reasons as follows:

> Considerable re-writing would be necessary because Carole Ann Ford is leaving the cast, and I think also that the science fiction series that have been most successful in the past year have been those with mechanical or alien monsters in them. Mac's idea is based upon similarities of Earth and his invented planet. In the future we would rather give the audience more monsters and more truly science fiction creations.
>
> I am sorry about this after all the hard work Mac has put into it

and, of course, it is not his fault that climates of opinion and styles of approach change as a serial like *Doctor Who* progresses.

Another story rejected by Whitaker on this date is Victor Pemberton's *The Slide*, about which he sends Donald Wilson the following memo:

> This is rather a stew pot of all the other science fiction serials we have ever done, with bits of Nigel Kneale scattered about. I don't think the dialogue is very good and I am quite sure it is not right for *Doctor Who*.

(Pemberton will in later years go on to become *Doctor Who*'s script editor himself, and to write a highly-acclaimed six-part story entitled *Fury from the Deep* based in part upon *The Slide*. *The Slide* itself will meanwhile have been turned into a successful science fiction serial for BBC radio.)

Friday 25: *The Dalek Invasion of Earth: The Daleks* is camera rehearsed and recorded in Riverside 1. During the course of the day, Jacqueline Hill sustains a minor injury to her hand.

Monday 28: Four days' preliminary rehearsal begins for *The Dalek Invasion of Earth: Day of Reckoning*.
   David Whitaker briefs the Copyright Department to commission from writer Bill Strutton a six-part story entitled *The Web Planet*. The target delivery date is 13 November 1964.

OCTOBER 1964

Friday 2: *The Dalek Invasion of Earth: Day of Reckoning* is camera rehearsed and recorded in Riverside 1. William Hartnell is injured during camera rehearsals when the supports of the Dalek spaceship's entry ramp, down which he is being carried on a stretcher, suddenly collapse. He falls awkwardly on his spine, and for a while is paralysed, but X-Rays show no permanent damage and he recovers sufficiently to take part in the evening's recording. It is however agreed that he should be given the following week off to recover fully.

Monday 5: Four days' preliminary rehearsal begins for *The Dalek Invasion of Earth: The End of Tomorrow*, with William Hartnell absent. The episode is rewritten so that the Doctor – to be played by stand-in Edmund Warwick with his face out of vision – falls unconscious at the beginning and plays no further part in the action.

Tuesday 6: Dennis Spooner briefs the Copyright Department to commission from Terry Nation the scripts for a new six-part story with which it is intended to conclude the second production block. The target delivery date is 30 January 1965.

Thursday 8: Verity Lambert is sent a memo by Christopher Barry, who has been assigned to direct both *The Rescue* and *The Romans*. Barry requests a planning meeting with the production team before rehearsals begin; expresses the view that there has been insufficient rehearsal in the past, and that he would like therefore to rehearse from 10.00 am to 5.00 pm each day during the rehearsal period; and requests that the cast be asked to attend a script conference before work starts in earnest on *The Rescue*.

Friday 9: *The Dalek Invasion of Earth: The End of Tomorrow* is camera rehearsed and recorded in Riverside 1.

Verity Lambert replies as follows to the previous day's memo from Christopher Barry:

> As far as I am concerned I am quite happy to have planning meetings for the episodes you have prepared before you go into rehearsal.
>
> I think it is up to you to discuss with the actors a possible 10.00 am to 5.00 pm rehearsal period. I do not think that they are particularly against this. The only day that we have regularly had an 11 o'clock start is Monday, as Bill Hartnell travels up from the country on that day and cannot get to rehearsal before 11.00 am.
>
> I am afraid it is not possible to get the cast together for a script conference before we go into rehearsal. They have been working regularly for 52 weeks and I feel, from their point of view, they must have a complete break away from the show.
>
> I agree with you it is quite possible that we are, perhaps, rehearsing too little. Most directors during the past few weeks and months have not rehearsed on Thursday afternoons. The cast have now got to feel that Thursday afternoon is an afternoon free. However, this is not so and, if fact, should you wish to rehearse Thursday afternoons, with them, they are being paid for it.

As you know, we can, in fact, rehearse for six hours. If you are not with the actors till 11.30 am or 12.00 am on a Wednesday, you have an extension till 7.00 pm. There is no reason, in fact, not to rehearse after the script conference (or to have a late run-through, as discussed this morning).

Barry subsequently agrees that rehearsals can continue to begin at 11.00 am on Mondays.

Monday 12: Four days' preliminary rehearsal begins for *The Dalek Invasion of Earth: The Waking Ally*.

Friday 16: *The Dalek Invasion of Earth: The Waking Ally* is camera rehearsed and recorded in Riverside 1.

Monday 19: Four days' preliminary rehearsal begins for *The Dalek Invasion of Earth: Flashpoint*.

Tuesday 20: Verity Lambert sends Donald Wilson a memo informing him that the total fees paid out to Malcolm Hulke for his ultimately unused story *The Hidden Planet* amounted to £1,612 10s 0d.

Donald Wilson sends Sydney Newman the following memo:

> As spoken yesterday, I am arranging to reduce the four-part serial entitled *Planet of Giants* to three parts. This is the 'miniscule' story with which we must begin our new season and I am not satisfied that it will get us off to the great start that we must have if it runs to its full length. Much of it is fascinating and exciting but by its nature and the resources needed we could not do everything we wanted to do to make it wholly satisfactory. I would, of course, have preferred to start with the Dalek serial but at the end of this one Carole Ann Ford is written out and we cannot, therefore, have her appearing afterwards in *Planet of Giants*.

Wilson goes on to say that, to make up for the lost episode, the Terry Nation serial with which it is planned to end the new twenty-six week production block will be extended from six episodes to seven. This idea will later be abandoned, however.

The reduction of *Planet of Giants* from four episodes to three is subsequently accomplished by the editing together of the final two episodes, with around half the recorded material from each being discarded.

A party is held in the Bridge Lounge at Television Centre to celebrate the impending completion of the first 52 episodes.

Friday 23: *The Dalek Invasion of Earth: Flashpoint* is camera rehearsed and recorded in Riverside 1. The recording overruns its allotted time by some fifteen minutes, finishing at around 10.30 pm. This is due partly to the fact that around twenty minutes has to be spent resetting scenery during the course of the evening, and partly to a number of problems that arise during recording of the last few minutes of the episode: a brief camera failure; a longer sound failure; a retake necessitated by William Hartnell fluffing his lines in the final scene; and a further retake required to rectify an unsatisfactory inlay shot.

This is Carole Ann Ford's last regular episode as Susan, and she subsequently writes to Sydney Newman to express her gratitude for having been given the opportunity to appear in the series.

Wednesday 28: Sydney Newman replies to Carole Ann Ford's letter as follows:

> Are you kidding – expressing your appreciation for appearing in *Doctor Who*! Fact is, we are greatly indebted to you. You have done a fine job for us in the BBC and we are deeply appreciative of your work.
>
> May I wish you the very best of luck in your future career, and hope to see you time and time again on the BBC screen in roles other than that of the 'waif from Outer Space' (what a title!)

Saturday 31: *Planet of Giants: Planet of Giants* is transmitted on BBC1.

David Whitaker's engagement as story editor formally ends at this point as he completes his hand-over to Dennis Spooner. Writers currently under consideration to work on the series are: William Emms, who is due to meet Verity Lambert to discuss his ideas; John Lucarotti, who may contribute another historical story; Brian Hayles, who has had one submission rejected but been asked to submit another; Alex Miller, who has likewise had two ideas rejected but been asked to try again; Hugh Whitemore, a writer on the soap opera *Compact*, who is to visit the production office to discuss the possibility of submitting some storylines; and Keith Dewhurst, a Manchester-based writer who has been approached through his agent but has yet to respond.

Also on the point of leaving the series' production team at this time is Mervyn Pinfield. Verity Lambert is by now well able to cope with the demands of the producer's job, and there is now no need for an associate producer. Pinfield will however continue to be credited on screen for the first two stories of the new production block.

NOVEMBER 1964

Thursday 5: Verity Lambert sends Drama Serials Organiser Terence Cook the following memo:

> With the approach of Christmas and also the fact that we are doing another Dalek serial, I have the feeling that we are going to be inundated once again with requests from various organisations to borrow Daleks.
>
> I have spoken to Perry Guinness in Publicity, who has been handling, so far, all the correspondence re borrowing Daleks. He tells me that he was, at one time, going to have two made for publicity purposes. This project fell through because he could not get permission from his Head of Department to put an order in.
>
> However, we now have four Daleks stored at Ealing. I am perfectly prepared to loan two of these Daleks to be used for publicity purposes if we have a guarantee that the Publicity Department will make good any damage which is incurred at the time of their use for publicity purposes.
>
> It obviously is not a problem of copyright, because Publicity Department were going to make two. Anyway, I do not know whether this seems to be a reasonable solution to this whole problem from everybody's point of view, but perhaps you could deal with it.

Saturday 7: *Planet of Giants: Dangerous Journey* is transmitted on BBC1.

Thursday 12: Verity Lambert sends Dennis Spooner, Mervyn Pinfield and Christopher Barry a memo stating that the name now decided upon for the new companion is Lukki (pronounced Lucky). Aside from Tanni, other names previously considered for the character have included Millie (which has been discounted because of possible associations with the *That Was the Week That Was* comedienne Millicent Martin) and Valerie.

Friday 13: Christopher Barry returns to composer Tristram Cary three tapes of incidental music from *The Mutants*, two of which Cary has lent him and the other of which he has found in the recording studio. Barry intends to re-use a number of pieces of this music for *The Rescue*.

Saturday 14: *Planet of Giants: Crisis* – the amalgamated version of the original *Crisis* and *The Urge to Live* – is transmitted on BBC1.

A BBC Wales programme about automation features two Daleks – speaking in Welsh! They have been loaned out by the *Doctor Who* office and have drawn tumultuous crowds when paraded through the streets of Cardiff on 7 December, prior to the programme's recording on 11 December.

Monday 16: Two days' filming of model sequences for *The Rescue* begins at Ealing.

Tuesday 17: Two days' shooting of film inserts for *The Romans* begins on Stage 3A/B at Ealing. On the second day, Wednesday 18, the Doctor is played by stand-in Albert Ward, wearing a Roman toga and with his face kept out of shot.

Friday 20: By this time the name of Maureen O'Brien's character has been fixed as Vicki.

Saturday 21: *The Dalek Invasion of Earth: World's End* is transmitted on BBC1.

Tuesday 24: Dennis Spooner has been carrying out extensive rewrites on David Whitaker's scripts for *The Rescue*, and revised versions are now sent out to principal cast members.

Wednesday 25: Raymond Jones's incidental music for *The Romans* is recorded at Broadcasting House. It is played by five musicians, supplied by Alec Firman.

Thursday 26: Verity Lambert and William Russell record an interview for the BBC's *Points of View* programme.

Friday 27: Verity Lambert's secretary, Valentine Spencer, sends her the following note reporting some grievances on the part of two of the series' designers, Raymond Cusick and Spencer Chapman (the designer of *The Dalek Invasion of Earth*):

> Raymond Cusick would be most grateful if you would ring him.

He wants to talk about the exploitation of the Daleks. He is 'rather sore' about it, as he is not getting anything out of it.

He also told me that during rehearsal of Serial K, some people came into the studio and tried to start measuring up the Robomen's head pieces. Spencer Chapman found out they hadn't got permission to do this and asked them to leave. Ray thinks they may have been something to do with Press Department.

Design Department is worried about both the above and have been having a Departmental meeting about these two things.

Cusick is later paid a bonus of £100 for having designed the Daleks. He regards this sum as derisory.

Saturday 28: *The Dalek Invasion of Earth: The Daleks* is transmitted on BBC1.

Monday 30: Four days' preliminary rehearsal begins for *The Rescue: The Powerful Enemy*.

DECEMBER 1964

Tuesday 1: A photocall is held to introduce Maureen O'Brien as Vicki to the press.

Wednesday 2: Val Spencer writes the following note:

Derek Hoddinott in Publicity rang, asking Dennis Spooner to write a short piece on John Qualtrough, the 14 year old Liverpool boy who sent in the story *Doctor What Strikes Again*, to give to the press, as the boy may be appearing on *Points of View* tomorrow.

Dennis Spooner wrote the following:

'The *Doctor What Strikes Again* script (subtitled *Doctor What and the Luxury Liner*) is a very funny send-up of the *Doctor Who* show.

'I'm certain that if the *Doctor Who* series runs long enough, Stephen John Qualtrough will become a serious contributor to the *Doctor Who* series – unless *That Was the Past That Was* claims him first.

'The dialogue, and the joke construction are near perfect, and it is astounding to find that somebody so young has such a penetrating sense of humour, and the ability to get it across.'

The above was dictated over the telephone to Derek Hoddinott. He asked if he could quote Dennis Spooner as having said this. Dennis Spooner agreed.

Thursday 3: At Publicity's request, William Hartnell attends a photocall with schoolboy Stephen John Qualtrough in studio Presentation A at Television Centre.

Friday 4: *The Rescue: The Powerful Enemy* is camera rehearsed and recorded in Riverside 1. Sound recordings of Jacqueline Hill screaming and of Ray Barrett (as the character Bennett) delivering the line 'You can't come in!' are made at 3.00 pm, as these are required to be played in on tape during the episode.
  The Government's Central Office of Information borrow two Daleks to appear in one of their programmes.
  Earlier in the year, David Whitaker approached John Wyndham to see if he would be interested in writing for the series, and today his agent replies that he is too busy working on a book.

Saturday 5: *The Dalek Invasion of Earth: Day of Reckoning* is transmitted on BBC1.
  A number of Daleks appear on the BBC light entertainment programme *The Black and White Minstrel Show*.

Monday 7: Four days' preliminary rehearsal begins for *The Rescue: Desperate Measures*.

Friday 11: *The Rescue: Desperate Measures* is camera rehearsed and recorded in Riverside 1.

Saturday 12: *The Dalek Invasion of Earth: The End of Tomorrow* is transmitted on BBC1.

Monday 14: Four days' preliminary rehearsal begins for *The Romans: The Slave Traders*.
  Two Daleks appear on the BBC magazine programme *Late Night Line-up*.

Wednesday 16: The six-part story commissioned from Terry Nation on 6 October 1964 has been abandoned. However, Dennis Spooner now briefs the Copyright Department to commission from Nation a replacement story, again a six-parter, featuring the Daleks. The target delivery date remains 30 January 1965. The story has the working title *The Pursuers*.

Friday 18: *The Romans: The Slave Traders* is camera rehearsed and recorded in Riverside 1.

Saturday 19: *The Dalek Invasion of Earth: The Waking Ally* is transmitted on BBC1.

Monday 21: Dennis Scuse, Ronald Waldman's successor as General Manager of Television Enterprises, sends Sydney Newman a memo informing him that the recent sale of *Doctor Who*'s first fifty-two episodes to CBC in Canada was placed in jeopardy by the substandard telerecordings made from the 405-line videotapes:

> As you may or may not know, we have recently concluded a fairly substantial deal in Canada for the *Dr Who* series. The correspondence which I attach is largely self-explanatory and the problems which are mentioned arise from a considerable amount of low-key lighting used in the production. This is extenuated by the inevitable degradation of tape transfer and 16mm telerecording.
>
> There may not be very much that can be done but I would be grateful if these problems could be brought to the attention of the producer and the situation borne in mind for the future.
>
> I need hardly add that a success with *Dr Who* in Canada could be extremely lucrative not only directly but also indirectly through merchandising activities.

Wilson subsequently brings this memo to Verity Lambert's attention.

Tuesday 22: Lambert sends Wilson a memo about future plans for *Doctor Who*. She notes that the last scheduled recording in the series' second, twenty-six week production block is due to take place on 4 June 1965, and the last scheduled transmission on 26 June 1965. She goes on:

> Should *Doctor Who* be continued after this date, I would like to suggest that we break transmission throughout July and

August. This would involve nine weeks (Weeks 27 to 35 inclusive). We could then start transmission again on 4 September 1965 (Week 36).

We could start recording on 30 July (Week 30), which would give us five weeks in hand and a break of eight weeks in recording.

I know that nine weeks seems a long break in transmission, but I think that July and August are bad months from our point of view.

Saturday 26: *The Dalek Invasion of Earth: The End of Tomorrow* is transmitted on BBC1.

Monday 28: Four days' preliminary rehearsal begins for *The Romans: All Roads Lead to Rome*.
Carole Ann Ford makes a public appearance at a *Doctor Who* exhibition at the *Daily Mail* Boys and Girls Exhibition at London's Olympia.

JANUARY 1965

Friday 1: *The Romans: All Roads Lead to Rome* is camera rehearsed and recorded in Riverside 1.

Saturday 2: *The Rescue: The Powerful Enemy* is transmitted on BBC1.

Monday 4: Four days' preliminary rehearsal begins for *The Romans: Conspiracy*.
Pre-filming begins for *The Web Planet* on Stage 2 at the BBC's Television Film Studios in Ealing. It is scheduled to be completed by Friday evening but overruns so that a number of scenes have to be held over to the following Monday. The only member of the regular cast required for the filming is Jacqueline Hill. Most of her scenes are shot on Wednesday 6 January and the remainder on the following day, and she is released from rehearsals for *The Romans: Conspiracy* to enable this to be done.

Tuesday 5: Three days' shooting of film inserts for *The Web Planet* begins at Ealing.

Friday 8: *The Romans: Conspiracy* is camera rehearsed and recorded in Riverside 1. The total cost of the episode is £2,383.

Saturday 9: *The Rescue: Desperate Measures* is transmitted on BBC1.

Monday 11: Four days' preliminary rehearsal begins for *The Romans: Inferno*.

During the course of this week, David Whitaker draws up a revised schedule for the series' second production block, which indicates that the planned running order for the stories after *The Romans* is now: *The Web Planet* (six episodes) by Bill Strutton; a historical story (four episodes) by Whitaker himself; *The Space Museum* (four episodes) by Glyn Jones; and Terry Nation's new Dalek story (six episodes). No recordings are planned for 25 December (Week 52) or for 2 April (Week 13), as these are public holidays.

Shortly after this, the proposals in Verity Lambert's memo of 22 December 1964 to Donald Wilson are rejected. It is agreed instead that the closing episode of *Doctor Who*'s second season should be transmitted on 24 July 1965 and the opening episode of the third on 11 September 1965, leaving a six week break in between. The series' second production block is to be extended from twenty-six episodes to thirty-five, with the last recording taking place on 6 August 1965, so that there will still be five episodes in hand when the break occurs. There will however be only a five week break in recording, with the first studio session of the third production block taking place on 17 September 1965.

Friday 15: *The Romans: Inferno* is camera rehearsed and recorded in Riverside 1. The total cost is £2,221.

Saturday 16: *The Romans: The Slave Traders* is transmitted on BBC1.

Monday 18: Four days' preliminary rehearsal begins for *The Web Planet: The Web Planet*.

Thursday 21: Christopher Barry sends the following memo to Raymond Cusick, who after *The Romans* is ending his regular assignment as a *Doctor Who* designer:

> Thank you for such lovely sets on *Dr Who*. I hope you enjoy your other work that you have now gone on to.
>
> Don't breathe a word but there's a vague chance that I may do another Dalek serial later in the year and if so I hope you would not mind working on it if it can be arranged.

Cusick will later work on three further *Doctor Who* stories, all featuring the Daleks, but from this point onwards it will generally be the case that scenic designers are asked to handle stories on a one-off basis rather than as part of a longer-term attachment to the series.

Friday 22: *The Web Planet: The Web Planet* is camera rehearsed and recorded in Riverside 1. The total cost is £3,033.

Saturday 23: *The Romans: All Roads Lead to Rome* is transmitted on BBC1.

Monday 25: Four days' preliminary rehearsal begins for *The Web Planet: The Zarbi*.

Friday 29: *The Web Planet: The Zarbi* is camera rehearsed and recorded in Riverside 1. The total cost is £2,428. The recording overruns its allotted time by sixteen minutes.

Saturday 30: *The Romans: Conspiracy* is transmitted on BBC1.

FEBRUARY 1965

Monday 1: Four days' preliminary rehearsal begins for *The Web Planet: Escape to Danger*.

Tuesday 2: Verity Lambert sends Serials Department Organiser Terence Cook a memo explaining the reasons for the overrun on the previous Friday's recording. After describing the seven retakes required, she concludes:

> This was an extremely difficult episode to do technically, in that there had to be a tremendous amount of scenery in the studio, and apart from the breaks necessary because of scene changes, there was the added problem that we had not used the Zarbi, except briefly in episode one, and it was impossible to tell until we got into the studio the kind of difficulties we would run into with dressing them and moving them from one scene to another. As it turned out we had to put in sufficient recording pauses to allow them to reposition from scene to scene.
>
> Finally, I would say that this was probably the most difficult episode of any we have attempted so far, and it certainly was the most complicated one of this particular six.

Hilary Bateson of the BBC's Publicity Department writes to D D'Vigne of Belle Vue Zoo Park (Manchester) Ltd to inform him that two Daleks which have been loaned to him for promotional purposes must be returned rather earlier than expected, on either 1 or 2 March. This is because they will be required for the new Dalek story, which is to begin recording in May.

Friday 5: *The Web Planet: Escape to Danger* is camera rehearsed and recorded in Riverside 1. The total cost is £2,196. This studio day proves to be one of the most problematic since the series began, and the recording overruns its allotted time by thirty-seven minutes. The start of camera rehearsals is delayed until 11.10 am as two sets – the TARDIS laboratory and the landscape of the planet Vortis – have yet to arrive in the studio, and a third – the Zarbi's Carsenome base – has yet to have its floor painted. This leads to further problems as the lighting supervisor has been unable to light the sets in advance and has to continue repositioning lights right up to and even during the evening recording period. Further delays occur during recording owing to a number of technical faults – one camera breaks down altogether and has to be dispensed with – and to the resultant nervousness of the cast.

Saturday 6: *The Romans: Inferno* is transmitted on BBC1. This is the last episode on which Mervyn Pinfield receives a credit as associate producer. The episode is followed by a short trailer for *The Web Planet*, consisting of a compilation of shots from the early episodes of the story and an accompanying voice-over.

Monday 8: Four days' preliminary rehearsal begins for *The Web Planet: Crater of Needles*.

Director Richard Martin sends Verity Lambert a memo about the trailer transmitted the previous Saturday for *The Web Planet*. He protests that, particularly in its use of long shots, it gave away too much, leaving him feeling 'like a conjurer about to do an elaborate two and a half hour trick when all the audience know the secrets already.' Lambert responds that she was responsible for the way in which the story was promoted, and that it was 'done with the specific purpose of taking the curse out of the Zarbi'; i.e. making them seem less horrific.

Tuesday 9: Lambert sends Martin the following memo headed 'Rewrites':

> I am very concerned about the amount of *line changing* that is going on during rehearsal of *Dr Who* scripts. I am not against rewrites, particularly if they improve the finished product. If, however, artists are continually changing lines purely because they can't remember what they are supposed to be

saying this does not end up as an improvement. I feel that it is your responsibility as a director to exercise control over this.

We have a reading on Wednesday, at which major points should come up. Odd line changes should take place on the Monday when you are blocking the show. By the Monday evening, save in exceptional circumstances, the script should be set and no changes should be made after that time. In this way the artists have a chance of learning their lines and going into the studio in control of the situation. If you allow them to keep on changing lines they will do so, and we have nobody but ourselves to blame if they don't know the script. As you know, Dennis is always available to come down to rehearsal for rewrites, and if you do have major problems of course he can come after the Monday, but in general all script changes should be made by Monday evening.

This note is for you to act on as you think fit, but I would strongly advise against making any kind of general announcement of its contents to the cast; as you know already, this only causes unpleasantness. I suggest possibly trying to have a chat with Bill on his own if you find it difficult to stop the constant changing in rehearsal.

If you would like to discuss this with me, or if you would like me to put the point to Bill, I would be delighted to do so!

Friday 12: *The Web Planet: Crater of Needles* is camera rehearsed and recorded in Riverside 1. The total cost is £2,850.

Saturday 13: *The Web Planet: The Web Planet* is transmitted on BBC1.

Monday 15: Four days' preliminary rehearsal begins for *The Web Planet: Invasion*.

Tuesday 16: Three days' shooting of film inserts for *The Crusade* begins at Ealing.

Friday 19: *The Web Planet: Invasion* is camera rehearsed and recorded in Riverside 1. The total cost is £2,676.

Saturday 20: *The Web Planet: The Zarbi* is transmitted on BBC1.

Monday 22: Four days' preliminary rehearsal begins for *The Web Planet: The Centre*.

Thursday 25: Verity Lambert sends the draft scripts for Terry Nation's new Dalek story, *The Chase*, to Richard Martin, who has been assigned to direct it. She notes that she is 'really very happy with it as far as the movement and action in the story are concerned,' and that 'it is slightly tongue-in-cheek and obviously is purely an adventure story, but ... there are lots of opportunities for imagination and for excitement.' She does however have a number of reservations. She is concerned about how two new monsters – the Mire Beast and the Fungoid – will be realised, particularly in view of problems experienced with the design of the Slyther creature in *The Dalek Invasion of Earth*, and considers that another alien race, the Aridians, are too 'unpleasant looking' as described by Nation. She feels that an episode involving Frankenstein's monster is out of keeping with *Doctor Who*'s usual style and could suggest a lack of imagination, and is considering asking Nation to replace it with something else – a suggestion to which he is quite amenable.

It has by this point been established that William Russell will be leaving *Doctor Who* when his contract expires at the end of *The Chase*. Terry Nation has therefore introduced in the final episode of his story a new character, an astronaut called Bruck, who will become the Doctor's new male companion.

Nation has meanwhile been discussing with Verity Lambert and Dennis Spooner ideas for a further six-part Dalek story to be made during the series' third production block. They agree that this new story should be preceded by a single episode 'trailer' in which none of the regular characters appear, allowing the cast a week's holiday. Spooner briefs the Copyright Department to commission from Nation the script for this trailer, referred to as *Dalek Cutaway*.

Friday 26: *The Web Planet: The Centre* is camera rehearsed and recorded in Riverside 1. The total cost is £3,342.

Dennis Spooner briefs the Copyright Department to commission from writer Brian Hayles a storyline for a story entitled *The Dark Planet*. This will ultimately be rejected.

Saturday 27: *The Web Planet: Escape to Danger* is transmitted on BBC1.

Monday 29: Four days' preliminary rehearsal begins for *The Crusade: The Lion*.

MARCH 1965

Wednesday 3: Richard Martin has gone on holiday abroad following completion of *The Web Planet*. Verity Lambert sends him a memo to see on his return, listing the scenes from *The Chase* that she has agreed with the Design Department should be done as film inserts. She ends:

> Your filming schedule will be heavy, although it will not involve location shooting, but your model making etc will be most expensive. I do implore you to keep your studio settings down in cost. I shall be away on your return, but you will no doubt find out that you have exceeded your budget on the Zarbi story by something in the region of £1,000. I do not want this to happen again.
>
> Will you please work to a budget of £2,750 per episode. If you should require more on this serial, will you please notify my office.

The budget allocated to *The Chase* is higher than the standard £2,500 as it is regarded as one of the more prestigious stories of this production block; savings will have to be made on some of the other stories to compensate.

It will later be decided that story should in fact have one day of location filming for some scenes set on the planet Aridius in the first two episodes.

Friday 5: *The Crusade: The Lion* is camera rehearsed and recorded in Riverside 1. The total cost is £3,515.

Saturday 6: *The Web Planet: Crater of Needles* is transmitted on BBC1.

Monday 8: Four days' preliminary rehearsal begins for *The Crusade: The Knight of Jaffa*.

Thursday 11: One day's shooting of film inserts for *The Space Museum* takes places at Ealing.

Verity Lambert has by this time decided to leave *Doctor Who* at the end of the second production block and move on to other work, but her successor has yet to be chosen. She sends Donald Wilson the following memo, headed '*Doctor Who*: Serial S', requesting permission to take the unusual step of commissioning story editor Dennis Spooner to write the story that will follow *The Chase* in the season's running order:

> As you know, I agreed with you last week that we should

contract Dennis Spooner to write this serial. This is because we will not have, at this point, finalised negotiations with Jacqueline Hill and Maureen O'Brien. This it will make it impossible to commission an outside writer.

This serial has to be ready for design information by the last week in April and, as I mentioned to you, we will not know about Jacqueline Hill until the new producer has been decided upon.

I think it would be a great risk to try an outside writer on this serial for the following reasons:

> 1) He will not be able to start writing it until he knows the characters.
>
> 2) None of the writers we have used so far are available and this would mean trying a completely new writer.
>
> 3) Of necessity, this serial has to be written fairly economically and I would not have the same control over an outside writer.
>
> 4) I also have had to agree with Bill Hartnell's agent to let him have one week out of this serial. Obviously this complicates matters still further.
>
> 5) Using an outside writer, it could quite well be that the serial will necessitate some considerable rewriting. This will put us in a very awkward position as far as design information is concerned.

Because of these points, I will be most grateful if you can confirm to me that I can commission Dennis Spooner to write this serial.

Friday 12: *The Crusade: The Knight of Jaffa* is camera rehearsed and recorded in Riverside 1. From this episode, *Doctor Who*'s budget per episode is increased from £2,330 to £2,500. The total cost of *The Knight of Jaffa* is £2,300.

Saturday 13: *The Web Planet: Invasion* is transmitted on BBC1.

Monday 15: Four days' preliminary rehearsal begins for *The Crusade: The Wheel of Fortune*.

Verity Lambert begins two weeks' holiday.

Donald Wilson agrees that Dennis Spooner can be commissioned to write Serial S.

Friday 19: *The Crusade: The Wheel of Fortune* is camera rehearsed and recorded in Riverside 1. The total cost is £2,150.

Saturday 20: *The Web Planet: The Centre* is transmitted on BBC1.

Monday 22: Four days' preliminary rehearsal begins for *The Crusade: The Warlords*.

Friday 26: *The Crusade: The Warlords* is camera rehearsed and recorded in Riverside 1. The total cost is £2,065.

Saturday 27: *The Crusade: The Lion* is transmitted on BBC1.

Monday 29: Four days' preliminary rehearsal begins for *The Space Museum: The Space Museum*.

APRIL 1965

By the beginning of this month, Dennis Spooner has – like Verity Lambert – decided to move on from *Doctor Who* when his contract expires later in the year. Spooner's replacement is to be Donald Tosh, a BBC staffer who has just completed an eighteen month assignment as story editor on *Compact*. Although he will be present during production of *The Chase*, his first on-screen credit will be for the following story, Dennis Spooner's four-parter, now entitled *The Time Meddler*. Lambert's successor has also been chosen now and is to be John Wiles, who has been on the staff of the BBC since the early fifties as a writer/adaptor and story editor and who has recently been promoted to producer by Head of Serials Donald Wilson.

To help acquaint the newcomers with the background to the series, Lambert and Spooner provide them with a note headed 'The History of *Doctor Who*', which gives a brief story-by-story summary up to the end of the second production block. The introduction reads as follows:

You will find listed below a thumbnail sketch of the serials transmitted and/or commissioned for *Doctor Who*. I think it is a point to bear in mind that any stories that are commissioned and are set in the future will have to be checked from their date point of view. Serials G, K and L involve the Earth in some way, so any given date must not clash with these. The Dalek serials have also to be watched with this in mind, as in the first Dalek serial (Serial B) Doctor Who did in fact wipe out the Dalek race. With a time machine at his disposal this is not as disastrous as it sounds, as he can go back to any point in their history; but one has to be careful in Serial B, K, R and in the Dalek story to come that they are true to the Dalek history calendar.

Another further note is that most writers call Doctor Who 'Doctor Who'. In fact he does not admit to this name, just the 'Doctor' part, and is never referred to as 'Doctor Who'. This is just the title of the show.

Doctor Who comes from a planet that we have never named. Various references to it have been made in the scripts as the show has gone along, but I personally have not gone back looking for them all.

Vicki's background was covered in Serial L, should you wish to go back and find this, and our new character, tentatively called Michael, was covered in episode six of Serial R, and further developed in Serial S.

Friday 2: *The Space Museum: The Space Museum* is camera rehearsed and recorded in TC4. The total cost is £2,643.

Dennis Spooner rejects Malcolm Hulke's *The Hidden Planet* and *Britain 408 A.D.*, which Hulke has re-submitted to the production office following David Whitaker's departure.

Saturday 3: *The Crusade: The Knight of Jaffa* is transmitted on BBC1.

Monday 5: Four days' preliminary rehearsal begins for *The Space Museum: The Dimensions of Time*.

Friday 9: *The Space Museum: The Dimensions of Time* is camera rehearsed and recorded in TC4. The total cost is £2,394.

One day of location filming for *The Chase* is carried out in Camber Sands, East Sussex.

Saturday 10: *The Crusade: The Wheel of Fortune* is transmitted on BBC1.

Monday 12: Four days' preliminary rehearsal begins for *The Space Museum: The Search*.

Four days' shooting of film inserts for *The Chase* begins on Stage 3A/B at Ealing.

Friday 16: *The Space Museum: The Search* is camera rehearsed and recorded in TC4. The total cost is £2,028.

Saturday 17: *The Crusade: The Warlords* is transmitted on BBC1.

Monday 19: Four days' preliminary rehearsal begins for *The Space Museum: The Final Phase*.

Tuesday 20: The first of two sessions is held between 2.00 pm and 6.00 pm at the Olympic Sound Studios to record Dudley Simpson's incidental music for *The Chase*. Simpson conducts an ensemble of five musicians, and the instruments used are: an electronic organ; a celeste; three tymps (one pedal); a xylophone; a marimba; and a vibraphone.

Director Richard Martin and film editor Norman Matthews begin three days' film editing work on sequences for *The Chase*.

Thursday 22: The second of the two music recording sessions for *The Chase* is held between 1.30 pm and 5.30 pm at the Olympic Sound Studios. The personnel and instruments used are the same as on Tuesday.

Friday 23: *The Space Museum: The Final Phase* is camera rehearsed and recorded in TC4. The total cost is £1,636.

Writer Robert Holmes meets Donald Tosh to discuss possible story ideas for *Doctor Who*. Tosh explains that he and John Wiles are intending to bring a new, more sophisticated style to the series.

Saturday 24: *The Space Museum: The Space Museum* is transmitted on BBC1.

Sunday 25: Following their meeting the previous Friday, Robert Holmes sends Donald Tosh a letter containing a storyline for a proposed four-part story. (Nothing comes of this idea now, but Holmes will resubmit it five years later under the title *The Space Trap* and it will eventually be made as *The Krotons* in *Doctor Who*'s sixth season.)

Monday 26: Four days' preliminary rehearsal begins for *The Chase: The Executioners*. Rehearsals this week and next take place in a Drill Hall at 58

Bulwer Street, London W12.

The film sequences for *The Chase* are dubbed with music and sound effects.

It has by this point been decided that the new companion character introduced in *The Chase* should be called Michael rather than Bruck.

Friday 30: *The Chase: The Executioners* is camera rehearsed and recorded in Riverside 1. The total cost is £6,083. Recording overruns its allotted time by ten minutes. This is a knock-on effect from delays caused earlier in the day by the fact that a special effect commissioned from Shawcraft was unavailable; the Shawcraft effects man had been asked to make a short trip back to their workshop on *Doctor Who* business but failed to return, having been sent out for the rest of the afternoon on another job. Verity Lambert later asks designer Raymond Cusick to register a protest with Shawcraft, as they are paid to have a man working on *Doctor Who* for the whole of the studio day.

MAY 1965

Saturday 1: *The Space Museum: The Dimensions of Time* is transmitted on BBC1.

Monday 3: Four days' preliminary rehearsal begins for *The Chase: The Death of Time.*

Wednesday 5: Graphics and Effects Manager Tony Foster sends Verity Lambert a memo informing her that he has taken up with Shawcraft 'in the strongest possible terms' their failure to provide a proper service for the previous Friday's studio work, and that he has received an assurance that it will not happen again. Shawcraft's labour charge for the episode is to be reduced accordingly.

Thursday 6: Director Douglas Camfield and a BBC photographer meet Jacqueline Hill and William Russell at 2.00 pm in the main reception area at Television Centre. They then visit a number of London locations, including Trafalgar Square and Hyde Park, to take stills for inclusion in a montage sequence showing Barbara and Ian back on Earth after parting company with the Doctor at the end of *The Chase* – Hill having by this point decided, like Russell, to leave the series when her current contract expires.

Friday 7: *The Chase: The Death of Time* is camera rehearsed and recorded in Riverside 1. The total cost is £2,441. The recording overruns its allotted time, almost entirely due to problems cutting from telecine film to live action and the time needed to rewind the telecine for retakes.

Saturday 8: *The Space Museum: The Search* is transmitted on BBC1.

Monday 10: Four days' preliminary rehearsal begins for *The Chase: Flight Through Eternity*. This week and next, rehearsals take place in the Territorial Army Centre at Artillery House, Horn Lane, London W3.

Two further film inserts for the final episode of *The Chase* are completed at Ealing. The first, shot on Stage 3A/B in front of a back-projection screen, shows Ian and Barbara on a double decker bus following their return to Earth at the end of the story. The second, shot between 2.00 pm and 3.30 pm just outside a maintenance garage behind Stage 3A/B, is a slightly earlier scene of the two companions running away from the building where the Daleks' time machine has deposited them, with an explosion (in truth a simple lighting effect) then occurring beyond the garage doors. These scenes are directed by Douglas Camfield and designed by Barry Newbery, effectively being made as part of the following production, Dennis Spooner's *The Time Meddler*. Ealing film inserts for the latter story, showing the TARDIS on a beach beside a rugged cliff-face, are also shot on this date.

Friday 14: *The Chase: Flight Through Eternity* is camera rehearsed and recorded in Riverside 1. The total cost is £2,614. The recording again overruns its allotted time, for the same reasons as did the previous week's. During the course of the day, Verity Lambert and Dennis Spooner ask Peter Purves, who has been cast as the American hillbilly character Morton Dill, if he would like to play the Doctor's new companion, Michael Taylor, who is to be introduced in the final episode of the story. Purves readily agrees.

Terry Nation has by this point delivered his script for the *Dalek Cutaway* episode and started work on the new six-part Dalek story it foreshadows.

Saturday 15: *The Space Museum: The Final Phase* is transmitted on BBC1.

Monday 17: Four days' preliminary rehearsal begins for *The Chase: Journey into Terror*.

Friday 21: *The Chase: Journey into Terror* is camera rehearsed and recorded in Riverside 1. The total cost is £2,658. The recording overruns its allotted time owing to its exceptionally complicated nature and to the fact that the start of camera rehearsals was delayed by the need to wait for paint to dry on a piece of scenery.

Saturday 22: *The Chase: The Executioners* is transmitted on BBC1.

Monday 24: Four days' preliminary rehearsal begins for *The Chase: The Death of Doctor Who*. Rehearsals this week take place in the Drill Hall at 239 Uxbridge Road.

Wednesday 26: Verity Lambert sends a memo to Barry Learoyd, Chief Designer (Drama), complaining about the poor quality of the walls for the Empire State Building set featured in the *Flight Through Eternity* episode.

Thursday 27: The Copyright Department is briefed to commission from writer Paul Erickson the scripts for a four-part story entitled *The Ark*.

Friday 28: *The Chase: The Death of Doctor Who* is camera rehearsed and recorded in Riverside 1. The total cost is £2,529. A fight scene between the Doctor and his robot double (played in some shots by Edmund Warwick) is pre-recorded between 3.00 and 3.30 in the afternoon as William Hartnell finds such scenes tiring and needs time to recover before the main recording in the evening.

Gerald Savory, Donald Wilson's successor as Head of Serials, has now asked Verity Lambert to make the next season's Dalek story a twelve-parter rather than a six-parter. Lambert sends Savory the following memo in response:

> Re your request to make Serial V (Dalek serial) a twelve-part serial instead of a six. I have put into motion the following, subject to negotiations with Terry Nation's agent and Dennis Spooner's agent. It will be possible to have a twelve part Dalek serial written jointly by Terry Nation and Dennis Spooner. The first recording for this will be on 15 October 1965 (Week 41) and it would continue up to and including 7 January 1966 (Week 1). At the moment we have one week's filming allocated to us in Week 39. We shall now require two weeks' filming and this ideally should be in Weeks 38 and 39.
>
> I am not able at this point to say if these serials can be done for less than £3,000 an episode, which as you know is what we have spent on the last two Dalek serials. I have asked Terry and Dennis to try to keep the overall cost as low as possible. However until they have been able to get together and work out a storyline it is not possible for me to commit myself.

The start of the third production block will subsequently be put back by one week. Recording of the twelve-part story will therefore begin on 22 October, and pre-filming at Ealing will take place over Weeks 39 and 40.

John Wiles later confirms that it will be impossible to mount the story on the usual budget of £2,500 per episode. An additional, one-off allocation of £3,500 is then made to the programme, which he elects to split equally between the first two episodes of the story.

Saturday 29: *The Chase: The Death of Time* is transmitted on BBC1.

Monday 31: Four days' preliminary rehearsal begins for *The Chase: The Planet of Decision*.

JUNE 1965

Friday 4: *The Chase: The Planet of Decision* is camera rehearsed and recorded in Riverside 1. The total cost is £2,285.

Saturday 5: *The Chase: Flight through Eternity* is transmitted on BBC1.

Monday 7: Four days' preliminary rehearsal begins for *The Time Meddler: The Watcher*. This story's rehearsals take place in the Drill Hall at 239 Uxbridge Road.

Wednesday 9: Director Richard Martin sends the following memo of appreciation to designers Raymond Cusick and John Wood for their work on *The Chase* and, in Wood's case, also *The Web Planet*:

> Thank you both very much for a highly successful six episodes of *Dr Who*. As we all know the difficulties under which this programme labours – the impossible task of its visual realisation – and as you are seldom there when the bits are swept up late on a Friday and congratulations seem in order, I would like it on record that you both worked extremely hard and contributed in a very great measure to any success that the programme may have obtained.
>
> For Mechanoids and mizzens; not to mention ants and animi of foregone worlds; for the sweat of your brows and the sweep of your brushes, my thanks.

Barry Learoyd replies to Verity Lambert's memo of 26 May, saying that the Empire State Building set looked satisfactory to him on transmission and pointing out that continual late information from the production office and consequent late design drawings mean that construction work is often rushed, leaving additional tidying up for the designers and studio staff to do on the recording day.

Incidental music for *The Time Meddler* is recorded in Lime Grove Studio R, featuring drums played by Charles Botterill. (Other music for this serial is to come from stock.)

Friday 11: *The Time Meddler: The Watcher* is camera rehearsed and recorded in TC4. The total cost is £1,949. The recording overruns its allotted time by seven minutes. This is due partly to the fact that a technical fault causes it to start four minutes late and partly to the fact that an entire sequence has to be reshot as it has used more stock music than can be cleared for copyright purposes – a fact not discovered until the end of the day.

Saturday 12: *The Chase: Journey into Terror* is transmitted on BBC1.

Monday 14: Four days' preliminary rehearsal begins for *The Time Meddler: The Meddling Monk*.

Wednesday 16: Verity Lambert replies to Barry Learoyd's memo of the previous Wednesday, asserting that the only reason the Empire State Building set looked satisfactory was that the director changed some of his shots to disguise its deficiencies, and that scripts and design discussions for *The Chase* were on time.

Friday 18: *The Time Meddler: The Meddling Monk* is camera rehearsed and recorded in TC3. The total cost is £1,803. A fight scene featuring stuntmen Fred Haggerty and Tim Condren is recorded out of sequence before the main recording of the episode.

Saturday 19: *The Chase: The Death of Doctor Who* is transmitted on BBC1.

Monday 21: Four days' preliminary rehearsal begins for *The Time Meddler: A Battle of Wits*.

During the course of this week, shooting of film inserts for *Galaxy 4* is carried out at Ealing.

Thursday 24: A photocall for *Galaxy 4* takes place at Ealing featuring the Drahvins and Chumblies.

Friday 25: *The Time Meddler: A Battle of Wits* is camera rehearsed and recorded in TC4. The total cost is £1,677. During camera rehearsals, actor

Michael Miller, playing Wulnoth, is asked to make a sound recording of one line of dialogue to facilitate cueing in the main recording that evening.

Saturday 26: *The Chase: The Planet of Decision* is transmitted on BBC1. This is the last episode on which Dennis Spooner is credited as story editor.

Monday 28: Four days' preliminary rehearsal begins for *The Time Meddler: Checkmate*.

JULY 1965

Friday 2: *The Time Meddler: Checkmate* is camera rehearsed and recorded in TC4. The total cost is £1,728.

Saturday 3: *The Time Meddler: The Watcher* is transmitted on BBC1.

Monday 5: Four days' preliminary rehearsal begins for *Galaxy 4: Four Hundred Dawns*. By this point, John Wiles has in effect taken over the day-to-day production of *Doctor Who* from Verity Lambert.
    Donald Tosh briefs the Copyright Department to commission from Dennis Spooner the scripts for his six scripts for the new twelve-part Dalek story, now entitled *The Daleks' Master Plan*. (Spooner has still not fully relinquished the story editor's post but is unable to commission himself as this would breach BBC restrictions on story editors writing for their own shows.)

Friday 9: *Galaxy 4: Four Hundred Dawns* is camera rehearsed and recorded in TC4. The total cost is £3,100.
    Donald Tosh briefs the Copyright Department to commission from John Lucarotti a new four-part historical story about the massacre of the Huguenots in Paris, 1572. This subject matter is the production team's suggestion; Lucarotti originally proposed to write a story about Eric the Red discovering Newfoundland.

Saturday 10: *The Time Meddler: The Meddling Monk* is transmitted on BBC1.

Monday 12: Four days' preliminary rehearsal begins for *Galaxy 4: Trap of Steel*.

Friday 16: *Galaxy 4: Trap of Steel* is camera rehearsed and recorded in TC4. The total cost is £2,094.
    Dennis Spooner briefs the Copyright Department to commission from

Terry Nation his six scripts for *The Daleks' Master Plan*.

Saturday 17: *The Time Meddler: A Battle of Wits* is transmitted on BBC1.

Monday 19: Four days' preliminary rehearsal begins for *Galaxy 4: Airlock*.

Tuesday 20: Douglas Camfield, who has been assigned to direct the forthcoming twelve-part Dalek story now entitled *The Daleks' Master Plan*, writes to composer Tristram Cary to ask if he would be willing to provide the incidental music for it:

> As a matter of interest, we met when I was production assistant to Waris Hussein on the *Marco Polo* story …
>
> My serial – to be written by Terry Nation and Dennis Spooner – will range far and wide in Space and Time. The basic idea is one concerning the Daleks' attempt to conquer the Universe in the year 4,000 AD. but we shall take in the Planet of Mists, a planet which is a kind of galactic Devil's Island, Ancient Egypt, Hollywood in the '20s, the Daleks' outer planet of Varga and so on and so forth. Being a twelve-parter, the story will be a complex and far-ranging one.
>
> One thing we shall be doing is to give back to the Daleks their former menace, plus trying, in general, to sharpen up the pace of the storytelling.
>
> The music, I think, should be largely electronic – weird and compelling. The first episode is to be called *The Nightmare Begins* and that should give some indication of the feeling I'm after. For the historical episodes, we could lose the electronic music and go after something else. Without scripts I cannot be more specific than that!
>
> I do hope that you will agree to work on this project. I thought your music for *Marco Polo* was excellent and I think this serial is right up your street!

Friday 23: *Galaxy 4: Air Lock* is camera rehearsed and recorded in TC4. The total cost is £2,293.

Saturday 24: *The Time Meddler: Checkmate* is transmitted on BBC1.

Monday 26: Four days' preliminary rehearsal begins for *Galaxy 4: The Exploding Planet*.

Friday 30: *Galaxy 4: The Exploding Planet* is camera rehearsed and recorded in TC3. The total cost is £2,463.

AUGUST 1965

Monday 2: Four days' preliminary rehearsal begins for *Dalek Cutaway: Mission to the Unknown*.

Friday 6: *Dalek Cutaway: Mission to the Unknown* is camera rehearsed and recorded in TC3. The total cost is £2,440.

SEPTEMBER 1965

Wednesday 1: One day of location filming is carried out for *The Myth Makers*.

Tuesday 7: John Wiles sends Terry Nation the following letter conveying comments by director Douglas Camfield and others on the draft scripts for the early episodes of *The Daleks' Master Plan*:

> Douglas has come up with some very exciting ideas for the serial which I do hope you will consider. One of his fears is that as far as he himself is concerned he would like to try to get more into the production indicative of the year 4,000 AD.
>
> We have had a lot of talks about this and some of the things we feel for example concern names of people. We both feel that, just as our names have changed a great deal since the time of Christ, so too in another 2,000 years a lot of names, now in use (and, in fact, used in your script) will have been corrupted into something else. This might happen by the dropping of consonants or the changing of vowels, e.g. ROALD instead of RONALD, VYON instead of WALTON. He also feels – and I think this is an interesting idea – that we may return to a kind of heraldry whereby the basic names in English reappear, e.g. BORS for one of the convicts on Desperus.

In this connection also, it seems possible that words will emerge meaning 'SPACE VESSEL'. Donald has suggested a vehicle called a *FLIPT* (Faster than light inter-planetary transporter) and a *SPAR* (Space car): terms like this can easily be explained in the scripts and will add to the possible vernacular of the period. We are a little worried also about Vitaranium. Bill Hartnell will certainly have great difficulty in saying it. May we for certain occasions change it to VX 2?

Some of the people who have read the scripts have also been a little worried by the reference to New Washington. They feel that in the year 4,000 the world will possibly be a single country owing allegiance to nothing that we know today. One suggestion is that we refer to it as Communication Centre Earth, which gives us the feeling that the whole world may be one giant built-up area where nationalities have ceased to exist.

How do you feel about these ideas?

This possibly sounds as if my only reaction to the scripts is to suggest amendments – far from it! I think there are some most exciting things in the story. But if we can help Douglas realise his ambitions for it we will get an even more exciting result.

Terry Nation replies later in the week indicating that he has no objection to most of the changes suggested by Wiles. He dislikes the substitution of 'VX 2' for 'Vitaranium', however, and suggests 'Vita' as a possible alternative. He also asks that the names of two of his characters, Mavic Chen and Sara Kingdom, be left unchanged.

Saturday 11: *Galaxy 4: Four Hundred Dawns* is transmitted on BBC1.

Monday 13: John Wiles writes again to Terry Nation, thanking him for his co-operation over the changes suggested the previous week and assuring him that there is no intention to change the names Mavic Chen and Sara Kingdom. He continues:

'Vita' and its derivatives worries us slightly because of its association with vitamins. Would you wear TARANIUM as a contraction of your original word? I am sure the Daleks would make it sound most sinister.

Four days' preliminary rehearsal begins for *The Myth Makers: Temple of Secrets*. This story's rehearsals take place at North Kensington Community Centre.

Maureen O'Brien, returning from holiday for the start of the new production block, is taken aback to learn that she is to be dropped from the series at the end of *The Myth Makers*. John Wiles' intention has been to replace Vicki with a new character, Katarina, whom he has had written into the last two episodes of the story as a late addition. He and Donald Tosh have quickly realised however that this character, a handmaiden to the prophetess Cassandra, would pose enormous difficulties for the series' writers, owing to her lack of modern knowledge. They have therefore decide to kill her off in the following story, *The Daleks' Master Plan*, and to use as another short-term companion Terry Nation's character Sara Kingdom, who will also be killed off at the end of that story. Adrienne Hill is subsequently cast as Katarina, and Jean Marsh as Sara.

Friday 17: *The Myth Makers: Temple of Secrets* is camera rehearsed and recorded in Riverside 1. The total cost is £3,327.

Saturday 18: *Galaxy 4: Trap of Steel* is transmitted on BBC1.

Monday 20: Four days' preliminary rehearsal begins for *The Myth Makers: Small Prophet, Quick Return*.

Friday 24: *The Myth Makers: Small Prophet, Quick Return* is camera rehearsed and recorded in Riverside 1. The total cost is £2,566.

Saturday 25: *Galaxy 4: Air Lock* is transmitted on BBC1.

Monday 27: Four days' preliminary rehearsal begins for *The Myth Makers: Death of a Spy*.

Five days' shooting of film inserts for *The Daleks' Master Plan* begins on Stage 3A/B at Ealing. The first scene to be shot is the death of Katarina for episode four – ironically, actress Adrienne Hill's first work on the series. As the story's scripts are still undergoing revision, director Douglas Camfield has to improvise some of the action based upon the agreed storyline. Problems occur all week due to the late delivery, and in some cases non-delivery, of props and scenery. A number of model shots due to be done on Friday are held over for completion the following Monday.

PRODUCTION DIARY

OCTOBER 1965

Friday 1: *The Myth Makers: Death of a Spy* is camera rehearsed and recorded in Riverside 1. The total cost is £2,230.

Saturday 2: *Galaxy 4: The Exploding Planet* is transmitted on BBC1.

Monday 4: Four days' preliminary rehearsal begins for *The Myth Makers: Horse of Destruction*.

A further five days' shooting of film inserts for *The Daleks' Master Plan* begins on Stage 3A/B at Ealing. The morning of the first day is spent completing the model shots held over from the previous Friday. Filming then continues with scenes of a battle between Daleks and Ancient Egyptians. Extras hired from the Denton de Gray agency to play non-speaking Egyptian soldiers are judged by director Douglas Camfield and production assistant Viktors Ritelis to be very poor, and a number of shots involving them are dropped. Problems again arise with scenery, and in particular with a model pyramid that takes one-and-half hours to erect on the morning of Wednesday 6 October after Shawcraft have worked all through the night to complete it. Bill Roberts, the manager of Shawcraft, tells Ritelis that he would be happy for some of the specialist prop and model work on *Doctor Who* to be put out to some other firm in future, as his team are overstretched.

Friday 8: One of the final pieces of filming for *The Daleks' Master Plan* at Ealing is a model shot of an erupting volcano, utilising steam and compressed air to achieve the effect of the magma. This proves unsatisfactory, however, as the volcano is out of scale with the model TARDIS required to materialise on it. A decision is taken to remount it at a later date.

The Myth Makers: Horse of Destruction is camera rehearsed and recorded in Riverside 1. The total cost is £2,091.

Saturday 9: *Dalek Cutaway: Mission to the Unknown* is transmitted on BBC1. This is the last episode on which Verity Lambert receives a credit as producer.

Wednesday 13: Composer Tristram Cary's incidental music for the first six episodes of *The Daleks' Master Plan* is recorded between 6.30 pm and 10.30 pm at the IBC Studios, at 35 Portland Place, London W1A. The instruments, played by an ensemble of musicians led by Eddie Walker, are: horn, cello, percussion, flute, oboe and vibraphone.

Friday 15: *Doctor Who*'s budget is set for the financial year beginning 1 April 1966 at an average of £2,750 per episode.

Saturday 16: *The Myth Makers: Temple of Secrets* is transmitted on BBC1.

Monday 18: Four days' preliminary rehearsal begins for *The Daleks' Master Plan: The Nightmare Begins*. The venue for this story's rehearsals is the Drill Hall at 58 Bulwer Street.

The volcano model shot initially attempted on Friday 8 October is remounted on Stage 2 at Ealing, this time using a high speed camera to increase its effectiveness. Again however it proves unsuccessful, this time because the rushes show strobing and an occasional sideways kick on the picture. It will therefore have to be remounted again.

John Wiles prepares a memo to be given to all the series' directors and their teams, setting out some standing orders for the production. Reiterating the contents of two earlier notes used by Verity Lambert for the same purpose, it stipulates that in order to facilitate overseas sales, each episode must have a 'fade to black' included immediately after the opening titles, or alternatively immediately after the reprise from the previous week, and another around half-way through (this is so that commercial breaks may be inserted); and that no more than five recording breaks should normally be scheduled for each episode. It goes on to state that artists who have appeared in previous *Doctor Who* stories should not be used again without approval first being obtained from Wiles; and that, in accordance with a ruling by Sydney Newman, no episode should have a duration of more than 24' 45" or of less than 23' 45". It also sets out the standard billing for *Radio Times* and explains the circumstances in which credits may be given for designers and members of the technical staff.

Thursday 21: The volcano model shot is again attempted at Ealing, but once more proves unsuccessful as the same picture fault occurs as on Monday.

Friday 22: *The Daleks' Master Plan: The Nightmare Begins* is camera rehearsed and recorded in TC3. The budget is initially set at £4,250 – the standard £2,500 plus half the additional one-off sum of £3,500 allocated to this story. It is subsequently increased to £4,310. The total cost is £5,318.

A press photocall takes place at 3.45 pm on the set, featuring William Hartnell and the actors playing characters called Technix, who are required to have their heads shaved for the production.

Saturday 23: *The Myth Makers: Small Prophet, Quick Return* is transmitted on BBC1.

Monday 25: Four days' preliminary rehearsal begins for *The Daleks' Master Plan: Day of Armageddon*.

Tuesday 26: John Wiles sends make-up supervisor Sonia Markham a memo pointing out that in *The Nightmare Begins*, the beard worn by actor Brian Cant, playing the character Kurt Gantry, differed noticeably between the pre-filmed inserts and the studio recordings, and that the hair-lace on William Hartnell's wig was showing badly in close ups. He concludes:

> I would be grateful if you could look into these points. The make-up on the whole in the programme is so good that I think it a pity when something lets it down.

Wednesday 27: Sonia Markham replies as follows to John Wiles's memo of the previous day:

> Thank you for your memo of 26 October. I have noted the contents. I appreciate your remarks and can only apologise for the lack of continuity on the make-up of Brian Cant.

> Regarding the hair-lace on Mr Hartnell's wig, owing to different lighting and change of positions on various sets, this does sometimes occur, especially in big close-ups, and this is almost unavoidable.

Friday 29: *The Daleks' Master Plan: Day of Armageddon* is camera rehearsed and recorded in TC3. The budget for this episode is £4,250, the total cost £4,031.

Saturday 30: *The Myth Makers: Death of a Spy* is transmitted on BBC1.

NOVEMBER 1965

Monday 1: Four days' preliminary rehearsal begins for *The Daleks' Master Plan: Devil's Planet*.

Friday 5: *The Daleks' Master Plan: Devil's Planet* is camera rehearsed and recorded in TC3. From this episode, the budget reverts to £2,500 per episode for the remainder of the story. The total cost of *Devil's Planet* is £2,268.

Saturday 6: *The Myth Makers: Horse of Destruction* is transmitted on BBC1.

Monday 8: Four days' preliminary rehearsal begins for *The Daleks' Master Plan: The Traitors*.

Friday 12: *The Daleks' Master Plan: The Traitors* is camera rehearsed and recorded in TC3. The total cost is £2,448.

Saturday 13: *The Daleks' Master Plan: The Nightmare Begins* is transmitted on BBC1.

Monday 15: The volcano model shot attempted on 8, 18 and 21 October is remounted again on Stage 3B at Ealing, and finally proves satisfactory.

Four days' preliminary rehearsal begins for *The Daleks' Master Plan: Counter Plot*.

Tuesday 16: Donald Tosh briefs the Copyright Department to commission from writer Brian Hayles the storylines for two stories, entitled *The White Witch* and *The Hands of Aten*.

Wednesday 17: John Wiles sends Serials Department Organiser Terence Cook the following memo:

> I have been told by our designer, Barry Newbery, that when the large SFX units arrived at Ealing for storage after last week's recording, they were found to be so seriously damaged that one of them, required for this week, cannot be used at all, and repairs to both are going to be very extensive. Enquiries have not elicited who or what was responsible for the damage; all that is certain is that a most valuable piece of SFX equipment, costing a great deal of money, has been smashed by inefficiency and indifference, and another considerable amount will be needed to put it right, in the meantime creating immense difficulties for the director and his designers. I am told that there is great uncertainty as to whose is the responsibility for the safe transportation and storage of all special effects, but may we register a very strong protest at having to be the ones to suffer for it. It is unforgivable that a director should be deprived within three days of recording of a vital piece of equipment because of inefficiency for which nobody will answer.

Friday 19: *The Daleks' Master Plan: Counter Plot* is camera rehearsed and recorded in TC4. The total cost is £2,194.

Barry Learoyd, the Chief Designer (Drama), sends John Wiles the following memo:

> *Dr Who* Serial V is proving a near disaster. I understand that the director is doing all possible to meet his dates but that his commitment to twelve consecutive episodes has made this virtually impossible. Scripts or near-complete scripts are often available but planning the design and shooting arrangements for these is entirely haphazard. The director has declared his availability to the designers, but in practice this means the designer designs to the script, presents the prepared design and gets an OK from the director in a meeting lasting perhaps five minutes. The result being that when he (the director) reaches the stage where he can plan his shots, he must use what is done – or whatever 'bits' of what is done that now fit in with his production ideas. This very often means large areas of unwanted and wasted scenery.
>
> I give you this summary, despite the fact that this Serial V will almost certainly continue in this same way, in order that you may make quite sure that the following four episode parts allow proper planning with the designers and directors together and so that you may fight wholeheartedly against any recurrence of more than six episodes being given to one director and in order that you take some action to ensure that the addition of the Christmas holiday period to the problem does not lead to real disaster.

Saturday 20: *The Daleks' Master Plan: Day of Armageddon* is transmitted on BBC1.

Monday 22: Four days' preliminary rehearsal begins for *The Daleks' Master Plan: Coronas of the Sun.*

Tuesday 23: John Wiles responds as follows to Barry Learoyd's memo of 19 November:

> Thank you for your memo. Once again I am sorry that script difficulties on the … serial have caused so much trouble to our designers. Nevertheless, I have no hesitation in affirming that I think the results to date have been first class, and a credit to all concerned with the programme. I am sorry that you consider some of the director's shooting to be wasteful as far as sets are concerned, this hadn't occurred to me, nor do I

believe I agree with you. Your point about any director working for more than six consecutive episodes is valid and I agree. Personally, I am planning no serial of more than four episodes. The director of Serial W joins me at the end of this week and will be available for discussions with her designer thereafter, and the director of Serial X will join me when he returns from leave in about two weeks' time. Consequently, I am hopeful that the same situation will not arise in the immediate future.

Wiles also sends Douglas Camfield a memo expressing his gratitude for the fact that the early episodes of *The Daleks' Master Plan* have been achieved within budget.

Friday 26: *The Daleks' Master Plan: Coronas of the Sun* is camera rehearsed and recorded in TC4. The total cost is £1,914.

Saturday 27: *The Daleks' Master Plan: Devil's Planet* is transmitted on BBC1.

Monday 29: Four days' preliminary rehearsal begins for *The Daleks' Master Plan: The Feast of Steven*.

DECEMBER 1965

Friday 3: *The Daleks' Master Plan: The Feast of Steven* is camera rehearsed and recorded in TC3. The total cost is £2,562.

Saturday 4: *The Daleks' Master Plan: The Traitors* is transmitted on BBC1.

Monday 6: Four days' preliminary rehearsal begins for *The Daleks' Master Plan: Volcano*.

Friday 10: *The Daleks' Master Plan: Volcano* is camera rehearsed and recorded in TC3. The total cost is £2,265.

Saturday 11: *The Daleks' Master Plan: Counter Plot* is transmitted on BBC1.

Monday 13: Four days' preliminary rehearsal begins for *The Daleks' Master Plan: Golden Death*.

Friday 17: *The Daleks' Master Plan: Golden Death* is camera rehearsed and recorded in TC3. The total cost is £2,398.

Saturday 18: *The Daleks' Master Plan: Coronas of the Sun* is transmitted on BBC1.

Friday 23: An extra day's shooting of film inserts for the final episode of *The Daleks' Master Plan* takes place on Stage 2 at Ealing.

Saturday 25: *The Daleks' Master Plan: The Feast of Steven* is transmitted on BBC1.

Monday 27: Four days' preliminary rehearsal begins for *The Daleks' Master Plan: Escape Switch*.

Friday 31: *The Daleks' Master Plan: Escape Switch* is camera rehearsed and recorded in TC3. The total cost is £2,391.

JANUARY 1966

Saturday 1: *The Daleks' Master Plan: Volcano* is transmitted on BBC1.

Monday 3: Four days' preliminary rehearsal begins for *The Daleks' Master Plan: The Abandoned Planet.*
Four days' shooting of film inserts for *The Massacre of St. Bartholomew's Eve* – John Lucarotti's four-part historical set in Paris 1572 – begins at Ealing.

Wednesday 5: Chief Designer (Drama) Barry Learoyd sends John Wiles a memo following on from their correspondence the previous November about *Doctor Who*'s scenery requirements:

> I was sorry to learn from the designer in the studio that there has been a bit of misunderstanding about our attitude to 'wasted' scenery. It is never our contention that a director should 'show the set' except where this is an integral part of his conception of the production.
>
> Our only interest in this respect is that he does not ask for more set than he is going to use. In Serial V, where the director had not the time available to plan productions with the designer in advance, and had no alternative therefore but to accept what was given to him, our interest was that he should shoot his action within these bounds, to the best advantage of the production.

Friday 7: *The Daleks' Master Plan: The Abandoned Planet* is camera rehearsed and recorded in TC3. The total cost is £1,919.

One day of location filming is carried out for *The Massacre of St. Bartholomew's Eve.* This is for a scene at the end of the story where a young girl named Dodo enters the TARDIS, subsequently to become the Doctor's new female companion. The production team's original intention was that the Huguenot character Anne Chaplet, played by Annette Robertson, should be taken on board the TARDIS at the end of this story. However, they have now reached the conclusion that to have a companion originating from Paris 1572 would pose the same problems of lack of modern knowledge as had been envisaged with Katarina. They have therefore decided to introduce instead a present-day character, Dorothea 'Dodo' Chaplet, descended from Anne. The actress cast as Dodo is Jackie Lane.

Saturday 8: *The Daleks' Master Plan: Golden Death* is transmitted on BBC1.

Monday 10: Four days' preliminary rehearsal begins for *The Daleks' Master Plan: Destruction of Time.*

Friday 14: *The Daleks' Master Plan: Destruction of Time* is camera rehearsed and recorded in TC3. The total cost is £1,888. The recording overruns its allotted time owing to the fact that the roller caption for the closing credits keeps sticking, requiring numerous retakes of the final scene. A further retake proves necessary when a stage hand appears in shot during the roller caption sequence, incurring director Douglas Camfield's wrath.

During production of *The Daleks' Master Plan*, John Wiles and Donald Tosh have both decided to quit the *Doctor Who* production team early in the new year. Wiles has never been entirely happy working as a producer, feeling more at home as a writer and a director, and he has had a very strained working relationship with William Hartnell. He has indeed proposed replacing Hartnell with another actor, but this has been overruled by Head of Serials Gerald Savory. Tosh has decided to leave partly out of loyalty to Wiles and partly due to a desire to move on to other work.

The man appointed as Wiles' replacement is Innes Lloyd, who has been on staff at the BBC since 1953 and has worked on a wide variety of different programmes. He has been chosen for the job by Sydney Newman, but accepts it with some reluctance as he is not a fan of science fiction. Tosh's successor is Gerry Davis, who has asked to be transferred to *Doctor Who* after a stint on the football team soap opera *United!*.

A number of stories have already been commissioned for the latter part of the third production block, including *The Ark* by Paul Erickson, *The Toymaker* by Brian Hayles (Tosh having now decided against using Hayles' other submissions, *The White Witch* and *The Hands of Aten*) and *The*

Gunfighters by Donald Cotton. Accomplished writer Ian Stuart Black is also due to submit a storyline to the production office. *The Toymaker* – the story in which it was proposed that Hartnell might be written out – is currently being heavily rewritten by Tosh from Hayles' scripts as, partly because of their extensive special effects requirements, these were considered unsuitable for production. It will therefore be some time before the influence of Lloyd and Davis will be fully felt.

Saturday 15: *The Daleks' Master Plan: Escape Switch* is transmitted on BBC1.

Monday 17: Four days' preliminary rehearsal begins for *The Massacre of St Bartholomew's Eve: War of God*. This story's rehearsals take place in the Drill Hall at 58 Bulwer Street.

Donald Tosh has by this point left the production office after completing his rewrites on Brian Hayles's *The Toymaker* (which will shortly undergo a change of name first to *The Trilogic Game* and then to *The Celestial Toymaker*). In consultation with John Wiles and director Bill Sellars, he has removed a number of impractical effects sequences – including some scenes set in a maze – and substituted two new games of his own, one of these being the Trilogic Game.

Tosh has now also formally rejected Hayles's storylines for *The Witch Planet* and *The Hands of Aten*; but Gerry Davis will subsequently commission from the writer a four-part historical adventure entitled *The Smugglers*, which will be made as the last story of the series' third production block.

Davis himself has meanwhile rejected an idea entitled *The New Armada* by the series' first story editor, David Whitaker, and returns it to him with the following letter:

> Enclosed please find your storyline entitled *The New Armada* which was passed on to me by Donald Tosh.
>
> Sorry, but I don't feel that this is quite in line with the direction set down by the Head of Serials for *Doctor Who*.
>
> We are looking for strong, *simple* stories. This one, though very ingenious, is rather complex with too many characters and sub-plots. To simplify it, as it stands, would reduce the plot to the point when it would virtually be a new creation.
>
> I should very much like to hear from you. Perhaps we could meet for a chat in the near future. Could you bring over a number of storylines in embryo form we could take a look at?

217

Tuesday 18: John Wiles sends the following letter to Donald Tosh:

> I have now had a chance of reading episode four of *The Toymaker* and I think it goes extremely well. Bill Sellars is also very pleased with it and a set of the scripts is now with the designer to start preliminary work. It is possible that it may be a bit short and I have agreed with Bill that I will look at all the episodes: in the event of one, three and four I'll try and work in sufficient business to give us an extra two or three minutes per episode and for episode two I will try and find another four minutes. I have discussed all this with Innes and Bill; I hope to do this as painlessly as possible, anyway don't worry, I shall respect the 'fabric' as if it were of Westminster Abbey itself. I gather … that you are sending back the Hayles versions of episodes one and two. I do appreciate this as it may help me to find the extra stuff, which I want to do early next week.

> Things go well here. Ian Stuart Black has brought in a very exciting synopsis and we are going ahead with Serial AA. Douglas has even finished his editing and has lost ten years!

> In conclusion I must thank you for everything you have done for the programme, not only in the immense amounts of rewriting which you have done, always so cheerfully and efficiently, but also for your constant encouragement and support in everything we have undertaken. Your help to me personally was quite fantastic and deeply appreciated and I hope that we shall continue to work together many times in the future. Have a splendid holiday and come and see us as soon as you get back.

Friday 21: *The Massacre of St Bartholomew's Eve: War of God* is camera rehearsed and recorded in Riverside 1.

The production team have now formally adopted a system of setting a budget for each episode according to its own particular requirements, rather than using the standard budget figure throughout. In future, the opening episode of each story will always be allocated a larger proportion of the total budget than the others, as this is the episode for which the new sets, monsters etc have to be made. It will however remain the case that if the total cost of a story exceeds the standard budget for the number of episodes it contains, savings will have to be made on other stories within the same financial year so that, at the end of the day, the books balance.

The budget for *War of God* is £2,825, the total cost £3,576.

Saturday 22: *The Daleks' Master Plan: The Abandoned Planet* is transmitted on BBC1.

Monday 24: Four days' preliminary rehearsal begins for *The Massacre of St Bartholomew's Eve: The Sea Beggar.*

Wednesday 26: Innes Lloyd sends copies of the draft scripts for the first two episodes of Donald Cotton's *The Gunfighters* to Rex Tucker, who has been assigned to direct it. The third episode is currently being rewritten as it 'came through with precious little action and nine sets,' and the fourth has yet to be delivered.

Friday 28: *The Massacre of St Bartholomew's Eve: The Sea Beggar* is camera rehearsed and recorded in Riverside 1. The budget is £2,425, the total cost £2,041.

Saturday 29: *The Daleks' Master Plan: Destruction of Time* is transmitted on BBC1.

Monday 31: Four days' preliminary rehearsal begins for *The Massacre of St Bartholomew's Eve: Priest of Death.*

FEBRUARY 1966

Friday 4: *The Massacre of St Bartholomew's Eve: Priest of Death* is camera rehearsed and recorded in Riverside 1. The budget is £2,425, the total cost £2,632.

Saturday 5: *The Massacre of St Bartholomew's Eve: War of God* is transmitted on BBC1.

Monday 7: Four days' preliminary rehearsal begins for *The Massacre of St Bartholomew's Eve: Bell of Doom.*

Friday 11: *The Massacre of St Bartholomew's Eve: Bell of Doom* is camera rehearsed and recorded in Riverside 1. The budget is £2,425, the total cost £2,019.

Saturday 12: *The Massacre of St Bartholomew's Eve: The Sea Beggar* is transmitted on BBC1.

Monday 14: Four days' preliminary rehearsal begins for *The Ark: The Steel Sky*. Although John Wiles will receive the on-screen credit as producer of *The Ark*, Innes Lloyd has by this point taken over full responsibility for the day-to-day production of the series.

Friday 18: *The Ark: The Steel Sky* is camera rehearsed and recorded in Riverside 1. The budget is £2,700, the total cost £5,678.

Saturday 19: *The Massacre of St Bartholomew's Eve: Priest of Death* is transmitted on BBC1. This is the last episode on which Donald Tosh is credited as story editor.

Monday 21: Four days' preliminary rehearsal begins for *The Ark: The Plague*.

Tuesday 22: Director Rex Tucker has by this time received draft scripts for all four episodes of *The Gunfighters*, but has expressed to Gerry Davis a number of reservations about them. Innes Lloyd sends him the following letter:

> Gerry Davis has told me that he was able to talk to you yesterday about episodes three and four of *The Gunfighters*, and he will look at them again in the light of your criticisms.
>
> Whilst they are not the greatest scripts, I believe and hope that there is a great deal of humour and adventure that can be got out of them. I am sure you will agree that it would be absurd to try and make a traditional western – I would suggest that the approach might be more on the lines of *Cat Ballou* – tongue in cheek – heroes and villains well defined. Perhaps before you do the casting we could have a talk about it. One of the things I believe we should look for is either American actors in London suitable to play parts in it, or English actors with really authentic accents.
>
> We will let you have the revised scripts as soon as they are available. I look forward to seeing you after you have finished editing *A Farewell to Arms*.

Friday 25: *The Ark: The Plague* is camera rehearsed and recorded in Riverside 1. The budget is £2,400, the total cost £1,945.

Gerry Davis has by this point completely rewritten the scripts for *The Celestial Toymaker* as Head of Serials Gerald Savory has objected to Tosh's inclusion of two characters, George and Margaret, whom he himself created for his successful West End play *George and Margaret* (the gimmick of which was that the title characters never actually appeared). On seeing the rewritten scripts, John Wiles sends a memo of protest to Savory, pointing out that he might otherwise be open to criticism for wasting money on Hayles's originals. He stresses that the story was supposed to have been one of great menace – although arising from a battle of wills between the Doctor and the Toymaker character, rather than from ray guns and monsters – and that this was what had given it its relevance to *Doctor Who*. He expresses the view that this has now been lost, as the Toymaker has been reduced virtually to a bystander and his conflict with the Doctor downplayed. He ends by expressing his regret that the story is going ahead at all now that the producer and story editor who commissioned it have both left.

Saturday 26: *The Massacre of St Bartholomew's Eve: Bell of Doom* is transmitted on BBC1.

Monday 28: Four days' preliminary rehearsal begins for *The Ark: The Return*.

MARCH 1966

Thursday 3: One day's shooting of film inserts for *The Celestial Toymaker* takes place at Ealing. Also carried out is a sound recording of William Hartnell for the scenes in episode two where the Doctor is invisible and heard only as a disembodied voice. Hartnell himself will be on holiday for the studio recording of that episode and of episode three.

Friday 4: *The Ark: The Return* is camera rehearsed and recorded in Riverside 1. The budget is £2,400, the total cost £1,939.

Saturday 5: *The Ark: The Steel Sky* is transmitted on BBC1.

Monday 7: Four days' preliminary rehearsal begins for *The Ark: The Bomb*.

Tuesday 8: Gerry Davis briefs the Copyright Department to commission from Brian Hayles the storyline for a story entitled *The Nazis*.

Friday 11: *The Ark: The Bomb* is camera rehearsed and recorded in Riverside 1. The budget is £2,400, the total cost £1,597.

Saturday 12: *The Ark: The Plague* is transmitted on BBC1.

Monday 14: Four days' preliminary rehearsal begins for *The Celestial*

Toymaker: The Celestial Toyroom. This story's rehearsals take place in the Drill Hall at 58 Bulwer Street.

Tuesday 15: Gerry Davis briefs the Copyright Department to commission from Ian Stuart Black the scripts for a further four-part story, working title *The Computers*, which will be transmitted immediately after *The Savages*. The basic scenario for this story, involving an attempt by a computer to take over the world from its base in the newly-constructed GPO Tower, has been suggested by scientist Dr Kit Pedler in discussion with Davis. It has been further developed in a storyline accepted from writer Pat Dunlop, who has since had to withdraw from the project as the proposed delivery dates for the scripts clashed with work he was already committed to doing on another BBC serial called *United!* Dunlop will subsequently be paid £50 for his contribution to the story. Pedler will meanwhile strike up a firm friendship with Davis and become *Doctor Who*'s unofficial scientific adviser.

It has by this point been decided that Steven will be written out of the series at the conclusion of *The Savages*. Peter Purves has been dissatisfied for some time with what he sees as a lack of development of Steven's character, and Innes Lloyd and Gerry Davis feel that the time is right for a change. The intention is that *The Computers* will introduce a replacement character called Richard, or Rich for short, who will join the Doctor and Dodo on their travels after meeting Dodo at a discotheque.

Friday 18: *The Celestial Toymaker: The Celestial Toyroom* is camera rehearsed and recorded in Riverside 1. The budget is £2,700, the total cost £3,686.

Saturday 19: *The Ark: The Return* is transmitted on BBC1.

Monday 21: Four days' preliminary rehearsal begins for *The Celestial Toymaker: The Hall of Dolls*.

Tuesday 22: Rex Tucker views the cinema film *Gunfight at the OK Corral* as part of his preparatory work for *The Gunfighters*.

Friday 25: *The Celestial Toymaker: The Hall of Dolls* is camera rehearsed and recorded in Riverside 1. The budget is £2,350, the total cost £2,535.

Saturday 26: *The Ark: The Bomb* is transmitted on BBC1. This is the last episode on which John Wiles is credited as producer.

Monday 28: Four days' preliminary rehearsal begins for *The Celestial Toymaker: The Dancing Floor*.

Four days' shooting of film inserts for *The Gunfighters* begins on Stage

3A/B at Ealing.

Thursday 31: Innes Lloyd sends Drama Serials Organiser Terence Cook a memo in which he reports that Barry Newbery's design drawings for episodes two and three of *The Gunfighters* will be unavoidably late. There are two reasons for this: first, the production team have 'had much trouble with scripts, due to rewrites and an uncontactable author'; and, secondly, Newbery has been tied up with work on *The Ark*, due in particular to the unusually extensive special effects requirements of that story.

APRIL 1966

Friday 1: *The Celestial Toymaker: The Dancing Floor* is camera rehearsed and recorded in Riverside 1. The budget is £2,475, the total cost £1,716.

Saturday 2: *The Celestial Toymaker: The Celestial Toyroom* is transmitted on BBC1.

Monday 4: Four days' preliminary rehearsal begins for *The Celestial Toymaker: The Final Test*.
    Gerry Davis rejects two storylines, *The Ocean Liner* and *The Clock*, submitted to the production office by David Ellis, and one, *The Evil Eye*, by Geoffrey Orme.

Tuesday 5: A sound recording session takes place between 1.30 pm and 6.00 pm at Riverside Studios for *The Ballad of the Last Chance Saloon* – a song, written by Tristram Cary and Donald Cotton, which is to be featured throughout all four episodes of *The Gunfighters*. The singer is Lynda Baron and the pianist Tom McCall. The recording goes badly, however, as Baron has difficulty mastering the tune, and it is decided that a further session will be required the following week.

Friday 8: *The Celestial Toymaker: The Final Test* is camera rehearsed and recorded in Riverside 1. The budget is £2,475, the total cost £1,449.

Saturday 9: *The Celestial Toymaker: The Hall of Dolls* is transmitted on BBC1.

Monday 11: Four days' preliminary rehearsal begins for *The Gunfighters: A Holiday for the Doctor*. Rehearsals for this story take place in the Drill Hall at 58 Bulwer Street.

Tuesday 12: A further sound recording session takes place between 7.00 pm and 11.00 pm at Riverside Studios to finish work on *The Ballad of the Last Chance Saloon*.

Friday 15: *The Gunfighters: A Holiday for the Doctor* is camera rehearsed and recorded in TC4. The budget is £3,205, the total cost £4,065.

Saturday 16: *The Celestial Toymaker: The Dancing Floor* is transmitted on BBC1.

Monday 18: Four days' preliminary rehearsal begins for *The Gunfighters: Don't Shoot the Pianist*.

Friday 22: *The Gunfighters: Don't Shoot the Pianist* is camera rehearsed and recorded in Riverside 1. The budget is £2,575, the total cost £2,142. Rehearsal is delayed by the late arrival of the prop guns required for the action.

Saturday 23: *The Celestial Toymaker: The Final Test* is transmitted on BBC1.

Monday 25: Four days' preliminary rehearsal begins for *The Gunfighters: Johnny Ringo*.

Michael Ferguson, the director assigned to handle *The War Machines*, visits Theatre 3 at Lime Grove Studios from 10.30 am to 11.30 am to view a film entitled *Machines Like Men*, which he hopes may provide some inspiration for his realisation of the story.

It has by this point been decided that Dodo will be written out of the series in the second episode of *The War Machines*, Innes Lloyd and Gerry Davis having concluded that a younger and more sophisticated female companion is required. *The War Machines* will therefore introduce two new companions, whom the production team have decided to call Ben (replacing the character Rich in writer Ian Stuart Black's original storyline) and Polly.

The latest version of *Doctor Who*'s format document, sent out to prospective writers to explain the background and approach to the stories, describes the newcomers as follows:

> *General notes about Ben and Polly:*
>
> They must have a *positive* and *active role to play in any story.* (From a production practicability point-of-view – they should be written *to share quite a proportion of the stories with the Doctor* – this is so that the load isn't so great!)
>
> They are not merely *the Doctor's acolytes but thinking human beings from this age, capable of individual thought and action.* They

do not always agree with one another or with the Doctor – they are people with all the *strengths and frailties – inhibitions and forms of expression of which individuals are capable*. They are thrown together with the Doctor – Ben as a reluctant traveller, who feels that he has been Shanghaid into the TARDIS and *always trying to get back to the present day and the Navy*; Polly, also reluctant, but *enjoys the excitement of the unpredictable* travel although *when very frightened wishes herself back in the security of her friends and London*. NEITHER OF THEM MUST EVER LOSE A SENSE OF AWE AND AMAZEMENT AT THE FORM OF TRAVEL THEY FIND THEMSELVES UNDERTAKING. e.g. *They are real people transported into real situations in incredible adventures in Space and Time.* They are ordinary people, with whom we sympathise, to whom extraordinary things happy.

As a general rule, Polly should find herself in dangerous situations from which either Ben or the Doctor, or both, rescue her. *She is our damsel in distress.*

BEN:

24, Able Seaman (Radar), Cockney. Father, now dead, was wartime sailor and peacetime dock-crane driver. Mother married again to unsympathetic step-father. Ben trained at sea school from age of 15, having previously stowed away on cargo ship for adventure to get away from unhappy home. He enjoys the Navy and all it has to offer. Enjoys all sport, especially boxing and athletics – interested in all things mechanical and electrical and in true Navy fashion can turn his hand to most things, including basic cooking and sewing.

Temperament:

A realist, down to Earth, solid, capable and cautious. Inclined, on occasions, to be shy. He is slow to anger but somewhat thin skinned about his Cockney accent. (He thinks, mistakenly, that Polly looks down on him because of this.) He is also sensitive to Naval allusions made in fun – such as 'What ho, my Hearties' – 'Shiver me timbers' etc. He is intensely loyal and will risk anything for his two companions but won't take any nonsense from either.

Attitudes:

Wants to get back to his ship in Navy and resents Doctor Shanghai-ing him in the TARDIS – also resentful of Polly for getting him into TARDIS in the first place. Apart from this he respects Doctor but thinks him impractical – i.e. the way he cannot predict where the TARDIS is going in Time and Space. Rises to Polly's jokes about the Navy and the Doctor's cracks about his 'quaint accent.'

POLLY:

21, Private Secretary to scientist. Father, country doctor in Devon, four brothers (one older – three younger). Happy and conventional middle class background, she has never been tied to her mother's apron strings – they never know when to expect her home but when she arrives they are happy to see her. Has been, in turn, a travel courier, done a small amount of modelling (which she found irksome to her intelligence and feet) and when we meet her she is secretary to chief scientist on computer programme. She lives in a self-contained Gloucester Road flat.

She loves sports cars, watching motor racing, ski-ing, clothes, swimming – pet hates: pomposity, deb's delights, conforming and officials (police to ticket collectors). She is always ready to lose herself in a new pursuit – if it offers excitement.

Temperament:

Intelligent, imaginative, impulsive, inclined to act first, think later. Gets terribly frightened by unimportant things but is stoic about larger dangers. Sometimes forgetful and unpredictable. She is a sucker for lame ducks. Her warm-hearted sympathy for the under-dog, coupled with her impulsiveness, sometimes lands her and her companions in trouble. She is totally undomesticated – cannot sew, knit or cook.

Attitudes:

Has sisterly affection for Ben, though relies on him when they are in a tight spot. Teases him about the Navy. Resents Ben's domestic practicability. The Doctor represents a father figure but irritates her at times when he is being pompous or mysterious. She is also inclined to tease him as well.

A number of actresses have attended auditions for the role of Polly, at which they have been required to read the following speech:

(SENTENCES IN CAPS SPOKEN TO PERSON IN ROOM)

POLLY: (INTO PHONE) Hello, yes right I'll hold on. (TO FRIEND IN ROOM) A LONG DISTANCE CALL – DUNDEE. NO HAVEN'T THE FOGGIEST. WHO LIVES IN DUNDEE ANYWAY? (TO PHONE) Oh, yes. (TO ROOM) HE'S COMING ON NOW!

Who's that? Doctor? Doctor, who? I didn't catch your last name, oh, I see. (TO ROOM) I WASN'T MEANT TO. (MAKES A FACE) Look are you sure you haven't got the wrong number of something?

Yes, my name is Polly Wright. But?… Oh, I see, a friend of my uncle's. But which uncle? Charles? Haven't seen him for ages – don't think he quite approves of me.

What! He's been kidnapped! You're joking! Who'd want to kidnap Uncle Charles? Oh I see!

(HAND ON PHONE – TO ROOM) HE SAYS THAT UNCLE CHARLES HAS BEEN KIDNAPPED BY DALEKS OR SOMETHING. HE MUST BE A NUT OF SOME KIND

Look, I think you'd better tell the police hadn't you, I mean … Oh!

(TO ROOM) HE SAYS I'M HIS ONLY HOPE

I'm very flattered Doctor whatever your name is but … Oh. He's in danger. You don't know Uncle Charles. They're in danger not him. He'll bore them to death. What's that? I'm in danger as well. Oh now, a joke's a joke but this … (TO ROOM) HE SOUNDS QUITE SINCERE ABOUT IT

But who is threatening me? – What! But he's right here I

(BACKING AWAY PHONE IN HAND) ROGER DON'T FOOL AROUND WITH THAT KNIFE. STAY WHERE YOU ARE …

On the basis of these auditions, the role of Polly is this month awarded to Anneke Wills, who began her acting career in 1954 at the age of eleven and has since appeared in several films and numerous TV plays and series. She came to the production team's attention earlier in the year when her husband, actor Michael Gough, portrayed the Celestial Toymaker. Michael Craze, who began acting as a boy soprano in the fifties and has since won a number of TV parts, is cast as Ben. Contracts have been agreed under which Wills is to receive £68 5s 00d per episode and Craze £52 10s 00d per episode. (William Hartnell is by this point receiving £315 per episode.)

Wednesday 27: Two day's shooting of film inserts for *The Savages* begins at Ealing.

Friday 29: *The Gunfighters: Johnny Ringo* is camera rehearsed and recorded in Riverside 1. The budget is £2,575, the total cost £2,196.

Saturday 30: *The Gunfighters: A Holiday for the Doctor* is transmitted on BBC1.

MAY 1966

Sunday 1: Rex Tucker carries out one day of location filming at Virginia Water for a scene in episode four of *The Gunfighters* where a fur-clad Savage is seen on the TARDIS scanner screen. The Savage is played by walk-on John Raven.

Monday 2: Four days' preliminary rehearsal begins for *The Gunfighters: The OK Corral*.

Friday 6: *The Gunfighters: The OK Corral* is camera rehearsed and recorded in Riverside 1. The budget is £2,575, the total cost £2,012. Rehearsal is again delayed by the late arrival of prop guns, causing vociferous complaints from members of the cast required to use them.

Saturday 7: *The Gunfighters: Don't Shoot the Pianist* is transmitted on BBC1.

Monday 9: Four days' preliminary rehearsal begins for *The Savages* episode one.

Friday 13: *The Savages* episode one is camera rehearsed and recorded in Riverside 1. The budget is £3,205, the total cost £4,542.

Saturday 14: *The Gunfighters: Johnny Ringo* is transmitted on BBC1.

Monday 16: Four days' preliminary rehearsal begins for *The Savages* episode two.

Friday 20: *The Savages* episode two is camera rehearsed and recorded in Riverside 1. The budget is £2,575, the total cost £2,806.

Saturday 21: *The Gunfighters: The OK Corral* is transmitted on BBC1.

Sunday 22: Location filming for *The War Machines* takes place between 10.00 am and 5.00 pm in Berners Mews, Newman Passage, Fitzroy Square, Charlotte Place and Bedford Square, all in the vicinity of the GPO Tower in central London. A prop police box is set up in Bedford Square for scenes of the TARDIS arriving at the beginning of the story and leaving again at the end. The GPO have refused permission for filming to take place from the Tower itself – this is the first weekend after the public opening of the Tower and they are concerned that there would be too much disruption – so panoramic high angle shots of the area are taken instead from the Centre Point building on Tottenham Court Road and the Duke of York pub in Charlotte Place.

Monday 23: Four days' preliminary rehearsal begins for *The Savages* episode three.
     Three days' shooting of film inserts for *The War Machines* begins at Ealing. The first two days are spent on Stage 3A/B, filming scenes of a warehouse where the War Machines are constructed. Wednesday 25 May sees the crew moving outside onto the studio lot for scenes of army troops storming the warehouse.

Thursday 26: A second day of location filming takes place for *The War Machines*, this time in the Covent Garden and Kensington areas, including Cornwall Gardens. Some high-angle shots are taken from a house at 50F Cornwall Gardens.

Friday 27: *The Savages* episode three is camera rehearsed and recorded in Riverside 1. The budget is £2,575, the total cost £2,252. Also recorded today are the first eight scenes of episode four, which involve smoke effects.

Saturday 28: *The Savages* episode one is transmitted on BBC1.

Monday 30: Four days' preliminary rehearsal begins for *The Savages* episode four.

JUNE 1966

Friday 3: *The Savages* episode four is camera rehearsed and recorded in Riverside 1. The budget is £2,575, the total cost £1,931.

Saturday 4: *The Savages* episode two is transmitted on BBC1.

Monday 6: Four days' preliminary rehearsal begins for *The War Machines* episode one. Rehearsals for this story take place in the Drill Hall at 58 Bulwer Street.

Friday 10: *The War Machines* episode one is camera rehearsed and recorded in Riverside 1. The budget is £3,205, the total cost £5,098.

Saturday 11: *The Savages* episode three is transmitted on BBC1.

Monday 13: Four days' preliminary rehearsal begins for *The War Machines* episode two.

Wednesday 15: Gerry Davis rejects the following storylines: *The Nazis* by Brian Hayles, *The People Who Couldn't Remember* by David Ellis and *The Herdsmen of Aquarius* by Donald Cotton.

Friday 17: *The War Machines* episode two is camera rehearsed and recorded in Riverside 1. The budget is £2,575, the total cost £2,355.

Saturday 18: *The Savages* episode four is transmitted on BBC1.

Sunday 19: Five days' location shooting for *The Smugglers* begins in Cornwall. The regular cast are needed only for the first day. They then return to London to continue work on *The War Machines*.

Monday 20: Four days' preliminary rehearsal begins for *The War Machines* episode three.

Innes Lloyd sends Jackie Lane a letter following her departure from the series:

> I'd like to thank you for all the hard work that you have put
> in since you have been playing Dodo. I am very sorry that

because of the background etc., you were a victim of circumstance. Anyhow, let's hope that your time with us has not been wasted, and that from it you may receive a tempting offer.

Should you want any photographs or anything, please do not hesitate to contact us; do come in and see us when you can.

Thursday 23: Michael Craze and Anneke Wills are presented to the press at a photocall beginning at 2.30 pm in Television Centre.

Friday 24: *The War Machines* episode three is camera rehearsed and recorded in Riverside 1. The budget is £2,575, the total cost £2,069.

Innes Lloyd sends Gerry Davis a memo confirming that William Hartnell will be unable to appear in episode three of Serial HH (yet to be commissioned), which is due to be recorded on Saturday 11 February 1967.

By this point, however, moves are afoot to write Hartnell out of the series altogether and replace him with another actor. Hartnell has been finding his role as the Doctor increasingly taxing and has now become extremely difficult to work with. Lloyd has decided that a change would be good both for the series and for Hartnell himself, and has won agreement to this from his superiors. He is already in discussion with well-known character actor Patrick Troughton to establish if he would be willing to take over from Hartnell. Other actors previously considered for the role of the second Doctor have included Michael Hordern and Patrick Wymark.

Saturday 25: *The War Machines* episode one is transmitted on BBC1.

Monday 27: Four days' preliminary rehearsal begins for *The War Machines* episode four.

Wednesday 29: Michael Craze carries out a sound recording for *The War Machines* episode four at Lime Grove R.

JULY 1966

Friday 1: *The War Machines* episode four is camera rehearsed and recorded in Riverside 1. The budget is £2,575, the total cost £2,090.

Saturday 2: *The War Machines* episode two is transmitted on BBC1.

Monday 4: Four days' preliminary rehearsal begins for *The Smugglers* episode one.

Friday 8: *The Smugglers* episode one is camera rehearsed and recorded in Riverside 1. The budget is £3,213, the total cost £4,261.

Saturday 9: *The War Machines* episode three is transmitted on BBC1.

Monday 11: Four days' preliminary rehearsal begins for *The Smugglers* episode two.

Friday 15: *The Smugglers* episode two is camera rehearsed and recorded in Riverside 1. The budget is £2,580, the total cost £2,299.

Saturday 16: *The War Machines* episode four is transmitted on BBC1. William Hartnell – having as usual returned for the weekend to his family home at Old Mill Cottage, Old Mill Lane, Mayfield, Sussex from his weekday digs at 98 Haven Lane, Ealing – tells his wife Heather than he has agreed to give up the role of the Doctor and that his final appearance will be in October. This will be in a story entitled *The Tenth Planet*, written by Kit Pedler with story editor Gerry Davis, which will be the first of the series' fourth production block.

Monday 18: Four days' preliminary rehearsal begins for *The Smugglers* episode three.

Friday 22: *The Smugglers* episode three is camera rehearsed and recorded in Riverside 1. The budget is £2,580, the total cost £1,552.

Monday 25: Four days' preliminary rehearsal begins for *The Smugglers* episode four.

Friday 29: *The Smugglers* episode four is camera rehearsed and recorded in Riverside 1. The budget is £2,580, the total cost £2,369. This brings to an end the recording of *Doctor Who*'s third production block.

AUGUST 1966

Monday 22: Director Derek Martinus sends the scripts for *The Tenth Planet* to William Hartnell, who is currently on holiday in Cornwall:

We've done quite a lot of work on these and I think the end result moves along at a real pace and has a lot of action. We've got a very good supporting cast for you headed by Bob Beatty as General Cutler. It would be very useful indeed if we could have a read through of all four episodes on the first Tuesday morning so that any inconsistencies can be ironed out and the new people get a perspective on the development of their characters. If we do this, it shouldn't be necessary for you to come in until after lunch on succeeding Tuesdays. I know you'll want to come up from the country, so can we say 10.45 for the first Tuesday morning (13 September)?

I hope you are having a wonderful rest in Cornwall, I very much look forward to working with you once more.

Rehearsals for this story are to start on the Tuesday of each week rather than, as in the past, on the Monday due to the fact that *Doctor Who*'s regular studio recording day has now been changed from Friday to Saturday, and the rest of the schedule has had to be adjusted accordingly.

Wednesday 24: Martinus holds a planning meeting for *The Tenth Planet*.

Hartnell replies as follows to Martinus's letter of 22 August:

The script arrived safely, thank you indeed.

I am extremely glad to hear that we have Bob Beatty with us, a good actor and an extremely pleasant fellow.

Forgive the repetition. We know each other well.

One important factor to me, at this boy's club, there are two ping-pong tables in the outer room where I would like to sit and compose my thoughts, therefore, I would ask you to forbid the rest of the cast playing at these tables during our working hours.

I find it most distracting trying to concentrate.

It will be my last four weeks with, or as, Dr 'Who', then I turn to pastures new.

My wife and I are certainly enjoying the rest together with

beautiful surroundings and perfect peace.

Tell Innes, the fishing is superb.

Finally, let me add my thanks to you for the considerate after lunch calls, so much easier at that awkward place.

My affection and regards to all those concerned.

Tuesday 30: Four days' shooting of film inserts for *The Tenth Planet* begins on Stage 3A/B at Ealing. The first day is devoted to model shots.

SEPTEMBER 1966

Tuesday 6: Martinus sends a further letter to Hartnell's holiday address in Cornwall:

Thank you very much for your nice letter – I am glad you think Bob Beatty is a good idea. I have worked with him myself before in the theatre and, as you say, he is both a very good actor and a very nice chap.

I am still not completely happy with the scripts though we are in the process of making one or two minor changes. However, I shall do my utmost to let you have a complete corrected set by the end of the week.

You will be glad to know that we have found a much better rehearsal room at St Helen's Hall. I very much look forward to seeing you on Tuesday at 10.45 am.

Saturday 10: *The Smugglers* episode one is transmitted on BBC1.

Tuesday 13: Four days' preliminary rehearsal begins for *The Tenth Planet* episode one at St Helen's Hall, St. Helen's Gardens, London W10.

Saturday 17: *The Smugglers* episode two is transmitted on BBC1.
The Tenth Planet episode one is camera rehearsed and recorded in Riverside 1. The budget is £3,215, the total cost £4,835.

Tuesday 20: Four days' preliminary rehearsal begins for *The Tenth Planet* episode two.

Saturday 24: *The Smugglers* episode three is transmitted on BBC1.

The Tenth Planet episode two is camera rehearsed and recorded in Riverside 1. The budget is £2,585, the total cost £2,355.

Tuesday 27: Four days' preliminary rehearsal begins for *The Tenth Planet* episode three. William Hartnell fails to arrive, informing the production team that he is ill. Story editor Gerry Davis rewrites the script so that the Doctor is unconscious for the entire episode and seen only briefly from behind, played by a double, Gordon Craig.

Thursday 29: Derek Martinus sends Hartnell the following letter:

> Very sorry to hear you are so poorly, but please don't worry about the show. Gerry has been very clever and managed to write around you.
>
> Everybody sends their warmest regards and we all hope you will be fit to do battle on the last one.

OCTOBER 1966

Saturday 1: *The Smugglers* episode four is transmitted on BBC1.

The Tenth Planet episode three is camera rehearsed and recorded in Riverside 1. The budget is £2,585, the total cost £2,171.

Tuesday 4: Four days' preliminary rehearsal begins for *The Tenth Planet* episode four.

Saturday 8: *The Tenth Planet* episode one is transmitted on BBC1.

The Tenth Planet episode four is camera rehearsed and recorded in Riverside 1. The budget is £2,585, the total cost £2,453. The transformation from William Hartnell to Patrick Troughton is recorded first, from 6.30 pm to 7.00 pm, having earlier been rehearsed for an hour. Following the dinner break from 7.00 pm to 8.00 pm, the remainder of the episode is then recorded between 8.30 pm and 10.00 pm. Recording slightly overruns its allotted time as Anneke Wills, Michael Craze and Gregg Palmer (playing a Cyberman) are required to do a retake of one scene in which technical problems occurred. This takes place between 10.00 pm at 10.15 pm.

After completion of the recording, the principal cast and members of the production team attend a farewell party for William Hartnell at Innes Lloyd's flat. Lloyd later drives Hartnell home.

Tuesday 11: Video editing is carried out between 7.30 pm and 10.30 pm on episode four of *The Tenth Planet*, bringing to an end the production of the first Doctor's era.

In the months between July and October 1966, following Patrick Troughton's agreement to take over from William Hartnell, the production team carried out a considerable amount of work on formulating the new Doctor's character and commissioning and developing scripts for the remainder of the fourth production block.

The Tenth Planet episode two was transmitted on BBC1 on 15 October 1966, episode three on 22 October 1966 and episode four on 29 October 1966, concluding the first Doctor's era on screen.

From Script to Screen
The Ark

INTRODUCTION

To try to analyse comprehensively the development of a *Doctor Who* adventure is not an easy matter. A television production is the result of many months' work by a large number of people, and what is ultimately seen on screen may have been affected and influenced in greater or lesser degrees by all of them.

Unless one is afforded a fly's eye view of every meeting and every aspect of the creative process, then any attempt to try to dissect the production is limited by the memories and personalities of those people to whom one speaks.

Bearing all this in mind, this chapter presents an in-depth look at just one of the first Doctor's stories. In doing so it reveals the process of making *Doctor Who* at this point in the series' history and – a factor common to every story – some of the behind-the-scenes discussions and thought which go into a production.

The production chosen for this case study is *The Ark*, a story transmitted mid-way through the third season in 1966.

The Ark was made during a period of transition for *Doctor Who*. Producer John Wiles and story editor Donald Tosh were both on the point of leaving the series, and their respective successors Innes Lloyd and Gerry Davis had yet to take over full responsibility from them. Consequently, Wiles, Tosh, Lloyd and Davis were all left with very few memories of this particular production. The story's writer, Paul Erickson, died in 1991, and as far as we know, never gave an in-depth interview about his work on it. For our view of the production we have therefore turned primarily to director Michael Imison – giving his first ever *Doctor Who* interview – and to designer Barry Newbery, who recall, scene by scene, the work that went into it. We have however incorporated a few comments from other participants, including some recollections from Paul Erickson taken from on-stage interviews given at two *Doctor Who* conventions in the eighties.

THE SCRIPTS

Every *Doctor Who* adventure that appears on screen starts life as an idea. This idea may be in the mind of a writer, it may come from the producer or the script editor, or, as is more often the case, it may develop out of a discussion between two or more of these people.

Once the initial contact has been made, a story outline or synopsis will generally be commissioned from the writer. Assuming that all is well when that is delivered, one or more of the actual scripts themselves will then be commissioned. Depending on the status of the writer, these stages may be compacted or expanded accordingly. In the case of *The Ark*, the idea of setting a story on board a giant travelling spaceship was one that the producer, John Wiles, was keen to develop. 'I loved the idea of the Ark,' Wiles remembers. 'It's always been one of my joys to imagine the world as a giant spaceship travelling on and on and on.' Wiles discussed this idea with story editor Donald Tosh who contacted Paul Erickson to see if he would be interested in submitting a story outline based on the concept. Tosh and Erickson then worked on the story outline together to develop the idea into final scripts.

Erickson was formally commissioned to write *The Ark* on 27 May 1965, at which time the story was assigned serial code 'Y'. Erickson was required to deliver the scripts for the first two episodes on 1 September 1965 and for the final two on 1 November 1965, for a production date of 5 March 1966. Erickson was paid through his agents a fee of £250 per episode.

There seems to have been a degree of wariness on the part of Erickson and his agents over the precise terms of the agreement to provide the scripts. Their concern revolved around whether or not there would be any fee payable if the scripts were ultimately rejected by the BBC. On 9 June, Erickson's agents arranged for a revised schedule of delivery dates, together with an assurance from Donald Tosh that he would advise promptly of the acceptance/non-acceptance of each script as it was delivered. The necessity for this assurance was that Erickson did not wish to work on any further episodes unless he was happy that they would be accepted. The revised delivery dates made provision for this. Episode one was now due on 18 August, episode two on 1 September, episode three on 30 September and episode four on 1 November.

Meanwhile, plans for the season as a whole were shaping up, and the extension of *The Daleks' Master Plan* from a six-parter to a twelve-parter meant that one story was effectively lost from the production order. Therefore, on 4 June 1965, *The Ark* was assigned the new serial code 'X'.

Erickson signed his writer's contracts on 14 June 1965 and subsequently delivered his draft scripts for episodes one and two on 7 September. John Wiles and Donald Tosh then discussed them with him, and the latter requested that he make some revisions. The revised versions of these first two episodes, together with the first drafts of episodes three and four, were all delivered on 18 November.

On 4 January 1966, Tosh accepted the scripts and authorised the full payment of all the moneys due to Erickson.

On 20 January 1966, Erickson's agent then contacted Tosh to ask that the final writer's credit be shared between Erickson and a woman named Lesley Scott, although he accepted that no further money would be due as a result. Up to this point, Erickson's had been the sole name on all documentation pertaining to the writing of the story. When asked about this in later years, Erickson replied that Scott – who was in fact his wife at the time – made no contribution whatsoever to the scripts. 'It was a personal arrangement I had with her,' he explained, 'which was my own personal business at the time. The circumstances went into history. I need say no more than that.'

The scripts for the first two episodes had a number of amendments made to them by Donald Tosh, and further input into all four episodes was made by the director, Michael Imison.

'I was brought in and given the scripts,' recalls Imison. 'Then I worked with the scriptwriters on them.'

Imison was not particularly impressed with the scripts at first. 'I didn't think they were wonderful! The Monoids were my idea. I can't remember what they were called originally. They were fairly indefinite creatures, but I had this idea, which I thought was brilliant, of having actors with ping pong balls in their mouths so that they could play these one-eyed creatures that would appear to have a living eye. I thought this would be a great thing for BBC Enterprises to market, but of course it was a total damp squib! I don't remember what else I got them to change. Having worked quite a lot as a script editor, I was quite happy to get people to rewrite.'

PRE-PRODUCTION

Michael Imison was a director new to *Doctor Who*, who had started his career at the BBC working for the Script Department.

'I applied for a general trainee scheme, which took half a dozen people straight from university and circulated them around the BBC with the idea of training top administrators. I thought that I would possibly be an administrator because my university experience, on the whole, though I'd done some directing, was as a student administrator. I didn't get the job, but I think they felt they ought to do something for me, and as I was clearly interested in drama, they sent me to the Drama Department in 1961. They employed me, first of all, as a script editor, and I worked on various plays and programmes under the overall control of Donald Wilson as Head of

Script Department and Michael Barry as Head of Drama.

'There was pool of us who, when we weren't working on a particular programme, carried out a sort of general survey of what writing was available. It meant for instance that I could go to the theatre a good deal at the BBC's expense! Which I was very happy to do as the theatre has always been my main love.

'I worked on a programme called *Compact*, which I was script editor of for quite a time, and was getting a bit fed up with this when a directing course became available. After I'd done the course, I started by directing some poetry programmes, which were a sort of summer replacement for the arts programme *Monitor*. Then I became one of the regular directors on *Compact*. From there, I went on to do classic serials, the most important of which was a version of *Buddenbrooks* by Thomas Mann. That was really quite a big undertaking, nine episodes, of which I was rather proud, but at that time the departments were split up and there was a new department head and he didn't like what I'd done on *Buddenbrooks*.'

Buddenbrooks was the third classic serial that Imison had directed, and then out of the blue he was assigned to work on *Doctor Who*, a job he saw as being a kind of penance. 'I thought I'd gone on to bigger things!'

Also assigned to the production was designer Barry Newbery, who had worked on *Doctor Who* since the very beginning, initially alternating on stories with Raymond P Cusick. Newbery had yet to design a science-based story for the series, although he had handled some episodes of *The Daleks' Master Plan*, and *The Ark* was to be his first such *Doctor Who*.

Unfortunately, Newbery does not have very happy memories of working on this story. 'One of the problems was that I didn't feel that the director was happy directing science fiction. Looking at it now, I can see that Michael was into the story and understood it and did a good job. You had so little time designing *Doctor Who* in those days, and you needed a director who was really proactive when it came to the nitty gritty of getting the programme made. When you're working to such a tight deadline, you've got filming and studio work to plan and you give a director an outline that you hope he will understand. You do sketches and plans of the sets for him, and you want to know which he wants to shoot in the studio and which on film. The clock goes round ever so quickly, and you need someone who comes up with the answers you want and need quickly.

'I was usually terribly enthusiastic about my work, and I probably gave myself too much to do in the allotted time. When you've got all the balls in the air and at the same time are trying to get sense from the director, and he is likewise trying to get sense from you and doesn't understand what you're talking about, then you get a terrible feeling of frustration. And I got that with Michael Imison. Mind you, I am talking about my troubles, but he had his troubles too.'

A part of this frustration was no doubt due to the fact that Imison was not happy to have been assigned to *Doctor Who* in the first place, but that he was nevertheless determined to make his mark with the show.

'I think I was deliberately trying to show off,' he admits. 'I can see I had a pretty ambitious camera script, not all of which was achieved! I did feel that one of the things *Doctor Who* should be doing was to have as much science and as many effects as one could manage. It was very complex, and I think over-ambitious.

'I remember vividly, because of the circumstances, that while I was recording the first episode, the Departmental Organiser, Terry Cook, appeared in the gallery and sat behind me. As a courtesy I said, "We're on page twelve," and indeed we'd been on page twelve for quite a time. "I was beginning to wonder if there was any other page!" he commented. So yes, it was quite complex.'

The Ark was the first full story for Jackie Lane, who played Dodo. Michael Imison remembers having to introduce her, as well as working with William Hartnell and Peter Purves, 'I had quite a lot to do with deciding what she was going to be like. Bill of course was very set in his ways and, as you can see in the finished episodes, was never very certain of his lines, and had to be handled with kid gloves. It was made very clear to me that I had to be very careful with him. Peter was very jolly. I liked him.'

The costumes for the Monoids were designed by BBC costume supervisor Daphne Dare and constructed by freelancers Jack and John Lovell. Dare recalls that the costumes were particularly challenging for the actors who had to wear them: 'The Monoids were a classic example of a monster that came together on the day. You see, we had so little time to practice the make-up and putting things together. The Monoids' Beatle wigs were more or less there to conceal the air holes in their heads. The costumes were very hot and uncomfortable, as they were made from latex and rubber. The actors would always wear cotton T-shirts underneath, which were absorbent, and then would put the costume on only at the last moment before rushing onto the set so that they were less likely to faint or expire!'

The novel aspect of the creatures was, as Michael Imison points out, the fact that they had only one eye. This detail is recalled by Jack Lovell: 'The eye was a ping-pong ball level with the actor's tongue. The actors looked out through holes in the mask, which is maybe why the upper part of the mask was covered with hair to conceal the holes, because I'm certain they were originally never meant to have hair.' John Lovell further recalls that the hair was actually yak hair.

During the sixties, the use of stock rather than specially-composed incidental music was a common practice, and it was one that Imison elected to follow for *The Ark*.

The music chosen was a combination of extracts from Tristram Cary's score for the season one story *The Mutants*, some of which had been reused on *Doctor Who* twice since, and some stock drum music by Robert Farnon (the track was actually called 'Drum-dramatics No. 11'). The latter was used as backing for the Monoid funeral in episode two, and also in episode four.

All the music and the new sound effects – which were provided as usual by Brian Hodgson at the BBC's Radiophonic Workshop – were pre-recorded onto tape and then 'played in' during the actual recording of the episodes in the TV studio. This meant that the cast and crew could hear the music and effects as they performed; and if a re-take was necessary, the tapes would need re-setting accordingly. This is one of the reasons why recording tended to be continuous, as the complexity of fitting together all the elements often precluded a retake if the only thing that was wrong was an actor fluffing a line and then recovering from it.

IN STUDIO

Eventually, the programme went into the studio. By the time of the third season, recording of *Doctor Who* was being split between the facilities at Riverside Studios on the south bank of the Thames at Hammersmith and those at Television Centre in White City. *The Ark* was recorded entirely in Riverside Studio 1, with shooting of film inserts taking place beforehand at the BBC's Television Film Studios in Ealing.

The four episodes of *The Ark* were camera rehearsed and recorded on 18 February, 25 February, 4 March and 11 March 1966 respectively. There was also apparently a single piece of recording completed on 24 January (between the recording of episodes one and two of *The Massacre of St. Bartholomew's Eve*) with actor David Greneau playing a Guardian. It is not known exactly what this extra recording was, or why it was scheduled for a non-recording day rather than for one of the adjacent recording days. It is possible that it was a session with a photographer to take the still required for the shrinking sequence in episode one.

Rehearsals for *The Ark* took place in a Territorial Army Drill Hall at 58 Bulwer Street, London W12. The cast would start rehearsing each episode on a Monday morning with a read-through of the script. This would be followed by initial rehearsals, with full rehearsals taking place from Tuesday to Thursday. Wednesday morning would normally be devoted to a first read-through of the *following* week's episode, so that the story editor would then have time to take it away and, in consultation with the writer, iron out any problems identified.

On the Thursday morning there would be a 'producer's run', for which the producer and story editor would be present and any final adjustments would be made to the script and the performances before the cast and crew moved into the studio on the Friday morning.

During the day on Friday, a final series of rehearsals would take place on the sets (these having been erected overnight), for the benefit not only of the director and his cast but also of the cameramen, lighting and other technical personnel. By about 7.00 pm, all would have to be ready for the episode to be recorded. After an hour's dinner break, the half-hour between 8.00 pm and 8.30 pm would be spent on line up – i.e. making sure that that cast and crew were all in their correct positions and that all technical equipment was ready. The recording itself would then be scheduled to take place between 8.30 pm and 9.45 pm (although in the case of *The Ark* there were a few variations from the norm, as the recording of episodes one and three was scheduled to last from 8.30 pm to 10.00 pm, and that of episode two from 8.15 pm to 9.45 pm, the dinner break in the latter case having taken place between 6.45 pm and 7.45 pm and line-up between 7.45 pm and 8.15 pm.)

Recording had to finish by 10.00 pm if the production was not to go into overtime and incur additional costs. In the case of *The Ark*, this deadline was passed for some of the episodes.

'Producer's runs were very important,' confirms Michael Imison. 'I always liked to have several of them if I could. The problem was that it was all so fast-moving; people had to have the opportunity of remembering where they were supposed to be next. Very often, although there are scene breaks on the screen, we just carried on recording and the cast were rushing round behind the scenes getting ready for their next entrance.'

Typically in the sixties, stories would be recorded in the same scene order as would be seen on transmission. As videotape was very difficult to edit, recording breaks would be scheduled only if absolutely necessary – to allow cast to change costume or make-up for example, or to move from one set to another where this could not be achieved by way of a 'bridging' scene featuring other cast members. These scheduled breaks were kept to a minimum, with an upper limit of five normally permitted in any one episode.

In a complete departure from the normal course of events, however, *The Ark* saw the first use in *Doctor Who* of full out-of-scene-order recording. This was for the final episode of the story, and was required because of the difficulty involved in moving the single full-size space shuttle pod prop from one set to another.

The scenes in the final episode were recorded in the following order:

> - The closing TARDIS scenes were recorded first, with the cast in their costumes for the following story, *The Celestial Toymaker*. William Hartnell was on a separate set to allow him to fade from view as the episode ended.

- The closing credits for the episode were then recorded from the caption roller.

- There was then a recording break to allow the regular cast to change into their costumes for *The Ark*.

- Recording continued from the start of the episode up until the first scene in the Refusian castle. Then all later scenes in the castle were recorded together.

- The scenes involving the escape of Steven and the Guardians from the kitchen were then recorded, as were all the scenes on the Ark involving the launcher.

- Next, the launcher prop was moved to the Refusis II set and all the scenes of the launcher on the planet were recorded.

- Finally, the remaining scenes were recorded in order.

Michael Imison also remembers doing storyboards for the episodes, planning out what the shots would look like when recorded and cut together. These storyboards would be used to help the designers and technical personnel to understand what the director was expecting. They were produced prior to the rehearsals, and then amended, if necessary, during the rehearsal process.

To indicate some of the considerations involved in making a *Doctor Who* story during the William Hartnell era, what follows is a scene-by-scene summary of *The Ark*, with comments from Michael Imison and Barry Newbery as appropriate, together with some contributions from Jackie Lane taken from a video interview.

THE STEEL SKY

A forest floor. A lizard sits motionless. Suddenly, with a raucous cry, a toucan flaps in and alights by the lizard.

Michael Imison: That shot was a failure, I have to say. You can see that it's a lizard. I wanted it to look like a huge monster but the cameraman couldn't find a lens that would do that, or misunderstood what I wanted.

Nearby, a scaly humanoid figure (Eric Blackburn) stands. When the creature turns we see that it has only one eye, which restlessly surveys its surroundings. It moves off through the jungle.

MI: He did manage to move the eye a bit there. One of the problems was that a lot of the Monoids were extras and you're not allowed to give extras specific direction, so I wasn't allowed to get them to do the sort of Monoid-y things that I'd hoped would make it a popular monster.

Barry Newbery: This looks quite a big jungle, doesn't it? It filled more than half of one of the stages at Ealing. At the very back there is a painted cloth. It's from stock, painted with Dylon, and it's been used so often that it's faded. It worked exceedingly well because it gave the impression of a tremendous distance, which doesn't come over too well on the black-and-white recording.

The boles of the trees are constructed scenery. The tops go out of frame. But all the foliage is from real trees. There's a great mixture of plants and trees from England and from elsewhere in the world.

A smoke machine was used in the jungle as well, and dry ice too.

All the greenery was hired from a firm called Greenery who were based at Hampton. They'd supply all the raw materials and we'd put peat and sawdust on the floor, marsh grasses and grass sods around, and then place all the trees and leaves to complete the effect.

The animals were all hired from a specialist firm and then looked after by minders. They'd put them into the shots where we'd need them. I remember one shot where we had the camera mounted on a mole crane and tracked along about sixty foot of camera track, then came down and stopped in close-up on a python moving over some dead tree branches. The sequence must have been dropped because I don't see it in this recording.

Elsewhere in the jungle, the TARDIS arrives. Dodo (Jackie Lane) emerges and promptly sneezes. Steven (Peter Purves) follows her out and berates her for leaving the ship.

MI: I'm trying to remember if I did that high shot with a mirror; shooting up into a mirror and seeing the image reflected. I think I may have done. That was one way to get around using a camera mounted on a very high crane.

Jackie Lane: The black and white tabard costume wasn't my favourite. It wasn't very flattering. The idea was that Dodo was an inquisitive character and they'd got this vast wardrobe in the TARDIS that they could use for wherever they happened to be, and Dodo just picked what she wanted at that particular moment whether she was in the right setting or not.

Dodo thinks that they have arrived at Whipsnade Zoo, just outside London, but she doesn't remember it as being quite so noisy.

MI: The soundtrack of birds was played in live, so the jungle would really have been that noisy!

The Doctor (William Hartnell) emerges from the TARDIS and suggests that Dodo might be right about their landing point. He returns to the TARDIS to continue checking his instruments as an alien reptilian hand pushes aside the greenery by the ship.

In a large control room, a report comes off a machine and is handed by a reptile creature to the Commander (Eric Elliott) who is presiding over a court of judgment.

BN: What's the date of this recording? That's a fax machine!

The Commander pronounces the prisoner (David Greneau) guilty of extreme carelessness in leaving open a valve in a heat exchange unit. This threatened the safety of the ship, and also of the Monoids. He passes a sentence of miniaturisation, to be carried out immediately. The prisoner will be reconstituted in 700 years' time when he will be of no further threat.

The Commander's daughter, Mellium (Kate Newman), pleads for clemency, but the Commander states that the only other option would have been expulsion. The defence counsel Manyak (Roy Spencer) and prosecution Zentos (Inigo Jackson) – on behalf of the Monoids – accept the sentence, and it is carried out.

MI: There are children present on the Ark because this was meant to be a community travelling for many years through space and we wanted to suggest that.

BN: The costumes were pastel colours, pink and white stripes for the females and blue and white for the males. I think the Commander may have had some red in his costume to designate his rank.

The prisoner is taken to a minifier cabinet and placed inside. He crouches on the floor and suddenly shrinks until he cannot be seen. A tray is removed from the floor of the cabinet, and Zentos, on behalf of the Monoids, thanks the Commander for the care he takes of them all.

BN: That miniaturisation shot was achieved with inlay. The shot of the man had to be lined up with the base of the cabinet, and the base of the cabinet had to be lined up with the bottom of the screen. That was the only way that the effect of him shrinking could be done. In order to make him shrink, the camera pulls back while keeping him central at the bottom of the screen. Then, when that shot is married to the static shot of the cabinet, it looks as though he shrinks within the cabinet while remaining on its floor.

MI: We took a photograph of the actor crouching down and we got a camera on a track to focus on the photograph, and I said 'If you go on a 24 degree lens and tilt up 12 degrees, the photograph will sit on the bottom of the frame, and as you track back it will appear to reduce.' Which it did.

Back in the jungle, Dodo sees an elephant coming towards them. She finds some bananas hanging in a bunch and offers a couple to the elephant. The Doctor recognises the elephant as being from India, which just adds to the strangeness: all the animals here are from different countries.

JL: All the elephant's scenes were done in one day in a film studio. Her name was Monica and she behaved beautifully throughout.

BN: It's not a full-grown elephant, more of a baby really. I think the jungle was something like fifty feet wide. The banana trees are in tubs, with rhododendron-like foliage to hide the containers.

MI: I insisted that we had shots of the cast actually touching the elephant, because I'd gone to the trouble of getting a real animal in rather than using some stock footage. I actually had the elephant in a van outside my flat overnight because he had to be driven down from somewhere in the north of England and the BBC wouldn't give the driver anywhere to park on the premises. The driver fed it and then went off to some hotel and he asked if I could keep an eye on it.

The Doctor's puzzlement is complete when he points out that as well as the mixture of animals, there is no sky, and the ground is trembling slightly.

BN: For the shot when they look up and see the roof, I got a very nice bonsai plant and set it up in front of a scaled-down painting of the roof. With a wide-angle lens on the camera, the bonsai looked like a full sized tree and the effect was quite convincing. However, the shot we see here isn't the one I set up. I've no idea why.

The metal roof was also seen as a painted cloth. I asked the scenic artist to paint it in such a way that it appeared to curve downwards, giving the impression that the Ark was spherical. You see, I had decided – whether rightly or wrongly – that since the ship obviously had artificial gravity it must be spinning like a ball in order to create this. Actually, having since given it some further thought, I now realise that the characters would have had to have been standing on the inner surface of the sphere for this to have worked, so the roof/sky wouldn't have looked like that at all.

The Doctor postulates that they might be in an indoor nature park. Dodo sneezes again and the Doctor berates her for not using a handkerchief. They move off for a last look around. Behind them, a Monoid emerges from the foliage and follows them.

In the main control room, a Monoid arrives and communicates in sign language to Zentos. A group of children are dancing in a ring and another Monoid is driving an electric transporter across the floor. The place is bustling with activity.

MI: This is 'page 12'! There were problems in getting the high angle, and I seem to recall difficulties in steering the vehicle round the sets as well. It's also all one shot from the start of the scene, with the Monoid coming round the corner and the camera pulling back and up.

BN: The trolley was a BBC scenery trolley. They were used to take goods around from stores to where the carpenters and painters were working on the set, and I borrowed one for the show and used some additional dressing to disguise it.

Zentos informs the Commander that the Monoids have located some intruders in the jungle. An image of the Doctor and Steven is displayed on a large screen in the wall of the control room. The Commander asks for the humans to be found and brought to him – not arrested, but invited.

BN: That is a back projection screen. Since the two scenic artists' cloths at the very back of the set are mounted on curves, that meant there was room in the very corner of the studio for a projector and, in another corner, space for the back projection mirror, which was needed to reflect the projected beam because of the shortage of space.

MI: I think the picture on the big screen was provided using inlay, because if it had been back projection, then I would probably have had my camera moving.

Dodo has found some paintings on a rock face in the jungle, which appear to represent zebras with two heads! The Doctor and Steven look at her discovery. An alarm echoes through the jungle and Steven sees that a group of Monoids have found the TARDIS. Dodo points out a cave and the travellers hide inside. When the aliens have gone, they try to get back to the TARDIS and see a huge city or factory in the distance. The Doctor realises that they are on board a spaceship. Suddenly they are surrounded by Monoids.

BN: That's a bad bit of camera-work! [A shot of Steven has wobbled all over the place]. Now this must be in the studio because if it had been on film, they would have re-shot it.

In order to match footage shot on film with material recorded in electronic studios, you had to have something that linked and matched the shots together, allowing you to cut between them. In the days when this was made, you couldn't cut the film or tape together afterwards. The film sequences, or telecine, were 'run in' live and it took nine seconds for the film to get to the point when you could cut to it, so it had to be planned very carefully, timing the action so that the telecine was actually to speed and playing the required scene to make a successful cut.

This meant that different telecine sequences couldn't have less than nine seconds between them unless you had two telecine machines. Then it got very complicated and time consuming.

Steven has been taken to the main control room, where he tries to explain how he and his fellow travellers arrived. The Commander disbelieves his story about time travel. He explains to Steven that the spaceship is travelling to the planet Refusis II as the Earth is dying. The Doctor and Dodo arrive and assure the Commander that they are human, and not Refusian spies as Zentos suspects.

The Doctor has been telling of some of his recent travels, all of which occurred, according to the Commander, in the first segment of time. They are now in the fifty-seventh segment, which the Doctor estimates to be at least ten million years since their last adventure.

The Commander informs them that they will arrive on Refusis in 700 years time. None of them will live to see the new world – that is a privilege reserved for their children's children.

BN: All those control consoles and equipment are built onto stock rostra. The columns were from stock with bits stuck on them. All the equipment is made. I put small pea-lights in the control panels, which didn't do anything except light up and look good.

Other parts of this set were made from moulded PVC, which to me at the time was a brand new material and technique.

The Commander explains that the entire population of the Earth is held on the ship in a miniaturised form.

BN: It would have been far too expensive to have built a separate set for the shot of the cabinets containing the miniaturised humans, so I improvised. I used a couple of filing cabinets and two mirrors set up at angles to one another to give multiple reflections. The miniaturised humans were just painted cut-outs, made by a freelance designer called Peter Pegrum, who went on to manage the BBC's Visual Effects Department. However, these miniatures were not seen on screen and nor was a shot of a Monoid removing a tray. I don't know why, as I know it was recorded.

The Commander asks Mellium to show Steven and Dodo the spaceship's statue while the Doctor remains with their chief controller, Manyak, to talk about the ship itself. The statue is gigantic and is intended to be a human holding a globe. It is being constructed by hand from a material called gregarian rock, which will last forever.

BN: That platform upon which Dodo climbs to get a closer look at the feet of the statue is supposed to look as though it is hydraulic. There are nine sections and they were supposed to lift to about 2' 6" apart, giving a total lift of 22' 6". Despite that, Dodo has to get onto the hydraulic lift using a rather futuristic looking stepladder!

The feet of the statue went up about another three or four inches and were made from expanded polystyrene (jablite), which has been carved into shape.

An alarm sounds and the launching bay doors open.

BN: The door's on a hoist. All the scenery beyond the door is painted, all the landing shuttles and everything. There's no room round there, none at all.

A Monoid drives in, with another Monoid lying on the bed of the truck. A strange fever is spreading among the Monoids. The Commander suddenly collapses with the same fever, which Zentos proclaims to be a disease brought by the humans. Dodo asserts that it's just a cold. The Doctor points out to Steven that these people have no resistance to the cold virus and it might be fatal to them. The sick Monoid dies and Zentos has the strangers seized. He says that the strangers must be made to suffer for the crime they have committed. If they all now die, then it was pointless leaving the Earth in the first place.

On the monitor screen, the Earth is seen spinning past.

MI: That was a model of the Earth on a wire, I think. That is back projection this time.

End of *The Steel Sky*

THE PLAGUE

MI: Because each episode was recorded separately from the others, the reprise from the end of the previous episode was often re-recorded the following week. Therefore the camera shots and actions sometimes differ.

The Doctor, Steven and Dodo are placed in a cell. Dodo is feeling better but the Doctor is frustrated – if only the Guardians would release them, they might be able to help.

BN: This is a very simple set; a bench seat at the back. That's a good join between the two pieces of scenery making up the cell walls in the corner!

There was a firm, I think it was called Woollens, who stocked a lot of very modern and expensive furniture, and I would have gone to a place like that to choose the props. They also had some of the latest designs from Italy.

Back in the main control room, another Monoid death is reported. The Guardians watch on a monitor screen mounted in the control console as more Monoids collapse. No humans have died yet, but nothing their microbiologists try seems to work against the virus.

BN: I would have asked the Technical Operations Manager on the show for a rack of eight or ten small monitors. He would have supplied me with their measurements so that I could ensure that the set was constructed to fit them.

MI: To get the effect of going from seeing the Monoid and the TARDIS on the monitor, to the same shot full on the screen, we simply ran the film, showed it on the monitor on the console, and then mixed to the film. It was quite a simple effect to achieve; it was just like going to another camera.

The Commander is in a sick bay being tended to by Mellium and a doctor, Rhos (Michael Sheard). Rhos explains that the data for this type of fever were lost in the primal wars of the tenth segment. The Commander gets Mellium to promise that if anything should happen to him, she make every effort to reach Refusis.

BN: That set was constructed from dark brown lathes against a cyclorama cloth round the back, illuminated so all you see are the lathes against the light.

Solemn drum beats ring out as four Monoids carry the shrouded body of one of their dead through the control room. They place it on a transporter and it is driven to the launching bay by a fifth Monoid. A hatch in the side of the space ship opens and the body is consigned to a space burial.

Zentos calls for a trial of the strangers before the illness gets too bad. Baccu (Ian Frost) will put the charges. Mellium and Manyak offer to defend the travellers.

Steven goes to speak at the trial, leaving the Doctor and Dodo in the cell watching on a monitor. As the trial progresses, Steven gets weaker. He tells the Guardians that the Doctor could help them if they would let him. Manyak argues that this is a reasonable approach. Baccu arrives with the news that a Guardian has died from the fever – the first Guardian to die. Two of the assembled Guardians (Paul Greenhalgh and Stephanie Heesom) call for the death of the prisoners, and this is picked up as a general cry. Zentos therefore condemns them to be cast from the ship by the Monoids. As the sentence is read, Steven collapses from the fever himself.

The Doctor argues that as one of his party has the fever, then they are as much victims as the Monoids and Guardians. The Commander recovers sufficiently to send an order from his sick bed that the travellers are to be released and allowed to try to find a cure, using Steven as a guinea-pig. After Dodo and Baccu have fetched some equipment from the TARDIS, the Doctor develops an antidote from natural animal membranes collected from two of the ship's specimens. Steven is treated, but rather than wait for the results, the Doctor goes ahead and treats everyone else as well.

The treatment works after about an hour, and Steven starts to recover.

As the Doctor and Dodo give Zentos and the other assembled Guardians the good news, the scanner shows the Earth boiling away as it spins through space.

BN: I didn't provide that effect. I suspect they went to Jack Kine at the Visual Effects Department for that.

MI: That shot was done on film at Ealing, but I don't recall how they got the smoke to come out.

The Doctor says his goodbyes to the Guardians, and a Monoid takes them back to the TARDIS on a transporter.

BN: That transporter is so noisy. I couldn't overcome the noise!

The TARDIS dematerialises, but moments later re-appears in what seems to be a slightly different part of the forest. The Doctor, Steven and Dodo emerge, puzzled at the fact that they appear to be in the same place.

BN: You see that tree there, the slanting one behind the TARDIS, that's made from fibreglass. It was built for Paul Bernard, another designer at that time when *Doctor Who* began. I had used it before in part three of *100,000 BC*.

They head for the control room, and Dodo notices that the statue has been completed – but it has the head of a Monoid and not of a human.

BN: That's a model with a good painting of the roof behind it. John Friedlander built the model.

MI: I had that model for a long time. It was about two feet high but it got thrown out eventually.

End of *The Plague*

THE RETURN

The Doctor notes that 700 years must have passed as the statue is complete, and Steven deduces, by looking at a navigation chart displayed on the main screen in the control room, that the spaceship must be almost at Refusis II.

BN: The navigation chart is provided by back projection. If you wanted to use back projection, you had to book it in advance, as its availability was limited. Nowadays, you'd have to pay for it out of your programme budget, and you would have to work out whether you could afford it, but back then it was a 'below the line' cost.

The Doctor uses the monitor screens on the console to look at other parts of the ship.

BN: Those small monitor screens were just transparencies with lights behind them to give the effect.

The pictures appear on the large monitor as well, and the Doctor, Steven and Dodo watch as a Guardian, Maharis (Terence Woodfield), serves a drink to what appears to be a Monoid sitting in a high-backed chair.

BN: That's a BBC tea trolley there at the side of the Monoid's room!

Another image is of the kitchen where the Guardians are working. One of them accidentally knocks a pot to the ground and a scaly hand holding a gun is seen. The gun fires and the Guardian collapses to the ground.

MI: I cast all the smaller parts; that woman there [playing Venussa] was someone I had a personal connection with. She is Eileen Helsby, and her sister was my BBC secretary, Thelma Helsby.

The Doctor notes that the Monoids appear to have become overlords. His theorising is interrupted by the arrival of a group of Monoids and Guardians. One of the Monoids (Ralph Carrigan) – who wears a collar marked with the number two – demands to know who the travellers are, and Dodo notes that the creatures can now speak.

MI: The voices were created live in the studio using a similar process to that used on the Daleks. Obviously the voices were not spoken by the actors playing the Monoids as they had ping-pong balls in their mouths! There would have been a speaker on the studio floor so that the actors could hear the voices as well. The Monoid voices were all provided by Roy Skelton and John Halstead.

Monoid Two explains that his race are the masters, following a recent revolution. The Guardians work for the Monoids. Yendom (Terence Bayler), a subject Guardian, privileged to serve the Monoids directly, agrees with the Monoid's observation. Monoid Two takes the Doctor and his friends to see their leader, Monoid One.

MI: Terence Bayler was an actor I'd used before on other productions.

When they arrive, Monoid One (Edmund Coulter) views a recording of the travellers' earlier departure in the TARDIS.

MI: That is a film clip from the end of part two.

BN: I vaguely remember the chair that Monoid One is sitting in. I seem to recall slipping a false back over its existing back. I might even have had the chair made.

Monoid One has checked the ship's history scans and knows of the Doctor's previous visit, and of the illness. It transpires that a mutation of the fever sapped the will of the humans and allowed the Monoids to take over. Monoid One orders Monoid Two to take the travellers to the security kitchen.
In the kitchen, Dassuk (Brian Wright) and Venussa (Eileen Helsby) are discussing the new arrivals.

MI: I'd totally forgotten I'd cast Brian Wright as Dassuk. He was at Oxford with me, and I had used him in *Compact* and in one of the classic serials. He went on to write a series of very funny radio broadcasts called *The Penge Papers*.

The strangers are brought in to help with producing food for the Monoids. The Guardians also know the legend of the Doctor's previous visit, and are amazed that his party can travel in time.

BN: There's an upside-down telephone kiosk cover on the wall there. People wouldn't have recognised it at the time because that type of telephone was not common.

We were always having to break new ground. When doing science fiction, we all tried to make our designs look like the sort of thing that belonged to a different era. In addition, if you put commonplace items in a strange situation, then they tend not to be recognised for what they really are. For example, I used school desks in the kitchen, and they do look alien! Well, I hope they do!

You get to use a lot of different things in a kitchen. I'm pretty certain I used that thing, there in the corner on castors, in *Marco Polo*, where it was painted dark brown! It didn't have castors in the earlier story, it was just on the floor.

Back in the control room, the Monoids are discussing their imminent arrival on Refusis. Monoid One has a plan for when they finally settle there – a plan that will solve the problem of what to do with the Guardians. As an initial step, he intends to send a forward landing party to Refusis to see what is there.

In the kitchen, one of the Guardians throws a small capsule into a bowl and it transforms into a pile of potatoes.

MI: That transformation was done with overlay. You start with a picture of the bowl empty, then overlay a picture of it full. In fact, I think the empty bowl was overlaid first and when that image was removed, the potatoes were revealed.

The Doctor, Steven and Dodo discuss how they might overthrow the Monoids. Monoid Two arrives and, while it is distracted by Venussa, Steven tries to get the heat-prod weapon off it. Monoid Three arrives and the attempt fails, a Guardian being killed in the struggle.

MI: I think that effect of the gun firing was done by just turning up the contrast on the camera so the picture whited out. There was also a light at the end of the gun, and a small charge of flash-powder ignited to give a puff of smoke.

Monoid Two takes the Doctor and Dodo away. They are to make the first landing on Refusis, and Steven is to be held prisoner to ensure that they behave.

The launcher is prepared and the Doctor, Dodo, Yendom and Monoid Two set off for Refusis.

MI: This was a tiny model at Ealing. I went to Ealing myself and supervised all the filming of the models.

When the launcher arrives on Refusis, the door opens.

MI: That door was pretty awkward to open and shut.

BN: Yes, it was supposed to work smoothly but it ended up rather jerky.

The group leave the launcher and look around Refusis for the first time.

BN: All the bits of white draped on the trees are actually fibreglass rovings. At the time, we didn't know they are an irritant to the skin. Cotton wool would have been just as good, but rovings were fireproof.

This landscape had to have a totally different aspect, because it was a new world. The rocks were all carved from two inch thick jablite. I used lots of thin and spiky leafed plants as well as broom-type plants, on the stems of which I hung the fibreglass. My aim was to create a setting totally unlike any you could find on Earth. I also added some fibreglass rocks from stock and some grass and sawdust.

Behind them, an invisible entity enters the capsule. The controls appear to work themselves, and the door closes and opens by itself.

BN: The launcher prop was rigged up with wires and strings to make it seem to operate itself. There's actually someone underneath moving the switches.

Monoid Two is concerned that they haven't yet encountered any Refusians and wonders that perhaps their advance information was wrong. The Doctor suggests sending back a message to the ship to say that all is well, and Dodo agrees: the sooner they start getting the population down onto the planet, the better. Monoid Two comments that it may not take as long as they think. Dodo seizes on this statement, challenges the creature to admit that the Guardians will be left behind. Yendom is appalled – the Monoids promised that they would all settle on Refusis.
The Doctor has seen a castle-like structure in the distance. They decide to go there.

BN: That castle was a painted backcloth – it looks as though the structure is about twenty miles away!

Arriving at the castle, they find it lavishly furnished, but deserted.

BN: The main door has bits of hardboard stuck on it, and the floor has been painted with a stencil roller to create the pattern. Over at the back, you can see some wooden screens that I'd used previously in *The Crusade* for a part of Saladin's palace. The flowers in the vase on the table came from Japan. They were artificial, and I'd never seen anything like them before.

Monoid Two, by smashing a vase and throwing the flowers from a second vase to the floor, challenges the Refusians to appear. Suddenly a voice (Richard Beale) rings out, telling the Monoid to put the second vase down. Monoid Two's arm is grabbed and the vase is forced back to the table by an invisible presence. The flowers fly from where they have fallen on the floor and replace themselves in the vase.

BN: The flowers were filmed being pulled out of the vase on a wire, and then the film was reversed to give the effect of them leaping back into the vase like that.

Back on the ship, Monoid One and Monoid Three (Frank George) are plotting by the statue. They are concerned that they haven't yet heard from Monoid Two.

MI: That shot was done with a mirror to get the nice top-down angle.

Monoid One explains that a fission device has been hidden on the Ark to destroy the Guardians after the Monoids have left for Refusis. The bomb is hidden in the giant statue. Unknown to them, Maharis, another subject Guardian, has overheard them on a monitor screen, and he reports to Steven and the other Guardians in the kitchen. He admits however that he did not see where Monoid One indicated the bomb was hidden.

On the planet, the Doctor is chatting with the Refusian. The invisible creature explains that their incorporeal nature came about as a result of a giant solar flare. They cannot even see each other, although they can sense each other's presence. The Refusians would welcome the habitation of their planet once more and have built places like the castle for their visitors to enjoy.

Monoid Two kills Yendom when the human tries to prevent him from returning to the launcher. The Doctor and Dodo find the body. Monoid Two starts to make a report back to the Ark, but the Refusian approaches and the launcher explodes, killing Monoid Two.

MI: The explosion was done on film at Ealing, and we blew up a small model of the launcher.

Dodo is horrified. The Doctor states that the two of them will have to wait until another party arrives; and if no one does come, they will just have to stay on the planet.

End of *The Return*

THE BOMB

Monoid Three asks Monoid One what they should do now, and Monoid One says that they should prepare for the main landings. Monoid Four (Edmund Coulter) is concerned that they don't know what Refusis is like. Monoid Three warns Monoid One that Monoid Four is questioning the wisdom of his leadership. Monoid One replies that if there is any problem, Monoid Four will be got rid of.

MI: Each of the Monoids has a communicator device around its neck. They move a slider to reveal a black dot at the front when they are speaking. I think that was to try and show which one was speaking at any given time, because it's not obvious otherwise.

The Refusian is concerned at the arrival of the Ark. They wish to have peace on their planet and do not want a war between humans and Monoids. The Refusian agrees to give the humans and the Monoids one day to try to resolve their problems.

MI: I wanted a 'god-like' voice for the Refusian, and I knew Richard Beale, who was a very good Shakespearean actor. I would have cast him because I thought he had the right sort of voice.

On the Ark, Steven is trying to work out how to escape from the kitchen. He and the Guardians decide to use Maharis without his knowledge.

The Monoids are forcing the Guardians to load trays of miniaturised Monoids into the launchers for transport to Refusis.

When Maharis enters the kitchen, Steven and Venussa distract him while Dassuk manages to slip through the door behind him. When Maharis has left, Dassuk opens the door from the outside and releases the captive Guardians.

The Monoids leave for Refusis. In the launcher, Monoid One informs Monoid Three that the bomb is timed to explode in twelve hours' time.

The launchers leave the Ark and head for Refusis.

MI: All those model launchers are on wires, and they've got little lights in them.

With the Monoids now out of the way, Steven and the Guardians start looking for the bomb.

The launchers arrive on Refusis and the Monoids disembark. They find the wreckage of the earlier launcher. The Doctor and Dodo watch from the undergrowth as Monoid Four expresses to another Monoid his discontent at Monoid One's decision to come to Refusis. The Monoid determines to challenge Monoid One and get back to the Ark before the bomb explodes. When they have moved on, the Doctor and Dodo get into one of the launchers.

Steven is growing dispirited at the lack of progress. He receives from the Doctor a message warning him about the bomb. An image of the Doctor is seen on the main screen.

MI: That image of the Doctor is inlay. When some of the Guardians move across it, their heads get cut off by the image!

The Doctor explains that he intends to try to glean from the Monoids the location of the bomb. He suggests that the Refusian pilots the launcher back to the Ark.

When the Doctor and Dodo move away from the launcher, they encounter Monoid Two and Monoid Sixty-Three, who take them off to see Monoid One. Behind them, the launcher leaves.

MI: That's a good model shot of the launcher leaving.

The launcher arrives on the Ark carrying the Refusian.

In the Refusian castle, the Doctor is questioned by Monoid One and denies having seen any Refusians. Monoid Four confronts Monoid One. Monoid One says that any of his people who are unhappy can return to the Ark. He tells them that the bomb is in the statue.

Monoid Four leaves with a group of Monoids sympathetic to his cause. Monoid One then reveals that he intends to destroy the rebels in the open. He and Monoid Two go to set an ambush.

On the Ark, Steven suggests that some of the Guardians should go to Refusis to try to preserve a proportion of humanity. Steven elects to stay on the Ark with Vanussa to try to find the bomb. Maharis has no wish to die for an ideal his forefathers thought of, so Vanussa suggests that he goes down to the planet with Dassuk and with two of the other Guardians.

Down on Refusis, Monoid One and his fellows ambush Monoid Four and his band of rebels on their way back to the launchers. There is a gun battle.

BN: This is quite a good illustration of the terrain I built. The basic shape was built up with rostra, then that was covered with rocks and foliage. That gives you different levels on the set. It's a very cheap and simple set to create.

The launcher from the Ark arrives.

MI: That is a forced perspective model shot. It's effective because you see a Monoid moving in the background as well as the full-sized launcher as the model touches down.

Maharis is the first to leave the shuttle, and he is immediately killed by one of the Monoids. The other humans leave the capsule as the Monoids fight. Dassuk makes for the castle and rescues the Doctor and Dodo, who return to the launcher. When they arrive, the gun battle is over, and Monoid Four seems to have won. The Doctor calls Steven on the radio to tell him where the bomb is hidden.

Once it is known that the bomb is in the statue's head, the Refusian on board the Ark uses its great strength to move the statue into the launching bay.

MI: The model of the statue was lifted by someone holding its legs out of shot, and then shifting their grip to the head as it moved past the camera. That gave the effect of it being moved by an invisible creature.

Once it is in position, the statue is ejected into space where it explodes safely.

MI: The statue wasn't actually blown up as I kept it afterwards. The explosion was a separate piece of footage that was mixed in at the right point.

The danger over, the Refusian agrees to help the humans settle on Refusis, provided that they make peace with the Monoids first.

The Doctor, Steven and Dodo say their goodbyes and make their way on an electric transporter back to the TARDIS.

The TARDIS leaves.

MI: That dematerialisation is done with two photographs, as the background completely changes as the ship vanishes.

In the TARDIS control room, the TARDIS is arriving at a new destination. Dodo and Steven have changed their clothes. The Doctor coughs and vanishes from sight. Dodo postulates that this might have something to do with the Refusians, but the Doctor tells his companions it is something far more serious: it is some form of attack!

End of The Bomb

PART 5 – POST-PRODUCTION

While the recording of a *Doctor Who* adventure accounts for what is eventually seen on screen, the diary of a production does not end there. There is also post-production work carried out.

Far less time tended to be spent on post-production during the first Doctor's era than during later eras, simply because nearly all the work was done in pre-production and live in the studio. All that remained for the director to do was to supervise any editing required, and any final sound dubs. 'There would have been a certain amount of editing done the week after recording,' confirms Michael. 'That tended to take place on the Monday or Tuesday evening the following week.'

As previously mentioned, the number of edits tended to be minimised by having the story recorded in transmission order with few recording breaks – although *The Ark* was unusual in that it did involve a fair degree of out-of-order recording on the final episode. In addition, the recording of each episode was done only about two weeks' prior to its transmission. The director therefore had to split his time between the episode just completed, the episode to be rehearsed and recorded the following week, and, possibly, further episodes of the story being planned for subsequent weeks.

For Michael Imison, work on *The Ark* was overshadowed by the fact that he was told when he was mid-way through making the final episode that his services as a director were no longer required by the BBC.

'Before I went into the gallery to record the last episode,' he recalls, 'I was handed a note to say that my contract was not being renewed.'

Michael therefore went back to being a story editor. 'I had to find the job myself; I wasn't offered it. Some friends in the Plays Department employed me and, curiously, the fact that I had done *Doctor Who* helped. They were setting up a science fiction series called *Out of the Unknown* and needed someone who knew something about science fiction. I knew nothing about science fiction, but as I had done *Doctor Who*, they thought I might!

'After a crash course in science fiction, which I thoroughly enjoyed, I had a marvellous time. I attended the Trieste Science Fiction Film Festival in France as a BBC observer and was immediately put on the Grand Jury! They thought that to have someone English on the Jury would be a good idea. Then the next year we entered one of the *Out of the Unknown* episodes, *The Machine Stops*, and won, so that was rather fun.

'Then the man who had sacked me became Head of Plays, and I realised that my future at the BBC was going to be very limited. An actor friend whom I'd employed in *Buddenbrooks*, who was at the time represented by a large American agency in London, came to talk to me. His agency had lost their London agent to a rival company and they needed someone in a hurry to look after their American clients in England – the other agent had gone off with all the English clients!

'My friend arranged for me to be interviewed and they offered me twice the money the BBC was paying! So then I became an agent, and I must say I've never regretted it.'

TRANSMISSION

The Ark was eventually transmitted on consecutive Saturdays from 5 to 26 March 1966. It achieved ratings, in millions of viewers, of 5.5 (episode one), 6.9 (two), 6.2 (three) and 7.3 (four), all of which were lower than the season average of 7.65.

Although the third season of *Doctor Who* had started successfully, enjoying audiences around the 10 million mark for most of the epic twelve part *The Daleks' Master Plan*, *The Massacre of St Bartholomew's Eve* had proved particularly unpopular, the ratings dropping off dramatically from 8.0 to 5.8 million. *The Ark* went some way towards improving the situation, and this trend was continued by *The Celestial Toymaker*, but *The Gunfighters* and *The Savages* proved less popular. In terms of position in the weekly TV chart, *The Ark* fared poorly. The highest placing it could manage was for episode two, which clocked in at 70th. For episode one, it dropped out of the top 100 shows altogether; the first time that *Doctor Who* had failed to appear in the top 100 since it started.

Part of the reason for *The Ark*'s poor figures was that most ITV regions were showing the highly popular music magazine show *Thank Your Lucky*

Stars in the slot opposite *Doctor Who*. It seems that, against this competition, *Doctor Who* could command a really high audience only when the Daleks appeared.

Considering the problematic background of the third season as a whole, and also the limited technology and time available, *The Ark* stands up well as an example of *Doctor Who* in this period. It was a very ambitious project, achieved with much imagination and skill by all those involved.

CREDITS

Written by	Paul Erickson and Lesley Scott
Title Music by	Ron Grainer and the BBC Radiophonic Workshop
Title Sequence	Bernard Lodge
Incidental Music by	Tristram Cary (stock)
	Robert Farnon (stock)
Special Sound	Brian Hodgson
Production Assistant	David Maloney
Assistant Floor Manager	Chris D'Oyly-John
Assistant	Thelma Helsby
Floor Assistant	Ernest Skinner
TM2	Fred Wright
Grams	John Hurley
	Tony Bowes
Vision Mixer	Clive Halls
Crew	1
Film Cameraman	Tony Leggo
Film Editor	Noel Chapman
Costume Designer	Daphne Dare
Make-Up	Sonia Markham
Lighting	Howard King
Sound	Ray Angel
Story Editor	Gerry Davis (and Donald Tosh before his departure)
Designer	Barry Newbery
Producer	John Wiles (and Innes Lloyd after his arrival)
Director	Michael Imison

Selling the Doctor

MEDIA

One of the main bastions of public interest in *Doctor Who* was the BBC's own listings magazine, *Radio Times*. From the series' on-air debut in 1963 right through to the end of the first Doctor's era, each new story was heralded by a feature article, accompanied as often as not by a photograph. Occasionally features would appear part-way through a story's run as well. As *Radio Times* was published in regional editions, each giving details of programmes specific to its own particular region as well as of those transmitted nationwide, there would often be regional variations in the coverage given to the series. For example, the London edition might present a small feature while the Welsh one boasted a whole page plus a photograph.

The first story to be promoted with a front cover photograph in the magazine was *Marco Polo* in February 1964, although the Serials Department had been pushing for such coverage ever since the very first story. The same privilege was later accorded *The Dalek Invasion of Earth* and *The Web Planet* – the stories given perhaps the most publicity of any of the first Doctor's adventures.

Doctor Who's first mention in *Radio Times* was actually in the edition published the week *before* its debut episode was transmitted, when in the 'Next Week' preview column a photograph and 'teaser' text announced the start of the first story. The BBC's own in-house magazine, *Ariel*, also covered the event, this time with a photograph of associate producer Mervyn Pinfield, producer Verity Lambert and director Waris Hussein on the classroom set from *An Unearthly Child*. *Ariel* described *Doctor Who* as 'an ambitious space/time adventure serial consisting of a series of stories of a varying number of episodes. Each episode will end on a cliff-hanger.'

Clearly there was considerable interest in the new series but, as things turned out, the opening episode was transmitted in less than ideal circumstances. First, the assassination the previous day of US President John F Kennedy meant that many viewers were simply not in the mood to watch television – unless it was to see one of the special programmes hastily put together by the BBC and ITV to mourn Kennedy's passing. Then there was the fact that on that Saturday evening many viewers' homes were blacked out by a widespread power failure, denying them the opportunity to receive the transmission.

Those who did watch, however, apparently liked what they saw. 'William Hartnell, gazing from under locks of flowing white,' wrote Michael Gowers in the *Daily Mail* on 25 November, 'and the appealing Carole Ann Ford represent the Unknown Them, William Russell and Jacqueline Hill the ignorant, sceptical Us, and their craft is cunningly disguised as a police callbox. The penultimate shot of this, nestling, after a three-point touchdown, in a Neolithic landscape, must have delighted the hearts of the *Telegoons* who followed.'

It was due to the aforementioned power cuts that the first episode was repeated the following week, immediately prior to the second, launching *Doctor Who* on what had been announced as a fifty-two week odyssey through space and time.

The press were strangely silent during the run of the Daleks' introductory story, *The Mutants*, but the fact that Terry Nation's evil creations had caught the public's imagination did not go unregistered. On 4 February, just three days after the transmission of the story's final episode, Douglas Marlborough reported in the *Daily Mail*: 'Since the Daleks vanished from the series, hundreds of children have written to ask what would happen to them. Some suggested that they should be competition prizes. Now the future of two of the five-feet-tall fibreglass-and-wood robots has been decided. Today they go to children of Dr Barnardo's Homes.' Marlborough went on to explain that two more Daleks had been kept by the BBC in case they were needed 'for future TV appearances.'

Under the headline 'Do-it-yourself Daleks are coming,' the weekly newspaper *Reveille* reported on 2 April that the BBC was arranging for 'hundreds of do-it-yourself scale models of the robots to be put on the market.' The article went on to state that 'the eerie, clipped-voice robots which appeared in *Dr Who*, the BBC television serial, proved so popular that they are to be brought back to the screen again, probably in the autumn.'

During 1964 and 1965, the Daleks became a national cult, but they were not the only race of *Doctor Who* monsters that the BBC tried to promote. Another first season menace that received a fair amount of coverage was the Voords, who were revealed to the public by the *Daily Mail* on 11 April – the same day as the first episode of *The Keys of Marinus*, the story in which they featured, was transmitted.

'They bounce across BBC TV screens today in the first episode of a new DR WHO space series – and could rival the dreaded Daleks,' wrote the reporter. The article was accompanied by a photograph showing Carole Ann Ford in the clutches of a rubber-clad Peter Stenson.

Other aspects of *Doctor Who* also started to attract attention. Writer John Lucarotti was interviewed by Elsie M Smith for an unknown newspaper, in which he revealed that writing *Doctor Who* was 'five per cent inspiration and ninety five per cent perspiration.' Designer Raymond Cusick was also interviewed for the same publication.

1964 drew to a close with another Dalek-related report in the *Daily Mail* – the paper that had given *Doctor Who* the most coverage over the previous year. Hot on the heels of the conclusion of *The Dalek Invasion Of Earth*, they reported that Terry Nation was being asked to bring back the aliens once more, but that he didn't want to do so. 'I don't want to bring them back,' he explained to Douglas Marlborough. 'They've hit such a level of popularity that nothing they do can be quite as popular again. The Beatles and pop groups in general have dropped a bit, and the Daleks seem to have filled the gap. I can't see them hitting this level for much longer. But what can one do? I don't want the Daleks back. The BBC does. They've insisted on it.' Perhaps the fact that, as Marlborough reported, Nation was speaking from a '15-room £15,000 Elizabethan mansion near Teynham, Kent' had something to do with his being persuaded to write another Dalek story.

During the series' second season, Nation's finances continued to fascinate Douglas Marlborough, who on 11 March 1965 reported: 'The man who invented the Daleks has made a fortune out of his science fiction mechanical monsters. Mr Terry Nation, their 34-year old creator, last night declined to say how much. But the TV and film rights are believed to be worth £300,000.' Nation was quoted later in the article as saying 'There was a sudden need for money and so I did the series. It turned out to be the shrewdest move I've ever made.'

Reveille carried an interview with Verity Lambert around the same time, and revealed that Carole Ann Ford was to be replaced with Margaret O'Brien (sic). The ever-dependable *Daily Mail* also interviewed Lambert on 28 November 1964, as the second Dalek story finished its run. On 2 April 1965, the *Daily Mail* reported that Jacqueline Hill and William Russell had both asked to leave the series by June.

Monsters other than the Daleks continued to be mostly ignored by the press, with two notable exceptions: the Zarbi, who received almost full-page coverage in the *Daily Mail*, and the Mechanoids, who were afforded similar treatment.

After *Galaxy 4* went into the studio, newspaper readers were treated to the sight of a trio of attractive women wielding rather large guns. 'Enter Dr Who's new foes: The ray-gun blondes' screamed the headline to Brian Bear's feature in the *Daily Mail*. This was followed by 'UGH! It's the TV monsters' after *Mission to the Unknown* was recorded on 7 August. On 23 October, a sextet of bald men peered from the paper as the Technix from *The Daleks' Master Plan* were unveiled. On 4 December, Jean Marsh hit the headlines as 'A Touch of the Avengers: The New Girl Linking Up with Dr Who Tonight.' The feature, with an accompanying photograph, revealed that Marsh had been given 'a woollen cat-suit, black leather boots, expertise in judo and karate and a ray gun for when that suits the script writers better.' The Beatle-wigged monocular creatures of *The Ark* also appeared in the press when Jackie Lane was announced as the latest addition to the TARDIS' crew.

On 3 December 1965, the Manchester *Evening News* speculated that William Hartnell might be giving up the role of the Doctor. 'I've had a good innings,' he apparently explained to their reporter. Hartnell's agent, Eric L'Epine Smith, denied any such thing: 'I can assure you categorically that William Hartnell is not giving up. I have plans for him when he finishes the series.'

Of course, Hartnell did eventually leave, and, on 6 August 1966, newspapers reported that the BBC was searching for a new actor to take the role of the Doctor. 'I think three years in one part is a good innings and it is time for a change,' Hartnell was quoted as saying in *The Times*.

OVERSEAS SALES

England was not the only country to enjoy the first Doctor's era. By the beginning of 1977, according to an internal BBC listing, the following overseas sales had been registered:

100,000 BC
New Zealand, Australia, Canada, Singapore, Nigeria, Rhodesia, Cyprus, Mexico, Hong Kong, Uganda, Lebanon, Ghana, Zambia, Jamaica, Kenya, Thailand, Mauritius.

The Mutants
Canada (episodes two to seven only), New Zealand, Australia, Nigeria, Singapore, Rhodesia, Cyprus, Uganda, Ghana, Zambia, Jamaica, Venezuela.

Inside the Spaceship
Canada, Australia, New Zealand, Singapore, Thailand, Nigeria, Rhodesia, Cyprus, Hong Kong, Mauritius, Ghana, Zambia, Jamaica, Kenya, Tunisia, Mexico, Morocco, Saudi Arabia, Iran, Ethiopia, Algeria.

Marco Polo
Australia, Canada, New Zealand, Nigeria, Singapore, Hong Kong, Uganda, Ghana, Zambia, Jamaica, Cyprus, Kenya, Thailand, Mauritius, Rhodesia, Venezuela, Bermuda, Ethiopia.

The Keys of Marinus
Australia, Canada, New Zealand, Singapore, Nigeria, Rhodesia, Uganda, Ghana, Zambia, Jamaica, Cyprus, Lebanon, Hong Kong, Kenya, Bermuda, Mexico, Thailand, Venezuela, Mauritius, Morocco, Saudi Arabia, Ethiopia, Algeria.

The Aztecs
Australia, New Zealand, Singapore, Hong Kong, Nigeria, Saudi Arabia, Trinidad and Tobago, Zambia, Uganda, Cyprus, Jamaica, Mexico, Rhodesia, Venezuela, Mauritius, Tunisia, Thailand, Iran, Ethiopia.

The Sensorites
Australia, New Zealand, Singapore, Nigeria, Iran, Hong Kong, Arabia, Trinidad and Tobago, Ethiopia, Zambia, Uganda, Cyprus, Mexico, Jamaica, Caribbean, Rhodesia, Mauritius, Tunisia, Venezuela, Sierra Leone, Morocco.

The Reign of Terror
Australia, New Zealand, Singapore, Nigeria, Hong Kong, Trinidad and Tobago, Zambia, Uganda, Cyprus, Jamaica, Rhodesia, Kenya, Mauritius, Thailand, Ethiopia.

Planet of Giants
Australia, New Zealand, Singapore, Nigeria, Hong Kong, Trinidad and Tobago, Zambia, Uganda, Jamaica, Venezuela, Mexico, Rhodesia, Kenya, Mauritius, Tunisia, Thailand, Mexico, Morocco, Saudi Arabia, Iran, Ethiopia.

The Dalek Invasion of Earth
Cyprus, Singapore, Nigeria, Zambia, Uganda, Hong Kong, Australia, Trinidad and Tobago, Arabia, Jamaica, Rhodesia, Kenya, Caribbean, Venezuela, Thailand, Morocco, Ethiopia, Algeria.

The Rescue
New Zealand, Australia, Singapore, Nigeria, Hong Kong, Trinidad and Tobago, Arabia, Zambia, Uganda, Jamaica, Mexico, Venezuela, Caribbean, Rhodesia, Kenya, Lebanon, Mauritius, Thailand, Saudi Arabia, Ethiopia, Algeria.

The Romans
Australia, New Zealand, Gibraltar, Singapore, Nigeria, Zambia, Caribbean, Mauritius, Sierra Leone, Jamaica, Ethiopia.

The Web Planet
Australia, Singapore, Nigeria, Zambia, Venezuela, Caribbean, Mauritius, Iran, Sierra Leone, Jamaica, Ethiopia.

The Crusade
Australia, Gibraltar, Singapore, Nigeria, Zambia, Caribbean, Mauritius, Sierra Leone, Jamaica, Ethiopia.

The Space Museum
Nigeria, Australia, New Zealand, Zambia, Venezuela, Caribbean, Mauritius, Mexico, Iran, Sierra Leone, Jamaica, Ethiopia.

The Chase
Australia, Gibraltar, Singapore, Nigeria, Zambia, Venezuela, Caribbean, Iran, Mauritius, Ethiopia.

The Time Meddler
Australia, New Zealand, Gibraltar, Singapore, Nigeria, Zambia, Caribbean, Mauritius, Jamaica.

Galaxy 4
Australia, New Zealand, Caribbean, Zambia, Sierra Leone, Singapore.

Mission to the Unknown
None.

The Myth Makers
Australia, New Zealand, Caribbean, Zambia, Sierra Leone, Singapore.

The Daleks' Master Plan
None.

The Massacre of St Bartholomew's Eve
Australia, New Zealand, Caribbean, Zambia, Sierra Leone, Singapore.

The Ark
Australia, New Zealand, Caribbean, Zambia, Sierra Leone, Singapore.

The Celestial Toymaker
Australia, New Zealand, Barbados, Zambia, Sierra Leone, Singapore.

The Gunfighters
Australia, Caribbean, Zambia, Sierra Leone, Singapore.

The Savages
Australia, New Zealand, Barbados, Zambia, Sierra Leone, Singapore.

The War Machines
Australia, New Zealand, Caribbean, Zambia, Sierra Leone, Singapore, Nigeria.

The Smugglers
Australia, New Zealand, Caribbean, Zambia, Sierra Leone, Singapore.

The Tenth Planet
Australia, New Zealand, Singapore.

On the basis of this list, therefore, *The Keys of Marinus* was the first Doctor story sold to the most countries in the sixties and early seventies, and *Mission to the Unknown* and *The Daleks' Master Plan* those sold to the least. (It appears that *The Daleks' Master Plan* may have been offered for sale only as an eleven-part story – presumably minus the off-beat Christmas Day episode *The Feast of Steven*.)

NEW ZEALAND
By Paul Scoones

New Zealand holds the distinction of being the first country outside the United Kingdom to screen *Doctor Who*. The New Zealand Broadcasting

Corporation (NZBC) acquired the first three stories, *100,000 BC*, *The Mutants* (a.k.a. *The Daleks*), and *Inside the Spaceship*, in June 1964. All thirteen episodes were rated Y, which meant they were considered unsuitable for screening before around 8 pm.

A single film print of each episode was held by the NZBC necessitating the staggering of the schedules so that the films could be transported between New Zealand's four regional channels: Auckland (AKTV-2), Wellington (WNTV-1), Christchurch (CHTV-3) and Dunedin (DNTV-2).

The episodes were first screened in the Christchurch region from 18 September to 11 December 1964, then in Auckland from 30 October 1964 to 29 January 1965, Wellington from 6 November 1964 to 5 February 1965 and Dunedin from 5 March to 28 May 1965. The episodes were screened on Fridays across all regions, usually at 7.57 pm, although from 19 March 1965 the screening time moved to 8.07 pm in Dunedin.

The New Zealand screening rights for this first batch of thirteen episodes expired 16 June 1966 and the episodes were sent on to Denmark on 26 March 1968.

Marco Polo was received 27 May 1966 was rated G, after censor edits to all but the first two episodes. The serial was first screened in the Auckland region on Thursdays from 27 October to 8 December 1966, then in Wellington on Tuesdays from 1 November to 13 December 1966, Dunedin on Thursdays from 15 December 1966 to 26 January 1967 and Christchurch on Mondays from 20 March to 1 May 1967. The start times were mostly around 6.50 pm. The New Zealand screening rights for *Marco Polo* expired 19 November 1968, by which time the NZBC were only the five edited episodes of the story as the first two uncut episodes had been dispatched to Iran on 20 October 1967. The five remaining episodes were still held at the Wellington Hill Street film store in April 1970; their fate after this date is unrecorded. However, the reused film can that had previously contained the last episode, *Assassin at Peking*, was discovered by Graham Howard at a Television New Zealand film storage facility in Wellington in 1990.

A BBC Enterprises document from 1977, detailing overseas sales of *Doctor Who* stories, notes *The Keys of Marinus*, *The Aztecs* and *The Sensorites* as having been sold to New Zealand, but if this was the case, there is no evidence that these stories were ever received.

A batch of seven stories was received on 19 September 1967, including *The Reign of Terror*, *Planet of Giants*, *The Dalek Invasion of Earth*, *The Rescue*, *The Romans*, *The Web Planet* and *The Crusade*, however three of these were omitted. All episodes of *The Dalek Invasion of Earth* were rated Y. Episodes 1 to 4 of *The Web Planet* and Episode 1 of *The Crusade* were also rated Y – although the remaining episodes of both stories gained G ratings. These three stories with Y-rated episodes were apparently held by the NZBC for some time with the intention of rescheduling them in a later post-8 pm timeslot, however this never eventuated.

The Reign of Terror, Planet of Giants, The Rescue and *The Romans* first screened in the Christchurch region from 26 January to 3 May 1968, then in Wellington from 8 March to 14 June 1968, Dunedin from 29 March to 5 July 1968 and Auckland from 24 May to 30 August 1968. The episodes played on Fridays across all regions, mostly around 5.30 pm.

After the transmissions, the episodes from this batch were retained at the Wellington Hill Street film store and were logged as held there on 1 April 1970. *The Reign of Terror* was subsequently destroyed on 18 June 1971 and *Planet of Giants* was destroyed on 14 July 1971. The first episode of *The Crusade, The Lion*, was still held in storage in Wellington in 1975, at which time it was scheduled to be destroyed. The 16mm film print was rescued from dumping by film collectors and was held in private hands until January 1999 when it was discovered in the collection of Auckland film buff Bruce Grenville by fans Neil Lambess and Paul Scoones, who arranged for the film to be loaned to the BBC.

A further batch of eleven Hartnell stories was received 23 September 1968, including *The Space Museum, The Time Meddler, Galaxy 4, The Myth Makers, The Massacre of St Bartholomew's Eve, The Ark, The Celestial Toymaker, The Savages, The War Machines, The Smugglers* and *The Tenth Planet*. Four stories were not purchased which were: *The Chase, Mission to the Unknown, The Daleks' Master Plan* and *The Gunfighters*. All eleven stories were rated G, however some censor edits were required to gain this rating. The film trims edited from *The Ark*, featuring several minutes of footage, were discovered by Graham Howard in New Zealand in 2002.

All eleven stories were screened in one transmission block and first aired in the Christchurch region from 27 October 1968 to 24 August 1969, then in Wellington from 24 November 1968 to 21 September 1969, Auckland from 5 January to 3 November 1969 and Dunedin from 12 January to 10 November 1969. The start time was initially mostly around 5.45 pm but later moved to around 6.10 pm in all regions from July 1969. The series screened on Sundays in all regions, however the series moved to Mondays in the Auckland region from 13 October and in Dunedin from 27 October 1969.

Following the transmissions, the episodes appear to have been stored in Wellington. The last recorded location of *The Space Museum* was at the Wellington Hill Street store in April 1970. *The Time Meddler* was sent on to Nigeria on 2 March 1973, from where the film prints were subsequently returned to the BBC in 1985. Government censor documentation indicates that the cuts present in these recovered episodes were made in New Zealand. *Galaxy 4, The Myth Makers, The Massacre of St Bartholomew's Eve, The Ark* and *The Celestial Toymaker* were sent to Singapore on 20 September 1972. *The Savages, The War Machines, The Smugglers* and *The Tenth Planet* had all previously been sent to Singapore on 10 January 1972. *The War Machines* film prints, which had had censor cuts made in New Zealand, were later found in Nigeria and returned to the BBC in 1984.

Having been omitted twenty years earlier, *The Dalek Invasion of Earth* finally aired on New Zealand television in November 1988 when it was scheduled to launch Television New Zealand's *Doctor Who* twenty-fifth anniversary 'Silver Jubilee' week. The story was presented in an omnibus format with all six episodes edited together, beginning at midday on Saturday 19 November 1988. The story gained a viewer rating of 3.6%.

The Dalek Invasion of Earth was repeated on TV2, broadcast from 17 February to 24 March 1991 on Sundays, mostly around 9.15 am. This time, the six episodes were screened in a single-episode-per-week format. This story was followed by a repeat of three Season Six Troughton stories and then the first two Pertwee seasons in several short blocks. Then, directly after the Pertwee story *The Daemons*, *The Time Meddler* screened from 9 May to 30 May 1993 on Sundays at 11.30 am on TV2. The version of *The Time Meddler* screened was the almost complete version restored and screened by the BBC in early 1992. This may have prompted the sale of this story to New Zealand.

In May 2000, the UHF and satellite channel Prime Television began a screening of every complete story in order from the beginning. The episodes were initially screened five nights a week (Monday to Friday), and after the first three weeks, an extra episode was added to the schedules on Sundays. The start time was 6.25 pm. The screenings commenced on Monday 15 May 2000. The Hartnell transmissions on Prime included six stories that had never before screened in New Zealand: *The Keys of Marinus*, *The Aztecs*, *The Sensorites*, *The Web Planet*, *The Chase* and *The Gunfighters*. *The Time Meddler* episodes screened on this occasion were the unrestored versions recovered from Nigeria with the cuts made by the New Zealand censor in 1968 still in evidence. Some of the Hartnell episodes screened on Prime were edited to remove 'Next Episode' captions and some had end credits that had been made for US syndication. The Hartnell era screenings ended Sunday 13 August 2000 with the last episode of *The War Machines*, but the series continued the following day with the first episode of *The Tomb of the Cybermen*.

AUSTRALIA
With Thanks to Dallas Jones

Doctor Who first aired in Australia at 7.30 pm on Tuesday 12 January 1965, when ABW Channel 2 Perth, part of the Australian Broadcasting Commission (ABC) network, transmitted the opening episode of *100,000 BC*. As in New Zealand, programmes were transmitted on a regional basis rather than nationwide, as the film had to be physically taken from one region to the next. *Doctor Who*'s debut in other regions therefore came a few days later.

In Sydney, for example, the first episode went out at 7.30 pm on Friday 15 January.

The Australian Censorship Board (ACB), by whom all TV programmes and films were required to be vetted and classified before they could be shown, had rated the first three *Doctor Who* stories as 'A', or Adults Only – hence the relatively late time slot. This initial batch of episodes had in fact been made available to Australia back in April 1964, but transmission had been delayed due to this unexpected hitch. When it came to *Marco Polo*, the ACB were prepared to rate some of the episodes 'G', or General, but only after certain cuts were made. This set a precedent whereby most of the other first Doctor episodes shown in Australia would be rated 'G' but subjected to minor cuts to remove supposedly objectionable shots.

Once weekly transmissions got underway, Australians were able to see *Doctor Who* regularly for sixty-seven weeks until the fourth and final episode of *The Crusade* was screened in Sydney on 22 April 1966 – one of the longest uninterrupted runs that *Doctor Who* has ever enjoyed anywhere in the world.

A further season began later in the year, on 3 October in Sydney, but now *Doctor Who* was being shown four nights a week (Monday to Thursday) rather than weekly, and at 6.30 pm rather than 7.30 pm. All the episodes in this season received a 'G' rating, but again cuts were made. Stories to suffer in this way included *The Chase*, *Galaxy 4*, *The Ark* (from which all close-ups of the Monoids were removed!) and *The Gunfighters*. *Mission to the Unknown* and three episodes of *The Daleks' Master Plan* were not cleared for transmission as it was considered impracticable to bring them within a 'G' rating by making cuts, the problem lying with the grim nature of the storyline itself. Consequently these two stories were not purchased for transmission in Australia.

The first *Doctor Who* repeat in Australia was of *The Reign of Terror*, beginning on 9 November 1966. This was followed by repeats of *Planet of Giants*, *The Romans*, *The Web Planet* and *The Crusade*. (*The Dalek Invasion of Earth* and *The Rescue* were omitted from this run due to their 'A' ratings.) After the repeats, the final batch of first Doctor stories were transmitted, starting on 31 March 1967 in Sydney. The final episode of *The Tenth Planet* – a story that, unusually, had escaped any cuts – went out on 14 June 1967.

CANADA

Another country that saw *Doctor Who* at a very early stage was Canada. The first episode was broadcast by the Canadian Broadcasting Corporation (CBC) at 5.00 pm on Saturday 23 January 1965. Transmissions then continued weekly (excluding *The Mutants: The Dead Planet*, and with a two week break after *100,000 BC: The Cave of Skulls*) until 21 April 1965, when the programme's slot was moved to 5.00 pm. on a Wednesday. The final five episodes of *The Keys of Marinus* were shown in a daily 5.00 pm slot from 28 June to 2 July. After this, CBC never aired *Doctor Who* again.

MERCHANDISE

The overwhelming success of *Doctor Who* in the sixties can arguably be traced back to the seven part Terry Nation-scripted story *The Mutants*, which added two new words to the vocabulary of schoolchildren everywhere: 'Dalek' and 'Exterminate'.

The BBC, as reported in the press, were bombarded with letters asking when the Daleks would return, and the interest continued unabated for the following three years. It is easy to look back and come to the conclusion that the Daleks were an overnight success, as they quite obviously were, but what has been less well-documented is the fact that their meteoric rise to become *the* merchandise item of the mid-sixties owed a great deal to one man, Walter Tuckwell.

In the early Sixties, the BBC created a licensing department, BBC Exploitation, whose job it was to exploit the varied and numerous rights in BBC-owned characters and settings. The department was very small and came into being partially because of the demand for Dalek-related products. The rights to market the Daleks were eventually given to a character-licensing company with whom the BBC had done business before, thus relieving the BBC of much of the work involved in such dealings. This company was Walter Tuckwell Associates.

'When they made their first appearance in about the fifth episode of *Dr Who*, late in 1963, I rang the BBC and asked if they were going to be a big thing,' Tuckwell explained in an interview at the time. 'They said: "Forget it. Dr Who is going to finish them off after six episodes and then he is off to China with Marco Polo."

'But like Dick Barton just after the war, this was a scary programme that the kids loved. They enjoy being frightened when they know the goodies are going to win in the end. Before the end of that first series, youngsters were running round their school playgrounds growling "Ex-term-in-ate". It was bingo and nobody knew it.'

Tuckwell's job was to approach manufacturers and publishers and try to interest them in buying a license to use the Daleks in conjunction with their products. As this involved the companies being approached and given the idea, rather than the companies independently deciding to approach the BBC, Tuckwell met with a very favourable response. By Christmas 1964, there were numerous companies gearing up to release toys and games the following year. When the BBC announced that they were planning another

Dalek story for Christmas 1965, interest grew even stronger, and by the end of 1965 around eighty-five different products had been released to tie in with *Doctor Who* and the Daleks.

This trend was reported by the press – how could they fail to notice? – and on 20 December the *Daily Mail* ran a story by Colin Reid discussing the problems parents faced in trying to keep Christmas presents secret from their kids: 'Have YOU ever tried to say "How much is that Dalek in the window?" just using your face and an occasional hiss? You have? That's the easy part.' The feature ended with Colin's kids finally finding the secret stash of Dalek toys and playing with them.

There was even a special BBC 'Interlude' film, set in a toyshop, during the course of which an army of Louis Marx Daleks was seen to be wiped out by a large, crawling doll.

Tuckwell's success at getting the Daleks into every toyshop, and from there into every child's Christmas stocking, was what really brought *Doctor Who* into the public eye. Without that marketing push, it is arguable that *Doctor Who* would not have become the hit it did.

There was even a fan following for the programme, and reviews of *Doctor Who* started to appear in science fiction fanzines of the period. A fan club for William Hartnell, concentrating on his role as the Doctor, was set up and run by a young fan who lived in Stoke-on-Trent. It provided occasional newsletters and sent out autographed publicity photographs of the regular cast members. This was the start of *Doctor Who* fandom, and fan organisations have continued to support and appreciate the series ever since.

SPIN-OFFS

Interest in *Doctor Who* spilled over into the theatre and onto cinema screens as the Daleks moved outside the boundaries of the television show that had spawned them.

24 June 1965 saw the release of the first full-length cinema film to feature the Daleks. *Dr Who and the Daleks* was an instant hit with people of all ages, and preparations started almost immediately on a follow-up, *Daleks Invasion Earth 2150 A.D.* This second film was released in June 1966, but as the Dalek craze was dying down by then, it fared less well at the box office. Although both films were based on televised scripts (for *The Mutants* and *The Dalek Invasion of Earth* respectively), the Doctor was played by Peter Cushing and his assistants by Roy Castle, Jennie Linden and Roberta Tovey (first film) and Bernard Cribbins, Jill Curzon and Roberta Tovey (second film).

Both films generated a large amount of media attention, which was boosted in 1965 by the Daleks paying a visit to the Cannes Film Festival and by a major display of props and sets that was mounted initially in London's

Selfridges department store and then went on tour around the country to other stores owned by the same parent company.

Producer Milton Subotsky's later claim that there were plans for a third film (reported to have been called *Doctor Who's Greatest Adventure*) seem to have no factual basis in the BBC documentation of the time, which indicates that although the contract for the first film allowed for the option on a second to be taken up, the contract for the second made no such provision for any further follow-ups.

Aside from the two cinema films, there was also a one-off stage play. *The Curse of the Daleks* was written by *Doctor Who's* story editor, David Whitaker, and featured neither the Doctor nor the TARDIS, concentrating instead on the Daleks themselves. The plot of the play picks up on the Daleks' immobilisation at the end of *The Mutants* and depicts the reactivation of the creatures by an unwary archaeological team, one of whose number has secret plans for them. The play was staged at the Wyndham's Theatre in London's Charing Cross Road and ran for two weeks from 21 December 1965.

Not content with taking part in the performing arts, the Daleks also had their own comic strip, which ran in *TV Century 21*, and their own annuals and books. They even made appearances at numerous promotional events and exhibitions, including the *Daily Mail* Boys' and Girls' Exhibition of 1964/65. This was the first major public appearance of the Daleks, and crowds packed the hall at London's Olympia exhibition centre to catch a glimpse of them as they patrolled the area, shrieking 'Ex-ter-min-ate' to general delight.

VIEWER REACTION

Doctor Who's first episode was watched by 4.4 million viewers. More and more people then tuned in as the weeks went by, until 10.4 million saw the end of *The Mutants*. The figure then hovered around the 9 to 10 million mark for a while before falling to around 7 million by the close of the first season.

The popularity of the Daleks peaked the following year, and it is perhaps unsurprising therefore to find that the second season gained the highest ratings for the series in the Sixties. It started well, with over 8 million viewers for *Planet of Giants*, but by the time *The Dalek Invasion of Earth* concluded, the figure had climbed to an impressive 12.4 million. The highest mark of the season, however, came with episode one of *The Web Planet*, which was watched by 13.5 million viewers.

From this point, the figures steadily fell, and the lowest audience of the first Doctor's era was recorded for episode three of *The Smugglers*, which managed only 4.2 million viewers.

Considering that far fewer people owned television sets in the Sixties than in later years, these ratings were not at all bad. *Doctor Who* was normally within the top fifty most watched shows each week, and *The Romans* episode one and *The Chase* episode six both climbed as high as number seven on the TV chart.

The series' audience appreciation figures were also generally good. These statistics were compiled by the BBC from a regular survey of a panel of viewers, whose comments would occasionally be used to write up more detailed Audience Research Reports on particular programmes. The Reports for *Doctor Who* provide a fascinating insight into how the series was perceived by the general public at the time of transmission.

'Tonight's new serial seemed to be a cross between Wells' Time Machine and a space-age Old Curiosity Shop, with a touch of Mack Sennett comedy,' commented one viewer, a retired Naval officer, after watching the opening episode of *100,000 BC*. There were occasional voices of discontent – 'A police box with flashing beacon travelling through interstellar space – what claptrap!' was one viewer's opinion – but on the whole the episode was regarded as 'an enjoyable piece of escapism, not to be taken too seriously, of course, but none the less entertaining and, at times, quite thrilling.'

By the time of *The Aztecs*, interest was apparently falling off. One viewer said he was 'afraid that this series has gone on far too long: the danger and escape there from fall into a never-varied pattern length and repetition – result, ennui.' And this was for the third episode of the sixth story to be transmitted! Others expressed a preference for the science fiction based adventures over the historical, but younger children seemed to have enjoyed *The Aztecs* more than their parents.

When the second season began with *Planet of Giants*, viewers welcomed the series' return – 'preposterous' though its concepts were. The most frequently-expressed view about the first episode of *The Dalek Invasion of Earth* was that there was not enough of the Daleks in it. Another comment was that the show was 'rather gruesome for young children to watch, with drowned bodies and daggered bodies.'

The Romans came under fire as being 'so ridiculous it's a bore!' Again there was criticism of the historical adventures in general, and one common comment was that the story lacked any realism – everything was 'transparently phoney.' *The Web Planet* was not liked either, being described as a 'third rate kiddies pantomime.' It was generally felt that the series had 'lost its entertainment value and should be either rested or "scrapped." Plainly, ideas were running out.' *The Space Museum* seemed to confirm this view as, after a promising start, it was thought to have deteriorated into 'a load of drivel.' Some viewers commented that William Hartnell seemed unsure of his lines – 'or,' said one, 'was it that Dr Who was given too many "um's", "ah-h-h's" and "er's" in the script?'

An interesting point to note here is that the stories that tended to attract the most criticism in the Audience Research Reports were those which received the highest ratings!

The Chase was very well received, with many positive comments being expressed. 'Full of adventure' and 'exiting, lively and quite convincing' were examples. However, a large minority seemed to hate *Doctor Who* with a vengeance, dismissing the programme as 'rubbishy, incredible and ridiculous – too ridiculous even for children.'

The Daleks' Master Plan elicited a wide variety of comments also, but the summation at the end of episode twelve was: 'It may be said that if adult viewers start by "tolerating" this serial for the sake of their children, it seems clear that they often find that it has its attractions and on this occasion there were, in fact, plenty who considered *Dr Who* excellent entertainment by any standards.'

Other, more ad hoc surveys of viewers' reactions were carried out from time to time by the BBC's audience researchers. During the run of *Marco Polo*, for instance, numerous comments were received to the effect that '*Dr Who* seemed to be a great favourite, apart from one or two younger children who find it frightening,' but that 'the punch and excitement of the Dalek period has given way to boring details of maps and commentary,' and more generally that 'several children and their parents have said they prefer this series to look into the future rather than the past.' Again, the occasional more disparaging comment was made. Two 'professional class' fathers, for example, thought that *Doctor Who* was 'a bad and pernicious programme' for the BBC to be putting out. However, these views were very much in the minority.

Overall, *Doctor Who* had been a great success, and from humble beginnings had risen to a position of prominence in British popular culture unparalleled by any contemporary TV series.

FIRST DOCTOR STORIES
IN ORDER OF AVERAGE VIEWING FIGURES
(Figures in millions of viewers)

The Rescue	12.5
The Web Planet	12.5
The Dalek Invasion of Earth	11.9
The Romans	11.6
Inside the Spaceship	10.15
Galaxy 4	9.9
Marco Polo	9.47
The Chase	9.4
The Crusade	9.38
The Daleks' Master Plan	9.3
The Space Museum	9.2
The Keys of Marinus	9.07
The Daleks	8.97
Planet of Giants	8.57
The Time Meddler	8.4
The Myth Makers	8.34
The Celestial Toymaker	8.3
Mission to the Unknown	8.3
The Aztecs	7.53
The Sensorites	6.92
The Tenth Planet	6.75
The Reign of Terror	6.73
The Ark	6.48
The Massacre of St. Bartholomew's Eve	6.43
100,000 BC	6.4
The Gunfighters	6.25
The War Machines	5.23
The Savages	4.91
The Smugglers	4.48

THE SECOND DOCTOR

David J Howe
Mark Stammers
Stephen James Walker

Foreword

For the legions of fans who had been glued to the adventures of this irascible old character for the previous three years, Hartnell was Doctor Who and it was impossible to imagine the series without him. Yet on 22 October 1966, their hero lay gravely ill on the floor of his TARDIS, his features blurred and were replaced by those of another. The unthinkable had occurred, Hartnell was gone but the series would continue. Whilst the credits rolled at the end of *The Tenth Planet*, viewers were left to ponder whether or not the series would have much of a future with its new star, Patrick Troughton.

Doctor Who had succeeded in popularising science fiction with the British viewing public. Hartnell had found renewed fame amongst a new generation of young fans. The dwindling numbers of 'real life' police boxes had suddenly become universally recognised as the exterior of the Doctor's TARDIS, and the Daleks had become a massive craze in their own right, spawning hundreds of pieces of merchandise and two feature films. Yet virtually all this success had taken place within the series' first two years, and despite the efforts of the production team, public interest had since waned.

Many within the BBC had doubted the series' appeal from the beginning, only grudgingly admitting the obvious success it achieved. When the viewing figures began to trail off during the third season, similar voices began to say it had run out of steam and that it was perhaps time for something new.

Britain and the world had changed a great deal since the series had begun. Beatlemania and the Mersey sound, Mary Quant and the arrival of the permissive society had changed people's perceptions. The growing conflict in Vietnam and the cold war dominated the news reports, whilst the Americans and the Soviet Union pushed onwards in the race to put a man on the moon. Science fiction was quickly turning into science fact. The mid-Sixties was a great time to be young. Teenagers were better paid and more independent than their parents had even been. Fashion, music and entertainment changed in style to attract the affluent youth market.

In the face of so much change, it was natural to expect that *Doctor Who* would need to adjust its format to continue to attract audiences. The series' production team were keen to aim its storylines at a slightly older viewing audience. This, however, caused problems between successive producers and Hartnell. The actor strongly believed that the show should stick with its tried and tested mix of fantasy stories and pseudo-historicals aimed at the younger end of the family audience. As the only survivor from the original cast and crew, he believed that he knew better than anyone else how *Doctor Who* should be made. Producer Innes Lloyd was determined, however, and he reached an agreement with Hartnell that the actor would not continue in the role. The search for a replacement ended with the announcement of Patrick Troughton as the new Doctor.

But how could such a change of actor be explained? Would the series' regular viewers accept Troughton in the role, or would they simply turn off? Would a greater emphasis on action in the plots attract new and bigger audiences? The production team could do nothing but wait for the public's reaction.

Join us as we travel back to examine a pivotal period of the series' history. The end of historical stories. An influx of new monsters, including several that would menace the Doctor in further adventures. A mammoth finale that would reveal the Doctor's origins. And an era packed with many stories that are still considered classics today.

Patrick Troughton
In His Own Words

ON HIS EARLY LIFE AND CAREER:

'I was born in Mill Hill, a suburb of London. I went to a sort of kindergarten there, and studied ballet dancing, under Pearl Argyle. She was in the film *Things to Come*. Anyway, I soon gave up the idea of becoming a ballet dancer – I must have been about six at the time. I went away later to boarding school at Bexhill-by-the-Sea. I did my O Levels at Mill Hill Public School, then my A Levels. Having got those, I went to the Embassy School of Acting. I was there for a couple of years, and received a scholarship to go to the school of the John Drew Memorial Theatre in East Hampton on Long Island in America. We did a whole lot of plays there, as well as a lot of hard work in our studies. I had a wonderful time; that is a wonderful part of the world.

'The day we broke up, we listened in to Neville Chamberlain announcing that we had declared war on Germany. My dad was a lawyer in a shipping firm, and he arranged me a trip back on a Belgian ship. We hit a mine off Portland Bill, coming back from Rotterdam. We had to take to the boats, and were picked up by a Greek steamer. We were taken into Weymouth, from where I phoned my dad to tell the family I was there. I was nineteen, so I did a bit of rep acting, to wait for my call-up. I had to wait till I was twenty-one, so I did some winter rep at Tunbridge with people like John Cullum, Googie Withers and others. I played Bottom in *A Midsummer Night's Dream*, apart from anything else! It was fun, but a bit sad really. One knew it was all coming to a grisly end when we joined up.

'I joined the Navy, and spent my first six months of the war up in the Highlands, at Loch Ewin. There, about five of us were chosen as commissioned candidates and sent to do three months' sea time before we could take our exams. We actually did six months, in fact, on the east coast convoy, on destroyers, working between Rosside and Sheerness. Then I was posted back to Scotland to train on Coastal Forces, which is what I wanted to do – small ships, motor torpedo boats, that sort of thing. I spent the rest of the war based in Great Yarmouth defending our convoys off the east coast against U-Boat and air attack. We also attacked the German convoys off the Dutch coast. We went generally looking for trouble, running up and down the convoy routes. That was all night work.

'Then we went down to Ramsgate, to bottle up the E-Boats off Ostend, to stop them coming out. I was given my own command, and sent back to Great Yarmouth. I spent the rest of the war picking Americans up out of the drink! This was when they returned in their Fortresses and Liberators. That was more or less my war ... It's very lovely having your own boat!

'After the war, I went back to rep work, in Amersham. I did three plays there, then I got into the Bristol Old Vic to do a whole season of Shakespeare and a few other plays. Then I decided that I didn't want to be away from home any longer, since I'd been away all the war. I was married by then, so I returned to London to try and find work. I went to the Mercury Theatre, where they were doing T S Eliot plays – *Murder in the Cathedral* and *Family Reunion* – and did those for about two years. Then I got into the film of *Hamlet*, playing the player king, with Laurence Olivier. Later on, I was in *Richard III*, where I was Olivier's acting understudy. I was in an identical costume, identical make-up. I had to watch him rehearse a scene, then do it for him – exactly as he had done it, or I was in trouble! This was so that he could compose the picture (he directed as well as starred), then he would do the scene. We went to Spain to film the battle – heaven knows why! It looked like the Crusades. It should have been a foggy, wet day in England. I can't think why he did it! I started then with television, in 1948. I got in on the ground floor, and I've never stopped. I did live television for about fifteen years, then taped – or telecine as it was in those days.'

Interviewed by John Peel in 1986 for *Fantasy Empire*.

ON PLAYING TV'S FIRST ROBIN HOOD:

'It was a bit primitive in those days. For the forest we had back projection. This was a slide, on a screen behind the actors. The projectionists were from Pinewood Studios, because they had a machine, and we had to hire it from them. It was all live, of course. We had this scene where I first met Little John. We came on for the scene, there was a noise behind us where the back projection machine was – and they put the forest in sideways! Then there was a sort of muffled conversation behind us while we were doing the scene, and the trees disappeared – there was a white screen – and then they went in the right way up! This was all being broadcast; it was live, you see, and you couldn't stop! That was quite fun ... It was a very good serial, though, despite that.'

Interviewed by John Peel in 1986 for *Fantasy Empire*.

ON WATCHING WILLIAM HARTNELL AS THE DOCTOR:

'We watched Billy as a family, and saw every single *Doctor Who* story through for his three years. We used to enjoy the ones where he went to the future and he met all kinds of creatures. We didn't so much enjoy the ones that were back in history, because they were so predictable. There was one, though, which explained the mystery of the *Mary Celeste* – which of course was Daleks! – that was rather fun. You can do anything you like on the show. You can move sideways, forwards or backwards in time. Billy was very keen, especially toward the end of his time, when there was some sort of alien presence or invasion, or when they were detected, to say in his character "Now, steady on. Don't let's think of them as a menace. Let's make contact with them". That's very important, really, because fear is a terrible thing.

'I tried to keep on Billy's idea that the aliens weren't necessarily enemies just because they were different.'

Interviewed by John Peel in 1986 for *Fantasy Empire*.

ON BEING CAST AS THE DOCTOR:

'[*Doctor Who*] had been going on about three years and I felt at the end of three years that, you know, it had gone on a long time and I didn't know how long the BBC were really thinking of keeping it. So, to be quite honest, I was very reluctant at first. To go and commit yourself to something out of the blue, which you really didn't know would go on ... I had a feeling that in a way the joke was over and that it had gone on too long.'

Interviewed by Richard Landen in 1983 for *Doctor Who* Magazine No. 78.

'I didn't think it was a particularly good idea of the BBC to replace Billy. I thought it was pretty silly, really! I didn't see how anyone could follow him. The only way that you could do that was to copy him, like Dickie Hurndall did in *The Five Doctors*. But to make him a completely new person ... I thought that the difficulties of selling it to the audience – apart from selling it to poor old Ben and Polly! – were enormous, almost insurmountable.

However, in the end, I was … persuaded, over a week of negotiations, and I thought, "What the heck, let's do this for a while and see what happens". Then, after a rather stop-start beginning while the audience wondered who the heck it was taking over, they settled down and started to like me, then to love me. I settled down and had the three best years of my life.'

Interviewed by John Peel in 1986 for *Fantasy Empire*.

'I was making a film called *The Viking Queen* when they tried to get me to play Doctor Who. We were in Ireland and it was while I was filming. The phone kept on ringing, and they were saying "Come and play Doctor Who". And I said "No, no, don't want to play Doctor Who". And they went on phoning up and I said "No, no, I don't want to play it out. It wouldn't last more than six weeks more with me!" In the end, they kept on pushing the money up so much every day that at the end of the week I said "What am I doing? Of course I'll do this part! Yes!" So I decided to do it, thinking "Well, perhaps a couple of episodes and then they'll finish with it; that'll be the end, but it'll be just one job and I'll move on to another". Little did I know …'

Interviewed by Ben Landman in 1984 for *Whovian Times* Volume 9.

ON HIS DOCTOR'S CHARACTER:

'We had to do something a bit different. My original idea was to black up, wear a big turban and brass earrings with a big grey beard; doing it like the Arabian Knights. The idea was that when I'd finished, I could shave the beard off and so on and no-one would know who I was and I wouldn't be type-cast'

Interviewed on *Pebble Mill at One* in 1973.

'The first idea was this windjammer captain with a sort of Victorian naval hat and brass buttons, but the Head of Drama Sydney Newman took one look at this costume and said "Whatever happened to the cosmic hobo?" He had the idea of making a sort of Chaplinesque character, a sort of tramp, in contrast to Billy Hartnell, and I suppose he must have known that I have a wicked glint in my eye for comedy, so we decided on that.'

Interviewed by Richard Landen in 1983 for *Doctor Who* Magazine No. 78.

'We went up to Bermans, the costumiers, and we just looked through all the old rubbish, really. We just got things out of hampers and had a look, and the costume evolved. It was sort of a ragged imitation of Billy Hartnell, I suppose, only a bit more way-out. To begin with, you see, I found myself playing it over-the-top, mostly because Sydney Newman kept on urging me to. But the Head of Serials, Shaun Sutton, who I think was a little bit wiser than Sydney Newman in many ways – in fact, considerably wiser! – said "No, no, just do it in your head, old chap, don't do all those stunts and so on". So I toned it down a bit after that, and it was warmer and a bit more successful.'

Interviewed on stage at the PanoptiCon VI convention in 1985.

'I had young children of my own when I was doing it. My daughter was about twelve and my son maybe ten, and my other son about eight, so obviously I had them in mind when I was playing it – and I tailored it to that, really. I think perhaps if I'd had a grown-up family, it might have been a different character that emerged; but with them being young, one had that in mind – you didn't want to make it too frightening and all that. You know, I heard the other day – having decided to be a sort of ineffectual, or apparently ineffectual, genius who seemed to get it all wrong until the very end when he got it right – apparently that scared the hell out of children far more than being absolutely certain you've got to win! Because all the time, the fear that I showed and the apparent bungling got them worried. They had no faith in the fact that I was going to solve it in the end, although of course we always did. That was just the reaction of one child I met – who's now grown up, of course.'

Interviewed by Ben Landman in 1984 for *Whovian Times* Volume 9.

'I don't think he was a goody. He was a bit naughty, wasn't he? Of course, you've got to be on the right side when there's a villain about, but he was naughty all the same. If you're going to be totally moral it's boring, so you have to colour it a bit. Let's face it, it's a smashing part!'

Interviewed by Richard Marson in 1984 for *Doctor Who Magazine* No. 102.

'It worked very well when I first took it on, because one was saying to everybody ,"This is the way we're going to do it. It's going to be different. If you don't like it, you can lump it." So we were exaggerating it a bit, and afterwards we toned it down as we got more confident in what we were doing. It became more subtle, and the script writers began to get on our wavelength, which made a hell of a difference. They began to write for you rather than you having to change the script to fit what you wanted to do.

Fortunately, that happened very quickly.

'As for the hat, well I think it was dear old Campbell Logan [a BBC producer], or it might have been Andy Osborn [the Head of Series], who said to me in the BBC club one evening, after they'd shown the first one, "Oh splendid. It'll go on for another three years. Have to get rid of the hat though." So the hat went!'

Interviewed by Richard Marson in 1984 for *Doctor Who Magazine* No. 102.

ON THE DEMANDS OF THE *DOCTOR WHO* SCHEDULE:

'We're not creative, we just do it. We rehearsed Monday, Tuesday, Wednesday and half Thursday, doing the show on Friday. At the beginning, we were filming every other weekend as well. You didn't have time to luxuriate in things like creativity and all that. By and large, though, the directors were all fine. Very nice. People like Gerry Blake, Douglas Camfield and David Maloney. They were all good.

'We got very tired about half way through the run, because they wanted us to film at weekends too. It was silly really, so we had a sort of sit-down strike and said "You've got to alter it". Our boss Shaun Sutton, bless his heart, said "OK, we'll change it," and it was arranged that before each story, we would do a week's work with the new director and new cast doing all the filming necessary. Then we would do the studio stuff in the normal way. It gave us a chance to catch our breath. You had so little time to think, you needed your Saturday and Sunday off to cope.

'You got into a pattern of doing it, and if anyone upset that routine, you were very distressed. If a director came along and started rehearsal half an hour late or quarter of an hour early, it threw you off balance straight away. Working like that, at that pace, for three years, was like doing weekly rep. You got extremely tired and you wanted a definite routine to keep you going and make sure you knew exactly what you were supposed to be doing. Anything that varied from that was awkward and you had to try and get it back to the old way of doing things.'

Interviewed by Richard Marson in 1984 for *Doctor Who Magazine* No. 102.

'We used to have four weeks off every August, and starting again was rather like jumping on a running bus. I remember that feeling when we were filming in Wales for *The Abominable Snowmen*.'

Interviewed on stage at the PanoptiCon VI convention in 1985.

'We had three and a half days' rehearsal, which was done in a church hall. When we were not actually rehearsing, Frazer Hines, Debbie Watling and eventually Wendy Padbury and I played a card game called Aggravation – non-stop for three years. For sixpenny stakes! It was a game you sort of won and lost as the years went past ... Then we would get called to do a scene. If we were left playing cards too long, we would poke our heads around the door and yell "What's going on? We want to work!" But the fun was purely by the way. We were like squirrels on a wheel.

'The problem was fatigue, really. In the end, you got the giggles, you were so fatigued. That can get very distressing, when someone gets the giggles. Not on the part of the artists so much, but the directors get a bit annoyed.'

Interviewed by John Peel in 1986 for *Fantasy Empire*.

ON HAZARDS ENCOUNTERED DURING PRODUCTION:

'On one occasion I went onto the set of *The Moonbase* at Lime Grove and they had this Gravitron hanging from the ceiling of the studio on a couple of wires and a hook. I normally wander about the set before the day begins to say "That's there, this is here, that looks like that," and generally become accustomed to the set. I stood under the Gravitron, had a good look and thought "Yes, that looks very nice". I took two steps off the set and the whole thing, which must have weighed about two tons, crashed down! I'd have been flattened! I remember the director, Morris Barry, deciding he didn't like the look of the set and having it rebuilt on the studio day. I admired him for that, but he was able to keep the show going only because he had very wide experience of live television.

'Explosions tended to be not so much dangerous as loud. There's a super photo of me from *The Invasion* being exploded at. One's nerve was fairly ragged after doing it nonstop, so those expressions were pretty realistic. The worst one was *The War Games*, which we filmed on Brighton rubbish tip. They'd used it for *Oh! What a Lovely War*, so there were already trenches and wire laid out. Visual Effects had these enormous explosions with great clods of earth all over the place. It was a bit alarming. By that stage we were all giggly, hysterical giggly. I just had to say "Jamie, Zoe" and we collapsed – that was it, finish.'

Interviewed by Richard Marson in 1984 for *Doctor Who Magazine* No. 102.

ON THE PLEASURES OF HIS TIME AS THE DOCTOR:

'My favourite role, I think, was Mr Quilp in *The Old Curiosity Shop* – but *Doctor Who* comes a very good second! I liked doing them all, but the first Yeti one was good fun.'

Patrick Troughton writing in November 1980 in a letter to fan Patrick Mulkern.

'It was a very happy show for a start. We were very fortunate in having super people like Frazer Hines. I acted with Frazer when he was twelve, a boy actor, so I've known him a long time. We just hit it off on the set, and when we ever had any time off the set, we liked each other there too. We found we could communicate acting-wise. He's a very good listener. Half the art of working with someone on a long-term basis was that you listened to what the other person was saying to you. This made a big difference to me.

'The producer, Innes Lloyd, was super too. Couldn't have a better producer than that – diplomatic, friendly and enthusiastic. Oh, we were very lucky.

'I'm sure Frazer has embellished a few of the stories that could be told. His favourite little jape was if we were off set or in the TARDIS, he'd say "cue" and I'd walk on, only to discover that it wasn't our cue at all. In fact, he's still doing that one!

'People do tend to romanticise, but it's part of our job to get people to do that. The more you do that the greater the compliment. In the end, of course, it's just a job. I'm a character actor, and I play a lot of characters. With *Doctor Who*, like a lot of work, you have enormous fun – more than usual even. But in the end it's still just a job.'

Interviewed by Richard Marson in 1984 for *Doctor Who Magazine* No. 102.

'It was a marvellous time. On a couple of occasions, standing in the TARDIS waiting for a cue to come on to the studio floor, Frazer Hines and I at a given signal would whip down Debbie Watling's pants just before we got the cue and then open the door and go out, and she'd be giggling away trying to struggle into her pants to get on the set! I don't know if that's printable, but there we are! That was the sort of thing – all very clean, you know, but great fun really! We had that sort of rapport, which was lovely.'

Interviewed by Ben Landman in 1984 for *Whovian Times* Volume 9.

'I loved playing the part! Playing one part for three years – I'd never done that in my life, you see. I'd gone from one character part to another, playing wildly different things: Saint Paul; Allan Breck in *Kidnapped*; the dwarf, Quilp, in *The Old Curiosity Shop*; the old Doctor Manet in *A Tale of Two Cities*; sometimes mad comedy; and just to come to one part for three years, which was happy, and people liked, was an absolute joy. It was wonderful! I had a young family at the time and it meant lots of pennies for them, and sending them to schools and that sort of thing. It was lovely, marvellous – just at the right moment, really!'

Interviewed by Ben Landman in 1984 for *Whovian Times* Volume 9.

ON MAKING SCRIPT SUGGESTIONS:

'One is inventing all the time, and it is either chucked out or accepted by the director. They have what is called a producer's run. This is the last run at a rehearsal. Peter Bryant was the producer after Innes and his little trick was that as the producer's run started, directly I opened my mouth, he started writing on his note pad. Frazer Hines and I had it down to a fine art. What we used to do was put in things we knew he wouldn't accept but at the same time slip in things he probably wouldn't see or notice. This way, he would chuck out the obvious ones and retain the more subtle ones, and that's how we did it. Another dodge we had was, if Frazer and I thought the script was over long, on reading it through we used to read it very slowly. There is always the lady with the stopwatch timing it to the end, and if it was too long, they had to cut it. That way we didn't have so much to learn. They could always pad it out with action if necessary.'

Interviewed by Richard Landen in 1983 for *Doctor Who* Magazine No. 78.

ON HIS DEPARTURE FROM THE SERIES:

'Three years was long enough. I didn't wanted to get "typed" and one had to get out while the going was good. Peter Bryant asked me way back how long, and I said "Three years, no longer". You see, say it had gone on for ten years and then the BBC had dropped it. I would have been sunk, because after ten years, you can't walk into another play. They'll all say, "Oh look, it's Doctor Who" straight away. Even though before I did *Doctor Who* I had done a long line of character parts, thirteen years of one part, Doctor Who, would have been suicide, professionally. Unless of course you can go on forever, then that would have been all right, but there was no guarantee that the BBC were going to keep it on forever. So I had to say, "How long? Okay, three years and I'll have to get out".'

Interviewed by Richard Landen in 1983 for *Doctor Who* Magazine No. 78.

'I resent giving it up from the money point of view – but not any other, even though I enjoyed doing it very much. One can't stay in one part forever, especially a success, and I saw the writing on the wall …!'

Patrick Troughton writing in January 1972 in a letter to fan Ian McLachlan.

ON *THE THREE DOCTORS*:

'Wasn't it for an anniversary of some sort? That was the reason I did it. They wanted us all together, and so I said "Yes, fine, great". And it was fun, it was lovely. Especially having Billy Hartnell there, even though he was only on film, trapped in a sort of bubble. A bit ga-ga, poor lad, but it was lovely seeing him there. Jon Pertwee and I developed quite a rapport, shall we say.'

Interviewed on stage at the PanoptiCon VI convention in 1985.

ON *THE FIVE DOCTORS*:

'It was wonderful! I fell into it at once! There's only one thing I regret, and that is that I didn't quite get the hair right – because my make-up lady, fifteen years ago, used to lift it with sort of curlers, you know, so it was fairly high, and I forgot that this time. So although the length and so on was right – it was my own hair, it wasn't a wig, although it looked like a wig I know – it wasn't quite the same. If I do it again, I'll lift it up a bit to look more like it used to.

'It was better than *The Three Doctors* in a way – it was more vivid. I don't know why.'

Interviewed by Ben Landman in 1984 for *Whovian Times* Volume 9.

ON *THE TWO DOCTORS*:

'*The Two Doctors* is a beauty. The Sontarans I'd never met on screen before, and they're splendid. Colin Baker is super too. And Seville was fantastic. It was very hot, but we had a lovely swimming pool we could fall into. I read my script and dressed accordingly – no way would I have that fur coat!'

Interviewed by Richard Marson in 1984 for *Doctor Who Magazine* No. 102.

ON HIS RELUCTANCE TO GIVE PRESS INTERVIEWS:

'You're press. I heard you were coming. It's no good. I never give interviews. Never.

'Just tell them that I am that mystery man of television, Doctor Who.

'You see, I think acting is magic. If I tell you all about myself it will spoil it.

'People talk about television being in the sitting-room and becoming an everyday thing. But it is not true, especially for the children. It is still magic, and I hope it always stays that way.

'I've only talked to you because you're a girl. And I like girls.'

Interviewed by Margaret Pride and Gillian Mills in 1966 for *Reveille*, edition dated 22-28 December.

'It's like a conjuror showing you how he does his tricks. If you can see how it's being done, it takes away all the magic. I don't want people to see me. I want them to see the person the writer's spent so much time creating, brought to life.'

Quoted in 1987 in *Doctor Who – An Adventure in Space and Time: Season Six Special.*

ON CONVENTION APPEARANCES:

'I don't want to become too associated again with the part – in this country. Not too much. In America, that's different, because I don't appear over there, except in repeats and things. I enjoy going to the American conventions very much – the travel and so on. But over here, I don't want to do it too much. I love doing it, though. It's lovely.'

Interviewed on stage at the PanoptiCon VI convention in 1985.

'It's an ego trip. They love you so much. When I was on the show, you didn't have time for such things. You didn't have time to do anything but go home and go to sleep! I went to bed at nine o'clock every night for three years! I couldn't have existed otherwise.'

Interviewed by John Peel in 1986 for *Fantasy Empire*.

ON THE RELATIVE MERITS OF STAGE, FILM AND TV WORK:

'I don't like acting on the stage, because I like to work during the day and I like to go home during the evening and put my feet up and watch the telly. Also, if I do the stage, I never see my wife Sheelagh because she works all day; she'd go to work and come back and I'd be going to work and it would be impossible. I much prefer the technique and intimacy of television or film. It's my style of acting. I can do both, though, and I'd love to do a while of farce or comedy on the stage – I think that's where it's most successful, because you've got to build on the audience for comedy; you've got to build on the laughs and so on. I wouldn't mind doing that, but it would have to be a very happy play and a very happy part, and for a limited time – six months or something, at the most. But I prefer television, and I've been in it now since 1948. It's given me all my chances, and you naturally stay with what you like.'

Interviewed by Ben Landman in 1984 for *Whovian Times* Volume 9.

ON HIS HOME LIFE:

'I like working with my hands, making things and home decorating, also gardening.

'I suppose, at heart, I am a country person. I would like to have been a naturalist as long as it didn't get me involved with snakes and spiders.'

Interviewed by Margaret Pride and Gillian Mills in 1966 for *Reveille*, edition dated 22-28 December.

ON RELIGION:

'I'm interested that you are studying theology. I don't think I could ever have done that – in a conventional church. There seem too many stumbling blocks to me – though I know the private views of churchmen are sometimes very different from the 39 Articles etc.

'But if only the great difficulties had not been there, I might well have been a professional churchman myself, though not in the Church of

England.

'It does seem to me that so much is just watered down medieval Christianity with no real attempt made to solve the problem, "Love or be damned". To me love can never reject, only fail to draw, and then only temporarily. I cannot get round the issue that Jesus seemed to believe in and advocate eternal torment – and that for no remedial reason.

'Either he's not the full embodiment of the Spirit of Christ of the Cosmos – or the record is sadly wrong. I think it is the latter; I think men may well get into torment and Jesus's reaction is always to get them out of it, but not, I'm afraid, in so many places in the Gospels. I wish he'd been a vegetarian too – not that I am – but Buddha was and I think that is more loving.'

Patrick Troughton writing in January 1972 in a letter to fan Ian McLachlan.

Character – The Second Doctor

These days, the fact that the Doctor can from time to time 'regenerate' – take on a completely new physical appearance in order to escape death – is well known to the general viewing public. It has indeed become an integral part of *Doctor Who*'s basic mythology, arguably as important an element of the series' format as the TARDIS or the Daleks, and each successive change of Doctor generates a wealth of speculation and publicity. This was not always the case, however.

From the time *Doctor Who* made its on-air debut in November 1963 up until the autumn of 1966, William Hartnell was the Doctor and the Doctor was William Hartnell – the two were effectively inseparable in viewers' minds. Hartnell's memorable portrayal of the character as a stern but kind-hearted grandfather figure, complete with long white hair and dignified Edwardian clothes, had endeared him to millions and helped to make *Doctor Who* the great national and international success it had become. While it was not unknown for a leading character in an important programme to be recast – each of the BBC's three famous Quatermass serials of the Fifties, for instance, had seen a different actor in the central role of Professor Bernard Quatermass – it was very unusual in an ongoing weekly series, and inevitably a risky and potentially unpalatable step to take.

Clearly, then, the decision to replace Hartnell with another actor was a brave one on the part of *Doctor Who*'s third producer, Innes Lloyd. Such a move had been considered by his predecessor, John Wiles, but had at that time been effectively overruled by the then Head of Serials, Gerald Savory. In announcements to the press, it was diplomatically suggested that Hartnell had left the series to resume his career in the theatre. In truth, however, according to many of those who worked with him, the actor had become increasingly difficult to work with – due partly to ill health and partly to an increasingly dogmatic and proprietorial attitude on his part – and Lloyd considered that the change would be beneficial not only for the series but also for Hartnell himself.

The concept of the Doctor undergoing a total physical transformation (a process that would not actually be termed 'regeneration' until 1974) provided a means of incorporating the change of actor into the ongoing narrative of the series itself. It is uncertain exactly who first came up with this idea – Wiles had proposed simply having the Doctor's appearance changed by the Celestial Toymaker after a period of invisibility in the third season story named after that character – but the likelihood is that it emerged in discussions between Lloyd and his story editor, Gerry Davis. Others who may well have been involved in the discussions were Head of Serials Shaun Sutton and Dr Kit Pedler, *Doctor Who*'s unofficial scientific adviser, with whom Davis was working closely on the scripts for the first Doctor's final story, *The Tenth Planet*.

Although a number of other possibilities, including Sir Michael Hordern, were considered, the man eventually chosen as Hartnell's replacement was 46-year-old character actor Patrick Troughton (who had at one time been a contender for the guest role of gunslinger Johnny Ringo in the third season story *The Gunfighters*). As Lloyd later recounted, this was a choice of which Hartnell himself very much approved:

'I recall him saying to me – though I don't know if he said it to anyone else – "There's only one man in England who can take over, and that's Patrick Troughton."'

Lloyd's own view was that Troughton was 'an absolutely ideal choice':

'He had versatility going for him – he was a distinguished character actor with a great many varied roles behind him. He was always in demand. He was a popular actor with a great following. Most important of all, I think, was that he had a leading actor's temperament. He was a father figure to the whole company and hence could embrace it and sweep it along with him.'

Troughton was offered the role of the new Doctor during the third week of June 1966, while he was on location in Ireland for the Hammer film *The Viking Queen*. Although he felt that *Doctor Who* had perhaps been 'done to death', he was eventually persuaded to accept, in part because he realised that the regular income would help to pay for his sons' education. He signed his initial twenty-two episode contract on 2 August.

In an article published on 2 September under the heading '"Tougher" Doctor Who is chosen', the *Daily Telegraph* reported the views of the BBC's Head of Drama Sydney Newman on the recasting of the Doctor:

'Our problem in choosing the new Doctor Who was very difficult, because we have decided to make considerable changes in the personality of the character. We believe we have found exactly the man we wanted.'

Troughton had initially harboured considerable doubts as to whether or not the audience would actually accept him as the Doctor. It had however been agreed from the outset that he should not even attempt to copy the style of Hartnell's performance but should instead endeavour to bring to the role his own, completely different characterisation. The big question was, what should that new characterisation be?

The production team set out their initial ideas in a short note (drawing in part on an early draft of the series' original format, dated 16 May 1963, which suggested that the Doctor had begun his travels as a fugitive from an unknown enemy during a galactic war). This read as follows:

The New Doctor Who

Appearance. Facially as strong, piercing eyes of the explorer or Sea Captain. His hair is wild and his clothes look rather the worse for wear (this is a legacy from the metaphysical change which took place in the Tardis). Obviously spares very little time and bother on his appearance. In the first serial, he wears a fly-blown version of the clothes associated with this character.

Manner. Vital and forceful – his actions are controlled by his superior intellect and experience – whereas at times he is a positive man of action, at other times he deals with the situation like a skilled chess player, reasoning and cunningly planning his moves. He has humour and wit and also an overwhelmingly thunderous rage which frightens his companions and others.

A feature of the new Doctor Who will be the humour on the lines of the sardonic humour of Sherlock Holmes. He enjoys disconcerting his companions with unconventional and unexpected repartee.

After the first serial – the Daleks – (when the character has been established), we will introduce a love of disguises which will help and sometimes disconcert his friends.

To keep faith with the essential Doctor Who character, he is always suspicious of new places, things or people – he is the eternal fugitive with a horrifying fear of the past horrors he has endured. (These horrors were experienced during the galactic war and account for his flight from his own planet.)

The metaphysical change which takes places over 500 or so years is a horrifying experience – an experience in which he re-lives some of the most unendurable moments of his long life, including the galactic war. It is as if he has had the LSD drug and instead of experiencing the kicks, he has the hell and dank horror which can be its effect.

The task of writing the new Doctor's debut adventure had been entrusted to David Whitaker, who as *Doctor Who*'s original story editor had been one of the small group of individuals responsible for developing the series in the first place. He had since contributed several stories of his own and had recently been discussing a number of new ideas with Davis; consequently, he seemed a natural choice to tackle this important project.

The storyline that Whitaker came up with was entitled *The Destiny of Doctor Who* – a reference to the Doctor's transformation – and, as suggested in the production team's note, featured the ever-popular Daleks (the hope being that their presence would help to reassure viewers that this was still *Doctor Who* that they were watching, even though the Doctor himself now looked different). Davis approved this storyline and on 22 July 1966 commissioned Whitaker to write the complete scripts for the six part story, for a fee of £300 per episode, with a target delivery date of 8 August. A separate fee of £15 per episode was paid to the Daleks' creator, Terry Nation, for their use in the story.

'This was around the time William Hartnell was leaving,' Whitaker later observed, 'and so, aware that the idea was to replace him with another actor, I wrote the Doctor's part as sketchily as possible, so that it could be easily altered. I then concerned myself with the rest of the story and delivered my scripts just before I was due to go abroad for a time.'

Mindful as he was of the need to keep the characterisation of the Doctor relatively vague, Whitaker was nevertheless influenced to a certain degree by the production team's note. Consequently he made him a somewhat verbose and arrogant type, with a sardonic wit akin to that of Sherlock Holmes. These draft scripts proved a source of some concern to Troughton, as he told a convention audience in 1985:

'We had script conferences and there was a first script, which was sort of written for Billy but in a way it was written for, it struck me reading it, a very verbose, autocratic Sherlock Holmes type – who never stopped talking! I thought, "That's not going to do for me over three years every week," so I said that I didn't see my Doctor quite like that: I saw him really as a listener. I thought that this Doctor listened to everyone and totted it all up and then made his own decision about things. Then in comes Sydney Newman and he starts talking about a "cosmic hobo", who obviously wouldn't talk like an intellectual, autocratic Sherlock Holmes type at all. So I leapt at it: I said "What a good idea! ... A man like that'd be more of a listener, wouldn't he? ..." I was very keen on the idea of doing it as a cosmic hobo.'

Newman had overall responsibility for literally hundreds of programmes each year and would not normally concern himself with the day-to-day production of *Doctor Who*. He did however keep a watchful eye on the series – all the more so, many people believed, because it was to a large extent his own brainchild – and he would always have to be consulted about important developments such as major format or cast changes. Hence his involvement in the initial discussions concerning Troughton's portrayal of the Doctor.

Davis later described how the detailed characterisation had been arrived at:

'We had to change the concept of the Doctor. We spent a whole day – producer, Head of Serials, Patrick Troughton, me and some others – at a meeting. As the morning went on, it became chaotic. Everyone was giving ideas, but there was no real cohesion. I could see that Troughton was getting very irritated. He was very uneasy about taking the job anyway, thinking that he might be type-cast. At the end of the morning, I realised we were getting nowhere, so I ejected everyone else from the meeting and just Patrick Troughton and I worked out the character.

'Really it came mostly out of Troughton's own personality. In an odd sort of way, he was playing himself. He was hard to pin down, shifting, always eluding the issue. This was very different from the positive, dogmatic character of Hartnell. So at the end of the day, we went back and I said I thought we had it.

'I thought it would be very interesting to have a character who never quite says what he means, who, really, uses the intelligence of the people he is with. He knows the answer all the time; if he suggests something, he knows the outcome. He is watching, he's really directing, but he doesn't want to *show* he's directing like the old Doctor.'

Davis was inspired in part by the character Destry portrayed by film star James Stewart in the popular Western *Destry Rides Again* (a 1939 production by Universal); someone who when asked a question would always reply by way of a parable rather than give a straight answer.

Once the new Doctor's character had been worked out, Whitaker's scripts for his debut story – which had now been retitled *The Power of the Daleks* – had to be amended accordingly. As this was a last minute job, and as Whitaker did not have the time to do it himself, Davis contacted another former *Doctor Who* story editor, Dennis Spooner, to perform the rewrite, beginning with the first episode over the weekend of 8-9 October 1966. Spooner's fee for this work was £75 per episode. Whitaker agreed to the rewrite on condition that neither his own fee nor his overseas rights were affected, that the characterisation of the Daleks was left unchanged, and that he still received sole writer's credit.

'I rewrote the story from David's scripts,' Spooner later confirmed. 'Terry Nation had the rights to write all the Dalek stories, but he was busy and couldn't do this one. So he handed the task over to David to write it. David wrote it as a straight piece for *nobody*. You see, he knew it wasn't going to be William Hartnell, and he didn't know *who* it was going to be. So he wrote it as "the Doctor", and "the Doctor" was really not written at all. Nothing the Doctor said was important to the development of the story. The Doctor was on the sidelines of the plot.

'When they cast Pat Troughton, Gerry Davis didn't feel that he, as story editor, could do the amount of rewriting that was going to be involved. As story editor, you've got to liaise with Make-up, Costume and all the other departments; you've got to look after your producer; you've got to take the director in hand. He knew that if he took this story, he would have to go home for three weeks to do the amount of rewriting it needed, so he asked me to do it.

'I went in and met Pat Troughton and I said to Pat, virtually, "How do you see yourself as the Doctor?" That was obviously so I'd be able to write it as he wanted to play it. Basically, he saw it as Charlie Chaplin. So we went through it together, and his part expanded to just the right size.'

When it came to choosing the costume and make-up that Troughton would wear, a number of outlandish ideas were mooted. It was thought, for example, that he might 'black up' and put on curly-toed slippers and a turban (an image that in later interviews he would often liken to the one adopted by German star Conrad Veidt in the 1940 London Films movie *The Thief of Baghdad*), or perhaps adopt the guise of a sea captain in full Victorian-style naval uniform. A number of these ideas were actually tried out in test fittings; and each time Troughton was kitted out in a new look, Newman would be fetched to pass judgment. Newman's reaction was invariably negative and, as Troughton would later attest, he eventually asked, 'But whatever happened to the cosmic hobo?' Consequently, Troughton's eventual costume, designed by Sandra Reid, was – as foreshadowed in the production team's original note – a tramp-like, Chaplinesque parody of Hartnell's, with stove-pipe hat, spotted bow tie, disreputable old frock coat and enormously baggy checked trousers. At one point during the rehearsal process, Troughton proposed playing the part wearing a frizzy, Harpo Marx-type wig. In the end, however, after this was objected to by his fellow regular cast members, his own hair was simply cut into a Beatle-style mop.

It was on 29 October 1966 that the series' followers were given their first glimpse of the new Doctor, at the end of the closing episode of *The Tenth Planet*. The production team had originally thought that it would be impracticable for the actual physical transformation to be depicted on screen – they had envisaged that the old Doctor would simply collapse to the floor of the TARDIS with his cloak covering his face – but they had changed their plans after discovering that a suitable electronic effect could be achieved by vision mixer Shirley Coward. Troughton had consequently been asked to sign a separate contract for this episode, and had done so on 16 September. After the transformation scene, viewers had to wait another week to begin to discover just how different from the original the new Doctor was going to be (although, due to the need to allow time for the last-minute rewrite, there had actually been a two week break in production between *The Tenth Planet* and *The Power of the Daleks*, recording for the former having been completed on 8 October and that for the latter having got underway on 22 October).

The director appointed to handle *The Power of the Daleks* was Christopher Barry. Barry was a long-standing contributor to the series, having worked on the very first Dalek story amongst others, and he also knew Troughton of old:

'Patrick Troughton took to *Doctor Who* like a duck to water. I don't think Sydney Newman was entirely happy with the first appearance of him during rehearsal. I think we had to tone it down a little, to try and incorporate more of Troughton's youth and humour and whimsy. Hartnell was always the old professor, grandfather sort of figure, which was good, but Troughton was a sort of whimsical figure, more musical, and advantage could be taken of that.

'Troughton, like Hartnell, was a very experienced actor and a very resourceful person. I think he found depths in his own personality. He nearly always played very straight, stern roles, like Cromwell in *A Man for All Seasons,* and I think he relished the idea of the Doctor. He was that sort of warm-hearted, lovely person himself, and it was seldom that he got a chance to play that sort of role in television.'

In the opening scenes of *The Power of the Daleks*, as the Doctor starts to recover from his transformation, his companions Polly and Ben see that underneath his cloak he now has on different clothes and is somewhat smaller in stature. Although Polly is prepared reluctantly to accept that this is the Doctor, albeit in a different body, Ben remains highly sceptical, suspecting that an impostor has infiltrated the TARDIS. Their uncertainty (which would doubtless have been shared by many viewers at the time) is in no way lessened by the Doctor, as he continually refers to himself in the third person and – as in the following exchange – will give only vague or oblique answers to their questions:

> BEN: (PICKING UP THE OLD DOCTOR'S RING) The Doctor always wore this. If you are him it should fit. (HE TRIES THE RING ON THE DOCTOR'S FINGER, BUT IT IS FAR TOO BIG) That settles it.
>
> DOCTOR: I'd like to see a butterfly fit into a chrysalis case after it spreads its wings.
>
> POLLY: Then you *did* change.
>
> DOCTOR: Life depends on change, and renewal.
>
> BEN: (SCEPTICAL) Oh, *that's* it, you've been renewed, have you?

> DOCTOR: (HALF TO HIMSELF) Renewed? Have I? That's
> it, I've been renewed. It's part of the TARDIS. Without it I
> couldn't survive.

The new Doctor is initially characterised by his unpredictability and his resorting to foolery when faced with a difficult situation. At moments of stress, he often delves into his pocket and takes out a recorder (an item liberated from the TARDIS's storage trunk), proceeding to play a jaunty tune on it – and even, on occasion, dancing a little jig. It is only as the adventure progresses that Polly and Ben, and with them the series' viewers, come to realise that the new Doctor's clown-like facade masks a keen intelligence and highly developed powers of observation, and that the strong sense of morality that the first Doctor always manifested is equally apparent in his successor.

This Doctor likes to create a smokescreen, so that no-one realises exactly what he is up to. His unassuming, sometimes outlandish behaviour is soon seen to be a tactic adopted to keep his adversaries – and sometimes even his allies – off balance. He deliberately leads people to underestimate his capabilities and intellect, but in truth has a keen analytical mind and knows exactly what he is doing. This is well illustrated by a scene at the end of *The Power of the Daleks* in which he appears somewhat bewildered and embarrassed at having 'accidentally' wiped out the colony's power supply in the process of immobilising the Daleks. 'Did I do all that?' he innocently asks, before whisking his companions back to the TARDIS. To Polly's later assertion that he *did* know what he was doing, his response is merely a wry grin and a chirpy tune picked out on his recorder.

While *The Power of the Daleks* was still in production, Lloyd and Davis amended their original note on the new Doctor's character to take into account the changes that had since been decided upon. The revised version, intended for the information of prospective writers for the series, was dated 28 November 1966 and read as follows:

THE NEW DOCTOR WHO

> (It must be emphasised that these notes are only a
> *supplement* to watching the Doctor in action on the screen
> and that *this* is the only way to a full understanding of the
> character.)

> The new Doctor is younger than the former (Hartnell)
> characterisation. He is more of an enigma, using humour to
> gain his ends rather than direct confrontation. His clowning
> tends to make his enemies underrate him and his obsession

with apparent trivialities, clothes, novelties of all kinds, etc, is usually a device merely to give him time to examine a newly-discovered clue.

With Ben, Polly and Jamie, he is cryptic, oblique and mysterious, preferring (like Sherlock Holmes) to keep his conclusions to himself and let the others theorise about the situation. However, we must feel that there is a keen purpose in all he does (if we can spot it!) and that he can flare into direct action and dominate the scene when necessary.

For some serials he uses disguise and appears in outfits ranging from an old woman to a German doctor of the 18th Century (these though must always be discussed with the story editor so we don't have him going into costume in every serial). His disguise is that of a Scarlet Pimpernell and used for the same purpose.

Perhaps his chief attribute is an avoidance of the cliché and obvious. His attitudes to any given situation are off-beat and unpredictable. Sometimes this leads to misunderstandings with his companions who consider him to be favouring the 'wrong side'. Ultimately we see his action to be the right one and understand his line of reasoning, but in the process he can revitalise many a familiar situation.

When he has achieved the desired result and is congratulated by the others, he invariably looks puzzled: Did he really do that? And if so 'how'? Perhaps the others can explain *how* he did it? His companions are therefore never quite certain if he has won a battle, etc, by accident or design and this sometimes leads to a 'Pied Piper' ending, with the people he has saved rejecting him because of his manner and his refusal to accept their gratitude. As with his fellow time travellers (and the viewers!), he wants them to think for themselves and stand on their own two feet, instead of putting a statue to their deliverer in the market place and making the same mistakes again.

The suggested disguises of 'an old woman' and 'a German doctor of the 18th Century' were actually seen to be adopted by the new Doctor in his second story, *The Highlanders*, which had been written by Davis himself (with a co-credit to Elwyn Jones, who had been originally due to write it). This story also saw the character taking on the guise of a Redcoat soldier; and the following one, *The Underwater Menace*, had him passing himself off as a gypsy musician in the Atlantean market place. Later, the season five story *The Enemy of the World* provided possibly the ultimate illustration of his talent for mimicry when he was seen to impersonate the tyrant Salamander, to whom he bore a remarkable physical similarly (not surprisingly, as this was a dual role for Troughton). By the time *The Enemy of the World* was transmitted, however, this character trait had been largely discarded. This was in line with the production team's rapidly-taken decision – based in part on adverse viewer reaction to *The Power of the Daleks*, as reflected in the BBC's internal Audience Research Report – to tone down the more outrageous aspects of the new Doctor's behaviour and make him an altogether less comical character. One illustration of this, as recalled by Sutton, is that the recorder prop played frequently by Troughton in his earliest episodes was hidden so that he was unable to use it.

The change of emphasis was reflected in the Doctor's costume, too, as the voluminous, loudly checked trousers in which he made his debut were altered and eventually exchanged for a much more conservative pair and the tall stove-pipe hat was dropped altogether, being seen for the last time in *The Underwater Menace*. Lloyd later claimed in interviews that the original trousers had in fact been taken in at the rate of an inch a week so that Troughton – who still feared type-casting and hoped that an outlandish costume would help him to avoid it – would fail to notice the difference. Troughton however denied this, arguing that he could not have been so easily fooled, and asserted that he was actually in full agreement with the overall mellowing of the character.

Following this change of approach, the second Doctor was still portrayed as someone who liked to fool people into underestimating his abilities – deliberately failing a simple intelligence test in the season six story *The Dominators*, for example – but the bizarre antics of his earliest episodes gave way to a gentle, quirky humour that counterpointed rather than eclipsed the drama and helped to diffuse the tension in some of the scarier scenes. Similarly, Davis's idea that the Doctor should achieve his objectives by subtle direction of others rather than by taking positive action himself was retained, but was now given a rather different slant whereby the character was seen to be somewhat manipulative.

Perhaps the prime illustration of this trait is provided by *The Evil of the Daleks*, the closing story of season four, in which the Doctor appears at times to be acting in a decidedly furtive and suspect manner. More so than at any other point since the early part of the series' first season, he seems an enigmatic and potentially dangerous figure with a distinctly dark side to his nature. His companion Jamie is on one occasion even moved to denounce him as being 'too callous' and to threaten to part company with him as soon as they reach their next destination – an echo of feelings expressed by the Doctor's original human companions, Ian and Barbara, in the early days of their travels in the TARDIS. The Doctor's dispassionate manoeuvring of individuals and events in order to bring about the Daleks' destruction – the sort of scheming now more commonly associated with his seventh incarnation than with his second – provides an effective reminder of his alien qualities. 'I am not a student of human nature,' he comments at one point, 'I am a professor of a far wider academy of which human nature is merely a part'.

Another notable instance of the Doctor's manipulation of others is offered by the next story, *The Tomb of the Cybermen*, in which he encounters a team of human archaeologists on the planet Telos and, largely without their realising it, gives them a crucial helping hand in gaining access to the base where the Cybermen are entombed – placing all their lives in considerable danger as a result. It would however be fair to acknowledge that these examples are somewhat atypical, and that the Doctor's knack of getting others to follow his agenda was generally portrayed in a rather less sinister light. This is certainly true of the numerous occasions on which the writers had him encountering inflexible authority figures – including Hobson in *The Moonbase*, the Commandant in *The Faceless Ones*, Clent in *The Ice Warriors*, Robson in *Fury from the Deep* and Bennett in *The Wheel in Space* – and gleefully confounding them with his shambolic manner and chaotic approach.

Troughton's interpretation of the Doctor became increasingly popular with viewers as time went by. The actor himself, though, found *Doctor Who's* gruelling production schedule more and more difficult to cope with, and seriously considered declining to renew his contract after completing a second year on the series. In the end, he decided to stay on – even though the BBC had turned down a request he had made, at the suggestion of *The Enemy of the World's* director Barry Letts, for a reduction in the number of episodes to be produced per season. The pressure on him was eased a little when he and his fellow regular cast members subsequently won an agreement that they should no longer be required to work at weekends as well as during the week. Early in his third year, however, Troughton made it known to the series' production team that he would not want to continue for a fourth. By this time, the strain of making the series was really beginning to take its toll.

'We were aware that Pat wanted to leave, of course,' says Derrick Sherwin, who worked as script editor and producer on his last season. 'He had had a hard slog – don't forget, we were doing about forty episodes a year in those days – and he was very, very tired. He had been consistently getting pretty shoddy scripts, too, and he was a perfectionist, he really wouldn't say poor dialogue. Consequently he was becoming very edgy towards the end, and there were a few rows. Eventually he decided that he had had enough. The Doctor had changed before, so we knew that we could change him again, and that's what we did.'

Director Paddy Russell also recalls the reputation that Troughton had acquired for being rather difficult to work with: 'Though I never directed a *Doctor Who* with Patrick Troughton, I knew him very well as an actor and had worked with him a lot … It was interesting, because I talked to Pat about *Doctor Who* much later, when he was doing a classic serial for me. Having found him a superb actor to work with and not at all difficult, I found it extraordinary when I heard that he had begun to give himself a very bad reputation on *Doctor Who*. We were chatting away one day and I said I couldn't believe these stories, and he said, "Well, I couldn't believe what I was doing. That's in the end why I left. The part overwhelmed me and it almost gave me schizophrenia".'

The production team decided that Troughton's final story ought to be a particularly memorable one and that, in order to achieve this, it should take the bold step of dispelling some of the mystery that had always surrounded the Doctor's background. Apart from occasional, invariably vague mentions of his alien origins – including, in *The Tomb of the Cybermen*, a rare and oblique reference to his family – very little had ever been revealed about his life prior to the televised adventures. Now, however, all that was to change. In *The War Games*, writers Malcolm Hulke and Terrance Dicks (then the series' script editor) came up with the explanation that the Doctor was in fact a renegade member of an awesomely powerful race of time travellers called the Time Lords. They also had him giving his companions Jamie and Zoe an explanation as to why he had first embarked on his journeys in the TARDIS:

DOCTOR: I was bored!

ZOE: What do you mean, you were bored?

DOCTOR: Well, the Time Lords are an immensely civilised race. We can control our own environment; we can live forever, barring accidents; and we have the secret of space-time travel.

JAMIE: Well what's so wrong in all that?

DOCTOR: Well, we hardly ever use our great powers. We consent simply to observe and gather knowledge!

ZOE: And that wasn't enough for you?

DOCTOR: No, of course not. With a whole galaxy to explore? Millions of planets? Aeons of time? Countless civilisations to meet?

JAMIE: Well, why do they object to you doing all that?

DOCTOR: Well, it is a fact, Jamie, that I do tend to get involved in things …

In order to explain Troughton's departure, Hulke and Dicks had the Time Lords in the closing episode of *The War Games* finally capturing the Doctor, placing him on trial for transgression of their law of non-interference in the affairs of other planets, returning his companions to their respective points of origin (in Jamie's case the Scottish Highlands in the aftermath of the Battle of Culloden, as seen in *The Highlanders*, and in Zoe's case the space station known as the Wheel, the setting of *The Wheel in Space*) and ultimately sentencing him to a period of exile on Earth – with a completely new appearance. Thus was the scene set for the era of the third Doctor …

Production Development

Production of the early part of the second Doctor's era was overseen by the same team as had handled the latter part of the first Doctor's – namely producer Innes Lloyd and story editor Gerry Davis. Lloyd, who had been assigned to *Doctor Who* by the BBC's Head of Drama Sydney Newman, had accepted the posting only reluctantly, as science fiction had previously been of no great interest to him. He had however grown to enjoy the genre as time had gone by – particularly after he had worked through a number of stories inherited from his predecessor John Wiles and started to make his own mark on the series. Davis, by contrast, had always liked science fiction, and had actually asked to be transferred to *Doctor Who* from his previous assignment on the football team drama series *United!*.

Lloyd had been keen from the outset to update the style of *Doctor Who* – which in his opinion had previously been rather old-fashioned and whimsical – and to make the Doctor's adventures more action-orientated and 'gutsy'. The first real fruits of this had become evident in the season three story *The War Machines*, which had seen William Hartnell's Doctor in the unfamiliar setting of contemporary London, working alongside the British armed forces to combat a megalomaniac super-computer situated within the newly-completed GPO Tower (which was renamed the Telecom Tower in the early Eighties). Lloyd had also taken this opportunity to change the image of the Doctor's companions. The original intention had been that Dodo (played by Jackie Lane) should continue as a regular, with a new character called Richard, or Rich for short, brought in to replace Steven (Peter Purves), who had been written out in the previous story, *The Savages*. In the end, however, Lloyd had decided that Dodo should also be written out, leaving the way open for the introduction of a completely new male and female companion team: seaman Ben Jackson (Michael Craze) and secretary Polly Wright (Anneke Wills) (whose surname was never given on screen) – two up-to-date, 'swinging Sixties' characters, very much in line with the aim of bringing a greater degree of realism to the series.

Indicative of the seriousness with which the production team viewed this aim was the fact that they had engaged the services of an unofficial scientific adviser in the person of Dr Kit Pedler. Pedler's first contribution to the series had been to propose the basic ideas for the story that had ultimately become *The War Machines*. He had then gone on to create, with assistance from

Davis, the Cybermen for the first Doctor's swansong, *The Tenth Planet* – which, with its suspenseful depiction of a multiracial team of scientists under siege in their advanced but isolated base, was typical of the type of story that Lloyd and Davis wanted to see presented in *Doctor Who*.

This basic scenario – an isolated community of humans, led by a strong-willed but misguided authority figure, being attacked and infiltrated by terrifying alien monsters – was indeed adopted as something of a standard format for Patrick Troughton's first two seasons as the Doctor. Stories that conformed to it to a greater or lesser degree included *The Power of the Daleks*, *The Moonbase*, *The Macra Terror*, *The Faceless Ones*, *The Tomb of the Cybermen*, *The Abominable Snowmen*, *The Ice Warriors*, *The Web of Fear* and *The Wheel in Space*. The perceived benefits of this approach were twofold: first, it made for some tense, claustrophobic and often very frightening dramatic situations; secondly, as Davis later explained, it meant that the series' relatively modest resources could be used particularly effectively:

'My basic premise for *Doctor Who* stories in that era of minuscule budgets was to forego the usual dozen tatty sets in favour of one major set around which we could concentrate all the money. This made a much more exciting and convincing central location for the drama.'

There were nevertheless a number of stories that departed from this approach. One of these was *The Highlanders*, Troughton's second outing as the Doctor, which was set in 18th-Century Scotland and – apart from the TARDIS and its occupants – featured no science fiction elements at all. This was to be the last historical story for many years, however, as the production team had decided that this genre – which had constituted an important part of the series' format since its inception – should now be dropped. One theory often advanced to account for this development is that the historical stories were less popular with viewers than the science-based ones. This indeed was the explanation given by Lloyd in a contemporary interview for the magazine *Television Today*:

'One change we have decided on is to drop the historical stories, because we found they weren't very popular. This doesn't mean we won't use historical *backgrounds* like those in *The Highlanders* by Elwyn Jones and Gerry Davis or *The Smugglers* by Brian Hayles, but we will not involve Doctor Who and his companions in events which cannot be changed because they really happened.'

An objective assessment of the series' ratings and audience appreciation figures in fact reveals very little evidence to support the contention that the historical stories were less popular than the science-based ones. The real reason for the dropping of the former may well have been not so much that they were unpopular with the viewing audience as that they were unpopular with the production team themselves, and out of line with their vision of the type of series that *Doctor Who* ought to be in 1967. Despite

Lloyd's suggestion to *Television Today* that stories with historical *backgrounds* might continue to be produced, this proved not to be the case.

The Highlanders was also notable for marking the debut of a new companion character, Jamie McCrimmon (Frazer Hines), who would continue in the series until the end of the second Doctor's era – making him the longest-running in the series' history. The production team prepared a detailed note to explain the character to potential writers. This was dated 28 November 1966 and read as follows:

FRAZER HINES in the part of JAMIE

He is a piper, and the *character must be that of a simple but engaging Scot*. Although his smile disarms opposition, he is on occasions a man of action who will defend his friends or principles fearlessly. *He is cheerful, open, manly, flexible –* more flexible in fact than Ben and Polly. *When either Ben or Polly are pulling his leg, he reacts with a grin.* Because of his romantic appearance, *he always wears the kilt –* his hair is longer and his shirt has a swashbuckling appearance: because of this and the attractive features of his character *he must assume the part of the Young Hero in each story.*

He must be constantly *AMAZED AND PERPLEXED* that he is wandering through Space and Time and is coming up against things, even common-place things, which he could never have dreamt of in his day. *The large things – planes, computers etc – rock him back on his heels –* he finds it hard to comprehend them all.

He brings many of the attributes of the Highlander of his period with him, being courageous, impetuous, superstitious and romantic. His impetuosity often provokes difficult situations for the time travellers, but his direct approach will sometimes help solve problems as well as create them.

His superstitious background enables him to relate the forces of evil fought by the Doctor to the witches, demons, goblins etc of his native land. Sometimes, in fact, this folklore gives him a deeper insight into the forces opposed to the travellers than the more scientific approach of the Doctor, Ben and Polly.

Attitudes to the Doctor, Ben and Polly.

TO THE DOCTOR:

The Doctor is a strange, loveable, wee chap to Jamie. He is obviously some sort of genial wizard or magician. He finds it hard to understand what his motives are or what he is doing when tackling a technical problem – but he knows he can help out with brawn, so he does. He doesn't question motives, he asks the question from interest and from a desire to know what is going on.

The Doctor enjoys Jamie as an oddity like himself. He also enjoys him as he knows that he has an appreciative and captive audience, and one that will laugh at his jokes. The Doctor is quick-witted with a supernatural intelligence, who will arrive at the answer to problems from the most unpredictable reasons ... Jamie has dash, but a scant education has only given him a sharpened instinct which he uses to approach a problem straightforwardly and solve it in a predictable way.

TO POLLY:

Jamie doesn't really know how to treat Polly. She is a girl and therefore all his experience tells him that she must be weak and gentle and therefore should be treated with chivalry. He goes out of his way to look after her, but is often confused by her 1966 attitudes and appearance. He is a little shy of her and all women, especially emancipated women. Polly is fascinated by Jamie's shyness and his Heroic aspect. She enjoys making Ben jealous, even though Ben's relationship has been that of bossy brother. She might have a 'thing' about Jamie if she didn't realise that it might make time travelling with her companions tricky.

TO BEN:

Ben has complexes, Jamie has none. Ben is nervy,

Jamie is calm. They both question ... Ben because he is suspicious of motives, Jamie because he genuinely wants to know. In adventurous escapades, they complement each other, Ben working out what a course of action should be and Jamie carrying it out. Ben is apt to take the mickey out of Jamie and is irritated when Jamie takes it good-humouredly – usually with a grin rather than a quip. Seeds of jealousy creep into Ben's character, having Jamie as a fellow time traveller. They don't always need to be seen to be negative emotions, but on occasions would motivate him to doing heroic actions to impress Polly and the Doctor and put him one up on Jamie.

After a period of relative stability for the series' production team, the end of May 1967 saw Davis relinquishing his post as story editor and going to work on another BBC show, *First Lady*. He had actually been asked to become producer of *Doctor Who* – Lloyd was now keen to move on, feeling that he had contributed all he could to the series – but had decided against this. Davis's departure also marked the end of Pedler's regular involvement as *Doctor Who*'s unofficial scientific adviser, although he would continue to provide storylines for Cyberman adventures throughout the remainder of the second Doctor's era. Davis and Pedler continued to work together as a team on other projects – most notably the highly popular *Doomwatch* series, which they created for the BBC.

Davis's successor as story editor was Peter Bryant – a former actor and radio writer, director and producer – who had been trailing him as an assistant since around January. Bryant was also seen as a potential replacement for Lloyd; he had looked after the show while Lloyd was on holiday for a week in January, and it had initially been thought that he would take the role of associate producer on the series, and he was actually credited as such on some episodes of *The Faceless Ones*. At the same time as he took over from Davis as story editor, Bryant brought in a new assistant of his own, namely his friend Victor Pemberton (who had previously had a small acting role in *The Moonbase*, at a time when he was working as a bit-part player while trying to obtain commissions as a writer).

The fourth season had been, all things considered, a successful one for *Doctor Who*. A critical change of lead actor had been well accomplished; a period of experimentation had led to the development of an effective new format; and, with the arrival of Jamie in *The Highlanders* and Victoria (Deborah Watling) in *The Evil of the Daleks*, two promising new companion characters had been introduced in place of Polly and Ben, who had made their final appearance in *The Faceless Ones*, a decision having been taken – apparently by Head of Serials Shaun Sutton – to write them out earlier than originally intended. The changes overseen by Lloyd and Davis had, in short, revitalised the series, which had won an increase in ratings from an average of around five million viewers per episode at the start of the season to an average of around seven million at the end, and an accompanying rise of around ten percentage points in its average audience appreciation figure, which now hovered at around the fifty-five mark. The task that Lloyd and Bryant faced for the fifth season was to consolidate and build upon that success.

Throughout this period, Lloyd remained keen to move on from the series, and it was not entirely coincidental that for the season opener, *The Tomb of the Cybermen* (which was actually made as the last story of the fourth production block), Bryant was temporarily elevated to the position of producer, while Pemberton took the story editor's credit. As Bryant later recalled, this came about after he simply asked Lloyd if could handle a story by himself:

'Innes knew that I wanted to be a producer, and by then I had a pretty solid background in the business, one way and another. I had all the qualifications one needs to be a producer. I'd done it all. So Innes said, "Yes, fine, sure". I think he may also have felt that since he wanted to leave the series at that point, if he had someone ready to take over from him, it would be a lot easier.'

The Tomb of the Cybermen was generally adjudged a great success within the BBC – Bryant recalls that Sydney Newman actually phoned him after the first episode was transmitted to say how much he had enjoyed it – but, nevertheless, the start of the fifth production block saw Lloyd continuing in the post of producer while Bryant reverted to story editor and Pemberton to uncredited assistant. Lloyd was still looking to leave the series at the earliest opportunity, however, and actively grooming Bryant as his successor.

One significant move that the two men made at this point was to start commissioning longer stories. During the previous production block, all but three of the stories had been in four episodes; for this one, six episodes was adopted as standard. The production team recognised that this extended length allowed for greater character development and a slower build up of suspense in the stories, but their motivation was nonetheless more financial than artistic. They knew that the fewer stories there were per season, the greater the proportion of the overall budget that could be allocated to each, and thus the higher the quality of the sets, costumes, visual effects and so on that could be obtained. The severe restriction of resources that had limited what could be achieved in the realisation of some of the stories of the fourth production block – most obviously those such as *The Underwater Menace* that had departed from Davis's favoured approach of having the action centred around a single main set and involving a relatively small cast – was therefore largely avoided during the fifth.

Location filming was also more affordable now, although the series' tight schedule still meant that only the first story to be made in the block could be accorded a major shoot; a whole week was spent in Snowdonia, North Wales, filming the exterior scenes for *The Abominable Snowmen*.

Another notable feature of the fifth production block was its conspicuous lack of Daleks – previously a staple ingredient of the series. Lloyd and Bryant did at one point toy with the idea of commissioning a story featuring both them and the Cybermen, but this was quickly vetoed by their creator, Terry Nation. Nation still harboured some hope of winning backing in the USA for the production of a separate series devoted to the Daleks (having failed to secure this from the BBC in discussions during 1966), and so in any case was unprepared to have them appearing in *Doctor Who* for the time being. It was this fact that had led to the development of the storyline in *The Evil of the Daleks* that had culminated in their apparent destruction at the end of the fourth season.

The unavailability of the Daleks left something of a vacuum, which the production team filled both by placing an increased reliance on the Cybermen – the series' second most popular monster race – and by taking steps to introduce a whole host of new creatures that they hoped would prove equally successful – an aim they came close to achieving with the Yeti and the Ice Warriors.

The Enemy of the World was Lloyd's last story as *Doctor Who*'s producer, as he had finally been granted his wish to move on to other projects. As planned, Bryant then took over from him. Pemberton, however, had by this time become aware that he was not cut out for the story editor's job, and had returned to freelance writing. That post consequently went instead to newcomer Derrick Sherwin, who had previously been an actor and a freelance writer. Terrance Dicks – another young freelance writer, who had previously worked for an advertising agency – was meanwhile invited by Sherwin, an acquaintance of his, to come in as a new assistant story editor.

'Sherwin had written to Shaun Sutton,' recalls Bryant, 'and Shaun had seen him and spoken to me about him. He'd said that there was this guy – an actor who'd done some writing as well – who wanted to come into the Beeb and work as a story editor, and would I like to meet him? So I did, and I said okay.'

It was in fact quite common for Sutton to put forward to the *Doctor Who* office the names of people that he thought might be suitable to work on the series – particularly directors.

'Shaun tried to encourage us to take people who possibly weren't getting the sort of beginnings or not getting quite as much work as they should have been. A lot of the first timers who came in, he wanted me to give 'em a go – and I did.'

The end of the fifth season saw another change occurring in the series' regular cast of characters. *Fury from the Deep* was Victoria's last full story (Watling having decided to bow out at this stage), and *The Wheel in Space* introduced a replacement in the person of Zoe Heriot (Wendy Padbury).

The making of season six was dogged by a number of behind-the-scenes problems. During this period, Bryant and Sherwin both became involved with other projects – perhaps most notably the military drama *S P Air*, produced by Bryant and written and co-produced by Sherwin, of which two pilot episodes were made in July and August 1969 and transmitted in November 1969 – and so were unable to give their full, undivided attention to *Doctor Who*.

On the scripting side, late changes were made to the number of episodes allocated both to *The Dominators* and to *The Mind Robber* (the former of which went out under the pseudonym Norman Ashby after writers Mervyn Haisman and Henry Lincoln demanded that their names be removed from it); and three of the seven transmitted stories – *The Krotons*, *The Space Pirates* and *The War Games* – were last minute replacements for others that had fallen through. The season did nevertheless achieve a far greater variety of settings and plots than the previous one, which had been largely Earthbound and, with its heavy reliance on the 'isolated group of humans infiltrated and attacked by alien monsters' scenario, somewhat formulaic. As opposed to the previous season, this time there were only three stories – *The Invasion*, *The Krotons* and *The Seeds of Death* – that could really be considered traditional monster tales. Again, however, this was not so much an artistic decision as a matter of economic necessity. Although the production team continued to spread the series' costs as far as possible by commissioning stories with relatively high episode counts – including the eight-parter *The Invasion* – they found that the budget would simply no longer run to creating large numbers of convincing alien costumes and environments.

Bryant was in no doubt that the commercial success of *Doctor Who* relied to a large extent on its monsters. Seeing that the first episode of *The Krotons* had gained an audience of nine million viewers, compared with an average of under seven million for some recent stories, he wrote a memo dated 21 January 1969 to BBC Enterprises bemoaning the cost of creating such alien creatures and explaining that, as he had no money remaining, the next six months' worth of the series had been planned with no monsters at all. His point was that if Enterprises wanted to be able to market the series, they should be prepared to make some financial contribution towards creating its most marketable assets. His memo provoked no concrete reaction.

Bryant and Sherwin had in any case concluded at an early stage of the season's production that *Doctor Who* was no longer working in its current format and needed to be revamped.

'I think people get bored with seeing monsters all the time,' says

Sherwin. 'They get bored with seeing funny planets and weird frogs and people with trees growing out of their ears. Going back into history as well – the historical bits were incredibly boring. The monsters were okay if you actually had a good monster, and the interplanetary stuff was fine as long as you had good models. But it was all expensive, and I personally felt that at that time it was absolutely essential to bring it down to Earth, to get the audience back and to make it a real show that they could watch; something that they could identify with.'

Bryant was very much in accord with this philosophy:

'I thought it was a good idea to do that, so that the kids could identify with what was going on. They'd know if a story was in the London Underground, because they'd know what an Underground station looks like. I didn't necessarily think there was anything lacking in the more fantastically-orientated stories, I just thought "Let's get back down to Earth again. Let's get somewhere where the kids can identify with the actors, with the characters".'

One of the main inspirations behind this idea was Nigel Kneale's three highly successful science fiction serials of the Fifties, in which Professor Quatermass and his scientific and military colleagues had been seen to battle a succession of alien menaces in near-contemporary England. In order to help meet his and Bryant's aim of remoulding *Doctor Who* in this image, Sherwin created the United Nations Intelligence Taskforce, or UNIT for short. This was to be an international military intelligence unit, established specifically to investigate UFOs and other strange phenomena, with which the Doctor could work while on Earth.

'The idea of it happening on Earth with real people who were involved in everyday lives was a good one,' asserts Sherwin, 'so I invented the United Nations Intelligence Taskforce and brought in some new characters.'

Having been impressed by the character Colonel Lethbridge-Stewart (played by Nicholas Courtney) in *The Web of Fear* – a story that had itself been somewhat influenced by the Quatermass serials – the production team decided (subject to the actor's availability) to bring him back as the commander of the British branch of UNIT.

'The character played by Courtney was a good foil for the Doctor,' observes Sherwin. 'A typical, type-cast, crass idiot from the Army, but nevertheless relatively intelligent and reliable and honest and straightforward. He was, well, limp.'

UNIT, with Lethbridge-Stewart promoted to Brigadier, made its debut in *The Invasion*; and, as Sherwin tells it, this was always intended as simply the first step in a process of moving towards a more permanent Earth-bound setting – something that he says would have happened even if Patrick Troughton had not made clear his intention to leave *Doctor Who* at the end of the season:

'The idea was always to bring it down to Earth gently and then to stay there for a long period of time. Quite apart from dramatic considerations, another factor was that budgets were being cut and we were being asked to do more. Don't forget that we were going from black and white into colour, which was an expensive exercise, and we had to have a run of productions that we could afford. We couldn't keep on creating spaceships and monster suits all over the place and going out to the back end of nowhere to film alien planets – it just wasn't on, with the financial restrictions that existed.'

By the time of the making of *The Invasion*, Sherwin had effectively become co-producer of *Doctor Who* with Bryant, leaving Dicks to take over as script editor (as the post of story editor had now been renamed). A young writer named Trevor Ray was later brought in to replace Dicks as assistant script editor. Bryant himself was now becoming less and less actively involved with *Doctor Who*, as he was in ill health.

Bryant's last credit as producer of *Doctor Who* was on *The Space Pirates*, for which Sherwin temporarily returned to script editing duties while Dicks was busy co-writing *The War Games* with Malcolm Hulke. The producer's credit on the latter story then went solely to Sherwin. At the beginning of October 1969, Bryant, Sherwin and Ray would all move on to troubleshoot an ailing BBC series entitled *Paul Temple*.

The conclusion of *The War Games*, with the Doctor being captured by the Time Lords and sentenced to a period of exile on Earth, was specifically designed to usher in the new format that Sherwin and Bryant had devised for *Doctor Who*. It was not to be until the following season, however, that that new format would finally come to fruition. The original intention had been that Bryant would return as producer for that season. In the end, however, he would be involved with only its first two stories and would then devote his time fully to *Paul Temple*. The producer's credit on the first story of the seventh season would go to Sherwin, and that on the second to Bryant's eventual successor – Barry Letts.

Visual Effects

Visual effects is an aspect of *Doctor Who*'s production that has always attracted particular attention. Sometimes this has taken the form of derogatory remarks and mocking comments, but from more well-informed commentators there has been a recognition that, given the technical and financial constraints within which it was made, the series overall actually achieved very high standards in this area. It was often, indeed, a pioneer of new visual effects techniques within television.

At the series' inception back in 1963, responsibility for its visual effects was assigned not to the BBC's own Visual Effects Department – which had been established as a separate unit within the Design Department in 1954 and cut its teeth on the controversial Nigel Kneale adaptation of Orwell's *1984* starring Peter Cushing – but to the scenic designers. Barry Newbery, who designed the first story, *100,000 BC*, explains how this somewhat surprising state of affairs came about:

'The original producer, Verity Lambert, had approached the Visual Effects Department at an early stage to see if they wanted to handle the series' visual effects work – of which there was obviously going to be quite a lot – but they'd said that they couldn't do it unless they had four more staff and an extra four thousand square feet of space. The powers-that-be weren't prepared to go along with that, and so it was declared that the set designers would have to be their own visual effects designers. The only exception was where fire or explosives were concerned, which is why the Visual Effects Department received a credit on *100,000 BC*.

'This wasn't just a case of political manoeuvring by Visual Effects to avoid getting involved with the series. Jack Kine and Bernard Wilkie, who ran the Department, weren't like that at all. They were really enthusiastic about their work, and I'm sure they would have loved to have done *Doctor Who*. I mean, they may have exaggerated their requirements a bit – and seen this as a good opportunity to boost their resources – but they certainly couldn't have coped with their existing resources.

'Mind you, in later years, when the Visual Effects Department got bigger, the situation changed, and I think there was a good deal of jealousy then. Their people were understandably keen to get in on the act!'

Raymond Cusick, the other principal designer for the series' first season and the man responsible for the Daleks' distinctive appearance, puts his own perspective on this:

'When the idea of *Doctor Who* was first put forward, Jack Kine, the Head of the Visual Effects Department, said that he would need three more visual effects designers to cope with the extra workload of doing the show. He was told that he couldn't have them, so he said, "Right, I don't want anything to do with it. The whole thing goes out to contract, to Shawcraft Models in Uxbridge". He was basically being obstructive. His assistant, a chap called Bernard Wilkie, was more helpful. I used to go and ask his advice on bangs and explosions, how we could do that sort of thing – because what happened was that Barry Newbery and I, although we had been booked simply to design the sets, ended up having to design the visual effects and the special props as well. Our workload was doubled! Having to go backwards and forwards checking sets was one thing, but having also to run off down to Uxbridge all the time to check with Bill Roberts, the manager of Shawcraft, well … Bill Roberts was a nice chap, mind you, and very helpful. We were both stuck with the situation, and neither of us knew what we were doing, quite honestly.

'I'm sure Jack Kine – like everyone else, really – thought that *Doctor Who* would die a death, and that the constant demand for visual effects would kill it off within the BBC. He was quite right about the amount of work involved; he really would have needed the extra people. I think he got upset when the show was a success. This sort of thing often happens at the BBC: if something's successful, all the producers and heads of department step forward and claim credit, whereas if it's a wash-out, they all step back, push the others forward and say "You take the blame". I've worked on productions where I've never even seen the producer, but later, when there's been a big ballyhoo, he's been the one to go and pick up all the awards.

'The truth is that Jack Kine and the BBC Visual Effects Department made no real contribution to *Doctor Who* until about five years after it started. I've read Barry Newbery's comment that they used to take responsibility for scenes involving fire or explosives, but I'm not sure about that. In the first Dalek story, there was a sequence of the Daleks cutting through a door with oxyacetylene, and that was done at Ealing under the supervision of a freelance chap who worked for Bill Roberts. There might have been someone from Visual Effects standing by, overseeing it, but if so, I can't remember who it was.'

This situation had changed little by the start of the second Doctor's era: the series' scenic designers remained responsible for meeting the visual effects requirements of the stories to which they were allocated and, while the Visual Effects Department was now prepared to service some of the more basic and straightforward of these requirements, anything complex or ambitious still had to be put out to contract.

At an early stage in the production of each story, the director, usually in consultation with the designer, would go through the scripts and decide which aspects of them would need to be realised by way of visual effects. These requirements would then be notified to the Visual Effects Department. On *The Moonbase*, for instance, director Morris Barry's production assistant Desmond McCarthy sent to Jack Kine the following memo dated 2 January 1967 and headed 'Visual Effects: "Return of the Cybermen"' (*The Return of the Cybermen* being the story's working title):

As spoken to your office, herewith list of visual effects:

EPISODE 1:

Page 4:	Models
" 19:	Meter needle flicks
" 23:	Electronic box – hospital
" 29:	Spark from Cyberman

EPISODE 2:

Page 10:	Oscilloscope

EPISODE 3:

Page 1:	Cyberman weapon?
" 2:	Smoke from man
" 20:	Model
" 25:	Squirt jets (studio)
	Chest units disintegrating (film)
" 29:	Weapon (as page 1) (film)
" 32:	Bottle bursts on Cyberman's chest unit
(film)	

EPISODE 4:

Page 6-7:	Bazooka (also 3/37) (film)
" 14-16:	Dot on monitor (film)
" 26:	Boiling fluids, exploding bottles
" 30:)	Laser torches
" 33:)	
" 37:	Saucer model

Scripts enclosed.

In subsequent discussions, it was decided that the oscilloscope effect proposed for the second episode should be dispensed with and that the shots of boiling fluids and exploding bottles destined for the fourth should be accomplished on film rather than in the recording studio. It was also established which of the effects could be handled internally by the Visual Effects Department and which would have to be bought in from an outside contractor – in this case, one of the series' regular suppliers, Bill King of Trading Post Ltd. On 12 January, McCarthy wrote to King at Trading Post's Factory Yard premises on the Uxbridge Road in London to detail what the commission involved:

> This is to confirm that we require the following visual/pyrotechnic effects for the above programme as discussed with our designer Colin Shaw:
>
> 1) Two Cyberman chest units to 'disintegrate/smoke' when fired upon by fire extinguisher – for film on 18 and 19 January and studio, episode three, on 18 February (discuss with designer how much needed for studio)
>
> 2) Bottle (from fire extinguisher) thrown at chest unit (as above) to burst and destroy it. For film on 18 January.
>
> 3) Smoke pours from the openings in man's clothes resulting from being fired upon by Cyberman's 'weapon' for studio, episode three, on 18 February (discuss with designer and wardrobe supervisor Miss Sandra Reid).

The series' continued reliance on outside contractors to meet requirements of this sort occasionally gave rise to problems. These came to a head during the filming of model shots for *The Faceless Ones*. Director Gerry Mill subsequently provided producer Innes Lloyd with a detailed note setting out what he considered to be a number of shortcomings in the work carried out for that filming by Shawcraft:

> *POINTS CONCERNING SHAWCRAFT*
>
> 1. The actual making of the aircraft was satisfactory, but when one is told that they are professionals and advised to use their staff to suspend and animate the model, one would have expected them to work out the suspension of the aircraft and the strength of the wires holding the model. They had done neither, and when at one point the model

was left suspended on one wire, the model fell and was broken. As it happened, they were able to mend it overnight and it did not hold up filming, as the aircraft shots had been completed for the day, but this need not have been the case.

2. As to the satellite, they knew this had to be flown, and once again we assumed they would give the matter some thought. We were amazed, however, to find their two suggested methods of suspension were:

a) an 'L' shaped tubular piece of scaffolding and

b) five or six strands of nylon thread, which was by no means a certified safe way of suspending the satellite and certainly from a filming point of view was completely unusable.

Eventually it was necessary, having used the scaffolding system, to take all light off the top of the model, thereby losing the whole effect of the satellite flying in space.

As to the finish of the satellite, the top section was reasonable, but the one and only working section, i.e. the 'bomb doors', was made of three-ply, which had neither been sand-papered nor sealed, and a MCU [i.e. medium close up shot] was taken of the doors opening, which has in fact proven to be unusable.

One's main complaint is that the Corporation appears to pay a large amount of money to Shawcraft for which one would expect a professional service, which is not forthcoming. Another small point, but very important nevertheless, is that at no time did they produce spare parts – e.g. when a lamp blew at the base of the satellite, at the end of a very frustrating day (i.e. waiting two and a half hours for the satellite to be slung), we then had to wait another half hour while the house electrician tried to find a suitable lamp!

This is not for my money a professional attitude. In addition, it is to be taken into consideration that we pay out of our budget an extra fee to the staff of Shawcraft to operate their special models (approx. £40 per day).

In addition, there is the added irritation that when a minor prop, for example the ray gun, was damaged on filming, there were no facilities for collecting or delivering the repaired ray gun from Shawcraft – and in fact there was a delay of three days, Shawcraft being 36 miles out of central London.

As a general point, it would seem to me that no one firm can be expected to make all the varying types of models that are needed for a programme like 'Doctor Who'.

Lloyd sent a copy of this note to Kine under cover of the following memo dated 17 March 1967:

On the serial being filmed at the moment – KK – the director, Gerry Mill, went to considerable trouble to find an aeroplane model making firm as he wanted a) to produce a more specialised model than Shawcraft b) at a more economical price. I understand that he consulted you about it and that Shawcraft were eventually given the order. At Ealing, due to mishandling by Shawcraft's men, shooting in the morning was held up two and a half hours and the first shooting in the afternoon was at five o'clock – added to which the model which was suspended was too heavy and fell, thus being damaged in consequence. Due to all these troubles, it was necessary to reshoot the model scenes today.

Whereas I understand that they give 'Doctor Who' a regular service, there have been gathering complaints recently by directors that their services are time consuming – things not working – or that their prices are exorbitant for the job they do. Is there a reason why we are not allowed to shop around to get better value for our money (we may not achieve this – but certainly in Gerry Mill's case he *found* such a company who were willing and able to provide the exact sort of model effect for the money he could afford from his budget)?

As far as cost is concerned, the MACRA – the monster featured in our current serial – cost £500+, the same price as a cheap car. It can be seen in studio on this Saturday or Saturday 25 March and I fail to see how the cost can be anything like the price they are asking.

The reshooting of the model scenes on 17 March, referred to by Lloyd in his memo, was abortive, and a further reshooting was scheduled for 11 April. On 21 March, Mill's production assistant Richard Brooks sent a letter to Bill Roberts setting out with the aid of a diagram a number of detailed improvements that the production team would like to see made to the satellite model. These were as follows:

> 1. A smoke feed (from smoke gun) through black piping (diameter to be decided) to be fed into satellite via one of the low arms near the base.
>
> 2. *Flying*: Satellite to be suspended by wire hawser (as thin as possible allowing for weight of satellite). Hawser to be painted with a black matt finish. *Very* thin wires to be attached to the ends of the other three arms and run through screw eyes on the floor to minimise swing of satellite.
>
> 3. 'Bomb doors' at base to be thoroughly refurbished, i.e. given a bright *metallic*, very smooth sheen – *NB* they have to be seen in close up.
>
> 4. Flashing lights in base rim – these must be able to be wired to a dimmer in order to achieve a pulsating light as against an actual flash.
>
> I shall be coming along to Shawcraft on either 3 or 4 April and any further details can be cleared up then.

Following the problems encountered on *The Faceless Ones*, it was agreed that the Visual Effects Department would finally take over responsibility for *Doctor Who*'s effects work. *The Evil of the Daleks* thus became the first story on which their designers received a credit since *100,000 BC*. The significance of this change was twofold: it meant first that the Visual Effects Department rather than the series' set designers would now carry out all effects design work for the series, working on the basis of a Visual Effects Requirements form agreed by the director, and secondly that although outside contractors would still sometimes be used to realise particular effects (as indeed was the case on *The Evil of the Daleks*, for which Shawcraft provided a number of models), it would now be Kine's staff rather than the production team who would carry out all direct liaison with them and be responsible for ensuring that their work was of an acceptable standard.

Unlike in later years, when a single Visual Effects Department designer would generally take charge of all the effects work for a given story, at this point in time, a number of assistants would usually collaborate to achieve the desired results. Hence, although one or two of these assistants would nominally have lead responsibility, the on-screen credit would always be to the Department as a whole rather than to any particular individuals.

The assistant with lead responsibility for effects on *The Evil of the Daleks* was Michealjohn Harris, who has particularly fond memories of the climactic civil war between the different Dalek factions:

'I know we had an absolutely marvellous time in that battle sequence, and we even had two radio-controlled model Daleks. We had a giant Mother Dalek in the studio, with a lot of hoses attached to it. We filled these up with all sorts of horrible mixtures, so that when they blew apart, the hoses swung through the air spewing filth. I know it caused a strike among the studio hands afterwards, clearing up the mess. In those days, we didn't have a model stage, and all those sequences were set up at Ealing. There was a model of the Dalek city seen from the mountains above; we did that as well. Compared with what was done in later years, it was fairly amateurish, but the great advantage was that it was on 35mm film, so what we lost in being amateurish, we gained in quality. I remember we built the whole city in various sorts of balsa wood and so on, and flooded it with dry ice fog as an opening sequence. We got a sort of rippling effect. Then the first explosions took place, and they were quite nicely sequenced using lines of running power ... Considering the circumstances under which it was made and how early it was, I don't think it was too bad. It wouldn't stand comparison today, though. It's a museum piece.'

Harris also worked on the following story, *The Tomb of the Cybermen*.

'We built models of the cryogenic chambers and they were used quite effectively. We filmed the model sequences at Ealing, because it was the business of the deep frost disappearing and the Cybermen coming back to life, a slight movement, and so on; it was a case of building up more frost and then reversing the whole sequence on film. Then we cut to the full-sized set at Lime Grove. We had to sew two or three of the Cybermen up with various pyrotechnic effects; smokes and fizzes and flashes and things out of their machinery.

'A number of techniques were used all at once for the Cybermats. That's the beauty of television; you can do all sorts of things. I remember our heroes had gone to sleep and the Cybermats were crawling up to them. Obviously there is no way in which you can do that forward, so again we did it in reverse. It was very, very effective because, curiously enough, when you do a thing in reverse like that, it starts slowly and then darts forward as though it has sort of made an effort, creeps forward and jumps, and the effect is very, very good.

'I've got a feeling we probably made about a dozen Cybermats. This was in the early days of television recording, when you weren't supposed to cut the tape – the tape was running on, so if you went from one side of the studio to the other, from one set to another, you ran like hell! – and I can remember very well, even to this day, running full tilt across the studio, holding the remote control in my hand, flinging myself down on one shoulder and sliding in on my shoulder and arm underneath the cameras to get to a control point. Oh, it was great fun in those days, it really was.'

This story involved some location filming for scenes in which a team of human archaeologists find the gates to the Cybermen's city.

'We did that in a grand quarry in Gerards Cross,' recalls Harris. 'We used a matte model; the gates to the city were matted in about six feet from the camera and lined up on a quarry face on the far side ... but of course you couldn't open the gates on that because you just got solid rock.'

The explosion that revealed the gates, though, was real.

'We had set up the charges quite early in the morning. We had pushed some of them down behind a great chunk of soft, gravelly sandstone, and there had been a delay – some reason why it couldn't be filmed – so we had gone on to do something else. The trouble was that, in the course of the day, with people walking past, the sand had dribbled in and dribbled in until it had filled the whole crack up – so it became a much more powerful explosion than was originally planned. It showered stone and sand and dust everywhere for miles!'

Harris's tasks for *The Abominable Snowmen* included creating the Yeti's metallic control spheres.

'The one that moved ran on two tiny trailing wheels, one single drive and one steering wheel that revolved around its own central axis. It was almost a complete sphere ... highly polished so that you couldn't tell whether it was rolling or not.'

The Yeti costumes were a joint effort between Visual Effects, who constructed the chest unit, and the Costume Department, who built the framework around the unit and covered the whole thing with fur.

'I remember the costumes being terrible things to wear,' says Harris. 'Awful. And the trouble was that there was filming in North Wales, and the actors inside them couldn't see their feet. They had to have three people to help them through each sequence! Terrible. The poor men kept falling down!'

Kine's resources were still very stretched during this period, and for season five's closing story, *The Wheel in Space*, it was decided that, in a throwback to the earlier system, all the required effects work should be handled by the set designer and bought in direct from an outside contractor – Bill King of Trading Post. It was however agreed that the extra costs that would inevitably result from this (given that such contractors naturally worked on a profit-making basis) would be underwritten by the Visual Effects Department rather than charged to *Doctor Who*'s budget. The same arrangement was then followed for *The Mind Robber*, *The Invasion* and *The Krotons*.

The *Doctor Who* production team were by this point becoming increasingly concerned with the situation. So too was the Drama Department's Chief Designer, Lawrence Broadhouse, who on 15 November 1968 sent to his boss, Head of Scenic Design Clifford Hatts, the following memo about the effects requirements for *The Seeds of Death*:

> The visual effects requirements in this 'Doctor Who' are extremely heavy and complicated. I have discussed with Jack Kine the situation arising from his statement to you that he cannot supply a visual effects designer at all, mainly owing to acute shortage of staff due to prior programme commitments and to sickness.
>
> The only solution he can offer is as follows: Bill King of Trading Post can undertake the work (I do not know if he has been told of the large amount required) but Jack Kine admits that King does not profess to design, although he says he has two 'designers'. The danger in this is that the scenic designer would have to devote considerably more time co-ordinating, if not actually designing, the visual effects than if an effects designer were allocated. But the scenic designer himself has a particularly heavy commitment in this serial.
>
> The whole situation is tricky because of the difficult type of effects required, and the large number.

Having considered this memo on the day that it was sent, Hatts noted:

> I agree with this memo and consider the situation extremely unsatisfactory and not acceptable to me.

Despite this, the effects for *The Seeds of Death* were eventually provided by Trading Post as Kine had suggested.

On 9 December, *Doctor Who*'s producer Peter Bryant sent the following memo to Kine about the effects requirements for the sixth season's last two stories, *The Space Pirates* and *The War Games*:

> I would like to request strenuously that the special effects in Serials YY and ZZ be serviced internally.
>
> YY is going to be complicated, and if not done internally very costly (even allowing for an underwrite). ZZ is a ten part serial, the last before the summer break in 1969, and again complicated.
>
> Both the shows are going to require a fair proportion of special effects *design* effort, and I would think too much for the set designer to be able to cope with in addition to his other work.

This provoked the following memo of reply dated 16 December from I Beynon-Lewis, the Head of Design Services Television:

> Further to your memo of 9 December and our telephone conversation, I am hopeful that the estimate to increase the staffing of Visual Effects Section will be presented to the Director of Television's Finance Meeting before the end of this month. At the same time, our accommodation problems should be considerably eased – at least on a temporary basis.
>
> Coming back to YY and ZZ in the light of the above, it is almost certain that we shall be able to cope with ZZ internally. YY we are not so sure about, since even after the establishment has been increased, we are still left with the problem of recruitment and training of new staff. We may be lucky in our recruitment – I hope so – but we must face up to the fact that training in our methods will still be essential. In the light of this, YY may have to be put outside, but I am asking Jack Kine to confirm this, or not, nearer the time.

In the event, it transpired that not only was the Visual Effects Department unable to service *The Space Pirates* internally, but Trading Post were also unable to undertake the assignment. This posed a considerable dilemma, which could eventually be solved only by having the design, construction and filming of the models undertaken entirely by freelancers. The designer from whom this work was commissioned was John Wood, who when previously employed by the BBC had been responsible for the sets for a number of Hartnell-era stories. The models were made by Ted Dove of Magna Models, and Wood then supervised the shooting of them by the Bowey Group's Nick Allder and assistant Ian Scoones at Bray Studios.

'That really arose out of internal BBC planning,' confirms Wood. 'At the time, an attempt was being made to convince the powers-that-be that there was a need for a new effects designer post within the Visual Effects Department – up to that point, you see, all the effects people had been at assistant level, and there wasn't a fully-fledged designer there. The scenic designer on *The Space Pirates* was Ian Watson but, mainly to help demonstrate the need for this new post, I was asked to go in and collaborate with the designer on the modelwork.

'I designed all the spaceships from scratch and had them purpose-built by an outside contractor, Magna Models. I wanted them to be clean-looking: simple and uncluttered, with sharp lines and angles. The models were quite large and detailed. The V-Ship, for instance, measured about eight feet across and had a transparent perspex panel at the top through which you could see the various levels and galleries representing the ship's interior. It also had hinged panels on the wings, which opened up to form launching bays for one of the smaller ships. I was particularly pleased with how that turned out.

'The actual filming of the spacecraft scenes was done by a firm called Bowey Films, and I went out to their premises in Slough to supervise it. I was asked by the director, Michael Hart, to handle these scenes due to the constraints of time.

'Bowey Films had been working on *Thunderbirds* with Derek Meddings and people like that, and they were specialists in their area, so I was able to rely quite a lot on their expertise.'

On 10 January 1969, Bryant sent the following memo to Beynon-Lewis:

> With reference to your memo dated 16 December 1968, I now gather from Jack Kine that it is not going to be possible to service ZZ internally, and on current form it rather looks as though we are going to be in exactly the same situation that we have been with Serial YY.
>
> With the greatest goodwill in the world, I really cannot accept a repetition of this alarming state of affairs, when, with the unavailability of Bill King, it became apparent that this programme could not be serviced either internally or externally, and days of very precious time were lost until Jack Kine was able to come up with a solution – and a very costly one at that as well. Had this been a programme

charge, it would have been quite impossible to have done the show at all, but being very properly charged as if serviced internally, the excess will be paid from a design source.

Serial ZZ is in ten parts and in its own way as complicated as YY. It is a very important serial since it will be Patrick Troughton's exit from the programme, and the last we do before colour. I would be most grateful for some thoughts on this matter. Filming on ZZ begins on 23 March 1969.

In the light of this protest by Bryant, it was eventually agreed that the effects for *The War Games* would, after all, be overseen by a member of Kine's team – namely Harris – although the majority of the work would still be subcontracted out.

'First World War battle scenes?' muses Harris. 'Yes, I did that down at Brighton on the rubbish dump there, just after they'd done Attenborough's *Oh! What a Lovely War* in the same place. I remember poor old Patrick Troughton being a bit nervous on that one, and laying down the law very strictly: "If he presses the button for that explosion while my head is above ground, I shall walk off the shoot and never come back!"

'There was quite an interesting control room in the studio scenes, which I can't remember very much about except that it had circular television screens. Funny, the details that come back. I've got a feeling that we built war game tables as well, with symbols on them. My goodness, the things that come back when you start to delve into the memory – things I'd absolutely forgotten about!'

The relationship between the *Doctor Who* production team and the Visual Effects Department continued to worsen as the costing of the effects work for *The War Games* became the subject of a heated dispute. Bryant's deputy Derrick Sherwin, who produced the story, made his feelings on the matter clear in the following memo of 17 March 1969 to Kine:

With reference to the costing of the special f/x commitment of the 'Doctor Who' serial ZZ, WAR GAMES.

Our conversations regarding the costing of these shows have been somewhat confused by your attitude towards the method of costing. As I previously mentioned to you in a memo (dated 6 March 1969), we have been working on the basis of our previous arrangement, i.e. that our special f/x programme costs shall not exceed the estimated cost of the show being serviced from within the organisation, whether or not we use external or internal services. This is a principle agreed upon some time ago and one which, to my knowledge, has not been superseded by any other arrangement.

On the telephone today, you were talking about 'new methods' of costing, and of applying these innovations to my show, Serial ZZ. This, it seems, is why the costs of this comparatively light show seem to be astronomically high! If this is the case, then I'm afraid I must object to these new costing innovations being thrust upon me at this critical stage of production. I am not arguing for or against this new system – merely the timing of it. If a new system is to be brought into operation, then I feel we need considerable advance warning. This we have not had. Consequently I must insist that our previous arrangement stands, and that we cost the show accordingly.

Our latest conversation regarding these costs, although your estimate dropped from the original £1500 to £900, is still to my mind well above reality. This is why, although I agreed to accept the latter figure as a basis for argument, I would like to see a *complete* breakdown of the f/x costing, so that we might judge each effect on its merit.

I'm sorry to be so insistent about this costing business, but on a show which has a very tight budget, I must watch every single penny that is spent.

I look forward to receiving the f/x costing breakdown from you.

This drew the following response of 20 March from Kine:

Thank you for your memo of 17 March. I have noted the contents and feel that in some degree I have contributed to your confusion by my reference to the new costing methods. As we stand at the moment, they are functioning *only* in Drama Plays, but will eventually cover all other productions. Basing the costings for 'Doctor Who' Serial ZZ on my original tariff, I enclose a breakdown showing actual external costings and internal costings.

Since costing is the purpose of this memo, I feel I must point out that over the past four 'Doctor Who's, Serials WW, XX, YY, ZZ, based on the internal-external differences in costing, the above four shows have cost Visual Effects £4,800. This shows that my own internal costing for *all* shows must have a built in loading in order that we can cover ourselves to pay for the difference in costing for all shows that we place to contract.

VISUAL EFFECTS BREAKDOWN FOR 'DOCTOR WHO' SERIAL ZZ

	Internal	External
1 Landing Stage, Control and Base.	£60 0s 0d	£140 0s 0d
2 Practical Stunguns.	£120 0s 0d	£265 12s 0d
4 Non-practical Stunguns.		
3 Battlefield Communicators.	£65 0s 0d	£130 5s 6d
1 Truth Machine.	£50 0s 0d	£110 10s 0d
4 Internal Alien Communicators.	£60 0s 0d	£150 0s 0d
1 Brain Washing Machine.	£52 0s 0d	£135 0s 0d
30 Map Symbols.	£22 0s 0d	£35 0s 0d
40 Magnetic Control Panel Symbols.	£15 0s 0d	£22 10s 0d
2 Perspex Maps for Cut-a-ways.	£35 0s 0d	£91 12s 0d
1 Sidrat Control Panel.	£15 0s 0d	£25 0s 0d
1 Fireplace Control Panel.	£32 0s 0d	£58 10s 0d
4 Gas Bottles and Valves.	£27 0s 0d	£60 0s 0d
Sonic Screwdriver Sequence.	£36 0s 0d	£59 15s 0d
Stop Motion Filming and Box.	£40 0s 0d	£95 10s 0d
Location Filming Battle Sequence.	£120 0s 0d	£200 0s 0d
Safe Explosion + 2 (effects).	£10 0s 0d	
	——————	——————
	£759 0s 0d	£1,579 4s 6d
Contingency for Repairs over Serial (10 part)	£100 0s 0d	
——————————		
Internal Total with Uplift	£920 0s 0d	£1,579 4s 6d
——————		
Difference to be paid by Effects	£659 4s 6d	

Sherwin wrote back to Kine later the same day:

Thank you for your memo of 20 March. I note your remarks concerning costing, but find your second paragraph still somewhat confusing.

If all shows are to have a built in loading to overcome the effects of your differences in costing, why then should this particular serial appear to cost far more in comparison with previous shows? Your costing breakdown appears to be comparatively reasonable with the exception of one or two individual items.

(1) *2 practical stun guns* at £120!? At £60 apiece this seems quite ridiculous! How can they cost this much internally?

(2) *4 gas bottles and valves* cannot cost £6 or £7 each!

(3) *Stop motion filming and Box*: We were assured that this would cost us merely the price of the box plus the stock! This surely can't come to £40!?

(4) *Location filming battle sequence*: Again, the price you personally gave us of £60 – how come it is now £120!?

These are the four items that immediately strike me. I have not in fact had time to go through your costing breakdown in detail. However, it does strike me that all costings are above average by 10% at least, and that this show is being *'loaded'* quite unfairly.

Despite your protestations that this set of shows is being treated on the basis of previous costing methods, I am still convinced that it is unrealistic. What, for instance, do you mean by *'uplift'*? The estimate of £100 for repairs to sf/x during the serial seems quite outrageous.

It does seem to me that if we are to agree on a final figure and cease argument, you could quite safely drop your estimates by at least £150 to £200 and still come out on the right side, despite your *'uplift'*!

I sincerely hope we can come to some mutually acceptable arrangement over this issue, and if you can review your estimate and bring it to within £700 to £750, we shall have no difficulty in reaching an agreement.

During the next two weeks I shall be away on location filming for this set of 'Doctor Who' stories. However, any comments or reaction to my suggestions will be communicated to me via my secretary. Should your reactions necessitate an immediate meeting, I shall of course return to London.

A rare note of harmony was sounded on 31 March when Michael Hart, the director of *The Space Pirates*, sent Kine a memo praising the effects work on that story. On 8 April, however, the dispute over *The War Games* continued, with Kine sending Sherwin the following memo:

I have now obtained a copy of your memo of 20 March; for some reason I never received one.

However, in brief I feel the time has come to wave the white flag. I could quite obviously do 'Doctor Who' or any show for the cost of the materials, but where would the capital come from to enable outside work to be paid for? This particular costing has been undertaken in close liaison with HDS Tel and I feel that I must refer to him before proceeding any further. He is at the moment on leave, but I should be able to contact him on his return on Monday 14 April. I imagine his reactions will be communicated to you via your secretary.

Sherwin, having heard nothing further in the interim, sent the following memo of 23 April to Beynon-Lewis:

I have recently been 'fighting' a battle with Jack Kine re the costing of special effects for the 'Doctor Who' serial ZZ, 'War Games'. Jack has now called a truce and referred the whole matter to you – hence this memo.

To attempt to put this matter in a nutshell is quite impossible, so you must bear with me whilst I go into it in some length.

The costing of special effects for this serial was, I presumed, going to be based on our previous agreements with you, i.e.

that if Visual Effects could not cope with doing the show 'inside' then we should not suffer financially, as a programme, from it being subcontracted.

However, this previous agreement appears to have been overlooked. When I tackled Jack about this, he murmured vagaries about there being a new costing system to allow for compensation of monies having been spent outside on subcontracts.

This was new to me – and certainly to Peter Bryant. It would seem that we are being asked to pay far and above the cost of our special effects to accommodate this departmental malady. Can this be the case?

In the case of the serial ZZ, I feel justified in insisting that costing methods should be as we previously agreed. Having budgeted a show on this basis, I feel it would be extremely unfair and indeed impractical to change your mind mid-stream.

I have agreed with Jack that £900 should be a 'talking point' re the costing of special effects on ZZ. This is a drop from the original estimate of £1,500!! Even so, £900 is still excessive for the internal costing effort. It should be no more than £750 at most. He insists that this excess is a result of these 'mythical' new costing methods!

What I want to know is: Do these new costing methods exist? If so, what are they? Why should they be suddenly applied to us without warning? Do they apply to the new series of 'Doctor Who' being formulated now?

Peter Bryant is I know concerned about this new departure affecting his new series of 'Doctor Who' stories.

In short, I do feel that if there are to be new costing methods, we should be briefed before the event.

I shall be delighted to discuss Serial ZZ with you in detail if this be necessary.

Beynon-Lewis's response to this memo is unrecorded, as is the eventual outcome of the dispute over *The War Games*. In any event, this whole issue of the cost of external contractors would soon be largely overtaken by events as the extra staff and resources for which the Visual Effects Department had been pressing would finally be granted to them, and they would in future be able to service the great majority of *Doctor Who*'s requirements internally. Even with the Doctor's exile to Earth by the Time Lords, these requirements would remain extensive, and the Visual Effects Department would thus continue to make a vital contribution toward the series' successful on-screen realisation.

Rewriting the Myth

One of the most major developments during the Patrick Troughton era was the exploration of the nature of the Doctor himself. The first, and arguably most important, aspect of this was the fact that the Doctor could physically change his appearance.

When the Doctor's body succumbs to the ravages of old age (or, as the Doctor himself puts it: 'This old body of mine is wearing a bit thin') at the end of *The Tenth Planet*, a mysterious force from within the TARDIS aids him to renew himself. He falls to the floor of his ship and his features visibly re-arrange themselves. He regains consciousness as a more youthful man who shares few physical characteristics with his former self. This change goes beyond his appearance, as his personality and mannerisms also have been affected by the metamorphosis. As the new Doctor tells a sceptical Ben at the start of *The Power of the Daleks*: 'I've been renewed. It's part of the TARDIS. Without it, I couldn't survive.'

This explanation is, however, ambiguous. The TARDIS's role in the process is never made clear, although during the Doctor's transformation the ship appears to operate itself – the levers and switches move of their own accord – and the central column in the main control console falls and rises. It could be argued that the use of the word 'renewed' is evidence that the new Doctor is merely a younger version of the original. However, given not only the physical differences between the two incarnations but the shift in personality as well, this seems unlikely. The Doctor himself likens the change to that of a butterfly emerging from its cocoon, when he attempts to explain to Ben why his ring no longer fits on his finger. This suggests some form of total bodily change, rather than just a turning back of time, and implies that the Doctor could potentially change his physical form and abilities as radically as a butterfly is different from a caterpillar. The term that has become more commonly connected with this change in the Doctor's appearance – regeneration – was not coined until later in the series' history.

The new Doctor's nature strikes the viewer as being a great deal more relaxed than before. Aloofness and irascibility are replaced by an often childish yet friendly demeanour with hidden depths. This Doctor later states that he is 450 years old (*The Tomb of the Cybermen*), the first time that an actual age in human terms has been established for the character. We also discover that the Doctor's new form is the spitting image of the would-be

Earth dictator Salamander (*The Enemy of the World*). The Doctor therefore manages to impersonate Salamander with ease, but is just as adept at taking on the guise of a German doctor (*The Highlanders*), a gypsy musician (*The Underwater Menace*) and an Earth Examiner (*The Power of the Daleks*), not to mention his vocal impersonation of the Karkus (*The Mind Robber*). The Doctor had previously assumed various roles during his adventures, and so perhaps this talent was always present, however it is within the era of the second Doctor that it comes to the fore.

With the fact that the Doctor is not human firmly established, we also learn in *The Tomb of the Cybermen* that he has a family. It had previously been stated that Susan was his granddaughter, and so the fact of the Doctor having other relations should come as no surprise. It is not, however, made clear whether he is referring to Susan or to a wife or even to parents. It is also possible that the Doctor's familial reminiscences are merely to ease his companion Victoria's pain following her father's recent death, and there may, in fact, be no family at all.

Susan's whole nature is called into question by the revelations during the Doctor's trial at the end of *The War Games*. She is not mentioned during the Doctor's trial, and this seems strange: the Time Lords are concerned to bring the Doctor to justice for his apparent interference in history, but appear happy to allow Susan to affect Earth's future development. One answer to this dilemma could be that Susan is not a Time Lord. Additional weight is given to this theory by the fact that, in the light of the Time Lords' longevity and ability to renew themselves, the Doctor's decision to leave Susan on Earth to marry the resistance fighter David Campbell in *The Dalek Invasion of Earth* seems in hindsight rather heartless. First, he would have known that she would outlive her future husband by centuries; and, secondly, without the TARDIS to aid her renewal, she would be condemned to die the first time she underwent this process.

Further revelations about the Doctor were to come, however. What had been shrouded in mystery from the very start of the series had been the reasons why the Doctor was travelling in his TARDIS in the first place. At the end of *The War Games*, we finally learn more about the Doctor's own people, the Time Lords, who had not previously been named.

We discover that the Doctor had the ability to contact his people whenever he chose to. The Doctor's reasons for fleeing his planet and its culture are also revealed. He simply became bored by his utopian world. The Time Lords had great powers but had strict laws against interfering with the affairs of others races. The Doctor therefore stole the TARDIS and left to see the wonders of the universe and to fight evil wherever he found it.

The Doctor's people appear to be very technologically advanced. We discover that they can live forever, barring accidents, can force a change of appearance upon another Time Lord, as they do to the Doctor, and that they can choose what their next incarnation will look like. The Time Lords also appear to have wide-ranging powers. The War Lord's and then the Doctor's trials are conducted without the aid of any visible control consoles: they can cause force fields to appear, can use a 'thought channel' to present images of what someone is thinking, and can affect the handling of a TARDIS at a distance. They are even able to remove a whole planet from time; and although they express a dislike of physical violence, they are ultimately prepared to erase life forms from history if their crimes are considered bad enough.

Along with revelations about the Doctor, his TARDIS too has several new facts established during this era. Up until this point, there had been only one ambiguous comment made by the Doctor (in *The Chase*) that suggested that he might have built the TARDIS himself; and Susan claimed to have named the machine from the initial letters of Time And Relative Dimension In Space. The Time Lords seen in *The War Games* also call their time machines TARDISes, which perhaps suggests, assuming Susan did devise the name, that she did so before her departure from her home world.

As well as previously established facts being confirmed – such as, for example, the ship's telepathic abilities, in that it can warn of danger by showing diverse images on the scanner (*The Wheel in Space*), and the use of mercury in the fluid links (*The Wheel in Space*) – other details are revealed, including the presence of an emergency exit out of the rear of the police box shell (*The Wheel in Space*), a power room (*The Mind Robber*) and a laboratory (*Fury from the Deep*) and the ability to present details of one of the Doctor's past adventures on the scanner (*The Wheel in Space*), this including events that the Doctor was not even present for and would therefore have no knowledge of. This could be explained as an extension of the TARDIS's telepathic abilities, which also allow it to show future events (*The Moonbase/The Macra Terror*) via the time scanner. Other minor revelations reinforce the invulnerability of the ship, in that it can temporarily survive being buried in hot lava (*The Mind Robber*) and that it has a special circuit called the Hostile Action Displacement System (HADS), which, if activated, will automatically move the ship if it is attacked (*The Krotons*).

At the conclusion of the Doctor's trial in *The War Games*, he is sentenced to exile on Earth, and Jamie and Zoe are, according to one of the Time Lords, returned to the point in time just before they started their travels in the TARDIS. It is also stated that they will remember only their first adventure with the Doctor. This can be interpreted in one of two ways: that their subsequent adventures with the Doctor never happened, or that they had their memories of the incidents wiped. The latter seems the more likely explanation. When the Doctor watches Zoe back on the Wheel, we hear the TARDIS leaving, suggesting that his companions were returned just *after* the TARDIS departed, presumably with them on board. Therefore the only way they would remember just their first adventure would be if the Time Lords had tampered with their minds. This idea is reinforced by the fact that Zoe has a vague feeling of having forgotten something important.

The Doctor meets his oldest enemies, the Daleks, only twice during this era, and not much more is revealed about them. In *The Power of the Daleks*, the Daleks on board the crashed spacecraft on Vulcan still need static electricity to move about, but the creatures are shown being created for the first time, and the organic Dalek mutants are somewhat similar in appearance to those seen previously in the season three story *The Daleks' Master Plan*. The Daleks that invade Earth in 1866, as seen in *The Evil of the Daleks*, are summoned by the use of static electricity, but appear not to need it as a motive force. They also have a time machine, with which they are able to transport the Doctor and Jamie from 1966 back to 1866 and from there to Skaro. In the Dalek city on Skaro, we see for the first time the Dalek Emperor – a huge motionless machine that sits within a mesh of pipes connected to the rest of the city. The Daleks manage to identify and isolate 'the human factor' – the aspect of humanity that has allowed the species to defeat the Daleks on numerous occasions. This discovery leads to the creation of 'the Dalek factor', a set of opposing impulses that, when introduced into human subjects, turn them into organic Dalek slaves. At the conclusion of the adventure, the Doctor manages to engineer a civil war on Skaro between Daleks that have had 'the human factor' implanted into them, and those Daleks still loyal to the Emperor. As the Dalek city is razed to the ground, the Doctor believes that he is witnessing the creatures' final end.

With the Daleks appearing only twice, other monster races come to prominence during this period – and none more so that the Cybermen, who first appeared right at the end of the first Doctor's era. The Cybermen develop significantly during the second Doctor's tenure – in particular in terms of their appearances and voices, which differ to a greater or lesser degree in each of their stories. These changes, however, are never explained or commented on in the dialogue.

The Cybermen who invade the Earth's lunar weather control station in *The Moonbase* are from an era subsequent to the destruction of their home planet, Mondas, and – perhaps surprisingly, given his change of appearance – recognise the Doctor. They make use of an effective neurotropic virus, and are able to hypnotically control human subjects. At some point, they have colonised the planet Telos as a new home. . It is in *The Tomb of the Cybermen* that the Doctor visits Telos and meets the Controller, a massive silver figure visibly different from his fellow Cybermen. The Cybermen are held in a state of suspended animation in their tombs by being frozen – a curious fact, when one considers that they have been seen to be capable of operating on the icy lunar surface (*The Moonbase*) and will later be seen active in space (*The Wheel in Space*). No explanation is given for this apparent discrepancy.

In later stories we see Cybermen being 'hatched' from egg-like shells (*The Wheel in Space*) and webbing cocoons (*The Invasion*). Various new weaknesses are also established for the creatures: along with being exposed to radiation (*The Tenth Planet*), their susceptibilities include being subjected to a gravity beam (*The Moonbase*), having their chest units sprayed with plastic solvents (*The Moonbase*) or liquid plastic (*The Wheel in Space*), being fired on by an x-ray laser (*The Tomb of the Cybermen*), having their chest units physically battered (*The Tomb of the Cybermen*), being subjected to intense electrical energy (*The Wheel in Space*), having pure emotion directed at them (*The Invasion*), and coming under fire from the mortars and shells of an army battalion (*The Invasion*).

Some variations on the standard Cyberman are also introduced. These included the Cyber Planner (*The Wheel in Space*) and the Cyber Coordinator (*The Invasion*), both of which appears as a computer-like brain, and the Cybermats (*The Tomb of the Cybermen*, *The Wheel in Space*), small metallic rodents that they use to carry out tasks of infiltration and attack.

The Tomb of the Cybermen confirms and re-emphasises a motivation for the Cybermen that was initially established in *The Tenth Planet*: specifically, to create more Cybermen by finding other humanoid species and altering them. Victims of this process include, in *The Tomb of the Cybermen*, the mute servant Toberman, who is partially converted into a Cyberman, including the replacement of one of his arms; and, as seen in *The Invasion*, the industrialist Tobias Vaughn, who has his body replaced, while his head, brain and hands remain human, and several workmen at Vaughn's factory.

Despite their humanoid origins, the Cybermen also need power in order to survive, and their city on Telos contains a revivification room, which can be used to 'recharge' the creatures as they emerge from hibernation.

The second Doctor's era spawned some other enemies that would go on to become part of the series' established myth. Perhaps the most distinctive are the Ice Warriors, a race of humanoid bipeds with reptilian scaly green armour who originate from the planet Mars. The creatures' bodies are a curious mixture of organics and electronics, including an effective sonic weapon mounted into their arms.

In *The Ice Warriors*, they have been buried in a glacier on Earth for many centuries, having left Mars in search of a new planet to colonise, as their own was dying. They are discovered around the year 3000 AD; and yet, in *The Seeds of Death*, set in the 21st Century, Earth is again looked to by the creatures as suitable for colonisation. Presumably as the first expedition had failed to report back, the Martians felt it was worth another attempt.

In *The Seeds of Death*, the Martians have evolved a highly ordered society; a caste system is revealed in which the Warriors, who in the earlier mission had commanded in their own right, are now commanded by unarmed Martians of smaller stature and with a different style of helmet. Above these commanders is a Grand Marshal.

There was a final element in *Doctor Who*'s mythos that was introduced during the latter part of the Sixties, and that was to form the basis for many of the adventures in the following decade. This was an organisation called the United Nations Intelligence Taskforce, or UNIT for short.

The seed from which UNIT grew was established when the Great Intelligence attempted a second invasion of Earth, as told in *The Web of Fear*, this time using the London Underground system as the means to attack. Leading the regular army during this adventure is a soldier named Colonel Lethbridge-Stewart.

Lethbridge-Stewart is a somewhat straight-laced army man, who operates by the book on most occasions. After his success at freeing London from the attentions of the Intelligence, he is promoted to Brigadier and placed in charge of the British arm of UNIT, a specialist force created to handle any future alien insurgencies on Earth.

UNIT has control of numerous pieces of impressive hardware, including jeeps, helicopters and a flying control centre. Their artillery contains everything from hand-guns to rocket launchers, and they appear to have almost limitless resources.

The creation of UNIT in the story *The Invasion*, together with the revelations about the Doctor, were arguably the most important developments during the second Doctor's era. They paved the way for the continuation of *Doctor Who* as an Earth-based adventure series, and introduced new regular characters into the format who would become almost as important as the Doctor and his companions themselves.

From Script to Screen
The Mind Robber

INTRODUCTION

This chapter presents an in-depth look at just one of the second Doctor's stories. In doing so it reveals the process of making *Doctor Who* at this point in the series' history and – a factor common to every story – some of the behind-the-scenes discussions and thought that go into a production.

The production chosen for this case study is *The Mind Robber*, a story in the series' sixth season in 1968. For our view of the production, we have turned primarily to director David Maloney, who recalls, scene by scene, the work that went into it. We have also had assistance from the main writer, Peter Ling; the designer, Evan Hercules; and the costume designer, Martin Baugh.

THE SCRIPTS

The Mind Robber started life as a story outline from Peter Ling, entitled *Manpower*.

Ling was a well known and respected television writer, children's writer and editor, who, with Hazel Adair, had devised one of the earliest television soap operas, *Compact*, and gone on to create the popular *Crossroads* series. He also worked on other popular shows including *The Avengers*, as well as productions for Associated Rediffusion and Lew Grade. The commission to write for *Doctor Who* was the result of a meeting on a train, as Ling recounted to *Doctor Who Magazine* in 1991:

'Terrance Dicks and Derrick Sherwin were working on *Crossroads* and *Doctor Who* at that time – although how they found time to do both, I don't know! During that time, when we were all commuting to Birmingham, I got to know them, and they suggested I write a *Doctor Who* story. My first reaction was, "Oh no, I couldn't possibly do that – it's not my cup of tea, and I don't know anything about science fiction." In the end, I did what must have been one of the least science fiction orientated stories they made.'

Of the initial ideas, Ling has only hazy memories: 'I outlined the vague notion of a planet inhabited by fictional characters, on the supposition that everything created has an existence of its own and must go on living somewhere, in some dimension of time, space, or thought. I suppose this arose from my own experience of soap-opera fans who have a strange kind of suspension-of-disbelief. They *want* to believe that somewhere there is a real Crossroads Motel. Sometimes we got letters from ladies applying for jobs not as actresses but as waitresses.'

Ling was commissioned on 21 December 1967 to prepare a detailed storyline and breakdown for a six-part *Doctor Who* serial, and the commission was agreed by his agent on 3 January 1968. Although the commissioning letter stated six episodes, Ling's initial, undated, breakdown was for the first episode of a four part story; and a letter of response from script editor Derrick Sherwin confirmed that Ling was indeed writing a four parter.

The original scene breakdown for the first episode of *Manpower* (which appeared as one word on the actual breakdown, although it also appeared as two words – *Man Power* – in other contemporary documentation) read as follows:

PART ONE: ANOTHER WORLD

The Doctor, Jamie and Zoe are travelling through space and time – there is a certain amount of friction between Jamie and Zoe, since he still misses Victoria and resents the newcomer who has taken her place. The Doctor tries to explain to him that Zoe's brilliant mathematical mind will be a great asset to them – her particular talent will be invaluable at plotting their course. Jamie is still not convinced, and when things start to go wrong, he immediately assumes that Zoe is at fault. The instruments are going haywire; Dr Who discovers that they are in the centre of a very powerful magnetic storm which makes the control of the Tardis impossible.

Worse is to come; first of all the spacecraft is lurching and shuddering badly, and then bits of it begin to disintegrate. This is no accident; they realise that some powerful force is moving in on them, and they are helpless to prevent it. Gradually the Tardis breaks up, and the three time travellers are whirled away into space, spinning off in different directions.

The Doctor tries to reach the others, but he too is floating in freefall, and soon he is alone – expect for a bright point of light that seems to be rushing towards him. It gets nearer and nearer, dazzling him with its brilliance, and he finally collapses.

Scene 2. THE FOREST

When he comes to, he finds himself miraculously unhurt, at the foot of what appears to be a tree, in a dense forest. But these are no ordinary trees; they are tall, smooth columns of various shapes, and he wanders through them as if in a maze.

There is no sign of Jamie or Zoe – he calls to them, and he can hear their voices in the distance, but cannot get through to them.

Suddenly he sees someone moving among the 'trees' , and finds a corner where he can take cover and watch.

The 'someone' turns out to be a strange semi-human monsters with a sinister, uniform appearance. (NB: The exact form of the new 'monsters' is obviously something to be decided in conference, but as a suggestion, what about a faceless head – a simple 'brain centre' – and enlarged, sensitive hands capable of 'seeing' or 'hearing' by turning towards a sound or an object like a radar scanner?).

The Creature is joined by some similar monsters; they are clearly a kind of army unit, methodically searching – and it becomes apparent that they are searching for the Doctor. They know he must be there somewhere, but they cannot find him.

The leader of the unit points his cupped hand at the trees, slowly 'scanning' the scene; and we cut to –

Scene 3. CONTROL ROOM

A TV screen picking up his field of vision, slowly panning across the forest. A man we cannot see – (over the shoulder shot) – is watching the screen; and he gives orders to move on to another area; they are not to give up their search until the Doctor has been found.

Scene 4. THE FOREST

The army obediently move away, and Dr Who emerges from his hiding place – to find himself face to face with s stranger; a man of about thirty, in 18th Century costume (leather coat, buckled shoes, Tom Jones wig) who carries a musket, pointed at the Doctor. He accuses the Doctor of spying – who is he? Where has he come from? The Doctor tries to explain as best he can; the stranger understands very little of the explanation, but is at least slightly mollified, and says that he's by way of being a sort of time traveller himself – his travels have taken him far and wide, ever since he was born in 1726.

The Doctor tells him he has to find Jamie and Zoe, and the stranger advises him which way to go, speeding him on his way with a warning that there are many traps hereabouts. Then he vanishes, as inexplicably as he had appeared.

The Doctor makes his way through the trees and is suddenly confronted by two of the army unit. They point their cupped hands at him, and we see –

Scene 5. CONTROL ROOM

As before, but this time the Doctor is picked up on two TV screens from the different angles of the two 'hands'.

The controller-figure gives his orders: 'Question him. You know the form of interrogation.'

Scene 6. THE FOREST

The two 'soldiers' fire questions at him – simple, childish riddles and catch-questions. Bewildered, the Doctor replies to the best of his ability – but when he tries to ask questions in his turn, the two figures will not reply. Instead, one of them suddenly produces a sword, and menaces him with it, asking: "What can you make of a sword?"

The Doctor is baffled, and the sword gets closer, the blade at his throat. 'What else can you make of it?' repeats the 'soldier'. 'Rearrange it!'

'S W O R D,' the other 'soldier' spells it out. 'This is your last chance – rearrange!'

The Doctor sees the sword lifted and poised to strike, and says desperately: 'S W O R D – well, it's an anagram of – of – W O R D S – *words!*'

And he lifts his hands to ward off the blow, only to find himself holding not a sword but a book – a dictionary … words …

'You have answered correctly. You may be a suitable candidate,' the 'soldiers' tell him, and move away.

It is getting dark now, and a thick mist is creeping up. The Doctor hears Jamie calling him, somewhere quite close, and thinks he sees him through the mist. But when he gets to him, he finds it is a lifesize cut-out portrait of Jamie. The mist is thicker, and there is an old-fashioned steel safe, beside a wishing well. The Doctor examines these objects warily; is this another trap?

Then, above his head, he sees two huge letters with diagonal strokes through them – an M and a T, floating in the mist; and between the safe and the well there is a giant hand, with a letter H in the palm, also crossed through.

The Doctor realises this is some form of rebus – picture-writing, as he called it when he was a child. He spells it out … 'Jamie' (the picture) – 'Mist', less the M and the T – that makes 'is' … 'Safe' … 'Hand' without the H – 'and' … 'Well' … 'Jamie is safe and well'.

And as he solves the puzzle, Jamie appears; another test has been completed successfully.

The Doctor is of course delighted, and Jamie wants to know what has been going on – where are they? The Doctor *[missing words]* expected here – they have been brought here as part of a plan, and the plan involves putting the Doctor through various intelligence tests, all of them involving words or a play on words.

They resume their search for Zoe, and hear her calling for help. They come up against –

Scene 7. THE WALL

A thick wall in the middle of the forest, with a heavy iron-studded door in it. On the other side, ZOE is trapped, begging them to rescue her. But when they go to open the door, they discover it isn't real – it's only painted on the wall. The Doctor says it reminds him of something – when he was very young … something is clicking at the back of his mind …

The door and the wall melt away, and there is Zoe, inside a huge glass jar, like a biology specimen.

'Got it!' The Doctor shouts triumphantly. 'When is a door not a door? When it's a jar …!'

And suddenly Zoe is free. Another test is over.

At least they are all together again; but the big problem now is where to go. With no Tardis, there seems to be no escape. Perhaps if they were to try and find a way through the forest.

Scene 8. THE FOREST

They set off together, but the 'trees' seem to go on forever. Jamie volunteers to climb one of them, to try and see from the top if there is a clearing anywhere. With their help, he shins up, & says this is a very odd pillar; the top of it is a letter 'E', like the drawn out letters in a stick of rock, only recognisable as letters from the end. In fact all the pillars are letters – we pull out and up and look down to see that our three travellers are in a forest of words; words on a giant page.

But at least there is a margin in sight in the distance – a way out.

Jamie climbs down again, and they head in the direction he tells them. They meet the 18th Century stranger again; he is more friendly now, and the youngsters take a liking to him.

He says he has been on this planet longer than he can remember, and he knows his way around. He explains to the Doctor that this period of initiation won't take long; 'they' have to test newcomers, so that everyone can be best fitted into the scheme of things. Who are 'they'? Oh – the master, up in the castle, and his assistants. There is really no need to be afraid of the Master – as long as you don't try to step out of line. Dr Who questions him about the 'Army' – are they human or electronic robots?

The stranger suddenly seizes up, and does not seem to understand. 'What army? I do not know what you mean.'

The Doctor tries to describe them – 'You must have seen them'.

But the stranger only says flatly: 'I cannot say more than I am given to know'. It is as if they were suddenly speaking different languages.

Then the 'Army' starts to come back; the Doctor hears them approaching, and asks the stranger to help them – to hide them. Our three heroes find a hiding-place, among the 'trees', and the stranger stays on guard.

The 'Army' moves in, still searching. The Stranger waits for a little, then turns to the Doctor's hiding-place and says calmly:

'You must have been mistaken. There are no soldiers here.'

At once the 'Army' rally round and encircle the Doctor and his companions, bringing them out of their hiding place. Jamie accuses the stranger of deliberate treachery – but he is bewildered and indignant. What soldiers? There are no soldiers.

The Doctor says 'Don't you understand, Jamie? He can't see or hear the soldiers. They are something he is not "given to know"!'

Sure enough, the stranger pleasantly wishes them a safe journey home and wanders off, leaving them in the hands of the enemy.

The 'soldiers' line up and advance, like beaters at a shoot, driving our heroes before them, until they reach the edge of the forest – now they have brought the trio out, it seems that their job is done. We cut to –

Scene 10. CONTROL ROOM

Where the 'Master' says approvingly: "Mission accomplished ... Now for the real test ..."

Scene 11. THE PLAIN

The trio are alone in the night. Where to go? Which way now?

In the distance they hear the sound of hoofs – galloping – coming nearer. A horse? No, not a horse; they see the creature at last, shining and white against the darkness ... A Unicorn. But no gentle storybook creature; its head lowered to charge, its sharp horn pointing straight at the Doctor – it comes on, faster and faster, and he is helpless to escape.

At the time that Ling submitted this outline, Sherwin and *Doctor Who*'s producer Peter Bryant were heavily involved in interviewing actresses for the part of the Doctor's new female companion to replace Victoria, played by Deborah Watling, who was leaving in *Fury from the Deep*, the penultimate story of the fifth season. The new actress was required imminently for the production of the fifth season's final story, *The Wheel in Space*. At this time a name for the new character had yet to be decided upon, and in his response to Ling's initial outline, dated 16 January 1968, Sherwin noted that he thought that they would gratefully adopt the name 'Zoe' for the companion. It therefore appears that this name was first suggested by Ling during early discussions about his story, or possibly by its inclusion in the outline.

Sherwin went on to give some suggestions and comments on the outline:

1) *Scene 1*: Before things start to go wrong with the Tardis, I think all three characters should be 'attacked' mentally, i.e. that they should suddenly start thinking and speaking erratically. The Doctor should be the last one to go 'under', insisting that they must all fight this

cerebral aggressor with all their might.

2) *Scene 2*: We discussed this before, but I think it is sufficiently important to reiterate. Is it wise to show the 'soldier' so soon? It is always better to use innuendo and keep the full visual impact of the physical threat until as late as possible, in this instance, towards the end of this first episode.

3) *Scene 4*: Gulliver should speak only phrases written by Swift – possibly only Gulliver's dialogue.

4) *Scene 5*: Another note we also discussed previously. It might be fun to use children as the Interrogators and not the early on 'soldiers'; then introduce a 'soldier' as the Warrior, but the 'soldier' could be an actual mythological or fictional soldier. Perhaps the Doctor should recognise this mythical image as part of the test. At the end of the test, the voice could be disembodied or perhaps actual words across 'ye silver screen'.

5) *Scene 7*: Zoe's imprisonment – they hear her voice behind the door on echo.

6) *Scene 8*: Gulliver: Once again, Gulliver should talk in Swift's actual words. Here maybe the Doctor could recognise him and also recall some of Swift. His questioning would fall down eventually as he runs out of quotes, hence Gulliver is unable to answer his questions concerning the 'soldier'.

These are my main points concerning the breakdown. Now for just an overall note concerning the actual construction and writing of the episode. It is essential to maintain the adventure element within the story, both particularly and as far as the visual aspect is concerned.

The Sets: As our studio facilities are at present limited, we must consider doing anything that isn't in the wood or on the plain, on film at Ealing. Therefore, the ensuing sequence in the Tardis, it's disintegrating and the noise within the Master's Control Hall must be considered to be part of our film effort. This will leave the entire studio free for the main body of the piece.

> Peter and I are very enthusiastic about the idea, and I
> suggest that you now go ahead and complete the
> breakdown of the three remaining episodes. When you
> have done that, we can talk further and proceed with
> the scripts if all else is equal.

Ling was eventually commissioned on 31 January 1968 to provide scripts for a four part story. Ling recalled that some of the ideas came, 'from my vague thought that Gulliver was a traveller outside the boundaries of space and time, and the idea of making him a real character. Having been a children's script editor for such a long time, I think I was soaked in children's literature and knew a lot about it.

'The central villain was "the Master", somebody who had been churning out boys' adventure stories. He was partly based on the famous Frank Richards, who used to write things like *Magnet* and Billy Bunter stories. I think he turned out more words than almost any other writer. He was also partly based on myself in a way, because for six years I wrote an endless school serial in the comic *Eagle*, so I was putting myself in that spot.'

Problems with *The Dominators*, one of the other stories for the sixth season, meant that that story, also originally conceived as a six part adventure, was reduced by one episode during editing of its scripts. This left the season potentially one episode short, and the production team decided to get around that problem by extending *Manpower* to a five parter. The problem was that there was no additional budget to cover this increase in length, so Derrick Sherwin took on the task of writing the additional episode himself.

'The only way to fill the slot was for me to write an extra episode,' Sherwin explained. 'But, because we'd already spent all the money, I had no sets, no visiting characters and no new monsters. All I had was a white cyclorama, lots of smoke, the three regulars, the TARDIS prop and what was left of the tatty TARDIS interior set – and out of that, I had to construct an episode. I also used some old robot costumes that I found dumped in a storeroom.'

These robots had, in fact, been created by designer Richard Henry for an episode of the BBC2 science fiction anthology series *Out of the Unknown* called *The Prophet*, which had been completed late in 1966 and transmitted on 1 January 1967. These costumes had therefore lain unused for over a year.

To create the new opening episode, Sherwin drew on his own idea of the TARDIS crew being attacked mentally before their arrival in the forest of giant letters.

Ling's four episodes were delivered in first draft (still numbered one to four) as follows: episode one on 26 February 1968 and episodes two, three and four on 26 March. Following the decision to allocate a further episode to the story, which was taken in late March 1968, Ling's scripts were renumbered on 4 April. On 7 April, Sherwin gained official sanction to write the new opening episode himself. On 22 April, the story's title was changed from *Manpower* to *The Mind Robber*, and Sherwin issued an internal memo informing all recipients of copies of the rehearsal scripts of this fact.

Ling's melding of fact and fiction continued as a theme throughout the scripts, and, upon receipt of revised drafts of episodes three and four on 17 April, Sherwin questioned the use of the character 'Zorro' – a black-masked and caped avenger created by writer Johnston McCulley for a serial called *The Curse of Capistrano*, which first appeared in 1919 in *All-Story* magazine – as it may have resulted in copyright clearance problems, and Ling's usage of the first verse of Walter de la Mere's *The Traveller*, for similar reasons. Ultimately neither was featured in the completed story.

PRE-PRODUCTION

The director assigned to handle *The Mind Robber* was David Maloney. Maloney had started out as an actor and had worked as such from 1954 until 1961. With a wife and a young child to support, he had then started to look for a job with more security.

'In 1960, I was working in the provinces doing repertory theatre, and I wanted something safer. I decided to join the BBC as a floor manager, and I rather cheekily told them that I'd done a lot of stage managing in repertory. I remember at my interview, when I was offered a temporary contract, they said to me, "Don't come in with the idea of ever directing. You will never be a director. Do you want to be a director?" And I said, "I want to work as a floor manager."

'After about 18 months as an assistant floor manager, BBC2 started up and I was promoted to a production assistant, a job that I did for the next six years. Over that period, I worked with a lot of interesting and exciting directors – both internal and freelance – and I gradually realised that some of these directors knew less about working with actors than I did. I started to think that maybe I could do this, and so when my chance came, I went on the BBC's director's course and started to direct. I enjoyed it. I got a lot of good opportunities to do costume work, as well as working on shows like *The Newcomers* and *Z-Cars*.

'When Shaun Sutton, the BBC's Head of Serials, said, "Do you fancy doing a *Who*?" I said, "Yes please!" and so I was allocated. This *Doctor Who*, *The Mind Robber*, was the first *Doctor Who* that I directed, although I had worked on the show as an assistant with William Hartnell. I remember that first episode was a sort of buffer episode that was shot on a white stage against a white cyclorama, which was difficult. We couldn't make coloured marks on the floor for the actors' positions. I can't remember how we resolved this, but we obviously managed it.'

Joining Maloney as director was another for whom this was to be a first – and, in this case, only – *Doctor Who*. This was Australian designer Evan Hercules.

'Originally I came over to England from Melbourne to work in the theatre, as I thought that that was what you had to do. This was the early Sixties, and I left Australia because there wasn't much scope left for me there designing in theatre and I had been told by quite an eminent director that if I went to London, did a couple of shows and then came back, then he'd give me a job instantly. So I headed off to London … where I stayed!

'At that time, the BBC was advertising for designers to work on BBC2, and I was lucky to be among the limited number chosen. We trained under Dick Levin, and one of the first things I did was *Doctor Finlay's Casebook*. As assistant designers, we were attached to a senior designer, and I was working with a wonderful lady called Fanny Taylor. Her voice would echo through the corridors of the BBC … a darling lady. I worked as an apprentice with her, and eventually took over her shows, which included *Doctor Finlay's Casebook*. It was fun and gave me a taste for the process of getting the designs together and the system of getting your ideas into reality. We'd learned this in theory, but doing it was another matter.

'Having worked in the theatre, for which all the designs tend to be three-dimensional, working for television was different, in that your work was seen in only two dimensions. Also, although we were working in reality, it was a compressed reality, where you had to try and bring over the feel of whatever the show was within the designs for it. We would interpret the reality into a number of symbols and images and then try and incorporate those in the sets and in the overall design.

'Working on *Doctor Who* was curious, because it presented me with a dichotomy. The story was set in a land of total fantasy, and so here was a chance to be extravagant and imaginative, but at the same time, you had to discipline yourself, because the story demanded specifics like a unicorn and Princess Rapunzel. I'd not done any science fiction before – and haven't since, as it happens – so this was a first for me, and was a great learning experience. The *Doctor Who* came up simply because it was my turn.'

The other key designers assigned to work on the story were Martin Baugh handling the costumes, and Sylvia James looking after the make-up. Both Baugh and James had worked extensively on *Doctor Who* before this point. Baugh had been responsible for the costumes for the bulk of the fifth season, and his designs for the show included the Yeti, the Ice Warriors, the redesigned Cybermen in *The Wheel in Space* and the Quarks.

CASTING

'My approach to casting was fairly standard,' explains Maloney. 'Particularly for young girls and boys, I would consider anyone put forward by agents, I'd go through *Spotlight* … see dozens of people for the parts. For main parts, I'd draw up a short-list. First of all, when you had some idea of who you might like to cast, you'd check on their fee, to make sure that they weren't so expensive that you couldn't afford them. This was done through the Contracts Department, and they'd tell you what the person was paid the last time they worked for the BBC. Sometimes you could afford to use an expensive actor if you made sure that it was balanced out elsewhere in the artists' budget by using a couple of less-expensive ones elsewhere. Then you'd contact their agent to check on availability. If the person was free, in the case of a well known actor, you'd send them a script. Then they might want to meet you to make sure you were all right, say, over lunch.

'Once, when I went to Scotland to direct a play, I was allowed only one hospitality meal on the production, and as I was about to engage Gregor Fisher – who is well known now for playing Rab C Nesbitt – I invited him to lunch. But he said he'd rather have a couple of pints. And that was the end of my hospitality allowance!'

For *The Mind Robber*, Maloney used only one well-known actor, Emrys Jones, along with Bernard Horsfall, who had played the detective Campion in 1959/60, while the remainder of his small cast were made up of newer, up and coming actors and bit-part players.

ON LOCATION

The location work for *The Mind Robber* was not extensive. There were two sequences that required the use of locations: one where Jamie clambers up some rocks to escape from a toy soldier, and a second where a white unicorn is seen to charge at the Doctor, Jamie and Zoe.

As was usual, the location filming all took place before any studio recording was started for the story.

The film was edited before the studio recording, and then transferred onto video by running it in during the recording breaks in each episode. One exception to this during this story was for episode five, all the material for which was, for reasons unknown, put straight onto film, in which form the episode was eventually transmitted. It is most likely that this was done due to the complex nature of the editing that would be required in the episode.

In order to transfer the electronic images from the studio cameras onto 35mm film, a Film Recorder (also known as a Telerecorder outside the BBC, and a Kinescope in America) was used. This was, in essence, a film camera that took pictures from a television screen; however, in reality, it was a complex, purpose-built device consisting of: a) a special high-resolution flat cathode ray tube (CRT) and shaped-filter assembly; b) a high precision clawbox to move, stop and position the film in an extremely short space of time; c) a high-quality optical system; and d) sophisticated electronics to synchronise the camera shutter to the television frame.

Film recording was the only way of preserving video material from around 1951 until the advent of the 2" video recorder at the BBC in about 1961, and it continued in use until much later. Shows that had a lot of editing work to be done in post production would often transfer to film because it was easier to edit than videotape (which had to be cut-edited until the late Sixties). Results were usually very good, with even 16mm systems managing to capture the full video bandwidth. Unfortunately, it is rare to see a first-generation recording, giving people the false impression that it was a poor-quality system.

IN STUDIO

At this time in *Doctor Who*'s history, the programme was being recorded at the rate of one episode per week. To indicate some of the considerations involved in making a *Doctor Who* story during the Patrick Troughton era, what follows is a scene-by-scene summary of *The Mind Robber*, with comments from director David Maloney and designer Evan Hercules.

EPISODE ONE

Standing outside the TARDIS, the Doctor and Jamie realise that lava from the volcanic eruption caused by the detonation of the Dominators' rockets on the planet Dulkis, is headed directly for them. They hurry inside and prepare the ship to leave.

The lava rolls over the TARDIS, and the fluid links start to overheat. The Doctor manages to stop the mercury from vaporising, but they are stuck. The Doctor suggests that he could use an emergency unit, which would move the TARDIS out of reality. He fetches it from a cupboard under the console and fits it to one of the panels. He hesitates about using it, but Jamie pushes the unit home and the TARDIS vanishes from within the lava flow.

When the Doctor asks Zoe to check the meters, none of them is showing anything. The Doctor goes to the power room to work on the controls, and when Zoe asks him where the TARDIS has brought them, he replies that they are 'nowhere'. Jamie and Zoe head off to change their clothes.

David Maloney: Because we were still making the programme almost as if it were live, with continuous shots, there are lots of tiny mistakes. There was a shot just now where we cut to a camera that wasn't quite settled on the TARDIS's monitor screen, and so the picture jerks as you see it ... Things like that. The vision mixer did all the cutting between the cameras. The model work of the lava was all shot earlier and played into the monitor at the right point. We also shook the camera to simulate turbulence as the ship took off. We did that a lot!

You can see how good Wendy Padbury is here. I didn't cast her, but she was brilliant. She had a sort of innocence. Simply marvellous. And Frazer was excellent for the children too. What's amazing is that Frazer's looks haven't changed in all these years. Witness *Emmerdale*. And I was a great admirer of Patrick. He was magical. In fact, after he had given up playing the Doctor, I cast him as an old sea-dog in a production of Fennimore Cooper's classic period story *The Pathfinder* for the BBC.

Zoe, who has changed into a glittery cat-suit, joins the Doctor in the power room. The Doctor claims that he isn't worried, and tries to warn Zoe not to go outside the TARDIS. He tells her they must stay in the ship.

DM: The instrumentation in the background looks as if it comes from an old electricity generating station – it probably did!

Evan Hercules: We just brought in a couple of extra flats to make the power room, and I expect the bits of electronic equipment came from Trading Post, a props company that was used quite extensively.

Back in the control room, Jamie's attention is drawn to the scanner screen by the skirl of Highland bagpipes. He sees an image of what he believes to be his home.

DM: The image of the Scottish Highlands was simply a caption slide that was mixed in at the appropriate place. The same technique was used for when Zoe sees her home. The slides were obtained from a company called G M Studios.

Zoe enters and the image disappears. Jamie is convinced that they have landed, and he checks the console, where there is a device that warns to go elsewhere if there is any danger. Zoe sees her own home on the scanner, but it too vanishes. They rationalise that they must have landed, and Zoe is all set to go outside. Jamie advises getting the Doctor, and goes to do this. When he's gone, the image of Zoe's home reappears and, calling for the Doctor and Jamie to follow, she opens the doors and runs out into a featureless white void. The image on the scanner vanishes.

DM: We were lucky on this serial, because we got the very best camera crew. Crew 5, run by Dave Atkinson. They were very, very creative, and that's something that we had on our side. The lighting co-ordinator, Howard King, was also splendid.

There's a lot of talk in this story, but I don't think that audiences at the time would have objected to talk. The point is that talk is cheaper than action and effects, and as *Doctor Who* was regarded as a 'children's' series, it was never given the budget it needed.

EH: There was no dry ice there, where she runs out. She just fades away. Very nice.

Jamie finds the Doctor and tells him about the images. The Doctor hurries to the control room to find that Zoe has gone. The TARDIS sounds a 'first warning' and, despite the Doctor's protests, Jamie runs out after her.

DM: If you look at the side of the shot there, you can see that the camera is locked off and there's a mix to make Jamie fade from sight as the Doctor comes into shot.

The TARDIS sounds a 'second warning' and the Doctor becomes aware of a presence in the ship. He sinks into a nearby chair and determines to fight.
   In a white void, Jamie and Zoe call to each other.

DM: The lighting for these scenes was excellent. Howard King managed to bleach out the background and leave the characters prominent without resorting to any electronic trickery. It's nice camera work as well.

EH: It's the camera crew again. When you have a good crew, they actively seek good shots, and the results are better.

DM: Crew 5 were a Plays Department crew, and we couldn't book them easily for serials. They were permanently 'not available'. But I'd worked with them as a floor manager on plays, and so I asked if they'd come and do this *Doctor Who*. They agreed almost as a joke. I can, however, see the quality of the camera-work in this.

EH: We had to use Studio 1 at Television Centre for this episode, because we needed the sense of space, and we also had to get the cameras a long way away from the actors.

[NB: Although both Maloney and Hercules recall recording episode one in Studio 1 at Television Centre, and episode two in a smaller studio, both are documented as having been recorded in TC3. The original recording was due to take place in Lime Grove Studio D, but this was changed at a late date, possibly to accommodate the large white set and distant camera positions that Maloney wanted for the opening episode.]

Jamie and Zoe find each other but realise that they are lost. They decide to call out to the Doctor.

In the TARDIS, the Doctor hears them calling, but believes it to be a part of the attack against him.

Jamie and Zoe start to feel that they're being watched; and, unseen by them, several robots (John Atterbury, Ralph Carrigan, Bill Weisener, Terry Wright) are closing in on them through the void.

DM: Those robots make a noise like a slowed down fart! I wonder what it was really.

Zoe and Jamie see their homes again, but resist the temptation. They suddenly see the robots approaching.

DM: Wendy was excellent at being afraid, at acting scared. She was a great screamer as well.

The robots cluster round the two travellers, and Zoe screams as she sees images of herself and Jamie, dressed in white, beckoning them away. The Doctor, still in the TARDIS, also sees the images, and mentally warns them not to go.

A voice (Emrys Jones) in the TARDIS tells the Doctor to follow them, but he refuses.

The robots aim their chest-mounted guns at Jamie and Zoe and open fire.

EH: The effect of the robots firing their weapons was created by simply spinning a wheel, on which had been painted a pattern of concentric lines, in front of a camera, and the vision mixer combining that image with the main image of the gun. It was done live, at the time we wanted the effect.

The voice tells the Doctor that there is still time to save his companions, and he realises that he can't let them remain in peril. He leaves the ship, and finds himself standing outside a completely white police box exterior.

EH: We had to paint the outside of the police box white for these scenes, and, when we'd finished, we had to clean all the white paint off again.

The Doctor calls to Jamie and Zoe, and he sees the white-garbed versions coming towards him, followed by the robots. He urges his companions into the TARDIS, and when they won't move and the robots open fire once more, he pushes them in with his hands.

Once inside, they are suddenly wearing their normal clothes again, and the Doctor closes the doors and initiates dematerialisation. Jamie settles down for a rest and Zoe apologises for going out. The Doctor tells Zoe about the voice he heard, but he can't explain what happened. Jamie hears a horse neighing in his sleep. The Doctor finds the power booster on the console and operates it. Jamie awakens from a dream about a unicorn.

As Zoe notes the power rising, the Doctor notices a buzzing sound that seems to be getting more intense. Jamie and Zoe become aware of it too. The Doctor tells Zoe to continue to read off the readings as the sound gets louder and louder. He slips into a chair and closes his eyes to try and fight off the mental attack.

The TARDIS, floating in space, suddenly bursts apart, and Jamie and Zoe are left clinging to the spinning console. They see the Doctor floating away from them, still sitting in the chair, as the console descends into a bank of mist.

DM: This was done in the model studio at Ealing. There was a model TARDIS and a model console and we cut between them and the real ones to get the effect. The smoke was overlaid on as well.

End of Episode One

EPISODE TWO

DM: Looking at this today, there seems to be too much re-capping between episodes; however, at the time, with a week in between, you could get away with it. The re-cap made up minutes of an episode that we had to take into account when timing the new story portions. We made the re-cap shorter or longer to adjust the overall time of the episode.

Jamie finds himself in a strange forest.

EH: The 'trees' were made from polystyrene, which was very expensive in those days. It was known by its trade name, jablite. It's a shame that you can't see that they're letters.

He suddenly spots a Redcoat (Philip Ryan) and attacks him with his knife.

DM: It's interesting here that Jamie has a knife. I doubt he would be allowed that in a serial like this today. The hero would simply not be permitted to carry such a weapon.

The soldier fires at point-blank range, and Jamie freezes into a photographic cut-out.

DM: When we started rehearsals for this episode on the Monday – each episode was rehearsed on the Monday to the Thursday and then recorded on the Friday – Frazer came in and said that he'd got chicken pox, and that they'd told him that he had to be in quarantine for a week and so he couldn't work. The first episode had been made, and so Derrick Sherwin came up with the very clever idea that in order to rescue Jamie, the Doctor had to make the face up from some cut-out parts, and he would get it wrong. He would build a different face, and out would jump another Highland warrior: not Jamie, but someone else. So we cast a substitute, a Scottish actor who simply played Jamie for the period that Frazer was not available. Then, later in the story, Jamie was again turned into a cut-out with a puzzle-face, and this time, the Doctor got it right and Frazer, having recovered from his chicken pox, took over playing Jamie once more.

EH: It's the sheer boldness of the idea as well. It's so full of interest, and an unexpected and interesting boldness.

Meanwhile, Zoe finds herself trapped by some castle walls where a door creaks open in front of her. Stepping through, she falls into darkness with a scream as the door closes behind her.

EH: I hired that door from Pinewood Film Studios.

In a control room, monitor screens show images of the castle door and the frozen Jamie. A figure (Emrys Jones) sitting before the screens, orders that the Doctor be found.

EH: We made the walls and ceiling out of mesh, as we wanted to get a sense of the galaxy around this fellow as he looks at his screens. The walls were a painted cyclorama cloth, and we also put a cloth over the top to give us a ceiling. The starfield was painted in black, blue and white. For this episode, we were in a smaller studio than for the first episode.

DM: The scenes being shown on the three monitors would have been fed through from the other cameras in the studio. We had five cameras available, and so the images from three of them would have been relayed to the monitors as the fourth camera shot the scene – notice it's all one take – and the fifth was positioned on Troughton for the following scene. All camera positions were plotted beforehand.

Emrys Jones, who played the Master, had been an absolutely first class juvenile actor in British films in the thirties, forties and fifties. I can't remember how I came across him, but I remember persuading him to take on the Master, which was really a character part for someone who had been a leading man in British films. I enjoyed working with him enormously, because he was a name and gave us such a marvellous character.

The Doctor awakens to find himself in the same forest as Jamie. He hears Jamie and Zoe calling to him, but he cannot find them.

Watching on the monitors, the Master requests that the lights be put on. The Doctor can now see what he's doing. The Doctor hides in one of the 'trees' as a squad of clockwork soldiers (Paul Alexander, Ian Hines, Richard Ireson) pass by, searching under the direction of the Master.

DM: Notice that the Master is wearing little devilish horns. I think that's the effect the producer intended to convey until we know more about him.

I can't imagine that we would have had the money to have constructed the costumes for the clockwork soldiers for this story.

When they have gone, the Doctor emerges, to be confronted by a stranger (Bernard Horsfall) who speaks an odd language. Settling on English, the Doctor makes friends with him after an initial misunderstanding.

Peter Ling: When I was writing the scripts, for the dialogue spoken by the stranger, I researched *Gulliver's Travels*. It wasn't something I knew backwards or anything, I just found the right dialogue. I did cheat a bit, however, and put together phrases quite unconnected in *Gulliver's Travels*. Most of the phrases were accurate, though.

DM: This was the first time that I cast Bernard Horsfall. I used him on two further occasions in *Doctor Who*, first as the Thal leader in *Planet of the Daleks* and then as the Doctor's opponent in *The Deadly Assassin*, because he was one of the few actors that I knew that was big enough to counter Tom Baker. I wanted a physical opponent who could match him. Here, playing Gulliver, it's interesting to note that all his lines are from the book, so whatever he's asked, he only quotes from the novel.

The stranger accuses the Doctor of being a traitor and claims that, by order of the Master, he is not permitted to help. He abruptly leaves.

The Doctor is suddenly surrounded by a group of children (Timothy Horton, Martin Langley, Sylvestra Le Touzel, Barbara Loft, Christopher Reynalds, David Reynalds), who shout riddles at him.

DM: The children came from the Barbara Speake stage school, and one of them was Sylvestra Le Touzel, now quite a well-known actress. I'd forgotten where I had worked with her. Then she mentioned it to me years later, and I couldn't remember her as the child.

Having solved the riddles, one of the children holds a sword at the Doctor's throat –

he realises it's another test, and rearranges the letters in 'sword' to make 'words'. The sword, thrown into the air, falls as a dictionary. The children run off.
    Jamie calls once more, and the Doctor finds the cardboard cut out.

EH: We took a photograph of Jamie and then blew it up to life size, which was something we used to do on *Z-Cars* quite a lot. We then mounted it on board and lit it so that at first you might think it was a real person.

The Doctor also finds a locked safe and a wishing well: it's a word puzzle, which he solves as 'Jamie is safe and well', at which point a jigsaw-type puzzle of Jamie's face appears. The Doctor completes the puzzle and Jamie returns to life, but with a different face (Hamish Wilson) – the Doctor got it wrong!

DM: One of the cut-up pictures of the faces on the puzzle was of me, one was of Frazer and a third was of the new actor playing Jamie, Hamish Wilson. I think the fourth might have been of the director Douglas Camfield. Hamish Wilson is now a well known radio producer in Scotland. He was an actors' union representative for a long time. Hamish has an authentic Scots accent, unlike Frazer, who had an assumed accent.

The Doctor shows Jamie his face in a hand mirror to prove to him that he has changed. They head off and, solving yet another puzzle, find Zoe trapped in a giant jam jar.

DM: That shot of Zoe in the jar was on film. In the studio, you don't actually see the glass jar at all – just the rim of it.

EH: We couldn't have done a giant glass, as it would have been too expensive to have created a large, curved perspex surface.

They rescue Zoe and try and find a way out of the wood. Jamie suggests climbing one of the 'trees' to see if there is a way out. He does so, and discovers that what they thought was a forest of trees is actually a forest of letters and words that spell out proverbs and sayings.

EH: I had a great deal of trouble with the forest of words. They were never really what I wanted. They never had the graphic quality that they should have had, because you should be able to see letters and words from above, and we were not able to pull that off.

DM: We couldn't see the letters. We couldn't get up high enough, because the studio was too small. We should have got the camera above the set – maybe using a mirror – and seen everything widely. We could do something better these days with electronic effects.

Jamie is, however, able to see a way out.

EH: We contrived that shot so as to get a low-angle on Jamie, while not seeing any of the studio ceiling. We rigged it so that there was a backing cloth behind him as the camera looked up.

Jamie descends and, as they move off, they once again meet the travelling stranger. The Doctor tries to question him, but the answers make no sense. The Doctor mentions the army of soldiers, but the stranger appears not to know what he means. They hear the soldiers returning and, as the Doctor and his friends hide in the letters, the stranger keeps guard. However, once the soldiers arrive, the stranger calls to the Doctor that there is no army present. The Master orders the soldiers to round up the Doctor and his friends. The soldiers herd them off through the forest of letters.
    When they arrive at the edge of the forest, they stop, and the soldiers vanish. The Doctor, Jamie and Zoe are left in a black void.

EH: The blackness was created with black velvet: on the floor and on a surrounding cyclorama.

Suddenly they hear a horse galloping and see a white unicorn coming towards them. Jamie remembers it from his dream. As the unicorn charges at them, the Doctor tells them not to run.

DM: We were assured by the property department that they had found a white circus horse for use as the unicorn. We intended to strap a horn on the horse's head. As we had such limited film time, we ended up at about one o'clock in the morning at an airfield south of Croydon on a very black night to film the sequence.

EH: The horn kept coming off. At first we tried to stick it on, but every time the pony shook its head, it came off. I can't remember how we ended up attaching it – perhaps by a strip around the pony's head.

Sylvia James: What we wanted was a white horse onto which we planned to attach a horn, which had been supplied by another department; and I had a small goatee beard to put on as well. When we got to this airfield in the middle of the night, the horse turned out to be a dark gold colour. Luckily someone had the idea of getting some 'blanko' from the RAF people stationed nearby, which was ideal as it was washable and would not harm the horse.

DM: This is a prime example of how we used to work in those days. We were so conscious that the thing wasn't working that, during the editing, we cut it as subliminally as we could, so that the viewer barely had a chance to see what was charging at the Doctor.

[The pony, whose name was 'Goldy', was supplied for filming on Sunday 9 June 1968 by Joan Roslaire of Willougby Farm in Essex. The hire cost was 50 guineas]

End of Episode Two

EPISODE THREE

The Doctor shouts to Jamie and Zoe to deny the existence of the unicorn, and it freezes into a cardboard cut-out.

DM: Of course, we couldn't get the unicorn and the actors in the same shot together, so the effect of it being there and charging at them was created through the editing.

The Master is watching on the monitors, and decides that the Doctor was 'a good choice'.
  The soldiers reappear, and the Doctor and his friends run off. The Master lets them go, as they have no way of escaping.
  The Doctor, Jamie and Zoe find themselves walking through a cobweb-strewn forest of twisted wood.

DM: I remember Evan being very clever with all this, and using the cobweb stuff. It looks quite nasty and eerie, and I remember being impressed with what Evan had done.

They come to a building where a Redcoat shoots at Jamie once more. The Doctor knows what to do, and re-creates his face – correctly this time – causing the real Jamie to come back to life.
  They enter the building, which is full of cobwebs and lit with candles.

EH: The spider-web there, with the spider in situ, was brilliant! We had a little wooden frame on which the web had been knitted. I think it'd been provided by Visual Effects. The idea behind the candles was a wonderful film by Jean Cocteau called *La Belle et la Bete* (*The Beauty and the Beast*), where there was a hand coming out of the wall holding the candelabra. These were very rich, rococo designs in brass. The effect of the candles being all melted down was achieved by us working with the candles beforehand.

The Doctor finds a ball of twine, and they realise that this is a labyrinth. Jamie ties the string to the door handle and they move into the maze, watched by the Master.

DM: The maze that the Master is looking at was simply a piece of perspex with three torches moving behind it to create spots of light.

The twine runs out, but Zoe believes she has worked out how to complete the maze. Jamie stays with the end of the twine while Zoe and the Doctor explore further. They eventually arrive at the centre of the maze, where there are piles of bones and animal tracks. Suddenly, roars ring out and the Minotaur (Richard Ireson) appears.

[The head of the Minotaur came from stock.]

Jamie hears the noise and runs to help, but is intercepted by a clockwork soldier. Realising that the solider 'sees' through a light on its hat, he covers it with his jacket. While the soldier (and therefore the Master) is blinded, he runs off.
　　The Doctor and Zoe shout that the Minotaur does not exist, and it vanishes. They return to where they left Jamie, but find that he has gone. The stranger appears once more, and the Doctor realises that he is Lemuel Gulliver, and that he can speak only the words that Swift wrote for him.

DM: Those lines are actually the opening lines of the book.

Jamie, still chased by the soldier, finds himself by some rocks, which he climbs to get away from it.

[The soldier was played by Ian Hines, Frazer Hines' cousin.]

DM: This location was south of Tunbridge Wells, and was the nearest place to London where you actually get rock that can be climbed. It was a youth training activity adventure centre with a rock face. We had to get a whole sequence – this – and the night filming of the unicorn completed in one day. So, we went down in the late morning, quickly shot the sequences of Jamie climbing the cliffs, and then, after an evening meal break, we travelled to Croydon to film the unicorn.

Looking up, Jamie wonders how he will ascend, when a rope is dropped down to him. He climbs the rope to a window in a castle turret, where he is met by a girl – he has actually been climbing up her hair! This is Princess Rapunzel (Christine Pirie).

S J: As the responsibility of the Make-up Department extended to the wigs and hair, we had to create this enormous long plait for Rapunzel. We got hold of a vast length of what must of been some sort of nylon hair, which we plaited and then sprayed with a blonde hairspray. This plait was so long that it went all the way round the make-up area – it was simply enormous. The actress, Christine Pirie, also had a blonde wig, and we attached this plait to the wig.

Rapunzel reluctantly agrees that Jamie can climb in the window. He does so, and finds himself in a hi-tech control room.

EH: This is perhaps the worst example of being able to see the joins in the set. I can't understand why it's so bad in these scenes. Perhaps I didn't have the time in studio to go round and cover up all the cracks.

On a large monitor is a page from the book **Treasure Island**, *while a ticker-tape machine prints out the continuing story of what the Doctor and Zoe are doing.*
    The Doctor and Zoe return to the heart of the labyrinth, where they find a statue of the Medusa (Sue Pulford). It starts to come alive. Jamie reads of their predicament. If they look at the Medusa's eyes, they'll be turned to stone.

[Sue Pulford played the Medusa only in long-shot in studio and for the scenes where her hand was seen approaching Zoe's face. All the animated shots of the head and shoulders of the creature were created in the visual effects studio by John Friedlander.]

The Doctor tries to get Zoe to disbelieve in the Medusa, but she cannot.

End of Episode Three

EPISODE FOUR

The Doctor remembers the mirror in his pocket, and they look at the image of the Medusa in that. It returns to stone.
    Jamie reads that the Doctor and Zoe have escaped, and tries to run himself, but an alarm sounds and he is trapped. Gulliver appears, closely followed by the robots from the void. Jamie hides, and the robots pass by.
    The Doctor and Zoe have left the labyrinth and see the citadel perched on top of a mountainous crag.

EH: That painting of the citadel came from the Design Department, but I didn't paint it myself.

Before they can make their way up, there is an explosion behind them, and the costumed figure of the Karkus (Christopher Robbie) appears in a flash. He challenges the Doctor, and Zoe informs him that the Karkus is a fictional character. The Karkus brandishes an anti-molecular ray disintegrator, which the Doctor claims is scientifically impossible, making it vanish. Enraged, the Karkus attacks the Doctor, and Zoe tells him that the Karkus has superhuman strength.

Zoe defends the Doctor and ends up beating the Karkus. He submits, and says he'll help them.

DM: I was most unhappy with this fight. I think I was sloppy on the day that we recorded it, and I should have had it re-taken, but I didn't.

[The fight arranger, B H Barry, was booked to coach Wendy Padbury in judo from 8 to 12 July 1968.]

Zoe explains that the Karkus appears in a strip cartoon from the hourly telepress in the year 2000. Reaching the door to the citadel, the Doctor rings the bell and imitates the Karkus to gain entry.

The Doctor and Zoe find Jamie, and he warns them about the alarm system – a photoelectric cell. The Doctor intends to see the Master, but Gulliver warns against this. The Doctor says he'll think about it, and Gulliver leaves. However, when he's gone, the Doctor says he intends to fight on. Jamie shows the Doctor the machine that was telling the story. The Doctor realises that the Master has been trying to turn them into fiction. Zoe is horrified, and accidentally activates the alarm. The robots arrive and silently herd them towards a doorway, where a voice welcomes them in.

EH: The sets are a lot better on this episode. I expect we'd had more time to get them set up properly.

They find themselves in the Master's control room. He is an old man who greets them warmly. He is connected from a skull-cap to a large, spinning computer behind him. He explains that he left England in the summer of 1926, having dozed off over his desk. He was writer of the adventures of Jack Harkaway which, for 25 years, appeared in the Ensign *magazine. It was because of this that he was selected to work in the Land of Fiction. His brain keeps the operation going. The Master explains that the Doctor is required to take his place in the running of the Land.*

Jamie and Zoe decide to sneak away as the Doctor keeps the Master talking. They find themselves in a huge library. They cannot get out, and the robots arrive, trapping them.

The Doctor refuses to cooperate, and the Master alternates between a harsh computer-voice (that of the Master Brain) and his own voice as he reveals that he has already written the fate of Jamie and Zoe, which has happened as predicted. He points to a screen, where the friends are seen to be fired upon by the robots before backing into the pages of a giant book. The book starts to close, squeezing them within.

EH: The book was mounted on enormous castors, and we had a couple of scene hands pushing it closed.

End of Episode Four

EPISODE FIVE

The Master explains that Jamie and Zoe have been turned into fiction. The Doctor still refuses to cooperate, and climbs up a bookshelf to escape. He arrives on the roof of the citadel.

EH: That set was based on Knowle House, a marvellous piece of architecture.

Jamie and Zoe appear, and the Doctor realises that they are now trapped.
The Doctor sees the master tape through a skylight and inadvertently calls on the Karkus to remove the glass panes. He then uses Rapunzel's hair to climb down to the typewriter, so that he can start to alter the fiction to his advantage.
The Master watches as the Doctor types in the next instalment: '... the enemy had been finally defeated by the Doctor'. Just in time, the Doctor realises that he cannot put this without turning himself into fiction. He climbs back onto the roof, where Jamie and Zoe have gone. The Karkus and Rapunzel are joined by Gulliver and the children, who all talk at once. Meanwhile, the Master writes that Jamie and Zoe realise that the Doctor is evil and must be punished. He sends them off to trap the Doctor.
The children are playing when they suddenly notice the TARDIS, from which Jamie and Zoe emerge. They usher the Doctor inside, and the external walls fall away to reveal that he is trapped within a perspex box, which fades away.
The Master writes the children out of the story, and the Doctor re-appears in the control room. The Master now intends to take over the planet Earth with the Doctor's co-operation, and has linked the Doctor to the Master Brain.
The Doctor realises that he now has equal power with the Master. He frees Jamie and Zoe from the book as the Master Brain calls for the white robots to enter the control centre. The Master orders the clockwork soldiers to destroy Jamie and Zoe.

DM: The monitor that they are watching this action on is called an Eidophore. It threw the picture onto a very large screen. We would book the Eidophore when we wanted a large, projected image in studio. It was used until the advent of Colour Separation Overlay (CSO), or Chromakey, when it was superseded.

EH: It was effectively a back-projection screen. We used them on *Z-Cars*. It had an arrangement of mirrors, which bounced the image about and made it larger.

DM: The difference was that a back-projection screen could take only a filmed picture, whereas the Eidophore could take a feed from one of the studio cameras and enlarge it. This process wasn't conceived by the Drama Department. It probably originated in one of the topical programmes or even *Top of the Pops*. We used to watch *Top of the Pops* regularly to pick up ideas and translate them into *Doctor Who*.

The Doctor calls on the Karkus to destroy the soldiers, which he does. The Master turns the Karkus on Jamie and Zoe, but the Doctor relates that his gun's energy has been used up. The Master then calls up Cyrano de Bergerac (David Cannon), and the Doctor counters this with D'Artagnan (John Greenwood). The two fictional swordsmen fight up on the roof.

DM: As an assistant, I worked on *The Spread of the Eagle*, three Shakespeare plays for the BBC, and John Greenwood arranged the fights. John and Bernard Hepton also did the fights for the Laurence Olivier film of *Richard III*. Greenwood was an excellent swordsman, and I cast him because of this.

Jamie and Zoe escape as the battle continues. The Master cancels Cyrano and substitutes Blackbeard the Pirate (Gerry Wain) instead. The Doctor cancels D'Artagnan and puts in Sir Lancelot (John Greenwood) in full armour.

DM: We used a real horse here for just one scene.

The Master Brain orders the Doctor destroyed, but the Master protests – the Doctor is the only person who can take his place. The Master Brain changes the white robots' weapons to destructor beams and sends them to remove the Doctor. The Doctor cannot save himself without writing himself into fiction. Jamie and Zoe decide to attack the computer in order to save the Doctor. They start pressing buttons at random, and the Master Brain overloads. The Doctor unplugs the Master from the computer as the robots open fire on Jamie and Zoe, who duck. The computer is hit.

DM: This is the point where we should have gone off in a new direction and done something fresh for the climax, but of course the endings are often forced on these *Doctor Who*s. You can see we're regurgitating some of the same effects again here. This is due to there being no more money and nowhere else to go except to blow the set apart.

The Doctor, Jamie and Zoe help the Master from the control room and out into a black void. A mist starts to appear and the Doctor hopes that the destruction of the

computer will send them all back into reality.
The TARDIS re-forms in space.

DM: That was a reverse of the film sequence of the TARDIS breaking up.

End of Episode Five

[As an addendum to the story of *The Mind Robber*, the start of the script for the first episode of the following story, *The Invasion*, contains the following stage direction:

> THE CAM. IS DEFOCUSED AND AS ITS PICTURE
> SHARPENS WE SEE THE DR SEATED IN HIS CHAIR
> WHERE WE LEFT HIM BEFORE THE TARDIS
> BROKE UP IN THE PREVIOUS STORY

This suggests that, aside from episode one of *The Mind Robber*, the remainder of the story was intended to be some sort of dream, or perhaps to have taken place only in the minds of the characters involved.]

POST-PRODUCTION

After the recording, very little remained to be completed on the show. 'One of the things that Sydney Newman changed when he became Head of Drama was the overruns in the studio,' explained Maloney. 'Many shows used to overrun their schedules, which cost money in overtime. So Sydney insisted there be a maximum of five recording breaks in a half-hour of drama. This meant that after recording the studio show, there were only five joins to make in the tape. That cut down editing time to the point where some directors didn't go to the editing – they just sent their assistant.

'This *Doctor Who* was a little more complex than that, however.'

One of the reasons for this was the way that the story had been constructed, both in planning and out of necessity.

The first thing to be completed for the story was the location filming, followed by all the model work (which included the stop-motion animation of the Medusa's head). Then, filming took place at Ealing Film Studios for sequences of the robots in the white void for episode one, plus several sequences for episode five including all the fights between the fictional characters.

Finally, selected sound recordings had to be made for the episodes, in particular for episode one, where the Doctor's thoughts were vocalised as he battled the Master Brain's invasion of the TARDIS. These took place at various times during the period of the recording of the episodes.

A final complication was Frazer Hines contracting chicken pox and having to be totally absent from the recording of the second episode. As a result of this, Hines' scenes at the very start of the episode were recorded before the scheduled start of recording for episode five.

Due to set requirements, the first three scenes of episode three (featuring the black void and the cut-out unicorn photograph) were recorded at the end of episode two. This allowed more space in studio for the other sets required for the second episode.

All this resulted in considerably more post-production editing and audio dubbing than was usual at this point in *Doctor Who*'s history.

Another note with regard to *The Mind Robber* is that, aside from in the final episode, there was no incidental music. Most stories of this era made use of stock music, while a few had scores especially provided by composers. The stock music in *The Mind Robber* was used only during the fight sequence between the fictional characters in the final episode and was a one minute and twenty-five second excerpt from Bruchner's 'Symphony No 7 in E Major'.

Perhaps the last word should go to David Maloney: 'Considering the crude conditions under which it was made, it's really quite slick.'

TRANSMISSION

The Mind Robber was transmitted on BBC1 from 14 September to 12 October 1968 and received an average audience rating of 6.86 million, which was just above the overall season average of 6.37. The ratings tailed off alarmingly at the end of the season, giving Troughton a less than auspicious end to his era.

The BBC also commissioned an audience research report for the final episode of *The Mind Robber*. There were 238 people surveyed to produce the report, and the compiler concluded that the overall reaction was not favourable.

'It seemed that this episode only served to confirm the growing feeling that the element of fantasy in *Dr Who* was getting out of hand,' the report said. 'This was one of the most far-fetched they had yet seen, most of the sample said, and, with the exception of a few who considered the ending a "bit of a letdown" to a promising adventure, the remarks of those reporting also applied to the story as a whole.

'For many, *Dr Who* was clearly something watched "for the children's sake" rather than from personal inclination. Never one of their favourite programmes, it had now deteriorated into ridiculous rubbish which could no longer be dignified with the term science fiction, they declared. This latest adventure, with its weak story line, was too silly for words and, in their opinion, *Dr Who* had had his day.'

Only a third of those spoken to felt that the story was enjoyable, and these people also liked the idea of a 'master mind' having the ability to fictionalise real people. However, the report also had a down side to this: 'On the other hand, several who welcomed the theme as a refreshing departure from "the more usual punch-up" between the Doctor's party and their current enemies thought the action terribly disjointed and difficult to follow and, although they personally found the story one of the best for a long time, ended by condemning it as far too complicated for younger viewers – who were, after all, its main audience.'

The report went on to detail the reactions of those children who were among those surveyed.

'Among the children whose comments were reported, some of the older ones welcomed this adventure as "one of the best ideas ever thought of in this series", and there was plenty of evidence that *Dr Who* still had a legion of devotees among younger viewers, from the five-year-old for whom it was "a Saturday-evening ritual" to the rather older boy who dismissed it as "tripe" but, according to his mother, "secretly rather enjoys it". Nevertheless, the doubts expressed by some members of the sample regarding children's ability to follow the idea behind this story were confirmed to a certain extent by the reported comments of the youngsters. Although many parents said that *Dr Who* was a viewing "must" with their children (even if his fascination was "of the horrible variety"), they quite often added that, on this occasion, it was fairly obvious that they were rather "at sea" as far as the plot was concerned. The under-tens, especially, were reported as saying that they much preferred the episodes with "monsters" (Daleks, Yeti and so forth), and, although a few criticised it as "childish", it would seem to have been the lack of action which mainly accounted for their disappointment.'

All these comments would no doubt have been of particular interest to producer Peter Bryant and script editor Derrick Sherwin as they formulated plans to take *Doctor Who* in a new, more adult direction in the early Seventies.

CREDITS

Director	David Maloney
Producer	Peter Bryant
Script Editor	Derrick Sherwin
Assistant Script Editor	Terrance Dicks (ep 4)
Writer	Derrick Sherwin (ep 1)
	Peter Ling (eps 2-5)

Designer	Evan Hercules
Costume Designer	Martin Baugh (did not supervise ep 5 recording)
	Susan Wheal (ep 5)
Make-Up Artist	Sylvia James
Visual Effects	Jack Kine
	Bernard Wilkie
Production Assistant	John Lopes
Assistant Floor Manager	Edwina Verner
Assistant	Judy Shears
Floor Assistant	Gavin Birkett
Vision Mixer	Geoff Walmsley
Fight Arranger	B H Barry (ep 4)
	John Greenwood (ep 5)
Typist	Trish Phillips (ep 5)
Film Editor	Martin Day
Film Cameraman	Jimmy Court
Grams Operator	Pat Heigham
Crew	Five (eps 1-3)
	Six (eps 4-5)
Sound	John Holmes
Lighting	Howard T King
TM2	Fred Wright (eps 1-4)
	Neil Campbell (ep 5)
Title Music	Ron Grainer and the BBC Radiophonic Workshop
Title Sequence	Bernard Lodge
Telesnaps	John Cura
Special Sound	Brian Hodgson

Selling the Doctor

MEDIA

By the autumn of 1966, press interest in *Doctor Who* was waning. Newspaper and magazine editors had seemingly grown tired of reporting the show's many changes of cast, and the unexpected and extensive interest in the Daleks over the previous couple of years had now abated, leaving everyone looking for something new to report on.

The BBC's own listings magazine, *Radio Times*, was still a staunch supporter of the show, and during Patrick Troughton's time with the series, afforded three front covers to it (the first publicising *The Power of the Daleks*, the second doing likewise for *The Tomb of the Cybermen* and the third, which appeared while *The Enemy of the World* was being transmitted, prefacing an internal feature looking at *Doctor Who*'s monsters). Small internal articles continued to appear on a regular basis, usually accompanied by a photograph, and readers were never in doubt when *Doctor Who* was around. *Radio Times* continued to be published in regional editions with occasional differences to the amount of coverage given to the show by each edition. The issue carrying the feature on the monsters was also heavily promoted, with clips of Troughton, Frazer Hines and Debbie Watling appearing in several TV trailers advertising the issue.

William Hartnell's forthcoming departure from the show was announced to the public on 6 August 1966, and a small item was carried by *The Times* indicating that the search was on for a new actor to play the Doctor. This actor was publicly named as Patrick Troughton on 2 September 1966. 'Actor Patrick Troughton, 46-year-old veteran of many "heavy" roles on the stage and TV, is to be the new Dr Who on BBC TV,' explained the *Daily Mirror*. 'He is taking over from William Hartnell who has given up the part of the long-haired scientist after three years. Troughton – he has twice played the part of Hitler in the theatre – will be seen battling the Daleks on Guy Fawkes Night. Dr Who will also have a changed personality – but the BBC is keeping this secret.'

When *The Power of the Daleks* made its debut on 5 November 1966, there was some coverage from the newspapers, most notably the *Daily Mail* and *The Times*, both of which ran short stories about it. Other items that gained press coverage included the return of the Cybermen in *The Moonbase*, the fish people in *The Underwater Menace*, and the Ice Warriors in *The Ice Warriors*.

Troughton has been described as an elusive and mysterious actor, and those newspapers that tried to give coverage to *Doctor Who* and its star found this to be the case. Troughton's dislike of interviews and publicity resulted in an almost total dearth of press coverage for the show. *Reveille* ran a full-page feature on *Doctor Who* in their Christmas 1966 edition, and found that while Anneke Wills, Frazer Hines and Michael Craze were happy to chat about their lives and what it was like to star in *Doctor Who*, Troughton was far more of a slippery customer. At the end of the interview, the reporter claimed that he said 'I've only talked to you because you're a girl. And I like girls,' before vanishing off to work. The piece ended with the reporter musing that Troughton was not the Doctor at all, but a leprechaun in disguise.

Kenneth Baily, writing in the *People* in September 1967, had more of a problem. He wanted to interview Troughton, but ended up being able to speak only with the people Troughton worked with. Baily claimed that in 20 years of appearing in TV roles, Troughton had never granted an interview – not strictly true, given that he had, at least, spoken to *Reveille* the previous year. The picture he painted was of a reclusive yet dedicated actor, much loved by all who worked with him.

Troughton maintained his privacy to the end of his time spent playing the Doctor, and beyond. The first 'major' interview about his time on the show came on the BBC's *Pebble Mill* programme in an interview to publicise *The Three Doctors*, a story celebrating *Doctor Who*'s tenth anniversary. Even in this interview, he said little, preferring to remain elusive when questioned about the series.

One rare occasion when Troughton did cooperate with publicity for the series came in December 1967, when he was pictured first helping to judge and then, in costume, with the winning entries to a competition launched by the BBC children's magazine show *Blue Peter* on 27 November to design a monster to beat the Daleks. According to *The Times* on 15 December 1967: 'BBC Television's *Blue Peter* programme received more than 250,000 entries when children were asked to design a blueprint for an original Dr Who-type monster. The winning designs were constructed by the visual effects department and went on parade at Lime Grove studios yesterday. Among top monster-makers were Stephen Thompson, aged 13, of Moira, near Burton-on-Trent, with his "aqua man", and Paul Worrall, aged eight, of Sheffield, with his "hypnotron".' Troughton's appearance in costume was actually at the *Daily Mail* Boys' and Girls' Exhibition over the Christmas 1967 period, at which event the winning entries were also displayed.

Because of Troughton's low profile, the newspapers and other media, on the rare occasions when they did cover the series, tended to concentrate on other aspects. The companions, the monsters and the effect of the show on children were all topics discussed at different points during the late Sixties.

MERCHANDISE

Compared with the first three years of *Doctor Who*, the Troughton era was largely forgotten by merchandisers and publishers alike. From a boom of around 100 items in 1965 alone, the years 1967 to 1969 saw only nine items of merchandise released: three editions of World Distributors' *Doctor Who Annual* (1967, 1968 and 1969), two records ('Fugue for Thought' by Bill McGuffie (1967) which featured music from the second *Doctor Who* film, *Daleks' Invasion Earth 2150 A.D.*, and 'Who's Dr Who?' by Frazer Hines (1968), at the time playing Jamie), a paperback edition of David Whitaker's novel *Doctor Who and the Crusaders* published by Green Dragon (1967) and two larger items: a Dalek Kiddie Ride produced by Edwin Hall and Co (1967); and a TARDIS climbing frame and playhouse produced by Furnitubes Associated Products (1968), of which only twelve are recorded as having been sold.

Perhaps the most significant activity for the era came when T Wall and Sons arranged a high profile *Doctor Who* promotion for their 'Sky Ray' ice lolly, which had just been re-launched in a 'new' shape. The promotion featured collectible cards given away with each lolly, and a special album could be obtained in which to keep them. There were television and cinema advertisements produced to promote the line (at least one of which was in colour) and in these, another actor appeared as the Doctor along with the Daleks. The Doctor was dressed in an outfit very similar to that worn by Patrick Troughton in his first few *Doctor Who* stories, and kept his face covered by his hands for the majority of his brief appearance. The 36 cards told the story of a Dalek invasion of the planet Zaos. The Doctor helps by bringing giant astro-beetles into the fray to fight against the Daleks. The album, called *Dr Who's Space Adventure Book*, contained 24 pages and, as well as a text story into which the collectible cards could be pasted, featured the 'inside secrets' of a Sky Ray Space Raider craft, pictures to colour, a cut-away Dalek into which readers could draw their own idea of what lived inside, and a 'mind mesmeriser'. The cover to the book was painted by Patrick Williams, who may also have painted the uncredited artwork that appeared on the cards themselves.

Only the Sky Ray promotion, the three *Doctor Who* Annuals and the ongoing comic strip in *TV Comic* featured the image of the second Doctor, and although there was some external interest shown in the Quarks (from *The Dominators*), a dispute between their creators and the BBC resulted in no products being licensed, although the robots did appear in several of the *TV Comic* strip stories. The Cybermen also appeared in the *TV Comic* strip.

OVERSEAS SALES

Continuing the practice of *Doctor Who* being sold for transmission abroad, the Troughton stories were picked up by several countries. These were documented in an internal listing produced by the BBC in February 1977. The listing is known to be incomplete – see the details of overseas transmissions in *New Zealand* that follow by way of example – and, in addition, prints would be passed on from one country to another, but what it presented was as follows:

The Power of the Daleks	Australia, New Zealand, Singapore
The Highlanders	Australia, New Zealand, Singapore, Zambia, Hong Kong, Uganda
The Underwater Menace	Australia, New Zealand, Singapore, Zambia, Hong Kong, Uganda
The Moonbase	Australia, New Zealand, Singapore, Zambia, Hong Kong, Uganda
The Macra Terror	Australia, New Zealand, Singapore, Zambia, Hong Kong, Uganda
The Faceless Ones	Australia, New Zealand, Singapore, Zambia, Hong Kong, Uganda
The Evil of the Daleks	Australia, New Zealand, Singapore, Hong Kong
The Tomb of the Cybermen	Australia, New Zealand, Singapore, Hong Kong
The Abominable Snowmen	Australia, New Zealand, Singapore, Zambia, Hong Kong, Nigeria, Gibraltar

Whereas Hartnell-era stories had been sold to as many as twenty three countries in total, during the Troughton era that number dropped to only eight, with only three countries – Australia, Singapore and Hong Kong – taking the majority of stories at the time.

No Troughton-era adventures were sold to the USA until around 1985. This was partly because in the late Sixties, the BBC undertook a systematic programme of wiping the master video tapes of any shows felt at the time to have no further commercial potential. These included the vast majority of *Doctor Who* stories made to that point. When this practice was eventually stopped, several Hartnell- and Troughton-era stories were found to be still in existence in negative format, and others were slowly returned from overseas and from private collectors. In 1985, a package of those Hartnell- and Troughton-era stories that had been recovered were made available to the USA for the first time.

AUSTRALIA
By Damian Shanahan

One of the main television providers in Australia is the Australian Broadcasting Corporation (ABC), the head offices of which are in Sydney. BBC Enterprises in Sydney would routinely provide the ABC with black and white 16mm film prints of *Doctor Who* serials as soon as they became available from the BBC in the UK. From there, stories would be sent to the Film Censorship Board (now the Office of Film and Literature Classification) for classification prior to transmission. The prints would then be passed around the country, eventually screening in all states, but not always premiering in the same region. When this circulation of material had finished, prints were either destroyed or passed on to other countries for further screening.

The following transmission details cover the screenings in Sydney, and while the dates differ considerably from those in other capital cities, the order of debut screening was essentially the same.

At 6.30 pm on Friday 21 July 1967, the first episode of *The Power of the Daleks* premiered in Sydney. This was followed by weekly transmissions up the end of *The Faceless Ones* on 26 January 1968. *The Evil of the Daleks*, the final story in Troughton's first season, was not purchased at this stage. Following transmission of *The Faceless Ones*, the ABC launched into an almost immediate run of repeats, starting on 12 February 1968, with all episodes from the William Hartnell story *The Chase* to *The Faceless Ones* (apart from *Mission to the Unknown* and *The Daleks' Master Plan*) shown Mondays to Thursdays at tea-time, and ending on 25 June. This effectively kept *Doctor Who* on Australian screens until the next season was ready to be shown.

At 6.05 pm on Friday 5 July 1968, Troughton's second season commenced its debut run. It continued until the end of *The Web of Fear* on 6 January 1969. The time slot had changed from Fridays to Sundays after the screening of *The Abominable Snowmen* concluded on 6 September 1968. This was followed by *The Evil of the Daleks*, which was screened weekly from 12 January 1969 to fill a gap created by delays in the censorship of *Fury from the Deep*, which was then screened from 2 March. *The Wheel in Space* was first transmitted from 13 April.

Meanwhile, the ABC took advantage of school holidays to utilise repeat rights, and *The Evil of the Daleks* was screened from 7 to 16 May. August school holidays saw repeats of *The Tomb of the Cybermen* and *The Abominable Snowmen*, and the Christmas vacation allowed for repeats of the remaining second season stories up to *Fury from the Deep*, concluding on 23 January 1970. *The Wheel in Space* was eventually repeated weekday afternoons from 31 August to 7 September 1970.

Troughton's third season commenced screening in April 1970 with *The Dominators*, which was followed by the remainder of the season up until *The Seeds of Death*. In January 1971, *The Dominators*, *The Mind Robber* and *The Invasion* were repeated. *The Space Pirates* and *The War Games* were eventually premiered from 11 April 1971.

The Space Pirates was repeated with *The Krotons* and *The Seeds of Death* in January 1972, while *The War Games* was repeated during the second week of May 1972, with the episodes shown in fifty minute blocks.

The was the last time that Troughton-era episodes were screened in Australia in the Seventies. Fourteen years later, in February 1986, *The Krotons* and *The Mind Robber* were repeated, following the first run of season twenty-two, and led into a complete run of Pertwee stories. The transmission of these two stories was the first time black and white episodes of *Doctor Who* had been screened since Australian television switched over to colour in 1975. While rights for two screenings of each of these stories were purchased, due to expire in 1988, they were not repeated. Clips from the first episode of *The Mind Robber* were used in promotional advertisements for the ABC shop throughout 1986.

Although all Troughton's stories had been screened, Australian viewers had not actually seen some of them as originally transmitted by the BBC. Because of the early time slot provided for the show by the ABC, each story was required to be rated 'G' – for General Audience. Hence, all stories had to be screened by Government censors who would make recommendations as to cuts required in certain episodes in order to bring them in line with the 'G' rating.

The following detail the cuts made to the stories.

•   *The Highlanders* was classified 'G' (for General) with minor cuts required to episode one. Reductions were made to Alexander McLaren's battle with a Redcoat at the beginning of the story, and to a hanging sequence featuring the Doctor, Ben, Jamie and Colin McLaren toward the end of the episode – about thirteen seconds in all.

•   *The Underwater Menace* had a total of 50 seconds of material removed, with each episode individually rated 'G with cuts'. The bulk of censoring concentrated on the sequences involving Polly's artificial gill operation from the first two episodes. Zaroff's spearing of Ramo in episode three and his own drowning sequence from the end of episode four were also reduced considerably.

•   Four separate cuts were made to *The Macra Terror* on 31 October 1967. Three of these were from the same scene, in which Ben and Polly first confront the Macra beast, with deletions made to Polly's screams and her being attacked by the creature. A small edit of a Macra claw approaching the Controller's neck was made to the end of episode two, and also to the reprise of this scene at the beginning of episode three. A total of just under half a minute of footage was excised from the story.

• *The Faceless Ones* was viewed by the Censorship Board on 4 October 1967, and its Certificate of Registration was issued after consideration some three weeks later. One of the censors remarked: 'In my opinion this series is not suitable for 'G' classification, but could be passed 'A' with no cuts. I am sure that this would not please the ABC so I am referring at this stage to all episodes screened so far. I will review episode 6 later.' *The Faceless Ones* was eventually passed for general viewing with only episode 1 requiring cuts in order to grant it a 'G' rating, bringing it in line with the rest of the episodes. Five cuts totalling approximately half a minute were made, mainly to close-up shots of the faceless creatures.

• *The Tomb of the Cybermen* was viewed at the Film Censorship Board on 10 January 1968 by three government censors, two of whom rated the serial 'A' (for Adult). One censor remarked that 'the serial is not suitable for children as it is violent, shows no regard for human life (or robot life) and is likely to terrify young children.' Another referred to *The Tomb of the Cybermen* as 'typical of the *Doctor Who* series – weird and wonderful! There are a number of aspects of the story which I would not want shown for General Exhibition so my opinion would be "A with cuts". There are a number of shots of deliberate violence or threats of violence.' Irritated by this attitude (which saw Hartnell's *The Daleks' Master Plan* rated 'unsuitable for general viewing' and hence unable to be screened), BBC Enterprises sought to appeal against this rating, which would as a consequence preclude a sale, as the ABC was only interested in purchasing *Doctor Who* that could be rated 'G'. BBC Enterprises issued a Notice of Appeal on 20 March 1968, which argued that the producers of *The Tomb of the Cybermen* 'took care to ensure that the material was in no way injurious to the psychology of children ... This series of programmes was viewed by two world authorities on child psychology, Drs Pedler and Himmelweit, and both pronounced the series to be quite harmless.' The Appeals Censor informed the BBC that the appeal would be heard on Monday 6 May and that the films were required for viewing on that day. On 15 May, the BBC were informed that *The Tomb of the Cybermen* was now passed as 'G' with no cuts required, and that the Appeal fee of three guineas was refunded. This was an unusual back down by the Film Censorship Board, and a delighted Enterprises made use of this as a case study in later appeals (most notably for the third Doctor story *The Daemons*). It could however be said that the appeal was, in part at least, somewhat disingenuous, as the 'Dr Pedler' referred to was the story's co-writer, Kit

Pedler, who, although a respected scientist, was not a world authority on child psychology! The appeal in fact seemed to be referring to a debate that had taken place on the BBC viewers' comment programme *Talkack*, in which both Pedler and Himmelweit had been involved (see below for further details).

• *Fury from the Deep* had been offered to the ABC on 26 June 1968. The prints were auditioned and then sent to the Censorship Board for classification, but weren't viewed by the Board until late January 1969. One of the three censors rated the serial as 'A' throughout, which would have precluded screening in the allotted late afternoon timeslot. He was out-voted, however, and the episodes passed as 'G with cuts'. A total of seven cuts were required in episodes two, four and five in order to grant the 'G' rating. The longest of these lasted 54 seconds and involved the deletion of the entire sequence where Mr Oak and Mr Quill enter Mrs Harris' bedroom and breathe out toxic fumes, which cause her to collapse. The total time removed from the story was just under two minutes.

• The ABC received audition prints of *The Wheel in Space* in August 1968. Censors viewed the story in March 1969 and rated it 'G and cut', ordering that the death sequence of the Australian character Duggan in episode four be reduced by four seconds, to edit his screams.

• *The Dominators* was offered to the ABC as early as 29 August 1968, and auditioned by the Director of Drama and Controller of Programming within weeks, but it was not viewed by the Censorship Board until 10 April 1969. The Censorship Board passed *The Dominators* as 'G' with a total of three cuts required to episode four. The Quark's execution of Tensa, torture of Teel and the extended murder sequence of Educator Balan were removed from episode four, reducing it by approximately twenty seconds. The tail end of Balan's death was also excised from the beginning of episode five.

• *The Invasion* created headaches for BBC Enterprises when the censors gave it an overall 'A' rating. Offered for purchase to the ABC on 24 December 1968, the films weren't sent for classification for almost a year. After some delay, the ABC indicated an urgency to have the material classified. The Censors replied, 'As you are aware, the Censor must see all episodes of a serial at one screening – the next *Doctor Who* serial VV *The Invasion*, has eight parts; we have tentatively scheduled it for censorship on 24th, 25th or 26th of February; i.e. the Censorship Schedule to be issued on 16th February. Please be assured that each serial will be scheduled for censorship as expeditiously as other programme pressures permit.' When BBC Enterprises learned of the 'A' rating, another appeal was lodged, and as with *The Tomb of the Cybermen* the serial was successfully, reclassified 'G'. This time, though, cuts were required in episodes five, six and seven. A total of over thirty seconds was edited, which included the killing of a policemen in the sewers by a Cyberman and reductions to the sequence in which Professor Watkins fires a gun at Tobias Vaughn. Vaughn's sinister appraisal of the Professor as being '... our insurance' was also removed.

• *The War Games* was classified 'G' with two minor cuts required to reduce throttling and strangle holds in a battle sequence in episode four, which totalled ten seconds.

In 1984, Australian fan Dallas Jones first received information on the Film Censorship Board's cuts made to *Doctor Who*. In October 1996, following more research by Jones along with several other researchers, most notably Rod Scott, fellow Australian Damian Shanahan uncovered more detailed information relating to all the cuts made by censors, as well as locating the actual footage. Commensurate with Australian Government requirement to retain edited material, the strips of 16mm film physically removed from those episodes had been kept. On 8 January 1997, the BBC received a digital copy of these segments of film, in many cases from episodes of *Doctor Who* at that point missing from the BBC's archives.

NEW ZEALAND
By Paul Scoones

The Patrick Troughton era began on New Zealand television in August 1969 with *The Power of the Daleks*, which was the latest in a long uninterrupted run of stories that had commenced with *The Space Museum* in October 1968. The first three Troughton stories, *The Power of the Daleks*, *The Highlanders* and *The Underwater Menace* were acquired in March-April 1969.

A single film print of each episode was held by the New Zealand Broadcasting Corporation (NZBC) necessitating the staggering of the schedules so that the films could be transported between New Zealand's four regional channels, Auckland (AKTV-2), Wellington (WNTV-1), Christchurch (CHTV-3) and Dunedin (DNTV-2).

Christchurch was the first region to screen Episode 1 of *The Power of the Daleks*, on 31 August 1969, followed by Wellington on 28 September, Auckland on 10 November and Dunedin on 17 November 1969. In the Christchurch and Wellington regions the series initially screened on Sundays, but moved to Mondays from 6 October (in Wellington) and 20 October (in Christchurch). In the Auckland and Dunedin regions episodes screened on Mondays from the outset of the Troughton era. Start-times were mostly around 6 pm.

The Moonbase and *The Macra Terror* screened in Christchurch and Wellington, but for viewers in the Auckland and Dunedin regions the series stopped after *The Underwater Menace*. This staggered break in the schedule allowed for all four regions to stop screening the series within the space of a month, between 26 January and 23 February 1970. The film prints for both *The Moonbase* and *The Macra Terror* were then stored in Auckland until the two serials screened several months later; in Auckland from 26 June to 14 August 1970 and in Dunedin from 10 July to 28 August 1970, on Fridays at around 6 pm.

Some information is available on the fate of the first five Troughton stories. NZBC records show that following transmission, the 16mm film prints were stored at a facility in Hill Street in Wellington. *The Power of the Daleks* was sent on to a television station in Singapore in January 1972. *The Highlanders* film prints are noted as having been destroyed at some point after April 1970, the fate of *The Underwater Menace* is unrecorded and records show that *The Macra Terror* episodes were destroyed on 27 June 1974. The fate of *The Moonbase* is also unrecorded, but the reused film can that had previously contained Episode 3 of this story was discovered by Graham Howard at a Television New Zealand film storage facility in Wellington in 1990.

The next four Troughton stories were purchased from August to October 1969. *The Faceless Ones* was rejected by the censor as unsuitable for broadcast and as a result the story was returned to the BBC in July 1970. The remaining three stories, *The Evil of the Daleks*, *The Tomb of the Cybermen* and *The Abominable Snowmen*, were screened, first in Wellington from 19 June to 9 October 1970, then in Christchurch from 3 July to 23 October 1970, Auckland from 21 August to 11 December 1970 and finally Dunedin from 4 September 1970 to 1 January 1971. In these last two regions the new episodes followed on directly from the delayed screenings of *The Moonbase* and *The Macra Terror*. The episodes screened on Fridays at around 6 pm on all channels.

According to NZBC records, the screening rights expired for the three stories in May, July and August 1973 respectively. The seven episodes of *The Evil of the Daleks* are all noted to have been destroyed, but the fate of *The Tomb of the Cybermen* and *The Abominable Snowmen* is unrecorded.

The remaining five stories from Season Five were all purchased between October and December 1970, however two of the five were not screened as *The Ice Warriors* and *Fury from the Deep* were rejected by the censor and the programme purchasing viewing committee respectively. *The Enemy of the World*, *The Web of Fear* and *The Wheel in Space* were approved by the censor for viewing, although some cuts were made to all three stories. Film trims of some of the censored sections from the latter two stories were discovered by Graham Howard in New Zealand in 2002. These three stories screened first in Wellington from 3 May to 30 August 1971, then in Auckland from 10 May to 6 September, Christchurch from 17 May to 13 September and finally Dunedin from 24 May to 20 September 1971. All of the episodes screened on Mondays mostly around 5.45 pm. The rights to these stories expired by May 1974 and the fate of the film prints is unrecorded.

Following the screening of *The Wheel in Space* no episodes of the series were broadcast in New Zealand for three and a half years and when the series did return in March 1975 it was with Jon Pertwee's first story as no stories from Season Six had been purchased by the NZBC.

Episodes from Season Six were first screened in 1985. *The Mind Robber* and *The Krotons* were selected to begin a long run of a mix of first-run and repeated *Doctor Who* stories on Television New Zealand (TVNZ)'s second channel, TV2. *The Mind Robber* was billed as both "the very first *Doctor Who* story" and a repeat in promotional material, when in fact it was neither. The story was transmitted on Fridays from 12 April to 26 April 1985, followed by *The Krotons* from 26 April to 10 May 1985. Two episodes were screened back to back each week, from 6.30 pm. The middle closing and opening credits were removed, and the opening titles of the first episode screened were edited to remove the episode number, usually replaced by a still frame of the series logo. The closing credits of the last episode of *The Mind Robber* were removed, with a continuity announcer coming on to explain that the first episode of *The Krotons* would follow after the commercial break. Viewer ratings for these screenings show that the series got off to a strong start, with *The Mind Robber* rating 11.1%, making it the seventh most watched *Doctor Who* story between 1985 and 1989. *The Krotons* however saw a drop to 8.1%.

A third previously unscreened story from Season Six was first aired in 1988 as part of TVNZ's *Doctor Who* twenty-fifth anniversary 'Silver Jubilee' week. The Troughton era was represented by an omnibus version of all six episodes of *The Seeds of Death* on 19 November 1988. Placed in a 2.40 pm Saturday slot on TV2, the story gained a viewer rating of 2.4%. As had been the case with *The Mind Robber* and *The Krotons*, the story was billed as a repeat, when in fact this was its first-time appearance on New Zealand television. *The Seeds of Death* was advertised in some publications with a synopsis for *The War Games*, prompting a voiceover correction at the beginning of the story.

The Seeds of Death, *The Mind Robber* and *The Krotons* were repeated in this order on TV2, broadcast from 31 March to 30 June 1991 on Sundays, initially at 9.15 am and then at 9.35 am for *The Krotons*. This time, the stories were screened in an unedited, single-episode-per-week format, with the exception of the last two episodes of *The Krotons*, which were broadcast back-to-back on 30 June 1991 as a late change to the schedules. Episode Four had been scheduled to screen on 7 July 1991.

Every complete surviving Troughton story screened as part of a run of

Doctor Who stories on the UHF and satellite digital channel Prime Television, in 2000. The episodes were screened six days a week (Sunday to Friday) at around 6.30 pm from 14 August to 21 September 2000. Following on directly from *The War Machines*, the Troughton stories began with *The Tomb of the Cybermen* followed by *The Dominators* – making its New Zealand television debut – *The Mind Robber*, *The Krotons*, *The Seeds of Death* and finally *The War Games*, also screening on New Zealand television for the very first time, more than thirty years after this story first screened in the UK.

JUNKING
By Andrew Pixley and Jan Vincent-Rudzki

It was during Patrick Troughton's tenure as the Doctor that the destruction of *Doctor Who* material began at the BBC. During the 1960s, it was policy to retain the master 405 line videotapes of programmes for a while, to allow for possible repeats. Then they would be erased by an electromagnet for re-use recording another show. Some episodes would be retained, however, generally as 16mm film recordings of the type used to sell BBC programming to other countries (film being an international standard whereas videotape was not).

On 13 December 1966, a Retain Order from Television Enterprises Sales was placed on all the *Doctor Who* serials up to and including *The Gunfighters* – this included the untransmitted pilot and a number of episode such as *The Waking Ally* that had been made on film. Around this time, Retain Orders were sent to the Videotape Library on an almost weekly basis to ensure that the most recently screened episodes – such as *The Power of the Daleks* and *The Highlanders* – were not wiped, at least not before 16mm films could be made of them. Although the paperwork is inconsistent (some episodes are listed for wiping more than once), it would appear that the first *Doctor Who* tapes to be wiped were those for *The Highlanders*, soon after 9 March 1967, barely a month after their BBC1 transmission. (*The Underwater Menace* episodes 1 and 2 were similarly labelled for wiping, but seem to have escaped erasure at this point.)

The first mass erasure of *Doctor Who* tapes appears to have been on 17 August 1967, less than a year after the initial Retain Order was issued. 80 episodes from the pilot to *The Gunfighters* were targeted for wiping (although probably only 78 of these were erased at this point). Some entire stories were deleted at this time (e.g. *Marco Polo*, *The Romans*, *The Ark*) while others were partially wiped (e.g. *The Reign of Terror*, *The Dalek Invasion of Earth* and seven episodes of *The Daleks' Master Plan*, including *The Feast of Steven*). Part of the reason for this may have been the arrival of new technology; *Doctor Who* would be recorded on the higher definition 625 line tape from late 1967 onwards, starting with *The Enemy of the World* episode 3. BBC1 would continue to transmit on 405 lines up until November 1969, with the 625 line tapes standards converted for broadcast.

The only episode to be marked for wiping in 1968 appears to have been *The Abominable Snowmen* episode 4, on a document dated 4 March – although the wiping does not actually seem to have occurred at this time. However, other paperwork shows that the tapes of *The Evil of the Daleks* were erased in August 1968, just after their BBC1 repeats (and despite a Retain Order issued on 1 August that year). Most of the remaining Hartnell tapes were destined for the same fate on 31 January 1969, when 25 more were wiped (including the second episode of *Inside the Spaceship*, the fourth episode of *The Reign of Terror*, *Planet of Giants*, the third episode of *The Dalek Invasion of Earth*, the first and last episodes of *The Crusade*, the third episode of *Galaxy 4* and the first episode of *The Myth Makers*). Nine Troughton episodes were also marked for deletion, along with *The Tenth Planet* episode 4, yet it seems that all these tapes in fact survived for a few more months.

17 July 1969 saw authorisation to wipe *The Chase: The Executioners*, the last three episodes of *The Daleks' Master Plan*, and *The Mutants: The Expedition*. On 21 July, the tapes and films for a number of Troughton instalments from *The Underwater Menace* through to *The Space Pirates* (i.e. both 405 and 625 line tapes) were listed on a junking document – a sign that the age of monochrome for BBC1 was shortly to come to an end. September saw a few Troughton episodes that had escaped the July purge re-assigned to a new list (editions of *The Underwater Menace*, *The Faceless Ones*, *The Abominable Snowmen*, *The Ice Warriors*, *The Web of Fear* and all *The Tomb of the Cybermen*), with eight other shows joining them in October (*The Tenth Planet* episode 4, *The Ice Warriors* Five and Six, *The Enemy of the World* episode 1 and episodes 1, 3, 5 and 6 of *The Web of Fear*).

By the end of 1969, it appears that the only monochrome episodes of *Doctor Who* to exist on their original tapes were both versions of *100,000 BC: An Unearthly Child*, *Mission to the Unknown*, *The War Machines*, *The Macra Terror*, *Fury from the Deep* and *The War Games*. Thankfully, at this point, although the tapes had gone, the 16mm films for most episodes were generally still in circulation around the globe from BBC Enterprises.

VIEWER REACTION

During the late Sixties, viewers were increasingly given opportunities to comment on television in general. This was through the letters pages of the *Radio Times*, through internal BBC 'audience research' surveys, and also on several television talk shows designed to air comment about television itself.

Reaction to the changeover of William Hartnell to Patrick Troughton was mixed, at least from readers of the *Radio Times*, whose views were printed in the magazine's 'Points from the Post' column. For example, G Howard from Leeds commented: 'I would like to send my heartiest congratulations to the production team of BBC1's *Dr Who*. Patrick Troughton and the superb character he has created have dragged the programme out of the unfortunate mess it had degenerated into. Given sensible scripts the programme could possibly emerge as one of the real successes of television science-fiction. I look forward to the time when *Dr Who* is performed for adults only.'

Mrs Estelle Hawken from Cornwall was, however, less impressed: 'What have you done to BBC1's *Dr Who*? Of all the stupid nonsense! Why turn a wonderful series into what looked like Coco the Clown? I think you will find thousands of children will not now be watching *Dr Who* which up to now has been the tops.'

Comments on the third episode of *The Power of the Daleks* from the BBC's viewing panel were recorded in an internal audience research report. 'Viewers in the sample who were enthusiastic about this episode ...' said the report, 'were confined to a minority, less than a quarter ... finding it appealing to an appreciable degree'. Amongst this group, it seemed the Daleks were the main attraction. 'This is supposed to be for the "kids",' commented a 'senior clerk', 'but I must confess that I found the programme quite gripping. As an ardent sci-fiction fan, I think the Daleks are the most sinister "aliens" I've come across'.

More often, though, 'viewers in the sample reported a very moderate degree of enjoyment, and a number were scarcely interested at all'. For some, even the Daleks had lost their appeal. 'They have made their impact, served their usefulness,' commented one malcontent, 'now they just seem hackneyed and more unreal than usual'.

If the production team had hoped that Patrick Troughton's arrival would give *Doctor Who* a boost, the initial signs were not encouraging. 'The series in general,' continued the report, 'is not as good as it used to be, in quite a few opinions – "At one time we used to hate to miss it; now we are quite indifferent"'.

Comments on the change of Doctor were more scathing: 'Once a brilliant but eccentric scientist, he now comes over as a half-witted clown,' complained a teacher. 'The family have really "gone off" Doctor Who since the change,' noted another viewer. 'They do not understand the new one at all, and his character is peculiar in an unappealing way'.

There was criticism, too, of Troughton's performance – although one person conceded that he 'seemed to be struggling manfully with the idiotic new character that Doctor Who has taken on since his change'. Typical opinions were that he was overacting, 'playing for laughs,' and making the Doctor into 'something of a pantomime character'. 'I'm not sure that I really like his portrayal,' was one verdict. 'I feel the part is over-exaggerated –

whimsical even – I keep expecting him to take a great watch out of his pocket and mutter about being late like Alice's White Rabbit'. A number stated that they had preferred William Hartnell in the role.

There was however a recognition from a minority that Troughton had yet to settle down and that there was still time for him to become 'fully acceptable'. Perhaps the most positive comment came from a student, who said that 'Patrick Troughton, a brilliant actor, had improved the programme greatly'.

In the mid-Sixties, there was an increased awareness of the role of the viewing public as a commentator on the programmes that the BBC produced. With this in mind, two series started transmission that gave the public the chance to air their views. *Junior Points of View* and *Talkback* gave *Doctor Who* a significant amount of coverage in the Sixties, in particular starting and then developing debates about whether or not the programme was too frightening for children.

'Please bring back the old Doctor Who. We don't like the new one, he looks as though he might be bad and never says "Now, now, my child,"' one concerned party wrote to *Junior Points of View*. Another commented: 'As *Doctor Who* is a programme for intellectuals, I suggest that the scriptwriter is replaced or forced to write something sensible for an actor on a great programme, too good to be wasted.'

The general feeling on this edition of *Junior Points of View*, which aired on 11 March 1967, was that 'it's not Patrick Troughton you don't like; it's the way he's made to play the part.' Some, however, did like Troughton, and favourable comments were reported along with the negative.

By 12 May, the show reported that 'letters praising far outnumber those against and it's now quite common to receive this sort of view from Corinna Duerden in Camberley: "We think the new Doctor Who is much better than the old one. At least he has more character and lets Polly and Jamie join in. Also it's not him alone who has the ideas. He's not such an old crank as the other Doctor Who."

When, in September, *Junior Points of View* transmitted comments from three Wiltshire schoolgirls who believed *Doctor Who* should be taken off air, the feedback the following week was swift and to the point. Viewers were horrified that no counter-argument had been presented, and continued to say that 'the lassies who objected to *Doctor Who* should have their minds brainwashed' and '*Doctor Who* is Dalektable'. They concluded with a brief poll: 'Let's see how the final voting went: for *Doctor Who* … 278; against *Doctor Who* … 31. And so by a substantial majority, *Doctor Who* is voted a hit!'

Concern over the horror content raised its head with the transmission of *The Tomb of the Cybermen*. The BBC programme *Talkback* covered this in its first transmitted edition on 26 September 1967. (It had also featured *Doctor Who* in its untransmitted pilot.) The transmitted edition was analysed by Trevor

Wayne in issue 37 of the fan reference work *Doctor Who: An Adventure in Space and Time*. He related one mother's complaint thus: 'I was horrified at the violent scene on *Doctor Who* last Saturday evening,' she said, referring to the final episode of *The Tomb of the Cybermen*, 'where the coloured man, Toberman, bashes into the Cyberman with his metal claw and the camera concentrated on the Cybermen's innards oozing out. I can't think of anything more disgusting and revolting and unsuitable for children, and this programme is put out at a time when even small ones might be around.' Kit Pedler was in the studio to try and defend the show by placing it in context: '... horror perpetrated by non-human beings ...,' he said. However Wayne went on to report that the show featured many 'excitable' contributors from the general public, and that no one seemed too concerned to defend either *Doctor Who* or the BBC, although those contributors who were parents seemed to place all responsibility on what their children watched on the BBC, and responded badly to suggestions that there might be an element of parental control required as well. The show concluded with input from Doctor Hilda Himmelweit, who came down in favour of the BBC, *Doctor Who* and the concept that 'children like to be frightened – but not too much.'

Junior Points of View on 6 October featured comments on the *Talkback* show in defence of *Doctor Who*. 'One lady criticising *Doctor Who* said that she was disgusted when she saw the Cyberman killed by the coloured man and all the white liquid oozing out of the Cyberman's body. I am sure the lady would not complain if a man was shot and he had blood oozing out of his body,' wrote one ten-year-old. Another correspondent commented, sagely: 'The adult does not know how a child's mind works.'

Most of the audience research reports conducted during the Troughton period noted *Doctor Who*'s continuing strong appeal to children. For instance, the one commissioned for the final episode of *The Moonbase* revealed:

'Whether they enjoyed it or not, a number supplying evidence made it plain that *The Moonbase* – not to speak of every *Dr Who* story – delighted their children: "My daughter is a firm fan of the programme" (housewife); "Like the Gravitron – had pulling power for the children" (planner); "The children love every minute of it. They prefer the science fiction adventures to the historical ones"'.

The report on the final episode of *The Evil of the Daleks* continued this positive trend. The most commonly expressed view was that the story had been 'as amusing and exciting as ever'. For those who held this view, 'the entire *Dr Who* series, if undoubtedly "pure escapism", was nevertheless "good fun" and certainly utterly harmless'. It seemed however that there remained some amongst the 180-strong sample who harboured very negative feelings towards the series: 'A not inconsiderable minority ... hoped that, as this episode suggested, this was indeed the last of the Daleks – and, for that matter, Dr Who, the TARDIS and "the whole stupid, childish, silly boiling lot".

In their opinion the series, which had always struck them as being "rubbishy" to a degree, had been "done to death"'.

The concluding instalment of *The Wheel in Space* drew very much the same cross-section of opinion from its sample of 214 viewers. 'The overall response to *The Wheel in Space*,' the report concluded, 'was favourable. There were, certainly, those who thought the whole thing ridiculous in the extreme and who could not imagine either children or adults finding much in it to appeal to them. Another group enjoyed it fairly well but felt that invention was, perhaps, beginning to flag. The stories were becoming repetitive; the series needed new ideas and new antagonists for Dr Who rather than Daleks, Cybermen and the like. This was a rather tame adventure, it was said, and there was too much use of pseudo-technical jargon that would be over the heads of most younger viewers. Whether they took it seriously or not, however, the bulk of the sample enjoyed Dr Who's encounter with his old enemies, two or three going on to say that they preferred his science fiction adventures to the historical ones'.

Attitudes seem to have changed, however, during the break between seasons five and six. A clear majority of the 185 viewers who commented on the opening episode of *The Dominators* considered that 'the continuing story of *Dr Who* had ceased to hold any interest or appeal. At first quite original and entertaining, it had been running far too long, they thought, and was now very much in a rut'.

'In the opinion of dissatisfied viewers,' it was noted, 'this particular episode ... was typical of the recent trend in the series, by which the idea of going backwards in time to various historical events (which several much preferred) had been largely discarded in favour of concentrating on the science fiction stories. Consequently, in order to maintain interest, the non-human characters had become more and more fantastic and improbable, it was said, and at least three in ten of those reporting dismissed this latest story as absolute rubbish. The series had long since lost all element of surprise, they declared, as, apart from minor details, each adventure followed the same pattern ("they arrive, separate, someone gets captured and the rest of the story is taken up with their rescue"); the new Quarks were nothing but "square Daleks"; and the development of the plot was much too slow: "this sort of thing needs to get off to an exciting start"'.

Only just over a third of the sample, who had long enjoyed *Doctor Who* as 'an entertaining "escapist" serial', felt that it 'continued to maintain a good level of inventiveness'; and some who had previously been regular viewers were now apparently starting to lose interest. 'Although I am a *Dr Who* fan of many years standing,' ran one typical comment, 'my enjoyment is steadily decreasing every week'.

It was the final episode of *The War Games* that attracted the most uniformly positive report for some time. Notwithstanding the story's epic length, the reaction of those viewers – roughly two thirds of the sample of 179 – who had seen all or most of the ten episodes was 'decidedly favourable'. Some were admittedly 'inclined to damn with faint praise', but the only really negative comment was that children seemed disappointed by the lack of monsters – and even this was balanced by the observation that 'not a few adult viewers' considered the story 'all the better for the absence of "inhuman creatures"'.

'Although there was little evidence of any great enthusiasm for this final episode of *The War Games*,' the report noted, 'nevertheless it is clear that the majority of the sample audience were very well satisfied. Certainly there were those, but in minority numbers only, who dismissed it as "the usual rubbishy nonsense", while others apparently found it disappointingly inconclusive. According to most, however, this exciting and action-packed episode had not only brought this adventure on the planet of the Time Lords to a most satisfactory ending, but also cleared up the mystery surrounding Dr Who's origin besides (most ingeniously) setting the scene for the "new" Dr Who'.

Despite these positive and reassuring comments, the show was failing badly in the ratings, and some possible reasons for this are discussed in the next section of this chapter. Despite the falling ratings, the memories that many adults today hold of the programme hail from this era of the show's history: Yeti in the Underground, Cybermen in the sewers, stinging seaweed and hissing Ice Warriors. This perhaps indicates that while fewer people were watching, the show was having a greater impact on those who did.

From a media point of view, it might be argued that *Doctor Who* needed this period of quieter contemplation. This allowed the initial furore created by the Daleks to die down, and for the show to establish itself as gripping and sometimes controversial teatime entertainment in which the Doctor was seen as the champion of good and order against all manner of monsters and creatures from space.

What is most interesting, however, is that just as mankind reached for the stars, and sent men to walk on the moon's surface in 1969, so *Doctor Who* was undergoing a re-vamp and was being planned as an Earth-bound series, forsaking the travels in space and time, for a far more fixed and recognisable setting.

RATINGS

Towards the end of the Hartnell era, the viewing figures for *Doctor Who* were at their lowest since the series began. From a peak of around 12.5 million in the second season, they had slumped to 4.5 million for *The Smugglers*, and, with the exception of the final Hartnell story, *The Tenth Planet*, which saw an upturn to 6.75 million, all the stories at the tail end of the era received the lowest ratings that the series had yet seen.

The reasons for this can be partially explained by looking at the shows that were being scheduled against *Doctor Who* on the regional ITV channels. During most of the Hartnell era, the ITV regions tended not to schedule like against like, and so science fiction and adventure fans tended to watch *Doctor Who* rather than the light entertainment fare that was on at the same time opposite it. In addition, *Doctor Who* had the hook of being a continuing serial and thus demanding some degree of viewer loyalty, which one-off films and cartoons did not. It wasn't until the transmission of *Galaxy 4* in 1965 that ITV finally placed a science fiction show opposite *Doctor Who*. This was the imported Irwin Allen space adventure series *Lost in Space*, and *Doctor Who*'s ratings suffered a dip from the eleven million mark of *Galaxy 4: Air Lock* to 9.9 million for *Galaxy 4: The Exploding Planet* and 8.3 million for the single-episode Dalek story *Mission to the Unknown*.

When *The Power of the Daleks* began on 5 November 1966, ITV's 'secret weapon' in the ratings war was another imported American series called *Batman*. As the Troughton era continued, ITV offered *Doddy's Magic Box* (a variety show featuring comedian Ken Dodd), *Mike and Bernie's Music Hall* (more variety, this time with Mike and Bernie Winters), *F Troop* (an American film series) and *Opportunity Knocks* (a popular talent show hosted by Hughie Green). The net result of these opponents (although *F Troop* actually made no impact at all) was that *Doctor Who* lost two million viewers (although there is no proof that the ITV competition was the sole cause of this).

The following year, ITV continued to place a diverse array of material opposite *Doctor Who*. There were repeats of *Sir Francis Drake*, *Just Jimmy* (comedy with Jimmy Clithero), cartoons, another swashbuckling adventure series called *Sword of Freedom*, and, in one region, *Captain Scarlet and the Mysterons*.

When *The Dominators* started, however, there was minimal competition from the regions due to a strike by the technician's union ACTT, which had begun on 2 August 1968. However, once the strike ended, the ITV service began to attack *Doctor Who* with renewed vigour. Gerry and Sylvia Anderson's *Joe 90* was transmitted against *The Mind Robber* on the London Weekend Television (LWT) region, while Granada presented Irwin Allen's *Voyage to the Bottom of the Sea*, and Yorkshire and Anglia Television (ATV) brought an imported high adventure series called *Tarzan* to the small screen. The cumulative effect of science fiction and adventure against *Doctor Who* contributed greatly towards a dramatic downturn in the BBC ratings.

Early in 1969, ATV and Southern transmitted Irwin Allen's *Land of the Giants*, and *Doctor Who* promptly lost a million viewers. A further million defected over the next fortnight. By 1 February, Yorkshire had started transmitting *Voyage to the Bottom of the Sea*.

As the sixth season of *Doctor Who* progressed, viewers appeared to forego

Doctor Who, preferring the regional ITV fare of *Voyage to the Bottom of the Sea*, *Land of the Giants*, *Tarzan* and an imported series from Australia, *Woobinda*, *Animal Doctor*. At the end of the sixth season, individual episodes of *The Space Pirates* and the ambitious ten-part *The War Games* received the lowest ratings so far in *Doctor Who*'s history, with the final story not even managing on average to break the five million mark, and episode eight managing only 3.5 million, making it the lowest rated episode to date.

As the Doctor spiralled off into the void at the end of *The War Games*, the show's traditional Saturday evening slot was filled by a brand new imported American series. This was, like *Doctor Who*, a science fiction drama series, with regular characters, monsters and a distinctive spacecraft. It was called *Star Trek*.

SECOND DOCTOR STORIES
IN ORDER OF AVERAGE VIEWING FIGURES
(Figures in millions of viewers)

The Moonbase	8.33
The Macra Terror	8.20
The Krotons	8.00
The Power of the Daleks	7.80
The Web of Fear	7.62
The Underwater Menace	7.48
The Enemy of the World	7.42
The Faceless Ones	7.38
The Ice Warriors	7.33
The Wheel in Space	7.25
The Seeds of Death	7.22
Fury from the Deep	7.20
The Highlanders	7.05
The Invasion	6.91
The Mind Robber	6.86
The Abominable Snowmen	6.85
The Tomb of the Cybermen	6.75
The Evil of the Daleks	6.43
The Dominators	6.16
The Space Pirates	5.93
The War Games	4.94

THE THIRD DOCTOR

David J Howe
Stephen James Walker

Foreword

The close of the Sixties was an exciting time. Technological advances seemed to be coming thick and fast. No sooner had people become used to having black and white television, than colour television was just around the corner. Cars were becoming more sophisticated and, to cap it all, we put a man on the moon on 21 July 1969 – surely the greatest acknowledgement of our technological superiority.

With this final conquest of space, thoughts were again turning outwards. Were we drawing attention to the Earth from alien beings? The moon was proved to be dry, dusty and dead, but what of Mars? Or Venus? What wonders might we be able to witness on those worlds?

With this new attitude, the science fiction shows of the past started to look very dated. The concept of rockets travelling across the vast reaches of space powered only by a firework could no longer be sustained. The idea of alien creatures crawling out of every nook and cranny of every planet – and many of them looking like humans – was also a dated one.

Things had changed, and *Doctor Who* had to change with them.

Co-producers Derrick Sherwin and Peter Bryant had several problems on their hands during the making of the series' sixth season. They knew that for the following season, the show was to be made in colour – even though there was no additional budget to cover this – and the alien monsters and creatures that had been *Doctor Who*'s staple for many years were becoming prohibitively expensive to realise.

Faced with having to solve these problems, Sherwin felt that moving *Doctor Who* to a more Earth-bound setting was a sensible approach. It was easier and cheaper to go out on location to film something that was supposed to be on Earth than something futuristic or alien. In addition, the menaces fought by the Doctor could be more home-grown, removing the need for complex alien make-up and costume requirements.

With this in mind, Sherwin introduced the concept of UNIT in the sixth season story *The Invasion*. UNIT was a military organisation that was dedicated to the protection of Earth from alien forces, and that would deal with any situation that seemed out of the remit of the regular Army. Even if Patrick Troughton had not left the show, the Doctor would still have been exiled to Earth, with UNIT effectively becoming the Doctor's 'home'.

As it was, Troughton stepped down and Jon Pertwee was chosen to play the third incarnation of the Doctor. A popular radio comedian and character actor, Pertwee was to bring a sense of style and flair to the show, and update its image from an eccentric tea-time series to an engaging action/adventure romp, with gadgets worthy of James Bond, and a dynamic Doctor with a sexy young woman in mini-skirt and boots as his companion.

With the new format in place, Sherwin and Bryant left *Doctor Who* in the hands of new producer Barry Letts, while they moved on to look after another BBC serial, *Paul Temple*. Letts' vision for *Doctor Who* was not too dissimilar from that of Sherwin and Bryant, and he delivered an action packed show that allowed for alien invaders and visitors, whilst still keeping the Doctor more or less trapped on this planet.

Other events at the time included the capture of the Manson 'family' for the killing of Sharon Tate; famine in Biafra; the first publication of the New English Bible, which sold at over 20,000 copies a week; the splitting up of the Beatles; and the Tories' return to power led by Edward Heath.

During the era of the third Doctor, the public saw the introduction of decimal currency to the UK, hot pants were all the rage in the fashion scene, the first heart and lung transplant was carried out, the miners went on strike over pay and blacked out large portions of the country, Nixon surrendered to the scandal of Watergate, Princess Anne was married to Mark Phillips, and Harold Wilson and Labour were swept to power after the fiasco of the miner's strike, ousting Edward Heath, who was himself replaced by Margaret Thatcher as leader of the Tory party.

Jon Pertwee was a radical change from Patrick Troughton, and his era saw the introduction of several new foes. Foremost among them was the Master, played by Roger Delgado. This evil renegade from the Doctor's own race appeared several times to try to conquer the Earth and to destroy the Doctor. Viewers were introduced to also introduced to a number of new monster races, including the Axons, the Sea Devils, the Mutants and the Sontarans, and saw the return of some old ones, in the forms of the Daleks and the Ice Warriors.

In the following chapters, we look at the development of *Doctor Who* during the third Doctor's era. *Day of the Daleks* is examined as a typical example of *Doctor Who* during this period in the show's history. We look at Jon Pertwee through his own words, and explore the art of costume design. We also look at the series' developing mythology, and examine the promotion and marketing that surrounded the series.

Join us as we revisit the era of the third Doctor.

Introduction
Jon Pertwee

As an actor, it is impossible to keep up with the many and intricate points of continuity that may occur when working on a long running drama show like *Doctor Who*. For a start, while I was working with the director on one story, the next couple of stories were already being discussed and planned by other directors. By the time I actually came to record a story, my main concern was to learn the lines, and if any major crimes of continuity had been committed, assuming I could spot them in the first place, I would usually try and suggest some easy way round them.

David J Howe and Stephen James Walker have bravely stepped through this continuity minefield and have pulled together an incredible number of facts and figures about my time as the Doctor. There are things in this book that I never knew and some, I'm sure, that no-one ever knew! Here you can discover in which story Nick Courtney wore that infamous eye patch; how and where I met the Drashigs, the Ogrons and the Ice Warriors; how my great friend Roger Delgado came to join us on the show; and many other fascinating and obscure pieces of information about the period when I played the Doctor.

In my book *I Am The Doctor,* I tell the story of that time from my own point of view. In this Handbook, you can find out more about the events that I was not party to.

It's an impressive book and I hope you enjoy it.

Jon Pertwee, April 1996

Jon Pertwee
In His Own Words

ON HIS EARLY LIFE:

'I was born in the Chelsea area of London on 7 July 1919. I have mixed blood. My father came from a French Huguenot family, and my real name is Jean Roland Perthuis de Leillevaux. We were Huguenots, who during the French Revolution escaped from France and set up in Essex. Anybody with the name Pertwee is a relation. There's Guy Pertwee in the Navy, and Admiral Jim Pertwee is my cousin. Bill Pertwee, the comedian from *Dad's Army*, is my cousin. Michael Pertwee, the playwright, is my brother. My father was Roland Pertwee, a famous actor, playwright, screenwriter – one of the top screenwriters in the world in the heyday of the movies.

'My father influenced me a great deal. He taught me to stand on my own two feet, to go out and earn my own living when I was sixteen and a half. He gave me a very good education, which I was hopeless at – I was expelled from a couple of schools, because I rebelled against ludicrous authority. I rebelled against spotty boys calling me back from my music lesson when I'd have to run about a quarter of a mile to their little rooms where they'd say: "Make me a piece of toast". I would say, "Why can't you make it yourself, are you crippled?", for which I'd be soundly beaten. I finally rebelled at the end of term after being beaten very unjustly and said to my fag master, "You threaten me with beating once more and I'll beat you within an inch of your life". He didn't believe me and sent me down into the quad, so I managed to grab a cane and, as he came round the corner, I gave him one across the face and opened it up like Errol Flynn slashing Basil Rathbone. That, of course, was the end of my career as a public schoolboy, because they did not "give the sucker an even break". It was tradition, tradition, play with a straight bat. Games were all-important. Human relationships and personality meant nothing. I was influenced by my father, a brilliant conversationalist and a wonderful man with words. He was intensely interesting, he could do anything … fisherman, actor, painter, writer.'

Interviewed by John Hudson and Stuart Money in 1975 for *Jon Pertwee Fan Club Newsletter* Issue 3.

'My parents always told me I was born in Innsbruck, Austria, and then when I got my birth certificate I found I wasn't – I was born in Chelsea. My mother was an Austrian and my father was of a French family, so we were a slightly mongrel family.'

Interviewed by Simon M Lydiard in 1984 for *Skaro* Volume IV Number 3/4.

'I had a strange sort of childhood. My mother and father parted just after I was born, and my father, who was a writer and originally an actor with [Sir Beerbohm] Tree and [Sir Henry] Irving, was rather wrapped up in himself and his own life. I was the youngest of three brothers and always felt a bit left out.

'We were brought up in the country, at Dulverton in the Exe Valley, near Tiverton, and I wish I'd appreciated how lucky we were in that. My father was a keen sportsman, and we had our own horses and rode to hounds and fished and shot. We had enormous physical freedom. Like my father, I had an ear for dialect and, living in the West Country, soon picked up the accent I now use for Worzel Gummidge.

'I went to several boarding schools, none of which I liked except the last, Frensham Heights in Surrey. That was better because it was co-educational and being of French extraction … I was interested in girls from an early age. I was offered a wonderful education and I wish I had taken advantage of it, but I've never liked the role of student. I've always had a thirst for adventure though.'

Interviewed by Pamela Coleman in 1983 for the *Sunday Express*.

'I joined a circus and had to drive a converted Austin Seven on the Wall of Death, with a lion sitting on a platform behind me.

'It was a very old lion, mark you. So old, you'd have had to kick it where it hurt to make it roar. Only the boss didn't want it roaring. "Folks'll see it ain't got no teeth," he used to moan.

'Anyway, the act ended one afternoon when we were having a break inside the base of the Wall. You know, sort of "take five" – only the lion took forever. We had to dismantle the Wall to get rid of it!'

Interviewed in 1972 for *Motor Cycle*.

'My father was an overpowering man. He had so many talents. As well as his acting and writing abilities, he knew all sorts of quaint, unexpected things. For instance, he was a great fly-fisherman and he invented his own kind of imitation fly, which is still sold commercially.

'I admired him intensely, but he seemed to find it terribly difficult to show love.

'I will always remember the night of my first professional performance in rep in Brighton. My father had promised to be there, and when I looked through the curtains before the performance, there he was in the fifth row. "He'll be round after the performance," I told my friends. But he never came, and the others said he couldn't have been there.

'But I had seen him. So the next day I rang him up and asked him why he didn't come round. He said, "I'm terribly sorry, I was too busy, I couldn't get there." But I had seen him ...

'Yet he would work at being a father in his own strange way. One day, my brother and I were due to go fishing, and we understood the tackle would be waiting for us in a fishing hut by the river. When we arrived there was none, but by using our imaginations a bit, we were able to improvise tackle from things lying around the hut – bits of cane, twine etcetera.

'Then, later, it dawned on me that my father had carefully left everything necessary to build tackle in the hut. It was a planned exercise in initiative.'

Interviewed by Ian Cotton in 1974 for *TV Times*.

ON HIS TIME AT THE ROYAL ACADEMY OF DRAMATIC ART (RADA):

'I had a teacher of Greek drama who wanted me to be a Wind. She wanted me to stand on the side of the stage and make wind noises – go "Woooh". This was such a load of rubbish that I really couldn't be bothered with it and didn't take it seriously, so I was very much reprimanded by the principal. On top of that, I was accused of writing rude remarks about the principal and this teacher on the lavatory walls – something that I denied categorically, because I had *not* written rude remarks on the lavatory walls. I told my father, who was absolutely furious. He rang the principal up, saying that he was going to sue him for defamation of character, for libel and every other charge you can think of. He said he was going to employ the greatest graphologist – handwriting expert – he could find to prove that it was not my writing. The principal then realised that he'd bitten off more than he could chew and dropped the charges. But he hated me, and soon afterwards I was given my cards, so to speak, and told that I was not the sort of person they wanted.

'It was after this, just before I left RADA, that we were doing an end of term play. In the first act I was a man who was murdered, and in the second I was a detective who came in and found out who did the murder. Noel Coward was judging, so when the play was over, they asked him if he'd seen anyone he liked. He said, "Yes, there were two very, very promising performances, from the murder victim in the first half and from the detective in the second. Who were the two people who were playing them?" So they had to tell him it was actually *one* person, and I was introduced to him. He said, "Ah yes, Pertwee. You're Roland's son, no doubt." Which of course I was. "Very good, very promising." And this was about the person they'd just expelled because, as they said, I wasn't cut out for the theatre!'

Interviewed by John Hudson and Stuart Money in 1975 for *Jon Pertwee Fan Club Newsletter* Issue 5.

ON THE START OF HIS ACTING CAREER:

'After RADA came a tremendously happy period when I joined a travelling theatre company. We went round in an old bus and I drove it, put up the theatre, got the water to put in the carbide lights that dripped onto the crystals that made the gas that lit the stage. It was as primitive as that.

'Then I went into rep. The name Pertwee certainly opened doors, but it didn't get me jobs. My father didn't give me a lot of encouragement, and now I think that that is probably what motivated me. I took on anything and grossly overacted.'

Interviewed by Pamela Coleman in 1983 for the *Sunday Express*.

'I was 19 in 1938 and had just joined the Rex Leslie-Smith Repertory Company at the end of the West Pier in Brighton, a job that marked the end of a lean time.

'The company paid me the splendid remuneration of three pounds ten shillings a week, and I stayed with a Madame Penison in the Victoria Road. I had a very comfortable room with crisp, clean French linen and, because this was the summer season, fresh flowers by the bed. My room and board cost me thirty shillings a week.

'From the residue of my earnings, I ran a superb Ariel Square-Four motorcycle, paid for on HP at a few shillings a week. I smoked five Woodbines a day, drank a quantity of rough cider and found I still had enough left over to escort "lady friends" out for cups of tea, ice cream and to take them dancing at Sherry's Dance Hall and generally lead the life of Riley.'

Quoted in 1996 in the *Daily Mail*.

ON HIS RADIO ROLES:

'I was in Naval intelligence during the War, and they sent me down to see a radio show that Lieutenant Eric Barker was doing. It was rumoured to be insulting to leading figures in the Government, and I was sent to put a stop to any risqué jokes. I sat in the auditorium, and Eric said, "I want somebody to shout out these lines". I said, "I'll do it". He looked at me and said ,"Who are you?", and I replied, "I'm a spy!". I told him that I'd been sent to check up on him, but if he let me say the lines I'd be a very bad spy. So he let me say the lines. The lines were [in a broad Cockney accent], "Leave him alone, you're always picking on him, the poor perisher!". Eric's actress wife Pearl Hackney would then walk in and say, "Who's that?", to which Eric would reply, "That's the Minister for Education!" (who was a Cockney at the time) – it was precisely the sort of joke I was supposed to stop!

'After this, Eric asked me if I wanted to go back the following week, which I did, and that was my big break in show business. That was my stepping stone from straight theatre to light radio, which was all-important then. I stayed with Eric for eight or nine years after that. We bought the rights to the show called *Mediterranean Merry-Go-Round*, and there were three versions for Army, Navy and Air Force. The Air Force one became *Much Binding in the Marsh*, the Army version became *Stand Easy* with Charlie Chester, and we became *Waterlogged Spa*, in which I played a postman (on whom I based the voice of the Worzel Gummidge character I play now).

'Much later, we did *The Navy Lark*, and I asked for two *names* alongside myself to appear, as I'm a great believer in teams. We got, originally, Leslie Phillips and Dennis Price. We took it in turns to top the bill each week. My voice man was Ronnie Barker. Michael Bates, Richard Caldicott and Heather Chasen were all beginners in radio and part of my team. Ronnie left after a while because he hadn't the time to keep doing it. He was becoming much too important in the business.'

Interviewed by Sheldon Collins, Robert Cope and Gary Leigh-Levy in 1988 for *Dream Watch Bulletin* Number 64.

'In spite of all my "voices" – and I used to use forty-two different ones in *Waterlogged Spa* – they aren't imitations. I adapt them from people I know. The "er, er, um, um-er" stutter is taken from the lady who used to serve in my school tuck shop. She used to try terribly hard to remember everybody's name as we all surged in for our daily bun and bottle of pop, and she'd mumble away to herself until she obviously couldn't go on saying "er, um" any longer, and she'd shout, "Next".

'Commander Highprice, my confidential spy, is based on my cousin. Cousin Hugh has a slight impediment to the roof of his mouth and he speaks quietly and confidentially to you as if every word were top secret. So I "borrowed" him.'

Interviewed by Val Marriott in 1973 for *Leicester Chronicle*.

'The BBC suggested doing a new comedy series based round the armed forces. They suggested the Air Force, but I said no, if it was any of them it had to be the Navy, and besides I was a Navy man. I did six years during the last war.

'A Navy man can get away with things that the other armed forces can't.

'The only people who've left *The Navy Lark* over the past fifteen years have been the late Dennis Price, who went after the first series, and Ronnie Barker. I'm rather glad that Ronnie left, not because I don't think that he is a super person – I do – but because it has given me a chance to do all the funny voices and not just the part of the Chief Petty Officer.

'The show has a sort of humour that doesn't really change. I've nostalgic feelings for it as well now.

'We do work to a script, but we're always flying off the page. This is a fantasy thing.

'I find it easy to imitate accents, but I can't copy people's voices. I have a set of gramophone records at home, and if I'm required to learn an accent, I put them on. It takes me only about fifteen minutes to pick up the way of speaking.'

Interviewed by John Kelleher in 1974 for *Cambridge Evening News*.

ON HIS FILM ROLES:

'My earliest film of any merit was *Murder at the Windmill*, which I made, I suppose, in the late forties, with Garry Marsh and Jimmy Edwards. It was about the Windmill Theatre and I played a detective. It was a very good little film and made an awful lot of money – in fact it's still making money in America.'

Interviewed by Simon M Lydiard in 1984 for *Skaro* Volume IV Number 3/4.

'I doubled for Danny Kaye in a film called *Knock on Wood*. Danny was double booked. He'd signed for something else in America. I didn't want to do it, but the film company were very persuasive. "This is a great opportunity," they said. "We'll get a lot of you on camera!" "You'll get my arse on camera!" The only way to put people off is to be ridiculously demanding. So I said to my agent, "I want a suite at the Savoy, I want a Rolls Royce hired, I want a Berkely caravan to use on location – the most expensive one you can buy – and at the end of the shooting I want it given to me. I want no publicity, I want all the clothes that I wear in the picture ..." – and everything else I could think of! I asked "What are they offering?" and when told replied, "Don't be ridiculous, I want five times that!" I did everything I could to get them to say "Is he out of his mind?" They took one look at my demands and said, "OK. Agreed." So I hoisted myself on my own petard.

'On the opening night, the film was very well received. A little Irish journalist went up to Danny Kaye and introduced himself. "I thought Jon Pertwee did very well for you," he said. "Yes, Jon did a great job," came Danny's reply. "Thank you!" That was all he needed! A quote from Danny Kaye. "Danny's Double" next day in the headlines!

'The part that I had originated in the stage version of *A Funny Thing Happened on the Way to the Forum* was that of the brothel keeper, Lycus, but it was played in the film by Phil Silvers! "Jon Pertwee" meant nothing to the general public abroad, so they gave me a tiny part instead. My wife Ingeborg and I went out to Madrid, lazing around for a month. It would take only about a day to film, so this was a sort of sop to my ego, because 20th Century Fox felt sorry for me. I felt sorry for myself! I got out there and they said, "Could you play the brothel keeper tomorrow? Phil Silvers has got religious mania! He's jumping up and down on his bed relating the Lord's Prayer because nobody recognises him in Spain!" But a second assistant director – I could kill him when I come to think of it! – went to the director Dick Lester and said, "I can get Phil Silvers on the set for you tomorrow". "You can? Go to it, son! The world will be yours if you can do it!" So he went off and said to Phil Silvers, "Jon Pertwee is in town", to which Phil replied, "Who?" "He's the man who played Lycus on Broadway and in London, and if you aren't on the set by half-past six, he's taking over!" He was there! I could have killed that guy, because I don't think he would have appeared otherwise.'

Interviewed by Andrew Knight and Martin Guarneri in 1985 and transcribed by Paul Mount for *Doctor Who – An Adventure in Space and Time: Season Eight Special.*

ON HIS SECOND WIFE, INGEBORG:

'I met her in a place called Kitzbühel, an Austrian ski resort. I was there on holiday, and I broke my leg in half – a compound fracture – when I was out skiing. That's why I was hobbling around Kitzbühel doing nothing but sitting around in the sun, drinking cups of tea and coffee and chatting in the market. Anyway, when I got back, a married couple, friends of mine, wrote to her and invited her to come over to England and stay with them and get to know me. So that's how it all happened. Her name was Ingeborg Rhoesha, and her father was a very eminent financier in the West German government; she was born and bred in Berlin and later lived in Bonn.'

Interviewed by John Hudson and Stuart Money in 1975 for *Jon Pertwee Fan Club Newsletter* Issue 3.

ON HIS PORTRAYAL OF THE DOCTOR:

'I asked Shaun Sutton, Head of Drama at the BBC and an old friend of mine, how he wanted me to play Doctor Who. He said, "Well, as you". I said, "Yes, that's the problem: what is me?" Like Peter Sellers, I had always hidden myself under what's known in the theatrical business as a green umbrella. I'd always played character parts and eccentrics, I'd never allowed myself to be just myself ... So eventually I just decided to play him as I felt, so really what the Doctor liked was just an extension of what I like. I like rather outrageous clothes, speed-boats, gadgets, karate and so on. I don't know how he struck me as a man ... I don't think I went into it that deeply, to be frank.'

Interviewed by John Hudson and Stuart Money in 1975 for *Jon Pertwee Fan Club Newsletter* Issue 3.

'I said, "Why have you hired me if you don't want me to do what I've learnt to do over the years – and act?" The producer Barry Letts, bless his soul, said that it was the ultimate test of my acting ability, to see if I could take these predominant elements of myself and turn them into a character for the Doctor.

'If you think about it, it does take a lot of confidence to play as up-front a figure as the Doctor. Most of the time, actors can safely hide behind their art. With this part, I didn't have that kind of easy protection – there was no fall-back.'

Interviewed by Richard Marson in 1986 for *Doctor Who Magazine* Number 113.

'I got away with murder on *Doctor Who* ...

'I was just playing me for the first time really, and I made him a dashing bloke dressed in pretty clothes. This was in the Seventies when people were very clothes conscious and wore frilly shirts and colours. All that hooked at the right time. I put in the martial arts and my love of gadgetry, motorcycles, cars, Bessie, helicopters – these were things that I liked anyway, so I just adapted them into *Doctor Who*. Apart from being hard work, it was a piece of cake!'

Interviewed by Andrew Knight and Martin Guarneri in 1985 and transcribed by Paul Mount for *Doctor Who – An Adventure in Space and Time: Season Eight Special*.

'I leave Doctor Who in the studio. But Doctor Who *is* me.

'He is an extension of myself, a complete extension and therefore a completely believable character.

'I can't bring him home with me, though. Otherwise I'd be besieged by vast hordes of Daleks.

'And I'd be arriving home in the middle of the sitting room in a blue box. Whatever would Ingeborg say!

'Playing Doctor Who is a job. I am a working actor. But people see certain eccentricities in him which, as I've said, are extensions of myself.

'I suppose he shows a certain amount of intolerance to others on occasion, plus a keenness to get on with the job in hand and not just wait about.

'And I love playing him because he's so active and adventurous. Like me in many ways, I suppose.

'For example, I love gadgets. I've got a new machine in the kitchen that can turn out instant cold drinks. I'm all for anything new and extraordinary.'

Interviewed by John Deighton in 1973 for *New Reveille*.

'I've got the best job on television and I wouldn't drop it for the Royal Mint. For a major movie I'd drop it, but for the Royal Mint, certainly not.

'Of course the income is very nice. I get nine months a year steady work and I can carry on as long as I like.

'It may not be the heaviest show on TV, but then I'm far too old to worry about artistic integrity and all that.

'I play it for real … A send-up would be unforgivable.'

Interviewed by Patrick Stoddart in 1973 for *Evening Echo*.

ON HIS DOCTOR'S COSTUME:

'They asked me what I wanted to wear for *Doctor Who* and I had all sorts of ideas. Then I got an early photo call, so I found my grandfather's old Inverness cape, a smoking jacket I had, and a frilly shirt from Mr Fish. They thought it was marvellous. I said, "How can we explain the change from Pat Troughton's rags?" and that's why, in

Spearhead from Space, they had me steal all the bits of clothing from the changing room in the hospital.'

Interviewed by Stuart Money in 1977 for *TARDIS* Volume 2 Issue 3.

ON THE *DOCTOR WHO* MONSTERS:

'I'm sure there must be things that would attract attention like the Daleks have, and we have tried hard to find them, but so far without success.

'The kids always go for something mechanical. They don't want to be a maggot, but they do want to be a machine. It's very easy to go around saying "Exterminate, exterminate", and great fun for them.

'The conditions inside the rubber suits we use for the monsters are almost intolerable. We almost killed one little midget gentleman who had a bad heart and all sorts of things wrong with him, and we didn't know and we put him in one of these things and he almost died.

'It gets so hot and so uncomfortable inside them that actors are allowed to wear the suits only for five minutes at a time, which poses a big problem for the director.

'We were doing one episode in which the Sea Devils appeared, and they were in full costume with big lizard heads. They were supposed to be sea creatures, and in one sequence they had to swim out to sea and submerge. But the costumes were so bulky that they couldn't. The director was screaming at them to dive, but they just couldn't get under the surface. They were all wallowing and floundering about, and with the heads coming off and floating around it was a shambles.'

Interviewed by John Curzon in 1973 for *Western Mail*.

'I can't bear the Daleks. I find them very boring, because they're tatty. But the public loves them. Whenever we had a Dalek story, the ratings went straight up. I like the Draconians, which had marvellous warts all over their faces, and cock-comb tops. I like the Ogrons, the half-masks. I like the things that are humanoid. Alpha Centauri, the one with the tentacles, had that very bad eye-lid. I enjoyed the one where the spaceship landed outside the power station at Dungeness – *The Claws of Axos*. Remember the monsters they had in that one – fantastic rubberoid things that looked as if they were inside out. They were marvellous. I like the Exxilons, though the reflective material on the costumes didn't work as well as we'd hoped. To me, the Cybermen, although I've never seen them on the screen, always seem as if they were pieces of tin and pipe – don't they lack reality in some way?'

Interviewed by John Hudson and Stuart Money in 1975 and quoted in *TARDIS* **Volume 1 Issue 3.**

'Often a *Doctor Who* monster that looks good on screen will be laughably bad off it. The production team were always scratching something together from nothing. I remember one of the worst were the Primords in *Inferno*, which was partly directed by Douglas Camfield. The whole filming was going very nicely, we all thought, the script was a good one, full of frightening bits for the audience and lots of action for the Doctor. Then they unveiled these ridiculous werewolf things with great false teeth and fur-covered rubber gloves. They were *awful*.

'I remember asking Douglas if he was serious about using them, and although I don't think he was very happy about it, it was too late to do anything about it. Olaf Pooley, who was playing the main villain in the story, caused a great stir when he refused point blank to be made up as one of these things, and I have to admit, I saw his point.

'It's well known now, but my other pet hate is the Daleks. Couldn't bear the things and can't imagine how they could be so popular. They looked so primitive to me, trundling around in the studio, and it was a great fight for our directors to make them look anything more than a heap of old plywood on castors.

'It was just my luck that we did several Dalek stories, and I squirmed through each and every one of them.'

Interviewed by Richard Marson in 1986 for *Doctor Who Magazine* **Number 113.**

ON THE *DOCTOR WHO* STUNTS:

'I frequently hurt myself because I take risks, and I take tumbles.
    'My latest injury is a punctured vein in the hip.'

Interviewed in 1972 for the *Sun.*

'It's the stuntmen themselves who bear the brunt of this. In *Inferno*, I hit Alan Chuntz – I hit him with Bessie at about forty miles an hour and put eighteen stitches in his leg! He didn't get out the way quick enough, and it opened him right up from the knee down to the ankle-bone. And he never said a thing! He knew I was upset, so he came out of hospital back onto location saying, "I'm all right". We said, "Come on Chuntzy, don't be silly, go home". But he stood up and managed to get through about three shots before he passed out. He's such a tough guy, and a very fine stuntman. Black belt karate, as well. We had a fight in *The Green Death* where some guards attacked me in a sort of corridor, and these guys – Alan Chuntz and Billy Horrigan – fought each other and tried to make each other cry out, pinch each other, twist an arm. The amount of punishment they take is incredible. They do a superb job, and never really get a mention. They're some of the most dedicated guys in the business.'

Interviewed by John Hudson and Stuart Money in 1975 and quoted in *TARDIS* Volume 1 Issue 3.

'What we did in my *Doctor Who* was to try to combine two approaches. The Doctor would use physical violence only when and if he had to, but if he had to then, boy, did he sock it to them. I was very lucky to be backed by one of the best stunt teams in the business – men like Stuart Fell and my usual double Terry Walsh.

'Where I could, I would always do my own stunts, but on occasions one of the boys would take me to one side and say, "Look mate, this one is really too dangerous, let us do it, okay?", and then I would give way, because you just don't argue with the professionals.

'My other problem was my bad back. I've suffered any awful lot from it over the years, the result of all the wear and tear I've subjected it to during the course of my career, both in the Navy and in show business. When we were making *Doctor Who*, it was Katy Manning who used to come up with the best solution – massage. She had a very light touch, and before long I'd be back on the set, so when she left, I really felt it!'

Interviewed by Richard Marson in 1986 for *Doctor Who Magazine* Number 113.

ON THE WHOMOBILE:

'I'd suggested to Barry Letts that the Doctor ought to have a space age car that could fly, hover and so on, but Barry had said, "Forget it, the show wouldn't stand the budget". I still liked the idea, though, and consequently when I met Peter Farries – who designs custom cars – at a Ford Main Dealers shop opening in the Midlands, I put it to him. Together we worked out a practical design that would be both outer spaceish and street legal. Before that, everyone had estimated that the mould needed for the fibreglass body would need to be in at least eight sections. Pete did it in two. When fitted to the Bond Bug chassis, the car had a top speed of over 100 miles per hour.

'One of the great joys of driving the Whomobile was watching the astonished expressions on the faces of policemen who would periodically stop the car, surround it with tape measures and then have to go away nonplussed because, despite its shape, all the dimensions were in accordance with the law.'

Interviewed by Richard Landen in 1982 for *Doctor Who Magazine*'s Winter Special.

ON HIS FAVOURITE *DOCTOR WHO* STORIES:

'Undoubtedly the one we filmed at Aldbourne in Wiltshire – *The Dæmons*. That was a marvellous story, and Chris Barry's direction was really something. And it was an ideal length – five episodes. I've always thought if you can't tell a story in five episodes, you can't tell it at all. But then of course, you've got to consider the budget of the show.'

Interviewed by Stuart Money in 1977 for *TARDIS* Volume 2 Issue 3.

ON MAKING AN INPUT TO THE SERIES' SCRIPTS:

'I didn't have any input at all into the storylines. There wasn't the time. If I'm going to finish shooting one story at the end of next week, and two days after that I'm going to be starting a new story – now that story's already been produced, cast, they've got the director, special effects men, make-up, and all these people are different from the ones I'm working with on the story I'm doing now, so that's all prepared. Come Monday, there are the director and the producer who come in and say, "We've discussed all this months ago – here we go". So naturally I can't have any input, because I can't work months ahead and do a show as well. The only thing that could happen was on the Monday read-through. I'd read the script through and, being a very perspicacious man, I could see where the flaws were, which scenes I didn't like and wouldn't be happy with. I'd say, "I don't like this, I'd rather do this, that or the other". The writers would be there with the okay, or they would say "No", and then we'd have little verbal punch-ups, but in the main they would see my reasoning and would go away in a corner and rewrite over the lunch hour. Then it's fixed, and from the Tuesday onwards you stick to the script as arranged on the Monday. So that's the only input on the script.

'On the other hand, if I went to the Boat Show, as I did, and saw a miniature hovercraft, I would say to the fellow, "I play a character called Doctor Who. How would you like to have one of your machines on television?" The answer was usually, "You don't have to tell me, I know – and yes, anytime!" So this is why, right throughout my era, we had those jet-ski boats and so on – I mean, I own all of them, I've got them all out in my place in Spain. I no longer have the Whomobile, I gave that to a very sweet young man, but he lets me use it whenever I need it for events and things, and Bessie of course was BBC property, but all the jet-boats and motorbikes I bought. Of course, after giving them big publicity, I got them very cheap!'

Interviewed by Guy Wainer, Greg Jones, Neil John and David Greenham in 1990 for *Skaro* Volume 5 Number 2.

ON THE APPEAL OF HIS ERA AS THE DOCTOR:

'Like every other programme, *Doctor Who* has had to move with the times. The problems with which he now finds himself faced are very different from the ones he had when the programme first started.

'When *Doctor Who* began, no-one ever thought a man would walk on the moon, but that has now become commonplace, and people are much more aware of scientific terms and phraseology.

'Frequently I have to memorise pages and pages of long involved scientific explanations and, believe me, that's no joke when you've no idea what it's all about.

'But I am very fond of gadgets and love all the ones we use in the programme.

'*Doctor Who* appeals to all ages and all classes. A man might come up to me in the street and say, "My daughter always watches *Doctor Who*". I then ask him, "But what about you?"

'And he will say, "Oh, I never miss it either".'

Interviewed by Norrie Drummond in 1973 for *South Wales Argus*.

'One of the remarkable things about *Doctor Who* is that although it might occasionally seem a little banal, a little infantile, it is very seldom wrong. It is always scientifically true, and writers spend a great deal of time making sure of this. Every idea put forward is checked in our reference library or with scientists.

'I met a gentleman recently, the president of the British Boxing Board of Control, in Jamaica. He was a man of about 65, and his wife said that he was a most crashing bore because every Saturday night, no matter where they were or who they were with, he had to get to a television set to watch *Doctor Who*, and there are a lot of people in that age group like that.

'It's not a children's programme, it is a family show. Some of the dialogue is so technical and complicated that the kids can't follow it, in fact half the time I don't understand it myself. I've spouted two whole pages of script and I haven't the faintest idea what I'm talking about.

'But the kids have a much greater fantasy than we have and they can accept it overall without understanding every detail. I've got an eight year old boy and he's often confused scientifically but he gets the story dead right, and he asks a lot of pertinent questions that I just don't know the answers to, so I have to give him 50p to shut him up.

'I have a theory, which I use, that there's nothing more alarming than coming home and finding a Yeti sitting on your loo in Tooting Bec. If you find a Yeti in the Himalayas that's where you expect it to be, but if it's on the loo in Tooting Bec that's a real surprise. People didn't like us finding these creatures on Earth, they preferred us travelling about in time and space.'

Interviewed by John Curzon in 1973 for *Western Mail*.

'The standard of the stories was one of consistent excellence, rather than occasional peaks among the dross. There were very few poor stories – the odd script might have needed a bit of reworking in rehearsal, but generally I was very well served.

'Barry Letts was very keen on the moral message, and a lot of our scripts incorporated that philosophy so that we became instruments of different political and social arguments. We did one about sharing the planet we inhabit, we did one about pollution, and they all had a kind of truth that our directors would seek out and enlarge. I think this is the main reason why audience figures went up so significantly when I was on – I'd like to think it was solely because of me, but in reality it had a lot to do with the twin appeal of the scripts – they had the crash bang wallop for the kids and the inner message for the mums and dads. And, of course, they had Katy Manning in a mini-skirt!'

Interviewed by Richard Marson in 1986 for *Doctor Who Magazine* Number 113.

ON *DOCTOR WHO'S* SUITABILITY FOR CHILDREN

'*Doctor Who* does not harm children. It is pure fantasy. Children love fantasy. The monsters scare them a bit but only in the short term.

'I recently judged a competition for children's drawings of monsters. Some of them were utterly horrific.

'And you should have seen the hair-raising stories they wrote about them.

'Children do have this kind of imagination.

'You never actually see anyone stabbed with a spear or anything like that in *Doctor Who*. You just see somebody throwing the spear.

'It's the explicit James Bond kind of violence, messy and bloody, that I think is bad.'

Interviewed by Hilary Bonner in 1972 for *Reveille*.

'We admit our errors. But I am irritated by parents who complain that their children have nightmares after watching the serial. All they have to do is bend forward at an angle of 45 degrees and turn a knob.

'You've never seen me hit anyone to bloodlet, have you?

'There is no pain inflicted. People just disappear or wilt when I place two fingers on their chests. But that goes down as violence. For a time I was stopped from doing karate, or anything that could physically defeat Doctor Who's enemies.

'It got to the point where we were allowed only to trip up monsters. In the end, we said we could not carry on like that. It was just too ridiculous for words.

'Things are better now. I had a glorious wrestle in slow motion with the devil the other day. But it was not violent.

'We kept out all the karate chops to the neck, and that sort of thing, in case the kids try it. I feel that in comparison with other programmes, we are not in any way violent.'

Interviewed in 1973 for *Gloucester Citizen*.

'*Doctor Who* has been described as the most violent programme on television. That's rubbish. We're out to scare children because they love being scared. They'll hide behind settees with their hands over their faces – but they're still watching.'

Interviewed in 1973 for *Newcastle Journal*.

ON NICHOLAS COURTNEY AS THE BRIGADIER:

'Nick was and is one of the finest actors available for that mix of English reserve and pure irony. He was great to work with, because he was a lot of fun beneath a very cool exterior and he would always play the most serious of scenes with a detectable twinkle in his eye.

'I remember when we were on location filming for *The Dæmons* there were a series of delays, and it looked as if we might have to call it a day without getting what we wanted in the can. This would have been frustrating in itself, even had it not been for the long time we had all been standing around waiting for the command to do the scene. Well, on hearing this I hit the roof, using the most colourful language at my disposal and generally behaving in a most unprofessional manner. Nick was marvellous in fraught situations. He came up and stopped me in my tracks and made me laugh, which cooled the situation down. You can't resist a man with his sort of charm, and he was a super colleague to have in all those *Doctor Who* episodes we made together.'

Interviewed by Richard Marson in 1986 for *Doctor Who Magazine* Number 113.

ON ROGER DELGADO AS THE MASTER:

'Roger was one of the most gentle men I've ever known. He was the most courteous person – he had a temperament, but always pointed it at himself in rehearsals. He would go absolutely berserk with anger if he couldn't get something right, but always at himself, never at anyone else. He was charming, polite, kind and considerate. He and his wife Kismet were very close friends to Ingeborg and me, and we loved them very dearly. I was desperately shaken when he was killed. We looked after Kismet until she managed to get herself together, and we still see a lot of her. Roger played villains because of those marvellous, hypnotic eyes, and that beard – he always had the beard like that. He played villainous Arabs, villainous policemen in the Far East, villainous crooks.

'As time went on, the Master appeared less regularly in the series. We decided his regular appearance was a mistake, because I was always defeating him, which just made him look stupid. I think sometimes the Master should have defeated me temporarily at the end of a story – such as in *The Sea Devils*, but on a grander scale. It was suggested once by Nick Courtney that the reason we didn't kill each other was that fundamentally we knew there was some connection between us. Then we wanted it to turn out by a Time Lord giving the game away that we were, in fact, brothers, which would have been a rather clever idea. So Roger gradually faded from the scene a little. We brought him into only about two stories per season, which we found was better. I loved working with him, and still miss him tremendously.'

Interviewed by John Hudson and Stuart Money in 1975 for *Jon Pertwee Fan Club Newsletter* Issue 3.

ON HIS *DOCTOR WHO* COMPANIONS:

'In my opinion, Caroline John didn't fit into *Doctor Who*. I couldn't really believe in Liz as a sidekick to the Doctor, because she was so darned intelligent herself. The Doctor didn't want a know-all spouting by his side, he wanted someone who was busy learning about the world. Although Caroline and I worked well together, I don't think it did the series any harm when she left.

'Katy Manning was far and away my favourite girl, and she fitted in perfectly with the way I wanted to do the show. It was funny, Katy was by no means conventionally attractive, she was really quite a funny mix, but I still think she was incredibly sexy in the part, and certainly off-screen too.

'They tried to turn her into a bit of a swinging teenager in the series, but no way could they have shown the real Katy! She was enormous fun and exceptionally generous to work with, always a good steadying influence on my rather volatile temper. It was a very sad day when she married Stewart Bevan and left us.

'Lis Sladen was a very talented lady with tremendous looks and a smashing figure. I remember Barry Letts saying to me, "Come along and meet Lis," and as they were casting for Katy's replacement, I instinctively knew that this was the girl Barry had in mind. Anyway, he led me into his office and introduced us. We all stayed for coffee and some general conversation and little did Lis know that every time her back was turned, I was making thumbs-up signs to Barry who, when given the opportunity, was frantically returning them to me.'

Interviewed by Richard Marson in 1986 for *Doctor Who Magazine* Number 113.

ON LEAVING *DOCTOR WHO*:

'I felt the team was breaking up. It all seemed to be changing and I decided I would change with it.

'Perhaps it's a bad decision – *Doctor Who* would have been a certain bread ticket for another year. It's a gamble that I hope doesn't come amiss.

'I've enjoyed doing the part, but I like to keep in lots of media – a jack of all trades but a master of none.

'What I really want is a break. It doesn't mean to say I'll never be Doctor Who again. I would if the BBC wanted me.

'I have been out of the theatre for five years. It is time I went back.'

Interviewed by Tim Ewbank in 1974 for the *Daily Mail*.

'I have no vertebra between the fifth and sixth lumbars. I have been in permanent pain for the last two *Doctor Who* series and there are now certain things I cannot do, such as twist around easily or bend properly.

'I don't believe in pain killers. I have trained myself to live with the pain – to rise above it.

'The back business wasn't the only reason I left *Doctor Who*. I felt I had run the gamut for the time being, although if the chance ever came I would love to go back.

'*Doctor Who* was a marvellous experience. I became the godfather to groups of autistic children, under-privileged kids – all sorts of youngsters who needed the strength and protection Doctor Who personified.

'Nothing I could do in the future could give me the same kind of pleasure.'

Interviewed by Patrick Stoddart in 1974 for an unknown newspaper.

'For one thing, Roger Delgado, who played the Master, was a very dear friend of mine. We he died, I was terribly upset. Then the producer, Barry Letts, decided to leave. So did the script editor.

'And while Lis Sladen, who took over as my leading lady, is a lovely and very talented girl, it just seemed that the old team was falling apart. It was the end of an era.

'It has left me time to do *Whodunnit?*

'And I think it is a good idea to appear just as myself, so that people will stop thinking of me as Doctor Who.

'I hope to be back on television in about eighteen months. It's going to be an adult adventure serial with a difference.'

Interviewed by Margaret Forwood in 1974 for the *Sun*.

'I get rather sad sometimes when I think that it's all over and that I shan't be there for the new series.

'The following for the programme has been fantastic. I get hundreds of letters a week, many from underprivileged and autistic children who seem to have identified Doctor Who as a father figure.

'Schoolmasters have told me that the programme has a tremendous influence for the good, because the Doctor inspires confidence and trust – qualities children really need to understand.'

Interviewed by Graham Johnston in 1974 for *Lancashire Evening Post*.

ON *THE FIVE DOCTORS*:

'I was delighted to appear in *The Five Doctors* and I thought it was a great shame that Tom Baker declined to take part. Of course, it would have been nicer to have had a bit more to do, but that was necessarily a problem, considering the amount of characters Terrance Dicks was trying to cram into his script.

'Generally, I thought I was done justice, and I told the producer Nathan-Turner then that I wouldn't mind coming back again to do the odd special – only occasionally, as I'm a bit long in the tooth now for the kind of physical demands *Doctor Who* makes of one ...'

Interviewed by Richard Marson in 1986 for *Doctor Who Magazine* Number 113.

'One occasion that comes to mind is coming down a mountain at about eighty miles per hour. I was icy cold and my eyes were scarlet. (There's a BBC postcard of me from that show which, if you look, has got red eyes!) Then a cameraman said to Lis Sladen, "Would you mind slapping Jon's face?" She said, "Yes, I would, I'm very fond of him, why should I do that?" He said, "Jon's face has turned blue and that's the only way of getting some colour back into him!"

'How they got that whole story together, I'll never know. The director did an amazing job trying to control all of us, and it must have been very difficult trying to control Pat Troughton and me.'

Interviewed by Sheldon Collins, Robert Cope and Gary Leigh-Levy in 1988 for *Dream Watch Bulletin* Number 64.

'When we did *The Five Doctors*, Lis Sladen and I were concerned about how we were going to work together, not having done so for some years. We went up on top of a mountain in Wales and did our first scene and reeled it off in one take, with absolutely no problems at all. It was as if we had never stopped working. It was just an instinctive thing.'

Interviewed by Joe Nazzaro in 1991 for *Doctor Who Magazine* Number 170.

ON *THE ULTIMATE ADVENTURE* STAGE PLAY:

'I enjoyed the tour very much, but twelve weeks was plenty for me. At my age, living out of suitcases gets very exhausting after a bit. Luckily I had a wonderfully enjoyable company to work with, a lot of youngsters for whom this was their first job and who were superbly enthusiastic. They worked very well with very little kudos – because if you're in a Dalek or a Cyberman skin nobody can see your face, and thus nobody can say "Wasn't he good?".

'During its run, the play changed enormously. In a morning, we'd rehearse a whole new scene that would appear in that afternoon's performance. When you're doing a tour like that, all the time you're chopping and changing, and I would be making suggestions to the company manager and then we'd do ahead and do 'em.

'There were plans to take the show to Australia and the West End. I was going to have a couple of months off and then go on tour again for three months in Australia, then come back and do a Christmas season in London. But I wouldn't have gone to Australia – my wife decided that for me. "I hope you enjoy yourself in Australia," she said, "because I'm not going. I don't want to travel around anymore." I've been dragging her around like a gypsy for years! I work a lot in America, a lot in Australia, and the last few years in New Zealand doing *Worzel Gummidge Down Under*. She said, "I've got a home and I'm never in it – what the hell's the point?" She's a writer, my wife, and at the time was working on a novel with a historical tone – a big book, taking an awful lot of work. I wasn't going on my own, so that was decided.

'Then the plan was to have a lovely long holiday and come back if we had a West End theatre. Whilst we were at Bristol, Ruey Benjamin, who runs the Palladium, sent his daughter to report on the play. Typically with someone really important like that, she arrived ten minutes late, which does not give one a very good opportunity of showing what the play is like. It just doesn't mean anything unless you see the beginning. The producer Mark Furness already had '*Allo, 'Allo!* on, which was an enormous success at the Palladium, and I think *Doctor Who* would have done great business during the Christmas season. I'm sure of it. But it didn't happen.'

Interviewed by Guy Wainer, Greg Jones, Neil John and David Greenham in 1990 for *Skaro* Volume 5 Number 2.

'The performance had to be enlarged for a live audience. It couldn't be played down in the way I do on television. I work to a television camera very much like I work to a cinema camera, but the theatre technique is quite different. The performance had to be bigger, in this show particularly, because we were playing very big theatres.

'We had a short rehearsal period really, so we had to get the script right before we went to rehearsals. I got a very early copy and made copious notes, suggestions and cuts. The writer Terrance Dicks and I have worked closely for years, so that presented no problem. We agreed on many things.

'The script evolved as the show went on, but not a lot as I was hardly ever off the stage and so certainly didn't want to do any rehearsing when we were on the road. The kids in the cast did, because they were doubling up and playing five or six roles each. If somebody got sick, then somebody would step in and take over, but I didn't rehearse on the road at all. We got it more or less right.'

Interviewed by Joe Nazzaro in 1991 for *Doctor Who Magazine* Number 170.

ON SPARE TIME PURSUITS:

'Anything that is beautiful and pleases the eye appeals to me. That is why I collect paintings and antiques – and love my garden.

'My only regret is that my acting career takes up seven days a week and finding time to enjoy the treasures around me is a problem.

'Our favourite varieties of rose are "Blue Moon", "Peace" and "Piccadilly", but last year we bought some bushes of "Opera".

'Design is very much my forte and what I have in mind is to put all the beds at one end and have a large lawn where our children Dariel (11) and Sean (8) can play without fear of damaging something important.'

Interviewed by Brian Gibbons 1973 for *Garden News*.

'I used to take my wife hunting around junk shops for antiques but she so obviously hated it that I always felt I was keeping her from something she'd much prefer to be doing. It inhibited me, so now I no longer drag her along on shopping jaunts. I make snap decisions and they usually turn out right. If she makes a suggestion, "Let's paint this wall orange", I say, "Tell you what, darling, let me paint a bit of it and leave it for a week to see if you like it". Never fails. Once she sees the result, she knows it's wrong, whereas I can usually judge without seeing the whole thing. We are both perfectly happy with the way things are.

'She wanted this house in Barnes very much. I was not immediately attracted to it. I like "cottagey" houses with low beams which make me feel secure, but Ingeborg loved the space, the high ceilings, the tall windows of this house. I agreed for her sake and grew to love it.

'I had always been mad on this village. It's the Beverly Hills of London, all the pros live here, West End only minutes away. It still retains all the little shops, delivery boys come round on bicycles and the milkman passes on messages: "Oh, when you get along to Sylvia Syms, do tell her ..." – and he does.

'We made one mistake here. We put orange hessian on the staircase wall, which was good when the doors were painted white, but ghastly when the doors had been stripped down to the pine. We changed it to green instead of orange.

'And I'm not good at lighting. I find it difficult to achieve exactly the effect I want. Lighting and lamp-shades still present me with problems.

'My main love is primitive design, old oak furniture, simple classic things. I find some modern designs interesting. I don't like Victoriana or Edwardian things. I am really drawn to anything that smacks of antiquity and age.

'In most homes there has to be a compromise between appearance and practicability. I think a dishwasher, and gadgets like that, are essential to a happy home, and I wouldn't expect to burden my wife with endless chores on my behalf.

'Coming from a theatrical family, I have never had the desire to hang on to the theatrical way of life, as do many actors who come into the profession from outside and can't get over congratulating themselves for having made it. When I am not working, I like to get right away from everything connected with acting. I'm a great hobbies man.'

Interviewed by Shirley Flack in 1974 for _tvlife_.

'Relaxation is riding a motorbike, a bit of water-skiing, or a nice burn-up in the jet-boat. My wife thinks I'm demented.

'I was with some friends a few years ago in Australia, water skiing on the Hawkesbury River near Sydney, and I seem to remember that most of the people involved had been having a very good lunch and were well smashed. The pilot of a shark-spotting plane was there, complete with plane, and someone suggested I try for the world water ski speed record – towed by the plane.

'So we put eight ropes on and the pilot muttered something about it being all right as long as we avoided thermals, and off we went.

'We got up to about 60 mph and then we came to a bend in the river where the pilot hit a thermal and the plane went straight up in the air. This presented a problem: did I let go and risk breaking every bone in my body or did I hang on, take off, follow the pilot over the bank and try a water ski touch-down on land?

'I chose the river, let go and bounced along for about a mile. To my considerable surprise, I survived.'

Interviewed by Ian Cotton in 1974 for _TV Times_.

'There was recently an incident in Spain when I nearly lost my leg. It was badly cut by the prop of a speed boat. My mate would never listen to the instructions I gave him, the boat kicked and threw him out.

'I was worried the boat would go rogue and run down a lot of kids, so, I tried to swim into the middle of its circle and grab ahold of the rope hanging from the bow and get into the boat.

'It didn't work, with the result I got myself into the splits with one foot one side and one foot the other with the engine in the middle and me hanging on. I had three choices: one was to be drowned, because the water was pouring over my head; another was to let go – the boat would come straight over and disembowel me.

'I took the third, which was to risk letting this foot go and pushing the boat off course. As soon as I let it go, my foot went straight into the prop. I nearly copped it that time.

'When I was about fifteen or sixteen, I bought myself an SOS two-stroke, a trial bike, which was a swine of a bike that never went properly. The very first day I took it out, I drove it straight into a flint wall, and I've still got the scars to prove it.

'After the War, I got the bug for motor racing, but I realised that I wasn't cut out to be a really ace man. If you're not going to be an ace, don't touch it. So I started racing hydroplanes. I belonged to the British Outboard Racing Club, and I'm still an honorary president or something.

'I raced hydroplanes for quite a few years until that again became big money, and then I started messing around in karts before it all became very pricey and the sport feeling went out of it. I always get out when the thing becomes too heavy.'

Interviewed by John Bryan circa 1974 for an unknown magazine.

ON OUTER SPACE:

'I'm a great believer in all things being possible. I shouldn't be in the least disconcerted if I came face to face with a bug-eyed monster from outer space – I hope I do – and I've met ghosts and poltergeists many times. I'm convinced there is life on other planets.

'I only hope I'm around when they come visiting.'

Interviewed by Val Marriott in 1973 for *Leicester Chronicle*.

Character – The Third Doctor

The principal responsibility for casting a new leading man to succeed Patrick Troughton in *Doctor Who* rested with the series' then producer Peter Bryant, in consultation with his deputy and script editor Derrick Sherwin.

'I went through *Spotlight*, the casting directory,' recalls Bryant, 'and thought and thought and thought about it. My first choice was Ron Moody, who had played Fagin in the musical *Oliver!*. I felt he would bring something special to the role. When I approached him, though, he turned it down.

'The other person I had in mind was Jon Pertwee. Again, that was on the basis that he was somebody who had the personality to bring something to this difficult, nebulous part, which on paper means nothing.'

'I was in a radio programme called *The Navy Lark*,' Pertwee later recalled, 'and one day one of the other actors, Tenniel Evans, said "Why don't you put yourself up to play Doctor Who? I understand that Patrick Troughton is leaving." I said "Why the hell would they want me? I'm a sort of eccentric character actor." He replied, "I think you would make a very good Doctor Who." So I rang my agent and told him, and there was a terrible pause. I said, "All right, forget it, I suppose it wasn't a very good idea." He answered, "No, no. It comes as a bit of a shock, that's all. I'll ring them up."

'He phoned the BBC, told them he had heard that Patrick Troughton was leaving and that he wanted to suggest one of his clients to take over. The producer said, "Who's that?" When my agent told him, there was a long pause. My agent said, "Sorry, we'll forget all about it!" The producer then said, "May I read you our short list?" So he read the list, and my name was second – and none of us had any idea! That was how I got the job.

'I went to see Shaun Sutton, who was Head of Drama at the BBC and a very old friend – we'd started in the business together. I said, "How do you want this played?" and Shaun replied, "Well – as you." I said, "What is me? I don't know what I am!" You see, I had always "hidden under a green umbrella" – meaning one has always played character parts. I had never played "me". He told me, "We know what you are, that's why you've been cast, and if you play it as you, it will come out all right." So Doctor Who was me!'

Bryant's expectation was that Pertwee would give the Doctor a lighter, more whimsical quality:

'I hadn't met Jon Pertwee before I cast him, but I knew a lot about his work and thought he would bring some comedy into the programme. It had been getting a bit heavy towards the end of Patrick Troughton's stint and I felt it badly needed lightening. He was such a multi-talented man, Jon. He could sing, he could play the guitar, he could do funny voices and he looked very good. All these things I thought he would contribute to *Doctor Who*. He had great authority, too, when he wanted to use it. He'd been in the business a long time; he knew his way around.'

In the event, although a few touches of whimsical humour would be apparent in his earliest episodes, Pertwee ultimately played the Doctor in a predominantly straight, serious vein, and his interpretation of the role was not at all as Bryant had envisaged.

Pertwee signed his contract for his debut season – *Doctor Who*'s seventh – on 21 May 1969, and was presented to the press at a special photocall held at the BBC Pictorial Publicity premises in Cavendish Place, just across the road from Broadcasting House in London's West End, on 17 June, four days after the recording of Troughton's final episode and four days before its transmission.

An early priority was to decide upon the new Doctor's regular outfit, a task that fell to BBC costume designer Christine Rawlins in consultation with Pertwee and the production team. The costume was made by distinguished tailor Arthur Davey, and the final details worked out in two fittings, which took place on 27 August and 4 September 1969 respectively.

New producer Barry Letts, who took over from Bryant and Sherwin shortly after this, had no involvement in Pertwee's casting but was nonetheless delighted with it, as he told *Doctor Who – An Adventure in Space and Time* in 1986:

'The role of Doctor Who demands an actor who genuinely possesses that much over-used, and often erroneously attributed, phrase "star quality". Jon would be the first to admit he is no classically-trained actor. He isn't another Laurence Olivier. But what he does have is an enormous amount of that "star quality", both on screen and off, and it's what I believe made him so absolutely perfect for the role.'

Letts was also completely in favour of the idea of Pertwee drawing to a large extent on his own personality in his portrayal of the Doctor, as he noted in a 1983 interview for *Doctor Who Monthly*:

'No actor playing the Doctor should be acting *all* the time. There has to be enough of his own personality showing on the screen. It makes life easier for him, for the script writers, in fact for everybody.'

In keeping with Pertwee's love of energetic sports, fast modes of transport and stylish clothes, the new Doctor's image was certainly much more dashing and action-orientated than those of his predecessors. This was also very much in line with the production team's general desire to steer

Doctor Who in a more adult direction, away from science fantasy and toward science fiction, to which end they had already decided to change the series' format by having the Doctor exiled to near-contemporary Earth by his own people, the Time Lords.

Just as the rather quaint police box exterior of the TARDIS was abandoned for most of the seventh season in favour of the relatively technological-looking central control console, so the more whimsical aspects of the Doctor's character were gradually played down. He was placed in the position of being an expert or an adviser, a brilliant scientist called in to deal with problems too difficult for others to handle, and his standard costume was frequently discarded in favour of more commonplace clothing such as lab coats, space suits and overalls. Once his alien credentials had been established in his debut story *Spearhead from Space* – in which he is admitted to hospital after his arrival on Earth and the doctors discover that he has two hearts (later revealed in *Inferno* to have a normal beat rate of 170 per minute), an inhuman blood type and cardio-vascular system, and the ability to enter a self-induced recuperative coma – subsequent references to his origins usually took the form of humorous asides providing light relief from the action. Examples include his ability to communicate in Delphon by wiggling his eyebrows, as also demonstrated in *Spearhead from Space,* and his frequent name-dropping references to meetings with famous historical figures such as Raleigh (*The Mind of Evil*), Mao Tse-Tung (also *The Mind of Evil*), Napoleon (*Day of the Daleks*) and Nelson (*The Sea Devils*).

Parallels can indeed be drawn between the style of Pertwee's Doctor and that of the distinctly down-to-earth Jason King, the flamboyant, frilly-shirted author who was one of the central characters in ITC's *Department S* and who in 1971 would be given his own eponymous series. Another contemporary hero to whom Pertwee's Doctor bore some similarities was Simon King of the *Counterstrike* series, transmitted on BBC1 in 1969. King, an alien observer sent to Earth to monitor the activities of hostile invaders, attracts attention when he is admitted to hospital and is found to have non-human blood.

Programmes within the same genre often draw on the same stock settings, scenarios and character types, and similar hospital scenes can also be found in the opening episode of the 1966/67 BBC series *Adam Adamant Lives!,* the costume of whose central character was one of the main inspirations for the third Doctor's regular attire.

Much of the characterisation of the third Doctor during the early part of his era derived indirectly from the exile scenario, and in particular from the fact that this involved him entering into an uneasy alliance with the British branch of UNIT – the United Nations Intelligence Taskforce – under the command of Brigadier Lethbridge-Stewart. The writers had him making frequent attempts to escape from Earth – including stealing the TARDIS key back from the Brigadier after the latter confiscates it (*Spearhead from Space*);

trying to repair the TARDIS control console (*The Ambassadors of Death* and *Inferno*) and its dematerialisation circuit (*Terror of the Autons* and others); and enlisting the help of his arch-enemy the Master to overcome the Time Lords' grounding of the ship (*The Claws of Axos*) – and much of his dialogue with the Brigadier consisted of verbal sparring signifying his resentment at being confined to one place and time and effectively being reduced to the level of, and worse still having to rely upon, humanity.

There are indeed times, particularly during these early stories, when the Doctor is depicted as a somewhat aloof and arrogant character. He is gratuitously rude and insulting – he calls the Brigadier a 'pompous self-opinionated idiot' in *Inferno*, for instance, and frequently rails against UNIT's military solutions to problems – and at times is blatantly patronising toward his assistant Liz Shaw and her successor Jo Grant. This serves both to point up his superiority over others – a purpose to which he also (somewhat hypocritically) puts his UNIT connections on some occasions when dealing with civilians, such as in *Doctor Who and the Silurians* when he states at one point "I have the authority to do precisely as I please" – and to emphasise the frustration he feels at his exile. On the rare occasions when he does actually manage to leave Earth, it is only on the Time Lords' terms, because they want him to carry out a mission on their behalf – a fact that appears if anything to add to his frustration. "It seems that I'm some sort of a galactic yo-yo," he fumes in *The Claws of Axos*, on learning that the Time Lords have programmed the TARDIS always to return him to Earth.

The production team's decision to have the Doctor's sentence of exile lifted in *The Three Doctors*, the opening story of the tenth season, meant that the character and the nature of his association with the Brigadier and UNIT had to change. There was now nothing to prevent the Doctor from leaving Earth if he wanted to do so. This presented less of a problem than it might have done, as during the course of seasons eight and nine the writers had in any case gradually mellowed the Doctor's attitude toward the Brigadier – and indeed his demeanour generally. Originally depicted as one of uneasy mutual convenience, their relationship was by this point being presented as one of obvious trust and respect. There was consequently no great strain placed on viewers' credulity by the suggestion that a bond of friendship had grown up between the two men, and that the Time Lord was now quite content to spend a proportion of his time on Earth voluntarily helping UNIT to defend the planet against alien attacks and other menaces. The implication was that his previous desperate attempts to get away had owed more to the fact that the Time Lords had removed his freedom to do so than to any positive desire on his part to sever his connections with UNIT.

In these later stories, the Doctor no longer insults the Brigadier but instead just occasionally pokes fun at him – as for example in *Planet of the Spiders* when he learns of his one-time romantic liaison with a woman called

Doris. He even sometimes speaks in the Brigadier's defence when he is criticised by others, such as Professor Rubeish in *The Time Warrior*.

Similarly, the Doctor's attitude toward the Time Lords, initially depicted as one of great hostility and resentment, is by the latter part of his era being more commonly presented as one of allegiance and loyalty.

Certain aspects of the third Doctor's characterisation remained constant throughout. One example is his love of unusual modes of transport, first evidenced in *Spearhead from Space* when, as a condition for his continued co-operation with UNIT, he insists on being bought a vintage roadster similar to the one he appropriated from the hospital where he was treated after his arrival on Earth. In addition to this car, which he nicknames Bessie, he is also seen driving – amongst other things – a motorbike (*The Dæmons*), a three-wheeled trike (*Day of the Daleks*), a jet-ski (*The Sea Devils*), a Land Rover (*Day of the Daleks, Invasion of the Dinosaurs*), a milk float (*The Green Death*), a hydraulic lift (*The Green Death*), a futuristic hovercraft-like vehicle (*Invasion of the Dinosaurs* and *Planet of the Spiders*), a gyrocopter (*Planet of the Spiders*) and a miniature hovercraft (also *Planet of the Spiders*).

Gadgets are also a great source of fascination to this Doctor – another character trait drawn from Pertwee's own personality. Most notable is his trusty sonic screwdriver, which he presses into service far more frequently than in the past and uses for a variety of different purposes, including not only opening numerous doors but also hypnotising the planet Peladon's sacred beast Aggedor (*The Curse of Peladon*), detecting and detonating land mines (*The Sea Devils*), detecting anti-matter (*The Three Doctors*) and causing marsh gas explosions (*Carnival of Monsters*).

The third Doctor also retains throughout a notable pride in his appearance, which in *The Three Doctors* leads his first incarnation to brand him 'a dandy'. Typically he sports a velvet jacket over a frilly shirt and cravat or bow tie, sharply-pressed trousers and well-polished slip-on shoes. Frequently he also dons a cloak or a cape when venturing outdoors. Such is his concern with his appearance that in *Planet of the Daleks* he even finds time to change his clothes when trapped alone in the TARDIS faced with imminent suffocation! In keeping with his image of sartorial elegance, he is also a connoisseur of food and wine (*Day of the Daleks*) and can at times can be said to show a degree of vanity.

An athletic and physically active man, he is proficient in the use of Venusian aikido and – as seen in *The Sea Devils* – an excellent swordsman. Other previously unsuspected abilities include fluency in Hokkien (*The Mind of Evil*) and an apparent degree of precognisance, such as in *The Time Monster*, when he has a nightmare foretelling some of the events that are to occur later in that story, and in *The Dæmons* when he appears to realise that there is a problem at Devil's End before there is any indication of this.

Like his previous incarnations, the third Doctor has a strong sense of morality, is highly protective toward his human companions, and invariably exhibits great compassion for the oppressed and those in need of assistance.

The question of the Doctor's motivation was one to which the production team gave a great deal of thought, as Letts told *Doctor Who – An Adventure in Space and Time*:

'Terrance Dicks and I are great talkers and great listeners, and throughout our years together we were constantly striving to find a "rationale" for *Doctor Who*; an "ethic" if you prefer. I was very clear in my mind about what the Doctor would do and what he wouldn't do. He was a flawed knight in shining armour, but flawed only insofar as he was "human". In other words, he was a knight who had left part of his armour at home and had knocked the rest up out of old tin cans.

'In *The Time Monster*, the Doctor talks about his old teacher on the hillside who inspires him with his greed, a greed to experience all the wonders of these new worlds he goes to. There's nothing wrong with experiencing such wonders as an end, but what *is* wrong, and what is thus wrong in the Doctor's character, is the craving for it. *The Time Monster* paints him as an only semi-enlightened being – someone who sees more clearly into reality than we do, who sees more clearly into his own motivations than we see into ours, because he is further along the path, so to speak, but who is by no means fully enlightened. Unlike the old hermit, he is no Parsifal, no Buddha. On the contrary, the very fact that he stole the TARDIS in the first place, to escape and to satisfy his craving, is the key to the flaw that makes him fallible.'

This was a theme to which Letts returned in the third Doctor's swansong *Planet of the Spiders* – which, like *The Time Monster*, he co-wrote on an uncredited basis with Robert Sloman. On this occasion, the whole story was consciously conceived as a Buddhist parable addressing the Doctor's thirst for knowledge.

'There is nothing wrong with the acquisition of knowledge in itself,' noted Letts, who also directed the story. 'Indeed it is the goal of any being who travels along a path of meditation towards enlightenment. What is wrong is having a greed for that knowledge, as greed presupposes a preoccupation with the self, the ego. We know that in the beginning the Doctor stole a TARDIS to satisfy his greed for knowledge, and in *The Green Death* he stole one of the blue crystals for precisely the same reason.

'The spiders in *Planet of the Spiders* represent the aspects of the ego – the false self with which we identify, including all the greed and the avarice, which causes us suffering in Buddhist terms. The individual spiders latch onto people like that, exteriorising the ego. Then, at the end of the story, the Doctor goes right inside the blue mountain. That symbolises him going right inside himself, even though he knows it will destroy him; just as somebody going right to the end of Zen is willing to allow himself to be destroyed, the false ego being destroyed to find the real self. He knows he will be destroyed, but knows also that he will be regenerated.

'What he is going to find is the Great One – the core of egoism, the central motivator of our lives, which wants to be in control of the world. The way it wants to do this is to increase the power of the thinking mind, as opposed to the experiencing mind. In other words, the mind is trying to become the Buddha, is trying to become the Uncreated, the Unborn, the Whole, which is impossible. If anyone tries it, ultimately they're going to destroy themselves. So the Doctor goes in, confronts this, and sees that it is an impossibility. In fact he warns the Great One in scientific terms that it is impossible. The old man is destroyed and the new man is regenerated. Yes, it was all a quite deliberate parallel.'

On 8 February 1974, between transmission of episodes four and five of *Invasion of the Dinosaurs*, the production team held a press conference to announce that Pertwee would be leaving *Doctor Who* at the end of the series' eleventh season. Pertwee later stated in interviews that he was given no choice but to go when Head of Drama Shaun Sutton reacted unfavourably to a request he had made for an increase in his fee. Others, however, recall that he was keen to move on, fearing that if he continued to turn down offers of alternative work, they might soon dry up. In the press, he was quoted as saying that he wanted a break and that a major factor in his departure was the sadness he felt over the recent death of his friend Roger Delgado (who had portrayed the Master) and the gradual break-up of his team on the series (Manning having left the previous year, Letts and Dicks having both decided to quit the production team, and the apparent phasing out of UNIT).

So ended another era of *Doctor Who*'s history, with the departure of the dashing man of action who had been the third Doctor.

Rewriting the Myth

Plot continuity has always been a bug-bear of long-running television series. It could be argued that good continuity is essential in a popular soap opera for the sake of believability, but is it really so vital in a series such as *Doctor Who*? Certainly Barry Letts and Terrance Dicks, the production team who oversaw most of the third Doctor's era, had little interest in sticking slavishly to the precise details of what had been established in the past, particularly where to do so would get in the way of telling a good story. They were however keen to keep faith with the series' regular viewers by avoiding any major contradictions, and indeed to make use of and develop the series' mythology where to do so would be advantageous, for example in providing the basis for new adventures. In this they were assisted by the fact that the Doctor had until recently been presented as a highly enigmatic character of unknown origins – he had only just been disclosed to be a Time Lord in the closing story of the series' sixth season – leaving them a virtually blank canvass with which to work.

Created by Dicks and writer Malcolm Hulke, the Time Lords were to constitute one of the most important elements in *Doctor Who*'s development during the Seventies. Initially, however, little was revealed about them. In their debut story, *The War Games*, they had been restricted to a brief appearance, and been presented as a mysterious and rather aloof race possessing awesome powers – including the power to exile the Doctor to Earth and transform his physical appearance. Nothing more was then seen of them until season eight's opening story, *Terror of the Autons*, when a Time Lord emissary dressed in a supposedly inconspicuous business suit, complete with bowler hat and brolly, materialises in mid air to warn the Doctor of the presence on Earth of another of their race – a renegade known only as the Master.

With the exception of the Master, who was conceived by Letts and Dicks as a regular arch-enemy for the Doctor, the Time Lords' presence is more felt than seen during the remainder of the eighth season and the whole of the ninth. Although *Colony in Space*, *The Curse of Peladon* (at least, if the Doctor's assumption is correct) and *The Mutants* all involve them sending the Doctor on missions to other planets, only in the first of these do they actually make another brief on-screen appearance (when it is revealed that the Master has stolen some of their files – as also mentioned later in *The Sea Devils*).

The fact that they need the Doctor to carry out missions on their behalf makes the Time Lords seem rather less all-powerful than was suggested in *The War Games* – and arguably also somewhat hypocritical, given that their reason for exiling the Doctor to Earth in the first place was that he had broken their cardinal law of non-interference in the affairs of other planets. This impression is confirmed in *The Three Doctors*, the opening story of the tenth season, which constitutes their most extensive appearance to this point.

On this occasion, they are even seen to be vulnerable to attack, albeit by one of their own kind – namely Omega, the engineer who, by arranging the detonation of a star, gave them the power they needed for time travel. Omega (whose robes are reminiscent of those of his fellow Time Lords) was thought to have been lost in the super nova and has long been regarded as one of his race's greatest heroes. In truth however he became trapped in the universe of anti-matter, where he now survives purely by force of will. His attack on the Time Lords – which involves draining the universe's cosmic energy into a black hole – is motivated by a desire for revenge for his apparent abandonment.

The Three Doctors sees the Time Lords portrayed as an essentially technocratic race, heavily reliant on science for their position of power. They are also shown to have a hierarchy, with a President and a Chancellor (who apparently has the power to overrule the President) taking charge of the emergency – an emergency that they fear could leave them as vulnerable as those they are 'pledged to protect', a rather surprising sentiment for a race supposedly committed to a policy of non-interference.

Other information to be gleaned from *The Three Doctors* includes the fact that the Time Lords have some sort of time scanner capability that enables them to observe the Doctor during his first and second incarnations; that they are able to bring all three Doctors together, although to do so is in breach of the First Law of Time; and that they can communicate with the first Doctor even when he is stuck in a 'time eddy'.

Still *The Three Doctors* fails to reveal any great detail about Time Lord society, leaving a residual air of mystery surrounding them. It is not in fact until season eleven's opening story, *The Time Warrior*, that viewers even learn the name of their home planet, Gallifrey (amended slightly from Galfrey in writer Robert Holmes's original storyline).

The only other Time Lord seen during the course of this era is K'anpo Rimpoche, who features in *Planet of the Spiders* – the third Doctor's swansong. He appears initially to be a Tibetan Abbot in charge of a meditation centre in the heart of the English countryside, but the Doctor recognises him as his one-time Time Lord guru – possibly the same person as the old hermit he once mentioned to Jo in *The Time Monster*. K'anpo is apparently killed during the course of the action, but is almost immediately reborn in the form of his deputy Cho-je – a projection of his own future self. For the first time, the Time Lords' ability to transform their appearance in this way is referred to here as 'regeneration'.

Throughout his third incarnation, the Doctor works on a semi-permanent basis with the British branch of the United Nations Intelligence Taskforce, or UNIT for short, and its commanding officer Brigadier Alistair Lethbridge-Stewart – a scenario set up in the season six story *The Invasion*. The alliance is initially an uncomfortable one, forced on the Doctor by his exile to Earth, but it becomes gradually less so as time goes by, and ultimately continues even after he has had his freedom to travel in time and space restored by the Time Lords.

Starting with the Brigadier, a character established in the Sixties stories *The Web of Fear* and *The Invasion*, the production team gradually built up a small ensemble of UNIT regulars. First was Sergeant Benton, who had also appeared in *The Invasion* – then holding the rank of Corporal – and was reintroduced in season seven's *The Ambassadors of Death*. Then, at the start of season eight, Captain Mike Yates was brought in as the Brigadier's second-in-command, a function previously fulfilled by a number of one-off characters – Captain Turner in *The Invasion*, Captain Munro in *Spearhead from Space* and Captain Hawkins in *Doctor Who and the Silurians* – and even by the relatively lowly Benton in *The Ambassadors of Death* and *Inferno*.

Another new regular, Corporal Bell, was more short-lived, appearing in only *The Mind of Evil* and *The Claws of Axos*; and other UNIT personnel, such as Major Cosworth in *The Mind of Evil* and Sergeant Osgood in *The Dæmons*, continued to be brought in on a one-off basis. Lethbridge-Stewart, Yates and Benton, however, went on to feature in many stories during the third Doctor's era.

The Brigadier comes across as a soldier of the old school, a stickler for military correctness, and often shows a lack of imagination when dealing with alien menaces, choosing to shoot first and ask questions later. He has no doubt where his loyalties lie and is willing to do whatever is necessary to safeguard the world as he knows it. He does however mellow with age, his manner becoming less formal – as evidenced by the gradual lengthening of his hair – and his relationship with the Doctor becoming less abrasive. In *Planet of the Spiders*, the Doctor even learns of a romantic tryst he once had in Brighton with a woman named Doris.

Captain Yates seems initially to be very much in the 'Boy's Own' mould of dashing army officers, debonair and athletic, but it soon becomes apparent that there is a more sensitive, romantic side to his nature. This eventually leads him, in *Invasion of the Dinosaurs*, to ally himself to the idealistic cause of Operation Golden Age, and in the process to betray his friends at UNIT. Allowed to resign quietly when his misguided actions are revealed, he is later seen, in *Planet of the Spiders*, to be developing the more spiritual side of his nature at K'anpo's meditation centre. This is perhaps more in keeping with his character than was his previous military lifestyle, although he seems to slip back quite comfortably into the role of a hero in the ensuing fight against the giant spiders of Metebelis 3.

Benton, meanwhile, is a relatively straightforward character; a solid and ever-dependable soldier who displays a strong loyalty to UNIT, the Brigadier and the Doctor.

UNIT has its main headquarters in Geneva, and has to liaise with the regular Army when carrying out its British operations. The Army even has the power to arrest UNIT officers and personnel in certain situations, as seen for example in *The Claws of Axos* and *Invasion of the Dinosaurs*. The British branch of UNIT appears to have a number of different headquarters buildings, including at least two in central London (*Spearhead from Space* and *The Mind of Evil*), one beside a canal (*Terror of the Autons*) and one set in large grounds (*The Three Doctors*) – or possibly it is simply subject to frequent relocations. It also has mobile headquarters units (*The Claws of Axos* and *The Dæmons*).

It is never stated in which years the UNIT stories are set: in many respects they appear to be contemporary to the time of their transmission, but in many other respects they appear to take place in the future; Britain, for instance, has a space programme that has succeeded in mounting manned missions to Mars (*The Ambassadors of Death*).

Doctor Who and the Silurians introduces a race of intelligent reptiles who ruled the Earth before the rise of humankind. They went into hibernation when a rogue planet approached and threatened to wreak destruction, and failed to wake up again when this threat failed to materialise, as the rogue planet went into orbit and became the moon. *The Sea Devils* features an amphibious strain of these reptiles, who have lain dormant in a base off the English coast, and the Doctor states that they hail from the Eocene era (their previous identification as Silurians in *Doctor Who and the Silurians* being incorrect).

Other previously unknown information about the Earth's history revealed during the third Doctor's era includes the fact that by the twenty-fifth century it will have become a pollution-ravaged and overcrowded nightmare from which groups of people will flock to colonise other worlds (*Colony in Space*); that by the twenty-sixth century it will have a powerful empire spanning half the galaxy (*Frontier in Space*); and that around the thirtieth century that empire will decline and fall, with many of its subject planets being granted independence (*The Mutants*).

The third Doctor's era also sees a considerable amount of new information being disclosed about the TARDIS, including the fact that the central control console can be taken outside the ship and operated independently of it, as seen in *The Ambassadors of Death*, *Inferno* and *Day of the*

Daleks; that the dematerialisation circuit (a Mark I in contrast to the Master's Mark II) is vital to its function; and that the Time Lords are able to operate the ship by remote control. In *The Curse of Peladon,* the Doctor states that the TARDIS is indestructible. *The Time Monster* however brings the revelation that two TARDISes (in this case the Doctor's and the Master's) can materialise inside each other, and that if they are configured to occupy exactly the same position in space and time – a move known as time ram – this will result in their total annihilation.

The Time Monster introduces the TARDIS's telepathic circuits, by which the Doctor manages to communicate with Jo after being consigned to the time vortex. On the Doctor's instructions, Jo returns him to the ship by activating a unit marked 'extreme emergency' on the control console. In *The Three Doctors,* the Doctor uses this same unit to send a request for assistance to the Time Lords, and in *Planet of the Daleks,* he uses the telepathic circuits to send a further such request. Also in *Planet of the Daleks,* the control room is shown to contain a wall unit from which a medical bed can be made to slide out for use in an emergency; and the Doctor almost dies after the police box outer shell is completely coated in fungus and the emergency oxygen cylinders run out. In *Death to the Daleks,* the ship's power is drawn off by a living city on the planet Exxilon, causing its systems to shut down completely – even to the extent that the Doctor has to open the main doors with a mechanical crank handle.

A number of stories, including in particular *The Time Monster* and *Planet of the Spiders,* even give strong suggestions that the TARDIS might actually be akin to a sentient being.

In *Day of the Daleks,* the Doctor mentions to Jo the Blinovitch Limitation Effect – an idea devised by the production team to explain away the paradoxes they saw as inherent in the concept of time travel, and later mentioned again in *Invasion of the Dinosaurs.* Interviewed in 1983 for *Doctor Who Monthly,* Letts explained how the idea had come about:

'Terrance Dicks and I had endless discussions about this whole question of the time paradox. What happens if you go back in time and shoot your grandfather before he's met your grandmother? You can't be born because your father was never conceived and, if that is so, how then could you shoot your grandfather? In short, time travel is impossible, and so we had to think of reasons that would make it *seem* possible. This was particularly true where we had action taking place in two parallel times.

'In *Day of the Daleks,* guerrillas were coming back from the future to the present day in repeated attempts to blow up a peace conference. While this was going on, the Doctor had gone ahead into the future to try to sort things out there. So there was action going on it two places at the same time. Now why, we wondered, should these events be going on coincidentally? Why, if you travel forward in time for a day and then come back, do you find a day has elapsed in your own time too? It isn't necessary at all: you could come back the day before, if you wanted to, surely.

'In the end, this difficulty really got on top of us. Having had it at the forefront of our minds for so long, we eventually had Jo Grant say to the Doctor, in effect, "Why don't we go back to the day before and get it right this time?" There is no real answer to that, so what the Doctor said was something like "Ah well, that's the Blinovitch Limitation Effect." When Jo said that she didn't understand, the door opened and in came the guerrillas. So we never explained the Blinovitch Limitation Effect, but it provided us with a way out of time paradoxes.'

Arguably rather at odds with this concept, *Day of the Daleks* reveals that the Daleks have undertaken a second invasion of 22nd-Century Earth – the first having been seen in the season two story *The Dalek Invasion of Earth*. It also has them using a race of unintelligent ape-like creatures, the Ogrons, as guards for their human slave workers. They initially fail to recognise the Doctor as their old adversary (unlike when he previously changed his appearance, in *The Power of the Daleks*), but then confirm his identity by way of a mind probe that extracts images of his previous two incarnations.

The Ogrons appear again in *Frontier in Space*, and the Daleks turn out to be behind a plot by the Master to cause a war between the rival empires of Earth and Draconia – the two dominant powers of the galaxy. In the following story, *Planet of the Daleks*, the Daleks' huge army is seen held in suspended animation on the planet Spiridon, waiting for the invasion to begin – an event that, in the end, is forestalled by the Doctor. Amongst the new facts revealed about the Daleks in this story are that they have been experimenting with invisibility; that their casings emit an automatic distress signal if opened; and that they are susceptible to extreme cold.

Death to the Daleks, the last Dalek story of the third Doctor's era, sees the machine-creatures encountering problems with the same power drain that has affected the TARDIS. They remain able to move about – something that the Doctor puts down to the psycho-kinetic nature of their motive power – but their weapons are initially useless. They overcome this obstacle by fitting themselves with new projectile weapons, which they test out by firing at a small model police box!

The other established *Doctor Who* monsters to be brought back for return appearances during this era were the Ice Warriors, who had been previously seen in two second Doctor stories – *The Ice Warriors* and *The Seeds of Death*. *The Curse of Peladon* reveals them to have forsaken their traditional warlike ways and joined a peaceful planetary alliance called the Galactic Federation, which also counts Earth, Alpha Centauri and Arcturus amongst its members – although the Arcturan delegate on the committee to assess Peladon's suitability for admission to the Federation turns out to be a traitor. In the sequel, *The Monster of Peladon*, the Doctor encounters a breakaway faction of

Ice Warriors, led by Commander Azaxyr, who want their race to return to its old ways. With the Time Lord's help, however, they are eventually defeated.

The Time Warrior sees the introduction of the Sontarans, who would go on to become one of the series' most popular alien races. In this story, Linx, a Commander of the Fifth Army Space Fleet of the Sontaran Army Space Corps, crash-lands his golfball-like ship in Medieval England. It is revealed that his race – three-fingered clones with huge domed heads – are locked in a near-perpetual war with the Rutans. They are dedicated to military efficiency, but do have one weak point – the probic vent at the back of their neck – which proves to be Linx's downfall. The Sontarans know about and have carried out a military assessment of the Time Lords – who they have concluded would be unable to withstand a sustained attack – and have their own, albeit relatively primitive, time travel capability achieved through the use of an osmic projector.

All in all, the third Doctor's era saw some significant changes taking place in, and some important additions being made to, the *Doctor Who* universe; a legacy that would remain with the series and be further built upon in later years.

Costume Design

Television is an essentially visual medium, and it should therefore go without saying that the success or failure of any programme will depend to a large extent on the visual realisation of the ideas worked out by the writer, director and production team. This is arguably all the more so in the case of a series such as *Doctor Who*, which relies for its impact on the willing suspension of disbelief by its audience. The on-screen depiction of the Doctor's fantastic and other-worldly adventures must be sufficiently convincing to enable the viewer to accept them as real – an illusion that can be very easily shattered by, say, a false-looking visual effect or a poorly executed monster. All too often, though, the role of the series' designers is overlooked or undervalued. This chapter aims to help redress the balance by highlighting one particular area of design – costume – that, along with others such as make-up and visual effects, makes a vital contribution toward the presentation of every *Doctor Who* story.

The usual practice during the 1960s had been for a particular costume designer to be allocated to *Doctor Who* on a semi-permanent basis, to handle a run of consecutive stories. This approach was continued at the start of the 1970s as newcomer Christine Rawlins was assigned to provide the costumes for all four stories of Jon Pertwee's debut season, season seven.

This assignment was not an entirely welcome one for Rawlins, as she was no great fan of science fiction in general or of *Doctor Who* in particular.

'I don't think I've ever watched the series before or since!' she commented in an interview for a 1988 issue of *The Frame*. 'To be honest, science fiction doesn't interest me particularly. When I was told I was doing *Doctor Who*, I did look at a few episodes but, no, it wasn't something that I'd thought that I'd want to do.'

An early priority was to design the new Doctor's costume; and although Pertwee would often state in interviews that this had come together more or less by accident, when he had decided to wear some of his grandfather's old clothes to attend a photocall, in Rawlins' recollection there was rather more to it than that:

'Around that time, there was a series called *Adam Adamant Lives!*. Adam Adamant was dressed in period costume, complete with cloak, and I remember thinking that something rather "romantic" like this would be a good contrast to the previous Doctor. That Jon Pertwee was thinking along the same lines was an agreeable coincidence, though whatever Jon had wanted, I'm sure the producer would have endorsed.

'Jon was extremely positive and professional and cared very much about the "look" of the whole production.

'Arthur Davey – a brilliant tailor – made the outfits for Jon.'

With the Doctor now exiled to Earth, season seven saw the Brigadier and his UNIT troops appearing as regular characters in the series. This initially entailed little extra work for Rawlins – for the first two stories, *Spearhead from Space* and *Doctor Who and the Silurians*, the UNIT uniforms created by Robina 'Bobi' Bartlett for the previous season's *The Invasion* were simply brought out of storage and reused, with extra copies made where necessary. Rawlins did however have to design all the outfits for the other new regular introduced at this point – the Doctor's assistant Liz Shaw, played by Caroline John.

For *Spearhead from Space*, Liz wore a very distinctive jacket that Rawlins created with the benefit of experience gained during her earlier career as a teacher of fashion design.

'We'd been teaching our students about vacuum moulding, which the Royal College of Art were doing in quite a big way at that time. I designed Liz's jacket so that the panels at the front were vacuum-moulded, while the rest was a jersey material. The jersey eased, but the vacuum-moulded sections were rigid, so you got an interesting effect. I remember Caroline John was fascinated by the whole thing. She was lovely.'

It has often been suggested that the UNIT stories were supposed to be set at some point in the future, but this was not something that Rawlins was asked to reflect in her costumes.

'No. In fact, the general rule I worked to on this season was to make the costumes sort of indeterminate, so that you couldn't specify a time period. Take the Autons, for example, with their boiler suits. The thing about boiler suits is that they are simple, straightforward – dateless – and come in sizes to fit everyone. We put scarves on them to hide the awful join at the neck. The masks were made by Visual Effects, and of course Make-up was very much involved.'

A similar collaboration between departments took place on *Doctor Who and the Silurians*.

'I remember the Silurians quite well. The costumes were very uncomfortable to wear, and got very sweaty inside!

'Jim Ward of Visual Effects designed the heads and put the lights in, and I was responsible for the bodies. They were actually sent outside the BBC to be made. We were looking at dinosaurs and prehistoric animals, and so the scaly suit evolved.

'The costumes were made from sheets of moulded rubber – ghastly to wear! – and, as far as I remember, they weren't tailored to the individual actors. We just made some standard sizes and they had to fit: that was the only thing we could do, so far in advance.

'I remember Jon Pertwee being very anxious about the join between the head and the body, which he thought was too obvious. It wasn't absolutely ideal, but we had to be able to lift the actors out very quickly if anything went wrong, because they could hardly breathe in there. I think it looked better when we got into the more controlled situation of the studio, after the location work, because it could be covered up more easily there.'

For the following story, *The Ambassadors of Death*, one of Rawlins' main tasks was to design the advanced spacesuits worn by the astronauts.

'That was actually a problem, because the first moon landings had only just happened in 1969 – the idea of somebody actually walking on the moon was still considered astonishing – and yet for this story we had to assume that space travel was usual. The aliens' helmets and suits were supplied from outside the BBC by a freelance contractor, Jack Lovell. The suits were made of quilted material, so they were rather like protective jump suits or jogging gear. The helmets were simple, too, and the attachments were reduced to the minimum.'

'We did make those spacesuits that appeared in *The Ambassadors of Death*,' confirmed Jack Lovell's son John in a 1989 interview for *DWB*, 'although they were actually made for the film *Moon Zero Two* and the BBC hired them out from the costumiers Bermans and Nathans for that story.'

The next story, *Inferno*, had relatively straightforward costume requirements.

'There's nothing much to say about that one really,' noted Rawlins, 'except that I think it was a good story.

'I remember there was a requirement to put UNIT in battle dress type uniform. For the soldiers in the alternative world, we just used different epaulettes and so on. We also gave them a different, American-style beret.

'Olaf Pooley as Stahlmann wore a Nehru suit, with the high collar. I remember taking him to Bermans and Nathans to get that made. There again, it was dateless in a way, yet also rather fashionable at the time, with the Indian influences around.'

Looking back on her year with *Doctor Who*, Rawlins reflected that it was not a very happy experience. Quite apart from the fact that she encountered a rather strained working atmosphere on the series, she found it extremely problematic to have to design the costumes for four stories in succession so quickly.

'Just as you were getting into the studio with one story, you had to design the next one. You had two directors demanding your attention at the same time! It was tricky. I do think my design was pretty awful, for that reason. I was the last costume designer to do a whole year of *Doctor Who*. Afterwards, the BBC, in their wisdom, changed that policy.'

In line with this change of policy, the work on the five stories of season eight was split between four different costume designers. The season opener, *Terror of the Autons*, was handled by Ken Trew, whose tasks included creating costumes for two new series regulars: Roger Delgado as the Master and Katy Manning as Jo Grant.

'Roger and I sat down and talked about how he wanted to look,' recalled Trew in a 1989 interview for *Starburst*, 'and we developed the idea of a business suit with a difference. It was at the time that the Maharajah jackets were just coming in, so we based it on that design with an embroidered collar. With Katy Manning, there wasn't much actual designing as such. We would take her shopping for fashionable clothes, to places like Biba's.'

The Mind of Evil marked the return to *Doctor Who* of season six's principal costume designer, Bobi Bartlett.

'I actually had a very harrowing experience on that one,' she recalls. 'It was quite a nightmare! I had to provide an awful lot of costumes – hundreds in fact – including some traditional but modern Chinese uniforms, which had to be made up from scratch, for the delegates at the peace conference. Now, whenever I had needed to get military-style costumes made up for a programme in the past, I had always gone to a very talented young man at Bermans and Nathans. At this time, when I came to do *The Mind of Evil*, he had just gone freelance and set up his own business specialising in uniforms, and naturally I went to him just as usual – he had always done such a good job for me in the past. I gave him all my designs and instructions, and told him that he had about six weeks in which to get the job done. Unfortunately, it turned out that he was in dispute with his former employers, and actually ended up in prison! I could never get to the bottom of what the disagreement was about. All I knew was that he was making up these costumes specially from my designs, so he couldn't have been at fault there.

'I tried everything I could to get things straightened out, but without success, so obviously I was left with a big problem. The police had seized everything from the costumier's premises, so I had to go down to the police station and search through a whole pile of clothes in one of the cells, to try to find my costumes. I was saying, "Look, I'll have a heart attack if I don't find these costumes. I'm trying to dress a *Doctor Who* story and I really need them. They must be here somewhere!" I actually got the detectives to help me look for them, but we couldn't find them anywhere.

'In the end, I decided that the only other thing I could do was to go to the prison where the costumier was being held and try to get in to talk to him. So I took a taxi to the prison, told the driver to wait outside for me, and went up and banged on the door. At first they didn't want to let me in, as it wasn't visiting time, but I demanded to see the governor, and eventually they took me through to the yard and locked me in a sort of cage, which was normally used by press reporters. There were some phones in there, so I got permission to call the BBC and tell them what was happening. I was trying not to panic, and to give the impression that this was just an everyday experience for me. You know, I was determined not to be fazed by it! I expect the guards were having a good laugh at my expense, or else they simply didn't believe my story.

'Anyway, about ten minutes later, a guard came back, keys clanking, and let me out of this cage. He said that the governor had agreed to see me, and showed me into his office. The governor sat there, wide-eyed, as I told him "You're not going to believe this, but ..." I explained what had happened, and eventually he agreed that I could speak to the prisoner by phone from his office. So they let this poor man out of his cell and got him to a phone, so that I could speak to him! I said "I'm terribly sorry about what's happened to you, but I've got to ask you where those costumes are." And it turned out that he'd never actually had a chance to get them made up before he was arrested! This was now less than two weeks before filming was due to begin, and I had no costumes!

'Fortunately he was able to tell me where all the material was, so I cut the conversation short, thanked him, and said to the governor, "Look, can I make some more phone calls? I've got to arrange for these costumes to be made up immediately." I was taken back into the same cage with all the phones, and got in touch with another costumiers in Shaftesbury Avenue, who agreed to do it as a rush job. I had to pay over the odds, as they had to bring in extra people and work overtime – sometimes through the night – but fortunately they managed to get everything done in time. I remember that when filming finally got underway, everyone on the production was saying that I had performed a minor miracle – because by this time, of course, the story had got around about me going to this prison and making them let me in!'

To provide the Axon monster costumes for the next story, *The Claws of Axos*, producer Barry Letts went direct to an outside contractor, Jules Baker. The other costumes for *The Claws of Axos* were designed by Barbara Lane. This was her first assignment on the series, but she would go on to handle a further three stories – *The Dæmons*, *The Curse of Peladon* and *The Time Monster* – during the third Doctor's era. She recalled her *Doctor Who* work in 1973 in an interview for a special *Radio Times* publication to mark the series' tenth anniversary:

'I had done a little science fiction work before *Doctor Who*, with programmes like *Out of the Unknown*. But I like doing all sorts of design – everything from classic serials to light entertainment. *Doctor Who* always presents special problems. The script provides you with a framework to build your monsters round, so at least you know whether it's smooth or hairy, six-armed or two-armed. But the big problem is that the costume has to fit over a human shape and yet disguise the fact there's a man or a woman inside.

'Inspiration can come from many directions. Prehistoric monsters are always good for research, so I often go round the museums or look up books before starting a design. The people the Doctor found in Atlantis [in *The Time Monster*] were in costumes based on ancient Cretian wall-paintings.

'As for materials, I try to use anything new that comes on the market. Plastic materials normally used for industrial purposes prove very useful, because they can be moulded to many different shapes and they're light to wear. If you make costumes too heavy, you're likely to find people fainting in them – we had that with the early Cyberman costumes, which were so bulky they had to be held together with nuts and bolts. I often use latex rubber, and the large, solid costumes are usually hung around a cane frame. For hairy creatures I sometimes use a man-made fibre usually used for rugs.

'Costumes for the "ordinary" characters are easier. I wanted Katy Manning to look a little way out, yet be dressed in practical clothes because of all the chasing about she had to do. That's where a trouser suit comes in handy. Jon Pertwee came up with his own designs originally, but I wanted him to look a little trendier, so I designed him a rather smart smoking jacket and a tweed cloak – but still cut on Victorian lines.'

Four costume designers who notched up just a single credit each on *Doctor Who* were Michael Burdle for *Colony in Space*, Mary Husband for *Day of the Daleks*, Maggie Fletcher for *The Sea Devils* and Hazel Pethig for *Planet of the Daleks*. Far more significant was the contribution made by James Acheson, who handled a number of stories during the third and fourth Doctors' eras and later went on to a highly successful career in feature films, winning three Oscars in recognition of his achievements.

Acheson had long been an admirer of *Doctor Who* before he first came to work on it for the season nine story *The Mutants*. In general, however, the series was not highly regarded within the Costume Department.

'I think one of the reasons for that,' noted Acheson in a 1987 interview for *The Frame*, 'was that people were quite scared of doing it, because it asked you to be more imaginative. It also demanded that you worked not just with bits of silk chiffon and three yards of wool crepe, but with fibreglass and plastic. People got a bit wary if they'd been used to working with dress fabric all their lives. They thought fibreglass was a remote, chemical process that ought to be left to other people rather than embraced and used. I found that idea rather exciting.'

The Mutants offered plenty of scope to try out unusual techniques and materials.

'That was the first show I did on my own, god help me. How I got this break was that Barbara Lane, the costume designer who was doing it, fell ill. I think we had about three weeks to put it together.'

The biggest challenge on this story was posed by the Mutant creatures themselves, and Acheson decided to contract out the making of their head masks to freelancer Allister Bowtell.

'I got a call from Jim Acheson,' remembers Bowtell. 'I didn't actually recognise the name, but when he appeared at my front door, I realised that he had been a student at Wimbledon Art School when I had been a teacher there, and our paths had crossed then. Now here he was, working for the BBC, wanting to talk to me about making a *Doctor Who* monster.

'The nice thing about this job was that it was the first time I had discovered and used foam latex. It was very difficult to get hold of – we went direct to Dunlop. It consisted of a five part mix and involved a baking process, which we had to do in a domestic oven. It was all very crude, but the material was lovely and flexible and so we decided to use it. We had some success, although only a moderate amount as we had to cast something like ten masks to get four useable ones out.

'The carapaces and claws were done by the Costume Department; I just did the masks. I sculpted the head, made the mould and then cast the masks – the whole process. I also painted them, and Jim then repainted them. I think the total cost was about £60 each.'

'One of the loveliest things about *Doctor Who*,' noted Acheson, 'was the planning meetings, which were very extensive, often extremely complicated and involved all the departments. We would sit round a table and thrash out how we were going to create these miracles in the twenty-five minutes' screen time we'd got. One had to work very closely with the director, because everybody had to know all the elements that went into a story – whether it was Colour Separation Overlay, whether your monster could get through the door, and so on.'

These were still early days in Acheson's career and, despite receiving welcome support from Letts, he felt that he sometimes made mistakes – principal amongst which he considered to have been the four Gel Guards in *The Three Doctors*.

'What one had always been taught to believe in and to respond to was the script. I mean, that's your starting point. So if a writer writes down that strange, jelly-like blobs with an eye in the middle are devouring people at will, that's what you do. You go along with the author's conception. What one came to realise was that often a literary or mental idea of what a monster ought to look like is hugely impractical, and that often one has to throw out an author's concept. And that was where one learned one's lesson, because those particular monsters were a disaster – an absolute disaster.

'They were impractical from all points of view. You were asking somebody to blob along in rough terrain without showing their legs and wearing an extremely hot and uncomfortable costume. I'll never forget the first day – I think it was at Rickmansworth chalk pits – when the van arrived with these blobs. They were pulled out of the back of the van, and people just laughed. I mean people just laughed at these things. It's a terrible moment when something like that happens, because you then have to live with these mistakes for however long it takes to make a whole four part story. It's a chastening experience.'

As in the case of the Mutant masks, the Gel Guard costumes were contracted out to be made by Bowtell (who, on the strength of his work with Acheson, had been added to the BBC's list of *bona fide* suppliers, and would subsequently become involved in numerous other productions).

'The Gel Guards were basically tailored out of about two inch thick foam rubber,' explains Bowtell, 'covered with vacuum-formed hemispheres of different sizes and latex over the whole lot. The Effects Department made the special claw with lights running down it.

'We also made the mask for Omega, although not the costume.'

'For Omega,' noted Acheson, 'I looked at lots of Greek masks. It was sort of based on a Greek theatre mask. I remember there were some very nice Colour Separation Overlay tricks for the scenes where Omega takes the masks off and there is no head behind it. I loved learning about effects like that. There were a couple of real young boffins – Dave Jervis I think was one – who had managed to create a little department for themselves. When you think of what we have now, with the amount of video graphics and paint boxes – the whole development of video trickery – those guys were pioneers.'

Acheson used reference material to recreate the costumes of the first two Doctors, but decided to redesign totally the costumes of the other Time Lords.

'I can remember looking at some Time Lords from previous stories and not liking them very much. The cliché of costumes for *Doctor Who* – or *Star Trek*, *Star Wars*, you name it – is that everybody seems to wear what's called a patrol collar, a stand collar. I noticed that whenever anyone moved their head, the collar would always become very crumpled. So on the Time Lord costumes, we used a shoe lining material for the shoulder pieces. You soak this in acetate and can then mould it over bodies. In fact, we moulded it over dress dummies. It gave everybody a very clean, armoured look around the heads.'

Acheson had previously used the same material for the costumes of the Inter Minorians in *Carnival of Monsters* – which although transmitted immediately after *The Three Doctors* at the start of the series' tenth season had been made some months earlier at the end of the ninth production block.

'These gentlemen were originally going to be wearing grey masks covering the whole head,' he noted, 'but when they put them on, they couldn't talk or act, so they all ended up with bald heads! But that was a Visual Effects Department problem.'

The costume created by Acheson for the showman Vorg had posed an unusual difficulty: the transparent bowler hat had steamed up at regular intervals! The headgear for Vorg's assistant Shirna had proved more successful, however.

'These were supposed to be a couple of vaudeville entertainers lost in space. At the time, you could go into any kind of horrible gift shop and find these springy things with balls on the end. They were just decorative gifts, but I thought they looked like planets revolving around a solar system, so we made a silly head-dress out of them.'

Barbara Kidd was the costume designer assigned to *Frontier in Space* – the story made between *Carnival of Monsters* and *The Three Doctors*. Like Acheson, she was very pleased to have an opportunity to work on *Doctor Who*.

'*Doctor Who* was just brilliant,' she recalls, 'because you did drawings and actually designed things – things you thought up in your head rather than researched from books.'

Frontier in Space featured a number of different groups of characters, and consequently had relatively heavy costume requirements. Particularly memorable were the Draconians. The initial concept for the heads of these creatures was sketched out by director Paul Bernard, and the masks were then made by Visual Effects Department sculptor John Friedlander, who had previously worked on other creatures such as the Ogrons (for *Day of the Daleks*) and the Sea Devils. The rest of the costume, however, was Kidd's responsibility.

'There was just a pencil sketch of the head,' she confirms, 'and that was all I ever saw. The body of the Draconian was designed by me. The basis was a sort of Samurai look. Originally the shoes were made out of flip-flops; we stuck lots and lots together to give a platform effect. On the filming, though, they all broke, so we had to use something else. I can't remember what we used in the end.'

When designing futuristic costumes for human characters, Kidd tended to opt for simple, elegant styles reflecting a logical progression from contemporary fashions – a reaction against what she saw as the excesses of some other designers when assigned to science fiction productions.

'The futuristic costumes for *Frontier in Space* were inspired by the idea of comic book drawings,' she notes.

Kidd went on to work on three further third Doctor stories – *The Green Death*, *Invasion of the Dinosaurs* and *The Monster of Peladon*. The latter featured the return of the Ice Warriors, but their costumes were simply taken from stock and sent out to be repaired by Bowtell.

'The Ice Warriors were incredibly uncomfortable things,' observes Kidd. 'They were just fibreglass shells that were bolted together, and once the guys were inside them, they couldn't get out – there was no release mechanism. They were incredibly hot, too. When they sat down between takes – and they always seemed to have to wait a long time for their scenes to be done –

their heads disappeared into their bodies, and they would just sit there like that!'

Kidd's ambitious original design for the Vega Nexos character seen in the first episode of *The Monster of Peladon* had to be dropped in favour of a simpler approach when it proved too expensive to realise.

'I was always very disappointed with the BBC's attitude towards *Doctor Who*,' she asserts. 'It was watched by millions of kids and adults, but because it had already captured that audience, they couldn't see why they should spend any more money on it. That, to me, was just the wrong way of thinking. If you've got an audience of that size, then you should put money into it, because those people should have the best that's on offer.'

Season eleven's opening story, *The Time Warrior*, was another for which Acheson provided the costumes. The most notable innovation on this occasion was Linx the Sontaran, whose look he devised in collaboration with make-up designer Sandra Exelby.

'The Visual Effects people had designed the costume and the facial features of the Sontaran up to a point,' recalled Exelby in an interview for *The Frame*, 'but they couldn't do the whole thing, as they needed time to design the spaceship. At our first planning meeting, we all sat down and the director, Alan Bromly, tried to explain the kind of thing he wanted. I can't remember if it was I or James Acheson who suggested that he should look half man, half frog and have no neck. We thought the lack of a neck would enhance the impression of him being frog-like.'

'The head had been modelled by John Friedlander,' confirmed Acheson, 'I think before I joined the production. We just had this very silly idea that he should have a helmet and that, when he took the helmet off, the head should be almost the same shape.

'I often worked very closely with John. He was very, very clever. He was making people speak through rubber masks long before he had the right materials available.'

The Sontaran's helmet and collar were contracted out to be made by Bowtell, but not the mask itself.

'The actual making of the mask was the responsibility of Visual Effects,' explained Exelby, 'as at that time the Make-up Department didn't have any facilities for making prosthetics. (It can be classed as an early prosthetic as it did use a certain amount of foam.) They took a cast of the actor Kevin Lindsay's face, and I went to help them do this, as I don't think they had ever done face casting before. They then constructed the mask from latex and fibreglass (without the resin – just the glass matting used to build up the shape). The top lip actually went inside Kevin's own lip as a flap. The bottom lip was attached under his lip, so there was some movement there, and then I just painted his lip in the same sort of browny-green colour as the mask. I also had to attach the mask round his eyes, adding make-up there to blend it in.'

The final addition to the ranks of the series' costume designers during the third Doctor's era was L Rowland-Warne, who handled two stories – *Death to the Daleks* and *Planet of the Spiders*. One of his challenges on the former of these was to create the look of the Exxilons, as he recalled in a 1988 interview for *Starburst*:

'The script said that they came out of the rocks, so I went to the location with the director and took Polaroid photographs of the sand dunes. Lots of these dunes had little ridges where the water had run down, and so I tried to incorporate that into the costumes. They were made from calico, onto which I laid torn terylene wadding that had been dipped in latex and silica. I used wood dyes in with the latex to give it colour, then created the texture by spraying on plastic paints. I designed the masks, which were then made by John Friedlander just before he left the BBC.

'Barry Letts made sure there was a logical reason for everything: the underground Exxilons were smaller than those on the surface because they had split away from the rest of their species generations earlier. To make them look different, we tried painting them with fluorescent paint, but that didn't do anything. In the end, we achieved luminous patterns on their bodies using a process called front axial projection. I contacted a company that make reflective road signs and got hold of some paint that reflects only when you are looking down the axis of the light. The studio cameras were fitted with a light source, which then lit up the fluorescent channels on the Exxilons' costumes.

'The subterraneans actually had to be glued into their costumes. There is a shot on the location filming of one of them looking over a hill, where we didn't glue the mask down, and you can see the back of it flapping in the wind. When we came to the studio, they were all sealed into their costumes, and were able to cool down only by removing the eye pieces.'

It was common practice for spare copies of costumes to be taken on location in case the originals became dirty or suffered unexpected damage, and Rowland-Warne recalled an incident during filming of the chase sequence for the second episode of *Planet of the Spiders* that illustrated the potential dangers of foregoing this precaution:

'The gyrocopter was being flown by a pilot wearing Lupton's jacket, which was tweed and I had found in BBC stock. Unfortunately the gyrocopter crashed. The pilot escaped without injury, but the jacket was in shreds on one side and I had no duplicate. I tried to buy another, but they had ceased to be made years before. So, on location, I had to make up the missing bits by taking out the turnings and sticking these onto the lining of an old anorak, which I then tacked onto the jacket. As it was a check jacket I joined all the pieces together and stuck them on with copydex.'

Rowland-Warne also recalled the recording of the regeneration scene at the story's conclusion:

'We had Jon Pertwee lying on the floor, which was then marked, and we moved in Tom Baker. The image was then rolled back and mixed. We always had a spare set of clothes for Jon in case one set got dirty, so Tom was dressed in these, as they were of similar build.

'I got on very well with Jon. We were both jokingly rude to one another, but he was lovely – a real professional. He took *Doctor Who* very seriously, but was wonderful with kids. We were filming the hovercraft chase from *Planet of the Spiders* never the Severn estuary, and he got very wet. We went back to the hotel and there were hundreds of kids who wanted his autograph. He got them all lined up, popped off to put on dry clothes and then came back down. We were all knackered, and yet he stayed and talked to them for an hour or so.

'Lis Sladen was also lovely. We mainly bought her stuff from Bus Stop, and we would go and choose from the new collection. I felt that she was an ordinary girl of the present day who would wear ordinary clothes.'

The arrival of the fourth Doctor marked the dawn of a new era for *Doctor Who* but, although many changes lay ahead, one thing would remain constant: the series' costume designers would continue to play a crucial role in the successful on-screen realisation of the Doctor's adventures.

Production Development

The start of the third Doctor's era coincided with a significant change of direction for *Doctor Who*, as co-producers Peter Bryant and Derrick Sherwin decided to have the Doctor exiled to Earth by the Time Lords and allied with UNIT under Brigadier Lethbridge-Stewart. In a contemporary interview, conducted toward the end of 1969, Sherwin explained his aims for the new format:

'What I want to do is to bring *Doctor Who* down to Earth. I want to mould the programme along the lines of the old Quatermass serials, which I found so compelling. I want to establish the concept of having things happen down on Earth, with people with everyday lives coming up against the unknown.'

The influence of writer Nigel Kneale's three ground-breaking BBC Quatermass serials – *The Quatermass Experiment* (1953), *Quatermass II* (1955) and *Quatermass and the Pit* (1958/59) – was certainly very apparent in the transmitted stories of season seven, which presented essentially the same scenario of a scientist (the Doctor) and his assistant (Liz Shaw) facing horrific alien threats, hindered by sceptical Earth authorities and with much of the action taking place in advanced laboratories, secret research establishments and sinister industrial complexes.

Of the four individual stories, *Spearhead from Space* is the one that most closely follows the narrative of a *Quatermass* plot. Here, just as in *Quatermass II*, a shower of hollow 'meteorites' brings to Earth a disembodied alien intelligence that takes over senior establishment figures and ultimately manifests itself as a hideous many-tentacled monster. *Quatermass* elements also feature in all the other stories. In *Doctor Who and the Silurians*, the discovery of aliens buried deep underground triggers a race memory in some human beings, a plot device also used in *Quatermass and the Pit*. *The Ambassadors of Death*, like *The Quatermass Experiment*, involves a missing space capsule later recovered with alien life on board. And in *Inferno*, as in *The Quatermass Experiment*, an infection gradually transforms men into vicious monsters.

The move to a near-contemporary Earth-bound setting and the conscious adoption of a more adult tone also gave *Doctor Who* something of the feel of a conventional action-adventure drama, the alien menaces encountered by the Doctor seeming all the more strange and unnerving for being seen in contrast with everyday settings – the 'Yeti on a loo in Tooting Bec' factor often cited by Jon Pertwee. Not only was this in accord with the artistic preferences of Bryant and Sherwin, but it also meant that the cost of creating fantastic alien settings and civilisations – something that had strained the series' budget to the limits during the latter part of the second Doctor's era – could be avoided. The increased use of location filming and the foregrounding of UNIT's military hardware, such as the 'Windmill' helicopter, also brought James Bond and war film connotations to the series, while UNIT itself recalled similarly-designated organisations such as UNCLE in the MGM/Arena series *The Man from U.N.C.L.E.*

The team of the Doctor, the Brigadier and Liz Shaw – a sophisticated assistant in contrast to the impetuous young companions of the past – followed the two-heroes-and-one-heroine set-up of many traditional action series, such as ITC's *The Champions, Randall and Hopkirk (Deceased)* and *Department S*, all of which were made at the tail end of the Sixties. Moreover, the fact that costume designer Christine Rawlins partly based the new Doctor's standard attire on Adam Adamant's period garb is only one of a number of respects in which the imagery of early-Seventies *Doctor Who* echoed that of the BBC's *Adam Adamant Lives!*. Another striking example lies in the fact that the Doctor was given a highly unusual car with a gimmick number plate, 'WHO 1', just as Adam Adamant had acquired a distinctive Mini Cooper S, number plate 'AA 1000'. In terms of its actual appearance, the Doctor's vintage roadster, Bessie, was very reminiscent of the cars driven by John Steed in *The Avengers*, the ITV series with which *Adam Adamant Lives!* had been designed to compete. The concept of the Doctor's exile to Earth, meanwhile, recalled the fate of comic strip superheroes such as DC's Superman and Marvel's Silver Surfer, a character who in his first adventure was deprived of his powers to travel through space and time and exiled to Earth for daring to defy his master.

Whilst acknowledging that the new format ushered in by Bryant and Sherwin dealt in the currency of conventional science fiction and fantasy-based action-adventure series, it would be wrong to suggest that it was completely dissimilar to Sixties *Doctor Who*, which had itself drawn on many of the same genres and traditions. It could indeed be seen as representing simply the culmination of a number of trends that had begun during the second Doctor's era, such as the increasing reliance on Earth as a setting and the proliferation of stories taking place in and around advanced scientific establishments presided over by misguided authority figures. The Quatermass influence had been very apparent in season five's *The Web of Fear*; and a number of late-Sixties stories, including *The Faceless Ones* and *The Enemy of the World*, had shown leanings towards a James Bond-type thriller style. UNIT itself had been carefully established in the season six story *The Invasion*, to which *Spearhead from Space* bore a number of similarities, even to the extent of including a near-identical battle sequence filmed at the same location. Season seven also followed the lead of season six in focusing on human evil as much as, if not more than, alien evil.

In terms of its realisation, too, this first season of the Seventies, despite boasting a higher location film content, had much in common with those of the late Sixties. Each of its four directors had worked on the series before, and had consequently become familiar with its techniques and conventions. Michael Ferguson's style of direction on *The Ambassadors of Death*, for instance, was very reminiscent of his work on the previous season's *The Seeds of Death*.

The departure of Bryant and Sherwin and the arrival of new producer Barry Letts, who formally took over with effect from *Doctor Who and the Silurians*, resulted in the series harking back even more strongly to its Sixties roots. Although pleased that the emphasis of the series had, as he saw it, moved away from science fantasy and towards science fiction, Letts disliked the stories being set almost exclusively on near-contemporary Earth and determined to have the Doctor journeying once more into space and time. In this, he was strongly supported by script editor Terrance Dicks, with whom he quickly developed a strong and effective working relationship. To achieve their aim, they came up with the idea of the Doctor being forced to undertake occasional missions for the Time Lords – a plot device first used in *Colony Space*. They also felt that the series should become rather lighter in tone than had been the case in the recent past, with a greater focus on characterisation.

One element of season seven with which Letts and Dicks had been particularly dissatisfied was the character Liz Shaw. They felt that the independent, self-confident scientist had little need to rely on the Doctor for explanations, and so failed to fulfil the required dramatic functions of aiding plot exposition and acting as a point of audience identification. They therefore decided to drop the character and to introduce in season eight's first story, *Terror of the Autons*, a replacement more akin to the naive young 'screamers' of the Sixties.

The new companion was Josephine Grant – or Jo for short – an impetuous young woman assigned to UNIT as a result of some string pulling by an influential relative. Jo would frequently run into danger and require rescuing by the Doctor, who could take her under his wing in a way that would have seemed condescending with her predecessor. At the same time, she would provide the writers with an easy-to-use cipher for any plot information that they needed to convey to viewers.

The production team also decided at this point to enlarge the UNIT team by giving the Brigadier a new second-in-command more suited to his status than the relatively lowly Sergeant Benton. This was Captain Yates, who was also envisaged as a possible love interest for Jo – although, in the event, little came of this in the transmitted stories.

Another, arguably even more significant, innovation in *Terror of the Autons* was the introduction of a new villain in the person of the Master – a renegade Time Lord dedicated to evil – who would appear in every story of the eighth season. Dicks and Letts, when recalling how they came to create this character, generally cite Sherlock Holmes's great adversary Moriarty as their chief inspiration. The fictional concept of the arch-enemy goes back much further than Sir Arthur Conan-Doyle's novels, however, and was firmly established in many of the genres and individual sources upon which *Doctor Who* drew in its seventh and eighth seasons.

In the James Bond films, for example, Bond almost always finds himself pitted against some deranged yet brilliant super-criminal, intent on taking over or destroying the world by means of a fiendish – if highly convoluted and improbable – 'master plan'. The name and individual traits of the villain might sometimes change from one film to another, but the character fulfils essentially the same function every time – to act as Bond's arch-enemy.

Superheroes, too, need supervillains to battle against; and just as a superhero always has characteristic powers and special abilities, so too must his adversary. Batman, for instance, is aided by Robin, has the use of his utility belt, travels in the Batmobile and can call on the resources of the Batcave, while each of his regular foes – the Riddler, the Joker, the Penguin, Catwoman *et al* – has his or her own particular special abilities and trademarks.

In early Seventies *Doctor Who*, the Doctor is aided by Liz or by Jo, has the use of his electronic gadgets, travels in Bessie and can call on the resources of UNIT. He also has his own special powers and abilities: mastery of Venusian aikido; the ability to converse fluently in obscure dialects; a high resistance to G-forces; and even, in *The Ambassadors of Death*, the power to make an object vanish as if by magic and reappear a few minutes later, without any apparent technological aid. The Master, filling the previously-vacant role of the Doctor's arch-enemy/supervillain, quickly establishes some of his own trademarks: the use of a matter-condensing gun; the power to hypnotise people and force them to do things against their will; and the expert use of disguises.

The Master's name is itself evocative of similar characters in other series, such as Batman's aforementioned adversaries and Adam Adamant's recurring foe, the Face; and it had been used once before in *Doctor Who*, for the mysterious controller of the Land of Fiction in the season six story *The Mind Robber*. As Letts and Dicks recall, however, their main reason for choosing this name was that, in common with the Doctor's, it corresponded to an academic qualification.

The only humanoid villain to have appeared in more than one story prior to the introduction of the Master had been the Time Meddler – also a member of the Doctor's own race – in the mid-Sixties. He however had been a very different type of character, motivated by a mischievous sense of fun and a desire to 'improve' the course of history rather than by a genuinely evil disposition. A much closer antecedent to the Master in terms of character traits can be found in *The War Games* in the person of the War Chief, an evil renegade Time Lord cynically exploiting his alien 'allies' as part of a scheme to gain power for himself – something the Master would also attempt in stories such as *Terror of the Autons*, *The Claws of Axos* and *The Sea Devils*.

The Doctor's relationship with the War Chief was quite different from those with his previous adversaries. The two Time Lords were seen to discuss the pros and cons of their situation in an academic, almost detached manner, and for once, the Doctor appeared to regard his opponent as an intellectual equal. When the War Chief tried to strike a bargain, offering the Doctor a half-share of power in return for his help, viewers were left with serious doubts as to what the Doctor's reply would be. This curious rapport – an indefinable bond, perhaps, between two members of the same race, outcast amongst lesser beings – was also very apparent between the Doctor and the Master. The Doctor seemed actually to relish each new encounter with his arch-enemy, admitting at the end of *Terror of the Autons* that he was 'almost looking forward to it'; a perhaps surprising sentiment, given the death and destruction that the Master had just caused.

While the War Chief can be regarded as a direct forerunner of the Master in terms of his motivation and his relationship with the Doctor, the War *Lord* – another character in the influential season six story *The War Games* – was a much closer parallel in terms of appearance, with his bearded, saturnine countenance and his plain black suit, complete with Nehru-style high-collared jacket. The hypnotic powers displayed by the War Lord's race, the Aliens, similarly foreshadowed those of the Master.

Quite apart from fulfilling the function of an arch-enemy, the Master also provided the production team with a means of lending credibility to a situation – a rapid succession of seemingly unconnected threats to Earth's security – that would otherwise have become increasingly unbelievable. All the various alien invasion attempts presented in the eighth season were seen to be due purely to the Master's intervention, and the Master's interest in Earth due mainly to the Doctor's own presence there. The workability of the exile scenario was thus preserved, although at the cost of a certain degree of predictability in the stories. The production team soon realised that viewers would eventually lose patience with the inclusion of the Master as the major villain in every story and with the long list of alien beings seemingly queuing up to attack the Earth. They therefore decided to limit the Master to one or two appearances per season from that point onwards, in conjunction with their policy of moving the series away from a totally Earth-bound setting.

Another shift of dramatic emphasis that occurred after *Terror of the Autons* sparked off a wave of criticism from some commentators about the levels of violence and horror in the series.

'There were big leading articles in several newspapers complaining bitterly about what we'd done,' reflected Letts in an 1990 interview for *Doctor Who Magazine*. 'We even had a letter from Scotland Yard about the policemen who turned out to be Autons, saying "Please don't do it again".

'I think we did go over the top but, when you think of it, the most terrifying things are ordinary things that can't be trusted. If it's a monster, it's a monster, and you know where you are. But if a toy comes to life and tries to kill you, it's not so funny.

'The BBC kept a very close eye on us after that, and we made sure we didn't do that sort of thing again, although in stories like *The Dæmons* we came close to it.'

Season eight had in many respects laid down a template for the remainder of the third Doctor's era. The gritty realism of the previous year's stories and been discarded, and *Doctor Who* had been steered back more towards a family audience. UNIT continued to represent an important element of the format, but characterisation and humour had now been given precedence over military hardware and action set-pieces; and while in season seven the Doctor's relationship with the Brigadier had been one of uneasy mutual convenience, during season eight it had become one of obvious friendship. The Doctor himself had also mellowed, losing the harder edges of his rather arrogant season seven persona and becoming a debonair and reassuring uncle figure, albeit still a man of action. There had now been established a group of reassuringly familiar regular characters – the Doctor, the Brigadier, Jo, the Master, Yates and Benton – and the actors who portrayed them had bonded together into a highly effective team, their *esprit de corps* readily evident from the transmitted episodes. All these developments would be carried forward and built upon.

Season nine consequently saw *Doctor Who* enjoying a period of relative stability. It had the same production team and main cast as season eight and was made in much the same style, continuing the mixture of stories set on near-contemporary Earth, where the Doctor operated as UNIT's scientific adviser, and occasional forays to other worlds, where he acted as an agent of the Time Lords. The less frequent use of the Master, however, left the way clear for stories devoted to other adversaries; and the production team took this opportunity to bring back some of the traditional monsters for which *Doctor Who* had become famous in earlier years – a further nod toward the series' roots. The season thus saw stories featuring the Daleks, the Ice Warriors and the Sea Devils – amphibious counterparts to season seven's Silurians.

Season nine also saw the production team increasingly using the series as a vehicle to highlight some of their own interests and to comment obliquely on issues of current concern to them. Examples included *The Curse of Peladon*'s allegory of the UK's accession to the European Community (generally referred to at the time as 'the Common Market'), *The Mutants*' commentary on ecology, colonialism and apartheid, and *The Time Monster*'s exploration in one scene of the Doctor's motivation in Buddhist terms (Letts being a devotee of Buddhism). Letts, in particular, was keen that the stories should work on more than one level and have a moral message underlying the action.

'The morality question was important to me from two points of view,' he told *Doctor Who Monthly* in 1983. 'First, I believe television does exert a strong influence on people. I disapprove strongly of any sort of show – film or television – that says there is no morality; that it is purely accidental whether you're on the side of the goodies or the baddies, and the person who wins is the one who hits the hardest. Secondly, I feel something of the moral passion that George Bernard Shaw talks about. Now that's nothing to do with whether you're religious or not. I think that all humankind is looking for an order and a meaning to life, and a facet of that search is this quest for morality; finding it and then trying to live by it.

'To give you an example of this in *Doctor Who*, one of the first things I did editorially on the show was to alter the ending of *Doctor Who and the Silurians*. If you remember, it was the sequence where the Brigadier blows all the Silurians up. Now, in the script, after the Brigadier has done this act, the Doctor says something like, "What a terrible thing to do. Think of all the science they've got that we haven't," and so on. To me that was wrong, and I had it changed to, "But that is murder. Just because a race has green skin doesn't make them any less deserving of life than we are."

'Now talking about moral passion might sound a bit pompous, but being aware of it also makes for good storytelling. When people used to come up with a story, or Terrance and I thought of a story, and we couldn't quite see where we were going with it, we would say, "Let's go back to the basics and ask ourselves: what is the story about; what point is the story making?" If it's just an adventure chase-about, then it's very difficult to make a good story, because all you're doing is just inventing new incidents. On the other hand, if you go back to brass tacks and say to yourself, "The point of this story is, for instance, that just because a chap has green skin doesn't mean he should be treated as an inferior," then immediately things start to fall into place, so that if an incident arises within the plot, you can ask "Is this leading the story in that direction?" It is an enormous help in the structuring of stories to have a point or theme to the whole thing.'

The tenth anniversary season again saw *Doctor Who* looking back to and celebrating its own history. This was most readily apparent in the opening story, which continued the production team's practice of aiming to launch each new season with some sort of 'gimmick'. Previous gimmicks had been the introduction of the Master in *Terror of the Autons* and the return of the Daleks in *Day of the Daleks*. On this occasion, it was the teaming up of the third Doctor with the first and second in a story entitled, appropriately enough, *The Three Doctors*. This was also the point at which Letts and Dicks finally contrived to bring the Doctor's exile to Earth to an end, having the Time Lords restore his freedom as a reward for defeating the renegade Omega.

'A lot of people have asked me how we came to do *The Three Doctors*,' noted Letts in a 1981 interview for *Doctor Who Monthly*, 'but really, if you think about it, it's the most obvious plot device of all: to have a serial where all three of them come together. While I was producer of *Doctor Who*, hardly a week went by without somebody coming up to me and suggesting this idea. So, when we actually came to do the story for the anniversary year, it was more a case of bowing to pressure than divine inspiration.'

Other anniversary elements within season ten included the return of the Daleks, again aided by the Ogrons, in two linked six-part stories, *Frontier in Space* and *Planet of the Daleks*, which together made up an epic tale recalling the twelve-part first Doctor story *The Daleks' Master Plan*.

This season was also notable however for marking the beginning of the end of the relatively stable period that the series had enjoyed since *Terror of the Autons*. The death of actor Roger Delgado shortly after the completion of the season's production meant that *Frontier in Space* would be the last third Doctor story to feature the Master – and there had in any event been plans to kill the character off after just one further appearance, to enable Delgado to pursue other work – while *The Green Death* saw the departure of Jo Grant as behind the scenes factors culminated in actress Katy Manning's exit from the series.

Season eleven's opening story, *The Time Warrior*, introduced a new regular character, Sarah Jane Smith, to accompany the Doctor on his travels. A different companion had originally been envisaged to fulfil this role but, as rehearsals began with the actress concerned (whose identity is currently unknown), it became clear that a rethink was called for. The production team then devised Sarah, who, as a freelance journalist, would have a plausible reason to get involved in dramatic situations and would also be capable and independent – attributes that Letts was particularly keen to see maintained, as he felt that the portrayal of earlier companions had left the series open to criticisms of sexism.

Sarah proved a worthy successor to Jo, but her introduction did nothing to stem the gradual break-up of the third Doctor's established behind-the-scenes team as Letts, Dicks and then finally Pertwee himself all decided to quit the series. Letts and Dicks both felt that they had contributed about as much as they usefully could on the production team, and that it was time for them to move on to other projects. They had already produced the adult science fiction series *Moonbase 3* for the BBC, and had indeed initially considered leaving *Doctor Who* some two years earlier, but had been persuaded by their BBC superiors to stay on and continue their highly successful run on the series.

'I think we did change the face of *Doctor Who* quite dramatically over the period when Jon Pertwee was the Doctor,' observed Letts in 1981. 'Certainly we attracted a much older age group to the show, as was proved one year when I had an audience survey conducted. The results showed that out of our total audience figure of nine million, 58% were over the age of fifteen. We pushed the technology of the BBC to its limits, using every new process we could lay our hands on, and, I think, introduced quite a few new elements into the stories.'

By the end of season eleven, however, it was clear to all concerned that *Doctor Who* would benefit from an injection of new blood; and that this would come with the appointment of a new producer and script editor and the casting of a new Doctor to take the series into the second half of the decade.

From Script to Screen
Day of the Daleks

INTRODUCTION

This chapter presents an in-depth look at just one of the third Doctor's stories. In doing so, it reveals the process of making *Doctor Who* at this point in the series' history and – a factor common to every story – some of the behind-the-scenes discussions and thought that go into a production.

The production chosen for this case study is *Day of the Daleks*, the story that introduced the series' ninth season in 1972 and that saw the return of the Daleks to *Doctor Who* for the first time since their apparent demise at the end of *The Evil of the Daleks* in 1967.

For our view of the production, we have turned primarily to director Paul Bernard and to designer David Myerscough-Jones, who recall, scene by scene, the work that went into it. We have also spoken to producer Barry Letts and script editor Terrance Dicks.

THE SCRIPTS

The initial idea for *Day of the Daleks* came in the form of a story outline from Louis Marks entitled *The Ghost Hunters*.

Marks had already written one story for *Doctor Who*, *Planet of Giants*, transmitted in 1964, and since then had been busy working on other assignments, including as writer and story editor on *No Hiding Place* and subsequently on a series that he himself had created, called *Market in Honey Lane* (latterly *Honey Lane*). As it happened, Paul Bernard, the eventual director of *Day of the Daleks*, had also been working on *Market in Honey Lane*, as had regular *Doctor Who* writer Robert Holmes.

Bernard had started his career as a theatrical designer in the Fifties, working on opera, ballet and musicals. He was employed by the theatrical manager Emil Littler to work on several of his productions, including a version of *Kiss Me Kate*, and a number of pantomimes. His theatrical career culminated with an approach by Granada Television in 1958, when he was offered a contract with them. Bernard therefore moved to Granada and worked in television design until 1960, when he left to become a freelance television designer. He subsequently worked for Thames Television on productions such as *The Avengers* and *Armchair Theatre* and for the BBC on numerous plays, including the *20th Century Theatre* series, and also on the detective series *Maigret*.

He had worked for Granada on a series called *The Verdict is Yours*, a complex courtroom production that was transmitted live. This involved the planning and choreography of six cameras, as he had to ensure that the entire production ran smoothly and that his designs incorporated the requirements and the potential requirements of the director. This resulted, by 1962, in Bernard achieving a high profile as a designer who also understood the technicalities of television. He was therefore asked by the BBC, in 1963, if he would consider training as a director in order to work on the embryonic BBC2 channel. Bernard accepted this offer, and in 1965, following his training and working on shows such as *Z-Cars*, again returned to freelance work, this time as a director.

He accepted a rolling contract with ATV during which he worked on shows including *Love* Story, *Emergency Ward 10* and *This is ... Tom Jones*. It was while working on *Honey Lane* that Bernard had introduced both Marks and Holmes to his own literary agent, who took them on. 'Robert, Louis and I had a very close working relationship on *Honey Lane*,' commented Bernard. 'We knew each other well and had a strong professional bond.

'Unknown to me, Louis had submitted a story idea to Barry Letts, who had just taken over as producer on *Doctor Who*. And both Robert and Louis knew that I was ambitious. I had spent some seven years at ATV as a drama director and was now looking for new challenges elsewhere. Obviously between Robert and Louis meeting Barry, and my coincidentally having directed a play written by Barry three or four years before, meant that he knew of my work. All this ultimately led to my getting a call from Barry asking if I would be interested in joining him on *Doctor Who*. Of course I said that I'd be delighted, as I knew that the challenge of working on *Doctor Who* would be more demanding of my creative talents.'

The outline for Marks' story underwent some discussion before Dicks was happy with it. In a letter to Marks dated 27 October 1970, Dicks commented that, 'the addition of the "going into the future" element gives it the added science fiction feeling that we need.' Dicks went on to explain that although he wanted to commission scripts, he was currently unable to do so because the go-ahead had not yet been received from 'the powers that be' for the season to be commissioned. He expected this to happen towards the end of 1970 or at the very start of 1971.

The storyline was eventually commissioned from Marks on 22 January 1971. Marks had at that time just started work for the BBC as script editor on a series called *Trial*. This caused some concern, in that he had worked out the storyline and it had been accepted by Dicks while Marks was still a freelance writer, and the terms and conditions for BBC personnel writing for a series like *Doctor Who* were different from those of a freelancer. Dicks pointed this out in an internal note dated 25 January, commenting that he and Letts were 'particularly keen to have this as our first 4-part serial of the next season.'

The storyline was scheduled to be delivered on 8 February, and by 23 February a four-part breakdown had been accepted by Dicks. Marks' four scripts for the story were accepted on 22 March 1971.

By this time, plans for the season as a whole were coming together, and, as with previous seasons, which had featured the introduction of the Doctor and the introduction of the Master respectively, Letts and Dicks were keen to make the most of the opening story for the ninth season.

'It's a curious thing about the Daleks,' explained Letts in a 1993 interview for Reeltime Pictures' *Myth Makers* series of video interviews. 'In general, directors don't like working with the Daleks – and writers as well. Even Terry Nation was finding it difficult to get new variations on the Dalek theme. The thing is that they are very limited, but everybody loved them. So we had quite happily made up our minds that we weren't going to have the Daleks. But then there seemed to be a groundswell of people wanting to know where the Daleks were, and when the Managing Director of television asked us where they were, we thought that it was about time that we had the Daleks.'

'We held them back until there was a definite demand for them,' agreed Dicks in the same interview.

Dicks remembers that the idea was always to add the Daleks into Marks' scripts. 'We got Louis' scripts in,' he recalled, 'and it was a fine story with nothing wrong with it at all. However, it still didn't have that certain something that we felt it needed in order to open the season. We then hit upon the idea of including the Daleks, and hurriedly set about doing this.'

Dicks then recalls that they were contacted by Nation's agents. 'They said that they had heard we were doing a Dalek story, and that we needed permission to proceed. So Barry and I went to see Terry down at Pinewood, where he was making *The Persuaders!* with Roger Moore and Tony Curtis, and, to try and get him on our side, asked if he would consider writing us a story for the following season. After some consideration, he was happy to do so, and we had no further problems on *Day of the Daleks*.'

Letts, however, believes that permission may have been sought before the Daleks were added, but that either way, he and Dicks were in contact with Nation, who gave his blessing to another writer using the Daleks.

On 14 April, Letts' secretary, Sarah Newman, wrote to the BBC's Head of Copyright, formally asking if they could check with Nation if it would be possible to include the Daleks in the season under preparation. On 22 April, ALS Management, replying on behalf of Nation, said that there was no problem about including the Daleks, subject to the usual negotiations as to this use.

As the decision had been made to include them in Marks' scripts, he was duly contacted about this.

'It simply meant putting the Daleks into the place of the other aliens I had envisaged ruling Earth in the future,' he explained in an interview for the fanzine *Matrix* in 1980. 'Once we got to work on it, we realised that the Daleks offered all sorts of other story possibilities.'

By this time, the story had been retitled *Years of Doom*, and around the start of June, Dicks produced a final scene breakdown, which featured the Daleks and which was all but identical to the story as it would be transmitted. He sent this breakdown to Marks on 8 June, so that the scripts could be revised accordingly. Letts confirmed that the Daleks were to be included in a memo dated 15 June to the BBC's Head of Copyright, asking them to formally clear the use of the Daleks with Nation. Nation was subsequently paid the sum of £25 per episode for their use.

On 5 July, Marks had revised and delivered all four scripts, and on 15 July, Dicks again wrote to let him know that the production team had decided to change the title from *Years of Doom* to *Day of the Daleks* – 'We thought we had better get them into the title,' he commented.

On the same date, Dicks sent copies of the scripts to Nation for his approval. In the accompanying letter, he mentioned that he was keen to set up a meeting to discuss with Nation the Daleks' *next* return in the following season.

Nation replied on 20 July, commenting that, 'It seems a very good and exciting batch of episodes.' He went on to say, 'I have a few suggestions for what (I think) will improve some of the Daleks' dialogue, and I'll let you have my notes quite soon. But you're the Script Editor and you can decide whether you think they're improvements or not.

'Look forward to talking to you about the second coming of the Daleks before very long.'

There is no record of what Nation's suggested changes were, or whether or not they were incorporated into the scripts.

'When I first saw the scripts,' Bernard recalled, 'the Daleks were definitely in. I never had any part in reinventing the storyline at all – in fact I never had any part in talking to Louis! Such was the lack of time. I was just delighted that my first script for *Doctor Who* was going to be by Louis Marks.

'I very seldom read a script all the way through and then go back and start again. As I read a script, I break it down into thumbnail sketches: either plan sketches from a directorial viewpoint as to what the mechanics of a scene are; or I do visuals – little scribbles. *Day of the Daleks* was made for these little visuals. My normal procedure would be that, having gone through the script and having linked it all together as a series of mechanics and visuals, I might then make some suggestions as to how certain scenes might be re-written to make them flow together. I can't be specific, but this is generally how I work.

'With this story, however, as I had been working with Louis and as he knew my style of directing, it is possible that there was not much that I needed to suggest as changes to the scripts.'

CASTING

'In those days,' explained Bernard, 'unlike today, the director did his own casting. Certainly at the BBC. They had a department that booked the artistes once you had chosen them, but they didn't have someone who went away and then came back with recommendations. You told them specifically who you wanted, and they went away and came back to tell you how much this person would cost, when they were available, and so on.

'As I read through the scripts, I start to think of people who would be good for the parts. Many directors liked to use their own group of people with whom they had worked, and I was no exception. Some people simply fitted in with the thinking of the script.

'Aubrey Woods was like that. He always had a reputation for being an oddball, outside the conventional, and that was exactly what I was after for the part of the Controller. I can't recall thinking of anyone else for that part.

'Anna Barry was a discovery. I saw a lot of girls for the part of the lead guerrilla, Anat. There were half a dozen agents that I would let know what I was doing, give them outlines of the three or four characters I wanted, and spontaneously they would supply me with suggestions. You could almost complete the casting of a production with literally two or three phone calls.

'Anna Barry was the result of a search through agents for a suitable actress. She was the daughter of the BBC's ex-Head of Drama, Michael Barry, and hadn't really done any major television. I liked to cast people who were unknown on television. Wanda Moore in *The Time Monster* was cast for similar reasons, in that she had done lots of stage work but not much television.

'The person that I wanted to get was Valentine Palmer, who played Monia. He was very popular at the time, but for some reason later dropped out of acting. He was very much in demand in the early Seventies, and was an excellent actor and very pleasant to work with.'

PRE-PRODUCTION

The designer assigned to work on *Day of the Daleks* was David Myerscough-

Jones, who had worked on two previous *Doctor Who* stories, *The Web of Fear* in 1968 and *The Ambassadors of Death* in 1970. He continued to work at the BBC up until 1991, when he left to work on the film *The Hawk* as well as other independent television and stage productions.

Myerscough-Jones had joined the BBC in the mid-Sixties as a designer, after spending time working in repertory theatres and at London's Mermaid Theatre as production designer.

'I always wanted to be a designer,' he explained. 'Ever since I was fourteen, I was influenced by film and theatre. I used to go to the theatre quite often in Liverpool and was passionate about theatre design – I still am. I was born in Southport in 1934 and, after the War, suffered a mixed education, but moved towards arts and design and spent three years at an arts school. Then I spent three years at the Central School of Arts, studying theatre design and painting. After finishing my studies, my first job was down at Perranporth in Cornwall, working in repertory theatre, and from there I travelled all over the country.

'I worked for three years at Glasgow's Citizen's Theatre, which was a marvellous experimental theatre. We had the ability to put on various plays in very adventurous ways, and it was a time of fermentation and great excitement. After that, I headed for London, and ended up working with Bernard Miles at the Mermaid Theatre for another three years. That too was adventurous and exciting, but my feeling at that time was that the nearer you got to London, the more conservative everyone was about theatre design. At the Citizen's, you could actually try things out, it was a great workhouse atmosphere, but in London everything seemed more standardised and economic. The Mermaid, however, was like a breath of fresh air, as Bernard was very supportive of anything new. I then got married, and realised that I needed to increase my income to live.

'I'd always had a fascination for television. It had a reputation among theatre-types of not being a 'true' medium, which I thought was rubbish. The regime that was there in the early Sixties was looking for a totally new concept of design for television. I have a huge admiration for Richard Levin, the BBC's Head of Design, who was an industrial designer, and yet he considered theatre and film sets to be some sort of invasion into television. An awful lot of people came into television whose backgrounds were in industrial design, and this resulted in a prejudice against certain design styles, which lasted for an awfully long time.'

Myerscough-Jones started at the BBC working for the Design Department as holiday relief, and was eventually made up to be a fully fledged designer around the mid-Sixties.

He was assigned to work on *The Web of Fear* as part of the normal allocations process, and among his work for that show were the Underground tunnel sets in which most of the action took place.

'We tried to get permission to use real London Underground stations for the story, but they wouldn't let us. We had to build them in the studios instead. They had to be multi-use sets, because there were so many different shots that had to be achieved. The set was constructed in sections so that they could be put together in different configurations to give the effect of the tunnels. We put them on rollers so that they could be swung round to form new curves and junctions and, with the addition of painted back-drops, we got the effect of tunnels going off into the distance.

'The tracks were made in lengths, and these too linked together and could be re-shuffled into different forms. One problem we had was that the contractor we used in London to make the tunnel sections couldn't cope, because they had also landed a theatre production for Covent Garden, and so we had to send out some of the sections to another contractor. The problem was that the two sets of sections didn't quite match up, and so we had to stick silver tape over the joins to try and get the lines continuous.'

Myerscough-Jones' next *Doctor Who* was *The Ambassadors of Death*. The opening scenes of this story demonstrated his desire to try and bring some wide-angle establishing shots into the programme.

'I always wanted to get away from the close-up and to open out the sets on a grand scale. There is an opening shot in *The Ambassadors of Death* of the interior of the Space Centre, where the director, Michael Ferguson, pulled the camera back into the farthest corner of the studio and shot the set with all the studio lights and equipment in the ceiling showing above. Then another camera was set up to point at a small model of the roof that we had constructed from straws and tracing paper cut into squares. It was a very laborious business to get the cameras lined up, and then the vision mixer combined the pictures from both cameras so that the model of the roof obscured the ceiling of the studio on the main picture. At that time, this sort of shot was rarely done, and many directors just went with standard shots of standard sets. It was a huge effort to try and get them to do anything else.'

For *Day of the Daleks*, Myerscough-Jones' work was divided into two distinct areas; the present day settings and those in the future, each of which posed particular and different problems for the designer and which are discussed in the detailed breakdown of the story.

'At that time, you tended to be allocated to work on productions, unless a producer or director specifically asked for you to work with them. We tended to be allocated to things that we were known for doing well, and I had been doing a lot of operas and more theatrical presentations. *Doctor Who* was something completely different, and was quite challenging and exciting to do. To work on *Doctor Who* was to be given a superb opportunity to extend the designer's range and vision. *Doctor Who* was a perfect vehicle for that, although, because of the way the stories were made, there was very little time to explore that aspect. Time in the studio was so tight that there was seldom the opportunity to experiment or to try something new.

'The whole time I worked at the BBC, I was always trying to extend the range of what we were doing in terms of design, and to try and get a different look to the productions. With *Doctor Who*, you could have a bit of fun and use materials and designs that you could not use elsewhere. It was a good show to do.

'When I got the scripts, the first thing I did was to look at the number of sheets of paper that made up the episode. *Day of the Daleks* had around 40 pages per episode, which was an incredible amount to get through in half an hour. Generally speaking, the more pages there were, then the more dialogue there was and the less action. Then I would look at the balance between dialogue and stage directions, and, again, *Day of the Daleks* had quite a lot of different locations.'

The next task of the designer was to break the script down into the different sets that were required and assess their complexity and importance to the story. For example, scenes set in the TARDIS were not normally a problem, as the sets already existed and the designer had only to consider if there was some specific prop or requirement for the console. In *Day of the Daleks*, the TARDIS interior was not required, but there were two main sets: Sir Reginald Styles' study and the hallway adjacent to it, and the main control room in the future. Less major, but nevertheless important, was the UNIT laboratory. Finally came less important sets, like the cellar in Styles' house, the interrogation room in the future, the tunnels through the railway arch and the guerrillas' hideout.

'I remember being generally very frustrated that I wasn't allowed to do as much as I wanted to do visually,' mused Myerscough-Jones. 'I think that's possibly a personal vanity, but it helps enormously to create shots that are visually impressive.'

In view of the fact that *Day of the Daleks* featured some complex effects work, and also in order to draw on Bernard's experience on previous shows, Letts took the unusual step of booking a studio for an experimental session to carry out some tests using Colour Separation Overlay (CSO). This practice was later repeated for several other stories during this period, when particularly complex effects were required.

'At the time of my being asked to direct *Day of the Daleks*,' explained Bernard, 'the BBC, like most studios, used a blue background to "key-in" a required background to a shot. At an early meeting with Barry, before I was commissioned to direct *Day of the Daleks*, I pointed out to him that we had experimented and worked with other colours on the series *This is ... Tom Jones* at Elstree for ATV. One of the most successful in these early exchanges was a yellow. When you used blue, you tended to get a trail behind the subject if they moved, which meant that you couldn't pan or move the camera. The main advantage with the yellow was that this "halo" effect was very much minimised, and we had found that we could pan and have the subject moving. We arranged for a full exercise with different yellows in the studio to gain engineering agreement. We tried different lighting situations and different yellows until we found one that "held" and created a genuine highlight. This was adopted, and used for the first time on *Day of the Daleks*. When I later went to Thames Television, I managed to gain approval to use it for *The Tomorrow People*.

'What it meant was a total rethink in wardrobe colours. Now, the actors could wear blue, but the costume designers had to be careful with yellow. However, the fidelity of the tone we used meant that near-yellows – orange, primrose, gold, caramel or pale yellows – could be used. It also meant that people with blue eyes no longer looked like something out of *Dracula* in close up!'

According to BBC documentation, the session was scheduled to take place in Studio 4 at Television Centre on Tuesday 7 September, although Bernard remembers that a full two days of studio were booked for the session.

'We were given a studio and use of the BBC's engineering department, but the session was not fully scheduled in the true sense of the word. We had to use whatever was available on the days: if we could record on video, then we did that, but if we had to wait because engineering or the mixing desks were in use by another production, we had to wait. We had to fit in with whatever else was happening.'

The main purpose of the session was to confirm whether yellow was a better 'key' colour for the CSO process than blue. Three colours were tested: green, purple and yellow. Although the test was not specific to *Doctor Who*, Bernard also took the opportunity to try out some special effects explosions, and also some optical effects for the sequences when Jo travels through the time vortex and for when the guerrillas travel through time.

For these tests, the UNIT lab set was erected in the studio; and actor and fight arranger Rick Lester (who played an Ogron in the story) and actress Wendy Taylor stood in for the Doctor and Jo for the CSO tests. Lester was also costumed and made-up as an Ogron for those sequences requiring the 'monster'.

The following sequences were carried out:

1. Involving 'monster' guard, Jo, guerrilla and guns
2. Unit lab scene with Doctor and Jo
3. Vortex sequence
4. Time travel sequence
5. Unit lab, gun/dummy sequence
6. Other CSO effects

The result of the test was that a colour called 'golden yellow' was found to be best for the CSO 'key' colour, and also that certain parts of the set would need re-painting as a result. They were too close to that colour, and would therefore cause problems on the final recording if left unchanged.

ON LOCATION

Much of the action in *Day of the Daleks* centred on three main locations: a railway arch; a large country house; and a futuristic work centre.

Bernard recalled that the railway arch was suggested by a friend who was always asking about his work. 'One day I mentioned to him that I was looking for a derelict area that had a bridge, maybe over water, maybe over railway lines, and he told me about this place called Bull's Bridge in Hayes, where he used to play as a kid. I went out there in the car, and it was perfect. It had been a shunting yard owned by British Railways, and they were tearing up the railway lines and turning the area into a vast wasteland. It also had some underground passages, so we could have the characters appear to be going into and coming out of underground tunnels.

'I got quite excited about this, because it meant that we didn't have to dig any holes in the ground.'

A large house to use as the country home of Sir Reginald Styles was found by the production team in Dropmore Park in Buckinghamshire. 'That one was not my doing,' commented Bernard. 'It was most probably found by my PA, Norman Stewart.'

Agreement was secured to use these locations: £160 was paid to use Bull's Bridge while £75 per day was agreed for the use of Dropmore Park.

The final location was the futuristic work centre.

'I had remembered,' explained Bernard, 'because I drove in from Roehampton, seeing a set of office blocks against the sky, and how, with the sun behind them, they looked rather ominous, and we agreed that they could be utilised.'

These office blocks were situated in Green Dragon Lane, just beside Kew Bridge in London. The building, called Harvey House, and its underground car park, were felt to be suitable as the factory where the Doctor sees women and children working before he is captured and taken for interrogation.

In order to document all the details relating to location filming on a story, a filming diary was prepared. This showed who was required on which locations and to film which scenes in which order. In the case of *Day of the Daleks*, the filming diary is different from Bernard's own notes. According to Bernard's notes, the following was filmed on each of the four days allocated. The number in brackets after the brief description is the episode number.

DAY ONE (Monday 13 September)

Dropmore Park (House): Guerrilla appears and runs (1); Dusk shot of House (1); UNIT troops deployed at house (1); Shura sees Doctor in house (1); Yates and Benton realise the Doctor is missing (2); Ogrons attack house (2); Daleks and Ogrons attack (4).

DAY TWO (Tuesday 14 September)

Bull's Bridge (Tunnel Area): Guerrilla attacked by two Ogrons (1); UNIT soldiers find body (1).
Harvey House (Underground Car Park): Doctor sees workers (3); Guerrillas fight Ogrons and Dalek (4).
Harvey House (Flats Area): Doctor & Jo escape and see trike (3).
Dropmore Park (House): Delegates arriving (4); Delegates leaving (4).

DAY THREE (Wednesday 15 September)

Bull's Bridge (Tunnel Area): Guerrilla put in ambulance (1); Anat's party appears (1); Shura kills UNIT soldiers (1); Shura arrives back at tunnel and is attacked by an Ogron (2); UNIT search unsuccessful (4); Doctor and Jo emerge from tunnel (4); Daleks and Ogrons emerge from tunnel (4).
Bull's Bridge (Devastation Area): Monia enters hideout (3); Trike chased by Ogrons (3).
Bull's Bridge (Desolation Area): Doctor exits from tunnel (3); Doctor passes security camera (3).

DAY FOUR (Thursday 16 September)

Harvey House (Flats Area): Doctor enters building (3); Ogrons chase Doctor and Jo from building (3).
Bull's Bridge (Devastation Area): Doctor and Jo return to tunnel (4); Final scene with Doctor and Styles (4).

After filming completed on 16 September, it was back to London to start rehearsals for the first studio recording, which took place on Monday 4 October and Tuesday 5 October.

IN STUDIO

At this time in *Doctor Who*'s history, the programme was being recorded two episodes every two weeks. This was a process instigated by Letts, in consultation with the production departments, from *Inferno* onwards. It meant that two episodes were rehearsed over a two week period, followed by a two-day studio recording block when all scenes for those episodes were recorded, often in transmission order. There were some exceptions. In the case of *The Dæmons*, for example, there were only three studio days (because there was a great deal of location filming for the story, reducing the amount of material that had to be recorded in studio) with material for episodes 1 to 3 being recorded on the first day, material for episodes 2 to 4 being recorded on the second, and material for episodes 4 and 5 being recorded on the final day.

To indicate some of the considerations involved in making a *Doctor Who* story during the Jon Pertwee era, what follows is a scene-by-scene summary of *Day of the Daleks*, with comments from some of those involved in the production.

EPISODE ONE

A sentry stands by a door in a hallway in Auderly House. Miss Paget (Jean McFarlane) emerges from the room and tells the sentry that Sir Reginald Styles is not to be disturbed.

[The name of the house underwent several changes over the course of the production. It started as Austerley House in the rehearsal scripts and was then changed to Aulderley House, and finally to Auderly in the transmitted version.]

Paul Bernard: What I used for these initial shots was a floor camera – literally a camera on mountings only, on the floor. The idea was to get a shot that was a little sinister and different.

In his office, Styles (Wilfred Carter) is working at his desk when a wind blows the curtains. When Styles goes to close the window, there is a man dressed in guerrilla attire there. The guerrilla (Tim Condren) points a gun at Styles but then vanishes into thin air. Miss Paget enters, and sees Styles is flustered. He explains what he saw to her.

PB: I cast Wilfred Carter because I wanted someone who could play Styles as a slightly pompous character. Again, I had worked with him before.

David Myerscough-Jones: To dress a set like this, you would brief the prop buyer on what you wanted and then they would go out and hire in all the numerous bits and pieces that were required. Just about all the elements in this set were hired in. The prop buyer is terribly important, but they tend to not be credited for their contribution.

At UNIT HQ, the telephone rings and the Brigadier (Nicholas Courtney) speaks to the Minister (unknown), who tells him what happened at Auderly House. The Brigadier assures the Minister that he was about to put his best man on it.

PB: I enjoyed working with Nicholas Courtney a lot. Very enjoyable. A very professional actor.

DM-J: The telephones were from stock. They are simply telephones that were in use in 1971, which is when the story was being made.

The Doctor is putting the finishing touches to the TARDIS' dematerialisation circuit. The TARDIS console is standing in his lab at UNIT HQ, and the Doctor ducks down to fiddle with it. Suddenly, a pair of doors at the back of the room swing open to reveal another Doctor and Jo. After a few moments, a component on the console explodes with a flash, and the 'other' Doctor and Jo vanish.

DM-J: That sequence was actually recorded at the start of the day – before we began on that opening scene. It was then played into this scene. I had a massive argument with Paul over this scene. If you look closely, you can see that the yellow background when the Doctor's and Jo's doubles are there, does not extend down far enough. There was a problem that we couldn't extend the cloth to mask the patch at the base. We also had to paint the backs of the doors so that they didn't pick up the CSO key colour.
   The cycloramas we used were made of felt so that they reflected an even colour.

PB: The problem with the floor was that I had to be able to see Katy, and so could not drop the camera down in order to hide the floor. The lesson learned was that we should have painted the floor yellow as well.

The Doctor explains to a perplexed Jo that this was a freak effect due to his tampering with the console. The Brigadier enters, and tries to persuade the Doctor to come and investigate the 'ghost' at Auderly House.

PB: Katy was very useful. She knew how to handle Jon Pertwee. I knew that at any critical moment on set, when there was some crisis going on, that I could sort things out and rely on Katy to calm Jon down. She was worth her weight in gold. Absolutely marvellous.
   I was warned by several people, when I was about to start this story, that Pertwee could be difficult. I think that was the generalised phrase. Now, I

had discovered in my working career, that those people who had been labelled like this, invariably I got on with. I found that it was no more than bloody-minded professionalism – and that, I respect. It turned out to be so. Pertwee was a perfectionist and a professional. It was difficult, but I eventually learned how to work with him and how to bend with him. All you had to do was to give him respect and understanding and he gave you a lot back.

Outside the house, the guerrilla appears once more.

PB: That pattern was simply projection of light onto a screen. We had no electronic effects in those days, and I had to invent these projected light effects. They were done by a company called EM-Tech, run by a young couple who had just come out of art school and who were putting on discos. I was introduced to them, and they had all these different light-projected patterns, and they went away and developed the patterns that I was after. The moving light pattern was then projected onto a screen about one metre by one and a half metres, and I then positioned a camera on the other side of the screen – like back-projection. We then mixed the image of the light with the image of the characters appearing and disappearing..

The guerrilla hears a whistling noise and runs. Just beside a railway arch, he is attacked and knocked to the ground by an Ogron (Rick Lester). Another Ogron (Maurice Bush) appears, and they head into the railway arch.

PB: The look of the Ogrons came about through sketches that I did while reading through the scripts. I showed these sketches to Barry Letts and told him that these were my initial ideas of what the Ogrons should look like. I do recall that the word 'Alsation' had been used in an earlier version of the scripts: that these creatures were the Daleks' guard dogs. I said that I didn't want to pursue that line, and that I saw them as more ape-like. I had this idea that they should be big men, and that the actors who played them should be, at a minimum, six foot six tall. I made that a condition. They were frightening by their size as well as by their make-up and their faces.

My intention with the monsters was always to frighten the kids. Their introduction in that scene was meant to be frightening. We had to be careful not to go too far with it, but the idea was to frighten the kids without being too grotesque.

[The rehearsal scripts describe the monsters – the name Ogrons does not appear – as 'Savage. Larger than life. They are humanoid in shape, with alien heads and hands.']

In Styles' study, the Doctor speaks with Miss Paget about the events of the previous night. Styles enters, and insists that nothing happened. The Doctor, however, has noticed muddy boot marks on the floor. Styles is preparing to leave for the airport and gives permission for the Brigadier's men to search the grounds.

DM-J: You can see in this scene that the chandelier has a braille line attached to it. Lighting technicians generally hate chandeliers; they have to be hung from the lighting bars in the studio, as the sets do not generally have ceilings. You indicate on your floor-plan where the chandelier is to be, and they then set it in that position. There is a diagonal wire, as well as the vertical one, used for positioning, and the cameraman would usually make sure that viewers can't see the wires holding up the chandelier.

PB: As a designer, I always used what are termed 'headers' on sets. These are ceilings and front pieces, things on top of the walls of the sets. I always insisted on seeing a ceiling where a ceiling should be seen. I wanted that study set to have a lot of depth to it, and I wanted it to have a visible ceiling. As to why the braille line is in shot … well … it shouldn't have been.

The guerrilla is found by the arch, and the Brigadier gets Captain Yates (Richard Franklin) to order an ambulance. There is a futuristic-looking gun beside the body, and Sergeant Benton (John Levene) finds a black box hidden 50 feet inside the tunnel.

In a control room in the future, the two Ogrons report to the Controller (Aubrey Woods). They claim to have found and destroyed the enemy. The Controller orders them to intensify their search for the guerrillas.

DM-J: The script gave only a very brief description for this set: 'a small austere room … control panels … a centre plinth'. I used the idea of the technicians sitting on seats attached to tracks so that they could move around. The whole set was up against a cyclorama, which had a dappled lighting effect thrown on it. The panels at the back were made from transparent perspex and were lit with coloured lights. The idea here was deliberately to give the idea of space, in contrast to Styles' study, which was very cluttered.

The Controller's chair was definitely hired from one of the more flamboyant hiring companies that we used. I think they were called Roy Moore and used to import the most extraordinary modern designs from Italy and the continent. You could never afford to build a chair like that. Even if you wanted to, it would have been very expensive. Again, it's prop-buying, and where you have to hire in a prop that is central and important to the overall design, then that single item can dictate how the rest of your designs may turn out. It's very important.

Back in Styles' study, the Doctor and the Brigadier report to Styles. He leaves for the airport. The unconscious guerrilla is put in an ambulance and, accompanied by Benton, taken to hospital.

Back in the Doctor's lab at UNIT HQ, the Doctor tests the gun. It is an ultrasonic disintegrator, however it was made on Earth. The Doctor shows Jo and the Brigadier the box found in the tunnel and explains that it is a crude time machine. He places a small circuit, which looks like a version of his TARDIS' dematerialisation circuit, in the box, and it starts to operate.

The guerrilla in the ambulance vanishes before Benton's eyes.

In the future, the Controller is advised by a technician (Deborah Brayshaw) that a time transference has taken place. It stops before they can track it. A Dalek orders the Controller to report.

[In the rehearsal script, this scene started with an exchange between the Controller and the Ogrons:

CONTROLLER: Well?

MONSTER: We are still searching.

CONTROLLER: You haven't found their headquarters?

MONSTER: We believe they are concealed in the tunnels beneath the city – the area is large…

CONTROLLER: I don't want excuses. Find them. Time is short.

This dialogue was cut from this scene and the earlier scene with the Controller and the Ogrons included to replace it.]

DM-J: The way that the technicians were operating their consoles was a deliberate attempt to be futuristic. We reasoned that there wouldn't be buttons and switches, but that all the controls could be worked by touch-sensitive panels.

I remember I wanted to get some long shots of that set. We put some sheets of moulded plastic, which glistened like coalite, under the technicians' seats. I wanted to get a feeling of interplanetary movement, and to have the technicians spinning around in space, but we never got round to it.

The Doctor notes that the machine has blown a fuse. Benton reports to the Brigadier that the guerrilla has vanished. The Doctor decides to spend the night at Styles' house, in case the attackers return.

At the house, the Doctor and Jo settle down for the night. Jo is nervous, but the Doctor enjoys the food and wine from Styles' cellars. Jo provides some food for

Benton, but Yates takes it instead, citing RHIP – Rank Has Its Privileges – as his excuse.

DM-J: The tapestries on the walls were hired in. We didn't have anything like that especially painted for this story. It's important when designing rooms to realise that hiring a tapestry is cheaper than building scenery.

The BBC used to have a substantial stock of furniture and drapes, which you used as much as possible because it was free. Nowadays you have to hire it all in, which is very expensive.

[The sequence where Jo offers Benton some cheese and wine only to have Yates take it instead is not in the rehearsal script but is present in the camera script.]

Outside the house, UNIT troops are all positioned. Down by the railway arch, three more guerrillas, Anat (Anna Barry), Shura (Jimmy Winston) and Boaz (Scott Fredericks) appear. Their leader, Anat, says that they will wait until light.
   At first light on 13 September, the Doctor pulls back the curtains, waking Jo up. Two UNIT soldiers patrolling by the railway tunnel are disintegrated by Shura.

PB: Because the tunnel was alongside a canal, I hired a barge and we used that to film some of the scenes from.

At UNIT HQ, a message is received by a radio operator (Gypsie Kemp) concerning the international situation, and it does not look good. All UNIT personnel are placed on maximum alert.

DM-J: The table in the foreground breaks the rules about the 'fourth wall' that you never see on television. You can see the edge of the table at the front, and the camera should have been closer so that you couldn't see it. There is supposed to be a wall there, and yet it looks like the table is, for no apparent reason, sitting in the middle of the room.

PB: I can't remember who I got to do the voices on the radio in that scene, or the Minister who speaks to the Brigadier on the telephone. As I had a sound booth in the studio to do the Dalek voices, it was most likely the same two people who did these other voices. That would have made economic sense.

Shura enters the house and fights with the Doctor. The machine is operating on the table.
   The Controller is advised that the time machine is operating again. The Controller reports to the Daleks that his underlings are trying to obtain the time/space co-ordinates.

PB: One of my requirements was to use CSO to key a picture onto a mock TV screen and then to be able to alter the composition of the shot with the screen in, without the image on the screen jumping all over the place. The engineers came up with a system – I think it was called Gaze – where two cameras were locked onto one master zoom control. They used it in *Top of the Pops* after us, and also in some sports programs.

The Daleks (Murphy Grumbar, Ricky Newby, John Scott Martin; voices: Oliver Gilbert, Peter Messaline) order that whoever is operating the time machine must be exterminated.

DM-J: One way to get over the fact that you can't build miles of scenery, is to use screens of reflective material. You reflect one into the other all the way down a corridor, and give the illusion of depth when there isn't any present. On this occasion, unfortunately, the use of all the reflective surfaces doesn't really work, and the room that the Daleks are in looks small and cramped.

[The original idea in the rehearsal script was that the Daleks' operations room should be a vast hall, with twenty or thirty Daleks operating the equipment.]

End of Episode One

EPISODE TWO

Anat and Boaz enter Styles' study with Jo, and order the Doctor to switch off the machine.
   The Controller enters the Daleks' room and tells them that the trace has gone. The Daleks order him to find the rebels.

PB: I like the door, because it's quite ominous in the way it takes a long time to open. Not like those very clever jigsaw things that slide apart in a flash. I remember I wanted something that took its time.

DM-J: All the camera script said was 'the big door opens', and I decided to use it opening like some great hydraulic thing rather than a standard door. It was attached to wires, which were attached to hoists in the studio and lifted up.

The guerrillas assume that the Doctor is Sir Reginald Styles and prepare to kill him, until the Doctor points out their mistake. They all hide in the cellar when Benton and Yates come looking for the Doctor and Jo.

DM-J: You can see a skylight above them in the cellar. That is known as 'doing things cheaply'. The skylight would have come from stock, and you can't alter it, all you can do is shine a light through it. It works to give the impression of a skylight, but it is a very cheap and simple effect.

When they have gone, the guerrillas tie the Doctor and Jo up and return to the study.

PB: I think this sort of scene where Jo and the Doctor simply chatted formed a part of the character of *Doctor Who,* particularly with Pertwee playing it. His character fitted in with this kind of loose Chinese philosophy on life.

In the future, the Daleks attach a time vortex magnetron to the equipment. Anyone using the time transfer machine will now be diverted to the control centre.

PB: When we went and looked in the BBC's storeroom where all the old props from the series were kept, we could find only three and a half Daleks. We refurbished three of them, and I used the half-Dalek several times as a 'blown up' one. We simply didn't have the money to make any more, so bravely I said that I could make it work.

At the house, Anat cannot make contact with her base, due to interference in the time vortex. Shura returns to the tunnel to try and make contact from there. He encounters an Ogron but manages to kill it before hiding himself.

[In the rehearsal script, Shura hid himself in the tunnels, but in the transmitted scene he runs off back towards the house.]

Unable to find the Doctor and Jo, Yates and Benton report to the Brigadier. He telephones the house, and Anat gets the Doctor to answer the call. The Doctor alerts UNIT to the fact that all is not well by using the phrase 'Tell it to the marines'.
Jo manages to free herself and grabs the box. It operates, and she is transported into the control centre in the future.

[The effect of the time vortex was achieved with a stock lens fixed to a camera. The lens was a multi-image lens-rotating prism, which had previously been bought by technical manager Bernard Fox for a previous *Doctor Who,* at which time the cost had been shared with *Top of the Pops.*]

PB: The effect of Jo spinning was done in the studio. It was done using a 20:1 zoom lens, and we got the distance by shooting into a mirror mounted on the lighting gantry. Katy was lying on a black covered rostrum, and she simply waved her arms and legs about as we zoomed out from her image in the mirror, rotating the lens as we did it. The lighting effect also served to cover up the image around Katy, as much of the studio was visible.

The Controller is cordial and friendly, and gets Jo to tell him exactly where and on which date she left her time.

DM-J: The set is actually a lot bigger than it looks on screen. As a designer, you try and provide something that will look good and that will also suit the requirements of the director. Unfortunately, there is no requirement that says he has to show all your set!

With this information, the Daleks prepare an ambush in the railway tunnel. They intend to go themselves to ensure there are no mistakes.
    The Doctor is tied up, but he frees himself. Anat and Boaz run as the house is attacked by Ogrons (Rick Lester, Maurice Bush, David Joyce, Frank Menzies, Geoffrey Todd, Bruce Wells).

DM-J: Visual Effects would have built the French windows and inserted them into the set for the scene where the Ogron smashes into the house. We had to make some effort to ensure that the interior of this room matched the windows on the outside of the house.

The Doctor manages to elude the Ogrons thanks to the timely intervention of the Brigadier, and follows the guerrillas to the railway tunnel, where he sees a Dalek.

End of Episode Two

EPISODE THREE

After seeing the Dalek, the guerrillas and the Doctor are transported 200 years into the future to the 22nd Century.

[According to the rehearsal script, the guerrillas had come from the 24th Century.]

PB: That effect was not quite as successful as the last one. It's a little off-centre. Today they would be able to correct something like that electronically, but we had no such facilities. They're really spoilt these days.

The Doctor tells them that he knows of the Daleks, and they explain that the creatures have ruled Earth for more than a century. The Ogrons attack, and they split up and run off.
    The Doctor finds a ladder and ascends out through a hatch onto an area of wasteland.

DM-J: I remember putting that hatch in. There was a hole in the ground, which was either dug for us or was there already, and the hatchway was made especially by us.

PB: We didn't dig the hole; it was there already.

The Controller reports to the Daleks that the rebels have escaped. When he mentions that Jo spoke of someone called the Doctor, the Daleks become agitated. They tell the Controller that he is an enemy of the Daleks and must be exterminated.

[The rehearsal script contains an additional scene prior to the above, in which two monsters give a report to the Controller that they have not found any of the rebels. One of the monsters also mentions that one of those who travelled to their time was dressed strangely and was called 'Doctor'.]

The Doctor makes his way to a work centre, where old men, women and children are toiling. He is seen on a security camera.

DM-J: The security camera was provided by Visual Effects. We supplied the huge door that the Doctor opens to get into the work centre.

Anat and Boaz are met by their leader, Monia (Valentine Palmer), at their hideout. Monia knows that Jo is in the control centre.

PB: Those were old buildings belonging to the abandoned British Rail goods yard. It was a wonderful location, with just about everything we wanted.

The Doctor is captured by Ogrons.

[According to the rehearsal script, just before the Doctor is captured, he sees one of the guards on a motor tricycle. This scene is emphasised in Bernard's own film schedule, but does not appear in the transmitted story.]

The Controller shares a meal with Jo. He is told that the Doctor has been captured, and assures Jo that he is safe and well.

DM-J: All those dishes and other tableware were especially made for the production. This is also the same set as the main control room, re-dressed and with different colours thrown onto the background.

The Doctor is being interrogated by the senior guard (Andrew Carr).

DM-J: The cell set is very simple. The bars at the back are standard stock set elements – something like P68 Stock Cell Units – which I positioned to give the idea of bars. Again, you can see the tops of the bars, and it would perhaps have been better if the shot had not been so wide, as it looks insecure.

The Centre Manager (Peter Hill) arrives and, once the senior guard has gone, tries to assure the Doctor that he is on the guerrillas' side. However, the Controller arrives and has the Doctor freed as his guest. The Manager transmits a report to Monia, telling him that the Doctor is important to the Daleks. Suddenly an Ogron smashes the Manager's transmitter.

Although the Controller is friendly, the Doctor is not prepared to listen to him. He knows that the Daleks rule in this time and that the Controller is a mere quisling. The Daleks plan to use a mind analysis machine on the Doctor to determine if he is their old enemy, as his appearance has changed. The Doctor and Jo knock their Ogron guard unconscious and escape on a three wheeled power-trike. They are, however, recaptured..

PB: Someone had told me about these little trikes that they were using on a 007 production at Pinewood – *Diamonds are Forever*, I think it was – and I thought this sounded like a great idea. I saw them on a documentary about the making of the film, and so we asked if we could get one. It was written in the script as a motor tricycle, and this balloon-wheeled vehicle was absolutely ideal.

During a publicity session for the story, Jon and Katy were like children. Every moment they could, they leaped onto it and drove it around. We all did.

DM-J: The trikes were brought into the production, and they really worked well. Although the chase is short, it is effective. It's all good, harmless stuff.

Monia decides that they must rescue the Doctor.
The Daleks place the Doctor under the mind analysis machine.

[Photographs of William Hartnell and Patrick Troughton were overlaid onto a sequence of graphics from the title sequence, representing the operation of the mind analysis machine on the Doctor. The image was keyed using CSO onto a yellow CSO board, which was suspended in the set.]

PB: I remember this scene being quite traumatic to do, because we had to make the image that appears on the CSO screen fit the picture. The image had to be created so that it filled the whole of the TV screen, but we were only 'seeing' a small strip of the image at the top. We had to make sure that the portion that was going to be seen had the correct patterns and pictures in it.

End of Episode Three

EPISODE FOUR

The Controller stops the Daleks from exterminating the Doctor and promises that he can get information from him.

[As scripted, the scene in which the Doctor is taken away starts with an extra exchange between the Doctor and the Daleks:

DR WHO: I've defeated you before. I introduced the human factor into the Daleks on Skaro. There was a rebellion …

DALEK 2: The rebellion was unsuccessful. The rogue Daleks were hunted down and exterminated.

DR WHO: I defeated you here on Earth too. Your invasion failed.]

Monia, Anat and Boaz work out how best to rescue the Doctor.

[This scene was completely restructured for the studio recording. The following is the camera script version:

(THE GUERRILLAS ARE PREPARING THEIR GEAR READY FOR THE ATTACK.

GUNS BEING INSPECTED)

BOAZ: (TO A GUERRILLA) Explosives?

(THE GUERRILLA HOLDS UP SOME POUCHES WHICH HE THEN PROCEEDS TO STUFF INSIDE HIS BATTLE DRESS)

Mind how you handle that stuff; it's still pretty unstable.

(BOAZ MOVES OVER TO WHERE MONIA IS DISCUSSING THE PLAN FOR THE ATTACK WITH ANAT. THEY HAVE VARIOUS PLANS LAID OUT BEFORE THEM

ANAT: Can't Jacob help us? He runs the Work Centre?

(BOAZ CROSSES TO JOIN THEM)

MONIA: Jacob was executed this afternoon.

ANAT: You mean when …

MONIA: That's right. They picked him up when he was contacting us about the Doctor.

ANAT: Oh no.

(A MOMENT)

BOAZ: Then how *do* we get through?

MONIA: The underground network of the old city. There's an exit just by this wall.

(THEY LOOK AT THE MAP)

ANAT: That network used to run under the whole town. Trains every few minutes. I've read about it.

BOAZ: Even as a ruin it has its uses.

MONIA: Come. Time is short.]

The Controller explains to the Doctor that Dalek rule started with 100 years of human war, which wiped out seven eighths of the population, leaving the Earth open to Dalek attack. The Daleks are using the Earth to provide raw materials for their ongoing war against all other life forms.
    The guerrillas attack the centre to try and rescue the Doctor.

PB: When we came to film this sequence at the car-park, that rubbish skip was there and we couldn't do anything about it. I may have asked for it to be painted, but we just had to work around it.

DM-J: I remember that horrible yellow dustbin there. I should have done something about it. At the time, you think that no-one will notice it and that maybe it looks slightly futuristic.

Boaz is killed, but the Doctor and Jo are freed. The Doctor insists that the guerrillas leave the Controller alive as they make their escape.

[A short extra scene appeared in the camera script following this sequence. It was of the guerrillas arriving back at their underground bunker.]

Back in the 20th Century, UNIT are searching for the Doctor and Jo, but to no avail.

[This scene featured a UNIT soldier with an Alsation dog. The dog was hired from a company called Zoo Animal Actors.]

[A scene where Shura emerges from hiding has been lost here.]

Monia and Anat explain to the Doctor and Jo that the wars started when Styles caused an explosion that destroyed the house in which the peace conference was taking place. The guerrillas therefore decided to kill Styles and allow the conference to go ahead. They now want the Doctor to return to kill Styles for them.

PB: I was pleased with this scene, because the guerrillas were being played by three good actors. As a director, it was satisfying to get them to settle down and emote rather than to just go through the motions and the lines.

Shura emerges from hiding and heads for the house. He breaks into the cellar and sets up the bomb he has been carrying.
    The Doctor realises that Shura is still in the past, and that Anat's party had some dalekanium explosive with them. It was Shura who caused the explosion – by trying to change history, they have created their own future.
    The Daleks set up an ambush in the tunnels to try and recapture the Doctor.

DM-J: Although this is the same set as in the earlier episode, the door to the section that the Daleks are in is completely different: it slides up on runners rather than being hinged at the top and hoisted on wires. The reason for this is that the sets for episodes three and four are in a different studio session from those for episodes one and two. Because of the need to put all the sets into the same studio, we didn't have room to put the full control room in: only a part of it was needed for these episodes, and the fabric of that set was being re-used for the area where the Doctor and Jo were being held. Therefore, what has happened is that the Daleks' room is there, but the control room is not. The door changed probably because there wasn't enough room in the studio to use the hinged door.

When the Doctor and Jo arrive in the tunnels in order to return to the 20th Ccentury to try and stop Shura, they are confronted by the Controller. The Doctor convinces him to let them go.
    The Doctor and Jo run from the tunnel in the 20th Century, and Benton reports to the Brigadier that they have been found.
    Unfortunately the senior guard witnessed the Controller's actions, and the Controller is exterminated by the Daleks.

[The Daleks' extermination effect, during which the picture goes into negative, was achieved using a technical device called a Complimentary Picture Amplifier (previously been known as an NPA within the BBC).]

The senior guard becomes the new Controller. The Daleks decide to invade the past themselves, to ensure that the conference is destroyed and that war breaks out.

[A short camera-scripted scene is missing here, showing Shura priming the bomb.]

A newscaster (Alex MacIntosh) announces the arrival of Styles and the delegates at the house.

PB: Alex MacIntosh was a real-life news presenter but had retired from being on the front-line and was freelancing at the time we made this story.

[According to the BBC's files, a Rolls Royce (MWF 435F) and a Daimler (AWP 633H) that had been hired for filming were damaged by adhesive signs that were affixed to the doors. The BBC's insurance did not cover this damage as it was not considered to be accidental, and the production had to foot the bill for repairs, which came to £239. However, there are no insignia or logos visible on either of the two cars in the footage used in the episode.]

PB: I put nothing on those cars except a small flag on the bonnet. I saw no need to.

The Doctor arrives and manages to convince the Brigadier to evacuate the house, and all the delegates leave.

[Jean McFarlane was originally to have appeared in this scene as Styles' secretary, but the actress had fallen ill and was unavailable. Her lines were given to an aide instead.]

Daleks and Ogrons emerge from the tunnel and storm the house.
UNIT troops fight them but cannot stop them. The Doctor finds Shura in the basement and explains what is happening. The Daleks enter the house. Shura tells the Doctor and Jo to leave. He intends to destroy the house and the Daleks with it.

PB: The worst thing about the design of the Daleks was that they could only run on smooth surfaces. We therefore had to lay boards down over the ground that the Daleks were to cross. This meant that I had to be very careful with how I placed the camera, so that we didn't see the boards. Considering that we had only six Ogrons, three Daleks and about ten UNIT guys, it was a hard battle to make work on screen. I did have the benefit of film editing, which allowed me to cut the shots together so that they had a lot of dramatic impact.

The Doctor tells the Brigadier to let the Daleks pass, and the troops fall back. The Daleks move through the house, looking for Styles and the delegates, and Shura detonates the bomb. The house is completely destroyed.

DM-J: That is an incredibly good model of the house, and it matches the real house superbly. It's a brilliant explosion.

The Doctor tells Styles that the peace conference has been saved.

PB: The explosion that they see in the distance was done on the waste ground that we had been using.

[There is a final scene in the camera script, which does not appear in the finished production. It starts with the Doctor and Jo walking towards the UNIT lab and pushing open the doors to see another Doctor and another Jo inside. There then follows exactly the same exchange as seen in episode one, ending with the Doctor and Jo in the lab vanishing. The scene then continues:

DR WHO: There you are, they've gone!

(THE BRIGADIER ENTERS)

JO: Doctor, what happened?

DR WHO: Very complicated thing, time. Once you've begun tampering with it, the oddest things start happening.

BRIGADIER: Doctor, what's going on here?

DR WHO: Nothing for you to worry about old chap.

BRIGADIER: For one ghastly moment I thought I saw two of you!

DR WHO: (NOW JOKING AGAIN) Exactly.

BRIGADIER: You mean there *were* two of you?

DR WHO: That's right.

JO: But which of us was the real us?

DR WHO: Both.

(THE BRIGADIER SHAKES HIS HEAD TRYING TO WORK IT OUT)

JO: Doctor – that future we went to – with Daleks ruling Earth. Is it going to happen or isn't it?

DR WHO: Well. It is and it isn't.

BRIGADIER: Oh come along Doctor.

DR WHO: First it is – then it isn't. There are all kinds of futures, you know.

JO: Futures with Daleks in?

(DR WHO STOPS WORK FOR A MOMENT)

DR WHO: It's possible Jo.

BRIGADIER: But surely the Daleks were all destroyed ...

DR WHO: I thought I'd destroyed them once before, but I was wrong. I must get the Tardis working again, Jo. I think I'm going to need it.

Although this scene was scripted, it is unlikely that it was actually recorded.]

PB: I was never one for an anti-climax. Once you had reached the end, then that was it. The ending that the transmitted story has is much more my style, and I think that the addition of that final scene in the script does create an anti-climax. I suspect it was removed before we started filming and recording the story. It may also have been omitted because of a lack of time

POST-PRODUCTION

In the early Seventies, episodes of *Doctor Who* were recorded two at a time, and all the scenes for one episode were generally recorded in the order they would be transmitted, or else grouped by set, depending on technical requirements or director preference. All the film sequences were prepared in advance and then 'played in' at the appropriate time onto the videotape master. Much of the videotape editing for *Day of the Daleks* was also carried out 'in-camera' at the time of recording.

'By the time we got to record in the studio, all the film sequences would have been edited together,' explained Bernard. 'The shots were filmed and edited together based on my film script, but you would go at the end of the rehearsal day to see the film editor in order to check and approve what had been done.

'By the time you got into studio, the film sequences were ready, and you played them in to add the effects and links to the recorded material live in the studio. You were expected to end up with the show pretty much as it would be transmitted. All that was missing was the music and sound effects, assuming that we hadn't added them in live as well.'

Dudley Simpson was hired to compose and create the incidental music – as usual at this point in the series' history.

'Dudley and I got on very well,' remembered Bernard. 'When I joined Thames Television, I took him with me, and he created the music for *The Tomorrow People*. We worked together very closely. I used to sit with him and go through the story in order to plan out where the music would fall.

'My feeling was that music had been used too often and too much in *Doctor Who*, but there was this philosophy that *Doctor Who* had to be supported by music. I don't think I overused it in *Day of the Daleks*. Dudley was very, very talented, and he could watch a story with me, and then thirty six hours later return with a finished score to start recording the music.'

On this story, Simpson hired two further musicians to create the music, and the score was recorded on 25 October 1971.

At the same time as Simpson was composing the music, Brian Hodgson from the BBC's Radiophonic Workshop was working on the special sound effects. These were added to the edited videotape, together with the music, at dubbing sessions that took place on the following dates: 28 October 1971 (episode 1), 29 October 1971 (episode 2), 3 November 1971 (episode 3) and 4 November 1971 (episode 4).

'I think *Day of the Daleks* stands up very well,' commented Bernard. 'I think it's slow in parts, but that comes partly from the indoctrination of television in the Nineties, which is very fast and furious.

'I look back on the two years I was involved with *Doctor Who* and *The Tomorrow People* as perhaps the most creative period of my career. I was firing on five cylinders, and had to be. The amount of creativity that needed to be generated was massive. It was a very exciting time, and I'm very proud to have been involved with it.'

THE THIRD DOCTOR

TRANSMISSION

Day of the Daleks was the first story in the ninth season, and was transmitted between 1 January and 22 January 1972.

It was heralded, as was each of the third Doctor's seasons, with a *Radio Times* cover. This was a painting especially commissioned from artist Frank Bellamy. Inside the magazine could be found a competition to win a Dalek of your own. The prizes were billed as 'mark 7' Daleks, and were in fact a number of specially commissioned Dalek toys. They were around two and a half feet tall and were operated by a control box mounted upon a stalk that projected from the rear of the Dalek. An edition of the BBC's regional news programme *Nationwide* on Tuesday 22 February 1972 featured a film report covering the delivery of a 'mark 7' Dalek to a winning junior school.

To enter the competition, readers were invited to complete a story that had been started by Terry Nation.

According to the *Radio Times*:

> Among the things that Dr Who most treasures is a crumpled and grubby piece of paper, a single page from the log of the Spaceguard patrol ship *Defender*. The edges of the page were charred by the fire that burned out the *Defender* when she re-entered the atmosphere of Earth too fast after returning from her mission on the planet Destron.
>
> The being who wrote these words is long dead of has not yet been born, for the event he describes may be in the past or the future. In deep space, time as we know it has no meaning.
>
> The events of which this single page tells intrigued the Doctor for many years. Finally his curiosity overcame his natural caution and he could resist no longer. He set the controls in the TARDIS, and with Jo started for Destron. The moment they were under way he handed Jo the page from the log. If all goes well, Dr Who and Jo will reach Destron. They may face the same dangers as the crew of the *Defender*. Perhaps become involved in the great battle. Anything might happen ...

The story started by Nation read as follows:

> ... and so little time, perhaps only a matter of hours. Because of my wounds, I can contribute nothing to the

action that is about to begin. Two of the crew members carried me to this high vantage point where I shall be able to observe the battle.

This planet, Destron, is like no other I have ever visited. Everything about it seems to have sprung from our worst nightmares. Every horror that my mind is capable of imagining is here, and many more beyond my imaginings. The very landscape is different and totally alien to any I have seen. Different in colours, shapes and textures. There are things that grow here. They are many and varied, but I hesitate to classify them as vegetation, for many of the species have the power of mobility. They hunt and feed upon one another. The animal life from the tiniest organism to the most gigantic monster, seem, to my eyes, hideous beyond description. All exhibit the most violent savagery and aggression.

That Destron was once inhabited by a creature of higher intelligence is certain. The buildings here, strange by our architectural standards, remain as monuments to their civilisation. The concern of our mission is in one particular building. We know that it was the arsenal of the creatures that lived here. An arsenal containing weapons so advanced, of such ingenuity, of such terrifying power, that no force in the seven galaxies could defend against them. How the Daleks learned of the weapons of Destron we do not know. But, they do know. They are here. Now. Our force is made up of units from all the planets that form the confederations of the seven galactic governments. Our mission: 'To prevent the arsenal on Destron falling into the hands of the Daleks, and to destroy all the weapons stored within it.'

We are on a hostile planet that favours neither side. If our force wins, the safety of all the colonised worlds is assured. If victory goes to the Daleks, they can fulfil their ambition to dominate all the known universe.

Something is happening. On the far side of the crater. The Daleks are beginning to move into position. Our force hasn't seen them yet. It's beginning and I …

Following this cliff-hanger, entrants had to take up the story, telling it as though they were there. The story was to be concluded in less than 400 words, and three drawings were also to be included: a landscape of Destron; some of the monsters that inhabit it; and the battle between the crew of *Defender* and the Daleks.

Some of the competition entries were displayed at the Ceylon Tea Centre in London during March and April 1972, along with a small exhibition of *Doctor Who* props, including an Axon, Alpha Centauri, Aggedor, Arcturus and, of course, a Dalek.. Everyone whose work was displayed received a special certificate to commemorate the fact.

A special trailer is reported to have been commissioned for *Day of the Daleks*, but no documentary evidence has been found to support this. This was allegedly filmed on location in central London and featured the Daleks patrolling many famous landmarks.

The story's transmission gained favourable ratings; the highest yet received by a third Doctor story. Despite this, the press were not kind in their criticism.

'Behind all the technological patter about ultrasonic disintegrators, *Doctor Who* appears to have been reduced to a single basic theme: the defeat of a world domination league,' complained Matthew Coady of the *Daily Mirror*, his feelings being echoed by Chris Kenworthy in the *Sun*.

Even Jon Pertwee made his dislike of the Daleks public, and subsequently singled out this particular show as one of the worst that he had done, although he was to revise this opinion shortly before his death in 1996.

Whatever the criticisms of the show, the Daleks had once more worked their magic, and the ninth season of *Doctor Who* was off to a flying start.

CREDITS

Director	Paul Bernard
Producer	Barry Letts
Production Assistant	Norman Stewart
Assistant Floor Manager	Sue Heddon
Assistant	Carolyn Driver
Floor Assistant	John O'Shaughnessy
Script Editor	Terrance Dicks
Production Secretary	Sarah Newman
Designer	David Myerscough-Jones
Costume Designer	Mary Husband
Make-Up Artist	Heather Stewart
Visual Effects	Jim Ward
Fight Arranger	Rick Lester

Film Editor	Dan Rae
Film Cameraman	Fred Hamilton
Assistant	Brian Easton
	Brian Johns
Sound Supervisor	Tony Millier
Sound Recordist	Chris King
Grams	Gordon Phillipson
TM1	Alan Horne
TM2	Derek Martin (eps 1, 2), Alan Arbuthnott (eps 3, 4)
Assistant	Norman Johnstone
Grips	Tex Childs
Vision Mixer	Mike Catherwood
Graphics	Sid Lomax
Crew	10
Title Music	Ron Grainer and the BBC Radiophonic Workshop
Incidental Music	Dudley Simpson
Special Sound	Brian Hodgson
Writer	Louis Marks
Daleks Originated by	Terry Nation

Selling the Doctor

MEDIA

Unlike any of the previous actors to have played the Doctor, Jon Pertwee was the media's darling. William Hartnell had neither the presence nor the trendiness, while Patrick Troughton had preferred to leave the character of the Doctor in the studio, and when he did consent to give an interview, it tended to be as an evasive and mischievous version of his on-screen persona.

Pertwee, on the other hand, actively courted the press. Here was an actor with many different facets to his character, whether they be in his profession as an actor, or his interest in gardening or motorcycling, or even a penchant for deep sea diving and an appreciation of moustache cups. When Troughton's intention to stand down from *Doctor Who* was announced in January 1969, there was minimal attention from the press. The previous changeover, from Hartnell to Troughton, had also been a low key affair; there had not even been a press call to announce the new Doctor, and therefore there had been few photographs and scant column inches given over to the event. With Pertwee's arrival, however, there was much more excitement over the change-over.

The press launch in June 1969 to announce Pertwee's appointment was very well attended, and the idea of bringing in a Yeti for the proverbial 'photo opportunity' was inspired. This resulted in coverage in many of the national newspapers the following day.

The press seemed initially interested in the change in direction that the series would be taking: a move away from the outer space adventures of the past, with the Doctor being brought down to Earth with a bang. Comments were made about the fact that the stories were going to be more adult, that the new companions – the Brigadier and Liz Shaw – were more aimed at an adult audience, and that Pertwee himself was going to play the Doctor as a serious character. He even noted in one early interview that, 'It will be set on Earth in the 1980s. I won't be wearing the Victorian clothes that the other Doctor Whos have used. I will be in a modern day suit.'

The producer, Peter Bryant, also said, in another interview, 'The new stories will be more realistic, with a sort of Quatermass flavour. We have an audience now which is adult sophisticated.'

Even Shaun Sutton, the BBC's Head of Drama, commented, 'The Daleks marching down Piccadilly is much more horrifying than anything up in space. This is real science fiction.'

This intention of making *Doctor Who* more adult and realistic resulted in an unexpected backlash. *Spearhead from Space* showed shop dummies coming alive and attacking shoppers, while *Terror of the Autons* depicted lethal plastic daffodils, a toy troll doll coming alive and strangling someone, and, worst of all, a policeman revealed to be a faceless killer robot rather than a trustworthy figure of law and order. These two stories managed to redefine the way in which the media perceived *Doctor Who*. Up until that point, it had been a curiosity. A show that was looked upon as providing gentle thrills and spills for viewers of all ages. Now it was a subject of national concern, as Mrs Mary Whitehouse of the National Viewers and Listeners Association repeatedly condemned the show as a bad influence on children's minds.

This criticism of excessive violence and horror was levelled at *Doctor Who* time and again during Pertwee's time as the Doctor, and the actor consistently countered these arguments by asserting that the ratings were very good, that parents did know that there was an 'off' switch on their television sets, and that he had personally met many hundreds of children to whom *Doctor Who* had done no harm whatsoever. In fact, the production team almost came to welcome Mrs Whitehouse's comments, as they always got covered by the press and ensured that *Doctor Who* was rarely out of the public eye.

Throughout the first half of the Seventies, it was the BBC's own listings magazine *Radio Times* that remained the strongest supporter of the show. The opening episode of every season was afforded a front cover on the magazine, something that no other Doctor could claim – Hartnell had been granted three covers, as had Troughton, but after the end of the Pertwee era, the coverage in the *Radio Times* would drop off to the extent that the only other cover to be granted while *Doctor Who* was regularly on the air was for the twentieth anniversary show, *The Five Doctors*, in 1983.

Not only were there covers, but there were also a great many features to be found inside the magazine. These ranged from fairly standard features on the cast, to a special feature on the making of the show, which ran as *Inferno* started transmission in 1970, and a three page comic strip painted by Frank Bellamy for the start of *Colony in Space*. Mid way through Pertwee's tenure, Bellamy started to provide small artwork images, which were included with the television listing each week, and occasionally larger pieces for specific stories, including *The Dæmons*. Occasionally other artists would be commissioned for pieces in a similar style, as for *The Time Warrior*.

As previously mentioned, Pertwee was a media magnet. This meant that there were numerous opportunities for 'lifestyle' pieces revolving around his love for motor bikes, gardening, lavishly decorated homes and his family. Pertwee was a true 'action man', and he seemed to be forever opening fetes and shopping centres, dressed in his *Doctor Who* outfit and driving, first Bessie, and then his special *Doctor Who* car that was later dubbed 'the Whomobile'.

Doctor Who found itself being promoted on a great many other shows. These included, in 1970, *Junior Points of View*, which made unfavourable comparisons with *Star Trek*. *Junior Points of View* became *Ask Aspel* and in 1971, after which it reported some children as saying that *Doctor Who* was not as scary as it used to be, and made a comparison by showing clips from the first Troughton story *The Power of the Daleks* and from *Terror of the Autons*. *This is Your Life* came knocking on Pertwee's door in 1971, and on 21 October 1971 the Daleks made an appearance on *Blue Peter*, hinting that they would be back in the new season. In December of 1971, the *Young Observer* magazine reported on an event at London's Planetarium, which featured Pertwee and Barry Letts talking about *Doctor Who* and displaying various props and monsters from the series. This event was hosted by *Blue Peter* presenter Peter Purves, who had himself, of course, appeared in *Doctor Who* as the Doctor's companion Steven Taylor back in 1965 and 1966.

Following up the 'Win A Dalek' competition in the *Radio* Times, the BBC's local news programme, *Nationwide*, carried a feature on 22 February 1972 on the delivery of a Dalek to one of the winning schools. Pertwee was the guest on *Ask Aspel* on 5 March 1972. In addition, the two Dalek cinema films from the Sixties made their debut on television during the Pertwee era. The first film, *Dr Who and the Daleks*, was shown on 1 July 1972, and the second film, *Daleks Invasion Earth: 2150 A.D.*, was shown on 19 August the same year. The BBC's Special Effects Exhibition at the Science Museum in London featured a *Doctor Who* display, and ran from December 1972 until June 1973. Its opening was featured on the 7 December edition of *Nationwide*.

On 10 Jan 1973, *Pebble Mill* had as its guests Troughton and Pertwee talking about *The Three Doctors*; and on 28 May 1973, Pertwee presented *Disney Time*. *Nationwide* also covered Katy Manning's departure from the show on 22 June 1973; Pertwee and a selection of monsters attended the Lord Mayor's show on 10 November 1973; *Blue Peter* on 5 November 73 covered the forthcoming season and unveiled the Whomobile to the public; while on *Nationwide* on 14 December 73, script editor Terrance Dicks appeared to talk about *Doctor Who* winning a BAFTA award for its scripts. Finally in 1973, on 21 December, *Pebble Mill* again featured *Doctor Who*, this time with Troughton and visual effects designer Bernard Wilkie demonstrating some monsters and effects. On 6 January 1974, Billy Smart's Circus featured a guest appearance by Pertwee with his Whomobile.

THE TENTH ANNIVERSARY

Doctor Who's tenth anniversary fell in 1973, and to celebrate it, the production team decided to commission a special story that would feature all three Doctors. This act established a precedent that was to last for the next twenty years, as each major anniversary would be marked with a special story in which the Doctor's past incarnations came together to defeat some evil menace. The Three Doctors resulted in less publicity than had been hoped, perhaps because the press had by now become bored with always reporting the same thing: that Doctor Who was too violent. The angle of 'sex in the TARDIS' had not yet been discovered by the tabloids, and so, whereas in later years if the Doctor's assistant wore something revealing then it became practically front page news, back in the early Seventies, the costumes worn by Katy Manning as Jo Grant barely raised an eyebrow.

The anniversary was also marked by the Radio Times releasing a special magazine. The only piece of factual writing readily available at this time was Malcolm Hulke's and Terrance Dicks' The Making of Doctor Who (which had been released as a paperback book by Pan in 1972), and therefore the Radio Times Tenth Anniversary Special was a milestone in the history of Doctor Who publishing. It collected together information and photographs from the entire history of Doctor Who, putting it all in context and including interviews with the Doctors and companions, as well as a new story by the creator of the Daleks, Terry Nation, and, for all those budding engineers who had written in to the BBC asking how to build a Dalek, plans for doing just that.

The magazine was very well received, and firmly established that the series had a history that was every bit as important as the current show. As this was the first piece of commercially available material that detailed the early days of the programme, there were a number of mistakes made, most notably in the titles given to some of the Hartnell stories, which had not been afforded overall titles on their transmission. (Up until The Gunfighters in 1966, all Doctor Who episodes had individual titles.) In compiling the special, in many cases the title of the first episode of a story was taken as being the overall title of the story itself, resulting in much confusion over subsequent years as to what the overall titles actually were.

Concluding the celebrations, the production team held a party on 10 December 1973, to which cast and crew were invited, along with selected members of the press.

MERCHANDISE

No new merchandise was released in 1970 to tie in with Pertwee's debut season. The first items associated with his Doctor started to appear in 1971, as merchandisers began to catch on to the potential of his Doctor. An early promotional tie-in was for a Kellogg's breakfast cereal, Sugar Smacks. The Doctor was shown on the front of all the boxes over the promotional period, and six small metal badges were given away inside the packs. The 'tag line' for the promotion was that Sugar Smacks endowed the consumer with: 'The Timeless Energy of Doctor Who'. The badges were particularly of interest, as they appear to have been the first examples of metal badges released to tie in with *Doctor Who*. The Doctor was also used as the basis of a promotion for one of Nestle's ranges of milk chocolate bars, with a series of 15 different wrappers being issued, collectively telling the story of the Doctor's battle against the Master's 'Masterplan Q'. The other items released in 1971 were a set of two *Doctor Who* jigsaws from Michael Stanfield Holdings, which featuring photographs of the Doctor, and an iron on transfer of a Dalek issued by Dodo Iron-Ons.

Although a *Doctor Who* Annual had not been produced by World Distributors for 1972 (the reason for this is unknown) it returned for a 1973 edition and featured a photographic cover showing the Doctor in the UNIT laboratory from *Terror of the Autons*. A further *Doctor Who* Annual was to be published for each of the remaining years that Pertwee played the Doctor.

1972 saw even more interest in the series, as a further two jigsaws were released in the Michael Stanfield Holdings range; *The Making of Doctor Who* by Hulke and Dicks was published by Pan through their children's imprint, Piccolo Books; a poster showing the Doctor menaced by a claw from *Colony in Space* was released, only to be hastily withdrawn at the request of Pertwee and replaced with a photograph of the Doctor and a Sea Devil instead; and the BBC Special Effects Exhibition at the Science Museum resulted in two more metal badges being issued, conferring on their wearer the rank of 'TARDIS Commander'.

Finally, in time for the Christmas market, Pertwee lent his vocal talents to a single called 'Who Is The Doctor', which was released on the Purple record label.

1973 saw the launch, in May, of the Target range of *Doctor Who* novelisations. Published by Allan Wingate in hardback and by Universal Tandem in paperback., the range kicked off with reprints of the three novels from the Sixties: *Doctor Who in an exciting adventure with the Daleks* (renamed to the simpler *Doctor Who and the Daleks*), *The Crusaders* and *The Zarbi*. These were followed in 1974 by newly commissioned novelisations of *Spearhead from Space* (called *The Auton Invasion*), *Doctor Who and the Silurians* (*The Cave Monsters*), *Day of the Daleks*, *Colony In Space* (*The Doomsday Weapon*), *The*

Dæmons, The Sea Devils, The Abominable Snowmen and *The Curse of Peladon.*
These books established the Target range and kicked off a publishing
phenomenon that was to last for as long as the original *Doctor Who* series
and beyond.

Also in 1973, the BBC finally re-issued the Ron Grainer *Doctor Who* theme
on a single. Also made available in this format was a track called *The World
of Doctor Who,* which appeared as the 'B' side to Dudley Simpson's title
music for the BBC series *Moonbase 3* and included music from *The Mind of
Evil* and the Master Theme from season eight. With the first of the BBC's
Doctor Who exhibitions opening at Longleat House, another metal badge was
released; another set of four jigsaws was produced, this time from Whitman
Publishing; World Distributors published a *Doctor Who* colouring book; and
the *Doctor Who* Space Mission Pad, a set of code sheets and carbon paper,
was made available by Naocraft Ltd.

Finally, Polystyle Publications, the publishers of *TV Comic,* which had
been running a *Doctor Who* comic strip for many years, released in 1973 a
Doctor Who Holiday Special. This featured *Doctor Who* comic strips and stories
and a look behind the scenes at the story *Frontier in Space.* A second special
was released in 1974.

FANDOM

There had been a *Doctor Who* Fan Club in existence since 1965, but by 1970,
its new secretary, Graham Tattersall, found that he was running it almost
single-handedly. The Club's magazine tended to range somewhat wider
than *Doctor Who* in its content. It was printed on a Roneo duplicator and, as
this method was expensive, Tattersall decided to abandon publication after
only a few issues.

'In the end,' Tattersall comments, 'I found the whole project of running
the Club not only expensive but also very time-consuming. My job was
taking up much of my spare time, and I had no option but to give up the
Club.'

This fact was discovered in late 1971 by a fourteen-year-old Edinburgh-
based fan called Keith Miller, who had written to the BBC asking about
Doctor Who fan clubs. Miller had tried to contact Tattersall, but to no avail,
and in the end he had written again to the BBC, who found out that
Tattersall was no longer interested in running the Club. On learning this,
Miller asked Barry Letts's production secretary, Sarah Newman, if he could
take over. Not realising how young he was, Newman agreed, and arranged
for a box of miscellaneous items, including the addresses of approximately
forty of Tattersall's members, to be sent to him.

Miller started up his revamped *Doctor Who* Fan Club on 30 December

1971, and initially the only service it provided was a monthly newsletter sent out entirely free of charge to the Club's members. After a couple of issues that Miller produced and published himself, he came to an arrangement with Newman that he would supply stencils and she would run off copies using the BBC's facilities. Miller feels that the Club would never have got off the ground if it wasn't for Newman's support and assistance.

Initially the newsletter was a relatively cheap publication, each issue consisting of a few A4 sheets of typewritten text duplicated on coloured pulp paper, stapled together in the top left-hand corner. From Issue 15 in April 1973, the newsletter – now called *DWFC Mag* – went bi-monthly, and Miller included more material on the history of the show and interviews with the cast. Although Pertwee was delighted that there was a *Doctor Who* Fan Club in existence, he encouraged a fan named Stuart Money to set up a Jon Pertwee Fan Club as well. Miller queried this arrangement, and Newman informed Money that the DWFC was the officially recognised club and that he should not set up a rival.

One of the most interesting aspects of Miller's newsletters were the frequent set reports that he presented. Although lacking in detail, the reports covered stories including *The Three Doctors* and *The Green Death* and were written with great enthusiasm.

OVERSEAS

1972 saw the first commercial sale of *Doctor Who* to America, with a batch of 72 episodes being made available by Time Life Films.

The original publicity brochure stated that *Doctor Who* was: 'Excellent access time programming – as a strip or once a week. Dramatising 13 complete, serialised adventure tales, each tale a complete story. Dr Who – part Who-dini, part Who-dunnit – travels around the universe encountering one incredible adventure after another – often aided by his capable, beautiful assistant, Jo Grant ... opposed by a cunning, sinister foe, the Master. Serialised dramas, each with gripping, cliff-hanging endings guaranteed to keep audiences coming back, again and again, to follow the adventures of ... Dr Who'

A page in *Broadcasting* magazine featured a photograph of Jon Pertwee from the show's title sequence with the heading: '72 half-hours with Dr Who and you're cured.' The main thrust of the advertisement was that *Doctor Who* could cure your TV station of flagging ratings 'and brings fast, fast, fast relief.'

The thirteen stories available were: *Doctor Who and the Silurians* (called *The Silurians* on the publicity brochure), *The Ambassadors of Death*, *Inferno*, *Terror of the Autons*, *The Mind of Evil*, *The Claws of Axos*, *Colony in Space*, *The*

Dæmons, *Day of the Daleks* (called *The Daleks* on the information brochure), *The Sea Devils*, *The Curse of Peladon*, *The Mutants* and *The Time Monster*. These were shown repeatedly on those channels that had purchased them, and no new sales of *Doctor Who* were made to America until a batch of 98 Tom Baker episodes was purchased in 1978.

TV Ontario in Canada started airing specially selected *Doctor Who* episodes in 1976. They aired two 'seasons' of Pertwee serials. Each story was introduced by commentator Dr Jim Dator, who discussed various philosophical and scientific elements of the show as well as continuity with previously aired stories. TVO also published an educational viewers guide to *Doctor Who* in 1976.

Their first 'season' was broadcast from 18 September 1976 to 12 March 1977 and consisted of *The Three Doctors*, *Day of the Daleks*, *The Curse of Peladon*, *The Claws of Axos*, *The Mutants* and *The Time Warrior*. All of these bar *The Claws of Axos* and *The Time Warrior* were repeated in 1979

Their second 'season' was broadcast from 16 September 1977 until 25 March 1978 and contained *The Time Monster*, *The Green Death*, *Death to the Daleks*, *The Monster of Peladon* and *Planet of the Spiders*. *The Time Monster*, *The Green Death* and *The Monster of Peladon* were repeated in 1980

NEW ZEALAND
By Paul Scoones

The Pertwee era commenced in New Zealand with *Spearhead from Space* and *Doctor Who and the Silurians*, which were shown on Television One from 14 March to 23 May 1975 on Friday at around 6 pm for the first three weeks, and then moved back to around 5 pm for the remaining eight weeks. Although colour television had been introduced to New Zealand in October 1973, these episodes were broadcast from black and white 16mm film prints, which had been acquired 24 January 1975.

Soon after the arrival of New Zealand's second national television channel, South Pacific Television (SPTV), the series returned on this new second channel. Because SPTV was still in the process of setting up its transmitters around the country, some regions missed out on seeing some of the episodes. From this point *Doctor Who* was transmitted in colour. The first story screened was *Day of the Daleks* followed by *Carnival of Monsters*, *The Three Doctors* and *The Time Warrior* in this order from 1 September to 16 December 1975. *Day of the Daleks* screened on Mondays at around 6 pm, and the rest of the stories screened on Tuesdays at around the same time.

Death to the Daleks was screened as a stand-alone story eight months later, on Fridays at 8 pm on SPTV from 6 to 27 August 1976. After another long break, the final two stories of the Pertwee era, *The Monster of Peladon* and

Planet of the Spiders, were screened on Sundays on SPTV at 6.35 pm for the first story and 6.15 pm for the second, from 20 March to 5 June 1977.

Well over half of the episodes from the Pertwee era were omitted during the initial screenings on New Zealand television. From Season Seven, both *The Ambassadors of Death* and *Inferno* had been omitted. All of Season Eight (*Terror of the Autons* to *The Daemons*) was unscreened, and *Day of the Daleks* was the sole transmitted representative of Season Nine. From Season Ten, *Frontier in Space*, *Planet of the Daleks* and *The Green Death* were all omitted. TVNZ programme traffic documents and a BBC Enterprises document from February 1978 listing overseas sales of all *Doctor Who* stories, both indicate that every purchased story was screened. It may be possible to attribute this to the BBC's junking of many Third Doctor episodes during the mid 1970s. Although as late as 1977 many of the omitted episodes were still screened in other countries, these appear to have been 16mm black and white film prints and colour NTSC video copies which were both unsuitable formats for PAL colour television in New Zealand.

The next Pertwee story screened was *The Green Death*, placed out of sequence between the Tom Baker stories *The Android Invasion* and *The Brain of Morbius* on Fridays at 6.30 pm on SPTV from 26 January to 2 March 1979. Jon Pertwee visited New Zealand in 1979 on a cabaret tour and his crime quiz show *Whodunnit* was popular with New Zealand viewers; these factors may have prompted the scheduling of *The Green Death* at this time.

A long run of *Doctor Who* stories on Television New Zealand (TVNZ)'s second channel, TV2 commenced in April 1985 with two previously unscreened Troughton stories, followed by an almost complete run of the entire Pertwee era. The episodes were initially screened on Fridays at 6.30 pm with two episodes back to back and the middle closing and opening credits removed. *Spearhead from Space* began on 10 May 1985, and the series ran without a break through to *The Three Doctors*. Most stories were screened in colour, except for: *Doctor Who and the Silurians*, *The Ambassadors of Death*, *Terror of the Autons*, *The Mind of Evil* and *The Daemons*. The last three episodes of *The Three Doctors* were screened back to back on 7 February 1986, followed by a month's break.

Viewer figures for this run of Pertwee episodes reveal that 12 July 1985 gained the greatest *Doctor Who* audience with *The Ambassadors of Death* Episode 7 rating 14.5% and its paired episode, *Inferno* Episode 1 increasing to 15%. 16 August 1985 received the second highest ratings, with Episodes Two and Three of *Terror of the Autons* both rating 13.5%. *Doctor Who and the Silurians* Episode 3, screened 31 May 1985, also rated 13.5%. *Terror of the Autons* was the highest-rated story with a 12% average.

Carnival of Monsters commenced on 11 March, now in a single episode per week format on Tuesdays at around 5.30 pm on Television One. *Planet of the Daleks* Episode Three was screened in black and white, and the first episode of *Invasion of the Dinosaurs* was omitted as TVNZ had been supplied with a re-edited five part version with renumbered episodes. The Pertwee episodes screened during this period were supplied by the Australian Broadcasting Corporation and consequently in many cases had cuts that had been made by the Australian censor. From 18 November 1986, during *The Monster of Peladon*, the series was screened on Wednesdays as well as Tuesdays at the same time. The Pertwee era ended 24 December 1986 with the screening of *Planet of the Spiders* Part Six.

The highest rated Pertwee episodes for this period were *Planet of the Daleks* Episode Six and *The Time Warrior* Episode Two, each with 13% of the potential viewing audience. *Planet of the Daleks* was the highest-rated story with a 10.8% average.

Stories from the Pertwee era were next broadcast in 1991, following on from repeat screenings of selected Hartnell and Troughton stories on TV2. *Spearhead from Space* Episode 1 screened 28 July 1991 (rescheduled at short notice from 14 July), and the whole of Season Seven played on Sundays at around 11.30 am, ending with *Inferno* Episode 7 on 12 January 1992. *Doctor Who and the Silurians* and *The Ambassadors of Death* were again screened in black and white.

After a one month break, the series resumed in the same timeslot for a further ten weeks, with *Terror of the Autons* and *The Mind of Evil*, from 16 February to 19 April 1992. All ten episodes were screened in black and white. Another much longer break preceded the screening of *The Claws of Axos*, *Colony in Space* and *The Daemons* from 24 January to 2 May 1993, again on Sundays at 11.30 am on TV2. *The Daemons* was screened in black and white. *The Daemons* was followed by a screening of the Hartnell story *The Time Meddler* in the same timeslot.

The thirtieth anniversary of *Doctor Who* was marked by TV2 with a screening of *Day of the Daleks* from 28 November to 19 December 1993 followed by the 1992 documentary *Resistance is Useless* on 26 December 1993. The timeslot was 11.35 am on Sundays, and each week's instalment was introduced by BBC Enterprises' thirtieth anniversary montage of the faces of the seven Doctors that appeared on BBC *Doctor Who* videotapes released during 1993.

Other than two screenings of the Paul McGann TV movie, it was more than six years before *Doctor Who* returned to New Zealand television. The UHF and satellite channel Prime TV began screening the series from the beginning in May 2000, and by September had reached the Pertwee era. At this time, Prime was screening the series at the rate of an episode a day, six days a week – excluding Saturdays – at 6.30 pm. Every Pertwee episode was screened in the correct sequence and without a break. This run saw the New Zealand debut of *Invasion of the Dinosaurs* Part One, and the rest of this story was broadcast with correctly numbered episodes for the first time and, in addition, a slightly longer edit of Part Three.

A number of episodes that had previously screened in New Zealand in black and white were broadcast for the first time in colour on Prime, including *The Ambassadors of Death* Episode 5, and all of *Terror of the Autons* and *The Daemons* – all of which had been successfully restored to transmission-quality colour by the BBC in the early 1990s. Although BBC held a colour version of Episode 1 of *The Ambassadors of Death* and a colour-restored version of all seven episodes of *Doctor Who and the Silurians*, black and white recordings of these instalments were supplied to Prime. Also broadcast in black and white were Episodes 2, 3, 4, 6 and 7 of *The Ambassadors of Death*, *The Mind of Evil*, *Planet of the Daleks* Episode Three and *Invasion of the Dinosaurs* Part One.

From *Death to the Daleks* onwards, Prime doubled their *Doctor Who* screenings from six to twelve episodes per week by moving the start time to 6 pm and running two episodes per night back to back. These were presented with the middle closing and opening titles and recap removed. The Pertwee era ended on Prime on 8 February 2001 with the screening of Parts Five and Six of *Planet of the Spiders*.

VIEWER REACTION

When one considers the ratings for the first of Pertwee's five seasons, it is a wonder that the change in format was considered successful. From just over 8 million for *Spearhead From Space*, the viewing figures dropped alarmingly over the season, finishing with around 5.5 million for *Inferno*. In fact, *Doctor Who* had not seen regular average ratings this poor since the last few stories of Hartnell's era (*The Savages*, *The War Machines* and *The Smugglers*), while the *War Games* had averaged out at 4.9 million.

The start of the eighth season saw a return to the 8 million mark, but this time the viewing figures were consistent over the whole season, with *Colony In Space* peaking at nearly 9 million (partly because of a new time-slot, which removed a scheduling clash with Gerry Anderson's *UFO* series on many ITV regions) and *The Dæmons* just behind it. Things were looking even better for the ninth season, with *Day of the Daleks* coming in at over 9.5 million viewers. After this, however, the season tailed off again, ending at about 7.5 million for *The Time Monster*. Repeating the success of previous season openers, *The Three Doctors* managed to pull in 10.3 million on average, with *Planet of the Daleks* not far behind. The figures for *Planet of the Daleks* were inflated by an extremely good figure for episode one (11.0), no doubt due in part to the FA Cup Final being shown immediately before it. *The Green Death* was the disappointment here, with just under 8 million viewers. The figures stayed pretty much the same for the eleventh, and final season, with, for the first time, the opening story not performing the best. *The Time Warrior* managed only around 8 million, while *Invasion of the Dinosaurs* and *Death to the Daleks* brought in around 9.5 million each. The Doctor's swan song in *Planet of the Spiders* saw about 9 million viewers tuning in on average.

Somewhat strangely, the highest rated third Doctor transmission was the repeat showing of *The Dæmons,* which achieved a figure of 10.53 million, followed by the repeat of *The Green Death,* which managed 10.45 million. Aside from these repeats, the highest rated Pertwee story was, perhaps not surprisingly, *The Three Doctors.*

In the media, the show seemed to be universally liked, with few negative comments to be heard. 'Wins my vote as the best in the series so far,' wrote Matthew Coady in the *Daily Mirror* about *Spearhead From Space.* 'What keeps *Doctor Who* forever young … is its absolute conviction,' Richard Last said in the *Daily Telegraph* about *The Three Doctors.* Writing about *The Green Death,* the same journalist later commented, '… an imaginative Christmas pudding script, taut direction, lavish filming and even a trendy ecological theme all contributed to the total effect, but what makes this venerable series tick is the complete conviction of all concerned.'

Where there were adverse comments, these tended to be inspired by the media's 'concern' for the violence and horror that was apparently contained within *Doctor Who*'s format – or else by a negative opinion of the Daleks. *Day of the Daleks* came in for some particularly harsh words: 'The series … is beginning to acquire an exhausted air, of which the return yet again of the mechanical monsters is an unmistakable symptom,' muttered Coady, again in *The Daily Mirror*; and, '…it's about time the BBC exterminated them once and for all,' declared Chris Kenworthy in the *Sun.*

The lasting appeal of the series was summed up by Richard Boston in *The Observer,* when he said of *Planet of the Spiders,* 'It is, I suppose, beyond dispute that *Doctor Who* is the best thing that has been done on television, and now that the programme is ten years old and that the current incumbent of the title role is about to be recycled, it seems only appropriate to pay tribute to its colossal achievement.'

But what of the viewers? In the BBC's internal audience research report for the omnibus repeat of *The Sea Devils,* it was stated that the story had been 'received with rather mixed feelings'. The report noted that 'a sizeable minority did not care for the series (which, in their opinion had "outlived its entertainment value") and found this story particularly corny and far-fetched, saying they "only watched for the children's sake". On the other hand, a considerable number said they thoroughly enjoyed Dr Who and the Sea Devils, despite having seen it before, and the series as a whole was considered imaginative and "good fun".'

For *Planet of the Spiders,* it was noted that the ending 'met with a tolerant rather than enthusiastic response from most of the … viewers who constituted the adult audience … a minority of about one in three found it very enjoyable.'

The report went on to state that Pertwee was, according to long term viewers, 'the most likeable and subtle Doctor so far' and ended with a selection of comments from children, which make for interesting reading:

'My 10-year-old son says: very entertaining, liked the story, marvellous effects (the spiders looked revolting), quite well acted, made you want to make sure of seeing next episode.'

'I thought it was good and scary.' (age 9)

'Three boys (14, 11 and 8) enjoyed it, but the spiders don't have the impact of Daleks.'

'My three year old was frightened of some parts but liked to listen to the music at the beginning and end.'

'My daughter (10 and a half) thought this last adventure was fabulous, but was very upset when the Doctor changed.'

'They seem to enjoy it immensely, with enough creepy monsters to keep them on the edge of the seat.'

'Two small boys rooted to their seats, tea forgotten, deaf to all talk by grown-ups, and nearly in the box with the horrors on the screen!'

'Exciting, frightening, a must for Saturday. When will it come back, Mum?'

THIRD DOCTOR STORIES
IN ORDER OF AVERAGE VIEWING FIGURES
(Figures in millions of viewers)

The Three Doctors	10.3
Planet Of The Daleks	9.7
Day Of The Daleks	9.6
Invasion Of The Dinosaurs	9.6
Death To The Daleks	9.4
The Curse Of Peladon	9.38
Carnival Of Monsters	9.2
Planet Of The Spiders	9.0
Colony In Space	8.5
The Dæmons	8.34
The Time Warrior	8.25
Spearhead From Space	8.2
The Sea Devils	8.17
Frontier In Space	8.0
Terror Of The Autons	7.95
The Mutants	7.8
The Green Death	7.72
Doctor Who And The Silurians	7.71
The Monster Of Peladon	7.7
The Mind Of Evil	7.6
The Claws Of Axos	7.4
The Time Monster	7.38
The Ambassadors Of Death	7.35
Inferno	5.6